This book must be returned immediately it is asked for by the Librarian,
and in any case by the last date
stamped below.

U.C.S.

3 0 OCT 1981

LIB

Swansea University
WITHDRAWN FROM STOCK
Information Services & Systems

U.C.S.

1 3 JAN 1995

U.C.S.

2 9 NOV 2001

hja

SWANSEA UNIVERSITY COLLEGE LIBRARY

D1135598

The Conduct of Linguistic Inquiry

5811

£8.50

FE

SWANSEA UNIVERSITY COLLEGE
LIBRARY

Classmark: P 158 Bot

Location:

Accession No:

10 0264384 8   TELEPEN

JANUA
LINGUARUM Series Practica 157

Studia Memoriae
Nicolai van Wijk Dedicata

endenda curat

C.H.van Schooneveld
Indiana University

MOUTON PUBLISHERS · THE HAGUE · PARIS · NEW YORK

The Conduct of Linguistic Inquiry

A Systematic Introduction to the Methodology of Generative Grammar

Rudolf P.Botha

MOUTON PUBLISHERS · THE HAGUE · PARIS · NEW YORK

Library of Congress Cataloging in Publication Data

Botha, Rudolf P.
The conduct of linguistic inquiry.

(Janua linguarum: Series practica; 157)
Translation of Generatiewe taalondersoek.
Bibliography: p.
Includes index.
1. Generative grammar–Methodology. I. Title.
II. Series.
P158.B6713 1980   415   80–25705
ISBN 90–279–3088–8 (casebound)
        90–279–3299–9 (paperback)

ISBN 90–279–3088–8 (casebound)
        90–279–3299–9 (paperback)

© 1981, Mouton Publishers, The Hague, The Netherlands
Printed in Great Britain

"... *the only excuse teachers have for teaching is ignorance*... *their own; their students' is taken for granted of course. If so, then teachers will do better to study than teach, since the more they will know the less they will wish to teach: which is all to the good. This is particularly true concerning methods*..."

Joseph Agassi 1976:11.

Preface for Instructors

As the student of linguistics progresses, he will be faced with questions such as the following: What kind of activity or enterprise is linguistic inquiry? What is a linguistic theory? What role do such theories play in linguistic inquiry? What is the difference between linguistic description and linguistic explanation? What is the function of predictions and postdictions in linguistic inquiry? How do linguists make discoveries about human language(s)? How are linguistic theories tested and justified? What types of argument do linguists use to justify their theories? How do linguists react to criticism of their theories? As far as I know, there is no textbook to which the student may be referred for well-founded and systematically integrated answers to these and other related methodological questions. The nonexistence of such a methodological textbook poses a serious obstacle to the intellectual development of the student seeking answers to the questions mentioned above.

There is, however, a good reason for the nonexistence of a methodological textbook of the kind in question. The demands made on the writer of such a textbook make the task quite discouraging. Not only should he possess the normal didactical skills. He should also be at home in two extremely complex fields: those of present-day linguistics and the philosophy of science. Contemporary linguistics is becoming more and more of a maze of highly technical controversies which tax even the most skilled scholars in the field. This is even more true of the modern philosphy of science. Attempting to write a textbook on linguistic methodology involves braving the dangers of both and the chances of survival appear to be slim.

A further obstacle to the writing of such a textbook is the fact that, under normal circumstances, writers of textbooks rely heavily on existing technical works in their particular field. In fact, most textbooks present little more than a simplified, specially compiled didactical representation of information from these technical works. As far as the methodology of linguistics – the field of study in which the two above-mentioned subjects intersect – is concerned, such technical works are extremely rare. This field is, in fact, poorly developed. Very little or no attention has been given to questions such as those raised in the introduction to this preface. As a result, much more is involved in writing a methodological textbook for contemporary linguistics than the mere representation of existing information. A considerable part of the contents of such a textbook has to be conceived by the writer.

In view of this, it is clear why no methodological textbooks for contemporary linguistics has been written as yet. However, the difficulties facing the writer do not, unfortunately, detract from the need for such a textbook. *The Conduct of Linguistic Inquiry* is the result of an effort to present students who have had a first, conventional introduction to generative grammar with a truly introductory textbook. As such it contains a limited amount of information on the general nature and individual aspects of linguistic inquiry as it is practised within the framework of generative grammar. The information contained in this book gives the student some first answers to questions such as those mentioned at the beginning of this preface. But it is not the ultimate aim of this book to give a mere representation of information on methodological aspects of generative grammar. Ultimately, the book aims at instilling in the student a consciousness of and sensitivity for these methodological or metascientific aspects. I am convinced that insensitivity as regards these methodological aspects is one of the main causes for the turmoil in contemporary linguistics.

Generative grammar, however, represents but one approach within modern linguistics. *The Conduct of Linguistic Inquiry* can therefore not really claim to be an introduction to the methodology of "contemporary linguistics". In my opinion, it is not didactically advisable to confront the student with the methodologies of various alternative approaches to linguistics within the confines of a single introductory textbook. I have chosen the approach within the framework of which the most and the most significant linguistic research has been done during the past twenty years. It would be senseless to introduce a student to "more recent", "deviant" approaches within contemporary linguistics while he is not yet thoroughly conversant with the substance and methodology of "classical" generative grammar.

In order to make *The Conduct of Linguistic Inquiry* useful to as large a public as possible certain measures have been taken. Thus, I have tried to keep the contents of the book as uncontroversial as possible, both from a linguistic and a philosophical point of view. As regards the linguistic aspect, the aims of generative grammar, the nature of linguistic theories, etc., I have concentrated on the Chomskyan approach. This does not mean that I am propagating this approach, nor does it imply that this approach does not have certain serious limitations. Moreover, this does not mean that other, "deviant" approaches within generative grammar are rejected as being sterile. Special status is accorded to the Chomskyan approach for the following reason: neither the origin and early development of generative grammar, nor the recent "deviant" developments within generative grammar can be understood when viewed in isolation from the Chomskyan approach. It is therefore clear that this approach should receive special treatment in an introductory textbook. As we proceed, it will become clear that, from a methodological or metascientific point of view, the Chomskyan approach is defined in terms of ontological realism, phenomenological rationalism, epistemological empiricism and methodological generality.

I have also tried to be uncontroversial in my choice of illustrative linguistic material. The material has been taken from the controversy between lexicalists and transformationalists, but the book does not purport to take sides in the controversy. Chomsky's work on nominalization in English and McCawley's reaction to it have furnished the greater part of the illustrative material. The material has been carefully selected so as to require a minimum of general linguistic erudition on the part of the student. At this point an explicit word of caution may be necessary. The accuracy of the metascientific characterization of the Chomskyan approach which is given in this book is in no way dependent on the correctness of the substantive linguistic principles presented as illustrative material. Among these principles are the $\overline{\text{X}}$-convention, the principle of neutral lexical entries, the recoverability condition on deletion transformations and the Coordinate Structure Constraint. Should linguists at any time abandon or drastically modify these and other substantive linguistic principles, they will not, by implication, alter the metascientific principles presented in this book.

As regards the metascientific aspect of the book: wherever possible, a serious effort has been made to steer clear of controversies such as those concerning the structure of theories, the ontological status of theories, the nature of scientific explanation, the mechanisms responsible for the growth of scientific knowledge, etc. If, for instance, the ontological status of linguistic theories is presented from a realistic viewpoint, it is not without reason. The realistic point of view happens to be descriptive of the Chomskyan view of the ontological status of linguistic theories and is presented as such. This policy has been followed throughout: concepts, hypotheses and theories from the philosophy of science are presented only insofar as they are descriptive of what is characteristic of generative grammar on a metascientific level. To further understanding it is highly desirable that the contents of a book such as the present one should be presented within the framework of a single, homogeneous, explanatory theory of philosophy of science. This, however, has unfortunately been impossible in the case of *The Conduct of Linguistic Inquiry*: such a philosophical theory, which is free from serious shortcomings, does not exist.

As far as the structure of the book and the presentation of the contents are concerned, I have also adopted certain measures to ensure that the book will be as useful as possible. For instance, an effort has been made to present the material in a maximally digestible form. For this purpose I have consciously chosen a pattern with certain redundant aspects. As far as the structure of the individual chapters is concerned: each chapter is introduced by a "Perspective" which contains a brief summary of the aims and contents of the chapter. At the end of (almost) every chapter bibliographic details of selected additional reading matter are to be found, in which certain important aspects of the contents of the chapter are discussed on a more advanced level. This has eliminated the need for footnotes and an abundance of disturbing references. In addition, the selected reading adds an extra dimension to the book for more advanced students. Through their further reading these students will gain insight into the problematic nature of certain metascientific aspects of generative grammar.

As regards the general nature of the discussion: this differs sharply from my other writings on methodological issues in generative grammar. Whereas these writings present in-depth analyses of small clusters of related methodological questions, the present textbook aims to be a more comprehensive, systematic discussion of a broad spectrum of topics. Moreover, whereas the general tenor of the discussion of the former writings is, on the whole, evaluative and critical, that of the latter work is of a neutral, non-evaluative, expository nature. These differences do not indicate that Saul has become Paul. It simply appears to me unwise to introduce a student to a complex set of (methodological) principles while simultaneously overwhelming him/her with what appears to be the serious limitations of these principles.

It may be appropriate at this point to say something about the status of *The Conduct of Linguistic Inquiry*. In its present form it is the translated version of a work which originally appeared in Afrikaans under the title *Generatiewe Taalondersoek: 'n Sistematiese Inleiding* (Kaapstad: Hollandsch Afrikaansche Uitgevers Maatschappij. 1978). The content of the English translation differs from that of the Afrikaans original on minor points only. A number of small errors have been eliminated and the bibliography has been extended to include publications which appeared up to 'the middle of 1978. The Afrikaans original, which was completed in 1976, also served as the basis for a Dutch adaptation by Ger J. de Haan, entitled *Inleiding tot Generatief Taalonderzoek: Een Methodologisch Handboek* (Groningen: Wolters-Noordhoff. 1978).

Despite efforts to ensure that *The Conduct of Linguistic Inquiry* will be useful to as many readers as possible, it is impossible to meet the requirements of all potential readers, as these requirements are far too varied. Constructive criticism of the contents of the book will not only make improvement possible, but will also have another beneficial effect, viz. stimulation of the inquiry into the methodological foundations of linguistics.

R.P.B.

Acknowledgments

This book owes its existence to the contributions of quite a number of people. Valuable criticism of the Dutch version was given by G. de Haan, E. Elffers-van Ketel, G. Koefoed, T. Pollmann, H. Schultink, M. C. van den Toorn, P. van Reenen and J. van Rijen. Similar comments on the Afrikaans version were received from A. de Kock, J. Dreyer, E. Loubser, M. Sinclair, A. Snyman, A. Ver Loren van Themaat, H. Waher and W. Winckler. The fact that the English translation accurately reflects both the content and tone of the original Afrikaans version is due to the skills of Cecile le Roux. Mrs. L. Gildenhuys was responsible for typing and retyping the various versions of the manuscript with endless patience and characteristic precision. All these people deserve my sincere thanks. They are of course not to be held responsible for the shortcomings of this work.

R.P.B.

Contents

CHAPTER ONE

Linguistic Run-up

1.0 PERSPECTIVE

The purpose of this study is to find out exactly what linguistic inquiry is all about. We shall do it by way of a systematic analysis of the general nature and individual aspects of this type of inquiry. More specifically, we shall be concentrating on linguistic inquiry as it is conducted within the framework of generative grammar. The first question we should ask ourselves concerning a study of the nature and aspects of linguistic inquiry is: for what reason(s) should this study form part of the student's training in contemporary linguistics? Chapter 1, "Linguistic Run-up", provides the answer to this question. The gist of the answer is simple: if we did not gain insight into the general nature and individual aspects of linguistic inquiry, it would be impossible to understand what present-day linguistics is all about. This main point is made concrete with reference to the generative study of the grammatical phenomenon of nominalization in English. We show that generative grammarians consider nominals to be related to sentences in various ways. This gives rise to a typical grammatical problem, viz. how can the relatedness of nominals to sentences best be accounted for within the framework of a generative grammar? Two possible solutions — which are alternatives in certain respects — have been proposed: the transformationalist hypothesis and the lexicalist hypothesis. The general features of each of these two hypotheses are outlined informally. Subsequently a brief exposition is given of one of the main arguments for preferring the lexicalist hypothesis to the transformationalist hypothesis. It is then shown that familiarity with the nature and aspects of linguistic inquiry is a prerequisite for understanding, evaluating and constructing these and other similar arguments. Finally, it is made clear how one should go about gaining knowledge of the nature and aspects of linguistic inquiry.

1.1 NOMINALIZATION

Our approach to the study of the nature and aspects of linguistic inquiry will be concrete, starting with a linguistic run-up. Let us consider some aspects of the generative study of nominalization in English. Compare the following three sets of expressions in English:

(1) (a)   *John has refused the offer.*
    (b)   *John criticized the book.*
    (c)   *John is eager to please.*

(2) (a)   *John's refusing the offer*
    (b)   *John's criticizing the book*
    (c)   *John's being eager to please*

(3) (a)   *John's refusal of the offer*
    (b)   *John's criticism of the book*
    (c)   *John's eagerness to please*

The expressions listed in (1) to (3) illustrate the linguistic phenomenon known as "nominalization". The term NOMINALIZATION denotes a particular kind of relatedness between two types of linguistic expressions: sentences and nominal expressions, or nominals for short. The nominals (2)(a)–(c) and the nominals (3)(a)–(c) correspond to the sentences (1)(a)–(c). The nominals (2)(a)–(c) are known as GERUNDIVE NOMINALS, while those of (3)(a)–(c) are known as DERIVED NOMINALS. The interrelatedness of the sentences (1)(a)–(c) on the one hand, and the gerundive nominals (2)(a)–(c) and the derived nominals (3)(a)–(c) on the other hand may be represented as follows:

(4) | GERUNDIVE NOMINAL | SENTENCE | DERIVED NOMINAL |
|---|---|---|
| *John's refusing the offer* | ↔ *John has refused the offer* | ↔ *John's refusal of the offer* |
| *John's criticizing the book* | ↔ *John criticized the book* | ↔ *John's criticism of the book* |
| *John's being eager to please* | ↔ *John is eager to please* | ↔ *John's eagerness to please* |

In the diagram (4) the double-headed arrow '↔' has the value "is related to".

We now ask ourselves: what is the relationship between sentences and corresponding nominals? This relationship can be described in terms of similarities and differences.   At this juncture we are chiefly concerned with the similarities. Traditionally, three types of similarities between sentences and corresponding nominals have been distinguished. Informally these can be shown to be similarities in morphological form, similarities in semantic interpretation and similarities in syntactic properties.

Firstly: consider the similarities in morphological form. The statement (5) describes such a similarity.

(5) *Refused* in the sentence (1)(a), *refusing* in the gerundive nominal (2)(a)

and *refusal* in the derived nominal (3)(a) have a common form element: "refus".

Shared form elements also characterize the other two sets of sentences, gerundive nominals and derived nominals given above, viz. "critic" in the (b) set and "eager" in the (c) set.

Secondly: consider the obvious similarities in the semantic interpretation of the sentence (1)(a) *John has refused the offer*, the gerundive nominal (2)(a) *John's refusing the offer* and the derived nominal (3)(a) *John's refusal of the offer*. Three of these similarities are described in (6) below.

(6) All three of the expressions (1)(a), (2)(a) and (3)(a) are so interpreted
    (a)   that the one who refuses is John,
    (b)   that what John does is to refuse, and
    (c)   that what is refused is the offer.

The statement (6) expresses a generalization about similarities in the semantic interpretation of the sentence, gerundive nominal and derived nominal in question. Similarities in semantic interpretation also characterize the series (1)(b) *John criticized the book*, (2)(b) *John's criticizing the book* and (3)(b) *John's criticism of the book* as well as the series (1)(c) *John is eager to please*, (2)(c) *John's being eager to please* and (3)(c) *John's eagerness to please*.

Thirdly: there are equally striking similarities in the syntactic properties of the sentence (1)(a) *John has refused the offer*, the gerundive nominal (2)(a) *John's refusing the offer* and the derived nominal (3)(a) *John's refusal of the offer*. Thus consider the expressions (7)–(9).

(7) (a)   *John has refused the offer.*   [= (1)(a)]
     (b)   **John has refused hope.*
     (c)   **Trouble has refused the offer.*

(8) (a)   *John's refusing the offer*   [= (2)(a)]
     (b)   **John's refusing hope*
     (c)   **Trouble's refusing the offer*

(9) (a)   *John's refusal of the offer*   [= (3)(a)]
     (b)   **John's refusal of hope*
     (c)   **Trouble's refusal of the offer*

A first, obvious fact is that the three expressions (7)(b), (8)(b) and (9)(b) are all unacceptable. For generative grammarians this fact indicated a shared syntactic property of the sentence (7)(a), the gerundive nominal (8)(a) and the derived nominal (9)(a). This shared syntactic property is expressed in the general statement (10).

(10)   In none of the expressions (7)(a), (8)(a) or (9)(a) can "refuse" co-occur with a noun such as *hope* in the object position.

A second striking fact is that the three expressions (7)(c), (8)(c) and (9)(c) are unacceptable as well. For generative grammarians this pointed to a second similarity in the syntactic properties of the sentence (7)(a), the gerundive nominal (8)(a) and the derived nominal (9)(a). This similarity is expressed in the general statement (11).

(11)   In none of the expressions (7)(a), (8)(a) and (9)(a) can "refuse" co-occur with a nonanimate noun such as *trouble* in the subject position.

Shared syntactic properties similar to those of (10) and (11) are to be found in the sentence (1)(b), the gerundive nominal (2)(b) and the derived nominal (3)(b), as well as in the sentence (1)(c), the gerundive nominal (2)(c) and the derived nominal (3)(c).

Within the standard theory of generative grammar, the syntactic similarities of (10) and (11) are similarities in selectional features. As will appear below, syntactic similarities can likewise exist with regard to strict subcategorization features. Today many generative grammarians will not regard similarities in selectional features as syntactic similarities. However, in our study, we need not take this into account.

The fact that English sentences and corresponding nominals show similarities gives rise to a typical problem for the generative grammarian: how can the linguistic similarities between sentences and corresponding nominals best be accounted for within a generative grammar of English?

Generative grammarians have proposed two types of solution to this grammatical problem. In certain regards these two types of solution are alternatives, and a choice has therefore to be made between them. Each type of solution will be outlined informally below. At this stage of our study it is neither possible nor necessary to enter into the technical details of these alternative solutions. We shall be concentrating mainly on those outlines which determine how each solution accounts for the syntactic properties which we considered above.

1.2   THE TRANSFORMATIONALIST HYPOTHESIS

The first, and historically earlier, type of solution which has been proposed is known as the TRANSFORMATIONALIST HYPOTHESIS. The prototype of the transformationalist hypothesis, of which several variants exist today, was developed by Robert Lees in his study *The grammar of English nominalizations* (1966). Basic to the transformationalist hypothesis is the following assumption: the relationship between a sentence and corresponding nominals is a transformational relationship. This assumption applies to the relationship between a sentence and a corresponding gerundive nominal as well as to that between a sentence and a derived nominal. According to the transformationalist hypothesis, therefore, the similarities between a sentence and the corresponding nominals are accounted for by deriving the sentence and the nominals from essentially similar underlying syntactic structures. The transformationalist hypothesis thus sets up a sentence-like underlying structure for both gerundive and derived nominals. The similarities between sentences and corresponding nominals exist on the level of the sentence-like underlying structure. Although there are significant differences between the properties of Lees-like syntactic underlying structures and those of standard theory deep structures, we need not concern ourselves with these in our study. Ignoring these differences enables us to use the term "deep structures" to denote both Lees-like underlying structures and actual deep structures.

Let us consider once again the sentence (1)(a) *John has refused the offer,* the gerundive nominal (2)(a) *John's refusing the offer* and the derived nominal (3)(a) *John's refusal of the offer.* In terms of the transformationalist hypothesis, the linguistic similarities between these three expressions are accounted for by firstly assigning essentially similar sentence-like deep structures to all three expressions and, secondly, deriving the surface structures of the three expressions by means of different transformations operating on these deep structures. A simplified, schematic illustration of this point is given in (12).

(12)   deep structure   surface structure

                                               ↗ *John has refused the offer*
John (has) refuse(ed) the offer → *John's refusing the offer*
                                               ↘ *John's refusal of the offer*

The sentence-like underlying structure of nominals has traditionally been assigned the status of an embedded sentence. This implies that a sentence containing a nominal is regarded as a complex sentence, i.e. it is transformationally derived from a complex deep structure, incorporating more than one sentential constituent.

This point may be illustrated with reference to the sentences (13)(a) and (b).

(13)(a)   *Sam applauds John's refusing the offer.*
     (b)   *Sam applauds John's refusal of the offer.*

The sentences (13)(a) and (b) respectively incorporate the gerundive nominal *John's refusing the offer* and the derived nominal *John's refusal of the offer.* On the basis of the transformationalist hypothesis, essentially similar deep structures are assigned to the sentences (13)(a) and (b). This deep structure can roughly be represented as follows:

(14)

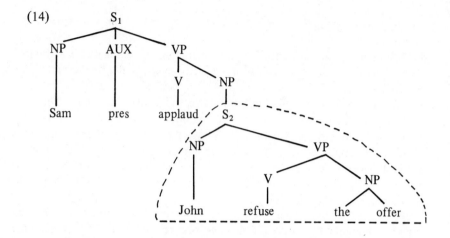

In the tree (14) the encircled embedded S_2 constitutes the sentence-like source of both the gerundive nominal *John's refusing the offer* in (13)(a) and the derived nominal *John's refusal of the offer* in (13)(b).

How then does the tranformationalist hypothesis account for the morphological similarity of (5), the semantic similarities of (6) and the syntactic similarities of (10) and (11) between the sentence *John has refused the offer* on the one hand, and the gerundive nominal *John's refusing the offer* and the derived nominal *John's refusal of the offer* on the other hand? Let us, first of all, consider the morphological similarity of (5). The deep structure of each of the three expressions in question contains the verbal element "refuse". It is therefore to be expected that the three expressions will have a shared form element. This acounts for the morphological similarity of (5).

This brings us to the similarities in semantic interpretation expressed in (6). The derivation of the sentence (1)(a) *John has refused the offer,* the gerundive nominal (2)(a) *John's refusing the offer* and the derived nominal (3)(a) *John's refusal of the offer* from essentially similar deep structures implies that the same set of grammatical relations occurs in each of these expressions. These grammatical relations – "subject-of", "direct object-of", etc. – form the basis of one aspect of the similarities in semantic interpretation expressed in (6). Therefore, since the three expressions all have the same deep structure subject, viz. *John,* all three of them are so interpreted that the one who refuses is John; because they have the same deep structure direct object, viz. *the offer,* all three the expressions are so interpreted that what is refused is the offer, etc. Moreover, the shared deep structure of (1)(a), (2)(a) and (3)(a) contains the same lexical items: *John, refuse, the, offer.* This accounts for a second aspect of the similarities in semantic interpretation: the similarity of the three expressions as regards lexical meaning. The tranformationalist hypothesis, therefore, accounts for the similarities of (6) in the semantic interpretation of the expressions in question in terms of shared grammatical relations and shared lexical items.

Finally, we have to consider the similarities in syntactic properties expressed in (10) and (11). The shared verbal element "refuse" and the shared grammatical relations also account for the similarities of (10) and (11) between the sentence (1)(a) *John has refused the offer* on the one hand, and the gerundive nominal (2)(a) *John's refusing the offer* and the derived nominal (3)(a) *John's refusal of the offer* on the other hand. Within the framework of the standard theory of generative grammar such similarities in syntactic properties are stated in terms of selectional features. The selectional features of linguistic units are specified in the deep structure. By assigning (nearly) the same deep structure to two or more linguistic units we state that these units have the same selectional features. This implies, moreover, that these linguistic units exhibit syntactic similarities of the type in question. In this way the syntactic similarities between the sentence (1)(a) on the one hand, and the gerundive nominal (2)(a) and the derived nominal (3)(a) on the other hand are accounted for by the transformationalist hypothesis. More specifically: on the level of deep structure these expressions contain the same verbal element "refuse" and, consequently, it follows that they have the same properties as regards the syntactic selectional restrictions for the subject and object positions. In other words, the similarity in selectional features, or syntactic selectional restrictions for the subject and object positions of these expressions can be reduced to the selectional restrictions of the verbal element "refuse". Within the framework of the transformationalist hypothesis these selectional restrictions need only be specified once in the form of a lexical entry in the lexicon. It is in this way that the generalizations of (10) and (11) about the similarities in the syntactic properties of *John has refused the offer, John's refusing the offer* and *John's refusal of the offer* are stated in the grammar of English.

1.3   THE LEXICALIST HYPOTHESIS

The second, more recent, solution which has been proposed for the grammatical problem of §1.1 is known as the LEXICALIST HYPOTHESIS. The core of the lexicalist hypothesis was expounded by Noam Chomsky in his article "Remarks on nominalization" (1972b). In the course of time, variants have also been developed for certain aspects of the lexicalist hypothesis. However, for the purposes of our study, we need not concern ourselves with the differences between the various versions. According to the lexicalist hypothesis, the relationship between a sentence and the corresponding derived nominal(s) is not a transformational but a lexical relationship. The essential difference between the transformationalist hypothesis and the lexicalist hypothesis concerns the status of derived nominals. According to the transformationalist hypothesis, derived nominals have the status of transforms, i.e. structures derived from sentence-like deep structures by means of transformations. According to the lexicalist hypothesis, on the other hand, derived nominals have the status of deep structures generated directly by base rules. More specifically, in terms of the lexicalist hypothesis, derived nominals are generated as NPs, i.e. noun phrases, in the base component. You will remember that, in terms of the trans- formationalist hypothesis, the relationship between sentences and corresponding derived nominals is specified by means of syntactic transformations. In terms of the lexicalist hypothesis, by contrast, this relationship is specified in the lexicon. In a grammar treating derived nominals in accordance with the lexicalist hypothesis, gerundive nominals are still derived transformationally. In other words, in such a grammar gerundive nominals still have the status of transforms.

Let us consider the lexicalist hypothesis with reference to the sentence (1)(a) *John has refused the offer* and the derived nominal (3)(a) *John's refusal of the offer.* In the article mentioned above, Chomsky proposes a single lexical entry for "refuse". This proposal accounts for the similarity in morphological form, as expressed in (5), between *refused* in the sentence (1)(a) and *refusal* in the derived nominal (3)(a). It is to be expected that two expressions containing the same lexical item will exhibit similarities in morphological form.

Chomsky's proposal of a single lexical entry for "refuse" also accounts for the syntactic similarities of (10) and (11) between the sentence (1)(a) *John has refused the offer* and the derived nominal (3)(a) *John's refusal of the offer.* In this single lexical entry are specified the fixed syntactic properties of "refuse", viz. those selectional and subcategorization features which "refuse" manifests in all expressions in which it occurs. The syntactic similarities of (10) and (11) between the sentence and derived nominal under consideration are accounted for in terms of such fixed syntactic properties. What is not specified in the single lexical entry for "refuse", however, is whether "refuse" is a verb or a noun. The lexical entry is neutral in that "refuse" is unspecified in terms of those syntactic properties which distinguish verbs from nouns. This entails that the lexical item "refuse" can be inserted in deep structures both under the node V and the node N. When "refuse" is inserted under the node V in a deep structure, it has the phonological form *refuse.* If, on the other hand, "refuse" is inserted under the node N, it will have the phonological form *refusal.* The nature of the rules, known as morphological rules, which specify the phonological form of "refuse", need not concern us here.

The deep structures assigned, within the framework of the lexicalist hypo- thesis, to the sentence (1)(a) *John has refused the offer,* the gerundive nominal (2)(a) *John's refusing the offer* and the derived nominal (3)(a) *John's refusal of the offer* can be roughly represented as follows:

(15) *John has refused the offer.*   [= (1)(a)]

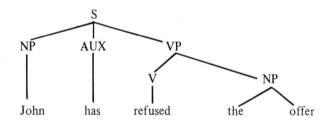

(16) *John's refusing the offer*   [= (2)(a)]

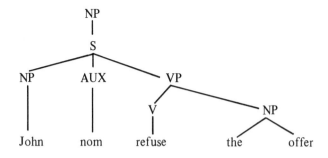

(17) *John's refusal of the offer*   [= (3)(a)]

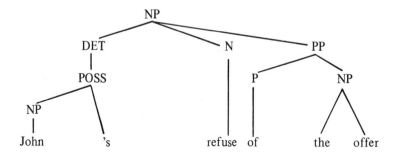

The trees (15)–(17) have been simplified in various ways which are irrelevant to our discussion. These trees clearly illustrate the fundamental assumption of the lexicalist hypothesis. Sentences and corresponding gerundive nominals have essentially similar sentence-like deep structures. The relationship between sentences and corresponding gerundive nominals is therefore a transformational relationship. Derived nominals, however, do not have a sentence-like deep structure, but the structure of an NP. The relationship between sentences and corresponding derived nominals is specified in the lexicon in the form of neutral lexical entries. The lexicalist hypothesis requires an additional device in order to express similarities, such as that of (6), in the semantic interpretation of sentences and corresponding derived nominals. It is not necessary, however, for us to consider the nature of this device.

Finally, the similarities and differences between the transformationalist hypothesis and the lexicalist hypothesis may be summarized schematically as in (18).

(18)

		transformationalist hypothesis	lexicalist hypothesis
gerundive nominals	status in deep structure	status of sentence	status of sentence
	relationship with corresponding sentences	transformational	transformational
derived nominals	status in deep structure	status of sentence	status of NP
	relationship with corresponding sentences	transformational	lexical

1.4   CHOMSKY'S CHOICE

Recall that both the transformationalist and the lexicalist hypothesis represents a type of solution to the grammatical problem of §1.1, viz. how the linguistic similarities between sentences and corresponding nominals can best be expressed in a generative grammar of English. We now come to the question of relative merit. Which hypothesis – the transformationalist or the lexicalist – offers the more adequate solution to the problem in question? In other words, which hypothesis would lead to a more adequate grammar of nominalization in English?

According to Chomsky, the lexicalist hypothesis has more merit than the transformationalist hypothesis. He justifies his choice of the lexicalist hypothesis by referring to three classes of linguistic differences between gerundive and derived nominals. Chomsky notes that the lexicalist hypothesis is more compatible with these differences than the transformationalist hypothesis. Let us consider how Chomsky uses one of these classes of differences in his argument for the lexicalist hypothesis. We shall return to the other two classes later on.

The class of differences between gerundive and derived nominals with which we are concerned includes differences in productivity. Chomsky points out that, in English, gerundive nominals can be formed freely from sentence-like deep structures. This is indicated by two facts: for almost every sentence there is a corresponding gerundive nominal and for every gerundive nominal a corresponding sentence can be found. In other words, the transformation that gives gerundive nominals applies almost unrestrictedly. On the other hand, there are numerous restrictions on the formation of derived nominals. This too is indicated by two facts: for many English sentences there are no corresponding derived nominals and for a large number of derived nominals no corresponding sentences can be found.

Chomsky cites the following expressions to illustrate that not all English sentences have corresponding derived nominals:

(19)(a)   *John is easy (difficult) to please.*
   (b)   *John is certain (likely) to win the prize.*
   (c)   *John amused (interested) the children with his stories.*

(20)(a)   *John's being easy (difficult) to please*
   (b)   *John's being certain (likely) to win the prize*
   (c)   *John's amusing (interesting) the children with his stories*

(21)(a)   **John's easiness (difficulty) to please*
   (b)   **John's certainty (likelihood) to win the prize*
   (c)   **John's amusement (interest) of the children with his stories*

Note that the sentences (19)(a)–(c) have corresponding gerundive nominals in the form of (20)(a)–(c). As is clear from the unacceptability of the expressions (21)(a)–(c), however, the sentences (19)(a)–(c) have no corresponding derived nominals.

The fact that every derived nominal in English does not have a corresponding sentence is illustrated by expressions such as the following:

(22)(a)   *John's doubts about their proposal*
   (b)   *the probability of John's leaving*
   (c)   *John's advice to Bill*

(23)(a)   **John doubted about their proposal*
   (b)   **It is probable John's leaving*
   (c)   **John advised to Bill*

It is clear from the unacceptability of the expressions (23)(a)–(c) that the derived nominals (22)(a)–(c) have no corresponding English sentences.

What is to be inferred from these facts about the relative merit of the transformationalist and the lexicalist hypothesis? In terms of the transformationalist hypothesis it should be possible to form derived nominals as freely as gerundive nominals. It follows that, in terms of this hypothesis, one would have expected the derived nominals of (21)(a)–(c) to occur in English as well. Every sentence should have had a corresponding derived nominal. For the syntactic structure underlying the sentences (19)(a)–(c) satisfies the structural description of the nominalization transformation that gives derived nominals. If the structural description of this rule is formulated in generalizing terms – as should be the case – then it will generate the derived nominals of (21)(a)–(c) from the deep structures in question. As we have seen, however, these derived nominals are unacceptable.

Chomsky now argues that, in terms of the lexicalist hypothesis, a grammar of English will not generate the unacceptable derived nominals of (21)(a)–(c). In such a lexicalist grammar, the lexical entries for *easy/difficult, certain/likely* and *amuse/interest* are such as to make it impossible for the grammar to generate these unacceptable derived nominals. These lexical entries contain a syntactic specification which prohibits the lexical insertion of *easy/difficult, certain/likely* and *amuse/interest* in the deep structures underlying the derived nominals of (21)(a)–(c).

This point may be illustrated with reference to (21)(a) **John's easiness to please.* The reason why this derived nominal is unacceptable, is that *easiness* occurs in combination with a certain sentential complement and this is impossible in English. The sentential complement has the approximate underlying form "someone pleases John". This underlying structure is transformationally reduced to the surface complement *to please John.* In a lexicalist grammar of English, the neutral lexical entry for "easy" will include a specification to the effect that it may not take such a sentential complement. Such a lexicalist grammar will therefore not generate a deep structure of the form $[_A easy]_A$ + S or $[_N easy]_N$ + S. As this structure is an important part of the deep structure underlying the unacceptable derived nominal (21)(a) **John's easiness to please,* a lexicalist grammar cannot generate such a deep structure. Consequently the unacceptable derived nominal cannot be generated by this lexicalist grammar.

This brings us to the main point of this linguistic preamble to our study of the nature and aspects of linguistic inquiry. Consider the following statements made by Chomsky (1972b:26) concerning the implications which the above-mentioned differences in productivity have for the relative merit of the transformationalist and the lexicalist hypothesis:

Summarizing these observations, we see that the lexicalist hypothesis explains a variety of facts of the sort illustrated by examples [19] through [21] · · · The transformationalist hypothesis is no doubt consistent with these facts, but it derives no support from them, since it would also be consistent with the discovery, were it a fact, that derived nominals exist in all cases in which we have gerundive nominals. Hence the facts that have been cited give strong empirical support to the lexicalist hypothesis and no support to the transformationalist hypothesis. Other things being equal, then, they would lead us to accept the lexicalist hypothesis from which these facts follow.

These statements by Chomsky give rise to two questions:

(24)(a)   What, precisely, is Chomsky asserting in each of them?
   (b)   Are these assertions true or false?

Consider, for instance, Chomsky's statement that the transformationalist hypothesis is consistent with the fact that the derived nominals of (21)(a)—(c) do not occur, but that this hypothesis would also be consistent with the conceivable "fact" that these derived nominals do occur. It is clear that the fact that these derived nominals do not occur and the conceivable "fact" that they do occur, are mutually incompatible. How, then, is it possible for a hypothesis to be consistent with both of two mutually incompatible facts? Is Chomsky's statement internally contradictory? And if it is not, then what precisely is being asserted? Is the assertion true or false? This brings us to a last question. According to James McCawley (1973:5) the nonoccurrence of the derived nominals of (21)(a) —(c) is inconsistent with the transformationalist hypothesis. Who is right: Chomsky or McCawley?

1.5   LINGUISTICS AND METASCIENCE

The questions formulated above clearly show that it is no simple matter to comprehend and evaluate the cited statements by Chomsky. But it is of crucial importance that the student and practitioner of linguistics should be able to do just this. The immediate consequence of failure in this regard would be that we are unable to come to grips with one of Chomsky's central arguments for the lexicalist and against the transformationalist hypothesis. From this it would follow that we cannot judge whether Chomsky was right in preferring the lexicalist hypothesis to the transformationalist hypothesis. The ultimate consequence would be that we simply do not understand what current generative grammar is all about, because Chomsky's lexicalist hypothesis is a fundamental thesis of his (revised) extended standard theory, and this theory is one of the major alternatives currently competing for supremacy in the field of generative grammar.

   For what reason(s) should anyone be unable to comprehend and evaluate the cited statements by Chomsky? Let us approach this question in a slightly roundabout way. Each of Chomsky's basic statements falls into one of two classes: a class of statements dealing with the transformationalist hypothesis or a class of statements dealing with the lexicalist hypothesis.

(25)   STATEMENTS ABOUT THE TRANSFORMATIONALIST HYPOTHESIS

   (a)   The transformationalist hypothesis is no doubt consistent with the facts.

(b)   The transformationalist hypothesis derives no support from the facts.

(c)   The transformationalist hypothesis would also be consistent with "other" facts.

(d)   The facts give no support to the transformationalist hypothesis.

(26)   STATEMENTS ABOUT THE LEXICALIST HYPOTHESIS

(a)   The lexicalist hypothesis explains a variety of the facts.

(b)   The facts give strong empirical support to the lexicalist hypothesis.

(c)   The facts follow from the lexicalist hypothesis.

(d)   The facts would lead us to accept the lexicalist hypothesis.

The expression "the facts", as used in (25) and (26), denotes Chomsky's observations about the occurrence of the gerundive nominals of (20)(a)–(c) and the nonoccurrence of the derived nominals (21)(a)–(c). In (25)(c) the expression "'other' facts" denotes the state of affairs which would have existed, had the derived nominals of (21) occurred.

Take a good look at the statements of (25) and (26). What are these statements about? They clearly do not make claims about human language in general, nor about English in particular. In other words, Chomsky is neither attributing properties to language in general, nor to any particular language. Thus, the statements of (25) and (26) are not statements about the objects of the study of linguistics. In this sense they are not LINGUISTIC STATEMENTS. The statements concern two classes of objects, hypotheses and facts, of which neither represents aspects of human language. Hypotheses and facts are not linguistic objects. It follows then that in the statements of (25) and (26) Chomsky attributes properties to nonlinguistic objects.

The properties attributed by Chomsky to these objects in the statements of (25) and (26) are nonlinguistic as well. Consider, for instance, the properties denoted by the expressions "being consistent with" [(25)(a), (c)], "deriving no support from the facts" [(25)(b)], "giving no support to the transformationalist hypothesis" [(25)(d)], "explaining a variety of the facts" [(26)(a)], "giving strong empirical support to" [(26)(b)], "following from" [(26)(c)] and "leading to accept the lexicalist hypothesis" [(26)(d)]. The properties denoted by these expressions are obviously features neither of language in general, nor of any particular language.

The nonlinguistic nature of the statements of (25) and (26) becomes even more clear if we compare them with the linguistic statements of (27).

(27)(a)   Corresponding to the sentence *John has refused the offer* are the gerundive nominal *John's refusing the offer* and the derived nominal *John's refusal of the offer.*

(b)   In none of the expressions of (27)(a) above can "refuse" co-occur with an object noun such as *hope*.

(c)   The relationship between a sentence and a corresponding nominal is a transformational relationship.

(d)   Derived nominals are deep structure NPs.

(e)   The lexical entry for "refuse" does not specify whether it is a noun or a verb.

The statements of (27) are linguistic statements: they represent assertions either about language in general or about a particular language. The objects to which these statements refer are linguistic objects: sentences, gerundive nominals, derived nominals, the lexical item "refuse", and so on. To these linguistic objects the statements of (27) attribute linguistic properties: the property of being a transformational relationship, the property of being an NP in the deep structure, the property of being a verb or a noun in the lexicon, and so on.

We have now established that the statements of (25) and (26) are not linguistic statements. But what are they then? They are METASCIENTIFIC STATEMENTS. How do metascientific statements differ from linquistic statements? Informally, the main difference can be said to be this: linguistic statements describe (a) language. Linguistic statements attribute linguistic properties to linguistic objects. Metascientific statements describe the nature, aspects and structure of (a) science or the conduct of (a) scientific inquiry. The objects with which metascientific statements deal are metascientific objects such as facts and hypotheses. The properties attributed to these objects in metascientific statements are metascientific properties such as the property of "being consistent with", "following from", and so on.

A general point is now clear. In order to appraise Chomsky's case for the lexicalist hypothesis as against the transformationalist hypothesis, we must be able to comprehend and evaluate two types of statements: linguistic statements and metascientific statements. And this holds not only for Chomsky's argumentation, but for generative grammar and linguistics in general. Metascientific statements such as those of (25) and (26) abound in the scientific discourse of linguists, in every serious linguistic publication and in every in-depth linguistic discussion. Without the ability to identify metascientific statements as such, the ability to understand them and the ability to judge their correctness, we cannot really understand generative grammar. It is in the absence of these abilities that Chomsky's metascientific statements become incomprehensible.

But the ability to critically follow the linguistic arguments of experts such as Chomsky is not the only skill needed in order to become a competent linguist. We should also be able to construct similar arguments for or against linguistic hypotheses. We should therefore be able not only to identify, comprehend and evaluate metascientific statements, but also to make similar statements and to integrate these in coherent argumentations.

What could we do, then, to acquire these abilities? The answer is simple. We must get to know the nature of the metascientific objects and properties with which these statements are concerned. That is, we must acquaint ourselves with, *among other things*,

(28)(a)   the nature and properties of hypotheses,
   (b)   the nature and properties of so-called facts,
   (c)   the circumstances in which hypotheses are (in)consistent with facts,
   (d)   the circumstances in which hypotheses derive (no) support from facts,
   (e)   the circumstances in which facts provide strong empirical support for hypotheses,
   (f)   the circumstances in which facts follow from hypotheses,
   (g)   the circumstances in which hypotheses explain facts,
   (h)   the circumstances in which facts lead us to accept hypotheses, etc.

The list of (28) is merely illustrative. There are many more metascientific objects and properties with which we have to familiarize ourselves in order to acquire the abilities discussed above.

What, then, is the most profitable manner in which to get acquainted with the nature and properties of this metascientific domain? Again, the answer is simple: through a systematic study of the general nature and individual aspects of linguistic inquiry. For it is in this general nature and these individual aspects that the metascientific domain manifests itself.

There are many forms of linguistic inquiry. In an introductory study such as this it is impossible to consider them all. We shall concentrate on the form of linguistic inquiry by means of which, in recent years, most insight has been gained into the nature of human language(s). This means that we shall be making a study of the general nature and individual aspects of linguistic inquiry as conducted within the framework of generative grammar. The type of study we are undertaking is known as a metascientific, or (general) methodological study. The discipline that provides the framework for such a study is known as METASCIENCE, PHILOSOPHY OF SCIENCE, or (GENERAL) METHODOLOGY.

SELECTED READING

Generative Study of Nominalization in English

Introductory/Summary

Baker 1978: ch. 18; Jacobs and Rosenbaum 1968:225—228; Stockwell et al. 1973:505 ff.

Advanced

Aronoff 1976; Bowers 1972:14–29; Chapin 1967; Chomsky 1972b; Fraser 1970; Fodor 1977:81–83, 125–126, 159; Jackendoff 1974a: §1.; 1974b; Lakoff 1967; 1970; Lees 1966; McCawley 1973.

Metascience/Philosophy of Science/(General) Methodology

Nature and Aims

Beerling et al. 1972: 9 ff.; Bocheński 1965:ch.2; Bunge 1959:ch.1; Botha 1971: ch.1; Caws 1966:ch.1; Hanson 1969:ch.1; Harré 1972:ch.1; Kaplan 1964:I.3; Losee 1972:1–4; Morgenbesser 1967b; Pap 1962: v–vi; Theobald 1968:ch.1.

Introductory Works

Beerling et al. 1972; Bocheński 1965; Bunge 1959; Caws 1966; Hanson 1969; 1971; Harré 1967; 1972; Hempel 1966; Kaplan 1964; Lambert and Brittan 1970; Rudner 1966; Theobald 1968; Toulmin 1965.

Distinction Science/Linguistics vs. Metascience

Botha 1971:13–17; Bunge 1959:ch.1; Scheffler 1963:5; Smart 1968:8–9.

CHAPTER TWO

Blueprint of Study

2.0 PERSPECTIVE

Before embarking on our study, let us consider in broad outline how the various parts of the study fit together. Chapter 2 gives the blueprint for this study of linguistic inquiry within the framework of generative grammar. The expression "linguistic inquiry within the framework of generative grammar" is exceedingly unwieldy and we shall therefore abbreviate it to LINGUISTIC INQUIRY for purposes of our study. Note, however, that wherever the term "linguistic inquiry" is used, it refers not to linguistic inquiry in general, but only to linguistic inquiry as conducted within the framework of generative grammar. Specifically, we will focus our attention on Chomsky's approach to generative grammar.

The content of this study is organized with reference to four guiding questions about the nature and aspects of linguistic inquiry, with reference to a distinction between nine main aspects of linguistic inquiry, and with reference to a further distinction between three fundamental angles from which linguistic inquiry may be viewed. In chapter 2, the four questions are formulated for which this study will provide the answers. Subsequently, an outline of the content of the study is given in terms of two summaries. The first is a summary of the general nature and aim of linguistic inquiry, as these will emerge from later chapters. The second is a list of nine main aspects which may be distinguished in linguistic inquiry. The distinction between an aspect of inquiry and a phase in a process of inquiry is elucidated as well. In conclusion, a description is given of the three angles from which each main aspect of linguistic inquiry may be studied: empirical inquiry in general, the study of language in general, and the study of specific individual languages.

2.1 GUIDING QUESTIONS FOR STUDY

We are directed in our study of linguistic inquiry by four guiding questions.

(1) (a) What is the general nature of linguistic inquiry?
    (b) Which main aspects can be distinguished in linguistic inquiry?
    (c) What does each main aspect of linguistic inquiry involve?

(d)   How are the main aspects of linguistic inquiry interrelated?

Satisfactory answers to these four questions should afford us a bird's-eye view of the metascientific domain within which linguists ply their trade.

The questions of (1)(a)–(d) are by no means the only interesting questions about linguistic inquiry. A fifth interesting and important question, for example, is the following:

(2)   What is problematic about the general nature and individual aspects of linguistic inquiry?

This question is interesting for a very special reason. A satisfactory answer to the question would indicate quite clearly the limits within which Chomskyan generative grammar constitutes a fruitful approach to the study of human language.

A satisfactory answer to (2), however, can only be sought when adequate answers to questions (1)(a)–(d) have been found. As our study is an introductory one, we shall concentrate on the questions of (1)(a)–(d) while pointing out, in passing, some of the problematic aspects of linguistic inquiry. It is impossible to discuss these problems exhaustively within the limits of our study. However, the selected reading provided at the end of each chapter will give an impression of these problems and what they involve. It must be stressed that the neutral, expository tone of the discussion is not meant to express the opinion that Chomskyan generative grammar is free from serious metascientific difficulties.

2.2   OUTLINE OF STUDY

It will gradually become clear that the aims of any type of inquiry determine the nature and main aspects of this type of inquiry. As far as the general nature and aims of linguistic inquiry are concerned, the following will appear from our study:

(3)   NATURE AND AIMS OF LINGUISTIC INQUIRY

   (a)   Linguistic inquiry is by nature an intellectual activity with the following guiding aim: to search for knowledge by means of which linguistic problems may be solved.

   (b)   Linguistic inquiry has the following "ultimate" objective: to gain insight into our understanding of that which is problematic with regard to human language(s).

   (c)   In linguistic inquiry this "ultimate" objective is pursued in terms of four more specific logical objectives:
      (i)   to give theoretical descriptions of the regularity, pattern, structure or mechanisms in an underlying linguistic reality;
      (ii) to give explanations of problematic linguistic data;

        (iii) to make predictions about an unknown linguistic reality (in the future);

        (iv) to make postdictions about an unknown linguistic reality (in the past).

(d)   Linguistic inquiry pursues its four logical objectives by formulating linguistic theories, i.e. hypothetical systems of concepts which represent an underlying linguistic reality.

(d)   Linguistic inquiry adopts the criteria that its theories must be
        (i) testable in principle, and
        (ii) justified in fact.

As will become clear in our study, the nature and aims of linguistic inquiry, as set out above, determine the nine main aspects of this form of inquiry.

(4)   MAIN ASPECTS OF LINGUISTIC INQUIRY

    (a)   choosing aims for linguistic inquiry,
    (b)   formulating well-formed linguistic problems,
    (c)   making linguistic discoveries,
    (d)   giving theoretical descriptions of an underlying linguistic reality,
    (e)   giving explanations of problematic linguistic data,
    (f)   making predictions and postdictions about ·unknown linguistic realities or parts of these,
    (g)   justifying linguistic hypotheses and theories,
    (h)   criticizing linguistic hypotheses and theories,
    (i)   reacting to criticism of linguistic hypotheses and theories.

The summaries in (3) and (4) above of the nature, aim, objectives and main aspects of linguistic inquiry serve only one purpose at this stage of our study, viz. to give a clear outline of what the study involves. In subsequent chapters the picture will be filled in with particulars about linguistic inquiry. However, for the sake of clarity, three general points concerning this outline need to be considered here.

Firstly, it will soon become clear that linguistic inquiry has many more aspects than the nine listed above. The choice of these nine as "main" aspects is, to a certain degree, arbitrary. We could have had ten main aspects, for instance, by regarding the making of predictions and the making of postdictions as two separate aspects. Or we could have had only eight instead of nine main aspects, for instance, by regarding the justification and criticism of linguistic hypotheses and theories as a single aspect. As we proceed, it will become clear that,.though there are no absolutely compelling reasons for the choice of nine main aspects, there are at least fairly good metascientific ones. Moreover, our choice of nine main aspects contributes in no small manner to the clarification and the justification of the way in which the study is organized.

Secondly, in the outline given above, a particular assertion is not made, viz. that every individual linguistic investigation pursues all the objectives of (3) and exhibits all the main aspects of (4). Jointly, the objectives of (3) and the main aspects of (4) present a maximal picture of linquistic inquiry. This means, on the one hand, that each of these aims and main aspects is reflected in at least some particular, individual linguistic investigations. On the other hand, not every individual linguistic investigation pursues all these objectives, and presents all these main aspects.

Thirdly, a clear distinction should be drawn between an aspect of something and a phase in something. This distinction may be illustrated with reference to the game of tennis. As a type of game, tennis is characterized by various aspects. These aspects include, for instance, the execution of various types of strokes; the use of rackets and balls; the use of a certain type of court; the use of a particular type of referee; the following of certain rules; the use of a particular scoring system; and the use of a division into matches, sets and games, etc. These aspects characterize tennis as a type of game. Let us consider, for the sake of comparison, the playing of a particular tennis match. Such a tennis match comprises a sequence of various distinct phases, viz. the sets and games actually played. Each game, in turn, comprises a sequence of shorter phases distinguished in terms of shots played by the players; positional changes made by the players on the court; rulings made by the referee; and so on. From this distinction between tennis as a type of game and the playing of a given tennis match, the following appears: an ASPECT is a distinguishable, nontemporal unit of content, while a PHASE is a temporal unit of action.

The nine main aspects of linguistic inquiry distinguished in (4) should not be regarded as nine consecutive phases in a process of inquiry. This distinction between an aspect as a distinguishable nontemporal unit of content and a phase as a temporal unit of action applies to linguistic inquiry as well. There is no direct correlation between the main aspects of linguistic inquiry as a type of intellectual activity, on the one hand, and the various phases of a given investigation as a series of consecutive acts on the other hand. Our study is concerned with the distinguishable aspects of the content of linguistic inquiry. A study of the phases within the process of linguistic inquiry falls beyond the scope of our study as it would have to show how nontemporal aspects of linguistic inquiry are realized in the temporal phases of individual investigations. It is obvious that we cannot consider the way in which aspects of inquiry are realized in the phases of a process of inquiry, if it is not yet clear what these aspects are. At this juncture, an explicit word of caution is not superfluous: the characterization of linguistic inquiry presented in this study will not make sense unless it is understood as a description of nontemporal, logically distinguishable aspects of content.

2.3   ANGLES OF STUDY

Each aspect of linguistic inquiry can be viewed from three different angles: that of empirical inquiry in general, that of the study of language in general and that of the study of specific individual languages.

Seen from the angle of empirical inquiry in general, the linguist is distinguished from, for instance, someone who lays bricks, someone who plays chess, someone who writes poetry, someone who makes mathematical calculations, someone who philosophizes, and so on. The first angle from which linguistic inquiry can be viewed reveals a first basic component of the linguist's research activity: the general empirical component.

The linguist's activity, however, is directed at a phenomenon known as "human language in general". In this aspect of his research activity, the linguist is distinguished from other scholars engaged in empirical inquiry which is not directed at language in general. Thus, from the point of view of the study of language in general, the linguist is distinguished from scholars such as those engaged in chemical, biological, sociological or ethnological research. This second angle from which linguistic inquiry can be viewed, that of human language in general, indicates the second basic component of the linguist's research activity: the general linguistic component. This component of the linguist's research activity may be called GENERAL LINGUISTIC INQUIRY. Viewed from the second angle, the linguist operates in the capacity of GENERAL LINGUIST.

However, the linguist's research activity is even more specifically directed in that he is always concerned with one or more particular, individual human languages. At a certain stage of his inquiry he will, for instance, be concentrating on English or Walbiri and not on French or Eskimo, or some other particular language. The third angle from which linguistic inquiry can be viewed, that of specific human languages, indicates the third basic component of the research activity of linguists: the grammatical component. This component of the linguist's research activity may be called GRAMMATICAL INQUIRY. Viewed from this angle the linguist operates as GRAMMARIAN.

The scholar engaged in linguistic inquiry is therefore active in three capacities simultaneously: that of empirical scientist, that of general linguist, and that of grammarian. Of course, in any particular investigation the linguist may concentrate either on language in general or on an individual language. But, as we shall see, in the former case his general linguistic inquiry will always be complemented by a grammatical component. In the latter case his grammatical inquiry will always have a complementary general linguistic component.

The question now is how each of the nine main aspects of linguistic inquiry is related to the above-mentioned three basic components. Schematically, the relationship between the main aspects and the basic components may be illustrated as follows:

(5)

		aspects of linguistic inquiry								
		(4)(a)	(4)(b)	(4)(c)	(4)(d)	(4)(e)	(4)(f)	(4)(g)	(4)(h)	(4)(i)
components of linguistic inquiry	general empirical									
	general linguistic									
	grammatical									

The diagram given in (5) represents the maximal framework within which a study of the main aspects of linguistic inquiry may be made. This diagram will form the framework of our study. However, the grammatical component of linguistic inquiry will be discussed in greater detail than the other two, as it is the most concrete of the three and therefore the natural focal point of an introductory study.

In order to prevent any misunderstanding, let us be quite clear about the content of the expressions "grammatical", "general linguistic" and "linguistic" as they will be used in this study:

(6)   (a)   GRAMMATICAL means 'language-specific', 'language-particular' or 'what is typical of an individual language';

       (b)   GENERAL LINGUISTIC means 'language-independent' or 'what is typical of human language in general';

       (c)   LINGUISTIC means 'both grammatical and general linguistic'.

SELECTED READING

Each of the claims made in this chapter about linguistic inquiry will be discussed more fully in later chapters. References for further reading in connection with these claims are therefore given in the chapters which follow.

CHAPTER THREE

Choosing Aims for Linguistic Inquiry

3.0 PERSPECTIVE

In chapter 3 of our study we shall consider the first main aspect of linguistic inquiry, viz. the choosing of aims to guide the inquiry. The contents of this chapter fall into three parts.

In the first part a characterization is given of the general nature and guiding aim of empirical inquiry in general. Subsequently the aim of this form of inquiry is characterized in terms of an object, abstractions and idealizations, objectives and criteria of adequacy.

In the second part of the chapter we take a look at what is involved in choosing an aim for grammatical inquiry. The four intellectual activities constituting the act of choosing such an aim are discussed. These are: the choosing of an object of inquiry; the selection of problematic aspects of this object for concentrated inquiry; the choosing of objectives to be pursued in the investigation of these problematic aspects; and the choosing of criteria for the knowledge which the grammarian wishes to gain. In the third part of the chapter it is shown that choosing an aim for general linguistic inquiry also comprises these four activities.

3.1 INTRODUCTION

In the introduction to this article "Remarks on nominalization" (p.11), Chomsky makes the following general statements about generative grammar:

(1)   The central task of descriptive linguistics is to construct grammars of specific languages, each of which seeks to characterize in a precise way the competence that has been acquired by a speaker of this language. The theory of grammar attempts to discover the formal conditions that must be satisfied by a system of rules that qualifies as the grammar of a human language, the principles that govern the empirical interpretation of such a system, and the factors that determine the selection of a system of the appropriate form on the basis of the data available to the language learner. Such a "universal grammar" (to modify slightly a

traditional usage) prescribes a schema that defines implicitly the infinite class of "attainable grammars"; it formulates principles that determine how each such system relates sound and meaning; it provides a procedure of evaluation for grammars of the appropriate form.

Chomsky's statements quoted in (1) above in fact represent a veiled, or meta-scientifically non-explicit, formulation of the aims of linguistic inquiry. "The central task of descriptive linguistics" refers to the aim of grammatical inquiry, while the expression "the theory of grammar [i.e. the general linguistic theory − R.P.B.] attempts to discover" refers to the aim of general linguistic inquiry. In (1), therefore, Chomsky in fact indicates a first main aspect of linguistic inquiry, viz. the choosing of aims of inquiry.

Schematically the first main aspect of linguistic inquiry may be represented as follows:

(2)

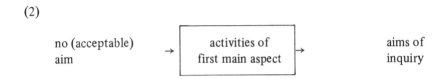

The content of the diagram (2) will be discussed in detail below. Our discussion will be directed by two general questions.

(3) (a)   What is the nature and guiding aim of scientific inquiry?

(b)   What does the activity of choosing aims of inquiry involve?

Note that question (3)(a) concerns the output of the diagram (2), while question (3)(b) concerns the content of this diagram. Initially these questions will be considered with reference to empirical inquiry in general. Subsequently they will be directed, first, at grammatical inquiry and, finally, at general linguistic inquiry.

3.2   INQUIRY IN GENERAL

3.2.1   General Nature and Guiding Aim

Scientific inquiry may assume various forms. Consider, for instance, principal forms such as natural science, mathematical inquiry, philosophical inquiry, historical inquiry, social inquiry and linguistic inquiry. Each of these principal forms of inquiry has several branches or divisions. Natural science, for instance, includes physical inquiry, chemical inquiry, biological inquiry, geological inquiry, astronomical inquiry, etc. In most cases each of these branches has even more specialized subdivisions. But what do all the various forms of scientific inquiry have in common? The answer to this question would reveal the general nature of scientific inquiry.

Firstly, to conduct any of these forms of scientific inquiry is to engage in an INTELLECTUAL ACTIVITY. Scientific inquiry thus has the general nature of a sort of intellectual activity or intellectual enterprise. Conducting certain forms of scientific inquiry also requires physical and verbal activity on the part of the scientist. One has but to think of the setting up of apparatus in experimental inquiry and the conducting of interviews in social inquiry. But even these are essentially a sort of intellectual activity. The planning of experiments, interviews, etc. and the interpretation of the data collected by means of such experiments and interviews are forms of intellectual activity.

Secondly, as a sort of intellectual activity, all these forms of scientific inquiry have a GUIDING AIM. This is the solving of problems. Scientific inquiry is undertaken because scientists find certain phenomena, events, states of affairs, etc. problematic. When a scientist considers something to be problematic it means that he cannot, within the framework of the existing store of knowledge, understand its occurrence, general nature or particular properties.

Thirdly, all the forms of inquiry mentioned above are primarily concerned with gaining KNOWLEDGE: knowledge within the framework of which whatever is problematic will lose its problematic character. The knowledge sought by scientists therefore has a very specific function: that of "deproblematizing" the world. A scientist is sometimes depicted as someone who seeks knowledge for the sake of knowledge itself. This is misleading, as the scientist is always in search of knowledge with which he can do something, viz. solve problems.

Fourthly, none of the above-mentioned forms of scientific inquiry will accept every piece of information as scientific knowledge. Scientific knowledge has certain properties which distinguish it from nonscientific information. Therefore, every form of scientific inquiry adopts certain CRITERIA which a piece of information must satisfy in order to qualify as scientific knowledge. We shall return to a number of these criteria below.

The general nature of scientific inquiry can thus be summarized as follows: SCIENTIFIC INQUIRY is a form of intellectual activity carried out by a scientist in search of a certain type of knowledge in terms of which problems may be solved. This characterization furnishes us with a general answer to the question (3)(a). Note that this characterization emphasizes the fact that scientific inquiry has a clearly defined guiding aim. It will gradually become clear that the nature of certain other main aspects of scientific inquiry are determined by this guiding aim.

3.2.2   Choosing Aims

All forms of scientific inquiry have the solving of problems as a general guiding aim. But one of the respects in which they differ is that they all give different content to this general aim. This is where the question, formulated as (3)(b) above, becomes relevant. What is involved in giving substance to the aim in question? It means that the scientist has to make four choices. Let us consider them individually.

3.2.2.1 *Choosing an Object*

In the first place, giving specific content to the guiding aim of scientific inquiry means choosing a specific OBJECT or DOMAIN OF OBJECTS at which the investigation is to be directed. Natural science, for instance, chooses "nature" as its object or domain of study; biological inquiry chooses "the flora and fauna"; astronomical inquiry chooses "the celestial bodies"; social inquiry chooses "the human society"; psychological inquiry chooses "the human mind"; and linguistic inquiry chooses "human language(s)". So the various forms of inquiry may differ with regard to, among other things, their object of study.

3.2.2.2 *Abstracting and Idealizing*

Forms of inquiry may differ, in the second place, insofar as each one of them singles out one or more different aspects of the chosen object or domain of objects for concentrated investigation. The chosen object of study or domain of objects normally has a variety of problematic aspects. As regards "human language(s)", for instance, the following aspects are problematic: how language originated; how children acquire language; what command of a language involves; why and in what ways language has changed over the centuries; why a language takes on various forms in a given society; how a language is mentally stored by the user; in what form a language is neurologically present in the human brain; and so on. The objects of investigation of nonlinguistic forms of inquiry present a similar variety of problematic aspects.

The practitioner of a particular form of inquiry now selects only one problematic aspect or a few problematic aspects of the object(s) of study on which to concentrate his investigation. In other words, the practitioner of a form of scientific inquiry ABSTRACTS only one or a few of all the problematic aspects of an object of study for concentrated investigation. The remaining problematic aspects are, to a significant extent, ignored within the framework of this form of inquiry. As a result, the object of study is IDEALIZED by the scientist. The object is considered to be problematic in only one respect or, at the most, in a few respects, while the object in fact has many problematic aspects.

It is for a very special reason that the scientist abstracts and idealizes. By doing this he simplifies his inquiry to a considerable extent. Should he try to consider all the problematic aspects of an object simultaneously, he would not make much progress. The constellation of problems with which he would have to deal as a result of such a comprehensive approach would make constructive research impossible. To avoid becoming bogged down the scientist therefore singles out one aspect or a few aspects of the object of inquiry, thereby adopting a policy analogous to the political one of divide and rule.

In many cases, of course, a given problematic aspect of an object can be understood only if a second or third aspect of this object is taken into account as well. The various problematic aspects of one and the same object of inquiry are inevitably mutually related and scientists have to take this fact into consideration. This does not compel them, however, to concentrate on all the problematic aspects of an object simultaneously or to pay equal attention to all these aspects right from the start. Initially they concentrate on one or a few aspects only and then gradually extend their inquiry to the other aspects which will facilitate understanding of the initially selected aspect(s).

As regards "human language(s)" the principle of abstraction is reflected in the fact that various forms of linguistic inquiry exist. For instance: generative grammar abstracts, among other things, the competence aspect of human language; psycholinguistic inquiry abstracts, among other things, the performance aspect; sociolinguistics abstract, among other things, the variety aspect, and so on. Various principal forms of inquiry – and the different branches of one principal form – may therefore also differ insofar as their practitioners single out different problematic aspects of one and the same object of inquiry and concentrate their research on the selected aspect(s).

3.2.2.3   *Choosing Objectives*

In the third place, giving specific content to the guiding aim of scientific inquiry means choosing certain OBJECTIVES which the scientist will pursue in his investigation of the selected aspect(s) of the chosen object(s). These objectives include: collecting and cataloging data about whatever is problematic; giving various kinds of explanations for that which is problematic; making predictions about nonobserved phenomena or events within the domain of study; gaining insight into or understanding of that which is problematic; etc. Various forms of inquiry may differ from one another with regard to, among other things, their choice of objectives of inquiry. A first form of inquiry, for instance, distinguishes itself in that its practitioners select as their primary objective the collecting and cataloging of data about the object(s) of study. This form of inquiry is known as TAXONOMIC or PRESCIENTIFIC inquiry. It is practised by certain biologists, certain ethnologists and, to give one more example, certain linguists. A second form of inquiry distinguishes itself in that its primary objective is that of description. Many historians consider historical inquiry to have this objective of description. A third form of inquiry has explanation as its primary objective. Many branches of natural science typically choose this objective of explanation. The search for insight into that which is problematic is generally accepted as the ULTIMATE OBJECTIVE of scientific inquiry.

3.2.2.4   *Choosing Criteria of Adequacy*

Giving specific content to the guiding aim of scientific inquiry means, in the fourth place, choosing specific CRITERIA for the knowledge which must be gained in terms of the objective(s) of inquiry. These criteria include, for instance: the criterion that the accuracy of the knowledge must be beyond reasonable doubt; the criterion that the knowledge must be systematic; the criterion that the knowledge must be lawlike; the criterion that the knowledge must be communicable; and so on. We shall return to these criteria in §3.3.1.4 below. At this stage it is sufficient to note that the various forms of inquiry may differ from one another with regard to the criteria which they adopt for the knowledge they are seeking. EMPIRICAL INQUIRY, for instance, adopts the following fundamental criterion: it must be possible to check the accuracy of the potential knowledge on the basis of experiential data. The natural sciences and, as we shall see later on, linguistic inquiry are regarded as forms of empirical inquiry. Mathematical inquiry, on the other hand, is a form of nonempirical inquiry as it does not adopt this fundamental criterion for the knowledge it seeks.

In retrospect it is clear that we have been looking at the intellectual activities which combine to constitute the first main aspect of scientific inquiry, viz. choosing aims for scientific inquiry. These activities can briefly be summarized as follows:

(4)   Choosing an aim of inquiry involves
  (a)   choosing one or more objects of inquiry,
  (b)   selecting one or more problematic aspects of the object(s) for concentrated investigation,
  (c)   choosing one or more objectives to be pursued in the investigation of the selected problematic aspect(s),
  (d)   choosing criteria which the knowledge to be gained in the inquiry must satisfy.

This background now enables us to define more accurately the nature of an aim of inquiry. Such an aim comprises one or more objects of inquiry, one or a few selected problematic aspects on which the inquiry will concentrate, one or more objectives of inquiry, and one or more criteria for the knowledge being sought.

3.3   GRAMMATICAL INQUIRY

3.3.1   Components of Aim

Let us consider the aim of grammatical inquiry. In view of what has been said in the preceding paragraph, this means that we have to consider the **object** of grammatical inquiry, its abstractions and idealizations, its objectives, and the criteria it adopts for grammatical knowledge.

3.3.1.1   *Object of Inquiry*

Grammatical inquiry is triggered by the fact that grammarians find certain aspects of people's linguistic performance, or behaviour, problematic. What are these aspects?

There are three fundamental ways in which native speakers of a language can perform linguistically. They can produce utterances, interpret utterances and make intuitive judgments about certain properties of utterances. These utterances and intuitive judgments about them constitute the PRODUCTS OF LINGUISTIC PERFORMANCE. On the one hand, the grammarian is puzzled by the fact that native speakers have the ability to produce and interpret utterances and, moreover, make intuitive judgments about properties of these utterances. How is it at all possible for a native speaker to effect these products of linguistic performance? On the other hand, the grammarian finds the nature and properties of these products of linguistic performance problematic. Why do utterances have certain properties and not others, and why do native speakers make certain intuitive judgments and not others about these utterances?

In order to understand the problematic aspects of linguistic performance and its products, grammarians make the assumption that people have a certain mental capacity which makes linguistic performance possible. This mental capacity is known as LINGUISTIC COMPETENCE and it constitutes the object of investigation of grammatical inquiry. It is on the basis of his linguistic competence that a native speaker of a language is able to produce utterances, to interpret utterances and to make intuitive judgments about the properties of utterances. Examples of such intuitive judgments are given in (8)(a)—(e) in §3.3.1.3 below.

The role that linguistic competence plays in linguistic performance may be schematically represented as follows:

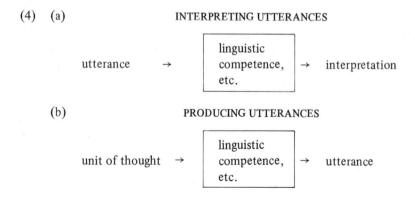

(4)   (a)   INTERPRETING UTTERANCES

            utterance   → | linguistic competence, etc. | →   interpretation

        (b)   PRODUCING UTTERANCES

            unit of thought   → | linguistic competence, etc. | →   utterance

(c)   MAKING INTUITIVE JUDGMENTS

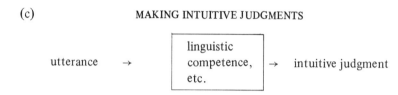

The representation of linguistic performance given in the diagrams of (4) has been simplified in various important respects. Apart from linguistic competence, various other abilities also play a role in linguistic performance. These abilities are represented by "etc." in the diagrams and we shall discuss them in greater detail in §3.3.1.2 below.

By his choice of an object for grammatical inquiry, the generative grammarian creates a complex linguistic reality. This reality is complex in that it comprises two levels: a surface level and an underlying level. Observable acts of linguistic performance and observable products of linguistic performance constitute the surface level. Acts of linguistic performance include the acts of producing and interpreting utterances and that of making intuitive judgments about the acceptability, ambiguity, etc. of utterances. Products of linguistic performance include utterances and intuitive judgments about these utterances.

The underlying level of the grammarian's linguistic reality takes the form of a mental capacity, a linguistic competence, which is unobservable and inaccessible to any form of direct investigation. An example of direct investigation is investigation which is carried out solely by using one or more of the senses. The problematic phenomena which trigger grammatical inquiry exist on the surface level of linguistic performance. The object of grammatical inquiry, however, is to be found on the underlying level of linguistic mental capacities. The linguistic reality of grammatical inquiry may be schematically represented as follows:

(5)   LINGUISTIC REALITY OF GRAMMATICAL INQUIRY

linguistic reality	surface level	linguistic performance and its products 1. directly given 2. observable	source of activating problem- atic phenomena
	underlying level	linguistic competence 1. not directly given 2. unobservable	object of inquiry

The generative grammarian thus assumes a two-levelled linguistic reality, with his object of inquiry existing on the underlying level of human mental capacities. This assumption is of crucial importance in a study of the nature and aspects of linguistic inquiry, as it will determine the content of various other aspects of this form of inquiry.

3.3.1.2   *Abstractions and Idealizations: The Ideal Speaker*

Abstraction and idealization play a fundamental role in the choice of aims for linguistic inquiry. What does this imply with regard to grammatical inquiry? In §3.3.1.1 above we saw that grammatical inquiry is triggered by judgments of grammarians to the effect that certain properties of linguistic performance and, especially, its products are problematic. Linguistic performance and its products are in fact complex phenomena. The nature and characteristics of a particular instance of linguistic performance and its product(s) are, in reality, determined by a combination of factors.

(6)   Some of the factors which influence linguistic performance are:
   (a)   the linguistic competence or unconscious linguistic knowledge of the speaker-hearer,
   (b)   the nature and limitations of the speaker-hearer's speech production and speech perception mechanisms,
   (c)   the nature and limitations of the speaker-hearer's memory, concentration, attention and other mental capacities,
   (d)   the social environment and status of the speaker-hearer,
   (e)   the dialectal environment of the speaker-hearer,
   (f)   the idiolect and individual style of speaking of the speaker-hearer,
   (g)   the speaker-hearer's factual knowledge and view of the world in which he lives,
   (h)   the speaker-hearer's state of health, his emotional state and other similar incidental circumstances.

Each of the factors mentioned in (6) is a variable in linguistic performance and, as such, may influence the nature and characteristics of a particular instance of linguistic performance and its product(s). Thus any of these factors may be responsible for what is problematic in a particular instance of linguistic performance or its product(s). It is therefore clear why the linguist regards linguistic performance and its products as complex phenomena.

In his choice of aims for grammatical inquiry, the grammarian tries to make his investigation more manageable by means of abstraction and idealization. Abstraction entails the following: the grammarian initially restricts his investigation to only one of the factors which influence linguistic performance, viz. the GRAMMATICAL FACTOR of linguistic competence. He therefore abstracts the factor of linguistic competence from the whole gamut of factors which underlie linguistic performance. Initially he tries as far as possible to understand whatever is problematic about linguistic performance and its products in terms of only one variable, viz. linguistic competence. The very choice of linguistic competence as the object of grammatical inquiry therefore already involves making an abstraction.

Initially the grammarian does not take the other, nongrammatical factors

(6)(b)—(h) into account. He therefore idealizes linguistic performance in that he assumes that linguistic performance is the product of linguistic competence alone. Linguistic performance and its products are thereby stripped of their complexity and become simpler phenomena than they in fact are. In terms of this idealization they are the result of only one factor. This, of course, represents an ideal state of affairs. The "etc." in the diagrams (4)(a)–(c) denotes nongrammatical factors such as those of (6)(b)–(h).

The idealization is formulated in terms of the assumption that the object of grammatical inquiry is the linguistic competence, not of an ordinary native speaker, but of an ideal speaker. But what is an ideal speaker? Chomsky gives the following answer to this question in his *Aspects of the theory of syntax* (1965:3).

(7)　An IDEAL SPEAKER-LISTENER
　　(a)　is a member of a completely homogeneous speech-community,
　　(b)　knows its language perfectly, and
　　(c)　is unaffected by such grammatically irrelevant conditions as memory limitations, distractions, shifts of attention and interest, and errors (random or characteristic) in applying his knowledge of the language in actual performance.

The effects of the factor (6)(e) of dialectal variation and the factor (6)(d) of social diversity on linguistic performance are eliminated by (7)(a). Similarly (7)(b) eliminates, among other things, the effect of the factor (6)(f) of idiolectal variation on linguistic performance. A variety of physical, psychological and accidental factors which may influence linguistic performance are eliminated by (7)(c): factors such as (6)(b), (c), (g) and (h). Consequently, the ideal speaker's linguistic performance is the product of his linguistic competence alone. If this were the case, it would be possible to fully understand the problematic aspects of linguistic performance and its products in terms of the nature and characteristics of linguistic competence. By means of this idealization the linguist strips linguistic performance of much of its complexity. As a result it is easier for him to gain significant insights into what is problematic.

In the end, of course, linguistic performance must be understood in its full complexity. Therefore, as the grammarian's understanding of linguistic performance – in terms of the grammatical factor of linguistic competence – grows, he gradually has to do away with his initial idealization. As his inquiry progresses, he has to start taking into account the nongrammatical factors of (6)(b)–(h) as well. It must eventually become clear how these nongrammatical factors interact with the grammatical one in actual linguistic performance. Lately grammarians have been taking a more serious look at the interaction of the various factors involved in linguistic performance. In particular, the interaction of the factors of social diversity and speech perception, on the one hand, with the factor of linguistic competence, on the other hand, has become the subject of serious study.

3.3.1.3   *Objectives of Inquiry*

In the preceding paragraph it was repeatedly stated that the grammarian wants to "understand" what is problematic in linguistic performance. By using an expression such as "understand" in this connection, we are in fact saying something about the objectives of grammatical inquiry. Our discussion of these objectives can be made concrete with reference to the grammatical investigation of nominalization in English.

The grammarian pursues the objectives of grammatical inquiry with reference to the two-levelled linguistic reality of (5) above. The object of grammatical inquiry exists on the underlying level of this reality in the form of a mental capacity, linguistic competence. As a mental capacity, linguistic competence cannot be subjected to direct investigation. That is, the grammarian cannot directly perceive linguistic competence. However, the nature and characteristics of linguistic competence are reflected to a certain extent in the linguistic performance of speaker-hearers. The primary data about linguistic competence are therefore to be found on the surface level of the grammarian's linguistic reality: the level of observable linguistic performance. These PRIMARY LINGUISTIC DATA take the form of products of linguistic performance, i.e. utterances and the intuitive judgments of speaker-hearers about the linguistic properties of these utterances. These intuitive judgments by speaker-hearers are conventionally called LINGUISTIC INTUITIONS.

Native speakers have intuitions about properties of utterances such as (non)-acceptability, (non)ambiguity, difference in meaning, similarity in meaning, etc. The following are five typical examples of linguistic intuitions taken from Chomsky's work (1972b) on nominalization in English.

(8) (a)   The expression *John's eagerness to please* is acceptable.
     (b)   The expression *John's easiness to please* is unacceptable.
     (c)   The expressions *John is easy to please* and *John's being easy to please* have similar meanings.
     (d)   The expressions *John's deeds* and *the things which John did* do not have the same meaning.
     (e)   The expression *John's picture* is ambiguous.

The intuitions given in (8) do not represent all the possible types of intuitions which native speakers may have.

This brings us to the objectives of grammatical inquiry, which are typically those of empirical inquiry: the search for insight into whatever is problematic; the description of the object of inquiry; the explanation of (classes of) problematic phenomena; and the making of predictions about nonobserved phenomena within the domain of inquiry.

The ultimate objective of grammatical inquiry is the gaining of INSIGHT into or UNDERSTANDING of the problematic aspects of individual human languages.

For example, according to McCawley (1973:9–10), the grammatical inquiry into nominalization in English should gain insight into the reasons for the existence or nonexistence of specific derived nominals; the nature of the relationship between derived nominals and their meanings, and the nature of the relationship between the selectional features of sentences and those of the various types of derived nominals. Grammatical inquiry pursues its ultimate objective, the search for insight, in terms of three more immediate objectives: description, explanation and prediction.

The first immediate objective of grammatical inquiry is that of DESCRIBING its object. This object is a mental capacity of the ideal speaker-hearer, viz. his linguistic competence. In grammatical inquiry, therefore, a description has to be given of an unobservable object on the underlying level of the linguistic reality. In technical terms such a description is known as a "generative grammar". We shall consider the metascientific properties of such a grammar in §6.3.2 below. All we need to note at this stage is that the transformationalist and the lexicalist hypotheses about nominalization in English are examples of two fragments of a grammar, or a grammatical description, of English.

The second immediate objective of grammatical inquiry is that of EXPLAIN-ING problematic grammatical phenomena. These problematic phenomena primarily consist of the intuitive judgments of the native speakers of a language about the properties of utterances of their language. The problematic phenomena can therefore be said to take the form of utterances as well as native speakers' linguistic intuitions about these utterances. For instance, according to Chomsky (1972b:19), the grammatical inquiry into nominalization in English should find an explanation for the discrepancies between the properties of derived nominals and those of gerundive nominals. In concrete terms, this entails, for example, that an explanation must be given for the native speaker's intuitive judgment that, whereas the derived nominals of (9) are unacceptable, those of (10) are acceptable.

(9) (a) *John's easiness (difficulty) to please
    (b) *John's certainty (likelihood) to win the prize
    (c) *John's amusement (interest) of the children with his stories

(10)(a) John's eagerness to please
    (b) John's certainty that Bill will win the prize
    (c) John's amusement at (interest in) the children's antics

In explaining the problematic properties of these utterances, the grammarian is giving explanations for phenomena on the directly given level of his linguistic real-ity. This point may be formulated more precisely: grammatical explanations are explanations not of the problematic properties of individual utterances, but of the problematic properties of classes of utterances. A CLASS OF UTTERANCES includes all those utterances which, intuitively, are repetitions of one another.

Thus, the grammarian is not interested in explaining, for instance, the unacceptability of the individual, specific utterance (9)(a) *John's easiness to please*, but rather in explaining the fact that the speaker-hearer intuitively finds this utterance, as well as all its repetitions, unacceptable. Utterances which are repetitions of one another realize one and the same SENTENCE of the language. This is why grammatical explanations are generally said to be explanations of the problematic characteristics of sentences. From now on the expressions "sentence" and "class of utterances (which are repetitions of one another)" will be used as synonyms.

The third immediate objective of grammatical inquiry is that of PREDICTING properties that nonobserved phenomena within the domain of inquiry must have. McCawley (1973:9) for instance, makes it quite clear that a grammatical inquiry into nominalization in English must not only make it possible to assign lexical entries to existing, i.e. acceptable, nominals. It must also provide a basis on which correct predictions may be made about the nonexistence, i.e. nonacceptability, of particular derived nominals. This means, on the one hand, that it must be possible to specify in which cases the nonexistence of certain derived nominals may be ascribed to accidental reasons. On the other hand, this means that it must be possible to specify in which cases their nonexistence may be ascribed to systematic reasons. These predictions are essentially concerned with the (non)acceptability of classes of utterances, i.e. classes of which the members are repetitions of one another. Thus, predictions are made about the linguistic intuitions of speaker-hearers. Generally speaking, the predictions of grammatical inquiry are predictions about the properties of classes of products of linguistic performance on the directly given level of the grammarian's linguistic reality.

To summarize:

(12)   GRAMMATICAL INQUIRY has
    (a)   the search for insight into or understanding of the problematic aspects of individual human languages, as its ultimate objective;
    (b)   the giving of descriptions of the linguistic competence of the ideal speaker, as a first immediate objective;
    (c)   the giving of explanations of the properties of sentences, as these are reflected by native speakers' linguistic intuitions about classes of utterances, as a second immediate objective;
    (d)   the making of predictions about the properties of sentences which have not yet been subjected to investigation, as a third immediate objective.

These objectives of grammatical inquiry are normally not formulated in such explicit metascientific terms as those of (12)(a)–(d). Their formulation is often opaque from a metascientific point of view. Compare, for instance, Chomsky's formulation in (1) above and the one given in (13) below:

(13)   Grammatical inquiry wants to determine

"(1)   the structure of particular sentences,
(2)   the grammar that characterizes all such structures for a particular language."

There is no essential difference between the content of this formulation –
recently given by Chomsky in his article "Questions of form and interpretation"
(1975d:172) – and that of the formulation given in (12). It is only from a metascientific point of view that the content of (12) is more explicit and determinate
than that of (13).

We have, so far, done little more than indicate the objectives of grammatical
inquiry. These objectives give rise to a variety of questions which have not yet
been discussed. For instance, why does grammatical inquiry choose these and not
other objectives?; how are the chosen objectives interrelated?; and how are these
objectives pursued? To be able to answer these questions, the various major
aspects of grammatical inquiry have to be studied in detail. This we will do in
the subsequent chapters of our study.

Let it suffice at this stage to point out that the grammarian pursues the
objectives of his inquiry by constructing a grammar for the language he is
studying. A GRAMMAR gives a description of the linguistic competence of the
ideal speaker. On the basis of this description it then gives the explanations and
makes the predictions which we considered above. As a description, a grammar
consists of a finite number of perfectly explicit rules which enumerate all and
only the grammatical sentences of the language, assigning to each one a proper
structural description. A completely explicit grammar is called a GENERATIVE
GRAMMAR. Such a grammar GENERATES the sentences of a language along
with their structural descriptions.

3.3.1.4   *Criteria for Grammatical Knowledge*

Let us call the scientific knowledge gained about individual human languages
GRAMMATICAL KNOWLEDGE. As a form of empirical inquiry, grammatical
inquiry does not accept any random piece of information as a fragment of
scientific knowledge. The grammatical knowledge which grammarians are after
must satisfy certain criteria. We shall briefly consider six of these criteria, which
are the same as those adopted by empirical inquiry for scientific knowledge in
general.

A first, primary criterion for grammatical knowledge is that its correctness
must be TESTABLE. Consider the following statements about nominalization in
English:

(14)(a)   The relationship between a sentence and a corresponding nominal
is a lexical relationship.
(b)   Derived nominals are not transforms.

(c)   In the lexical entry for "refuse", it must not be specified whether "refuse" is a verb or a noun.

The information contained in (14)(a)–(c) cannot be regarded as grammatical knowledge if it should prove to be impossible to test its correctness. There is no room for untestable speculations within the corpus of grammatical knowledge about a particular language. Generative linguists regard grammatical inquiry as a form of empirical inquiry for the very reason that it adopts the criterion of testability.

A second criterion for grammatical knowledge is closely related to the first. In order to qualify as grammatical knowledge, a given piece of information must not only be testable, but it must be clear from the testing of the information, that it is indeed WELL-GROUNDED or JUSTIFIED. The second criterion for grammatical knowledge is therefore that it should be well-grounded, or justified. Before the information contained in the statements (14)(a)–(c) can be accepted as fragments of grammatical knowledge about English, it must be shown that there are sound reasons why it should be regarded as probably correct. Should the information prove to be incorrect, it cannot be accepted as grammatical knowledge.

A third criterion for grammatical knowledge is that it should have an INTER-SUBJECTIVE CHARACTER. In terms of this criterion, a piece of information about a particular human language cannot be regarded as a fragment of grammatical knowledge if its correctness cannot be checked by *any* skilled grammarian. In other words, grammatical knowledge must be common property within the community of skilled grammarians. This presupposes that grammatical knowledge is communicable. A fragment of grammatical knowledge which exists only in the mind of an individual linguist is by nature subjective and cannot be included in the corpus of grammatical knowledge. If it were impossible for skilled grammarians to test the grammatical information contained in Chomsky's statements (14), this information would not be admitted to the corpus of grammatical knowledge – even if Chomsky were convinced in his own mind of its correctness.

A fourth criterion for grammatical knowledge is that it must be SYSTEMATIC. This means that a collection of unrelated, isolated fragments of grammatical information about a language do not have the status of grammatical knowledge about this language. Within the corpus of grammatical knowledge, the various units expressing fragments of knowledge – units such as those of (14)(a)–(c) above – must be systematically interrelated in terms of clearly discernible relationships. There are various reasons why grammatical knowledge should be systematic. Only two will be mentioned here. First, if grammatical knowledge forms an integrated system, gaps in this knowledge can be spotted more easily. Grammarians are constantly striving to gain knowledge which is as exhaustive as possible. Secondly, if grammatical knowledge forms an integrated system, it is easier to spot internal contradictions. Two or more pieces of information which are mutually contradictory cannot be part of the same system of grammatical knowledge.

The four criteria discussed above are interrelated in a specific way. Jointly they must ensure that the knowledge gained by grammatical inquiry is RELIABLE. In the last instance, the knowledge which scientists seek must be reliable. The search for knowledge which is reliable is expressed in these four complementary criteria.

A fifth criterion for grammatical knowledge is that it must, as far as possible, be GENERAL. In terms of this criterion, grammatical knowledge must, as far as possible, take the form of general principles or generalizations. It is not in the first instance the aim of grammatical inquiry to record individual grammatical phenomena in their unique, isolated form. The grammarian is primarily interested in stating the relationships which exist between classes of grammatical phenomena. In other words, grammarians try to establish what the underlying general principles are that relate seemingly unrelated individual phenomena. In (14)(a) and (b) above two typical grammatical generalizations are expressed. But if we look at (14)(c), we see that not all fragments of grammatical knowledge can be expressed in the form of a generalization. Information about unique, idiosyncratic aspects of human languages — such as the distinguishing properties of individual lexical items — especially, cannot be expressed in a general form. This is why we say that grammatical knowledge must be general *as far as possible*.

A sixth criterion for grammatical knowledge is that the generalizations in terms of which it is expressed must, as far as possible, be LAWLIKE. This criterion — to which we will return in §7.3.2.2.2.1 — stipulates that the generalizations concerned must specify what the properties of and the interrelationship between linguistic units must be. In other words, these generalizations must not express purely accidental correlations between classes of linguistic phenomena. A generalization must be lawlike in the sense of not being a mere summary of the properties of a limited number of studied utterances. To emphasize the lawlike character of the generalization (14)(b), it may be reformulated as follows: "If a linguistic unit is a derived nominal it cannot be a transform".

These six criteria for grammatical knowledge determine the nature and content of further aspects of grammatical inquiry. In our discussion of the other aspects, we shall therefore return to these criteria.

3.3.2   Choosing a Grammatical Aim

This brings us to the intellectual activities by which the generative grammarian conceives the aim of grammatical inquiry. These activities are analogous to those in terms of which scientists in general construct such aims. In §3.2.2 these activities were discussed in detail and at this stage we may merely point out that they include: choosing an object of inquiry, making abstractions and idealizations, choosing objectives to be pursued, and choosing criteria of adequacy.

3.4   GENERAL LINGUISTIC INQUIRY

3.4.1   Components of Aim

We come now to the components of the aim of general linguistic inquiry.

3.4.1.1   *Object of Inquiry*

General linguistic inquiry is undertaken because the generative grammarian finds certain aspects of language acquisition problematic. The expression "language acquisition" denotes the process by which a child gains command of a language as his mother tongue. Language acquisition therefore involves the construction by a child of the mental capacity which we identified as linguistic competence in §3.3.1.1.

But what are the problematic aspects of language acquisition which trigger general linguistic inquiry? In the first place, the nature of the process of language acquisition is problematic. Generative grammarians are particularly concerned with the following problematic aspects of this process: (a) of all the animals, only man has the ability to acquire linguistic competence; (b) a child can acquire any language with which he is in contact as his native language; (c) all normal children start acquiring language at more or less the same age, proceed at more or less the same pace, and complete the process of language acquisition within more or less the same period of time; (d) a child acquires his native language without making any systematic, conscious effort to learn it; (e) systematic instruction has little or no effect on the success of the process of language acquisition; (f) a child acquires his native language despite the considerable difference in quality between what he is acquiring – an abstract, complex mental capacity – and the available data on the basis of which he apparently has to construct this capacity, i.e., concrete utterances. In the second place, the linguist finds the properties of the products of language acquisition problematic. In other words, he finds it problematic that acquired linguistic competences or languages have the properties which they have.

In order to understand the problematic aspects of the process of language acquisition and its products, the generative grammarian assumes that human beings possess a certain mental capacity: a LANGUAGE ACQUISITION FACULTY, or LANGUAGE FACULTY for short. Man's language faculty is the mental capacity which enables him to acquire a language as his native tongue on the basis of his contact with a limited number of utterances of that language. Schematically this point may be illustrated as follows:

(15)   LANGUAGE ACQUISITION

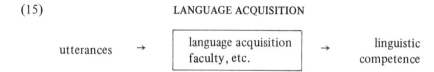

In addition to the language acquisition faculty, various other factors are also active in the process of language acquisition. These factors are represented by "etc." in the diagram (15). We will return to a few of these factors in §3.4.1.2 below.

What is important at this stage, is that the object of general linguistic inquiry is a mental capacity as well, viz. man's language acquisition faculty. The generative grammarian assumes that man innately possesses whatever is "common to" or "universal in" all possible human languages. Man's language acquisition faculty — as a species-specific, biologically-based mental capacity — is therefore realized in the universal, language-independent aspect of his linguistic competence.

As far as the generative grammarian's choice of an object for general linguistic inquiry is concerned, it is important to note that this type of inquiry also postulates a two-levelled linguistic reality. The surface level comprises aspects of the process of language acquisition and its products. By contrast, man's language acquisition faculty as an abstract mental capacity exists on an underlying level of this two-levelled reality and is, by its very nature, unobservable. It will be difficult to show that the process of language acquisition can be directly perceived. The six problematic aspects of this process which we pointed out earlier may, however, be discerned with relative ease. It requires no taxing mental effort to establish that the process of language acquisition has these problematic aspects. Thus the generative linguist regards these aspects of the process of language acquisition as "easily discernible". The problematic aspects of individual linguistic competences or languages are similarly relatively "easily discernible" in that they are described in the grammars of these languages. Schematically, the linguistic reality of general linguistic inquiry may be represented as follows:

(16)   LINGUISTIC REALITY OF GENERAL LINGUISTIC INQUIRY

linguistic reality	surface level	aspects of the process of language acquisition and its products 1. directly given 2. "easily discernible"	source of activating problematic aspects
	underlying level	language acquisition faculty 1. not directly given 2. unobservable	object of inquiry

It will gradually become clear that the generative grammarian's postulation of a two-levelled linguistic reality (16) has far-reaching implications for further aspects of general linguistic inquiry. Finally, as expected, the two-levelled linguistic reality (16) of general linguistic inquiry and the two-levelled linguistic reality (5) of grammatical inquiry are components of one larger, integrated linguistic reality. The nature of the interrelatedness of these two components within this integrated linguistic reality will be the topic of § 12.1.2.

3.4.1.2   *Abstractions and Idealizations: Instantaneous Language Acquisition*

Abstraction and idealization play a role in the choice of aims for general linguistic inquiry as well. Language acquisition, like linguistic performance, is quite complex in that it involves the interaction of a variety of factors. The child's language acquisition faculty is but one of the factors, or variables, in the process of language acquisition. Another important factor is the child's increasing linguistic experience. By LINGUISTIC EXPERIENCE is meant the child's contact with the utterances of a language.

The child does not acquire his ultimate linguistic competence in one single step as a result of his contact with one limited corpus of utterances of a language. In acquiring a language, the child constructs successive approximate versions of his ultimate linguistic competence on the basis of his linguistic experience, and with the aid of his language acquisition faculty. The child's earliest approximations of this linguistic competence are grossly oversimplified, but as the child gains more linguistic experience, he replaces these inadequate approximations with increasingly more adequate approximations of his ultimate linguistic competence. Language acquisition is in fact a gradual process in which the child's increasing linguistic experience plays an important role. How exactly linguistic experience contributes to language acquisition is not yet very well understood. In a recent article "A theory of core grammar" (1978:8), Chomsky attempts to minimize this contribution by postulating that language acquisition is a process of growth rather than a process of learning. It is easier to understand the six problematic properties of the process of language acquisition – mentioned earlier in this paragraph – in terms of a process of growth rather than of learning. Chomsky (1978:8), puts the matter as follows:

We should rather think of it [i.e. language acquisition – R.P.B.] as analogous to biological growth and maturation. In short, when a person knows a language, he knows vastly more than experience warrants, which indicates that the contribution of the innate endowment [i.e. the language acquisition faculty – R.P.B.] must be of overwhelming importance, much as in the case of the physical growth of the body.

As a gradual process, language acquisition is too complex a phenomenon to be subjected to systematic inquiry. The generative grammarian therefore tackles his inquiry by assuming that the language acquisition faculty is the only factor that plays a role in this process. From the constellation of factors which are jointly responsible for language acquisition, he abstracts the language acquisition faculty for the purpose of meaningful investigation. An important factor which, initially, is not taken into account is that of linguistic experience. The linguist therefore idealizes language acquisition by regarding it as an instantaneous process. In so doing he gives a drastically simplified, idealized representation of the process of language acquisition. This idealized representation implies that language acquisition occurs instantaneously as the child applies his language acquisition faculty to a single corpus of data about a language. The linguist will of course eventually have to abandon this idealization of instantaneous language acquisition and attempt to understand language acquisition as the product of an interaction between the language acquisition faculty and, among others, the factor of linguistic experience.

Note that this idealization also creates an ideal individual, viz. an IDEAL LANGUAGE LEARNER who is capable of instantaneous language acquisition. An ordinary, nonideal language learner is by nature incapable of instantaneous language acquisition. The status of the ideal language learner will be discussed in §6.4.2.3. The function of the idealization of an ideal speaker and instantaneous language acquisition in linguistic inquiry is the same as that of idealizations such as ideal gases, frictionless engines, completely rigid rods and perfectly elastic bodies in natural science. These ideal objects are created to enhance the possibility of gaining insight into complex actual objects. Idealizations therefore succeed insofar as they further the search for insight. Ill-chosen idealizations may seriously hamper or even completely block this search, a fact of which Chomsky (1975d:171) is well aware:

> Idealizations and abstraction are unavoidable in serious inquiry, but particular idealizations may be questioned, and must be justified on empirical grounds.

3.4.1.3   *Objectives of Inquiry*

The objectives of general linguistic inquiry, like those of grammatical inquiry, are typical of those of empirical inquiry: the search for insight via description, explanation and prediction. For a few generative grammarians, general linguistic inquiry has an additional objective, viz. postdiction. Let us consider these objectives individually.

The ultimate objective of general linguistic inquiry is to gain INSIGHT into, or UNDERSTANDING of, what is problematic about human language in general. General linguistic inquiry seeks this insight, or understanding, by determining the universal properties of human languages. It is with these universal properties, or LINGUISTIC UNIVERSALS, that human beings are innately endowed in the form of the language acquisition faculty. In attempting to determine these linguistic universals, linguists try to determine what a possible human language is and how a possible human language differs from something which is not a possible human language. Linguists pursue this ultimate objective by way of a number of more immediate objectives, viz. description, explanation, prediction and postdiction.

A first more immediate objective of general linguistic inquiry is to give a DESCRIPTION of its object. As this object is man's language acquisition faculty, a description is therefore given of a mental capacity on the underlying level of the general linguist's linguistic reality. Such a description is given in terms of linguistic universals. In (17) we have a typical component of such a description.

(17)   The grammars of all human languages are organized in terms of a syntactic, a phonological and a semantic component.

Another typical example of a component of a general linguistic description comes from Chomsky's inquiry into nominalization in English. Recall that in this inquiry he reaches the conclusion that lexical items such as "refuse" must have neutral lexical entries. This conclusion implicitly contains the following statement about human language in general:

(18)   The lexical aspect of human language in general is organized in terms of, among others, neutral lexical entries.

A second more immediate objective of general linguistic inquiry is the giving of EXPLANATIONS. At a general level this implies the explanation of problematic aspects of the process of language acquisition. At a more specific level it implies the explanation of problematic aspects of that which is acquired, viz. individual human languages. First of all, let us consider the objective of explanation at the specific level of the problematic aspects of individual human languages.

In §1.3 an outline was given of Chomsky's lexicalist grammar of nominalization in English. According to this grammar, English does not have a nominalization transformation or transformations for derived nominals. The question is whether the absence of such a transformation for generating derived nominals in English is accidental or not.

(19)   Why does the grammar of English fail to include a nominalization transformation for derived nominals?

To answer this question (19), is to give a general linguistic explanation of a problematic aspect of an individual human language. A possible answer to this question – and therefore an example of a general linguistic explanation – is given in §7.4.3.

This brings us to the more general level at which general linguistic inquiry attempts to give explanations, viz. that of problematic aspects of the process of language acquisition. Six of these problematic aspects were mentioned in §3.4.4.1. Consider, for instance, the sixth aspect as represented by the question (20).

(20)   How is it possible for a child to acquire an abstract, complex linguistic competence as the result of contact with a limited number of concrete utterances?

An answer to this question would in fact represent a general linguistic explanation of this particular problematic aspect of the process of language acquisition.

A third more immediate objective of general linguistic inquiry is the PREDICTION of the essential properties of individual languages which have not yet been subjected to inquiry. This objective is related to that of describing man's language acquisition faculty. We have seen that such a description entails the specification of which systems are possible human languages, and which systems are not. Giving such a specification involves the making of predictions. The generative grammarian has knowledge of a limited number of languages only. These languages he can describe in terms of universals. But insofar as these universals also apply to languages which were not investigated individually, the generative grammarian is in fact making predictions. The linguistic universals given in (17) and (18) above form the basis for predictions about the essential properties of individual languages which have not yet been subjected to investigation. Such predictions constitute an essential part of the generative grammarian's characterization of a possible human language.

A fourth, and more immediate, objective of general linguistic inquiry – for an increasing number of generative grammarians – is the making of POST-DICTIONS. Postdictions are "predictions" about phenomena, events, states of affairs, and so on in a past reality. Those linguists who pursue the objective of postdiction consider language changes to fall within the domain of study of general linguistics. They regard it as one of the tasks of general linguistic inquiry to determine what are possible changes in human language and what are not. We shall see later on that determining linguistic universals, and establishing what is a possible language change, are closely related.

To summarize:

(21)   GENERAL LINGUISTIC INQUIRY has
   (a)   the gaining of insight into, or understanding of, what is problematic about human language in general, as its ultimate objective;
   (b)   the giving of a description of man's language acquisition faculty, as a first more immediate objective;
   (c)   the giving of explanations for problematic aspects of the process of language acquisition on the one hand and, on the other hand, problematic aspects of individual human languages, as a second more immediate objective;
   (d)   the making of predictions about the essential properties of non-

investigated individual human languages, as a third more immediate objective;

(e)   the making of postdictions about possible language changes in
the history of human language, as a fourth more immediate
objective.

Generative grammarians generally do not formulate the objectives of general
linguistic inquiry in such explicit metascientific terms as we have done in (21)
above. They often resort to a synoptic formulation such as that of (1) in §3.1
and (22) below.

(22)   General linguistic inquiry wants to determine "the explanatory
principles of universal grammar that characterize the class of possible
grammars and in this way contribute to an account of how knowledge
of language can be acquired".

The formulation of (22) is a recent one given by Chomsky in his article
"Questions of form and interpretation" (1975d:172). It is in fact a "technical"
summary of the objectives of general linguistic inquiry specified in (21). As
regards the objectives of (21), we shall discuss the reasons for choosing them, the
various ways in which they are interrelated and what is involved in pursuing
them, further on in our study.

At this point, it is sufficient to note that the generative grammarian pursues
the objectives of general linguistic inquiry by constructing a GENERAL LIN-
GUISTIC THEORY. Such a theory describes man's language acquisition faculty
and forms the basis of the explanations, predictions and postdictions which we
considered above. The main components of a general linguistic theory take the
form of linguistic universals.

3.4.1.4   *Criteria for General Linguistic Knowledge*

The knowledge about human language in general which linguists seek may be
called GENERAL LINGUISTIC KNOWLEDGE. In order to qualify as a fragment
of general linguistic knowledge, a piece of information about language in
general must satisfy essentially the same criteria as have been adopted for
grammatical knowledge. In other words, general linguistic inquiry adopts the
criterion that the knowledge it seeks must be (a) testable, (b) grounded or
justified, (c) intersubjective, (d) systematic, (e) general and (f) lawlike.

The content of these criteria were explicated in §3.3.1.4 above and will not
be repeated here. Only one additional point should be made in connection with
these criteria: in terms of the criterion of testability, general linguistic inquiry
is regarded as a form of empirical inquiry.

3.4.2　Choosing a General Linguistic Aim

The intellectual activities performed by the linguist in choosing an aim for general linguistic inquiry are analogous to those involved in choosing an aim for grammatical inquiry. In other words, the choosing of an aim for general linguistic inquiry involves choosing an object of inquiry, selecting, or abstracting, aspects of this object for concentrated investigation, thereby creating a certain idealization, choosing objectives of inquiry and choosing criteria for the knowledge which is being sought.

3.5　RETROSPECT

In (23) a schematic survey is given for the preceding discussion of the aims of linguistic inquiry.

(23)　　　AIMS OF LINGUISTIC INQUIRY

	grammatical inquiry	general linguistic inquiry
object of inquiry	mental object: linguistic competence	mental object: language acquisition faculty
idealiza- tion	ideal speaker	instantaneous language acquisition
objectives of inquiry	gaining of insight into individual human languages VIA 1. description of linguistic competence 2. explanation of problematic properties of classes of products of linguistic performance (= sentences) 3. prediction of properties of classes of non-investigated products of linguistic performance (= sentences)	gaining of insight into language in general VIA 1. description of language acquisition faculty 2. explanation of problematic aspects of language acquisition and individual languages 3. prediction of essential properties of non-investigated languages 4. postdiction of possible language changes

	1. criterion of testability	1. criterion of testability
criteria for knowledge	2. criterion of groundedness 3. criterion of generality 4. criterion of lawlikeness 5. criterion of systematicity 6. criterion of intersubjectiveness	2. criterion of groundedness 3. criterion of generality 4. criterion of lawlikeness 5. criterion of systematicity 6. criterion of intersubjectiveness

From this scheme it is clear that, as far as the choice of aims is concerned, grammatical and general linguistic inquiry represent one and the same intellectual enterprise. Both adopt a two-levelled linguistic reality with the object of inquiry, a mental object, on the underlying level; both make certain abstractions and idealizations in their choice of aims; both pursue the fundamental objectives of empirical inquiry; and both accept the fundamental criteria for scientific knowledge adopted by empirical inquiry in general.

But the scheme also clearly shows the differences between grammatical and general linguistic inquiry, especially as regards their choice of a specific object of inquiry: linguistic competence versus the language acquisition faculty. As we progress, it will become increasingly clear how grammatical and general linguistic inquiry are integrated within the framework of generative grammar.

Finally, let us briefly look at the sense of the expression "science" as it is used, for instance, in the term "linguistic science". The expression "science" has more than one sense. Two of its more general senses are illustrated in (24)(a) and (b).

(24)(a)   "Smith practises (linguistic) science."
   (b)   "Smith derives the idea from (linguistic) science."

In (24)(a) the expression "science" is used to denote a process or an enterprise. In this context it is synonymous with "scientific inquiry" and denotes an ordered collection of activities. In (24)(b) the expression "science" denotes a result. In this context it is synonymous with "the products or results of scientific inquiry" and denotes an ordered corpus of knowledge.

SELECTED READING

Nature of Science/Scientific Inquiry

   Bocheński 1965:10–12; Kaplan 1964:7, Northrop 1966:ch.1–4.

Nature of and Criteria for Scientific Knowledge

   Bocheński 1965:3–5; Bunge 1967a:3–6; Caws 1966:ch.2; Harré 1972:ch.3;

Nagel 1961:ch.1; 1967:4–8; Woozley 1967:183–184.

Abstraction and Idealization in Scientific Inquiry

Benjamin 1965:103–106; Hanson 1971:1–8; Kaplan 1964:82–83; Rudner 1966:54–63.

Objectives of Scientific Inquiry

Insight/Understanding

Hanson 1971:44–45; Kyburg 1968:3, 5; Toulmin 1961:ch.2.

Description

Feigl 1965:477; Harré 1979:48ff.; Popper 1969:103–104; Theobald 1968:ch.3.

Postdiction

Hempel 1965:173–174; Hempel and Oppenheim 1953:322–323; Kaplan 1964: 349.

Problem-solving

Bunge 1967a:165–168; Kuln 1967:ch.4; Northrop 1966:ch.1; Popper 1969:ch.2.

Explanation

Caws 1966:91; Hanson 1971:39–45; Harré 1967:25–26; Hempel 1965:173; Kyburg 1968:3–5; Nagel 1961:4; 1967:13; Popper 1969:103ff.

Prediction

Caws 1966:91; Hanson 1971:45–46; Harré 1967:78ff.; 107–108; Hempel 1965: 173; Toulmin 1961:ch.2.

General Discussions of Aims of Generative Grammar

Chomsky

1957:ch.6; 1962a; 1964:ch.1, 2; 1965:ch.1; 1966:ch.1; 1967:397–408; 1968:ch.2; 1972b:11–12; 1972c:62–68; 1972d:125–129; 1974.

Others

Bach 1965; 1974a:ch.1, 10; Botha 1968: §§2.1.–2.4.; 1971: §2.2.5.1.; Fodor, Bever and Garrett 1974:ch.3; Lyons 1970:ch.4; Lakoff 1974a; Lees 1957; Maclay 1971; McCawley 1974; Postal 1966; Ruwet 1973:ch.1, Appendix II.; Searle 1974; Steinberg 1975.

Grammatical Inquiry

Abstraction and Idealization

Chomsky 1965: §1.; 1968:23–24; 1975d:171–172, 194, 1976:3–4; 1978:8–9; Derwing 1973: §7.4.

Criterion of Empirical Testing

Bach 1964: §8.4.; 1974a: §1.4.; Botha 1968: §3.2.3.4.; Chomsky 1962c:161; 1965:18–24; 1972b:13; 1975b:37; Chomsky and Halle 1965:104–106; Lees 1957:376.

Object of Inquiry

Chomsky 1957:56; 1965:3–9; 1967a:397–399; 1968:23–24; 1976:2–3, 13; 1978:7–8; Derwing 1973:ch.8; Ruwet 1973:4–7, 27–28; Steinberg 1975.

Objectives of Inquiry

Insight/Understanding

Bach 1974a: §1.2.; Chomsky 1965:20; 1968:ch.1.

Description

Botha 1971: §4.1., 4.2., 5.1.1.; Chomsky 1966:23n; 1968:24; Katz 1964; Kiparsky 1968a:171.

Explanation

Botha 1968: §3.2.3.3.; Chomsky 1962a; 1962b:158; 1968:23ff.; 1970; 1975b:11.

Prediction

Bach 1964:5–6, 176, 186; Chomsky 1957:49; 1962b:158; Lees 1957:380.

General Linguistic Inquiry

Abstraction and Idealization

Chomsky 1975c:119, 147; 1976: 3–4; 1978:7; Chomsky and Halle 1968:331–332; Derwing 1973:80–82.

Criterion of Empirical Testing

Bach 1974a;5–18; Botha 1971:176–177; Chomsky 1957:56; 1964:97–99; 1965: 53–56; 1972b:13; 1975b:11, 13–14, 38–39; Chomsky and Halle 1965:104–106; 1968:ix.

Object of Inquiry

Chomsky 1964:25–27; 1965:47–59; 1966:20–22; 1968:23–24; 1975b:9, 37; 1976:2–3, 13; 1978:7.

Objectives of Inquiry

Insight/Understanding

Bach 1974a: §1.2.; Chomsky 1965:20; 1968;ch.1.

Description

Bach 1974a:ch.11; Chomsky 1965:27–30, 35–38; 1967:400–408; Chomsky and Halle 1965:100; Fodor, Bever and Garrett 1974:139–140.

Postdiction

King 1969: §4.6.; Kiparsky 1968a.

Explanation

Bach 1974a:251–252; Chomsky 1968:23–24; 1975b:9, 11,37. See also "Explanatory adequacy" on p. 238.

CHAPTER FOUR

Formulating Linguistic Problems

4.0 PERSPECTIVE

In chapter 4 we shall consider the main aspect of linguistic inquiry which may be described as "the formulating of problems". The chapter is divided into three parts. In the first part a distinction is drawn, on a general level, between a problematic state of affairs on the one hand and a problem on the other hand. The formulating of problems is subsequently discussed with reference to this distinction.

The second part of this chapter is concerned with the problems of grammatical inquiry. First of all, a distinction is drawn between various fundamental forms and types of grammatical problems. The emphasis in this part, however, is on the various activities involved in the formulating of grammatical problems. Most important among these are the analysis of a problematic state of affairs, the description of the problematic state of affairs, the construction of problems and the evaluation of problems. The discussion of the analysis of a problematic state of affairs provides the basis for a characterization of the structure of such a state of affairs. Special attention is furthermore given to the status and characteristics that so-called pretheoretical grammatical descriptions have within the context of the formulation of grammatical problems. It is shown that giving such a description involves collecting, systematizing and symbolizing linguistic data. In clarifying these activities a more precise characterization of (primary) linguistic data is given. This characterization involves the drawing of a distinction between genuine and spurious linguistic intuitions.

The third part of the chapter firstly gives a general description of the nature of general linguistic problems. This is followed by a brief survey of the characteristics of the various types of problems which may be encountered in general linguistic inquiry.

4.1 INTRODUCTION

Consider the following three questions about nominalization in English:

(1) (a)   How should a grammar of English specify the fact that the express-

ions *John's deeds* and *the things which John did* are synonymous?

(b)   How should a grammar of English express the stylistic differences between derived and gerundive nominals?

(c)   How should a grammar of English specify the fact that gerundive nominals are logically more transparent than derived nominals?

(1)(a)–(c) are indeed questions about nominalization in English. And yet generative grammarians will not even try to find an answer to any of them. For, within the framework of linguistic inquiry, (1)(a)–(c) are not well-formed grammatical problems.

As a grammatical problem, (1)(a) is ill-formed because it is based on the incorrect judgment that the expressions *John's deeds* and *the things which John did* are synonymous. The ill-formedness of (1)(b) is the result of an incorrect general linguistic assumption, viz. that grammars must account for the stylistic properties of linguistic units. Within the framework of generative grammar, stylistic variation is not regarded as being part of the structure of human languages. The ill-formedness of (1)(c) may be attributed to its formulation in terms of the obscure, incomprehensible expression "logically more transparent". It is not at all clear exactly what it is that question (1)(c) singles out as being problematic.

In short, not every question about a human language represents a well-formed grammatical problem in generative grammar. Being exclusively concerned with the solving of well-formed grammatical problems, linguistic inquiry therefore has an aspect which involves the formulating of well-formed linguistic problems. These well-formed linguistic problems include problems concerning language in general and problems concerning individual human languages.

Schematically this aspect of linguistic inquiry may be represented as follows:

(2)

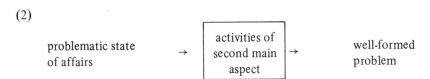

We shall consider three general questions in connection with this scheme.

(3) (a)   What is the general nature of problematic states of affairs?

    (b)   What is the general nature of well-formed problems?

    (c)   What are the activities involved in formulating whatever it is that is problematic as well-formed problems?

First of all, let us consider these questions from the point of view of empirical inquiry in general.

4.2   INQUIRY IN GENERAL

4.2.1   Nature of Problematic States of Affairs and Problems

The questions (3)(a) and (b) cannot be answered separately. A PROBLEMATIC STATE OF AFFAIRS represents something in reality which scientists do not understand. A state of affairs is problematic because there is a gap in the existing knowledge. This means that the fragment of knowledge, in terms of which the state of affairs could have been understood, is missing. A PROBLEM specifies what it is that is needed in order to resolve the problematic state of affairs. In other words, a problem makes clear what the scientist has to look for to fill the gap in the existing knowledge. The solution to the problem takes the form of a fragment of new knowledge. If the knowledge in question is scientific, the problem is a SCIENTIFIC PROBLEM.

A problem may be regarded from a logical, psychological and linguistic point of view. From each of these points of view, a different aspect of the problem is seen. From the logical point of view, the problem is interesting on account of its "anatomy". A problem is an entity consisting of mutually related concepts or units of thought. From the psychological point of view, the problem is interesting on account of the way in which it originates. A problem originates in the mind of a scientist when there is something which he finds he does not understand. From the linguistic point of view, the problem is interesting on account of its external form. Problems generally have the overt, i.e. linguistic, form of an interrogative or an imperative sentence. We shall be concentrating on the logical aspect of linguistic problems below.

4.2.2   Formulating Problems

This brings us to question (3)(c) which deals with the intellectual activities involved in the formulating of well-formed problems. We shall consider these activities in detail with reference to grammatical inquiry. At this point it is sufficient to indicate the four main activities involved in the formulating of problems: (a) analyzing the problematic state of affairs, (b) describing the problematic state of affairs, (c) constructing problems and (d) evaluating problems with regard to well-formedness and significance.

4.3   GRAMMATICAL INQUIRY

4.3.1   Nature of Grammatical Problems

The grammarian's inquiry is triggered and sustained by problems. This is why it is important that we take a close look at the nature of these problems. When investigating a particular language, the grammarian is confronted with various types of problems of which we shall consider two: substantive and metascientific.

4.3.1.1 *Substantive Problems*

In grammatical inquiry, SUBSTANTIVE PROBLEMS are problems concerning parts of the grammarian's two-levelled linguistic reality. In other words, substantive problems express fragments of ignorance about the native speaker's linguistic competence and, by implication, about the sentences and other types of linguistic units which are produced and interpreted on the basis of this linguistic competence. Substantive grammatical problems therefore represent gaps in the scientific knowledge about individual human languages. The problem of §1.1 about the nature – lexical or transformational – of the interrelatedness of sentences and corresponding derived nominals in English is a typical example of a substantive problem. The substantive problems of grammatical inquiry are commonly known as GRAMMATICAL or LANGUAGE-SPECIFIC PROBLEMS.

The substantive problems confronting the grammarian in the course of his inquiry may be reduced to a number of general types. Only the three most fundamental types will be considered here. Problems of the first fundamental type concern the properties of sentences or the classes of utterances in which the sentences are realized. In (4), a number of typical examples of this type of substantive, or grammatical, problem are given. The generalized format of these problems is given first, and is then illustrated by a concrete example.

(4) (a) GENERALIZED FORMAT: How should the property P of the class of utterances U be explained?
CONCRETE EXAMPLE: Why is the derived nominal *John's easiness to please* unacceptable?

(b) GENERALIZED FORMAT: How should the similarity S between utterances of the class C_1 and utterances of the class C_2 be explained?
CONCRETE EXAMPLE: Why are the derived nominal *John's refusal of the offer*, the gerundive nominal *John's refusing the offer* and the sentence *John has refused the offer* interpreted in the same way?

(c) GENERALIZED FORMAT: How should the difference D between utterances of the class C_1 and utterances of the class C_2 be explained?
CONCRETE EXAMPLE: Why is the derived nominal *John's emphatic refusal of the offer* acceptable, whereas the corresponding gerundive nominal **John's emphatic refusing the offer* is unacceptable?

Grammatical problems of the three subtypes indicated in (4) demand an explanation of the properties of classes of utterances (i.e. sentences or other linguistic units), of the similarities between related classes of utterances and of the differences between related classes of utterances.

The second fundamental type of substantive problem in grammatical inquiry includes problems concerning structural descriptions. Solving grammatical problems of the first fundamental type — those of (4) — entails assigning structural descriptions to the linguistic units underlying utterances which are repetitions of one another. From these structural descriptions it should be clear why the utterances have the problematic properties in question. The generalized format of the second type of substantive problem is shown in (5).

(5)   What structural description(s) should be assigned to the linguistic unit(s) U at the level of structure/representation L?

The levels of structure referred to in (5) include: syntactic structure such as surface structure, deep structure, lexical structure; phonological structure such as phonetic representation, phonological representation and lexical representation; and semantic structure such as logical form, semantic representation and lexical representation.

In (6) a typical example is given of a grammatical problem of the generalized format (5).

(6)   What deep structure(s) should be assigned to the derived nominal *John's refusal of the offer*, the gerundive nominal *John's refusing the offer* and the sentence *John has refused the offer?*

Note that the problem (6) corresponds to that of (4)(b). We shall return to this point below.

The third fundamental type of substantive problem in grammatical inquiry concerns grammatical rules. By definition, a generative grammar is a system of rules enumerating sentences along with appropriate structural descriptions. Therefore (7) represents a fundamental type of substantive problem in linguistic inquiry.

(7)   What are the rules that generate the sentences S along with their appropriate structural descriptions?

The rules referred to in (7) include, among others, syntactic rules such as lexical redundancy rules, base rules and transformations; phonological rules such as redundancy rules, readjustment rules and ordinary phonological rules; and semantic rules such as redundancy rules and various sorts of semantic interpretation rules.

In (8) a typical concrete substantive problem of the generalized format (7) is given.

(8)   What are the base rules which generate the categorial structures of the

linguistic units *John's refusal of the offer, John's refusing the offer* and *John has refused the offer?*

Note that an analogous question about the deep structures of these linguistic units would also have to refer to the lexical entries for the items in these units. The deep structure of a linguistic unit is its categorial structure into which lexical items have been inserted. Such an analogous question about lexical entries will have the same format as (6) above.

Note that grammatical problems in linguistic inquiry form tripartite series. A problem concerning the structural description of linguistic units, corresponds to a problem concerning the properties of these units. Compare the problems (4)(b) and (6) on this point. Moreover a problem concerning the rules specifying the structural description of linguistic units, corresponds to a problem concerning the structural description. Compare the problems (6) and (8) on this point. A typical substantive, or grammatical, problem therefore has a formulation in each of the three fundamental substantive types discussed above.

(9)

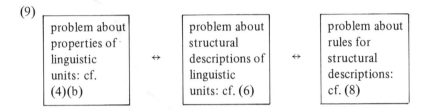

The most concrete type of grammatical problem concerns the properties of linguistic units as these units are realized in classes of utterances. It is often problems of this type that trigger a grammatical investigation. The most abstract type of grammatical problem concerns grammatical rules. Problems of this type concern the grammarian's actual object of study: the linguistic competence. A grammatical investigation is considered to be completed when the grammarian feels that he has found a satisfactory solution for one or more problems of this type. The type of problem concerned with structural descriptions for linguistic units provides the link between the more concrete problems of the former type and the more abstract problems of the latter type.

4.3.1.2 *Metascientific Problems*

METASCIENTIFIC PROBLEMS in grammatical inquiry represent difficulties encountered by the grammarian in connection with the nature, aspects and conduct of his inquiry as an intellectual enterprise. The following are typical metascientific problems which may be encountered in grammatical inquiry:

(10)(a)   Is the idealization I fruitful?
 (b)   Is the linguistic intuition LI correct or not?
 (c)   Is the pretheoretical grammatical description D adequate?
 (d)   Is the grammatical explanation E for the phenomena P adequate?
 (e)   Is the grammatical statement S correct or not?

Metascientific problems such as those of (10) may arise in connection with each aspect of a grammatical investigation; they crop up repeatedly in every individual investigation. Normally the grammarian need not solve these problems afresh every time he is confronted by them. The general approach to the study of language within the framework of which he is working — generative grammar in our case — should, in principle, offer a solution for every type of metascientific problem. In generative grammar the solving of such metascientific problems, in their general form, is the task of general linguistic inquiry. We shall return to this point in §4.4.2.2 below.

4.3.2   Formulating Grammatical Problems

In §4.2.2 we indicated very briefly the four main activities involved in formulating a well-formed problem in empirical inquiry. We shall now discuss each of these activities with reference to the formulating of grammatical problems.

4.3.2.1   *Analyzing the Problematic State of Affairs*

In the linguistic run-up of chapter 1 we considered a typical example of a problematic state of affairs in grammatical inquiry. Recall that what was found to be problematic was the nature of the relationship between sentences such as (11)(a) on the one hand and gerundive nominals such as (11)(b) and derived nominals such as (11)(c) on the other hand.

(11)(a)   *John refused the offer.*
 (b)   *John's refusing the offer*
 (c)   *John's refusal of the offer*

To be able to formulate a grammatical problem on the basis of this problematic state of affairs, the grammarian must satisfy a minimal requirement: he should know exactly what it is that is problematic. The grammarian therefore has to analyze the problematic state of affairs carefully to determine the exact nature of whatever it is that is problematic. This analysis has two aims, viz. to isolate each component of the problematic state of affairs and to determine how these components are interrelated. The analysis of the problematic state of affairs represents the first main type of activity involved in the formulating of well-formed grammatical problems.

4.3.2.1.1 *Determining the problematic data*
A problematic state of affairs typically has four components. The first component takes the form of data about linguistic units, or linguistic data. These data represent the PROBLEMATIC (LINGUISTIC) DATA. In this context a datum about a linguistic unit is a minimal amount of information about that unit. Generative grammarians often use the expression "facts" as a synonym for "linguistic data". In §4.3.2.2.2.2, however, it will be shown that a clear distinction can be drawn between data and facts.

The question which now arises is: what are the problematic data in the problematic state of affairs mentioned above? These data concern

(12)(a)   three types of linguistic units – sentences, gerundive nominals and derived nominals – and in particular

(b)   three linguistic aspects – the morphological, the semantic and the syntactic aspects – of these types of linguistic units and in particular

(c)   similarities and differences between these three linguistic aspects of the three types of linguistic units.

These data were problematic in that they indicated the existence of a relationship between sentences on the one hand, and derived and gerundive nominals on the other hand, but the nature of this relationship was not at all clear.

Of primary importance among these grammatical data were the linguistic intuitions of the native speaker of English: particularly his intuitive judgments about the morphological form, semantic interpretation and acceptability of the sentences, and the derived and gerundive nominals in question. Utterances and the intuitive judgments about their properties are therefore regarded in linguistic inquiry as PRIMARY (LINGUISTIC) DATA about a language. We shall discuss the nature of these data in §4.3.2.2.2 below. At this point it is sufficient to note that analyzing a problematic state of affairs, in the first place, implies that the grammarian should determine exactly what the problematic linguistic data are in terms of which a particular state of affairs is problematic.

4.3.2.1.2 *Determining the grammatical background assumptions*
The second component of a problematic state of affairs comprises background knowledge and/or background assumptions about the language about which problematic data exist. Knowledge and/or background assumptions about a particular language may be called GRAMMATICAL BACKGROUND ASSUMPTIONS for short. In the problematic state of affairs in question, Lees's ideas about nominalization in English represent the most important grammatical background knowledge and assumptions. The gist of Lees's ideas about nominalization may be formulated as (13).

(13)   Nominalization in English is a transformational syntactic process.

According to the grammatical background assumption (13), the relationship between sentences and nominals must be a transformational one. It appears, however, that with regard to three aspects of derived nominals data exist which cannot be reconciled with the existence of such a transformational relationship.

Firstly, there are data about the productivity of derivative nominalization. From these data — which we considered in §1.4 — it appears that not every sentence has a corresponding derived nominal. In terms of a transformational account of the relationship between sentences and derived nominals, there should have been a one-to-one correspondence between sentences and derived nominals. The absence of such a correspondence indicates that many derived nominals are syntactically irregular.

Secondly, there are data about the semantic interpretation of derived nominals which are incompatible with the existence of a transformational relationship between sentences and derived nominals. In terms of such a relationship, sentences and corresponding derived nominals would have had the same semantic interpretation. However, many derived nominals are semantically irregular in that their semantic interpretation contains an idiosyncratic element which is absent from the semantic interpretation of the corresponding sentences. Compare, for instance, the semantic interpretation of derived nominals such as *laughter, marriage, construction, actions, activities, deeds, belief, doubt,* etc. for an illustration of this point.

Thirdly, there are data about the internal structure of derived nominals which are incompatible with the existence of a transformational relationship between sentences and derived nominals. Derived nominals have an internal structure similar to that of NPs. In terms of a transformational account of the relationship between sentences and derived nominals, the internal structure of derived nominals should reflect that of sentences. However, there are a number of differences in internal structure between sentences and derived nominals. A few of these differences are presented in the following scheme.

(14) SYNTACTIC DIFFERENCES BETWEEN
      SENTENCES AND DERIVED NOMINALS

		sentences	derived nominals
	occurrence of aspectual verbs	John *has* criticized the book.	*John's *have(ing)* criticism the book
	occurrence of adverbs	John *sarcastically* criticized the book.	*John's *sarcastically* criticism of the book
	applicability of Subject Raising	it is certain that John will win ⟶ John is certain to win.	the certainty that John will win ⟶ *John's certainty to win
	applicability of Dative Shift	John gives the book to Bill ⟶ John gives Bill the book	John's gift of a book to Bill ⟶ *John's gift of Bill a book

The differences in the internal structure of derived nominals on the one hand and sentences and gerundive nominals on the other hand are discussed in detail by Jackendoff in his "Introduction to the $\overline{X}$-convention" (1974:1–3).

What is important to us is that the three classes of data about derived nominals mentioned above are problematic when considered in relation to a particular grammatical background assumption: Lees's assumption of a transformational relationship between sentences and derived nominals. Therefore, analyzing a problematic grammatical state of affairs also entails that the grammarian should determine what the grammatical background assumptions are in terms of which a particular state of affairs is problematic.

4.3.2.1.3 *Determining the general linguistic background assumptions*
The third component of a problematic state of affairs comprises background knowledge and/or background assumptions about language in general, or GENERAL LINGUISTIC BACKGROUND ASSUMPTIONS for short. The problematic state of affairs which we are considering includes, among other things, the general linguistic background assumptions of (15).

(15)(a) Sentences, derived nominals and gerundive nominals are significant units in the structure of a human language.

 (b) The similarities and differences observed with regard to the three types of linguistic units mentioned in (a) concern aspects of these units which are linguistically significant.

(c)   An account of the relationship between units of the three types in question must take the form of a system of rules.

(d)   In principle there are two types of rules which are referred to when giving an account of this relationship: transformational rules and base rules with associated neutral lexical entries.

Suppose we should refuse to make one or more of these general linguistic background assumptions. Then the problematic state of affairs we are considering would either change significantly, or would cease to exist altogether. Suppose, for instance, that we should refuse to make the assumption (15)(b). Then the similarities and differences in morphological form, semantic interpretation and syntactic structure which were observed to exist between sentences and gerundive and derived nominals, would become linguistically irrelevant. This would mean that a problematic state of affairs based on these similarities and differences could not exist within the framework of generative grammar. Each one of the general linguistic assumptions of (15) affects the existence and content of our problematic state of affairs in an analogous way. In the third place, therefore, the analysis of a problematic state of affairs implies that the grammarian should determine each of the general linguistic background assumptions in terms of which this state of affairs is problematic.

4.3.2.1.4   *Determining the assumptions about linguistic inquiry*

The fourth component of a problematic state of affairs comprises one or more background assumptions about the aims and nature of grammatical inquiry. These assumptions may be called METHODOLOGICAL or METASCIENTIFIC BACKGROUND ASSUMPTIONS. The problematic state of affairs under consideration, includes the following metascientific background assumptions:

(16)(a)   Grammatical inquiry is aimed at resolving problematic states of affairs.

(b)   Resolving a problematic state of affairs involves, among other things, the giving of explanations for problematic linguistic data.

(c)   Giving grammatical explanations involves, among other things, the specification of the relationship between linguistic units which are partly similar and partly different.

(d)   Linguistic intuitions of native speakers are the primary source of data about the similarities and differences referred to in (c).

Suppose we should refuse to make one or more of the methodological background assumptions of (16)(a)–(d). Then the problematic state of affairs which we are considering would either cease to exist or would change substantially. It is therefore important to determine all the metascientific background assumptions contained in a problematic grammatical state of affairs. Analyzing a problematic grammatical state of affairs therefore implies, in the fourth place, that the grammarian should determine every metascientific background assumption in terms of which this state of affairs is problematic.

4.3.2.1.5   *Structure of a problematic state of affairs*

Considering what has been said so far, it is clear that a problematic grammatical state of affairs is a complex entity. It contains (a) a data or factual element: data about linguistic units; (b) a grammatical element: background knowledge and/or assumptions about the individual language in which the linguistic units of (a) occur; (c) a general linguistic element: background knowledge and/or assumptions about human language in general; and (d) a methodological or metascientific element: background assumptions about the nature and aims of grammatical inquiry. Analyzing a problematic grammatical state of affairs involves isolating each of these four components of the problematic state of affairs and determining the ways in which they are interrelated, as we have done in preceding paragraphs.

With this description of the structure of a problematic grammatical state of affairs in mind, note that raw data about a human language are not problematic when viewed in isolation. They only become problematic when viewed against a certain background of knowledge and assumptions. This EPISTEMIC BACKGROUND includes knowledge and/or assumptions about individual human languages, about human language in general and about grammatical inquiry. Background knowledge and assumptions about a particular language usually take the form of a fragment of grammar of that language. Background knowledge and assumptions about human language usually take the form of a (fragment of) universal grammar or a general linguistic theory. In chapter 6 of our study, we shall see that both the grammar of an individual language, and a universal grammar, have the metascientific nature of scientific theories. At this point, it is sufficient to note that every problematic grammatical state of affairs contains a THEORETICAL COMPONENT. And, finally, the total system of grammatical, general linguistic and metascientific background knowledge and assumptions is often referred to as the grammarian's APPROACH TO THE STUDY OF LANGUAGE. This point will be discussed in greater detail in §11.2.1.

4.3.2.2   *Describing the Problematic State of Affairs*

The grammarian obviously needs to capture the results of his analysis of a problematic grammatical state of affairs in some permanent form. This he does by giving a description of this problematic state of affairs. In this description the grammarian specifies, as precisely as possible, each of the elements or components − factual, grammatical, general linguistic and metascientific − of which this state of affairs is composed. Giving such a description represents the second type of activity involved in formulating well-formed grammatical problems. However, as we shall see in §4.5, this description need not be presented by the grammarian as part of the published report on the findings of his inquiry. Moreover, in §12.2 it will be shown that, within the framework of generative grammar, there are certain types of investigation in which the analysis and description of problematic states of affairs do not play a central role. The content of §4.3.2 can be fully understood only if these two reservations are borne in mind.

An important aspect of the describing of a problematic grammatical state of affairs is the accurate recording of the data about classes of utterances that are problematic. The description which results from such recording of problematic linguistic data respresents an INFORMAL, PRESYSTEMATIC or PRETHEORETICAL DESCRIPTION of the linguistic units on which the data bear. Such a pretheoretical description of linguistic units should not be confused with the description of the ideal speaker's linguistic competence as presented in the form of a grammar. The latter is known as a "theoretical description". In §6.3 we shall consider in detail the nature and characteristics of theoretical descriptions as products of linguistic inquiry. At this point it is sufficient to note that these two types of description are directed at different levels of the grammarian's linguistic reality. On the one hand, pretheoretical grammatical descriptions describe classes of objects on the surface level, i.e. classes of products of linguistic performance. Theoretical descriptions, on the other hand, describe objects on the underlying level of mental capacities. Let us now take a closer look at the nature of pretheoretical grammatical descriptions, and at what is involved in constructing such descriptions.

4.3.2.2.1   *Pretheoretical grammatical descriptions*
In pretheoretical grammatical descriptions, claims are made about expressions such as the following:

(17)(a)   *John has refused the offer.*
   (b)   *John's refusing the offer*
   (c)   *John's refusal of the offer*
   (d)   **John has refused hope.*
   (e)   **John's refusing hope*
   (f)   **John's refusal of hope*
   (g)   **Trouble has refused the offer.*
   (h)   **Trouble's refusing the offer*
   (i)   **Trouble's refusal of the offer*
   (j)   *John is easy to please.*
   (k)   *John's being easy to please*
   (l)   **John's easiness to please*
   (m)   *John's deeds*
   (n)   *John has done/did things.*
   (o)   *John's doing things*
   (p)   *John has criticized the book.*

(q) *John's having criticized the book*

(r) **John's have(ing) criticism of the book*

The following claims are typical of those made in pretheoretical grammatical descriptions:

(18)(a) *refused* in (17)(a), *refusing* in (17)(b) and *refusal* in (17)(c) have a shared morphological element: "refus".

(b) All three the expressions (17)(a), (17)(b) and (17)(c) are interpreted so that

(i) the one who refuses is John;

(ii) what John does is to refuse; and

(iii) what is being refused is the offer.

(c) The expressions (17)(a)−(c) are acceptable, whereas the expressions (17)(d)−(i) are not.

(d) In none of the expressions (17)(a)−(c) can "refuse" be combined with a noun such as *hope* in the object position.

(e) In none of the expressions (17)(a)−(c) can "refuse" be combined with a nonanimate noun in the subject position.

(f) Whereas the sentence (17)(j) has a corresponding gerundive nominal in the form of (17)(k), it appears from the unacceptability of (17)(l) that (17)(j) does not have a corresponding derived nominal.

(g) Whereas all not too complex sentences have corresponding gerundive nominals, not all moderately complex sentences have corresponding derived nominals.

(h) The meaning of the derived nominal (17)(m) includes the element "fairly significant", whereas this element is absent from the meaning of the corresponding sentence (17)(n); the gerundive nominal (17)(o) and the sentence (17)(n), on the contrary, have the same meaning.

(i) In many cases the semantic relationship between sentences and corresponding derived nominals is irregular, whereas the semantic relationship between sentences and gerundive nominals is regular.

(j) Whereas a sentence such as (17)(p) and a gerundive nominal such as (17)(q) may contain an aspectual verb such as *have(ing)*, a corresponding derived nominal such as (17)(l) cannot contain such a verb.

Let us now consider the pretheoretical statements of (18)(a)−(j), first from the point of view of their content and then from the point of view of their formulation.

From the point of view of their content, the statements (18)(a)−(j) represent PRETHEORETICAL CLAIMS. We shall regard a CLAIM − or, more technically, a PROPOSITION − as a unit of content with a certain logical structure. Logically, a pretheoretical claim such as (18)(a) is composed of two parts: an argument and a function. In the pretheoretical claim (18)(a), the expression *"refused* in (17)(a), *refusing* in (17)(b) and *refusal* in (17)(c)" represents the argument. It is the task of the ARGUMENT to individuate or single out an object or class of objects. In the pretheoretical claim (18)(a), the function is represented by the expression "have a shared morphological element: 'refus' ". It is the task of the FUNCTION to ascribe a property to the (class) of individuated objects or to specify the type to which these objects belong. From the point of view of content, therefore, a pretheoretical claim individuates (a class of) objects to which a property is ascribed or a type is assigned.

As a unit of content, a pretheoretical claim must satisfy the following fundamental condition:

(19)   The accuracy of a pretheoretical claim must be beyond reasonable doubt.

The condition (19) implies that the individuated (class of) objects must, in all probability, belong to the type or have the property assigned to it.

From the point of view of formulation, the claims of (18)(a)–(j) represent declarative sentences. The expressions or terms of which these sentences are composed, are known as PRETHEORETICAL TERMS/EXPRESSIONS. In (18)(a)–(j) we find the following typical examples of pretheoretical terms: "shared morphological element", "expressions", "(are) interpreted", "(un)acceptable", "combined", "noun", "object position", "subject position", "sentences", "derived nominals", "gerundive nominals", "meaning", "semantic relatedness", "aspectual verb", etc. In principle any linguistic term with a meaning which is reasonably fixed, clear and nonambiguous may be used as a pretheoretical term.

The linguistic formulation of a pretheoretical claim must satisfy the following fundamental condition:

(20)   The linguistic formulation of a pretheoretical claim may not be obscure.

The condition (20) states that it must be clear from the formulation of the claim what is being propounded and what is not. This criterion presupposes that there is a fixed, clear correlation between pretheoretical terms and the individuated (classes of) objects, ascribed properties and assigned types which they denote.

This brings us to the question of what is involved in giving a pretheoretical grammatical description of the problematic properties of utterances. In other words, what activities have to be carried out in order to arrive at a pretheoretical grammatical description? It will emerge from our discussion that among these activities the following are basic: collecting data about whatever is problematic, systematizing the collected data and symbolizing the results of this systematization.

4.3.2.2.2   *Collecting data*
Recall that the primary problematic data of grammatical inquiry take the form
of classes of utterances and linguistic intuitions about these utterances. In
§3.3.1.1 we saw that both utterances and linguistic intuitions are products of
linguistic performance. LINGUISTIC INTUITIONS represent the non-reasoned
judgments of native speakers about the properties of utterances. These judgments relate to properties such as (un)acceptability, (un)ambiguity, similarity
and difference in meaning, and so on. Such judgments are called "intuitive" or
"unreasoned" because native speakers do not arrive at them by way of conscious
reasoning. They do not in fact know the grounds for their intuitive judgments,
with the result that they cannot justify these judgments. It is therefore senseless
to ask a native speaker to justify, for instance, his judgment that a particular
utterance is unacceptable.

The native speakers who have the ability to make intuitive judgments belong
to two classes. On the one hand, there is the class of native speakers who have
not had any linguistic training. Grammarians use linguistically untrained native
speakers as INFORMANTS: sources of linguistic intuitions. The intuitive linguistic
judgments of these linguistically untrained native speakers are often called
INFORMANT DATA. On the other hand, there is the class of native speakers who
have been linguistically trained, viz. the grammarians themselves. Grammarians
may, by way of introspection, consult or tap their own linguistic competence for
linguistic intuitions. The intuitive judgments of skilled grammarians are for this
reason known as INTROSPECTIVE DATA.

In order to give a satisfactory description of the problematic properties of
linguistic units, the grammarian must have sufficient data about these units at
his disposal. This implies that he should obtain an adequate number of data
about the problematic linguistic units in question. The activity by which these
data are obtained, is traditionally known as DATA COLLECTING. The result or
the product of data collecting is a CORPUS (OF DATA). But what is involved in
collecting a corpus of (primary) linguistic data? Data collecting has two main
aspects: recording and evaluating.

4.3.2.2.2.1   *Recording the data*   The first main aspect of data collecting in
grammatical inquiry is the RECORDING of primary linguistic data about whatever
it is that is problematic. The grammarian is especially interested in those data
which shed most light on the nature of the problematic state of affairs. Data
which are illuminating in this sense are relevant, while all other linguistic data
are, for the time being, irrelevant. To be able to distinguish between illuminating,
relevant data and useless, irrelevant data, the grammarian needs some sort of
clue. This clue is provided by the theoretical and metascientific elements in the
problematic state of affairs at which the investigation is directed. These elements
give the grammarian certain ideas about the kinds of linguistic data which would
reveal the nature of whatever it is that is problematic. An idea which guides the
grammarian in recording certain linguistic data as being relevant, while disregard-

ing other data as being irrelevant is often referred to as a (GRAMMATICAL) WORKING HYPOTHESIS.

Consider, for instance, the problematic nature of the relatedness of a series of expressions such as *John has refused the offer, John's refusing the offer* and *John's refusal of the offer.* The theoretical and metascientific elements – cf. (13), (15) and (16) above – of the problematic state of affairs in question, suggest the following to the grammarian of English:

(21)   Linguistic data about differences and similarities between the morphological, syntactic and semantic aspects of series of corresponding sentences, gerundive nominals and derived nominals should throw some light on the problematic nature of the interrelatedness of these expressions.

The idea expressed in (21) is a concrete example of an extremely general grammatical working hypothesis which guides the grammarian in his collecting of linguistic data. This working hypothesis may be made more specific by stipulating exactly what properties of the morphological, syntactic and semantic aspects are implicated. Such a more specific version of the working hypothesis (21) would induce the grammarian of English to record the linguistic data of (18) as being relevant. Without such a working hypothesis it would be quite impossible for the grammarian to distinguish between relevant and irrelevant linguistic data. We shall return to the general nature and function of working hypotheses below.

We have seen that the utterances and intuitive judgments recorded as primary linguistic data come from two sources, viz. linguistically untrained native speakers and the grammarian himself as a native speaker of the language he is investigating. The grammarian may obtain his primary linguistic data in one of two ways. Firstly, he may stumble across them, which means that he obtains them more or less accidentally without making a purposeful, systematic effort to find them. Or, secondly, he may try to obtain these data by consciously and systematically searching for them. The latter method is called ELICITING. In linguistic inquiry, the method of obtaining data by means of systematic elicitation is not widely used. The grammarian usually uses his own utterances and his own intuitive judgments about these utterances as his primary linguistic data. He normally supplements these with utterances and intuitive judgments made by other grammarians as these are presented in the literature. The primary linguistic data of grammatical inquiry are therefore mostly introspective data, supplemented in exceptional cases with systematically elicited informant data.

4.3.2.2.2.2   *Evaluating the data*   The result of the grammarian's data collecting – as we have seen in the previous paragraph – is a corpus of data. Let us assume for the sake of our study, that the corpus of data of a comprehensive grammatical investigation of English may include the following primary linguistic data:

(22)(a)   (i) *John's eagerness to please*
       (ii) *John's easiness to please*
       While the utterance (i) is acceptable, the utterance (ii) is unacceptable.

(b)   (i) *John is easy to please.*
       (ii) *John's being easy to please*
       The utterances (i) and (ii) have the same meaning.

(c)   (i) *John's deeds*
       (ii) *The things which John did*
       The expressions (i) and (ii) have the same meaning.

(d)   (i) *John's picture*
       The expression (i) is ambiguous. It could, among other things, mean "the picture that John has", "the picture of John" and "the picture painted by John".

(e)   (i) *The horse raced past the barn fell.*
       (ii) *The horse ridden past the barn fell.*
       The utterance (i) is unacceptable, whereas the utterance (ii) is acceptable.

(f)   (i) *Peter Piper picked a peck of pickled peppers.*
       (ii) *She sells seashells by the sea-shore.*
       Both the utterances (i) and (ii) are unacceptable.

(g)   (i) *Harry reminds me of himself.*
       The utterance (i) is unacceptable.

(h)   (i) *My toothbrush is alive and is trying to kill me.*
       The utterance (i) is unacceptable.

(i)   (i) *John's belief in ghosts*
       The utterance (i) is unacceptable.

(j)   (i) *The meat upset the dog.*
       (ii) *The dog was upset by the meat.*
       (iii) *The dog was upset at the meat.*
       (iv) *The dog was upset because of the meat.*
       (v) *The meat made the dog upset.*
       The utterances (i)–(iii) are more closely related to one another than they are related, as a group, to the utterances (iv) and (v).

(k)   (i) *Who must telephone her?*
       (ii) *Who need telephone her?*
       The utterance (i) is acceptable, whereas the utterance (ii) is unacceptable.

(l)   (i) *Larry reminds me of Winston Churchill although I perceive that Larry is not similar to Winston Churchill.*
       The meaning of the utterance (i) contains a contradiction.

(m)   (i) *The target wasn't hit by many arrows.*
       (ii) *Not many arrows hit the target.*

(iii) *Many arrows didn't hit the target.*
The utterance (i) is synonymous with the utterance (ii), but not with the utterance (iii).

Having compiled such a corpus of primary linguistic data, the grammarian has by no means finished his data collecting. Data collecting has a second main aspect, viz. the evaluation of the primary data recorded by the grammarian. By evaluation is meant that the grammarian determines whether the data in his corpus satisfy certain criteria. Three of these criteria are of primary importance.

(23)(a) The criterion of genuineness: the intuitive judgments included in the corpus should represent genuine linguistic intuitions.

(b) The criterion of correctness: the intuitive judgments which represent genuine linguistic intuitions should be correct.

(c) The criterion of comprehensiveness: the corpus as a whole should be sufficiently comprehensive.

Let us now consider each of these criteria with reference to the corpus of (22).

1. THE CRITERION OF GENUINENESS – The criterion (23)(a) is needed because not every intuitive judgment about an utterance represents a genuine linguistic intuition. In §3.3.1.2 we saw that linguistic performance is the product of the interaction of a variety of factors. The grammarian's investigation is directed at only one of these factors, the grammatical factor of linguistic competence. Therefore, his primary linguistic data should include only intuitive judgments which reflect the properties of linguistic competence. Intuitive linguistic judgments which reflect the properties of the underlying linguistic competence, represent GENUINE LINGUISTIC INTUITIONS.

Some intuitive judgments about utterances do not reflect the properties of linguistic competence, but are the products of the nongrammatical factors operative in linguistic performance. A number of these nongrammatical factors were given as (6)(b)–(h) in §3.3.1.2. Intuitive linguistic judgments which do not reflect the properties of linguistic competence represent SPURIOUS LINGUISTIC INTUITIONS and should not be included in the corpus of primary grammatical data. In terms of the grammarian's abstraction of an ideal speaker, it is not an objective of grammatical inquiry to account for the role of the nongrammatical factors in linguistic performance.

In the corpus of primary linguistic data (22) there are four spurious linguistic intuitions, viz. (22)(e)–(h). As regards the intuitive judgment (22)(e): the intuitive judgment that the utterance *The horse raced past the barn fell* is unacceptable is the result of the perceptual complexity of the utterance. In his article "The ascent of the specious or there's a lot we don't know about mirrors" (1974:181–182), Thomas Bever shows that the native speaker finds the perceptual processing of this utterance extremely difficult. The intuitive judgment that the utterance is unacceptable therefore reflects an aspect of the role of one or more perceptual strategies in linguistic performance and not a property of the linguistic competence. A grammar, therefore, need not account for the unacceptability of this utterance. We shall have something more to say about the spuriousness of the judgment (22)(e) in §7.4.6.

As regards the intuitive judgment (22)(f): the intuitive judgment that the utterances *Peter Piper picked a peck of pickled peppers* and *She sells seashells by the sea-shore* are unacceptable reflects a property of the native speaker's speech production apparatus. Bever (1974:191) shows that it is exceptionally difficult to articulate these utterances. It is therefore the articulatory complexity of these utterances, and not the linguistic competence, which is responsible for their unacceptability. The intuitive judgment of (22)(f) therefore represents a spurious linguistic intuition and need not be explained by a grammar of English.

As regards intuitive judgment (22)(g): the intuitive judgment that the utterance *Harry reminds me of himself*, is unacceptable, does not reflect a property of the linguistic competence. The unacceptability of this utterance may be attributed to the role of the situation or context in which the utterance was used. Yehoshua Bar-Hillel (1971: 404–405) argues that speakers who judge this utterance to be unacceptable, base their judgment on the fact that they have difficulty in imagining a situation in which such an utterance could be used. Their intuitive judgment therefore reflects the role of a nongrammatical, pragmatic factor in linguistic performance and need not be accounted for by a grammar of English.

As regards the intuitive judgment (22)(h): the intuitive judgment that the utterance *My toothbrush is alive and is trying to kill me* is unacceptable, also reflects the role of a nongrammatical factor in linguistic performance. In this case the judgment reflects something of the speaker's view of the world he lives in. More specifically, it reflects the speaker's view of his relationship with nonanimate objects. This judgment thus does not reflect a property of the linguistic competence. As such it represents a spurious linguistic intuition and need not be explained by a grammar of English.

The grammarian has the task of ascertaining the genuineness of every intuitive judgment in his corpus. Spurious linguistic intuitions must be excluded from the corpus, because a grammar does not have to provide an account of the role of nongrammatical factors in linguistic performance. This is no simple task, as it requires a considerable amount of knowledge of the role of these factors in linguistic performance. In §7.4.6 we shall consider a strategy which is used to assess the genuineness of intuitive linguistic judgments. At this point it is sufficient to note that it is the grammarian's abstractions and accompanying idealizations that determine which intuitive judgments about utterances are genuine and which are not.

2. THE CRITERION OF CORRECTNESS — The criterion (23)(b) is adopted because speakers may make mistakes in their intuitive judgments about the properties

of utterances. This is true both of linguistically untrained speakers and of skilled grammarians. Linguistic intuitions are not infallible. Consequently the fact that a particular linguistic judgment represents a linguistic intuition does not necessarily imply that the judgment is correct.

The corpus (22) contains two intuitive linguistic judgments which represent genuine linguistic intuitions, but which are, nevertheless, incorrect. The first is (22)(c). In English the expressions *John's deeds* and *the things which John did* do not have the same meaning. *John's deeds* means "*fairly significant* things which John did". The second incorrect linguistic intuition is (22)(i). The expression *John's belief in ghosts* is simply not unacceptable in English. Such incorrect or mistaken linguistic intuitions may not be included in the grammarian's corpus of data. In §4.3.2.4.1 below we shall see that incorrect linguistic intuitions give rise to the formulation of ill-formed grammatical problems.

At this point a distinction should be drawn between data and facts. A DATUM is a fragment of information which has not been thoroughly tested on the basis of some criterion of correctness. A FACT, on the other hand, is a fragment of information of which the accuracy, after careful testing, seems to be beyond reasonable doubt. In short, a fact represents what, in all probability, is actually the case. It is a tested and probably correct datum about reality. Many generative grammarians do not make this distinction, but loosely use the expressions "datum/a" and "fact(s)" as synonyms.

3. THE CRITERION OF COMPREHENSIVENESS – The criterion (23)(c) is adopted because there are many factors which may influence genuine linguistic intuitions. Linguistic intuitions may be influenced to such an extent that they give a misleading impression of the properties of the linguistic units under analysis. Thus a genuine linguistic intuition may be variable. It is the grammarian's task to ascertain whether the content of the genuine linguistic intuitions within his corpus was influenced in a misleading manner.

The corpus (22) contains four examples of linguistic intuitions of which the content was misleadingly influenced, viz. (22)(j), (k), (l) and (m). As regards (22)(j): Bever (1974:193–194) argues that the content of this linguistic intuition was influenced by the physical context in which the judgment was made. The physical context in which a speaker makes an intuitive judgment determines the measure of introspection of which he is capable. The judgment (22)(j) was made in a context which was not conducive to introspection. In a "more introspective" context, speakers judged differently about the relatedness of the expressions in question. Thus, placed in front of a mirror – a context which is highly conducive to introspection – speakers intuitively judged that the utterances (j)(i)–(v) are all mutually related to the same extent. This shows clearly that, when compiling a corpus of primary linguistic data, the grammarian should take into account the influence of the factor of physical context on linguistic intuitions. He should try to determine as far as possible to what extent the content of the linguistic intuitions in his corpus may have been influenced by this factor.

As regards (22)(k): Bever (174:193) maintains that the intuitive judgment that the utterance *Who need telephone her?* is unacceptable was influenced by the factor of perceptual contrast. This utterance is intuitively unacceptable when it is contrasted directly with the utterance *Who must telephone her?*. When the first utterance is contrasted with *Who want telephone her?*, it is intuitively acceptable, while it is the latter utterance which is intuitively unacceptable. It is clear, therefore, that the perceptual context in which an intuitive judgment is made may also have an effect on the resulting linguistic intuition. The grammarian should, once again, try to determine to what extent the content of the linguistic intuitions in his corpus was influenced by this factor.

As regards (22)(l): the intuitive judgment about the internal contradictoriness of the utterance *Larry reminds me of Winston Churchill although I perceive that Larry is not similar to Winston Churchill* is that of Paul Postal (1970:41). The content of this judgment was probably influenced by Postal's observational expectations. Within the framework of his inquiry he probably expected the utterance in question to contain an internal contradiction. Other linguists – for instance Bar-Hillel (1971:402–403) and Bowers (1970:560) – who did not operate within this framework, intuitively judged this utterance not to be internally contradictory. It is a well-known fact that the expectations of the scientist can, to a certain extent, determine the way in which he sees the world. The grammarian should therefore determine as far as possible to what extent the linguistic intuitions in his corpus could have been influenced by his observational expectations.

As regards (22)(m): not all speakers of English intuitively judge that, whereas the utterance *The target wasn't hit by many arrows* is synonymous with the utterance *Not many arrows hit the target*, it is not synonymous with the utterance *Many arrows didn't hit the target*. Only speakers of a particular dialect make this judgment. Speakers of a different dialect do not have these intuitions. Speakers of the latter dialect – for example George Lakoff (1969:12) – judge the first utterance (i) to be synonymous with the last utterance (iii) as well. The dialectal origin of the speaker may therefore influence the content of his linguistic intuitions. The grammarian should determine to what extent the content of the linguistic intuitions in his corpus may have been influenced by the factor of dialectal variation.

What is shown by these examples is how the content of genuine linguistic intuitions may be influenced by a variety of factors. It is the task of the grammarian to determine to what extent the linguistic intuitions in his corpus may have been subject to such influences. This is no simple task and it is one which is often neglected. The simplest way to set about the matter is to ensure that the corpus of data is sufficiently comprehensive. It is obvious that variations in the content of linguistic intuitions will be more conspicuous in a large corpus than in a small one.

When compiling his corpus of primary linguistic data, the grammarian should try consciously to take into account the influence of the factors of physical context, perceptual context, observational expectations and dialectal variation on the content of linguistic intuitions. Suppose, for instance, that the grammarian wishes to know whether a particular utterance and all its repetitions are acceptable to the native speakers of the language. To start with, he could try to obtain intuitive judgments about the acceptability of the utterance from informants in different perceptual contexts. This would enable him to determine the influence of perceptual contrast on the content of this particular linguistic intuition. He could also have the informants make their intuitive judgments in different physical contexts, thereby determining the influence of the factor of physical context on the content of the linguistic intuition in question. His next step could be to obtain intuitive judgments from informants speaking different dialects of the language, thereby determining the influence of the factor of dialectal variation on the linguistic intuition. Finally, the grammarian could try to elicit the intuitive judgment under consideration from grammarians who are not working within a framework that creates observational expectations similar to his own. This would enable him to determine the influence of his observational expectations on the content of this particular intuitive judgment.

The systematic collection of informants' linguistic intuitions is no easy task. To do this techniques are needed that are both valid and reliable. These techniques must be VALID in that they must make it possible to obtain only genuine linguistic intuitions – as opposed to irrelevant judgments – from informants. They may be said to be RELIABLE if they succeed time and again in accurately determining the linguistic intuitions of informants. Such valid and reliable techniques for obtaining informant data are not in fact available in linguistic inquiry. As a result, few grammarians make a serious effort to determine to what extent the linguistic intuitions in their corpus could have been influenced by factors such as the four mentioned above.

None of the intellectual activities involved in the evaluation of primary linguistic data is in any way simple. The grammarian's decisions as to genuineness, correctness and comprehensiveness often represent nothing but guesses or speculation. Often it only becomes possible at an advanced stage of an investigation to judge the accuracy of such guesses or speculation. In §7.4.6 we shall return to the question of how to reach firmer conclusions about genuineness.

4.3.2.2.3 *Systematizing the data*

A corpus of primary linguistic data such as that of (22) lacks internal organization. In other words, the members of this corpus are isolated entities of which the interrelationship is not at all clear. The second type of intellectual activity involved in constructing a pretheoretical grammatical description consists in making a first attempt at systematizing the collected primary linguistic data. In this context systematization involves a number of more elementary intellectual activities, viz. classifying, correlating, ordering and measuring.

4.3.2.2.3.1 *Classifying* In general terms CLASSIFYING comprises the grouping together of objects, phenomena, events, etc. on the strength of their having one or more properties in common. A CLASS therefore represents a collection of objects, phenomena, events, etc. with one or more common properties.

The data in a corpus of primary linguistic data may be systematized by classifying the objects to which these data refer. For instance, in order to systematize a corpus of data about nominalization in English, classes such as the following may be used:

(24)(a) A class of sentences:
 John is easy to please, John is eager to please, John has refused the offer, John has criticized the book, etc.

(b) A class of gerundive nominals:
 John's being easy to please, John's being eager to please, John's having refused the offer, John's having criticized the book, etc.

(c) A class of derived nominals:
 *John's easiness to please, John's eagerness to please, John's refusal of the offer, John's criticism of the book, etc.

(d) A class of expressions containing "easy" as form element:
 John is easy to please, John's being easy to please, *John's easiness to please, etc.

(e) A class of expressions containing "eager" as form element:
 John is eager to please, John's being eager to please, John's eagerness to please, etc.

(f) A class of expressions that are semantically regular:
 John's laughing, John's marrying Anne, John's converting X, John's doubting Y, John's believing Z, etc.

(g) A class of expressions that are semantically irregular:
 John's laughter, John's marriage to Anne, John's conversion of X, John's doubt about Y, John's belief in Z, etc.

(h) A class of expressions with (more or less) the same semantic interpretation:
 John has refused the offer, John's having refused the offer, John's refusal of the offer.

(i) A class of expressions with the same selectional features:
 John has refused the offer (/*hope), John's having refused the offer (/*hope), John's refusal of the offer (/*hope).

(j) A class of sentences with no corresponding derived nominals:
 John is easy (difficult) to please, John is certain (likely) to win the prize, John amused (interested) the children with his stories, etc.

(k) A class of expressions with the internal structure of sentences:
 John's being eager to please, John's being easy to please, John's having refused the offer, John's having criticized the book, etc.

(l) A class of expressions with the internal structure of NPs:

John's eagerness to please, John's refusal of the offer, John's criticism of the book, etc.

To establish classes such as those of (24)(a)–(l) is to impose a first sort of systematization on the corpus of unorganized linguistic data. A good classification results in a much more synoptic arrangement of the data within the corpus. This, in turn, makes it possible to refer to the linguistic data contained in the corpus in generalizing terms. Without such a classification, the grammarian can only refer to individual data. Once these data have been classified, he can refer to classes of similar data.

One may now ask why the grammarian chooses certain classes and not others? Or, why does the grammarian classify the linguistic units in question in one way rather than in another way? For instance, why is it that in (24) the classes chosen were those of sentences, gerundive nominals, derived nominals, expressions that are semantically regular, expressions with the internal structure of sentences, etc. rather than other conceivable linguistic classes?

In his choice of linguistic classes – just as in his collecting of primary linguistic data – the grammarian is guided by grammatical working hypotheses. He would, for instance, hypothesize that

(25)(a)   a class comprising sentences is both relevant and significant in the systematization of the corpus (22);

(b)   classes comprising derived and gerundive nominals are both relevant and significant in the systematization of the corpus (22);

(c)   a class comprising expressions with the internal structure of sentences/NPs is both relevant and significant in the systematization of the corpus (22); etc.

As in the case of data collecting, such grammatical working hypotheses are suggested to the grammarian by the grammatical and general linguistic background assumptions in the problematic state of affairs which triggered the inquiry. Recognition of these background assumptions as such is therefore also essential when it comes to classifying the primary linguistic data.

A second general question concerns the criteria for a good classification. An important criterion for a good classification is that of naturalness.

(26)   The classes into which the members of a corpus are grouped must be natural classes.

A NATURAL CLASS is one of which the defining property is associated with a significant number of other properties of its members. In other words, the members of a natural class exhibit clusters of common properties. An excellent example of a natural class is the class of vertebrates in biology. The defining property of this class – possession of a spinal column – correlates with a number of other properties of its members. Among these properties, for instance, are the presence of a particular type of circulatory system and the presence of a particular type of nervous system. The presence of the latter two properties can be predicted on the strength of the presence of the former, defining property of the class.

In the grammatical investigation of nominalization in English, gerundive nominals, for instance, represent a fairly natural class. The defining property of this class, the gerundive property, correlates with at least three other properties of the members of this class: syntactic regularity, semantic regularity and the presence of a sentence-like internal structure. In this investigation, a class of expressions of which the defining property is, say, that they all appear in a particular novel would represent an artificial class. The defining property of this class would, in all probability, correlate with no other properties of the members of this class.

The criterion (26) for a good classification may be called an EMPIRICAL CRITERION, as it is based on a kind of factual regularity in the interrelatedness of the properties of the members of a class. Logicians have also developed a number of FORMAL CRITERIA for good classifications. A first formal criterion requires that the division of a class into subclasses must be exhaustive. This impies that every member of the larger class should also be a member of one of the subclasses. A second formal criterion requires that the subclasses of a larger class should be mutually exclusive, i.e. subclasses may not overlap. A third formal criterion requires that, as far as possible, a single principle for dividing larger classes into subclasses should be used for the entire classification. Formal criteria such as these are logical criteria which are subordinate to an "empirical" criterion such as (26). The aim of the grammarian is not to arrive at a formally elegant classification, but to have a classification from which it is clear how the properties of individual objects are factually interrelated.

4.3.2.2.3.2 *Correlating*   In classifying his data, the grammarian imposes a first measure of systematization on an unorganized corpus of data. By performing a second elementary activity, that of correlating, the grammarian may take this systematization one step further. As we have seen in the discussion of natural classes, CORRELATING, or associating, involves determining for each member of the corpus all the classes in which it appears. The aim of correlating is to determine how the various classes include and/or exclude one another in terms of their members. Correlating thus entails that the grammarian attempts to establish how the distinctive properties of the members of a corpus are interrelated.

For instance, when systematizing a corpus of linguistic data about nominalization in English, the following correlations may be made:

(27)(a)   The expression *John's believing the President* is a member of the class of gerundive nominals, of the class of semantically regular expressions and of the class of expressions with the internal structure of sentences.

(b)   The expression *John's belief in the President* is a member of the class of derived nominals, of the class of semantically irregular expressions and of the class of expressions with the internal structure of NPs.

(c)   The expression *John's refusing of the offer* is a member of the class of nominals with a gerundive aspect and of the class of expressions with the internal structure of NPs.

On the basis of correlations such as (27)(a)–(c), the grammarian can now formulate generalizations such as the following:

(28)(a)   The majority of the members of the class of derived nominals are also members of the class of semantically irregular expressions and of the class of expressions with the internal structure of NPs.

(b)   The majority of the members of the class of gerundive nominals are also members of the class of semantically regular expressions and of the class of expressions with the internal structure of sentences.

(c)   No member of the class of gerundive nominals is at the same time a member of the class of semantically irregular expressions.

(d)   No member of the class of derived nominals is at the same time a member of the class of expressions with the internal structure of sentences.

By generalizing correlations as in (28) above, it becomes clear how the distinctive properties of the classes within the corpus are interrelated. For instance, the generalizations of (28) indicate the following relationships between the linguistic units of the corpus (22):

(29)(a)   The property of 'being a gerundive nominal' correlates with the property of 'being a semantically regular expression' and with the property of 'being an expression with the internal structure of sentences'.

(b)   The property of 'being a derived nominal' correlates with the property of 'being a semantically irregular expression' and with the property of 'being an expression with the internal structure of an NP'.

Correlating the members of a corpus therefore involves determining for each member in which classes it appears, generalizing the correlations which have been found and determining, on the basis of these generalizations, how the defining properties of the classes are interrelated. When establishing these correlations, the grammarian is once more guided by grammatical working hypotheses. For instance, underlying the correlation (27)(a) is a grammatical working hypothesis such as the following:

(30)   The interrelatedness of the linguistic properties of having a gerundive aspect, being semantically regular and having a sentence-like internal structure could be both relevant and significant.

Working hypotheses such as (30) may be suggested by the grammatical and general linguistic background assumptions present in a problematic grammatical state of affairs. If guided by fruitful working hypotheses, the activity of correlating may contribute largely to the effective systematizing of the corpus of grammatical data.

4.3.2.2.3.3   *Ordering*   A third type of activity in terms of which the data in a corpus may be systematized even further, is that of ordering. ORDERING involves determining, for a particular class, how the members of that class are mutually related. In its most basic form, ordering means determining the internal relationship of each pair of members of a class. The relationship between the members of each pair may be expressed in terms of an ordering relation. By ordering the members of a class, the grammarian assigns an internal structure to this class.

But let us make our discussion of ordering more concrete by considering what is involved with regard to a corpus of linguistic data about nominalization in English. One of the classes in terms of which such a corpus may be systematized, is the class (24)(g), the class of semantically irregular expressions. It would be possible to order the members of this class in terms of the relation "semantically more/less irregular than". Within this class a derived nominal such as, for instance, *John's laughter* could be ordered with regard to the derived nominal *John's deeds* in terms of the relation "semantically less irregular than". A second class in terms of which such a corpus may be systematized, is that of (24)(1), the class of expressions with the internal structure of NPs. The members of this class could be ordered in terms of the relation "more/less like an NP than". Within this class an expression such as *John's refusing of the offer* may be ordered with regard to an expression such as *John's refusal of the offer* in terms of the relation "less like an NP than". The former expression has a gerundive aspect which true NPs miss. We return to the nature of expressions such as *John's refusing of the offer* – so-called mixed nominals – in §6.3.3.2 below.

Finally, consider the class to which the unacceptable derived nominals belong. Most generative grammarians are of the opinion that not all unacceptable utterances are equally unacceptable. This is also true of unacceptable derived nominals. It is therefore possible to order the members of the class of unacceptable derived nominals in terms of the relation "more/less unacceptable than". For instance, the derived nominal *John's easiness to please* may be ordered with regard to the derived nominal *his criticism of the book before he read it* in terms of the relation "more unacceptable than"'. Some speakers of English, while judging that both these nominals are unacceptable, consider the latter expression to be less unacceptable than the former. The (relative) unacceptability of *his criticism of the book before he read it* will be discussed in §10.1 and §11.3.1.2.2.

Note that no ordering is possible without grammatical working hypotheses. The grammarian has to have some idea of which ordering relations may be linguistically significant. For instance, at the basis of the last example of ordering given above, is a working hypothesis such as (31).

(31)   With regard to two members of the same linguistic class it may be linguistically significant that the one is more/less unacceptable than the other.

The grammatical and general linguistic background assumptions are once again the source of such grammatical working hypotheses.

4.3.2.2.3.4   *Measuring*   In certain forms of inquiry a fourth type of activity plays a role in the systematization of a corpus of data, viz. measuring. MEASURING involves determining a quantitative value for a quality of an object or a class. In other words, measuring implies the quantification of a quality. Successful measuring may greatly enhance the preciseness of the data in a corpus. Linguistic inquiry differs from natural science and social inquiry in that measuring plays almost no rule in the former type of inquiry. This does not mean, however, that it would be senseless in principle to try and quantify linguistic qualities.

Consider, for instance, the linguistic quality expressed in terms of the relation "less unacceptable than". It would be quite possible to have a scale of degrees of acceptability in terms of which different numerical values could be assigned to this quality. It should be obvious that a quantitative statement such as (32)(b) is much more precise than a qualitative statement such as (32)(a).

(32)(a)   The derived nominal *his criticism of the book before he read it* is less unacceptable than the derived nominal *John's easiness to please.*

(b)   On the scale S of unacceptability, the derived nominal *his criticism of the book before he read it* has the value 3, while the derived nominal *John's easiness to please* has the value 10.

Measuring could therefore be quite useful in linguistic inquiry as a means of ensuring that a high level of precision is attained in systematizing data. Measuring, however, is a senseless activity in the absence of adequate measuring procedures, i.e. measuring procedures which consistently yield results that are both valid and reliable. A measuring procedure produces valid results when it in fact measures what it is intended to measure. It produces reliable results when its results are consistently accurate. Developing adequate measuring procedures is a highly complex enterprise. Generative grammarians generally do not spend much time on the development of such measuring procedures and the associated scales for the quantification or grading of qualities.

4.3.2.2.4   *Symbolizing*

The collection and systematization of data about linguistic units does not yet result in a pretheoretical description of the properties of these linguistic units. This requires a third type of activity, viz. symbolizing. Generally speaking, SYMBOLIZING implies representing something with the aid of symbols. In the case of a pretheoretical grammatical description, symbolizing involves the representing of the systematized grammatical data with the aid of symbols. Symbolizing is also commonly referred to as "describing".

The first two main activities involved in giving a pretheoretical grammatical description – viz. data collecting and systematization – are essentially intellectual activities. Symbolization, on the other hand, is essentially a linguistic activity, as it involves the use of some type of language – natural or artificial. In grammatical inquiry symbolization generally involves the use of a natural language. This results in linguistic statements such as those of (22), (24), (27), (28) and (29) about problematic linguistic units. In addition to expressions of natural languages, pretheoretical grammatical descriptions also contain special symbols, tables, figures, diagrams, etc. In (33) a few examples are given of the various means of symbolization.

(33)   MEANS OF SYMBOLIZATION

type	examples		
expressions of natural languages	"sentence", "utterance", "nominal", "gerundive", "acceptable", "is", "and", "not"		
special symbols	"S", "NP", "VP", "AUX", " * "		
diagrams	$[_S [_{NP} [_N]_N]_{NP} [_{VP} [_V]_V]_{VP}]_S$ S NP VP N V I see		
tables		semantically regular	internal structure of S	internal structure of NP
	derived nominals	no	no	yes
	gerundive nominals	yes	yes	no

The means used in symbolization, as part of the giving of pretheoretical grammatical descriptions, must satisfy certain criteria. Among these criteria are the criteria of sufficiency and of nonobscurity.

(34)(a)   The criterion of sufficiency: the symbolic means should make it possible to represent *every* part of the information about the corpus of systematized data.

(b)   The criterion of nonobscurity: a symbol must have a single, fixed value in all the contexts in which it is used.

The criteria of (34) are adopted to ensure that pretheoretical grammatical descriptions are maximally precise and unambiguous. The better the pretheoretical descriptions of the problematic properties of linguistic units, the greater the possibility of constructing well-formed problems on the basis of these linguistic units.

4.3.2.2.5   *Interrelatedness*

In conclusion, let us consider the interrelatedness of data collecting, systematization and symbolization as aspects of the giving of pretheoretical grammatical descriptions. These three activities do not represent successive phases in the giving of a pretheoretical description. In other words, it is not as though the grammarian *first* collects his data, *then* systematizes these data and *finally* symbolizes the systematized data. From a temporal point of view, these activities take place simultaneously when the grammarian is giving a pretheoretical grammatical description. While the grammarian collects his data, he is already attempting to systematize them, and the results of these preliminary attempts at systematization are simultaneously symbolized. In fact, data collecting is impossible without systematization, and systematization is impossible without symbolization. The distinction between these three activities is therefore a logical distinction. Data collecting, systematization and symbolization represent logically distinguishable aspects — not temporally distinguishable phases — of the giving of a pretheoretical grammatical description.

The various activities involved in the giving of pretheoretical grammatical descriptions are represented schematically in (35).

(35)

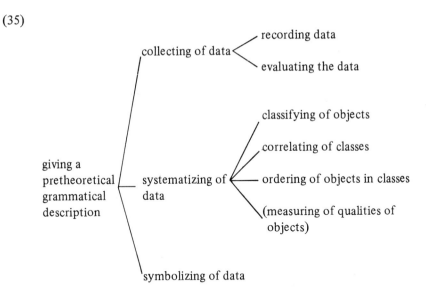

It is clear from (35) what a complex activity the giving of pretheoretical grammatical descriptions is, and this in itself is but one aspect of the description of a problematic grammatical state of affairs. The other aspects are: the specification of the grammatical background knowledge and/or assumptions by virtue of which the grammatical data are problematic; the specification of the general linguistic background knowledge and/or assumptions by virtue of which the grammatical data are problematic, and the specification of the metascientific assumptions about grammatical inquiry by virtue of which the grammatical data are problematic.

4.3.2.2.6 *Taxonomic linguistic inquiry*

Recall that the guiding aim of grammatical inquiry is the solving of grammatical problems. For this reason, pretheoretical grammatical descriptions cannot be the end product of grammatical inquiry. The information contained in such descriptions does not offer solutions for the grammatical problems which triggered the investigation. More specifically, such pretheoretical grammatical descriptions offer neither the insight nor the explanations in which the generative grammarian is interested. This applies not only to linguistic inquiry, but also to empirical inquiry in general. A. Cornelius Benjamin (1965:88) gives a striking formulation of this point:

The traditional positivists, therefore, seem to be wrong in insisting that description represents full-grown science. Facts must be collected, of course, before there can be science, and they must be classified and correlated. But a descriptive science is not a mature science; rather, it is a science in its youth — science still exhibiting the characteristics of childhood but showing also the promise of adolescence. When an inquiry has become descriptive it has taken on only the minimum features of genuine science. It gives us something to talk about — something which arouses our curiosity, like symptoms told to a doctor. But not until the facts have been accurately observed, reported, perhaps manipulated in various ways, and organized are we ready for the real task of science — that leap into the unknown which provides us with an explanation in terms of hypothetical and theoretical notions.

There does exist a form of linguistic inquiry which is essentially concerned with giving pretheoretical grammatical descriptions of corpora of linguistic units. This form of linguistic inquiry is known as "taxonomic linguistic inquiry". The main objectives of TAXONOMIC LINGUISTIC INQUIRY are the collecting of data about limited corpora of linguistic units, the systematization of the collected data, and the symbolization of the systematized data. Taxonomic linguistic inquiry is not concerned with gaining insight into or giving explanations for problematic grammatical states of affairs. It is essentially and exclusively interested in collecting and cataloging "facts" about linguistic units. A discussion of the metascientific aspects of taxonomic linguistic inquiry falls outside the scope of our study. In §11.4.2.1.2, however, we shall consider a few of the distinctive features of this form of linguistic inquiry.

4.3.2.3   *Constructing Problems*

In the preceding paragraphs we have dealt in detail with two of the four main types of activities involved in formulating well-formed grammatical problems. The first was the analyzing and the second the describing of the problematic grammatical state of affairs. The third main type of activity involved in formulating well-formed grammatical problems is the CONSTRUCTING of the problem. The constructing of a grammatical problem has two aspects: a conceptual aspect and a linguistic aspect. We shall consider these two aspects separately.

Recall that what is problematic in a given grammatical state of affairs may be regarded as a gap or a lacuna in the knowledge about a particular language. It should now be clear from the analysis and description of a problematic grammatical state of affairs what the nature and extent of this gap in the grammatical knowledge about the language is. The CONCEPTUAL ASPECT of the construction of a grammatical problem implies that the grammarian, in terms of concepts, gives as precise a representation as possible of the nature and extent of this gap in the grammatical knowledge. On the conceptual level, therefore, constructing a problem means precisely delineating a fragment of ignorance. From this delineation it must be clear what it is that the grammarian must come to know'in order to "deproblematize" the problematic state of affairs.

The concepts, or units of thought, used in this delineation refer to the various components of the problematic state of affairs. A first class of concepts —

PHENOMENOLOGICAL CONCEPTS – refers to factual data about problematic properties of linguistic units. These concepts are called "phenomenological" because they represent those properties of linguistic phenomena which may be intuitively known. A second class of concepts – GRAMMATICAL CONCEPTS – refers to the grammatical background knowledge and/or assumptions within the framework of which these properties are problematic. A third class of concepts – GENERAL LINGUISTIC CONCEPTS – refers to the general linguistic background knowledge and/or assumptions within the framework of which these properties are problematic. A fourth class of concepts – METASCIENTIFIC CONCEPTS – refers to the assumptions about the aims and nature of grammatical inquiry within the framework of which these properties of linguistic units are problematic.

In order to make these points more concrete, consider the following grammatical problem:

(36) How is the fact that, whereas the expression *John's eagerness to please* is acceptable, the expression **John's easiness to please* is unacceptable, to be explained on the transformationalist hypothesis?

Note that in constructing this problem, the grammarian has used the concepts 'acceptable', 'unacceptable' and 'expression'. The factual element of the problem is constructed in terms of these concepts. Another concept which is central to the constructing of the problem is that of 'explained'. This concept refers to the grammarian's acceptance of a particular objective of grammatical inquiry. In terms of the concepts referring to the factual element in the problematic state of affairs – 'acceptable', 'unacceptable' and 'expression' – and the metascientific concept 'explained', the problem (36) may be given a less specific formulation.

(37) How is the fact to be explained that, whereas the expression *John's eagerness to please* is acceptable, the expression *John's easiness to please* is unacceptable.

Note, however, that in constructing the grammatical problem (36) the concept 'transformationalist hypothesis' has been used as well. In the context of (36) this concept has two levels of content. On the first level, the concept represents a background assumption about a particular language: in English derived nominals are generated transformationally. By using the concept 'transformationalist hypothesis' in constructing the problem (36), the content of the problem has been made much more precise than that of the problem (37). In (36) an indication is given of the type of explanation – a transformationalist one – required for solving that which is problematic. On the second level, the content of the concept 'transformationalist hypothesis' represents a background assumption about human language in general: transformations are significant components in the structure of human language in general.

Thus the problem (36) has been constructed by relating to one another units of thought, or concepts, belonging to four different classes: concepts representing factual data about a particular language; a concept representing a background assumption about a particular language; a concept representing a background assumption about human language in general; and a concept representing an assumption about the objectives of grammatical inquiry. Grammatical problems are typically constructed in terms of concepts belonging to these four classes.

This brings us to the second aspect of the constructing of a grammatical problem: the LINGUISTIC ASPECT. This aspect involves the symbolization of the conceptual content of the problem. Grammatical problems are normally symbolized in terms of expressions of natural languages, i.e. they are "put into words". The problems (36) and (37) illustrate this point. The outward, or linguistic, form of a grammatical problem is often that of an interrogative sentence. This point also is illustrated by the problems (36) and (37).

The conceptual and linguistic aspects of the constructing of grammatical problems can be distinguished from each other, but not separated. In other words, when analyzed metascientifically, these aspects are found to have different characteristics. The conceptual aspect comprises the manipulation of concepts, while the linguistic aspect comprises the manipulation of linguistic symbols. In practice, however, it is impossible to construct a problem in terms of concepts, without simultaneously representing it by means of linguistic expressions. Even when the grammarian is still "conceiving" the problem, linguistic expressions are used for giving a form to the problem.

4.3.2.4   *Evaluating Problems*

In the preceding paragraphs we have seen that problems play a most important role in grammatical inquiry. They direct the grammarian's search for the knowledge which has to be gained in order to resolve problematic states of affairs. In view of the importance of this guiding function of grammatical problems, the grammarian does not accept just any problem. Only the problems which satisfy certain criteria are deemed fit for the task of guiding grammatical inquiry.

There are two fundamental criteria which a grammatical problem must satisfy in order to be a guiding factor in grammatical inquiry.

(38)(a)   A grammatical problem must be well-formed.
   (b)   A grammatical problem must be significant.

Evaluating problems in terms of the criteria of well-formedness and significance represents the fourth main type of activity involved in formulating grammatical problems. So let us take a closer look at these criteria.

4.3.2.4.1   *Assessing for well-formedness*
The obvious question, as far as well-formedness is concerned, is: what distinguishes

a well-formed grammatical problem from an ill-formed one? A well-formed grammatical problem is a problem which is, in principle, solvable. In other works, it is a problem which contains no element that precludes the possibility of gaining the knowledge needed to "deproblematize" the problematic grammatical state of affairs in question. Ill-formed grammatical problems, by contrast, are in principle insoluble. An ill-formed problem contains one or more elements which preclude the possibility of gaining new knowledge.

But what are the criteria in terms of which grammatical problems are to be assessed for well-formedness? Let us consider, first of all, a few typical ill-formed grammatical problems and try to determine the cause of the ill-formedness of each one of them.

Consider the following grammatical problem:

(39)   How should the fact that the expressions *John's deeds* and *the things which John did* are synonymous be explained by a grammar of English?

This grammatical problem is ill-formed because it is based on an incorrect linguistic intuition. The expressions in question are not synonymous in English. The problem (39) is the result of an error in the grammarian's data collecting. His assessment of the correctness of his primary linguistic data was inadequate. A mistake in any of the activities involved in the collecting of data may thus result in an ill-formed grammatical problem.

Now consider the grammatical problem (40).

(40)   How should a grammar of English account for the fact that the following gerundive nominals contain the preposition *of: John's refusing of the offer, John's proving of the theorem, the growing of tomatoes?*

This grammatical problem also is ill-formed. Its ill-formedness is the result of an error of classification. The expressions in question were wrongly classified as gerundive nominals. As regards their internal structure, these expressions have a number of properties characteristic of NPs: for instance, the possessive subject may be replaced by *the* as in the case of *the growing of tomatoes*. The problem (40) therefore wrongly suggests that the solution will be transformational instead of lexical. A mistake in any of the activities involved in the systematization of the data may therefore result in an ill-formed grammatical problem.

Incorrect symbolization of the systematized data may also give rise to ill-formed grammatical problems. The first class of factors at the root of ill-formed grammatical problems concerns mistakes made in the giving of pretheoretical grammatical descriptions. In other words, wrong factual assumptions, i.e. assumptions about grammatical data, result in the constructing of ill-formed grammatical problems. This is why it is so important that pretheoretical grammatical descriptions should be adequate: inadequate pretheoretical grammatical descriptions give rise to ill-formed grammatical problems.

Let us consider a grammatical problem which is ill-formed for quite a different reason.

(41)   Is the element *of* in the derived nominal *John's refusal of the offer* a postposition of *refusal* or is it a preposition of *the offer?*

The grammatical problem (41) is ill-formed because it has been constructed in terms of a mistaken background assumption about English, viz. that postpositions are a significant structural category in English. As a result of this assumption, (41) is an insoluble grammatical problem. Thus, incorrect grammatical background assumptions give rise to unsolvable problems in the same way as do incorrect factual assumptions. Unsolvable problems cannot guide the grammarian in his search for new knowledge about particular languages.

Let us assume for the sake of argument that there are clear stylistic differences between gerundive and derived nominals. The following grammatical problem is then ill-formed as well:

(42)   How should the stylistic differences between gerundive nominals and corresponding derived nominals be specified in a grammar of English?

Within the framework of linguistic inquiry, (42) is an ill-formed grammatical problem because it includes an incorrect general linguistic background assumption, viz. that stylistic differences between linguistic units are grammatically significant. In generative grammar, such differences are conventionally regarded as irrelevant to the description of human languages. No solution to the problem (42) therefore exists within the framework of generative grammar. In passing, it should be noted, however, that in his recent book, *A transformational approach to English syntax* (1976:9ff.), Joe Emonds creates a framework within which certain stylistic differences between linguistic units are indeed relevant to the description of particular languages.

Consider another example of an ill-formed grammatical problem.

(43)   Which mechanical procedure may be used for the classification of gerundive and derived nominals in English?

Within the framework of generative grammar (43) is an ill-formed grammatical problem because it has been constructed in terms of a mistaken assumption about the nature of grammatical inquiry. This is the assumption that the classification of linguistic units with the aid of mechanical procedures is an objective of generative grammar. A mechanical procedure is a procedure of which the application requires no mental effort worth mentioning on the part of the linguist. Generative grammar does not aim at developing such procedures for making grammatical analyses.

A final instance of an ill-formed grammatical problem is given in (44).

(44)   Is the higher productivity of gerundive nominalization in English a relative or an absolute phenomenon?

As a grammatical problem, (44) is ill-formed because it is not at all clear how it should be understood. Its ill-formedness is the result of its obscure, unintelligible formulation. Note that in (44) two expressions have been used of which the sense cannot be determined: "the higher productivity" and "a relative or an absolute phenomenon". A problem of which the formulation is obscure is unsolvable. On the one hand it is not clear what it is that is problematic, and on the other hand it is not clear what grammatical knowledge would represent a solution for this problem.

Let us return to the question about the criteria which a grammatical problem should satisfy in order to be well-formed. From our discussion of a number of typical ill-formed grammatical problems, five fundamental criteria have emerged.

(45)   In order to be WELL-FORMED, a grammatical problem should contain

   (a)   no incorrect factual assumptions, i.e. assumptions about linguistic data;

   (b)   no incorrect grammatical background assumptions, i.e. assumptions about the structure of a particular human language;

   (c)   no incorrect general linguistic background assumptions, i.e. assumptions about the nature and properties of human language in general;

   (d)   no incorrect metascientific assumptions, i.e. assumptions about the nature and aspects of linguistic inquiry, and

   (e)   no obscure elements, i.e. uninterpretable expressions, in its formulation.

A grammatical problem which fails to satisfy one or more of the criteria (45) (a)–(e) is ill-formed. Grammatical problems are evaluated with a view to identifying and eliminating ill-formed problems. A grammatical investigation which is triggered and guided by ill-formed problems cannot, in principle, yield insight into particular human languages.

4.3.2.4.2   *Assessing for significance*
A grammarian does not judge all well-formed grammatical problems to be interesting. He is interested only in problems of which the solution will significantly expand the existing knowledge about a particular human language. Not every solution of a well-formed grammatical problem contributes equally to the expansion of the existing knowledge. Well-formed grammatical problems of which the solution contributes significantly to the expansion of the scientific knowledge about a language are considered to be SIGNIFICANT GRAMMATICAL PROBLEMS. Well-formed problems of which the solution does not contribute significantly to the expansion of this knowledge are considered to be NON-

SIGNIFICANT GRAMMATICAL PROBLEMS. The second aspect of the evaluation of grammatical problems comprises the following: the grammarian attempts to judge which of the well-formed grammatical problems encountered in his investigation are significant and which are not. Obviously, in his inquiry he will concentrate on the solving of significant grammatical problems.

Let us consider the distinction 'significant-nonsignificant' with reference to a number of examples of grammatical problems. Consider, for instance, the following two problems which may be formulated within the framework of a grammatical investigation of nominalization in English:

(46)(a)   What is the nature of the relatedness between sentences and corresponding derived nominals: lexical or transformational?

(b)   What is the shared form element in the expressions *criticize, criticizing* and *criticism?*

Both these problems are well-formed. Within the framework of a grammatical investigation of nominalization in English, however, there is a marked difference in their significance. As a grammatical problem, (46)(a) is considerably more significant than (46)(b). In other words, the solution of (46)(a) would make a much larger contribution to the scientific knowledge about English than the solution of (46)(b).

Judging the significance of grammatical problems is no simple matter. Two factors in particular complicate matters. In the first place, the significance of a grammatical problem is a variable property which may change along with the circumstances. A first circumstance concerns the nature of the problem with which a given grammatical problem is being compared. For instance, the problem (46)(b) is relatively insignificant when compared with (46)(a). But in comparison with the problem (47), the problem (46)(b) becomes quite significant within the framework of a grammatical investigation of nominalization in English.

(47)   What are the features of the first phonetic segment of the expressions *criticize, criticizing* and *criticism?*

The solution of the problem (47) would contribute next to nothing to the knowledge about the process of nominalization in English. By contrast, the solution of the problem (46)(b) would make some contribution to this knowledge. The important point is that a judgment of significance is a relative judgment. A given grammatical problem is more or less significant only in relation to another grammatical problem.

The second circumstance in accordance with which the significance of a grammatical problem may vary, concerns the stage of inquiry which has been reached. This point may be illustrated with reference to the following well-formed grammatical problem:

(48)   Is the expression *his criticism of the book before he read it* acceptable or not?

In the initial stages of the grammatical investigation of nominalization in English, the problem (48) was relatively insignificant. After Chomsky had proposed the lexicalist hypothesis, however, (48) became a significant problem. According to this hypothesis, derived nominals have the internal structure of NPs. The expression *his criticism of the book before he read it* represents a derived nominal which contains a constituent of a VP in the form of *before he read it*. In terms of the lexicalist hypothesis, therefore, this expression should be unacceptable. But some speakers of English apparently find the expression acceptable. It is therefore of the utmost importance for the evaluation of the lexicalist hypothesis during the later stages of the investigation that a solution be found for the problem (48). In these later stages (48) therefore becomes a significant problem. In short: judgments concerning the significance of grammatical problems are also relative to the stage of inquiry that has been reached.

This brings us to the second factor which complicates the making of judgments about the significance of grammatical problems. The first factor was the variability of the property of significance. The second factor is the absence of clear criteria of significance. Grammarians' judgments about the significance of grammatical problems are generally based on their knowledge of the subject, their experience in conducting linguistic inquiry and their "feelings" as to how an investigation will or may develop. It is nearly impossible to formulate such considerations as simple criteria of significance. Yet the judgments of grammarians about the significance of grammatical problems are an important regulating factor in grammatical inquiry.

4.3.2.5   *The Formulating of Grammatical Problems*

It is clear from the discussion so far that the formulating of well-formed grammatical problems is a complex activity. It may therefore be useful to summarize briefly what has been said in the preceding paragraphs.

(49)   As an intellectual enterprise, the formulating of well-formed grammatical problems involves four main types of activities:

    (a)   analyzing a problematic grammatical state of affairs by determining the components representing

       (i)   the problematic linguistic data,

       (ii)   the grammatical background assumptions,

       (iii)   the general linguistic background assumptions and

       (iv)   the metascientific background assumptions;

    (b)   describing this problematic state of affairs by, among other things, giving a pretheoretical grammatical description of the

problematic linguistic units which are the result of
   (i) the collecting of primary linguistic data,
  (ii) the evaluating of these data,
 (iii) the systematizing of these data, and
 (iv) the symbolizing of these data;

(c)   constructing a problem by means of the manipulation of
   (i) phenomenological, grammatical, general linguistic and meta-scientific concepts and
  (ii) expressions which symbolize these concepts linguistically;

(d)   evaluating this problem with regard to
   (i) well-formedness and
  (ii) significance.

4.4   GENERAL LINGUISTIC INQUIRY

4.4.1   General

In the preceding paragraphs we considered a grammatical problem as a gap or a lacuna in the scientific knowledge about an individual human language. In an analogous way, a GENERAL LINGUISTIC PROBLEM may be seen as a gap in the scientific knowledge about human language in general. We had a detailed look at what is involved in the formulation of well-formed and significant grammatical problems. The formulating of well-formed and significant general linguistic problems is no different in any essential respect. Formulating general linguistic problems also involves four fundamental intellectual activities: (a) analyzing the problematic state of affairs, (b) describing the problematic state of affairs, (c) constructing a problem and (d) evaluating this problem.

As intellectual activities, (a) – (d) above are not essentially different in general linguistic inquiry from the corresponding activities in grammatical inquiry. Therefore it will not be necessary to consider the nature of these activities with regard to general linguistic inquiry. General linguistic inquiry does, however, differ from grammatical inquiry with regard to the import of the problems by which the inquiry is directed. Let us consider this point more closely.

4.4.2   Nature of General Linguistic Problems

The distinction between substantive and metascientific problems can be drawn with regard to general linguistic problems as well.

4.4.2.1   *Substantive Problems*

In general linguistic inquiry, SUBSTANTIVE PROBLEMS are concerned with linguistic universals. These problems represent gaps in the scientific knowledge about that which is "general", "universal" or "essential" in all natural languages. Substantive problems of this nature may take two forms which, in linguistic inquiry, are considered to be equivalent.

The first form that substantive general linguistic problems may take is that of problems about the class of possible human languages. In essence, this form of problem concerns the question of whether a given linguistic principle is language-particular or universal, i.e. language-independent. A language-particular linguistic principle is regarded as a component of only one or a few particular languages. At this juncture of our study a universal linguistic principle, i.e. a linguistic universal, can be regarded as a structural component of every possible human language. By implication, a universal linguistic principle should therefore form part of every existing human language. This may be illustrated by an example.

In § 1.3 it appeared that the lexicalist hypothesis provides for the existence of neutral lexical entries for pairs of items such as *refuse–refusal, easy–easiness, criticize–criticism,* etc. The following question arises with regard to such neutral lexical entries:

(50)   Do neutral lexical entries represent a type of structural element which is restricted to English or do these entries represent a type of structural element which is typical of every possible human language?

This is a typical example of a substantive general linguistic problem which takes the form of a problem about the class of possible human languages. General linguistic inquiry is concerned with giving as accurate a characterization as possible – in terms of linguistic universals – of the class of possible human languages.

The second, equivalent form which substantive general linguistic problems may take is that of problems about language acquisition and, in particular, problems about the properties of man's innate language acquisition faculty. The fundamental question is whether or not a particular linguistic principle forms part of man's language faculty. In this form, the general linguistic problem of (51) may be formulated as follows:

(51)   Does the principle of neutral lexical entries represent a linguistic principle which may be learned on the basis of experience of the utterances of a language, or does it represent an (innate) part of man's language acquisition faculty?

To regard a linguistic principle as an aspect of man's language faculty, is to consider it not to be learnable on the basis of experience of utterances. In other words, it is the same as regarding this principle as innate, or biologically endowed. Within the framework of linguistic inquiry, the problems (50) and (51) are equivalent. Their equivalence follows from two assumptions which generative grammarians make. The first is that linguistic universals exist as aspects of man's language acquisition faculty. The second is that language-particular linguistic principles exist as aspects of the linguistic competence which may be learned on the basis of experience of the utterances of the language in question.

4.4.2.2   *Metascientific Problems*

In conducting his inquiry, the general linguist encounters METASCIENTIFIC PROBLEMS of varying degrees of abstractness. We shall consider a few typical examples of these problems.

On the first and most concrete level, the general linguist is confronted with the problems which arise in the course of an individual general linguistic investigation. These metascientific problems represent difficulties in connection with the nature, aspects and conduct of the investigation. Consider the following typical examples:

(52)(a)   Is the idealization I which has been made for the purpose of the general linguistic investigation G a fruitful idealization?

(b)   Is the general linguistic explanation E for the phenomenon P adequate?

(c)   Is the statement S that U is a linguistic universal correct?

Metascientific problems such as (52)(a)–(c) in general linguistic inquiry correspond with metascientific problems such as (10)(a)–(e) in grammatical inquiry.

On the second, more abstract level, the general linguist encounters problems about metascientific problems. These more abstract metascientific problems concern both matascientific problems – such as (10)(a)–(e) – of grammatical inquiry, and metascientific problems – such as (52)(a) – (c) – of general linguistic inquiry. Consider, once again, the metascientific problems (10)(a) – (e) of grammatical inquiry. For the general linguist these problems give rise to more abstract metascientific problems such as the following:

(53)(a)   What criteria should an idealization in grammatical inquiry satisfy in order to be fruitful?

(b)   What criteria may be used to determine whether or not linguistic intuitions are correct?

(c)   What criteria should pretheoretical grammatical descriptions satisfy in order to be adequate?

(d)   What criteria should grammatical explanations satisfy in order to be adequate?

(e)   What criteria may be used to determine whether or not grammatical claims are correct?

The more abstract metascientific problems (53)(a)–(e) relate to the metascientific problems (10)(a)–(e) respectively. It appears, therefore, that every metascientific problem of grammatical inquiry gives rise to a more abstract metascientific general linguistic problem. The latter type of problem is not restricted to specific, individual grammatical investigations, but it concerns grammatical inquiry in general. It is therefore not the task of the grammarian of a particular language to solve these problems. It is a task for the general linguist.

Metascientific problems – such as (52)(a)–(c) – of a general linguistic inquiry also give rise to more abstract metascientific problems. On the second, more abstract level, the metascientific problems (52)(a)–(c) correspond with the more abstract metascientific problems (54)(a)–(c).

(54)(a)   What criteria should idealizations in general linguistic inquiry satisfy in order to be fruitful?

(b)   What criteria should general linguistic explanations satisfy in order to be adequate?

(c)   What criteria may be used to judge whether or not claims about linguistic universals are correct?

Compare the more abstract metascientific problems (54)(a)–(c) with those of (53)(a)–(e). It is clear that in both cases the same kinds of questions are being asked: questions about criteria of fruitfulness for idealizations; questions about criteria of adequacy for explanations; questions about criteria of correctness for claims; etc. It is therefore to be expected that these two sets of problems will have similar solutions.

4.4.2.3   *Problems vs. Mysteries*

With regard to grammatical inquiry, a distinction was drawn between well-formed and ill-formed problems. The class of well-formed problems was further divided into significant and nonsignificant problems. We now come to a third type of distinction: one which was made by Chomsky (1975c:ch.4) with regard to substantive general linguistic problems. This is Chomsky's distinction between problems and mysteries.

For Chomsky, PROBLEMS are questions for which it should be possible to find solutions within the framework of the existing approach to the study of language. Chomsky (1975c:138) cites the following examples of such general linguistic problems:

(55)(a)   What kinds of cognitive structures are developed by human beings on the basis of their experience, specifically in the case of the acquisition of language?

(b)   What is the basis on which these cognitive structures are acquired?

(c)   How do the acquired cognitive structures develop?

The domains on which problems such as (55)(a)–(c) touch are still largely unknown. Yet Chomsky considers it possible to reach satisfactory solutions for these problems in terms of the existing store of knowledge and within the framework of the existing approach to the study of language.

For Chomsky, MYSTERIES, on the other hand, are questions for which there seems to be no solution within the existing approach to the study of language. Mysteries represent questions in the investigation of which no progress seems to be made. Chomsky gives the following examples of such general linguistic mysteries:

(56)(a)   How do people use the cognitive structures, acquired in the process of language acquisition, in linguistic performance?

(b)   How do people succeed in acting appropriately and creatively in linguistic performance?

Chomsky is of the opinion that the "creative aspect of language use" in particular is just as much of a mystery today as it was for the Cartesians centuries ago.

It is important to note that Chomsky's distinction between problems and mysteries is not parallel to our distinction between well-formed and ill-formed problems. Mysteries, in particular, are not ill-formed problems. Ill-formed problems are unsolvable in principle, as they contain an element which precludes the possibility of gaining new knowledge about human language. Mysteries, on the contrary, are not in principle unsolvable in the sense that they contain such an element. They are unsolvable in the context of a particular phrase of development within the field of study: a phase characterized by inadequate knowledge and poorly developed approaches to the study of language. Nothing, however, precludes the possibility of this knowledge growing and these approaches being further developed, thus making it possible to find solutions to these mysteries. With regard to the distinction between significant and insignificant problems, the following may be said about mysteries: mysteries represent some of the most significant general linguistic problems. The most dramatic expansion of the existing store of general linguistic knowledge will be the result of the solving of mysteries.

4.5   STATUS OF THE FORMULATION OF PROBLEMS

In conclusion, a general point has to be elucidated in connection with the status of the formulation of problems in linguistic inquiry. Generative grammarians publish the results of their investigations in the form of technical research reports: articles, monographs, books, etc. These technical reports contain mainly two things. On the one hand, they specify the problems for which solutions are sought. On the other hand, the solutions for these problems are given and justified.

What these technical reports generally do not contain is a complete and true representation of the various kinds of activities carried out by the linguist in formulating and solving his problem. Even the products of these activities — analyses of problematic states of affairs, pretheoretical grammatical descriptions, etc. — are very rarely represented in detail in these technical reports.

From the fact that technical research reports give an incomplete picture of the activities and their products mentioned above, the following conclusion may not be drawn, viz. that these activities play no role in linguistic inquiry. It is not the function of technical reports to present a complete and true picture of the linguist's research activities. Their function is to offer elegantly formulated and well-reasoned solutions to linguistic problems. The highways and byways by which the linguist reaches these solutions are matters for his personal diary or for the metascientist's study of linguistic inquiry.

Finally, in § 12.2 it will be shown that, within the framework of generative grammar, a distinction may be drawn between various kinds of investigations. It will then be pointed out that the formulating of linguistic problems does not necessarily play a central role in every kind of investigation. Investigations directed at linguistic phenomena which have not been studied in any great depth and which, consequently, are still poorly understood represent the kind of investigation of which the formulating of problems is an essential part.

SELECTED READING

Not much that is useful has been published about the various aspects of the formulating of problems in empirical inquiry in general and in linguistic inquiry in particular. Only a limited number of readings which are really informative are given below.

General Nature of the Formulating of Problems

   Northrop 1966:ch.1–3.

General Metascientific Discussion of Problems

   Nature, Aspects, Properties of Problems
   Bunge 1967a:ch.4.

   Typologies of Problems
   Bunge 1967a:ch.4; Northrop 1966:ch.2.

Well-formedness of Problems

Bunge 1967a: ch.4.

Weighting of Problems for Significance

Laudan 1977:31ff., 64ff.

Pretheoretical (Grammatical) Descriptions

Recording of Data

Benjamin 1965:ch.2.

Evaluating of Data

Bever 1974; Botha 1973: §5.4; Katz and Bever 1974.

Systematizing of Data

Benjamin 1965:ch.4; Botha 1968: §3.2; Bunge 1967a: §§2.4., 2.5.; Caws 1966:ch.6; Northrop 1966:ch.3.

Symbolizing of Data

Benjamin 1965:ch.3; Bunge 1967a: §2.1; Caws 1966:ch.5; Harré 1967:ch.1, 3.

Taxonomic Linguistic Inquiry

Botha 1968: §3.2; Gleason 1969; Lyons 1970:ch.3; Searle 1974:1–8.

Laudan's study (1977) deserves special mention: it represents an attempt at developing a comprehensive new philosophy of science or "model of scientific progress" based on the view that science aims fundamentally at the solution of problems.

CHAPTER FIVE

Making Linguistic Discoveries

5.0 PERSPECTIVE

In this chapter we shall be considering the making of linguistic discoveries as a third main aspect of linguistic inquiry. The making of discoveries in empirical inquiry in general is the topic of the first part of the chapter. First of all we take a look at the nature of insight into or understanding of a problematic state of affairs, as this is what discovery is essentially about. The attention then shifts to the nature of discovery as an intellectual activity. Two general points of view about the nature of this activity are considered. The first is that discovery is essentially a nonrational activity; the second, that discovery is, to a large extent, a rational activity. Having taken note of these two points of view, discovery is considered from the point of view of the constructing of tentative hypotheses and theories. In conclusion, a number of strategies are discussed which are used by scientists to create more favourable circumstances for the construction of hypotheses.

The second part of the chapter deals with the nature of discovery in grammatical inquiry. A distinction is drawn between language-specific and language-independent discoveries. Examples are given to illustrate how the grammarian is guided by general linguistic assumptions in making language-specific discoveries.

The topic of the third part of the chapter is the nature of general linguistic discoveries. It is shown that, unlike grammatical discovery, general linguistic discovery is not a systematically guided activity. Some general linguistic discoveries, however, are in fact made in a nonaccidental way. It is then shown that the general linguist is directed towards such discoveries by the framework of linguistic knowledge within which he is working. Two of the directing aspects of this framework are singled out for special attention. The first takes the form of general linguistic principles of a "higher order"; the second, that of previously solved general linguistic problems.

5.1 INTRODUCTION

We have found three types of differences between gerundive and derived nominals which are problematic for the grammarian of English. The first type of difference concerns syntactic regularity, or productivity. For every gerundive nominal there is a corresponding sentence and for every – not too complex – sentence a corresponding gerundive nominal is to be found. But many sentences do not have corresponding derived nominals and for many derived nominals there are no corresponding sentences. The second type of difference concerns semantic regularity. The semantic interpretation of gerundive nominals may be predicted in terms of the meaning of their constituents and the relationships between these constituents. Many derived nominals, on the other hand, have unpredictable aspects of meaning. The third type of difference concerns internal syntactic structure. While gerundive nominals have the internal structure of sentences, derived nominals have the internal structure of NPs.

Against this background of facts and assumptions, the grammarian of English formulates the following problem:

(1)   Why is it that gerundive nominals and derived nominals differ from each other with regard to syntactic regularity, semantic regularity and internal syntactic structure?

To solve the problem (1) an explanation has to be given for the three types of differences between gerundive and derived nominals. Chomsky proposed the following solution for this problem:

(2)   Gerundive nominals are transforms of sentence-like deep structures, while derived nominals are deep structure NPs.

Chomsky regards (2) as an adequate solution for the grammatical problem (1). In terms of (2) it can be understood why the three types of differences mentioned above exist between gerundive and derived nominals. Transforms are essentially syntactically and semantically regular and must have the internal structure of sentences. Deep structure NPs do not necessarily have these properties. Let us assume for the purpose of our discussion that Chomsky's solution for the grammatical problem under consideration is correct.

The important question for us is: how did Chomsky conceive of (2) as a solution for the grammatical problem (1)? Or, how did Chomsky gain the insight in terms of which the problematic state of affairs in question was resolved? In other words, how did Chomsky discover that gerundive nominals are transforms while derived nominals are deep structure NPs? As far as their content is concerned, these three questions are equivalent.

Questions with the general tenor of the three we formulated in the previous paragraph – questions about scientific discovery – will be our concern in this chapter. These questions indicate the existence of a third main aspect of linguistic inquiry: the making of linguistic discoveries. We shall regard the making of scientific discoveries in general as follows: the making of a scientific discovery involves the gaining of insight, or understanding, in terms of which a well-formed

scientific problem can be solved. Schematically, the making of linguistic discoveries, as a third main aspect of linguistic inquiry, may be represented as follows:

(3)

| well-formed problem | → | activities of third main aspect | → | insight/understanding needed for solution |

Among the questions which may be asked in connection with this scheme, two
are fundamental.

(4) (a) What is the nature of the insight, or understanding, which is involved in scientific discovery?
(b) How does a scientist make a scientific discovery?

The first question, (4)(a), concerns the nature of the output of the diagram (3).
The second question, (4)(b), concerns the nature of the content of the square in
the diagram (3), i.e. the nature of the intellectual activity known as "scientific
discovery". We shall consider the questions (4)(a) and (b), first from the point
of view of inquiry in general and then from the point of view of linguistic inquiry.

5.2 INQUIRY IN GENERAL

5.2.1 The Nature of Insight

The question (4)(a) as to the nature of insight represents a complex philosophical
problem. A highly technical, philosophical discussion of this problem falls outside the scope of our study. Let us therefore approach the problem from another
angle and reformulate it as (5).

(5) Under what circumstances do scientists have the feeling that they have
(gained) insight into, or understanding of, a problematic state of affairs?

The circumstances referred to in (5) are described by scientists in terms of expressions such as "regularity", "pattern", "structure", "mechanism" and "cause". In
(6) a number of typical examples of descriptions in terms of these expressions
are given.

(6) To have INSIGHT into a problematic state of affairs involves
(a) being able to reduce whatever is problematic to – or to see it as
the manifestation of – an underlying regularity;
(b) being able to fit whatever is problematic into an underlying
pattern;

UNIVERSITY COLLEGE LIBRARY SWANSEA

(c)   being able to identify whatever is problematic as part of a structure, i.e. an ordered arrangement of parts;

(d)   being able to indicate the mechanism in terms of which whatever
is problematic "works"; or

(e)   being able to point out the cause of whatever is problematic.

The statements (6)(a)–(e) are overlapping, informal statements in terms of
which scientists often refer to insight. It is clear from (6) that many scientists
regard the search for insight as the search for the regularity, pattern, structure,
mechanisms or causes underlying that which is problematic.

Now consider Chomsky's solution (2) for the grammatical problem (1) about
the problematic differences between gerundive and derived nominals. Notice
that the solution consists in pointing out the regularity, pattern, structure or
mechanisms underlying that which is problematic. This is done in terms of the
expression "transforms", "sentence-like deep structures", and "deep structure
NPs".

In (6), circumstances are mentioned in which scientists *feel* that they have
insight into, or understanding of, a problematic state of affairs. The expression
"feel" has been used deliberately in connection with (6). Apparently, by using
this expression, we talk about insight, or understanding, in subjective psychological terms. It seems, then, that what was called the "ultimate objective" of
empirical inquiry in §3.2.2.3 is something subjective. Recall further that in a
subsequent paragraph, §3.2.2.4, we adopted the following criterion for scientific
knowledge: scientific knowledge should be intersubjective. But are we not now
faced with a contradiction? How can intersubjective knowledge be gained if the
ultimate objective of scientific inquiry is the pursuit of an apparently subjective
objective? A scientist whose ultimate objective is a certain feeling – the feeling
of having insight – , after all, appears to be pursuing something which is essentially subjective.

This, however, is only an apparent contradiction. Scientists in fact pursue this
ultimate objective of gaining insight in terms of a number of more immediate,
more specific objectives. These more immediate, more specific objectives are by
nature logical. We have already considered four of these nonsubjective, logical
objectives in terms of which scientists pursue the insight with which they are
ultimately concerned: (a) the giving of a description of the regularity, pattern,
structure, mechanisms or causes underlying that which is problematic; (b) the
giving of explanations for whatever is problematic; (c) the making of predictions
about an unknown future reality; and (d) the making of postdictions about
an unknown past reality. In subsequent parts of our study it will become clear
that descriptions, explanations, predictions and postdictions are by nature nonsubjective, logical objects. We shall also see that the giving of descriptions, the
giving of explanations and the making of predictions and postdictions are closely
interrelated.

It is now possible to characterize more precisely the circumstances in which scientists have insight into a problematic state of affairs.

(7)   To have INSIGHT into a problematic state of affairs involves
    (a)   being able to give a description of the regularity, pattern, structure, mechanisms or causes underlying it;
    (b)   being able to give an explanation for that which is problematic;
    (c)   being able to make predictions about similar states of affairs in an unknown reality of the future; and
    (d)   being able to make postdictions about similar states of affairs in an unknown reality of the past.

Within this framework lies the answer to the question (4)(a) – the question about the nature of insight. This framework will be filled in as our study progresses.

5.2.2   The Nature of Discovery

This brings us to the question (4)(b) concerning the nature of the activity of discovery. This question is often formulated as follows:

(8)   How do scientists discover the regularity, structure, pattern, mechanisms or causes underlying a problematic state of affairs?

The question (8) is obviously of crucial importance. On the one hand, an adequate answer to this question will reveal the nature of that with which inquiry is essentially concerned, viz. the making of discoveries. On the other hand, it is possible that an adequate answer to this question would enable scientists to develop all kinds of procedures for making discoveries. The development of such procedures would obviously contribute much to the advancement of science.

It will soon become clear, however, that the answers which are given to the question (8) are extremely disappointing. They are disappointing in the sense that they reveal preciously little about the nature of discovery. In their answers, scholars basically assume two points of view with regard to the nature of scientific discovery. According to the first point of view, discovery is essentially a nonrational activity. According to the second point of view, discovery is, to a fairly large extent, a rational activity. We shall discuss each of these points of view about the nature of scientific discovery in more detail.

5.2.2.1   *Nonrational Aspect of Discovery*

The majority of scholars, i.e. scientists and philosophers, hold that discovery is essentially a nonrational activity. According to a philosopher such as Popper

(1965:31) the conception of a new idea – be it a scientific theory, a musical theme or a dramatic conflict – is a nonrational activity. Popper and other like-minded scholars describe their attitude towards the nature of scientific discovery in terms of a distinction between the context of discovery and the context of justification in scientific inquiry.

In the CONTEXT OF DISCOVERY scientists conceive of the (new) ideas that give them insight into that which is problematic. In this context scientists "think out" new ideas. In the CONTEXT OF JUSTIFICATION, on the other hand, reasons are given why these ideas should, or should not, be accepted. In this context, then, the merit of these ideas is determined. The greatest merit an idea can have is that of being correct.

These scholars now argue that, in the context of discovery, empirical inquiry is a nonrational activity. This has two implications.

(9) (a)   No logical rules can be laid down for the thinking out of new ideas.
(b)   There are no mechanical procedures by means of which discoveries can be made.

As regards (9)(a): what is in fact being said is that no rules of thought or inference exist with the aid of which new ideas can be derived from existing ones. Informally, a logical rule is an instruction to deduce a unit of thought from another, existing unit of thought. According to (9)(a), there are no rules in terms of which the solution for a problem can infallibly be deduced from data about the problematic state of affairs in question. Therefore, no logical rules can be given in terms of which Chomsky "thought out" the solution (2) for the grammatical problem (1).

As regards (9)(b): the absence of logical rules for discovery excludes the possibility of developing mechanical procedures of discovery. For instance, true scientific problems can never be solved by computers. The possibility of programming a computer to devise such solutions presupposes the existence of logical rules for discovery.

For the scholars in question, scientific inquiry is a rational activity only in the context of justification. This has the following implication:

(10)   Logical rules exist which may be used to argue that a given idea has, or does not have, merit as a solution for a scientific problem.

What is being said in (10) is that it is possible, in a rational way, to give reasons why ideas gained by nonrational means should be accepted or rejected. In chapters 9 and 10 of our study, the implications of (10) for linguistic inquiry will be discussed in greater detail.

But what do we mean when we say that discoveries are made in a nonrational way? How are new ideas conceived as solutions for problems if there are no logical rules for discovery? In short, what is the nature of nonrational discovery? Scholars who subscribe to the point of view in question formulate their answers to questions such as these in terms of expressions such as "brain-wave", "imagination", "intuition", "ingenuity", etc. Discoveries are made in a nonrational way by scientists' "having brain-waves or sudden inspirations", "using their imagination", "having creative intuitions" or "showing great ingenuity". The activities enumerated here are all nonrational kinds of mental activity and are therefore not definable in logical terms. The scholars who resort to such definitions of the nature of discovery unfortunately have little to say about the nature of these types of mental activity.

They argue further that the study of these nonrational forms of mental activity does not fall within the domain of metascience. According to them, question (8) concerning the "how" of discovery is not a metascientific question at all. They consider this to be a question for the psychology and/or the history of science. As far as psychology is concerned: it could be possible to subject these forms of nonrational mental activity to empirical psychological study. The aim would be to determine the nature, functioning, limitations, possibilities, etc. of the mental processes and/or capacities which are indicated by expressions such as "brain-wave", "imagination", "intuition" and "ingenuity". As far as history of science is concerned: historians of science could make a detailed study of the circumstances in which famous scientists have made important discoveries. Such a study might reveal what combination(s) of circumstances – intellectual, emotional, pragmatic, etc. – would establish the kind of context which is conducive to the making of discoveries.

The gist of the matter is that these scholars have little to say about the nature of discovery as an activity. To say that it is an activity which (a) is essentially nonrational, (b) does not fall within the domain of study of the metascience, but (c) could possibly be subjected to psychological and/or historical study, does not throw much light on the nature of this activity.

5.2.2.2 *Rational Aspect of Discovery*

A smaller group of scholars regard discovery as an intellectual activity which is to a large extent rational. According to them, empirical inquiry is a rational activity both in the context of discovery and in the context of justification. The essence of their attitude to discovery is the following:

(11) There are logical rules which may be used in the making of discoveries.

As far as these logical rules are concerned, they emphasize two points. The first is that these logical rules of discovery are not the same as the logical rules that are used in the context of justification. The second point is that the logical rules for discovery are not of the same kind as the logical rules for justification.

We shall consider the second point as it is explicated by the philosopher Peter Caws in his article "The structure of scientific discovery" (1969:1376). He points out that the logical rules used in the justification of ideas are commonly regarded as effective procedures. An EFFECTIVE PROCEDURE is a procedure of which the application infallibly produces the correct results. According to Caws rules of discovery are not of the same kind. More specifically, they are not effective procedures. In other words, there is a finite possibility of their application producing the wrong results. Caws (1969:1376) summarizes the matter as follows:

> When people say 'there could be no rule for making discoveries', they generally have the first sense of the term in mind: there could be no way of *being sure* of making discoveries. But there might still be sets of rules which, if faithfully followed, would increase the chances of making them.

It is clear that Caws and those who agree with him give a much less restrictive meaning to the term "logical rule" than those scholars who maintain that discovery is essentially nonrational. In principle, both groups could therefore be right. The first group could be right in the sense that no effective procedures for making discoveries exist and that discovery is therefore essentially a nonrational activity. The second group could be right in the sense that noneffective procedures for making discoveries do exist and that discovery is therefore essentially a rational activity.

The second group of scholars regard question (8) concerning the "how" of discovery as a question which must be answered by metascience. The obvious question is: what details can these scholars give us about the noneffective procedures of discovery? In other words, what are the logical rules which are in fact used by scientists in thinking out new ideas, in gaining new insights and in making discoveries? The disappointing fact is that, as far as details are concerned, practically nothing is known about the logical rules which scientists are supposed to use for making discoveries. What is more, serious problems exist with regard to the logical rules for discovery which have been proposed. Let us consider, for instance, the logical rule called "abduction" by Peirce and "retroduction" by Hanson. We limit our discussion to Hanson's definition of this rule in his book *Patterns of discovery. An inquiry into the conceptual foundations of science* (1965:85ff.).

According to Hanson, an observed state of affairs which is surprizing, i.e. problematic, or anomalous, is central to empirical inquiry. In connection with such a problematic state of affairs, the scientist typically asks himself the following question: what, i.e. what idea, must I assume in order to explain this state of affairs? For Hanson, "explain" means 'to organize in an intelligible, systematic conceptual pattern'. According to him, the scientist "deduces" this idea from the problematic state of affairs. This "deduction" is made in terms of the logical rule of RETRODUCTION, or RETRODUCTIVE INFERENCE. Informally, Hanson's rule of retroduction (1965:86) may be described as follows:

(12)(a)   A surprizing phenomenon P is observed.
  (b)   P would be explicable as a matter of course, if the hypothesis (or idea) H were true
  (c)   Hence there is reason to think that it is true.

In terms of retroduction, the hypothesis (or idea) H is inferred as being probably true from a description of the surprizing phenomenon P. The reasoning, according to Hanson, is from the data to the hypothesis, not the reverse.

However, there is a serious problem in connection with Hanson's rule of retroduction. The philosopher Wesley Salmon (1967:111–112) points out that this rule is not used to think out an idea for the first time. It is used only after the idea has been thought out and then only to argue that the idea already devised is probably correct – because it explains the surprizing phenomenon. Hanson's rule of retroduction is therefore not a logical rule for making discoveries, but a logical rule for justification. This does not mean that all proposed logical rules of discovery are in fact rules of justification. What is disappointing is that this happens to be the case with one of the less obscure rules of discovery. Neither the scholars who emphasize the nonrational nature of discovery, nor those who emphasize the rational nature of discovery succeed in elucidating the nature of one of the most fundamental aspects of empirical inquiry.

5.2.3   Formulation of Hypotheses as a Modus Operandi

In §5.2.2.1 above we saw that the nature of discovery as an intellectual activity can, in all probability, not be described in terms of effective procedures for making discoveries. In §5.2.2.2 we saw that very little has been said about discovery in terms of particulars about noneffective procedures for discovery. The question we now have to ask ourselves is whether nothing more illuminating can be said, on the level of metascience, about discovery as a main aspect of empirical inquiry. Something can in fact be said, but then not in terms of "logical rules" or "procedures for discovery". The gist of what there is to say is the following: in empirical inquiry scientists make their discoveries by way of the construction of hypotheses. What does this statement imply?

A hypothesis is an assumption about something. Let us suppose that this "something" is a problematic state of affairs. To form a hypothesis about a problematic state of affairs is to make an assumption or a guess about "what might be the case" with this state of affairs. Within the context of the search for insight in empirical inquiry, a HYPOTHESIS is an assumption about what might be the regularity, pattern, structure, mechanism or cause underlying a problematic state of affairs.

For instance, Chomsky's solution (2) for the grammatical problem (1) in connection with the differences between gerundive and derived nominals, includes two hypotheses: the assumption that gerundive nominals are transforms of sentence-like deep structures and the assumption that derived nominals are deep structure NPs. In empirical inquiry, therefore, the ideas which give insight into problematic states of affairs take the form of hypotheses, or assumptions.

Calling an idea a "hypothesis" gives no indication as to how a scientist arrives at the idea. More specifically, to call an idea a "hypothesis" is neither to say that it was devised in a rational way, nor to say that it originated in a nonrational way. By calling it a hypothesis, two aspects of this idea are emphasized. The first is the functional aspect: the function of a hypothesis is to give a certain amount of information about an aspect of reality which is unknown and which cannot be known in any direct way. In this context, a direct way of getting to know something is, for instance, that of elementary sense perception. The second aspect is the epistemological one: the idea embodied in a hypothesis, or the information contained in a hypothesis, is by nature tentative. In other words, a hypothesis represents a unit of thought of which the correctness has not yet been established. To say that a hypothesis is "tentative", therefore, implies that it has to be tested and justified.

Thus, to make discoveries by forming hypotheses implies the following:

(13)   Scientists make their discoveries by
    (a)   making assumptions about the regularity, pattern, structure, mechanism or cause underlying that which is problematic,
    (b)   regarding these assumptions as tentative, and
    (c)   attempting to test and to justify these assumptions.

In order to solve a significant scientific problem, it is often necessary to construct more than one hypothesis. A number of interrelated hypotheses jointly form a THEORY. In the next chapter of our study we shall discuss in greater detail the nature, functions and properties of the theories constructed in empirical inquiry. One mere point which may be noted here is that empirical inquiry pursues the logical objectives of description, explanation, prediction and postdiction by constructing internally structured sets of hypotheses, or theories.

5.2.4   Heuristic Strategies

It is a historical fact that significant scientific problems often offer considerable resistance to attempts at solving them. In other words, it is often extremely difficult to form hypotheses in terms of which significant problems may be solved. Recall, for instance, the problems which were classified as mysteries in §4.4.2.3. The hypotheses in terms of which these mysteries might be solved have eluded linguists for many centuries.

Scientists have now developed a set of strategies to facilitate the forming of hypotheses in the case of such persistent problems. These strategies, called HEURISTIC STRATEGIES, have the function of creating circumstances which are conducive to the construction of hypotheses. Heuristic strategies are not logical rules or procedures for making discoveries. Their status is that of pragmatic measures. A heuristic strategy represents any means which may be systematically used to create more favourable circumstances for the construction of hypotheses. Heuristic strategies, of which there are quite a variety, differ from one field of study to another. We shall consider a few that are in common use in forms of empirical inquiry.

PROBLEM DECOMPOSITION is a first, widely used heuristic strategy. It involves trying to break up persistent problems into a number of elementary, more manageable problems. This strategy is based on the assumption that the solution for a complex problem may be developed step by step by solving each of its elementary parts.

The use of ANALOGIES represents a second general heuristic strategy. In terms of this heuristic strategy, the scientist looks for previously solved problems which are analogous to the one with which he is struggling. Should he find an analogous problem which has already been solved, he tries to determine whether its solution does not perhaps contain the germ of a solution for his own problems. It is obvious that the more similar the two problematic states of affairs, the better are the chances of successfully applying the heuristic strategy of analogy.

Consider, for instance, the problem of how light travels. This problem is analogous to that concerning the way in which sound is transmitted through the medium of air. The solution proposed for the latter problem was that sound is transmitted through air in the form of waves. By applying the strategy of analogy, a solution for the problem of the transmission of light was developed on the basis of the solution for the latter problem. It was proposed that light too is transmitted in the form of waves. In §5.4.2.2.2 we shall consider two recent cases in which the heuristic strategy of analogy was applied in general linguistic inquiry.

The use of ABSTRACTIONS and IDEALIZATIONS represents a third general heuristic strategy. In §3.2.2.2 we discussed the function of abstraction and idealization in the formulation of aims for empirical inquiry. In the context of discovery, abstractions and idealizations have basically the same sort of function, viz. that of simplification. In terms of the heuristic strategy of abstraction and idealization the scientist temporarily ignores certain facts about a given problematic state of affairs. In this way the scope of whatever is problematic is restricted.

Let us consider an example of the use of this heuristic strategy in natural science. Suppose a physicist found the relation between the length and the weight of the arms of a bar balanced approximately at its mid-point to be problematic. This physicist's problem is to express the relation in question in the form of a simple law. In an attempt to determine this relation he may start experimenting with a bar which he balances on a pivot. In his experiments he may vary two things: the respective lengths of the arms of his bar and the weight of each arm. He will probably find that his experimental data are too complex to be reduced to a simple law. Their complexity will be increased, for instance, by the fact that it is impossible to measure the length of the arms of the bar precisely; by the fact that the bar cannot move absolutely freely on its pivot; by the fact that the bar is not exactly homogeneous so that one arm may weigh more than the other, etc.

In order to formulate the law in question – and thus to solve the problem – the physicist may now simplify his data. He may do this by ignoring all the complicating factors such as data about the length, free movement and weight of the arms of the bar. This means that he is creating an idealization: an ideal bar or lever which is in equilibrium without being influenced by extraneous factors. He can then try to solve his problem with reference to this ideal lever. This idealization has in fact been made in physical inquiry. With regard to an ideal lever, a law has been formulated which specifies that the product of the weight and the length of the arm is a constant quantity.

The heuristic strategy of idealization is widely used in empirical inquiry. A few well-known examples are: ideal gases that are chemically absolutely pure; ideal individuals who are completely isolated; the ideal human being who lives perfectly economically; the ideal state with a perfect democracy; and so on.

5.3   GRAMMATICAL INQUIRY

5.3.1   General

In §3.3.1.1 we saw that the linguistic reality at which grammatical inquiry is directed is a complex two-levelled reality. The first, directly given level is that of linguistic performance and its products: utterances and linguistic intuitions. That which is problematic and by which grammatical inquiry is triggered exists on this directly given level in the form of puzzling intuitive data about the properties of utterances. The second level of the grammarian's linguistic reality is that of underlying mental capacities: the level of linguistic competence. The grammarian tries to understand whatever is problematic on the level of products of linguistic performance by forming hypotheses about the underlying linguistic competence. The insight with which grammatical inquiry is concerned is thus sought on the level of linguistic competence. That is why pretheoretical grammatical descriptions cannot give this insight. They describe the properties of classes of products of linguistic performance and do not have the status of hypotheses about the underlying linguistic competence. Typical grammatical hypotheses and theories aim at revealing the content and structure of the underlying linguistic competence. This point will be discussed in greater detail in §6.3.2.3.

The discoveries the grammarian has to make in order to solve his problems are, therefore, discoveries about linguistic competence. As we have seen in §5.2 there are no logical rules or effective procedures for making such discoveries.

Note in particular that the activities constituting the systematization of the corpus of primary linguistic data do not represent effective procedures for discovery. In other words the classification, ordering, correlating and measuring of primary linguistic data do not mechanically yield hypotheses about the underlying linguistic competence. The value of these activities lies primarily in their contribution to the formulation of well-formed grammatical problems.

5.3.2   Nature of Grammatical Discovery

The discoveries that have to be made in order to solve substantive grammatical problems fall into two classes: language-specific and language-independent discoveries.

5.3.2.1   *Language-Specific Discoveries*

Recall the grammatical problem (1) concerning the three types of differences between gerundive nominals and derived nominals. Chomsky proposed the solution (2) for this problem: gerundive nominals are transforms of sentence-like deep structures, while derived nominals are deep structure NPs. This solution has two aspects on the basis of which its discovery may be called a LANGUAGE-SPECIFIC DISCOVERY.

As regards the first aspect of the solution (2): in this solution nothing new is *directly* asserted about human language in general. For instance, it is not asserted in (2) that gerundive and derived nominals occur in all human languages; that in all languages in which they occur gerundive nominals will be transforms, or that in all languages in which they occur derived nominals will be deep structure NPs.

As regards the second aspect of the solution (2): in this solution nothing new is *indirectly* asserted about human language in general. What is true is that the solution is given in terms of a number of background assumptions about human language in general. Among these assumptions are those of (14).

(14)(a)   Human language is structured in terms of, among other things, a level of deep structure and a level of surface structure.

   (b)   The relationship between deep structure and surface structure is a transformational relationship.

Note that none of these general linguistic background assumptions is new. As part of the existing general linguistic background knowledge they were already available to the grammarian, in this case Chomsky.

This brings us to the significance of the two aspects of the solution (2) for the grammatical problem (1). To solve this problem it was not necessary to assert anything new, either directly or indirectly, about human language in general. In other words, the solving of the problem (1) did not necessitate the making of new discoveries about the nature and organization of human language in general. The solving of this problem required only a deepening of the grammatical insight into English. In other words, only a language-specific discovery had to be made in order to solve the problem. This is in fact the case with the majority of substantive grammatical problems. The implications of this point will be discussed in §5.3.3 below.

5.3.2.2   *Language-Independent Discoveries*

The solving of some substantive grammatical problems requires more than the making of language-specific discoveries. The solving of these problems necessitates a deepening of the insight into human language in general. In other words, in order to solve these substantive grammatical problems one or more LANGUAGE-INDEPENDENT DISCOVERIES have to be made. We shall consider a typical example of this type of grammatical problem.

In his investigation of nominalization in English, Chomsky found a significant parallelism in the internal structure of nominal constituents (NPs), verbal constituents (VPs) and adjectival constituents (APs). This parallelism becomes clear when the NP of (15)(a), the VP of (15)(b) and the AP of (15)(c) below are compared.

(15)(a)   *John's proofs of the theorem*
   (b)   *will prove the theorem*
   (c)   *even ignorant of the theorem*

The following parallelism is to be observed in the structure of the expressions (15)(a)−(c): each has a head which is preceded by a specifier and followed by a complement. Schematically this parallelism may be represented as follows:

(16)

SPECIFIER	HEAD	COMPLEMENT
John's	*proofs*	*of the theorem*
will	*prove*	*the theorem*
even	*ignorant*	*of the theorem*

For the grammarian of English, the following typical grammatical problem now arises:

(17)   How should the linguistically significant parallelism in the structure of NPs such as *John's proofs of the theorem,* VPs such as *will prove the theorem* and APs such as *even ignorant of the theorem* be specified in a grammar of English?

The grammatical problem of (17) is essentially a problem about the base rules of English. Chomsky wishes to specify the internal structure of the constituent categories in question in terms of base rules. The parallelism in the structure of NPs, VPs and APs must therefore be reflected in the similarity of the content of the base rules expanding NPs, VPs and APs. The base rules for each of these three categories will have to generate a specifier, a head and a complement, in that order. Thus, at the level of rules, the following problem will correspond with the grammatical problem (17):

(18)   How should similarities, of the kind in question, in the base rules expanding NPs, VPs and APs be expressed in a grammar of English?

The grammar of English would be seriously deficient if the problem (17)/(18) could not be solved, as this would mean that the grammar failed to express a linguistically significant structural property of English. The importance of expressing linguistically significant facts will be discussed in detail in §6.3.3.1.2.

In the late sixties, the existing knowledge about language in general did not include assumptions in terms of which the grammatical problem (17)/(18) could be solved. Within the framework of this knowledge it was impossible for a grammar of English to express a parallelism such as the one in question explicity in terms of base rules. The solving of this grammatical problem thus required a deepening of the insight into human language in general. In short, to solve this grammatical problem a language-independent discovery had to be made. In the present stage of development of linguistics this is the case with many grammatical problems.

The language-independent discovery in terms of which a solution for the grammatical problem (17)/(18) becomes possible, is embodied in Chomsky's $\overline{\text{X}}$-convention, read "X-bar-convention". The $\overline{\text{X}}$-convention is a notational convention which makes it possible to collapse the base rules for, among others, NPs, VPs and APs. These rules are collapsed in such a way that linguistically significant similarities of the kind in question between the rules are explicitly expressed. This also means that the linguistically significant parallelism in the structure of NPs, VPs and APs is explicitly expressed.

In terms of the $\overline{\text{X}}$-convention, X is used as a variable representing any lexical category. In the case of an NP, VP or AP the head – i.e. N, V or A respectively – is represented by X. An X with a bar, i.e. $\overline{\text{X}}$, is used to represent the node which immediately dominates X. The complement immediately following the head of an NP, VP or AP, is represented by the notation Comp_X. The linguistically significant fact that in an NP, VP and AP the head is immediately followed by a complement may be specified by means of the following rule schema:

(19) $\overline{\text{X}} \longrightarrow \text{X} - \text{Comp}_X$

The rule schema (19) is an abbreviation for, among others, the base rules of (20).

(20) $\overline{N} \longrightarrow N - Comp_N$
$\overline{V} \longrightarrow V - Comp_V$
$\overline{A} \longrightarrow A - Comp_A$

In terms of the $\overline{X}$-convention, the node by which $\overline{X}$ is immediately dominated is represented by an X with a double bar, i.e. $\overline{\overline{X}}$. This $\overline{\overline{X}}$ node also dominates the specifier immediately preceding X. In the $\overline{X}$-notation the specifier is represented as $Spec_{\overline{X}}$, or $[Spec, \overline{X}]$. The linguistically significant fact that in an NP, VP and AP the head is immediately preceded by a specifier may be expressed by means of the following rule schema:

(21) $\overline{\overline{X}} \longrightarrow Spec_{\overline{X}} - \overline{X}$

The rule schema (21) is an abbreviation for, among others, the base rules of (22).

(22) $\overline{\overline{N}} \longrightarrow Spec_{\overline{N}} - \overline{N}$
$\overline{\overline{V}} \longrightarrow Spec_{\overline{V}} - \overline{V}$
$\overline{\overline{A}} \longrightarrow Spec_{\overline{A}} - \overline{A}$

[As initial rule of this grammar, Chomsky proposes $S \longrightarrow \overline{\overline{N}} - \overline{\overline{V}}$.]
    The $\overline{X}$-convention thus embodies the discovert that in human language in general, constituents such as NP, VP and AP are structured as follows in the deep structure:

(23)

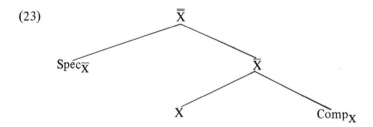

In terms of this discovery about human language in general, a solution can now be proposed for the grammatical problem (17)/(18).
    Note that in terms of the content which we have assigned to the term "grammatical" in this study, only language-specific discoveries are "grammatical discoveries". GRAMMATICAL DISCOVERIES are discoveries about the form and content of a certain mental capacity, viz. the ideal speaker's competence in a particular language. Language-independent discoveries are "general linguistic discoveries" in the terminology of our study. We shall consider the nature of general linguistic discovery in greater detail in §5.4.1.

5.3.3   Making Language-specific Discoveries

An important characteristic of grammatical discovery, such as language-specific discovery, which appeared from the preceding paragraphs is that it is a guided activity. Language-specific discoveries are made within the framework of a set of assumptions about language in general. The general linguistic assumptions guide or direct language-specific discovery in a very special way. We shall illustrate this point by means of an example.

In §5.3.2.1 above we saw that Chomsky's solution for the grammatical problem (1) makes use of, among other things, the two assumptions of (14)(a) and (b) about human language in general. This point could also be formulated as follows: Chomsky's search for a solution to the problem in question was guided in a certain direction by the assumption that human language is structured in terms of a level of deep structure and a level of surface structure which are transformationally related. Chomsky sought the solution to his problem in terms of these assumptions. The general linguist assumes that transforms and deep structures have the following relevant properties:

(24)   TRANSFORMS

    (a)   are syntactically regular,

    (b)   are semantically regular, and

    (c)   have the internal structure of sentences.

(25)   DEEP STRUCTURE CONSTITUENTS such as NPs

    (a)   are not necessarily syntactically regular,

    (b)   are not necessarily semantically regular, and

    (c)   do not necessarily have the internal structure of sentences.

The content of the expressions "syntactically regular" and "semantically regular", was explicated in §5.1 above.

Suppose that it appeared from the data about a given language that the language has a class of units which (a) are syntactically regular, (b) are semantically regular and (c) have the internal structure of sentences. The general linguistic assumptions of (24) then guide the grammarian towards the discovery that these linguistic units are transforms. Suppose also that the language in question has a second class of linguistic units which, as a class, (a) is not syntactically regular, (b) is not semantically regular, and (c) does not have the internal structure of sentences, but rather that of NPs. The general linguistic assumptions of (25) now guide the grammarian towards the discovery that these units are deep structure NPs. These two discoveries would not have been possible within a general linguistic framework which did not include the assumptions of (14), (24) and (25).

Note, however, that the general linguistic assumptions of (14), (24) and (25) could also guide the grammarian in a negative way: they could direct him away from certain other discoveries about the nature of these linguistic units. The general content of these discoveries would be that gerundive and derived nominals are objects of a kind that would not be able to co-exist with transforms and deep structure NPs within the same linguistic reality. General linguistic hypotheses, therefore, provide for a class of linguistic objects which could exist and, consequently, could be discovered. At the same time they exclude other logically conceivable objects which could not exist and, therefore, could not be discovered. Syntactic units existing within the framework of a general linguistic theory which did not distinguish between surface and deep structure would be examples of linguistic objects which could not be discovered within the framework of the transformational linguistic theory.

The guided nature of language-specific discovery enables the grammarian to argue in the following way:

(26)   According to the general linguistic assumption A, human language in general has the structural property P.

L (say English) is a human language about which problematic data exist which could be understood in terms of P.

Thus, L probably has the structural property P.

In §9.2.1.2.1 we shall see that (26) has the format of a particular form of argument. At this point it is sufficient to note that if language-specific discovery were a rational activity, the reasoning could take the form of (26). In other words, the form of argument represented by (26) could constitute a non-effective procedure for making discoveries. In §9.2.1.2.1 we shall see, however, that (26) is probably more a form of argument used in the justification of grammatical hypotheses.

The main point, in other words, is that the grammarian's set of general linguistic assumptions forms a matrix for possible solutions to a large number of substantive grammatical problems. Take, for instance, the assumption (24) about the nature of a transform and the assumption (25) about what a deep structure NP cannot be. Jointly, these two assumptions provide the following matrix for a possible solution to a substantive grammatical problem:

(27)   If a class of linguistic units does not have the properties (24)(a)–(c) but, in fact, has the opposite properties of (25)(a)–(c), then the members of this class are probably deep structure NPs.

A grammarian who knows the general linguistic assumptions (24) and (25) knows, in embryonic form, a possible solution to a substantive grammatical problem. Should he now be confronted in the course of his investigation with a concrete problem of this form, he need not wait for a solution to appear out of the blue.

Among the general linguistic assumptions by which the grammarian is guided in the making of language-specific discoveries, there is a subtype which should be specially mentioned, viz. Arnold Zwicky's (1973:468) "methodological principles". The function of these so-called METHODOLOGICAL PRINCIPLES "is to suggest what the most likely state of affairs is in a given situation, in the absence of evidence of the usual sort". Consider the following three examples given by Zwicky in his article "Linguistics as chemistry: the substance theory of semantic primes" (1973:468):

(28)(a)   The MAJORITY VOTE PRINCIPLE in comparative reconstruction: "if the majority of daughter languages agree in having a certain feature, then that feature is to be attributed to the protolanguage".

(b)   The CONTRAST PRINCIPLE in phonology: "if segments are in contrast, then they are underlyingly distinct".

(c)   The SURFACIST PRINCIPLE in syntax: "*ceteris paribus*, the syntactic structure of a sentence is its surface constituent structure".

Such general linguistic "methodological principles" come into play in the absence of the usual type of factual linguistic data which could indicate the direction in which a solution to a grammatical problem probably lies. In these circumstances "the methodological principle provides a kind of background assumption, a position taken when no other is especially supported", according to Zwicky (1973:468). In §10.4.3.3 we shall consider another interesting feature of Zwicky's "methodological principles".

It is clear, therefore, that general linguistic assumptions play an important role in the making of language-specific grammatical discoveries. There are also a number of other factors which operate in discoveries of this type. Among these are: the existing knowledge about the particular language; the metascientific criteria which an idea must satisfy in order to qualify as a hypothetical solution; the intellectual qualities of the grammarian, etc. We have singled out general linguistic assumptions in this paragraph because they are responsible for the special character of language-specific discovery, viz. that of a guided activity.

Note, in conclusion, that general linguistic assumptions also have a heuristic function in another aspect of grammatical inquiry, viz. that of the formulation of problems. In §4.3.2.2 we saw that the grammarian is guided by certain "ideas" when collecting and systematizing primary linguistic data. These "ideas" about what to collect, how to classify, how to order, how to correlate and how to measure we called "grammatical working hypotheses". The important point is that it appeared that the general linguistic background assumptions in a problematic state of affairs are an important source of these grammatical working hypotheses. General linguistic assumptions may therefore also guide the grammarian towards the discovery of fruitful grammatical working hypotheses.

5.4   GENERAL LINGUISTIC INQUIRY

5.4.1   Nature of General Linguistic Discovery

In §3.3.1 we saw that the linguistic reality of general linguistic inquiry is also a complex reality. In other words, this reality exists on two levels. The first, more direct level is that of individual human languages as these are embodied in the mental capacity of linguistic competence. That which is problematic, and which triggers general linguistic inquiry, exists on this level of individual languages. What the general linguist finds problematic is to determine which properties of the individual languages are language-specific and which properties are universal and, in addition, why the individual languages have the language-specific properties which they do have. The second level of the general linguist's linguistic reality is that of language in general as it is embodied in man's innate language acquisition faculty. Whatever it is that he finds problematic on the level of individual languages, the general linguist tries to understand by constructing hypotheses about the nature, content and structure of man's language acquisition faculty. These hypotheses are assumptions about linguistic universals, i.e. aspects of man's linguistic competence which are innate in the form of the language acquisition faculty. Thus the insight which the general linguist seeks and the discoveries with which he is concerned are to be found on the level of man's language acquisition faculty. To simplify matters we shall refer to discoveries about the nature, content and structure of the language acquisition faculty as GENERAL LINGUISTIC DISCOVERIES. General linguistic hypotheses and the general linguistic theories within which they are organized are hypotheses and theories about the nature, content and structure of the human being's language acquisition faculty. Up to now we have referred to these hypotheses and theories as "(background) assumptions" and "(background) knowledge about language in general".

5.4.2   Making General Linguistic Discoveries

We shall now consider a number of aspects of the intellectual activity by which the general linguist makes his discoveries.

5.4.2.1   *Nonguided Nature of General Linguistic Discovery*

General linguistic discoveries are by nature language-independent discoveries. Consequently, the activity of general linguistic discovery differs from that of language-specific, or grammatical, discovery in an important respect: the making of general linguistic discoveries is a nonguided activity. In other words, unlike grammatical discovery, general linguistic discovery does not take place within the framework of a set of guiding background assumptions.

An important implication of the nonguided nature of general linguistic discovery is that there is no form of argument in general linguistic inquiry analogous to that of (26) in grammatical inquiry. In other words, general linguists could not argue as follows:

(29)   According to the psychological assumption A, intellectual capacities in general have the structural property P.
Human language is embodied in a mental capacity about which problematic data exist which could be understood in terms of P.

Thus, human language probably has the structural property P.

To illustrate this point, think of Chomsky's discovery that the base rules of human languages are organized in terms of the $\bar{X}$-convention. Notice that no psychological assumption about the structural properties of intellectual capacities exists which could have guided Chomsky in making this discovery.

It is not impossible in principle that such psychological assumptions could exist and could play a role in general linguistic discovery. A significant deepening of the insight into the nature and characteristics of intellectual capacities in general could produce such an ordered set of assumptions. Within the framework of these assumptions general linguistic discovery, too, could become a guided activity. At the moment, however, such a framework does not exist, as is clear from the following observations by Chomsky (1976:22–23):

It remains an open question, and an interesting one, to determine whether there really are significant analogies between the principles of mental representation and mental computation that seem well motivated in the study of language, and other mental operations, in other domains. Personally, I am rather skeptical; I see no interesting analogies in other cognitive domains, but so little is known that we can really say very little.

5.4.2.2   *The Nonaccidental in General Linguistic Discovery*

It appeared from the preceding discussion that, at present, general linguistic discovery is not by nature a guided activity. This does not mean, however, that all general linguistic discoveries are made in a purely accidental way. General linguistic discoveries are made within the framework of the existing linguistic knowledge. This framework includes knowledge about human language in general and knowledge about individual human languages. It appears that this framework of linguistic knowledge can direct the general linguist towards certain discoveries. The "directing" role of the existing linguistic knowledge is rather limited, however. It is only in the case of a small number of discoveries that the general linguist is directed by this knowledge. These discoveries represent NON-ACCIDENTAL DISCOVERIES. We shall consider two ways in which the framework of linguistic knowledge may exercise this "directing" function.

5.4.2.2.1 *The role of higher-order principles*

Consider, once again, the content of Chomsky's $\overline{X}$-convention as it was discussed in §5.3.2.2. Notice that this general linguistic convention was proposed in order to make it possible to express a linguistically significant similarity between grammatical rules, in this case base rules. By nature this convention is a so-called abbreviatory notational convention. The convention makes it possible to reduce base rules exhibiting the similarities in question to only a few rule schemata. This means that the $\overline{X}$-convention is an example of the implementation of a particular general linguistic assumption. The general linguistic assumption in question may be represented as (30).

(30)   Partial similarities between sets of grammatical rules are made explicit by reducing these rules to one or a few rule schemata.

The general linguistic principle of (30) is a so-called HIGHER-ORDER PRINCIPLE because it specifies what properties other general linguistic principles of a lower order should have. The lower-order general linguistic principles concerned are notational conventions for the formulation of grammatical rules.

This brings us to the main point in connection with the $\overline{X}$-convention: Chomsky's proposal of an abbreviatory notational convention as a solution for the grammatical problem (18) is by no means accidental. He was "directed" towards a solution in terms of an abbreviatory notational convention by the higher-order principle (30) which was part of the existing linguistic knowledge. In other words, the discovery of the $\overline{X}$-convention *as an abbreviatory notational convention* was a nonaccidental general linguistic discovery. It is the "directing" role of higher-order general linguistic principles which is responsible for the non-accidental nature of a first class of general linguistic discoveries.

This point may be illustrated by another, fictitious, example. Suppose there were stylistic differences of a systematic nature between gerundive nominals and corresponding derived nominals. Suppose also that it was assumed that a grammar of an individual language should account for these differences. In order to account for these differences in a grammar, a certain general linguistic discovery would first have to be made, viz. how human language in general is structured stylistically. Suppose now that a general linguist A made the discovery (31) in this connection.

(31)(a)   Human language has a level of stylistic structure with the properties P_1, P_2 and P_3.

(b)   Stylistic structures are generated on this level by stylistic rules with the properties p_1, p_2 and p_3.

A would have made the general linguistic discovery that stylistic structures and stylistic rules are also significant components in the organization of human language.

This general linguistic discovery would be nonaccidental and nonsurprizing in a very important respect. The framework of linguistic knowledge within which it would be made would include the following higher-order general linguistic principle:

(32)   Linguistic differences (and similarities) of a systematic nature between linguistic units exist on some level of structure which is generated by some or other type of rule.

The higher-order general linguistic principle (32) would have directed A towards discovering a new level of structure and a new type of rule. For this reason A's discovery (31) would be a nonaccidental discovery. Note that higher-order principles do not determine the exact properties of whatever is discovered. They merely indicate the type to which that which is discovered will probably belong.

5.4.2.2.2   *The role of analogy*

There is a second class of general linguistic discoveries that are not purely accidental. This class includes discoveries that are made analogously to other discoveries. We shall consider, in outline, two examples of this type of general linguistic discovery. It is unfortunately impossible to discuss these examples in detail. More particulars will be found in a substantive course on generative grammar.

The first example concerns the cross-classification of syntactic constituents such as NP, VP, AP, PP (= Prepositional Phrase), AdvP (= Adverbial Phrase), PrtP (= Participle Phrase), ArtP (= Article Phrase), and others. In order to express certain syntactic generalizations about English it must be possible to refer to a class of syntactic constituents including as its members PP, PrtP, AP and AdvP. Let us call this class C_1. In order to express other syntactic generalizations about English it must be possible to refer to a class of syntactic constituents including as its members NP, ArtP, AP and AdvP. For the time being, this class may be called C_2. Notice that AP and AdvP are members of both class C_1 and class C_2. In other words, AP and AdvP must be cross-classified as members of both the class C_1 and the class C_2.

The general linguistic problem confronting the linguist is how such a cross-classification of syntactic constituents should be effected. In other words, how can it be specified in a natural way in the grammar of English that AP and AdvP are members of both the class of constituents C_1 and the class of constituents

C_2? Chomsky (1972b:48–49), followed by Jackendoff (1974a:12–13), proposed the solution of (33).

(33)   Syntactic constituents such as NP, VP, AdvP, AP, etc. should not be regarded as unanalyzable units. These constituents should rather be regarded as bundles of syntactic features. In terms of its various features a constituent could then, in a natural way, be a member of various classes of constituents.

Consider, for instance, the first class of constituents C_1 including as members PP, PrtP, AP and AdvP. This class may be denoted in a natural way in terms of the syntactic features of its members. Syntactic constituents of which the head does not have a subject in the surface structure of sentences would be members of this class. This class may therefore be denoted in terms of its defining syntactic feature [− Subj.].

The second class of constituents C_2 may also be denoted in a natural way in terms of the syntactic features of its members NP, ArtP, AP and AdvP. Syntactic constituents of which the head does not have an object in the surface structure of sentences are members of this class. This class may therefore be denoted in terms of its defining feature [− Obj.].

The solution (33) for the cross-classification problem in question, therefore, implies that a syntactic constituent such as AP and AdvP is composed of, among other things, the syntactic features [− Subj , − Obj]. In terms of these syntactic features, the fact that the relevant constituents are members of both class C_1 and class C_2 may be specified in a natural way. AP and AdvP are distinguished from one another in terms of a third syntactic feature, but we are not concerned with this distinction.

This brings us to the main point of the discussion of the cross-classification of syntactic constituents. The essence of the solution (33) to this problem is that these syntactic constituents are not unanalyzable units, but rather bundles of features. Chomsky (and Jackendoff) reached this solution by way of analogy. In the mid-sixties an analogous problem existed with regard to the cross-classification of lexical items. One and the same lexical item had to be classified as a member of more than one lexical syntactic category. For instance, the lexical item *boy* in English had to be classified as a member of each of the following lexical syntactic (sub)categories: Count Nouns, Common Nouns, Animate Nouns and Human Nouns. To solve the problem of the lexical syntactic cross-classification of lexical items, Chomsky made the proposal (34) in his *Aspects of the theory of syntax* (1965:79–83).

(34)   Lexical items should not be regarded as unanalyzable units, but rather as bundles of syntactic features. In terms of its various features a lexical item may then in a natural way be a member of various lexical syntactic classes.

Notice the similarity between (33) as solution to the problem of the cross-classificaion of syntactic constituents and (34) as solution to the problem of the cross-classification of lexical items. This similarity is not accidental, as the two problems are formally equivalent, i.e. of the same general form. Chomsky consciously used the solution (34) for the latter problem as model for the solution (33) of the former problem. In other words, he discovered the solution (33) by way of analogy. He was "directed" towards the solution (33) by the solution (34). Therefore, the discovery that syntactic constituents such as NP, VP, AP, etc. are not unanalyzable units, but are bundles of features, is in an important respect non-accidental.

But our illustration of the role of analogy in general linguistic discovery may be taken even further. The solution (34) to the problem of the cross-classification of lexical items was also discovered by way of analogy. Chomsky developed this solution by analogy to a solution which had been proposed for a problem of cross-classification in generative phonology. In order to formulate phonological rules in a maximally general way, a variety of categories of speech sounds have to be set up. And in terms of its behaviour in different phonological rules, a given speech sound may be a member of more than one phonological category. For instance, /p/ is a member of the category of consonants together with /b t k f v s x g/, a member of the category of voiceless speech sounds together with /k t f s x/, a member of the category of anterior speech sounds together with /b t d f v s l r m n j w/, etc.

The linguist's problem is to specify the cross-classification of speech sounds in the grammar in a natural way. The solution (35) was proposed for this problem.

(35)   Speech sounds should not be regarded as unanalyzable units, but rather as bundles of distinctive features. In terms of its various distinctive features, a speech sound may in a natural way be a member of various phonological categories.

Notice that the solution (34) for the problem of the cross-classification of lexical items is analogous to the solution (35) for the problem of the cross-classification of speech sounds. Chomsky (1965:80–81) consciously used the latter solution as a model for the former. In other words, he was "directed" towards the solution (34) by the solution (35) which, in the mid-sixties, formed part of the existing corpus of linguistic knowledge.

The second way in which an existing corpus of linguistic knowledge may direct a linguist towards general linguistic discoveries may therefore be characterized in terms of analogy. However, the "directing" function of analogy is limited in an important respect. Analogical "directing" takes place only when two or more general linguistic problems have the same form. The role of analogy in the making of general linguistic discoveries may be studied further with reference to a number of examples recently discussed by Chomsky in his paper "A theory of core grammar". Chomsky's (1978:11–12) first example shows how

· · ·we can think of base structures, transformational rules and surface forms as analogues resp. to abstract phonological representations, phonological rules and phonetic representations.

His second example (1978:23) concerns the way in which a syntactic theory of markedness may be developed by analogy to the existing markedness theory of generative phonology. A final example, not discussed by Chomsky, concerns the way in which the principle of cyclic rule application was extended by analogy from phonology to syntax. As all these examples show, it is generative phonology which has yielded the significant analogies for making nonaccidental discoveries in generative syntax.

In conclusion, note that general linguistic discovery is not a guided activity in the same sense as language-specific discovery. However, some general linguistic discoveries are nonaccidental by virtue of the role that higher-order principles and analogy play in these discoveries.

SELECTED READING

Insight/understanding

Nature of

Achinstein 1971:68–78; Hanson 1971:43–45; Scriven 1970.

Discovery

Heuristic Strategies

Benjamin 1965:102–108; Bunge 1967a:199–203.

Construction of Hypotheses

Barker 1957:ch.2, 8; Benjamin 1965:20–21, 117–122, Bunge 1967a:ch.5; Hempel 1966:ch.2.

Context of Discovery vs. Context of Justification

Caws 1969:1375; Rudner 1966:6; Salmon 1963:10–14.

Nonrational Nature of Discovery

Bunge 1959:68; Caws 1969:1375–1376; Hempel 1966:14; Popper 1965:31; Rudner 1966:6; Salmon 1967:18–19.

Rational Nature of Discovery

Caws 1969:1375–1376; Hanson 1965:ch.4; Holton 1973:17–20.

Retroduction

Achinstein 1971:117–119; Hanson 1965:85–87; 1971:63–67; Salmon 1967: 111–114.

Study of Discovery by History of Science

Gingerich (ed.) 1975; Holton 1973: especially ch.10; Hildebrand 1957.

CHAPTER SIX

Giving Theoretical Linguistic Descriptions

6.0 PERSPECTIVE

In this chapter we shall be dealing with a fourth main aspect of linguistic inquiry, viz. that of giving theoretical descriptions of the objects studied by generative grammar. In the first part of the chapter we take a brief look at the giving of theoretical descriptions in empirical inquiry in general. The discussion hinges on two questions: what is a theoretical description?; and what activities do scientists carry out in giving theoretical descriptions?

In the second part of the chapter, the same two questions are viewed from another angle, that of grammatical inquiry. The nature of grammatical theories and their various components are discussed first. Special attention is given to the nature of grammatical concepts and the ontological status of grammars. With regard to the ontological status, three questions are raised: which aspect of the ideal speaker's linguistic competence is described by a grammar?; what is meant by saying that theoretical (grammatical) concepts "represent" aspects of the linguistic competence? and how can a grammar describe a mental capacity of a nonexistent individual, an ideal speaker? Finally, the ontological status of grammars is placed in metascientific perspective with reference to the philosophical distinction "realism" vs. "instrumentalism". Secondly, this part of the chapter deals with the nature of grammatical description. Grammatical description is an intellectual activity comprising several parts. The parts singled out for discussion are: forming grammatical concepts, explicating the content of these concepts, integrating these concepts into hypotheses and theories, symbolizing the content of these hypotheses and theories, elucidating the content of grammatical theories and axiomatizing these theories.

In the last part of the chapter, the giving of theoretical descriptions in general linguistic inquiry is discussed in broad outline. The nature of general linguistic descriptions is discussed first, with reference to linguistic universals. Special attention is given to the nature of general linguistic hypotheses and the concepts of which they are composed. We take a look at the ontological status of general linguistic theories with reference to the nonexistence of an ideal language learner. Secondly, this part of the chapter deals with the nature of the activity known as "general linguistic description". Special attention is given to the forming of general linguistic concepts. The criteria for these concepts are viewed in their relation to the criteria for grammatical concepts, which are discussed in more detail in the second part of the chapter.

6.1   INTRODUCTION

In §1.3 we discussed the outlines of Chomsky's lexicalist hypothesis. This was done by pointing out, among other things, how this hypothesis accounts for certain syntactic similarities between the sentence *John has refused the offer* and the derived nominal *John's refusal of the offer.* The syntactic similarities in question were formulated as (10) and (11) in §1.3. The outlines of Chomsky's lexicalist hypothesis were expounded more or less as in (1) below.

(1)   The lexicon contains a single lexical entry for "refuse". In this single lexical entry are specified the fixed syntactic properties of "refuse", viz. those selectional and subcategorization features which "refuse" manifests in all expressions in which it occurs. What is not specified in the single lexical entry for "refuse", however, is whether "refuse" is a verb or a noun. The lexical entry is neutral in that "refuse" is unspecified in terms of those syntactic properties which distinguish verbs from nouns. This entails that the lexical item "refuse" can be inserted in deep structures both under the node V and the node N. When "refuse" is inserted under the node V in a deep structure, it has the phonological form *refuse.* If, on the other hand, "refuse" is inserted under the node N, it will have the phonological form *refusal.* Morphological rules specify the appropriate phonological form of "refuse".

What we have in (1) is in fact a fragment of a grammarian's theoretical linguistic description of an aspect of English. Thereby we have isolated a fourth main aspect of linguistic inquiry.

As a main aspect of linguistic inquiry, the giving of theoretical linguistic descriptions is closely related to the ultimate objective which linguistic inquiry has as a form of empirical inquiry, viz. the search for insight into, or understanding of, whatever it is that is problematic. This search for insight involves determining the actual regularity, pattern, structure, mechanism or cause underlying that which is problematic. The scientist's first logical objective is that of giving a description of this regularity, etc. It is in this context that the giving of a theoretical linguistic description represents a main aspect of linguistic inquiry. Schematically this main aspect may be represented as follows:

(2)

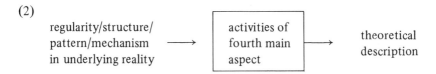

Two questions arise in connection with this diagram. The first question, (3)(a), concerns the "output" of the diagram, viz. theoretical descriptions. The second question, (3)(b), concerns the content of the box, viz. the activities involved in giving theoretical descriptions.

(3) (a)   What is a theoretical description?
    (b)   What activities do scientists carry out in giving theoretical descriptions?

These two questions will be considered from three angles: those of empirical inquiry in general, grammatical inquiry and general linguistic inquiry.

6.2   INQUIRY IN GENERAL

6.2.1   Biological Excursion

Since theoretical descriptions are by nature abstract objects, coming to grips with the fourth main aspect of linguistic inquiry is no simple matter. Our task is further complicated by the fact that the giving of theoretical descriptions involves the carrying out of several complex activities. A slight digression into biological inquiry will prepare us for this taxing part of our study. This biological excursion will illustrate in concrete terms what kind of object a theoretical description is.

For centuries scientists interested in nature were puzzled by the ability of bats to fly in the dark without colliding with the physical objects surrounding them. Within the framework of the then existing biological knowledge they could not explain this singular phenomenon. Spallanzani, an eighteenth century Italian biologist, formulated this fragment of ignorance in the form of the following problem: how does a bat control the direction of its flight in circumstances in which its eyes can be of no use? In order to solve this problem, Spallanzani and other biologists searched for the mechanism by which bats control their flight in the dark.

For biologists, the nature of the flight control mechanism of bats remained a riddle until after World War One. Then Hartridge, a physiologist and sound theoretician, recalled the use which had been made during the war of sound-detecting devices to determine the presence and position of objects which could not be directly seen. Hartridge speculated that the flight control mechanism of bats worked on essentially the same principle as these sound-detecting devices. More particularly, he hypothesized that bats are informed by the echoes of their own shrill cries of the presence and the position of physical objects in their immediate vicinity.

This idea of Hartridge's was further developed by the biologists Donald

Griffin and Robert Galambos. On the strength of their research, Griffin and Galambos gave the description (4) of the nature and functioning of the flight control mechanism of bats.

(4) (a) Flying bats emit supersonic cries.
    (b) These cries are reflected as echoes by the physical objects in the vicinity of the flying bats.
    (c) The flying bats record the echoes of their supersonic cries.
    (d) The properties of these recorded echoes inform the flying bats of the presence and the position of physical objects in their vicinity.

In (4) we have a concrete example of a theoretical description of a mechanism which actually underlies a problematic state of affairs. This theoretical description of the flight control mechanism of bats provided biologists with the coveted insight into the problematic flying ability of these animals. Extensive biological experiments confirmed the accuracy of this theoretical description beyond reasonable doubt.

6.2.2   Nature of Theoretical Descriptions

The expression "a theoretical description" may be paraphrased as follows: "a description given in the form of a theory". From this paraphrase it is clear that, in order to answer question (3)(a) regarding the nature of a theoretical description, two more fundamental questions have to be considered first.

(5) (a) What is a description in this context?
    (b) What is a theory in this context?

In §§4.3.2.2.1 and 5.2.3 we considered the nature of descriptions and theories on a general level. We shall now consider them in more detail.

6.2.2.1   *"Description"*

As regards question (5)(a): note that the flight control mechanism of bats, as described in (4), exists on the underlying level of reality. In other words, this mechanism cannot be observed directly, does not exist on the surface level of reality and is not accessible to direct investigation. This is a typical characteristic of theoretical descriptions, i.e. that which is being described exists on a deeper level of reality. A theoretical description gives an image, representation or replica of something which cannot be observed in any direct manner. Consequently, a theoretical description is not merely a summary of data collected by means of sense perception or other forms of direct recording. The theoretical description

(4) given by Griffin and Galambos is clearly not a summary of data about a number of observed cases of bats flying in the dark.

What type of information is contained in a theoretical description of the described object? To describe an entity, object, mechanism, etc. — "something", or S, for short — is to answer questions such as the following:

(6) (a) What kind of entity, object, mechanism, etc. is S?
    (b) What are the properties of S?
    (c) What parts does S have?
    (d) How are the parts of S interrelated?
    (e) Of what is S a part?
    (f) How is S related to the other parts of that of which S is itself a part?
    (g) How does S and its parts work?

A theoretical description need not provide answers to all questions similar to those of (6) in order to qualify as a description. However, it should be obvious that the more questions like those of (6) a theoretical description answers, the more informative this description is, and the more informative a theoretical description, the more exact the representation, image, or replica it offers of the underlying reality.

A theoretical description such as that of Griffin and Galambos is given in terms of DESCRIPTIVE STATEMENTS or PROPOSITIONS. This description consists of four propositions: (4)(a)–(d). Each of these propositions is composed of several CONCEPTS. Concepts such as 'supersonic', 'sound', 'echo', 'reflect', 'record', etc. are used to construct the propositions of (4)(a)–(d). The nature of these concepts will be discussed in detail in §6.3.2.2 below. In the meantime, think of a concept as a unit of thought representing an aspect of reality.

A proposition is composed of concepts following the logical pattern which we considered in §4.3.2.2.1. In other words, in the construction of a proposition, some concepts play the role of arguments, while other concepts play the role of functions. Recall that, in a proposition, the argument singles out an object or a class of objects, while the function ascribes a property to the (class of) individuated objects or specifies the type to which this (class of) objects belongs. For instance, look at the proposition (4)(b): "these cries are reflected as echoes by the physical objects in the vicinity of the flying bats". In this proposition, the concept 'these cries' constitutes the argument. It singles out a class of objects — supersonic cries emitted by flying bats — to which a property is ascribed. The conceptual content of the rest of the proposition in question plays the role of function. It ascribes a property to the individuated class of objects: the property of being an echo.

The content of the expression "description" in "theoretical description" may therefore be characterized as follows:

(7) A DESCRIPTION

(a) constitutes an image, representation, or replica of an entity, object, mechanism, etc. which exists on an underlying level of reality;

(b) does (a) by specifying the type, properties, parts and/or manner of functioning of the entity, object, mechanism, etc. in question.

(c) does (b) in terms of propositions which are composed of concepts according to the pattern 'argument-function'.

The essential function of theoretical descriptions is to describe. However, we shall see further on that grammarians also use theoretical descriptions for other important purposes such as the giving of explanations and the making of predictions and postdictions.

Notice that a description is a logical structure in two respects. On the one hand, it is composed of propositions which are in turn constructed according to a certain logical pattern. On the other hand, these propositions are combined in terms of certain logical relations to form a complete, integrated description. The giving of a description therefore involves the construction of a logical structure. This accounts for the fact that the giving of theoretical descriptions was characterized as a "logical" objective of empirical inquiry in §5.2.1.

6.2.2.2 *"Theoretical"*

This brings us to question (5)(b): what is a theory in this context? In §5.2.3 a theory was characterized as a set of interrelated hypotheses. Hypotheses were characterized as tentative assumptions about aspects of reality which are unknown and which cannot be known by any direct means. What more can be said about the nature of theories?

Scholars disagree fundamentally about the nature of theories. For instance, there are profound differences of opinion about what the functions of theories are, or should be, in empirical inquiry, about the relation(s) between theories and reality, and so on. There are two reasons for these differences of opinion. In the first place, the term "theory" has come to mean many different things in empirical inquiry. In other words, the class of objects denoted by the term "theories" is far from homogeneous. A variety of objects which differ from one another in several respects are all denoted by the same term. Consequently, it is rather difficult to specify exactly what the common distinctive properties of these objects are. In the second place, scholars view this variety of objects from several different philosophical angles. In other words, they try to determine the nature and properties of these objects in terms of various philosophical assumptions about what theories should or should not be. Each of these philosophical "theories" about theories gives a different picture of the nature of theories. The volume *The structure of scientific theories* edited by Frederick Suppe (1967a), gives an impression of how the two factors just mentioned contribute to the differences of opinion among scholars about the nature of theories.

Particulars of these differences about the nature of theories fall outside the scope of our study. For our purposes it will be sufficient to note a number of properties which theories seem to have according to the philosopher of science, Peter Achinstein. We shall consider the specific properties which theories may have with regard to their function(s), formal structure, and so on, when we discuss the theories used in linguistic inquiry.

In his book *Concepts of science* (1968:121ff.), Peter Achinstein claims that those objects which are called theories usually have five properties. A first property of theories is that they are composed of propositions which state what the case is. A PROPOSITION represents the content of a declarative sentence. The propositions of (4)(a)−(d) are examples of such propositions. A second property of theories is that they are not obviously true or false. Scientists believe that theories are probable, in other words that they will prove to be true rather than false. A third property of theories is that they offer, or might probably offer, the insight or understanding which scientists seek. A fourth property of theories is that their content cannot be deduced from other, more fundamental theories. In terms of their content, theories are therefore relatively fundamental. A fifth property of theories is that they are, to a certain extent, integrated. In other words, the tentative propositions constituting a theory collaborate in producing the insight the scientist seeks. These propositions are connected, they supplement one another, they hardly overlap and they are not mutually contradictory.

To call a description − such as the one given by Griffin and Galambos of the flight control mechanism of bats − "theoretical" is therefore to emphasize certain properties of this description.

(8)   A description is THEORETICAL in the following sense:
(a)   it is not obviously true or false, but is rather tentative;
(b)   it is probable, but must be carefully tested and justified;
(c)   it is relatively fundamental in terms of its content, and
(d)   the propositions of which it is composed form an integrated whole.

The expression "theoretical" has the meaning of (8) in the context of Achinstein's work. In (7) and (8) an answer has therefore been given to the question about the nature of a theoretical description.

6.2.3   Giving a Theoretical Description

This brings us to question (3)(b) about the activities carried out by scientists when giving a theoretical description.

(9)   Giving a theoretical description involves, among other things,
    (a)   forming theoretical concepts,
    (b)   explicating the content of these theoretical concepts,
    (c)   integrating theoretical concepts into hypotheses and theories,
    (d)   symbolizing the content of hypotheses and theories,
    (e)   elucidating the content of the theories, and
    (f)   axiomatizing the theories.

We shall discuss the nature of the activities of (9)(a)–(f) in detail with regard to the giving of theoretical grammatical descriptions. Among other things, it will become clear that the activities of (9)(a)–(d), unlike those of (9)(e)–(f), are essential components of the giving of theoretical descriptions.

6.3   GRAMMATICAL INQUIRY

6.3.1   General

In preceding parts of our study we have in fact considered examples of fragments of the theoretical descriptions constructed in grammatical inquiry. The first example – the outlines of Chomsky's lexicalist hypothesis – was given as (1) in §6.1 above. Notice that this description is given in terms of natural language. Neither the "neutral" lexical entry, nor the morphological rules which are of crucial importance to this description are formalized in terms of special symbols. Therefore, (1) represents a fragment of an UNFORMALIZED THEORETICAL GRAMMATICAL DESCRIPTION.

However, when we discussed the content of Chomsky's $\bar{\text{X}}$-convention in §5.3.2.2, we also considered a fragment of a FORMALIZED THEORETICAL GRAMMATICAL DESCRIPTION. Among other things, the following base rules of English were given in this paragraph:

(10) $\text{S} \longrightarrow \bar{\bar{\text{N}}} \underline{\quad} \bar{\bar{\text{V}}}$
       $\bar{\bar{\text{V}}} \longrightarrow \text{Spec}_{\bar{\text{V}}} \underline{\quad} \bar{\text{V}}$
       $\bar{\text{V}} \longrightarrow \text{V} \underline{\quad} \text{Comp}_{\text{V}}$
       $\bar{\bar{\text{N}}} \longrightarrow \text{Spec}_{\bar{\text{N}}} \underline{\quad} \bar{\text{N}}$
       $\bar{\text{N}} \longrightarrow \text{N} \underline{\quad} \text{Comp}_{\text{N}}$

In (10) we have a fragment of a formalized theoretical grammatical description. The base rules are given explicitly in terms of symbols which have been specially chosen for the purpose.

We shall consider two main points in connection with theoretical grammatical descriptions such as (1) and (10). On the one hand we shall take a look at the nature and properties of such descriptions. On the other hand we shall focus on the activities carried out by the grammarian in giving such descriptions. But let us first of all reconsider our terminology. What we have been calling "a theoretical grammatical description" is commonly known as "a grammatical description", "a grammatical theory", or "a grammar". We shall therefore be using these four expressions alternately as synonyms.

6.3.2   Nature of Grammars

6.3.2.1   *Technical Characterization*

In §3.3.1.3 it emerged that in linguistic inquiry a grammar has a descriptive function. Chomsky makes this very clear in his *Aspects of the theory of syntax* (1965:4): "A grammar of a language purports to be a description of the ideal speaker-hearer's intrinsic competence". In order to fulfil this descriptive function, a grammar must have certain properties. These properties are usually described in technical linguistic terms which are not metascientifically explicit.

(11)(a)   A GRAMMAR takes the form of a system of mutually related rules.
   (b)   These rules must be finite in length and in number.
   (c)   The rules must be completely explicit.
   (d)   The rules must enumerate all the grammatical sentences of the language and no ungrammatical sentences.
   (e)   The rules must assign an appropriate structural description to each enumerated sentence.
   (f)   In doing (d) and (e) the rules must express linguistically significant generalizations about the language.

Note that lexical entries are not mentioned separately in technical characterizations such as that of (11). In such characterizations lexical entries are regarded as a type of rule. Note also that (11) is a technical description of a formalized grammar or theoretical grammatical description. In (11)(a)–(c) properties of the form of a grammar are stated, while in (11)(d)–(f) properties of the content of a grammar are specified. The properties (11)(a)–(d) will not be studied *en bloc* below. We shall consider them in the course of our study as and where they become relevant in terms of their relatedness to other aspects of linguistic inquiry.

6.3.2.2   *Grammatical Concepts*

It is clear from what has been said so far that a grammar describes the ideal speaker's linguistic competence in terms of a system of rules and lexical entries.

These rules and lexical entries express hypothetical descriptive statements — GRAMMATICAL HYPOTHESES for short — about individual human languages. Five examples of such hypotheses are given below.

(12)(a)   Derived nominals are deep structure NPs.

(b)   Gerundive nominals are transforms of sentence-like deep structures.

(c)   On the level of deep structure, S consists of an NP and a VP.

(d)   In the deep structure the major constituents, NP, VP and AP, each contain a specifier, a head and a complement.

(e)   The lexical item "refuse" may be inserted under both the node N and the node V.

The grammatical hypotheses of (12)(a)–(e) are, of course, hypotheses about English.

Grammatical hypotheses such as (12)(a)–(e) are composed of concepts, i.e. units of thought. Most important among these concepts are those which may be regarded as THEORETICAL CONCEPTS. Typical examples of theoretical concepts are 'sentence', 'noun phrase', 'verb phrase' and 'adjective phrase'. The theoretical concepts which are used in the construction of a grammar may be called GRAMMATICAL CONCEPTS for short. Theoretical concepts, as units of thought, are linguistically represented by THEORETICAL TERMS. For instance, the theoretical concepts mentioned above are linguistically represented by the theoretical terms "S", "NP", "VP" and "AP" respectively. The theoretical terms representing grammatical concepts may be called GRAMMATICAL TERMS for short. Note that a concept is indicated by placing it between single inverted commas, '· · ·', while a term is placed between double inverted commas, "· · ·".

The main question for us is: what exactly is a grammatical concept? Let us consider grammatical concepts from the point of view of their content. The content of all grammatical concepts has two components, viz. an empirical and a systematic component. The content of certain grammatical concepts has, in addition, a third component, viz. a thematic component. These three components of the content of a grammatical concept may be illustrated with reference to the concept 'sentence' as it occurs, for instance, in a transformational generative grammar of English.

In terms of the EMPIRICAL COMPONENT of its content, the grammatical concept 'sentence' refers to objects in the grammarian's linguistic reality. Recall that we saw in §3.3.1.1 that this reality has two levels, viz. a directly given level of linguistic performance and an underlying level of linguistic competence. In terms of the empirical component of its content, the grammatical concept 'sentence' refers to objects on both levels of the linguistic reality. On the directly given level of linguistic performance, we have utterances and intuitive judgments about these utterances which may be explained by means of this grammatical concept. We shall return to this point in §6.3.3.1.1. On the underlying level of linguistic competence, there has to be a mental mechanism which is represented by means of this grammatical concept. The exact meaning of "represented" in this context will be discussed in §6.3.2.3.

To summarize: the empirical component of a grammatical concept has two sides corresponding to the two levels of the grammarian's linguistic reality. In §6.3.3.1.2 we shall see that, apart from the linguistic intuitions of native speakers, grammatical concepts may also refer to another type of intuition, viz. certain intuitions that grammarians have in their capacity as skilled linguists.

In terms of the SYSTEMATIC COMPONENT of the content of a theoretical concept, this concept is related to other theoretical concepts. The systematic component of the content of grammatical concepts also has two sides. Firstly, a grammatical concept such as 'sentence' is related to other grammatical concepts within the same grammar. For instance, in the grammar of English, the concept 'sentence' is related to other concepts such as 'noun phrase', 'verb phrase', etc. This relatedness is stated in the rules – and lexical entries – within which 'sentence' occurs along with the other grammatical concepts.

The four base rules (13), which Emmon Bach (1974a:106) proposes for English, show clearly how the concept 'sentence' (S) is related to, among other things, the concepts 'NP' and 'VP' in the grammar of English.

(13)(a)   S $\longrightarrow$ (Sentence-Adverb) NP AUX VP (Location) (Time)

(b)   VP $\longrightarrow$ $\left\{ \begin{array}{l} \text{V NP NP Adverb} \\ \text{Copula Predicate} \end{array} \right\}$

(c)   Predicate $\longrightarrow$ $\left\{ \begin{array}{l} \text{NP} \\ \text{Adjective} \\ \text{Location} \\ \text{Time} \end{array} \left(\left\{ \begin{array}{l} \text{NP} \\ \text{\# S \#} \end{array} \right\} \right) \right\}$

(d)   NP $\longrightarrow$ $\left\{ \begin{array}{ll} \text{NP} & \text{\# S \#} \\ \text{(Det)} & \text{N \ (\# S \#)} \end{array} \right\}$

The base rules of (13) are interpreted in the conventional way. Within the framework of these rules, the concepts 'NP', 'VP', etc. co-determine the content of the concept 'S'. The systematic aspect of the content of a grammatical concept therefore, in the first place, represents the relationships existing between this concept and the other grammatical concepts within the same grammar.

Secondly, a grammatical concept such as 'sentence' is related to concepts in the general linguistic theory. These general linguistic concepts occur in the grammarian's set of assumptions about the nature of language in general. Consider the following examples of such general linguistic assumptions:

(14)(a)   Sentences are the fundamental linguistic units, i.e. units in terms of which the structure of human languages must be described.

(b)   A sentence has three fundamental aspects: a syntactic aspect, a semantic aspect and a phonological aspect.

(c)   As far as the syntactic aspect is concerned: sentences are constructed in terms of a deep structure and a surface structure.

Notice how, in these three general linguistic assumptions, a relatedness is shown to exist between the content of the concept 'sentence' and that of concepts such as 'fundamental linguistic units', 'syntactic aspect', 'semantic aspect', 'phonological aspect', 'deep structure' and 'surface structure'. Specifically, the content of the latter concepts co-determine that of the former concept. The systematic aspect of the content of a grammatical concept – such as 'sentence' in the grammar of English – therefore, in the second place, represents its relatedness to general linguistic concepts such as those occurring in (14)(a)–(c). In §6.3.3.1.3 we shall see that a grammatical concept without a systematic component in its content is an undesirable element in a theoretical grammatical description.

In his book, *Thematic origins of scientific thought* (1973:56ff.), the philosopher and historian of science, Gerald Holton, shows that the content of many theoretical concepts used in empirical inquiry also has a third component, viz. a THEMATIC COMPONENT. This component represents a thema. In any field of study a THEMA is a fundamental presupposition which cannot be formulated as an empirical hypothesis. This presupposition, moreover, crops up repeatedly in historically successive phases in the development of the discipline. The content of certain grammatical concepts also has a thematic component. Such grammatical concepts are those of which the content includes a particular type of element: an element which, in the history of the study of the language, occurs repeatedly as part of successive grammars. The concept 'sentence', as it occurs in the grammar of English, is a good example of a concept of which the content also has a thematic component. In the history of the grammatical investigation of English, this concept crops up repeatedly with the content 'fundamental structural unit of English'. In the concept 'sentence' the thema is therefore the presupposition that the sentences of English are the fundamental structural units of this language.

Not every grammatical concept has a thematic component in its content. The content of new grammatical concepts cannot have such a component. For instance, in Chomsky's lexicalist grammar of English, the concepts represented by "nom" and "[+ NP]" do not have a thematic component in their content. In this grammar, the grammatical concept 'nom' represents the linguistic element which determines the morphological form of derived nominals, while the grammatical concept '[+ NP]' is the conceptual representation of a new (type of) syntactic feature.

The preceding discussion may be made concrete with reference to the following diagram:

(15)   linguistic theories

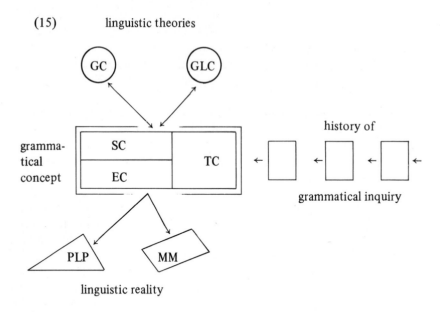

In the diagram (15) a schematic representation is given of the structure of the content of a grammatical concept such as 'sentence' in the grammar of English. The content of the concept is represented by the double-lined box. In this box "EC" symbolizes the empirical component. On the one hand, the empirical component refers to products of linguistic performance ("PLP"). On the other hand, the empirical component refers to an aspect of a mental mechanism ("MM"), viz. the native speaker's linguistic competence. "SC" symbolizes the systematic component of the content. On the one hand, the systematic component represents the relatedness of the concept in question to other concepts ("GC") in the same grammar. On the other hand, the systematic component represents the relatedness of the concept in question to concepts ("GLC") in the general linguistic theory. The third component, the thematic component, is symbolized by "TC". The boxes and arrows to the right of the TC represent the historical continuity of the thematic component of the content of the grammatical concept.

6.3.2.3   Ontological Status

In the preceding paragraph we distinguished two sides of the empirical component of the content of a grammatical concept. The one side is related to the products of linguistic performance of which the problematic properties may be explained with the aid of the concept in question. The other side represents an aspect of a mental mechanism, viz. a part of the ideal speaker's linguistic competence. This brings us to the crucial question: what do we mean when we say that a grammar describes the ideal speaker's linguistic competence by representing it in terms of theoretical concepts? This question may be broken down into three more specific questions.

(16)(a)   Which aspect(s) of the ideal speaker's linguistic competence does a grammar describe?

 (b)   What do we mean when we say that theoretical concepts "represent" the linguistic competence?

 (c)   How can a grammar describe a mental capacity of a nonexistent individual, an ideal speaker?

6.3.2.3.1   *Aspects of linguistic competence*

As a mental capacity, the linguistic competence has various aspects. Three of these are of importance to us.

A first aspect is the substantial or material aspect. The SUBSTANTIAL ASPECT of the linguistic competence represents the content, or substance, of the native speaker's unconscious linguistic knowledge by virtue of which he is capable of linguistic performance. Linguistic performance comprises the producing and interpreting of utterances and the making of intuitive judgments about properties of utterances. The content of the linguistic competence is therefore, to a certain extent, reflected in the products of linguistic performance.

A second aspect of the linguistic competence is the structural or formal aspect. The STRUCTURAL ASPECT of the linguistic competence represents the structure, or organization, of its content. This organization exists in terms of mental mechanisms, or mental structures. From the point of view of its structural aspect, Chomsky regards the linguistic competence as "the mentally represented grammar". In his article "Conditions on transformations" (1973:275, note 59), he formulates this point as follows:

> Surely · · · the natural assumption is that there is a mentally represented grammar expressing knowledge of a language and used in production, perception and prediction.

By "prediction" Chomsky here means "prediction of properties, especially (un)grammaticality, of sentences". According to Chomsky, the mental mechanisms in terms of which the linguistic competence is organized, or structured, must play a role in linguistic performance. In other words, as a structured unit, the linguistic competence in one way or another forms part of the speaker's speech production and speech perception mechanisms.

A third aspect of the linguistic competence is the physical aspect. As part of the mechanisms described above, the linguistic competence is localized in the human brain. In other words, the linguistic competence is physically realized as a part or parts of the speaker's neurological system. Chomsky and Jerrold Katz formulate this point as follows in their article "What the linguist is talking about" (1974:364):

> ... the grammar in the form that it would take in models of speech production and speech perception must structurally correspond to some features of brain mechanism.

The neurological realization of the linguistic competence in the form of brain mechanisms represents the PHYSICAL ASPECT of the linguistic competence.

We can now answer the question (16)(a) about the aspect(s) of the linguistic competence which the grammar describes. For the majority of generative grammarians a grammar must describe the substantial aspect of the linguistic competence. For a significant subgroup, this description must go even further: it must also describe the structural aspect of the linguistic competence. In his article "Questions of form and interpretation" (1975d:171), Chomsky states very clearly that

> study of language is part of a more general enterprise: to map out in detail the *structure* [the italics are mine – R.P.B.] of mind. On the assumption just noted, we might continue to regard a grammar as a separate component of this more general system and proceed to investigate its specific properties.

In short, a grammar should describe the structure, or organization, of the linguistic competence as well. Recall that for Chomsky the linguistic competence is the "mentally represented grammar" of which a characterization was given above.

Note that a grammar may represent the content of the linguistic competence without necessarily representing its structure as well. The contrary is not possible however. The organization of a given complex unit of content cannot be represented in terms of structural components without the content itself being represented at the same time. In short, representing the structure of the linguistic competence in a grammar implies representing its content.

Chomsky does not require a grammar to describe the physical aspect of the linguistic competence. A grammar therefore need not describe in neuro(physio)-logical terms the brain mechanisms corresponding to the "mentally represented grammar". In his book *Reflections on language* (1975c:91), Chomsky assigns this task to the neurologist:

> Studying the use and understanding of language, we [linguists – R.P.B.] reach certain conclusions about the cognitive structure (grammar) that is being put to use, thus setting a certain problem for the neurologist, whose task it is to discover the mechanisms involved in linguistic competence and performance.

6.3.2.3.2 *"Represent"*

This brings us to question (16)(b): how does a grammar represent the linguistic competence in terms of theoretical concepts?

Let us start with the representation of the substantial aspect of the linguistic competence. A grammar represents the content of the linguistic competence by enumerating all the grammatical sentences – and no ungrammatical sentences – of the language and by assigning appropriate structural descriptions to these grammatical sentences. Generative grammarians assume that the linguistic knowledge which a grammar "needs" in order to generate these sentences with their structural descriptions must be substantially the same as the unconscious linguistic knowledge by virtue of which the native speaker is capable of linguistic performance. In other words, if the ability of a grammar to enumerate sentences and to assign structural descriptions to these sentences is parallel to the ability of the native speaker to interpret, to produce and to judge sentences, it is assumed that the grammar represents the content of the linguistic competence.

This brings us to the representation of the structural aspect of the linguistic competence: what would it mean for a grammar to represent the structural aspect of the linguistic competence? Over the years, generative grammarians have come up with different answers to this complex question. The details of these answers – and the problems attached to them – fall outside the scope of our study. For our purposes, these answers may be divided into two classes: those which provide for a strong form of representation vs. those which provide for a weaker form of representation. A grammar gives a STRONG REPRESENTATION of the structure of the linguistic competence if there is isomorphism between the grammar and the linguistic competence. This happens when for each theoretical concept, rule and (sub)component of the grammar, a corresponding independent mental mechanism or structural component of the linguistic competence is to be found. In the mid-sixties Jerrold Katz characterized this strong form of representation as follows in his article "Mentalism in linguistics" (1964:133):

> Every aspect of the mentalistic theory involves psychological reality. The linguistic description and the procedures of sentence production and recognition must correspond to independent mechanisms of the brain. Componential distinctions between the syntactic, phonological and semantic components must rest on relevant differences between three neural submechanisms of the mechanism which stores the linguistic description. The rules of each component must have their psychological reality in the input-output operations of the computing machinery of this mechanism. The ordering of rules within a component must, . . ., have its psychological reality in those features of this computing machinery which group such input-output operations and make the performance of operations in one group a precondition for those in another to be performed.

Katz uses the expression "linguistic description" as a synonym for "grammar".

The kind of isomorphism between the grammar and the linguistic competence which is assumed by the strong form of representation is called RULE-FOR-RULE ISOMORPHISM or MICRO-ISOMORPHISM. The psycholinguist, Levelt (1974:69), characterizes this kind of isomorphism as follows:

> An implication of this point of view is that a given partitioning in the linguistic grammar must correspond to a parallel partitioning in the psychological process. As the input and output of every linguistic rule is copied psychologically, this must also hold for groups of rules. If, for example, the formal model is a transformational grammar, the distinction between the base grammar and the transformational component will be reflected in a parallel segmentation of psychological processes; the deep structures would be the output of one process, for example, and the input of another.

The strong form of representation, based on isomorphism between grammar and linguistic competence, was strongly advocated by generative grammarians in the mid- and late sixties. However, it appeared on investigation that a grammar cannot give such a strong representation of the structure of the linguistic competence. It was found, for instance, that for many transformational rules in the grammar of English no corresponding mental mechanism exists in the linguistic competence. These findings persuaded some generative grammarians to make provision for weaker forms of representation. Even Katz (1977) has abandoned his strong position on psychological reality quoted above.

Currently, generative grammarians provide for, among others, the following weaker form of representation: a grammar gives a WEAKER REPRESENTATION of the structure of the linguistic competence if the components or types of rules of the grammar correspond to independent mental mechanisms or structures within the linguistic competence. This weaker form of representation assumes a relation of SEMI-ISOMORPHISM between the grammar and the linguistic competence. In her recent article, "Toward a realistic model of transformational grammar" (1976:4), Joan Bresnan emerges as a supporter of this weaker form of representation:

> . . . we should be able to define for it [a realistic model of grammar − R.P.B.] a *realization mapping* to a psychological model of language processing. Such a realization should map distinct grammatical rules and units into distinct processing operations and informational units in such a way that different rule types of the grammar are associated with different processing functions.

According to Levelt (1974:69) supporters of such a weaker form of representation − based on semi-isomorphism between grammar and linguistic competence − maintain

the general agreement between the partitioning of the grammar and that of the psychological mechanism. For them, components of the grammar correspond to relatively independent processes in the language user (macro-isomorphism). In their details, these show little structural agreement with the rules of the grammar, but input and output remain linguistically defined entities, such as surface structure and deep structure. This school thus omits isomorphism on the microlevel, but retains it for the major steps.

Semi-isomorphism, therefore, implies that the linguistic structures generated by a grammar correspond to mental structures in the linguistic competence. This does not imply, however, that the individual rules – which generate linguistic structures – correspond to mental structures.

But what are Chomsky's views on the relation between a grammar and the structure of linguistic competence? Chomsky has nowhere formulated his views on the matter as explicitly as, for instance, Katz and Bresnan have formulated theirs. However, Bresnan (1976:2) argues that her views on the matter are in fact the result of an attempt to take Chomsky's view of transformational grammar seriously. There are indeed indications that Chomsky cannot be in favour of an extremely weak form of representation. Recall that Chomsky's "mentally represented grammar" not only characterizes the ideal speaker's knowledge of a language, but is in fact used in production, perception and prediction. For Chomsky (1975c:171) the function of the linguist's grammar is ". . . to map out in detail the structure . . ." of this mentally represented grammar, or linguistic competence. It is not clear how such a detailed "mapping out" would be possible if there were no or merely a trivial form of correspondence between the structure of a grammar and that of the linguistic competence. Further considerations which seem to corroborate the assumption that Chomsky accepts a nontrivial form of correspondence between a grammar and the linguistic competence are discussed in §§7.3.2.3, 9.3.2.4.3. It should be emphasized, however, that even Chomsky's latest expositions of his position on the relation between linguistic theories and mental language capacities are unclear in important respects. This point is illustrated by Botha's (1979a, b) discussion of Chomsky's article "On the biological basis of language capacities" (1976).

The relationship between a grammar and linguistic competence is commonly characterized in terms of expressions such as "psychologically real" and "psychological reality". A grammar, grammatical rule or grammatical (theoretical) concept which represents an aspect of the structure of linguistic competence is considered to be PSYCHOLOGICALLY REAL or to have PSYCHOLOGICAL REALITY. Whether or not a grammar or part of it is psychologically real is therefore commonly related to its ability to give a correct representation of an aspect of the *structure* of the linguistic competence. However, certain generative grammarians use the expressions "psychologically real" and "psychological reality" in a weaker sense. They relate the property of having, or not having, psychological reality to the role the grammar, or part of it, plays in the explanation of the linguistic intuitions of native speakers. For instance, Levelt (1974:70) maintains that "a linguistic concept is psychologically real to the extent that it contributes to the explanation of behaviour relative to linguistic judgments". In our study we shall not use the terms "psychologically real" and "psychological reality" in this weak sense. We shall use them to denote the ability of a grammar, or part(s) of it, to give a representation of structural aspects of linguistic competence.

6.3.2.3.3   *Nonexistence of ideal speaker*

Only question (16)(c) remains to be answered: how can a grammar describe a mental capacity of a nonexistent individual – an ideal speaker? We seem to be faced with a contradiction. A grammar must describe a mental capacity in an underlying reality. However, the individual who should possess this mental capacity does not in fact exist. The only speakers who do exist are ordinary, nonideal native speakers whose linguistic performance is subject to various physical and mental limitations.

However, it is not paradoxical to maintain that a grammar must describe the linguistic competence of an ideal speaker, as it is the same as saying that a grammar must give only an *approximate* description of the linguistic competence of the ordinary, nonideal native speaker of the language. This description is approximate in that it does not take into account those factors which are responsible for the fact that ordinary native speakers are nonideal speakers. These factors were discussed in §§3.3.1.2 and 4.3.2.2.2.

Aspects of the linguistic competence of the ordinary native speaker are co-determined by the factor of dialectal variation, the factor of social diversity, the factor of idiolectal variation and the factor of nonlinguistic physical and mental restrictions. A grammar describes the linguistic competence of the ordinary native speaker as if these factors played no role at all in determining the content and structure of his linguistic competence. In this sense the grammar gives only an approximate description of the ordinary native speaker's linguistic competence. In other words, it describes the ideal speaker's linguistic competence. The reasons why a grammar cannot describe the linguistic competence of a nonideal native speaker were discussed in §3.3.1.2.

6.3.2.3.4   *Metascientific perspective*

The relation between a grammar and linguistic competence may be seen in a wider metascientific perspective, viz. that of the ontological, or cognitive, status of scientific theories. The ONTOLOGICAL or COGNITIVE STATUS of a theory is determined by the type of relationship which exists between the theory and reality. We shall consider two metascientific views of the ontological status of theories: realism and instrumentalism.

REALISM, or the realistic point of view, hinges on two crucial principles. The first principle is that, in terms of their theoretical concepts and hypotheses, theories make claims about, or give a description of, an underlying reality. This reality underlies the directly given, observable, problematic phenomena, events, objects, etc. In terms of its first principle, therefore, the realistic point of view provides for a two-levelled reality: a reality with an underlying level and a directly given, observable level. The second principle of realism is that the descriptive statements which theories make about the underlying level of reality may be true or false. These two principles of realism are diversely articulated in the philosophical literature, with the result that several versions of realism exist. The differences between these versions fall outside the scope of our study.

INSTRUMENTALISM represents the point of view which opposes realism with regard to the two principles discussed above. The first principle of instrumentalism is that theories do not describe an underlying reality. Theories are regarded as means, or instruments, for the organization of data about (problematic) phenomena, events, objects, etc. which are directly given. Instrumentalism represents theories as means of making deductions about these phenomena, events, objects, etc. Instrumentalism therefore does not provide for a two-levelled reality. The second principle of instrumentalism is that theories, as means of organizing data, cannot be true or false. Theories can only be more or less adequate means of organization. More adequate theories have a wider range of applicability. They make it possible to organize a larger number and variety of data in a more economical way than less adequate theories.

But what is the ontological status of grammars? Chomsky and Katz (1974: 359) declare unambiguously that grammars have a realistic status: "The question now at issue is, in essence, the question of realism. Are we willing to postulate that our *dags*, and our linguistic theory, describe properties of the speaker-hearer? Is the mature speaker-hearer to be regarded as a "system" with the properties spelled out in detail in the postulated *dag*, and is the child to be regarded as a "system" with the properties spelled out in detail in the postulated linguistic theory? The standard account follows normal scientific practice in answering "yes" to both of these questions". *Dag(s)* is the abbreviation for "descriptively adequate grammar(s)". For our present purpose it may be taken to mean simply "grammar(s)". In §7.4.2.2 we shall take a closer look at what Chomsky considers to be a descriptively adequate grammar.

Grammars, therefore, describe an underlying linguistic reality, viz. a mental reality of mental capacities. This view that grammars describe an underlying mental reality is known as MENTALISM. It appears from the work of, among others, Foss and Fay (1975), Hutchinson (1974), Katz (1977), Ringen (1975) and Stitch (1975) that generative grammarians over the years have developed several versions of mentalism. These versions differ from one another, among other things, on the question of what it means for a grammar to *represent* an aspect of linguistic competence. Recall that in §6.3.2.3.2 above we drew a broad distinction between two forms of representation, a strong and a weaker form. This distinction is at the same time a distinction between what we could call STRONG MENTALISM and WEAK(ER) MENTALISM. The details of and problems associated with this distinction between the various versions of mentalism fall outside the limited scope of our study.

Note in conclusion that at present there is no leading generative grammarian who supports a nonmentalistic view of grammars. In terms of a purely non-mentalistic view, a grammar would not describe the structure of a mental capacity on an underlying level of the linguistic reality. A pure nonmentalist would regard a grammar as a mere means of economically organizing data about products of linguistic performance.

6.3.3 Giving a Grammatical Description

In the preceding section, §6.3.2, we considered the general nature and a number of particular properties of theoretical grammatical descriptions. We shall now take a look at some of the activities in terms of which the grammarian gives such descriptions, or constructs grammars. In other words, we shall consider the implications of question (3)(b) for grammatical description. In §6.2.4 the most important activities carried out by scientists when giving theoretical descriptions were indicated on a general level. These activities included: forming theoretical concepts, explicating the content of these theoretical concepts, integrating theoretical concepts in hypotheses and theories, symbolizing the content of the hypotheses and theories, elucidating the content of theories and axiomatizing the theories. Let us now consider these activities with reference to grammatical inquiry.

6.3.3.1 *Forming Theoretical Concepts*

Grammatical concepts represent the elementary components of theoretical grammatical descriptions. For instance, Chomsky's lexicalist grammar of English is composed of grammatical concepts such as 'sentence' ("S"), 'noun phrase' ("NP"), 'verb phrase' ("VP"), 'auxiliarium' ("AUX"), 'determiner' ("Det"), 'nominalizer' ("nom"), 'pluralis' ("pl"), 'causative' ("cause"), 'refuse', 'prove', and so on. Recall that a grammatical concept may be regarded as a unit of thought which represents an aspect of the linguistic competence of the ideal speaker.

A first activity involved in the giving of theoretical grammatical descriptions is that of forming the necessary "building-blocks", viz. grammatical concepts. It follows from what has been said so far that forming a grammatical concept entails the giving of a conceptual representation of an aspect of the ideal speaker's linguistic competence.

The question is: how does a grammarian form a grammatical concept? This question is, in actual fact, a different version of the question about the nature of grammatical discovery. The unit of thought, or idea, embodied in the grammatical concept must be "discovered" or "thought out". In §5.2.2 we saw that very little information is available about the logical mechanisms in terms of which such discoveries are made. When talking about the forming of grammatical concepts, therefore, we can do so only in very general terms.

The forming of a grammatical concept or conceptual representation is a complex activity. This becomes even more apparent if we compare the forming of such conceptual representations to the making of other types of representations. For instance, it may be compared to the making of a photographic representation of an object. To make a photograph of an object is to give a visual representation or image of an *observable* object. To form a grammatical concept, on the other hand, is to give a conceptual representation of an *unobservable* object. Giving a representation of an unobservable object is obviously more complex than giving a representation of an observable object.

The grammarian can gain insight into and represent the linguistic competence only on the strength of indirect data about it. These indirect data mainly take the form of primary linguistic data, i.e. utterances and linguistic intuitions as products of linguistic performance. In short, the grammarian can form grammatical concepts, or conceptual representations, of the linguistic competence only on the basis of what is known about the products of the use of linguistic competence. From the information about these products, the grammarian tries to form an image, or a concept, of the mental capacity which, when applied, yields these products. Central to the grammarian's attempts to form grammatical concepts, is the general question (17).

(17)   How must the linguistic competence be structured if its use yields products with the properties which are recorded in my pretheoretical grammatical description?

The ideas which the grammarian has in answer to this general question represent his grammatical concepts.

Let us make our discussion more concrete by giving specific content to the general question (17). In §1.1 we considered, among other things, the following data about English:

(18)(a)   The utterance *John has refused the offer* is acceptable.
   (b)   The utterance **John has refused hope* is unacceptable.
   (c)   The utterance **Trouble has refused the offer* is unacceptable.
   (d)   The utterance *John's refusal of the offer* is acceptable.
   (e)   The utterance **John's refusal of hope* is unacceptable.
   (f)   The utterance **Trouble's refusal of the offer* is unacceptable.

With reference to the data of (18) the general question (17) may now be given the specific content of (19).

(19)   How must the linguistic competence of the ideal speaker of English be structured if its use produces the utterances of (18)(a)–(f) with their particular properties of acceptability?

The answer to (19) must be given in terms of a grammatical concept which gives a conceptual representation of an aspect of the linguistic competence in question. Chomsky's answer to the question (19) has already been discussed.

(20)　The structure of the linguistic competence in question contains the neutral lexical entry "refuse"
　　　(a)　which has certain fixed selectional and subcategorization features, but
　　　(b)　which is left unspecified with regard to those syntactic features which distinguish between nouns and verbs.

The neutral lexical entry "refuse" represents the grammatical concept which gives a conceptual representation of the relevant aspect of the linguistic competence. The point is that if "refuse" were part of the linguistic competence in question, it would follow that the products of linguistic performance (18) (a)–(f) must have the properties which they do in fact have.

The data about the relevant properties of these products of linguistic performance are directly given. On the basis of these, the grammarian tries to form a conceptual image of how the linguistic competence must be structured to yield these products of linguistic performance. Chomsky and Katz (1974:364) give the following characterization of the essence of the forming of linguistic concepts:

> Clearly the linguist does not produce a priori pronouncements on the details of neural connections and pathways, but rather presents a modest inference from some very general features of effects to very general features of their causes, providing a sketch of what the causes would have to be like to be able of producing the effects.

In §7.3.2.3 we shall discuss the implications of this way of reasoning for the nature of grammatical explanations.

The method of forming concepts described above is not restricted to linguistic inquiry. In empirical inquiry in general this kind of "reverse" reasoning from the properties of the products of a mechanism to the properties of the mechanism itself is widely used. The following example should illustrate this point. The object of study of the geologist is the geological processes occurring far below the surface of the earth. These processes cannot be directly studied in any way. The data about these processes are indirect as they are data about the products of the processes. The products of these processes take the form of geological phenomena, events and objects which may be observed on the earth's surface, such as volcanic eruptions and their products, earthquakes and their products, etc. On the basis of the properties of the products of these subterranean geological processes, the geologist tries to form conceptual images or representations of the nature and properties of the hidden processes. The geologist's conceptual images represent the theoretical concepts of which geological theories are composed.

Schematically the grammarian's method of forming concepts may be represented as follows:

(21)

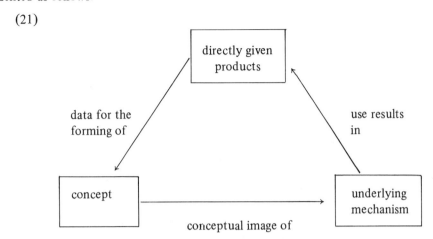

When forming grammatical concepts within the framework of (21), the grammarian takes into account special criteria which the final products must satisfy. Four of these are of crucial importance. Let us consider them individually.

6.3.3.1.1 *Explaining primary problematic data*

Consider the theoretical grammatical description (1) in §6.1 above. Note that the grammatical concept which is central to this fragment of a description of English is a neutral lexical entry for "refuse". Note further that this neutral lexical entry for "refuse" is initially included in the grammar of English because with the aid of this grammar, the grammarian must be able to explain certain linguistic data which are problematic. We considered these problematic data in §1.1. The crux of the matter is that it must be possible to explain why sentences such as *John has refused the offer*, and derived nominals such as *John's refusal of the offer* exhibit syntactic similarities such as those of (10) and (11) in §1.1. If the lexicon of English contained a neutral lexical entry for "refuse", with the properties indicated in (1) of §6.1 above, it would follow that these sentences and derived nominals must exhibit the syntactic similarities in question. To reason thus is to explain the relevant primary problematic data about *John has refused the offer* and *John's refusal of the offer* with the aid of the grammar of English. In other words, problematic properties of classes of utterances (= sentences) are explained by showing how these properties follow from certain aspects of the underlying linguistic competence. These aspects of the linguistic competence are represented by grammatical concepts. We shall return to the nature and properties of grammatical explanations in more detail in §7.3 below.

Every grammatical concept must play a role in the explanation of primary problematic data. To facilitate later reference, this first criterion for grammatical concepts may be formulated as (22).

(22)   Grammatical concepts must make it possible to explain the problem-
         atic primary linguistic data about the language with the aid of the
         grammar of that language.

A concept which does not play a role in grammatical explanation cannot be used
in the construction of a theoretical grammatical description. The criterion (22)
is a MINIMAL CRITERION for grammatical concepts. With a view to the discussion
of the second criterion, it should be noted that the linguistic data referred to in
(22) are data about utterances and linguistic intuitions.

6.3.3.1.2   *Expressing linguistically significant generalizations*

In §5.3.2.2 we looked at the internal structure of NPs such as *John's proof of
the theorem*, VPs such as *will prove the theorem* and APs such as *even ignorant
of the theorem*. Two points were made with regard to the structure of these
constituents. First, there is a parallelism in the structure of such NPs, VPs and
APs. In the grammar of English this parallelism is expressed in a similarity
between the base rules generating NPs, VPs and APs. Secondly, Chomsky is
of the opinion that this parallelism is linguistically significant. In other words,
for Chomsky this parallelism represents an essential, nonaccidental structural
property of English.

A grammar has to express these linguistically significant facts about a
language explicitly in the form of generalizations. In other words, a grammar
must express the LINGUISTICALLY SIGNIFICANT GENERALIZATIONS about a
language. This also implies that a grammar may not express any linguistically
nonsignificant generalizations, which present in a general form data about
accidental, nonessential properties of a language.

Whatever a grammar has to say about a language is stated in terms of grammatical concepts. For this reason grammatical concepts must satisfy a second
criterion in linguistic inquiry.

(23)   Grammatical concepts must make it possible to express the linguis-
         tically significant generalizations about a language.

In §5.3.2.2 we discussed the implications of the criterion (23) with regard to
Chomsky's opinion that the parallelism in the structure of NPs such as *John's
proof of the theorem*, VPs such as *will prove the theorem* and APs such as *even
ignorant of the theorem* is linguistically significant. In order to express this
linguistically significant parallelism, it was necessary to include the concepts
'specifier', 'head' and 'complement' in the grammar of English. This was achieved
by means of the $\overline{\text{X}}$-convention. In terms of these three concepts it could be
explicitly specified that the NPs, VPs, and APs mentioned above are all composed
of a head preceded by a specifier and followed by a complement.

In order to meet the criterion (23), the grammarian must be able to draw a
certain distinction. He must be able to distinguish between facts and generaliza-

tions that are linguistically significant, and facts and generalizations that are linguistically nonsignificant. The problem is that linguistic inquiry has no clear, objective criterion on the basis of which this distinction may be drawn. In other words, the grammarian has no clear, objective criterion for linguistic significance. For this reason the grammarian's judgments as to what is and what is not linguistically significant have an intuitive character. These judgments are the result of his extensive and profound contact with the language he is studying. However, these judgments cannot be justified on the strength of objective data or considerations. Because of their intuitive, nonobjective origin, these judgments about linguistic significance may be called "intuitions". Note, however, that these intuitions about significance are not of the same kind as linguistic intuitions. All native speakers of a language have linguistic intuitions about the properties of the utterances of their language, while only trained grammarians can have intuitions about linguistic significance.

Moreover, intuitions about linguistic significance are not intuitive judgments about such properties of utterances as acceptability, ambiguity, synonymy, paraphrase, etc. Intuitions about linguistic significance concern similarities, differences, parallelisms, (dis)symmetries and other forms of relationship holding between structures and rules. Such intuitions are typically rendered in terms of expressions such as "structures", "rules", etc.

(24)(a)   There is a linguistically significant similarity/difference between the structures S_1 and S_2/the rules R_1 and R_2.

(b)   The structures S_1 and S_2/the rules R_1 and R_2 exhibit a/no linguistically significant parallelism.

(c)   The symmetry/dissymmetry between the rules R_1 and R_2 is linguistically significant.

Linguistically significant facts and generalizations therefore concern forms of relationship between either structures or rules. As far as structures are concerned, the relationship is to be found in their make-up. As far as rules are concerned, the relationship is one of content, form or function.

The following example illustrates clearly the importance of grammarians' intuitions about linguistic significance in linguistic inquiry. McCawley (1973:74–75) rejects Chomsky's 'specifier' as a grammatical concept of English. He does so because, unlike Chomsky, he intuitively judges that there is no linguistically significant similarity between, for instance, *John's, will* and *even* in the NP *John's proof of the theorem*, the VP *will prove the theorem* and the AP *even ignorant of the theorem* respectively. According to McCawley, therefore, the inclusion of the grammatical concept 'specifier' in the grammar of English makes it possible to express an accidental similarity as if it were linguistically significant. In terms of this concept, there is a significant similarity between *John's, will* and *even*, viz. that they are all specifiers. According to McCawley, this similarity is purely accidental as it is by mere chance that these three constituents occur in the same position in the NP, VP and AP respectively. A grammar of English which includes the concept 'specifier' is therefore considered to be inadequate by McCawley. In §6.4.3.1.2 we shall see that McCawley regards it as a flaw in the $\bar{X}$-convention that it makes it possible to express such linguistically nonsignificant generalizations.

6.3.3.1.3   *Having systematic grammatical content*
In §6.3.2.2 it appeared that a grammatical concept has both empirical and systematic content. The systematic content has two aspects: a grammatical, or language-specific, aspect and a general linguistic, or universal, aspect. Against this background, a third criterion for grammatical concepts may be formulated.

(25)   The language-specific content of grammatical concepts must as far as possible be systematic.

The criterion (25) may be explicated in both negative and positive terms. In negative terms, this criterion implies that a grammatical concept may not be formed to account for only one or a few problematic data. Such grammatical concepts are by nature *AD HOC* and are less desirable elements in a theoretical grammatical description. They reduce the value of the description in which they occur. This point will be discussed in detail in §§9.3.2.2.5, 9.3.2.3.2, 10.3.2.1.4 and 10.3.2.2.

In positive terms, the criterion (25) implies that a grammatical concept must play a role in the formulation of as many structural descriptions and grammatical rules as possible. In other words, a grammatical concept should make it possible to express the greatest possible number of different (types of) grammatical generalizations about a language. Such a concept must therefore play a role in stating relationships between classes of apparently unrelated linguistic units. Further on in our study we shall see that such a grammatical concept has a degree of explanatory and predictive power, which is a highly desirable property for a grammatical concept to have.

An example will serve to illustrate what it means for a grammatical concept to have systematic content on a language-specific level. The concept 'NP' in the grammar of English is not only needed in the formulation of the hypothesis that derived nominals have the internal structure of NPs. It also plays a role in the formulation of a large number of rules in the grammar of English. Among these rules are the following:

(26)(a)   Base rules such as those given as (13) in §6.3.2.2.
    (b)   Syntactic transformations such as
        (i)   EXTRAPOSITION   Optional

$$\text{SD: X, } [_{\text{NP}} \text{ it, S] , Y]}_{\text{VP}}$$
$$\qquad\quad 1 \quad\; 2 \quad\; 3 \quad 4$$
$$\text{SC: 1} \quad 2 \quad\; \phi \quad 4+3 \Longrightarrow$$
$$\qquad\qquad\qquad\qquad \text{(cf. Bach 1974a:89)}$$

(ii) PASSIVE

SD: X, NP, AUX   V, (Prep), NP, by, Agent, Y
     1 2   3   4   5   6   7   8   9
SC: 1 6 3+be+-en 4   5 ϕ 7   2   9

(cf. Bach 1974a:90)

(c) Phonological rules such as

$$\begin{bmatrix} 1 \text{ stress} \\ V \end{bmatrix} \longrightarrow [1 \text{ stress}] \ / \ 1$$

$$V \ldots \text{———} \ldots] \text{ NP}$$

(cf. Chomsky and Halle 1968:17)

(d) Semantic interpretation rules such as the RULE FOR RECIPROCAL PRONOUNS: assign to *each other* the feature [+ anaphoric to i] in a structure contrining NP_i.   (cf. Chomsky 1976:3)

The grammar of English contains numerous rules, the formulation of which requires the grammatical concept 'NP'. This concept therefore fully satisfies the criterion that the language-specific content of grammatical concepts should be as systematic as possible.

We have seen that a grammatical concept which is formed to account for only one or a few problematic data is by nature *ad hoc*. Such concepts are undesirable elements in a grammar because they play no role in the stating of relationships, the expression of regularities, the giving of explanations and the making of predictions. But not all aspects of the ideal speaker's linguistic competence can be described in terms of non-*ad hoc* grammatical concepts. Every language has so-called idiosyncratic or exceptional aspects. The majority of idiosyncratic aspects of a language are concentrated in the lexicon. Lexical items often behave exceptionally with regard to the syntactic, phonological and morphological processes of the language. Take, for instance, the irregular plurals of the lexical items *ox, child, man* and *loaf* in English, or the irregular past tense forms of the lexical items *go, do, is* and *eat*. The grammatical concepts needed for the description of such idiosyncratic aspects of the linguistic competence must be *ad hoc* as they are formed to express nongeneralities in a grammar. Note, in conclusion, that the criterion (25) for grammatical concepts is related to the criteria of systematicity and generality for grammatical knowledge, which were discussed in §3.3.1.4. The criterion (25) realizes one aspect of the latter criteria.

6.3.3.1.4 *Having general linguistic content*

This brings us to the fourth criterion for grammatical concepts – one which realizes another aspect of the criteria of systematicity and generality for grammatical knowledge. Every individual language has two aspects. On the one hand, it has an aspect in terms of which it is something separate and individual; an aspect which distinguishes it from all other individual languages. On the other hand, it has an aspect in terms of which it is a manifestation of human language in general; an aspect in terms of which it is just like all other human languages. It must be quite clear from the grammar for an individual language, in what respects the language is individual. But the grammar must show just as clearly in what respects this language is a manifestation of language in general. This means that those respects in which an individual language is a manifestation of language in general must not be represented in the grammar as if they were unique properties of the language in question. In other words, a grammar must describe the linguistic competence in such a way that it is quite clear which aspects of the linguistic competence are innate in the form of the language acquisition faculty and which aspects are acquired on the basis of linguistic experience. This is the background to the fourth criterion for grammatical concepts.

(27)   The general linguistic content of grammatical concepts must be as large as possible.

The criterion (27) implies that grammatical concepts should, as far as possible, be formed in accordance with the linguistic universals of the general linguistic theory. [Recall that the term "general linguistic theory" refers to the grammarian's complete set of assumptions about language in general.]

On the one hand, the grammarian attempts to use as many substantive universals as possible as grammatical concepts in his grammatical description. Substantive universals represent the units, categories, rules, etc. which seem to occur in (almost) all human languages. Examples of such substantive universals are, or could be, the lexical categories N, V and A; the constituent categories NP and VP; the syntactic features [± _____ NP], [± count]; the phonetic features [± vocalic], [± consonantal]; the base rule S $\longrightarrow$ NP VP; the transformation Passive; and so on. By using a substantive universal as a grammatical concept the grammarian indicates a respect in which the language in question is a manifestation of language in general.

On the other hand, the grammarian tries to form those grammatical concepts that do not represent substantive universals in accordance with the proposed formal universals. The formal universals specify the *types* of units, categories, structures, rules, etc. in terms of which human language is constructed. The grammarian tries not to form grammatical concepts which are not typical of human language in general. To describe a language in terms of grammatical concepts which are not typically linguistic is to claim that the language in question is not a manifestation of language in general. To make such a claim within the framework of linguistic inquiry is to act in a completely nonrational way. Linguistic inquiry within the framework of generative grammar requires that grammatical concepts should have as large a general linguistic content as possible. This means that grammatical concepts must either represent substantive universals, or be formed in accordance with formal universals. This criterion elucidates another point which was discussed in §5.3.3, viz. that language-specific discovery is a guided activity. When forming a grammatical concept the grammarian is restricted – and thus guided – by linguistic universals. The concept is formed within the framework of the characterization, given in terms of such universals, of what a possible human language would be.

Suppose, however, that the data about a particular language were such that they could not be explained except by forming a concept which is not typically linguistic in terms of a given universal. The grammarian will then conclude that the universal in question is incorrect and that it gives an inaccurate representation of human language in general. However, he will reach this conclusion only if all the relevant data about the language force him to form the concept in question. The importance of the criterion (27) may not be underestimated. In his article "Avoiding reference to subject" (1976:168), Paul Postal spells out in no uncertain terms what the results of such an underestimation would be:

> Without viewing linguistic facts in the perspective of universal grammar, one is doomed to confuse accidental properties of rules with universal ones, to miss generalizations, to formulate as ad hoc restrictions properties that can be predicted, and to take as universal what are language-particular features.

This concludes our discussion of the four criteria for grammatical concepts. Further on in our study we shall look at additional criteria for these concepts, for instance, the criterion that the content of grammatical concepts may not be such that they preclude the possibility of making testable statements. This criterion will be discussed in § 10.3.3.2.1.

6.3.3.2   *Explicating of Concepts*

In order to be used in the construction of grammatical descriptions, grammatical concepts must have an explicit content. In terms of this criterion it must be completely clear what the content of a grammatical concept is in such a description. Suppose that the content of a given grammatical concept – say the concept 'nom' in Chomsky's grammar of English – was not completely clear. It would then be impossible to make precise, unambiguous statements about the linguistic competence of the ideal speaker. For this reason one of the important activities involved in giving theoretical grammatical descriptions is that of explicating, i.e. completely clarifying, the precise content of the grammatical concepts used.

There are various means of explicating the content of a theoretical concept. The most common way of doing this is to give a DEFINITION of (the meaning of) the theoretical term by which a concept is represented linguistically. Thus the explication of the content of theoretical concepts, as an aspect of empirical inquiry, often involves giving definitions. The nature, functions, logical structure, possibilities and limitations of the various types of definitions have been dealt with extensively in the philosophical literature. Within the narrow limits of our study we cannot even attempt to give a survey of this literature.

Let us first of all consider a number of examples of definitions by means of which grammarians typically attempt to clarify the meaning of grammatical terms. In his lexicalist grammar of English, Chomsky uses grammatical terms such as "nom", "copula", "by Δ", "[+ NP]", "[Spec, N̄]", "[Spec, V̄]" and "[Spec, Ā]". Comsky (1972b) gives the following definitions of these grammatical terms as they appear in the nonformalized version of his grammar:

(28)(a) "nom" :   "... *nom* is the element that determines the morpho-
                        logical form of the derived nominal ..." (pp.27–28)

(b) "copula" :   "... the copula serves as a kind of existential oper-
                        ator." (p.34)

(c) "by Δ" :   "... *by* Δ is an agent phrase, related, in ways that
                        are still unclear in detail, to adverbials of means and
                        manner." (p.41)

(d) "[+ NP]" :   "... [+ NP] is a feature (or a complex of features)
                        that can be part of a complex symbol introduced by
                        a transformation ..." (p.49)

(e) "[Spec, N̄]" :   "... [Spec, N̄] will be analyzed as the determiner
                        ..." (p.52)

(f) "[Spec, V̄]" :   "... [Spec, V̄] (will be anlyzed) as the auxilliary
                        (perhaps with time adverbials associated) ..." (p.52)

(g) "[Spec, Ā]" :   "... [Spec, Ā] (will be analyzed) perhaps as the
                        system of qualifying elements associated with
                        adjective phrases (comparative structures, *very*, etc.)."
                        (p.52)

How are definitions such as those of (28) constructed? Schematically a definition may be shown to consist of three parts:

(29) $x =$ df · · ·

The first part, represented by "x" in (29), is the DEFINIENDUM. It is the term being defined — for example, "nom" in the case of the definition (28)(a). The second part is represented in (29) by the symbol combination "$=$df". This combination has the value "is defined as". The third part is represented in (29) by the broken line "...". This represents the DEFINIENS, i.e. the expression in terms of which the definiendum is defined. In the definition (28)(a) the expression "... the element that determines the morphological form of the derived nominal ..." represents the definiens.

The definitions of (28) (a) – (g) may also be used to illustrate a distinction which has to be drawn between two important types of definitions of grammatical terms. A theoretical term has both an intension and an extension. The INTENSION of a term is specified by the list of essential properties which an object must have to be able to be denoted by the term. For instance, the intension of the term "living being" is the list of properties which an object must have in order to be called a living being. Among these would be, for instance, possession of a metabolism, manifestation of self-regulating behaviour, the ability to adapt, manifestation of purposeful behaviour, and so on. The EXTENSION of a term, on the other hand, is the class of all objects — in the past, present or future, known or unknown — which (should they exist) would be denoted by the term. The extension of the term "living being" is the class of all living beings — in the past, present or future.

A term may therefore be defined by specifying either its intension or its extension. An INTENSIONAL DEFINITION of a term specifies the essential property/ies of the object(s) denoted by the term. The definition (28)(a) of the grammatical term "nom" is a typical example of an intensional definition. Another example of this type of definition is the one given by Chomsky (1972b:58–59) for the term "mixed nominal".

(30)   "... (mixed nominals) appear to have the internal structure of noun phrases; thus the possessive subject can be replaced by a determiner, as in (56c). On the other hand, adjective insertion seems quite unnatural in this construction."

Chomsky gives the following three examples of such "mixed nominals": *John's refusing of the offer* (= (56a)), *John's proving of the theorem* (= (56b)) and *the growing of tomatoes* (= (56c)). In the intensional definition (30) two of the essential properties of "mixed nominals" are specified, viz. their apparently having the internal structure of NPs and the unnaturalness of adjective insertion in such nominals.

A serious limitation of intensional definitions such as that of (30) has to be pointed out. If the meanings of the expressions appearing in the definiens are not quite clear, an intensional definition contributes very little to the clarification of the definiendum. Suppose, for example, that it was not quite clear what the expressions "internal structure of noun phrases", "adjective" and "quite unnatural" meant. Then the definition (30) would be of little help in establishing unambiguously the meaning of the term "mixed nominals". An attempt could then be made to define these three expressions intensionally. But the same problem would arise: the meanings of the expressions used in the intensional definitions of these three expressions might also be rather vague. Further intensional definitions might all be inadequate as the same problem could arise every time.

Thus, to insist that *all* the terms in a theory must be defined intensionally creates a dilemma. On the one hand, this could result in infinite regression. Attempts to give an intensional definition of each term that occurs in an intensional definition would result in an infinite string of intensional definitions. On the other hand, the grammarian might find himself trapped in a vicious circle. In order to prevent the infinite regression which we pointed out above, the grammarian could attempt to define a term intensionally only in terms of expressions which have already been defined intensionally. However, for two terms A and B this would mean that B is used (indirectly) to define A, and A is then used (indirectly) to define B. In this way none of the terms is explicated unambiguously.

How do generative grammarians solve the problems connected with the intensional definition of grammatical terms? Note that the grammarian gives intensional definitions of grammatical terms as they occur in his unformalized theoretical grammatical descriptions. However, these terms also occur in generative grammars as formalized systems of rules. The grammarian solves his problem of definition within the framework of these formalized grammars in which grammatical terms are defined extensionally. Extensional definitions are not subject to the same limitations as intensional definitions.

An EXTENSIONAL DEFINITION of a term explicitly enumerates all the objects denoted by the term. For instance, consider the grammatical term "sentence" ("S") as it occurs in the grammar of English as a formalized system of rules. In the grammar the term "sentence" is defined extensionally in that the grammar explicitly enumerates all the (grammatical) sentences of English. The grammar of English also gives extensional definitions for other grammatical terms, such as "NP", "VP", "PP", "AUX", etc. In the formalized grammar of English these terms are not defined by specifying the essential properties of sentences, NPs, VPs, and so on. The formalized grammar defines them by explicitly enumerating all objects which are sentences, NPs, VPs, etc. respectively. In linguistic inquiry intensional definitions are approximate definitions of grammatical terms as they are used in unformalized grammatical descriptions. Extensional definitions, on the other hand, are explicit definitions of grammatical terms as they are used in formalized grammars.

Grammarians often use a form of definition in informal grammatical descriptions, which at a first glance appears to resemble extensional definitions. This form of definition is used when the grammarian tries to clarify the meaning of a term by giving a number of typical examples of the objects which the term denotes. The first, preliminary definitions which Chomsky (1972b:15) gave for the grammatical terms "gerundive nominal" and "derived nominal" are instances of this form of definition.

(31)   "... corresponding to the sentences of [2] we have the gerundive nominals of [3] and the derived nominals of [4]:
[2]   a. John is eager to please.
          b. John has refused the offer.
          c. John has criticized the book.
[3]   a. John's being eager to please
          b. John's refusing the offer
          c. John's criticizing the book
[4]   a. John's eagerness to please

b. John's refusal of the offer
c. John's criticism of the book"

This method of defining by giving examples represents a form of OSTENSIVE DEFINITION. To define a term ostensively is to indicate what it is that the term denotes.

At a first glance, ostensive definitions resemble extensional definitions. They both represent a means of defining by referring to the objects denoted by the term. However, there are a number of differences between these two forms of definition. An important difference is that in the case of extensional definitions, as they appear in formalized grammars, the objects denoted by the definiendum are enumerated exhaustively and systematically. In the case of ostensive definitions, on the other hand, only a few typical examples of the objects denoted by the definiendum are given. Ostensive definitions are therefore far less explicit than extensional definitions.

We can now summarize the activities involved in the formulation of definitions in linguistic inquiry.

(32)   To define a grammatical term,
    (a)   in unformalized grammatical descriptions, is
        (i) to give typical examples of the objects denoted by the term, thereby giving an ostensive definition of the term and/or
        (ii) to specify the essential properties of the objects denoted by the term, thereby giving an intensional definition of the term
    (b)   in formalized grammatical descriptions, is to give rules which explicitly enumerate all objects denoted by the term, thereby giving an extensional definition of the term.

6.3.3.3   *Integrating of Concepts*

The following grammatical concepts, among others, occur in Chomsky's lexicalist grammar of English:

(33)   'S', 'NP', 'VP', 'AP', 'Prep-P', 'Det', 'Article', 'POSS', 'AUX', ' [+ NP]', 'by Δ', 'noun', '[+ cause]' and "refuse".

As a theoretical description, a grammar does not represent an unorganized collection of grammatical concepts. A grammar is the result of the organizing of these concepts. In other words, within a grammar grammatical concepts are integrated. This brings us to a third activity involved in the giving of theoretical grammatical descriptions: the integrating of grammatical concepts.

The integrating of concepts has two fundamental aspects.

(34)   The construction of a theoretical grammatical description from gram-
       matical concepts involves
       (a)   integrating grammatical concepts into grammatical hypotheses,
             and
       (b)   integrating grammatical hypotheses into grammatical theories.

We shall consider the two aspects of the integration of grammatical concepts
individually. The activity of (34)(a) is commonly known as CONSTRUCTING
(GRAMMATICAL) HYPOTHESES, while that of (34)(b) is known as CONSTRUCTING
(GRAMMATICAL) THEORIES.

6.3.3.3.1   *Constructing grammatical hypotheses*
Consider the following concrete example of a grammatical hypothesis:

(35)   All derived nominals are units which, at the level of deep structure,
       have the internal structure of NPs.

The hypothesis (35) occurs in the unformalized version of Chomsky's lexicalist
grammar of English.

As regards the structure of the grammatical hypothesis (35), notice that the
hypothesis is the result of the integration of the grammatical concepts 'derived
nominal', 'unit', 'level', 'deep structure', 'internal', 'structure' and 'NP'. In order
to integrate these concepts, two other kinds of concepts had to be used. The
first of these other, nongrammatical concepts are RELATIONAL CONCEPTS. The
hypothesis (35) contains two relational concepts. These are represented linguistically by the expressions "are" and "have". Relational concepts such as 'are'
and 'have' represent the relations between the objects, properties, etc. represented by the grammatical concepts. Relational concepts may be seen as being
the cement used in the construction of grammatical hypotheses from grammatical concepts. Relational concepts, of course, are not used exclusively in linguistic
inquiry nor in empirical inquiry in general. They are used in the construction of
all kinds of ideas, nonscientific as well as scientific.

The second kind of nongrammatical concepts occurring in the hypothesis
(35) may be called QUANTITATIVE CONCEPTS. In (35) 'all' is a typical example
of a quantitative concept. The function of a quantitative concept is to specify
a value on a scale of quantity for each of the properties, objects, etc. represented
by the grammatical concepts. But quantitative concepts such as 'all', 'one', 'each',
'some' are not used exclusively in the construction of scientific ideas.

It has already been pointed out that (35) represents a grammatical hypothesis
within an unformalized grammatical description. In formalized grammars such
hypotheses take the form of grammatical rules and associated lexical entries. In
other words, in formalized grammars grammatical concepts are integrated into
grammatical hypotheses in the form of grammatical rules and lexical entries. By
implication, the integration of concepts is carried out within the framework

of the FORMAL UNIVERSALS which determine the abstract form of these rules and entries. Base rules such as those of (36), among others, will play a role in expressing the content of the hypothesis (35) in Chomsky's lexicalist grammar of English.

(36) $\bar{\bar{N}} \longrightarrow [\text{Spec}, \bar{N}] \underline{\quad\quad} \bar{N}$
       $\bar{N} \longrightarrow N \underline{\quad\quad} \text{Comp}_N$

In (36) the arrow represents the relational concept 'is composed of'.

When integrating grammatical concepts into grammatical hypotheses, the grammarian takes into account a number of general criteria which the hypotheses must satisfy when "completed". Three of these criteria are fundamental.

(37)(a)   Grammatical hypotheses must have a clear, precise content.
   (b)   Grammatical hypotheses must be well-formed.
   (c)   Grammatical hypotheses must be testable.

The first criterion, (37)(a), requires the content of a grammatical hypothesis to be nonobscure. It must be quite clear exactly what is being propounded in the hypothesis. The second criterion, (37)(b), determines that a hypothesis may have no logical defects. For instance, a hypothesis may not be internally contradictory. In terms of the third criterion, (37)(c), it must be possible to check whether the hypothesis is incorrect or probably correct on the basis of empirical data. This criterion will be discussed in detail in §10.3.3.2.1.

These three criteria are mutually related. A hypothesis cannot have a clear, precise content if it is not well-formed. Moreover, the content of a hypothesis must be quite clear if it is to be testable on the basis of new empirical data. Note that the criteria of (37)(a)–(c) are minimal criteria for the acceptance of grammatical hypotheses as scientific hypotheses. A grammatical hypothesis which fails in terms of one of the criteria of (37) can be included neither in an unformalized, nor in a formalized grammatical theory.

A last general point must be made in connection with the grammatical hypothesis (35). This hypothesis is an example of a REPRESENTATIONAL or MECHANISTIC hypothesis. In terms of its content, this hypothesis represents an aspect of an underlying mechanism: an aspect of the linguistic competence. Linguistic inquiry also involves the construction of hypotheses which are not representational in this sense. These NONREPRESENTATIONAL or PHENOMENOLOGICAL hypotheses represent assumptions about linguistic data. But what exactly is the role of nonrepresentational hypotheses in linquistic inquiry?

To answer this question we must go back to §4.3.2.2.2.2 where we discussed the evaluation of primary linguistic data. It appeared that these data must satisfy various criteria in order to be included in the corpus of problematic data. One of the important criteria was that of genuineness. To be included in the corpus of primary linguistic data an intuitive linguistic judgment such as (38) must represent a genuine linguistic intuition.

(38)   The utterance **John's easiness to please* is unacceptable.

We have seen that it is not always easy to judge whether a given intuitive linguistic judgment is genuine. In such cases the grammarian can but assume that
the judgment in question is, or is not, genuine. Such an assumption about a
property of a linguistic datum represents a nonrepresentational, or phenomenological, grammatical hypothesis.

The following are examples of phenomenological grammatical hypotheses:

(39)   The intuitive judgment that the utterance **John's easiness to please* is
         unacceptable is genuine/spurious.

As phenomenological grammatical hypotheses, the hypotheses of (39) are not
in the first place descriptive of the linguistic competence. They are directly
concerned with a product of the application of the linguistic competence. In
§7.4.6 we shall see how grammarians argue for or against the correctness of such
phenomenological grammatical hypotheses.

6.3.3.3.2   *Constructing grammatical theories*

We now come to the second aspect, (34) (b), of the integrating of concepts as an
activity involved in the giving of grammatical descriptions. This second aspect
of the integrating of grammatical concepts involves the integrating of individual
grammatical hypotheses into grammatical theories. Theoretical grammatical
descriptions typically comprise more than one grammatical hypothesis. These
grammatical hypotheses are mutually related in terms of logical relations.
The fundamental relation is that of conjunction which is expressed linguistically by "and", "as well as", etc. Consider, for example, the first two hypotheses in the unformalized description (1). They are repeated here as (40)(i) and
(ii) for easy reference.

(40) (i)   The lexicon contains a single lexical entry for "refuse".
     (ii)   In this single lexical entry certain fixed syntactic properties are
            assigned to "refuse", viz. those selectional and subcategorization
            features which "refuse" exhibits in all expressions in which it occurs.

The two grammatical hypotheses (40)(i) and (ii) express supplementary statements about the linguistic competence of the ideal speaker of English. They may
therefore be combined by "and" to form one complex hypothesis. To integrate
grammatical hypotheses into a grammatical theory involves, among other things,
such a combining of hypotheses.

Consider, once again, the formalized grammatical description (10). In such a
description grammatical hypotheses are expressed in terms of rules and associated

lexical entries. This means that in a formalized grammatical description the integrating of grammatical hypotheses is taken a step further. This is done in accordance with the general linguistic principles which specify how rules are ordered with regard to one another, how rules are organized in components and how rules are applied. These general linguistic principles may be called ORGANIZATIONAL UNIVERSALS for the sake of convenience. Conventional introductions to generative grammar present and illustrate many such principles of rule ordering, componential organization and rule application. Consider the following typical examples of a principle of rule ordering (41)(a), a principle of componential organization (41)(b) and a principle of rule application (41)(c).

(41)(a) Phonological rules are ordered linearly.
   (b) Phonological rules form a block with regard to base rules: there is no mutual interpenetration between phonological and base rules.
   (c) Phonological rules, such as those assigning stress, are applied cyclically.

The integrating of grammatical hypotheses, formalized by means of rules and lexical entries, is done in terms of such organizational universals.

As ordered sets of grammatical hypotheses, grammatical theories must satisfy the same minimal criteria as individual grammatical hypotheses. This implies that the content of grammatical theories may not be obscure, that grammatical theories may have no internal logical defects and that grammatical theories must be testable. A grammatical theory which fails in terms of one of these criteria is considered not to be a scientific theory.

Finally, a possible misunderstanding has to be cleared up. Neither the construction of grammatical hypotheses from concepts, nor the construction of grammatical theories from hypotheses is a simple activity which can be carried out mechanically. In both cases it is a question of gaining insight and making discoveries. From this point of view the integrating of grammatical concepts is analogous to the forming of these concepts. In both the integrating of concepts and in their formulation, the grammarian guesses at the unknown properties which an underlying mental capacity must necessarily have in order to yield products with certain known properties. In §6.3.3.1 we discussed the nature of this form of guessing in detail.

6.3.3.4 *Symbolizing the Content*

In §3.3.1.4 we considered a number of criteria for grammatical knowledge. The third of these was that grammatical knowledge must be intersubjective. This implies that grammatical knowledge must be common property. It may not exist only in the mind of one or a few grammarians. In order to be common property grammatical knowledge must be captured in a form in which it is accessible to all skilled grammarians. This brings us to the fourth activity involved in giving theoretical grammatical descriptions: the symbolizing of the content of grammatical hypotheses and theories. By capturing it in terms of symbols, the knowledge which is potentially contained in the content of these hypotheses and theories becomes common property.

The content of grammatical hypotheses and theories may be symbolized in two ways. It may be symbolized either in terms of natural language, or in terms of a special system of symbols. Let us consider these two methods of symbolization individually.

The result of the symbolizing of the content of grammatical theories and hypotheses in terms of natural language is an UNFORMALIZED THEORETICAL GRAMMATICAL DESCRIPTION. We have already considered a number of fragments of such descriptions. The largest fragment was presented as (1) above. An unformalized grammatical description is given in terms of special theoretical terms and other expressions of natural language.

The result of the symbolization of the content of grammatical hypotheses and theories in terms of a special system of symbols is a FORMALIZED THEORETICAL GRAMMATICAL DESCRIPTION. In (10) above an example was given of a fragment of such a description. Giving such a formalized description presupposes the existence of notational conventions. A NOTATIONAL CONVENTION is an instruction always to represent a certain fragment of information in terms of a particular symbol or combination of symbols. To illustrate this point, four examples of notational conventions are given in (42).

(42)(a)   Symbolize the content "rewritten as/replaced with" by means of the arrow "———→".

(b)   Symbolize the fact that an element is optional by placing it between parentheses, "( )".

(c)   Symbolize the boundaries of syntactic constituents by means of labelled brackets such as " [NP]NP".

(d)   Symbolize the syntactic features of units with the aid of combinations of symbols such as " [+ wh]".

To represent the content of grammatical rules and lexical entries explicitly with the aid of such notational conventions is to FORMALIZE these grammatical rules and lexical entries.

Formalized grammatical descriptions are better than unformalized grammatical descriptions in important respects. A first respect in which formalized grammatical descriptions are better than unformalized grammatical descriptions has to do with the fact that the former are more explicit and therefore more precise than the latter. The special symbols of formalized grammatical descriptions are chosen in such a way that they are absolutely clear and unambiguous. By contrast, the expressions in terms of which unformalized grammatical descriptions are given are typical expressions of human language and therefore often ambiguous. Formalized grammatical descriptions generally comply better with the criterion of (37)(a) than unformalized grammatical descriptions. The criterion (37)(a) was that of absolute clarity of content. Moreover, the fact that formalized grammatical descriptions are more precise and more explicit ensure that they are more readily testable. The more precise and explicit a given statement, the easier it is to check whether this statement is incorrect or probably correct. We shall return to this point in §10.3.3.2.6.

A second respect in which formalized grammatical descriptions are better than unformalized grammatical descriptions concerns the presence of internal contradictions. Contradictions in grammatical statements and the inconsistent use of grammatical concepts are more easily spotted in the former than in the latter descriptions.

A third, related respect in which formalized grammatical descriptions are better than unformalized descriptions concerns the presence of gaps and hidden assumptions. In a formalized grammatical description every available fragment of relevant information about the language in question is explicitly represented. Consequently, if there are gaps in this information these are immediately apparent. But what is more, formalization forces the grammarian to represent explicitly every assumption which he makes about the language in question. In unformalized grammatical descriptions, on the other hand, gaps in the information and implicit assumptions remain hidden more easily.

To ensure that formalized grammatical descriptions are better than unformalized grammatical descriptions in the three respects mentioned above, the grammarian consciously has to take certain measures. Firstly, he must choose the special symbols to be used in the formalization with special care. Each symbol must have only one fixed value. And every distinct element of content must be represented by only one fixed symbol. Secondly, the grammarian must ensure that the notational conventions in terms of which the symbols are used are absolutely clear and that they are applied with strict consistency.

One important point remains to be dealt with in connection with formalization. Formalization cannot transform an ugly duckling into a beautiful swan. In other words, formalization cannot change a superficial, trivial impression about a language into a profound, significant insight into this language. Formalization does not represent a simple, mechanical procedure for making significant grammatical discoveries.

We can now give a synoptic characterization of the activity of symbolization.

(43)   As part of the giving of theoretical grammatical descriptions, symbolizing involves
   (a)   giving unformalized descriptions by representing the content of grammatical hypotheses and theories in terms of expressions of natural language;
   (b)   giving formalized descriptions by representing the content of

grammatical hypotheses and theories in terms of special symbols and notational conventions.

We have now considered four essential, indispensable activities involved in the giving of theoretical grammatical descriptions: forming grammatical concepts, explicating the content of grammatical concepts, integrating grammatical concepts into hypotheses and theories and symbolizing the content of grammatical hypotheses and theories. In addition to these four essential activities, there are two activities which are not essential: elucidating the content of grammatical theories with the aid of analogies, etc. and axiomatizing grammatical theories. These two nonessential activities may, but need not necessarily, form part of the giving of theoretical grammatical descriptions. For this reason they are regarded as nonessential parts of the giving of such descriptions.

6.3.3.5   *Elucidating the Content*

The ideas about reality which are contained in a theory are often highly complex and difficult to understand. Even if these ideas are presented in the theory in a completely explicit and coherent way, linguists often have great difficulty in understanding them. Linguists therefore often consider it necessary to make use of special means in order to present the content of their theories in a more accessible, comprehensible, lucid or striking manner than it is done in the theory itself. Presenting the content of a theory in a more accessible, comprehensible, lucid or striking manner may be called ELUCIDATING THE CONTENT OF THE THEORY. The elucidation of the content of theories may constitute a fifth activity in the giving of theoretical descriptions.

One of the means commonly used in empirical inquiry to elucidate the content of theories is that of constructing analogies. Some of the more striking analogies used in natural science are well-known. A first example is the analogy between an atom and a solar system. In terms of this analogy the nucleus of an atom is compared with the sun and the electrons in the atom with the planets moving around the sun in elliptical orbits. A second example is the analogy between the waves of light, sound and water. Huygens (1945:4) formulates this analogy as follows:

> I call them [light and sound] waves from their resemblance to those which are seen to be formed in water when a stone is thrown into it, and which present a successive spreading as circles, though these arise from another cause, and are only on a flat surface.

A third example is the analogy between a gas and a container filled with billiard-balls. In terms of this analogy the molecules in the gas are likened to perfectly elastic billiard-balls striking the sides of the container as well as each other.

According to the philosopher Peter Achinstein (1968:205–209), the following is typically the case when a scientist S draws an analogy between two objects X and Y:

(44)(a) S is suggesting the existence of certain similarities between X and Y. An analogy cannot be drawn between two completely different objects.

(b) Despite various similarities X and Y are, in other respects, unlike. An analogy cannot be drawn between two completely identical objects.

(c) When S draws an analogy between X and Y, he suggests that X can be thought of and described from the point of view of Y and by employing concepts appropriate to Y.

(d) In drawing the analogy between X and Y, S typically has the following aim: he intends to illuminate X, to help provide some, or a better, understanding or grasp of X and he believes that Y will be considered more familiar, better understood, or more easily grasped than X.

To draw an analogy between X and Y is therefore to indicate similarities between the otherwise nonidentical X and Y. On the basis of these similarities, X may be thought of or described from the point of view of Y. The result is that X is more easily grasped. We have thus revealed a second role of analogy in scientific inquiry: analogy furthers understanding of the content of theories and of the concepts from which they are constructed. The first role of analogy, that of heuristic clue, was discussed in §5.4.2.2.2.

Analogies are also used in the giving of grammatical descriptions to elucidate the content of grammatical theories. One of the better known analogies is the one which is used to elucidate the difference between a psychologically real and a psychologically nonreal grammar of a language. This analogy is constructed with the aid of the parallel distinction between a psychologically real and a psychologically nonreal description of somebody's arithmetical abilities. In his article "Linguistic universals and linguistic change" (1968a:171), Paul Kiparsky presents the following condensed version of this analogy:

Suppose that someone succeeds in writing a grammar which correctly enumerates the sentences of a language and assigns them the right structural descriptions. Such a grammar would ipso facto correctly represent the substance of a fluent speaker's knowledge of the language. But it would not necessarily represent the form of this knowledge in the sense of actually corresponding to the system of rules which is internalized by the speaker and constitutes part of what enables him to produce and understand arbitrary utterances in the language. Similarly, the knowledge of someone who has learned arithmetic, that is, the infinite set of correct arithmetical computations, could be defined by many different systems of rules, including both psychologically incorrect ones, such as certain axioms of set theory, computer programs, and so on, and the psychologically correct one, namely whatever knowledge is actually used in arithmetical performance, such as the rules of school arithmetic and the multiplication table.

This analogy is worked out in more detail by Robert King in his book *Historical linguistics and generative grammar* (1969:8ff.). A similar analogy is developed by Larry Hutchinson in his article "Grammar as theory" (1974: 45—48).

Analogies such as Kiparsky's can only succeed if they satisfy a certain criterion, viz. that Y — compare (44) above — must be better understood than X. It would be senseless to try and elucidate X by comparing it to Y if Y were understood no better, or even worse, than X. For example, if linguists understood mathematics no better than they understood grammars, Kiparsky's analogy would fail.

To give an analogical representation of (an aspect) of the content of a grammatical theory is, briefly, to elucidate this content by pointing out similarities between it and an object which is better understood. However, note once again that the drawing of such analogies is not an essential, indispensable part of the giving of theoretical grammatical descriptions. Analogies neither add to, nor detract from, the content of these descriptions. The only function of such analogies is that of elucidation.

6.3.3.6 *Axiomatizing of Grammars*

Some scholars — philosophers of science and scientists — insist that theories should be axiomatized. To AXIOMATIZE a theory is to present its content in the form of an axiomatic system. Axiomatic systems and the axiomatization of theories are exceptionally complex topics. Within the limits of our study it is impossible to discuss the question of what axiomatic systems are or how theories are axiomatized in any detail. Following Peter Achinstein (1968:149), we can but briefly indicate in broad outline what is involved in the axiomatization of a theory.

The axiomatization of a theory is done in four basic steps. The first step is to determine which assumptions of the theory cannot be derived from other more fundamental assumptions. These nonderivable, fundamental assumptions of the theory represent the AXIOMS. The second step is to state the axioms in terms of an initially agreed-upon vocabulary. The members of this vocabulary fall into two classes: primitive terms and defined terms. PRIMITIVE TERMS are terms which are not defined directly; DEFINED TERMS are terms that are defined with reference to the primitive terms. The third step is to indicate what propositions may be inferred from the axioms by means of logical or mathematical rules. These derived propositions represent the THEOREMS. The fourth step is to show explicitly how the theorems are inferred from the axioms. To do this is to give the (logical or mathematical) PROOFS of the theorems. "In short, to present a theory axiomatically it is necessary and sufficient to supply a vocabulary of primitive and defined terms and to cite axioms, theorems, and proofs", according to Peter Achinstein (1968:149).

Scholars who are in favour of axiomatization point out various advantages of the axiomatic presentation of theories. A first advantage is that every assumption made by the proponent of the theory is explicitly represented. A second advantage is that the logical structure of the theory becomes more transparent. It becomes possible to determine precisely from which fundamental assumptions other less fundamental assumptions are inferred and in terms of what principles the inference is made. A third advantage is that the various terms of the theory are clearly organized. Each term can be recognized either as one whose definition can be given by using (some of) the other terms in the theory, or else as a primitive term. Scholars who advocate the axiomatization of theories on the strength of these advantages therefore provide for a sixth activity in the giving of theoretical descriptions: the axiomatizing of theories.

Certain generative grammarians regard a formalized grammar as an axiomatic system. They consider S, the initial symbol of the phrase structure rules, to be the (only) axiom in this system. The sentences generated by the grammar represent the theorems. The phrase structure rules and transformational rules represent the principles of inference in terms of which the theorems are inferred from the single axiom. The proofs of these theorems are the derivations resulting from the application of the phrase structure and transformational rules. The various grammatical terms constitute the vocabulary of the axiomatic system.

For grammarians who regard a generative grammar as an axiomatic system, giving theoretical grammatical descriptions involves a sixth activity: axiomatizing grammatical theories. Two general points have to be noted in connection with the axiomatization of grammatical theories. On the one hand, generative grammarians equate the axiomatization of grammatical theories with the axiomatic presentation of the syntactic component of a grammar. This follows from the description given above of the axioms, theorems, rules of derivation, and so on in such an axiomatic system. On the other hand, "axiomatize" and "formalize" should not be regarded as synonyms. To formalize a fragment of grammar means strictly one thing: to present the rules constituting that fragment of grammar in a maximally explicit form. Axiomatizing a grammar involves much more than giving formalized rules. Axiomatizing involves giving axioms, theorems and derivations as proofs.

6.4   GENERAL LINGUISTIC INQUIRY

6.4.1   General

In this section we shall consider in broad outline what is involved in giving theoretical descriptions in general linguistic inquiry. Let us start by looking at a fragment of such a description. The example (45) is taken from the introductory section of Chomsky's study (1972b:12) on nominalization in English.

(45)   I will assume that a grammar contains a base consisting of a categorial component (which I will assume to be a context-free grammar) and a lexicon. The lexicon consists of lexical entries, each of which is a system of specified features. The nonterminal vocabulary of the context-free grammar is drawn from a universal and rather limited vocabulary, some aspects of which will be considered below. The context-free grammar generates phrase-markers, with a dummy symbol as one of the terminal elements. A general principle of lexical insertion permits lexical entries to replace the dummy symbol in ways determined by their feature content. The formal object constructed in this way is a DEEP STRUCTURE. The grammar contains a system of transformations, each of which maps phrase-markers into phrase-markers. Application of a sequence of transformations to a deep structure, in accordance with certain universal conditions and certain particular constraints of the grammar in question, determines ultimately a phrase-marker which we call a SURFACE STRUCTURE. The base and the transformational rules constitute the syntax. The grammar contains phonological rules that assign to each surface structure a phonetic representation in a universal phonetic alphabet. Furthermore, it contains semantic rules that assign to each paired deep and surface structure generated by the syntax a semantic interpretation, presumably, in a universal semantics, concerning which little is known in any detail. I will assume, furthermore, that grammatical relations are defined in a general way in terms of configurations within phrase-markers and that semantic interpretation involves only those grammatical relations specified in deep structures (although it may also involve certain properties of surface structures).

THEORETICAL GENERAL LINGUISTIC DESCRIPTIONS are usually given in the unformalized form of (45). We shall consider a number of points in connection with the nature and construction of such descriptions below. We shall be concentrating on the main points only. Moreover, we shall deal quite cursorily with these main points, as our only purpose will be to indicate the main similarities and differences between such descriptions and theoretical grammatical descriptions. In our discussion the terms "(theoretical) general linguistic description" and "general linguistic theory" will be used alternately as synonyms.

6.4.2   Nature of General Linguistic Theories

The object which the general linguistic theory describes is, as we saw in §3.4.1.1, the language acquisition faculty of an ideal language learner. Recall that the language acquisition faculty is a cognitive structure, or mental capacity: the capacity to acquire language on the basis of experience of utterances of the language.

In his article "On cognitive structures and their development" (1975e:4), Chomsky compares the general linguist's investigation of this cognitive structure to an anatomist's/biologist's investigation of an organ such as the eye or heart. For the purpose of this comparison he calls the language acquisition faculty a "mental organ". In the case of both this mental organ and a physical organ such as the eye or heart, the scientist tries to determine

(46)(a)   the nature of this organ in a particular individual;
    (b)   the general properties of the organ which are invariable within the species;
    (c)   the position of the organ within a system of various similar structures;
    (d)   the phases of development of the organ in the individual;
    (e)   the genetically determined basis underlying the development of the organ in the individual; and
    (f)   the factors which, in the course of evolution, gave rise to the development of the organ.

We saw above that the description of the mental organ in question – man's language acquisition device – is presented in the form of a general linguistic theory.

In the technical terms used in this field of study, the content of the claims which the general linguistic theory makes about the language acquisition faculty is known as LINGUISTIC UNIVERSALS. The general linguistic description represents an organized system of linguistic universals. These universals may be divided into various types.

SUBSTANTIVE UNIVERSALS represent a limited class of structural elements – such as linguistic units, categories and rules – from which all languages choose their "building blocks". For instance, the phonetic features proposed by Chomsky and Halle (1968:298ff.) represent a set of substantive universals. Similarly, the claim that all languages include a passive transformation expresses a substantive universal.

FORMAL UNIVERSALS represent aspects of the formal structure which the various types of rules and lexical entries have in all languages. The claim in (45) that a lexical entry is a system of specified features expresses such a formal universal. A second example of a formal universal is expressed in (45) by the claim that the rules of the base are context-free.

ORGANIZATIONAL UNIVERSALS represent aspects of the structure/organization of grammars in terms of components and subcomponents. Chomsky's claim in (45) that the base consists of a categorial component and a lexicon expresses such an organizational universal. His claim that the base and the transformational rules constitute the syntax is another example of the expression of an organizational universal.

General linguists characterize linguistic universals in three equivalent ways. Firstly, linguistic universals are represented as aspects of the language acquisition faculty. As such they represent those aspects of the linguistic competence which cannot be acquired through linguistic experience and must therefore be genetically determined and innate. Secondly, linguistic universals are represented by the majority of generative grammarians as being aspects of all possible human languages. This view will be elaborated in § 10.4.2.1.3. Thirdly, linguistic universals are represented as conditions which must be met by the grammatical theories of all human languages. This is the view expressed in (45). As far as the general linguist is concerned, the expressions "language in general", "all (possible) human languages", "language acquisition faculty"/"language faculty" and "genetically determined and innate aspect of the linguistic competence" all denote one and the same object: the object described by the general linguistic theory.

6.4.2.1   *General Linguistic Hypotheses and Concepts*

From a metascientific point of view, the propositions in terms of which linguistic universals are expressed represent hypotheses. In (47) five typical examples of GENERAL LINGUISTIC HYPOTHESES are given.

(47)(a)   All human languages include a passive transformation.
   (b)   Base rules are context-free.
   (c)   The base comprises a categorial component and a lexicon.
   (d)   Among the lexical entries of a language there is a class with the properties of neutral lexical entries.
   (e)   Major class constituents such as NP, VP and AP are composed of a head preceded by a specifier and followed by a complement.

General linguistic hypotheses are constructed from theoretical concepts, or GENERAL LINGUISTIC CONCEPTS. Among the theoretical concepts constituting the five hypotheses of (47) are 'passive', 'transformation', 'base', 'rule', 'context-free', 'component', 'lexicon', 'lexical entry', 'neutral', 'major class', 'constituent', 'head', 'specifier', 'complement', 'NP', 'VP', and so on. These general linguistic concepts represent minimal units of thought which are linguistically expressed by GENERAL LINGUISTIC TERMS.

The content of general linguistic concepts – such as 'neutral lexical entry' – is similar to that of grammatical concepts in that it has various components. A first component is the EMPIRICAL COMPONENT which has two sides. On the one hand, the empirical component represents an aspect of the language acquisition faculty on the underlying level of the general linguist's reality. On the other hand, the empirical component refers indirectly to utterances and linguistic intuitions as products of the use of the individual languages. For instance, the concept 'neutral lexical entries' refers indirectly to all utterances and linguistic intuitions which are explained in terms of this concept in the grammars of particular languages. The reference is indirect in that it occurs via the grammars of the individual languages. In §1.3, for instance, we saw that syntactic similarities between a sentence such as *John has refused the offer* and a derived nominal such as *John's refusal of the offer* may be accounted for in terms of the concept 'neutral lexical entry'. This concept refers in an analogous way to the utterances – and intuitions about them – in other human languages of which certain properties may be explained in terms of this concept. This point will be further elaborated in §6.4.3.1.1. In §6.4.3.1.2 it will appear that general linguistic concepts also refer indirectly to another kind of intuition: the intuitions grammarians have about the linguistic significance of grammatical facts and generalizations.

A second component of the content of a general linguistic concept is the SYSTEMATIC COMPONENT. This component, too, has two sides. In terms of its first side the systematic component represents the relationship between the concept and other concepts within the hypotheses of the general linguistic theory. On the one hand, the concept is related to the general linguistic concepts in terms of which its content is characterized. For instance, in (48) the concept 'neutral lexical entry' is related to the concepts 'fixed syntactic properties', 'lexical items' and 'free'/'unspecified'.

(48)   A neutral lexical entry includes
    (a)   a number of fixed properties of the lexical items which it represents and
    (b)   a few syntactic properties which are free, or unspecified.

On the other hand, a general linguistic concept is related to those general linguistic concepts in the characterization of which it is used. In addition, it is related to the other general linguistic concepts with which it is combined for use in these characterizations. For instance, in (49) the concept 'neutral lexical entry' is related to the concepts 'lexicon', 'ordinary lexical entry' and 'lexical redundancy rules'.

(49)   The lexicon includes ordinary, nonneutral lexical entries, neutral lexical entries and lexical redundancy rules.

In terms of the second side of the systematic component of its content, a general linguistic concept is related to grammatical concepts. More particularly, it is related to the grammatical concepts by which it is realized or instantiated in the particular languages. The general linguistic concept 'neutral lexical entry' is realized in all neutral lexical entries occurring in the grammars of the individual languages. In the grammar of English, for example, this concept is realized in, among others, the grammatical concepts 'refuse', 'amuse', 'easy', 'eager', 'critic', and so on.

The content of some general linguistic concepts has a third component as well: a THEMATIC COMPONENT. The thematic component of such a concept is represented by that element of its content which represents a nonempirical presupposition occurring repeatedly in various, historically successive general linguistic theories. The content of the general linguistic concept 'sentence' contains such a thematic component. In the history of the scientific study of language in general, this concept crops up repeatedly with the content 'funda-mental structural unit of human language'. The content of the general linguistic concept 'neutral lexical entry' does not have such a thematic component. The latter concept is a new theoretical concept with no corresponding predecessors in the history of linguistics. Note that in linguistic inquiry, a set of theoretical concepts exists which are, in a certain sense, both general linguistic and gram-matical concepts. These concepts form part of both individual grammars and the general linguistic theory. They are the concepts which we called substantive universals in §6.4.2.1: properties, units, categories, rules, etc. which occur in the structure of (almost) all human languages. Among these concepts are universal phonetic, semantic and syntactic features, universal syntactic categories such as 'sentence', 'NP', 'VP', 'N', 'V', etc., universal rules such as the passive transforma-tion, and so on. When they form part of an individual grammar, these concepts in a certain sense represent grammatical concepts. But when they form part of the general linguistic theory they in a certain sense represent general linguistic concepts.

Note, in conclusion, that general linguistic hypotheses such as those of (47) must satisfy the same minimal criteria as grammatical hypotheses. In other words, general linguistic hypotheses, too, must have a clear, precise content, must be well-formed, and must be testable. These criteria also apply, *mutatis mutandis*, to the systems into which general linguistic hypotheses are integrated, viz. general linguistic theories.

6.4.2.2   *Ontological Status*

In linguistic inquiry the general linguistic theory has the same kind of ontological status as an individual grammar. The general linguistic theory, too, describes an underlying mental capacity: the language acquisition faculty of the ideal language learner. More specifically, the general linguistic theory describes the substantial and the structural aspects of the language acquisition faculty, but not its physical aspect. It describes the substantial aspect by specifying precisely what linguistic knowledge is innate. It describes the structural aspect by specifying the compo-nent parts which constitute this innate linguistic knowledge as well as the way in which these parts are organized. However, the general linguistic theory does not describe how the innate linguistic knowledge is realized neurophysiologically in the brain.

Chomsky requires the general linguistic theory to be psychologically real as well. This is clear from his characterization of the concepts from which the general linguistic theory is constructed. Chomsky (1975d:166–167) has the following to say about the status of general linguistic concepts such as 'subjunctive', 'irrealis', 'imply', 'synonym', 'significant', 'subject', 'verb', 'phonological unit', 'grammatical transformation':

> In the best case, some of these concepts can be taken as primitive and others defined in terms of them, with other principles serving as axioms of the theory. Each primitive notion should ideally be assigned a set of tests and criteria for applying it to data. Taking seriously the task of explaining how the structures of grammar 'come into existence in the mind of a speaker', we can add further conditions on the choice of primitives. A particular choice of primitives can be considered an empirical hypothesis as to the preliminary analysis of data that serves for acquisition of language. Thus we assume (under appropriate idealization) that the learner analyzes utterances and the situations and events in which they are embedded in terms of these primitive notions, and 'abstracts some notion of [the] structure' of linguistic expressions by applying the explicit and implicit definitions that constitute linguistic theory, the latter now being taken as a theory of a certain 'faculty of mind'. The primitive notions of the theory, so construed, provide the analysis of data in terms of which knowledge of language is acquired and verified.

What Chomsky is saying is, in essence, that general linguistic concepts must be psychologically real.

The general linguistic theory gives a description of a mental capacity of a non-existing individual: the ideal language learner. Chomsky's depiction (1975c:15) of the ideal language learner may be reconstructed as in (50).

(50)   The IDEAL LANGUAGE LEARNER
    (a)   acquires his native language instantaneously;
    (b)   acquires his native language on the basis of a cumulative record of all the data about the language to which he has been exposed up to this instant;
    (c)   is unaffected in his acquisition of his native language by non-linguistic psychological, physical and other random factors.

By contrast, an ordinary language learner acquires his native language over a period of several years. In addition, he does so on the basis of an ever expanding record of data about the language. Furthermore, in his language acquisition there is constant interaction between his language acquisition faculty on the one hand and nonlinguistic factors of a psychological, physical and random nature on the other hand. The latter, random factors would include, for instance, the educational and cultural stimulation which he receives during the period of language acquisition. The possibility also exists that the ordinary language learner's language acquisition faculty does not remain constant during the period of language acquisition, but that it may, for instance, deteriorate.

To give a description of the language acquisition faculty of the ideal language learner is to give only an approximate description of the language acquisition faculty of the ordinary language learner. More specifically, in describing the language acquisition faculty of the ideal language learner, the grammarian does not take into account the interaction between this language acquisition faculty on the one hand and, on the other hand, any of the following factors: the factor of the duration of the process; the factor of increasing linguistic experience; the factor of the role of nonlinguistic psychological, physical and other random circumstances; and the factor of changes in the language acquisition faculty.

Chomsky emphasizes that he accords a realistic status to the general linguistic theory as well. The quotation from the article "What the linguist is talking about" by Chomsky and Katz (1974:359), which was given in §6.3.2.3.4, may be considered again on this point. Notice that this quotation postulates a realistic status not only for grammars, but for general linguistic theories as well. Like a grammar, the general linguistic theory gives a description of an object in an underlying reality. And like the claims of a grammar, those of the general linguistic theory may be either true or false. By implication, a general linguistic theory is not merely a means of economically organizing large corpora of data about the individual human languages.

6.4.3   Nature of General Linguistic Description

As an intellectual enterprise, the giving of general linguistic descriptions involves essentially the same activities as the giving of theoretical grammatical descriptions. However, the two kinds of description involve two distinctly different objects. In the case of theoretical grammatical descriptions, this object is the linguistic competence of an ideal speaker. In the case of general linguistic descriptions, by contrast, this object is the language acquisition faculty of the ideal language learner.

The giving of general linguistic descriptions may also be characterized in terms of forming theoretical concepts, explicating the content of these concepts, integrating theoretical concepts into hypotheses and theories, symbolizing the content of the hypotheses and theories, elucidating the content of theories and axiomatizing theories. We shall only consider the criteria which apply to the formulation of general linguistic concepts.

As far as the other activities are concerned, only a few points need to be mentioned. Intensional definitions are commonly used to explicate the content of general linguistic concepts. These concepts are defined extensionally only insofar as they are realized as grammatical concepts in individual grammars. As a rule therefore, the symbolization of the content of general linguistic theories is not done by way of direct formalization. The content of these theories is conventionally presented in terms of natural language. Finally, no systematic attempt is generally made to axiomatize general linguistic theories.

6.4.3.1   *Forming Theoretical Concepts*

General linguistic theories are structures of which the elementary components are theoretical concepts such as 'base', 'rule', 'transformation', 'deep structure', 'lexicon', 'neutral lexical entries', 'selectional features', 'sentence', 'major class', 'phonetic representation', and so on. Such GENERAL LINGUISTIC CONCEPTS may be regarded as minimal conceptual units which represent the content and structure of the language acquisition faculty of the ideal language learner. Because the language acquisition faculty cannot be subjected to any form of direct investigation, the general linguist can form such concepts in an indirect way only.

The general linguist investigates the language acquisition faculty via its products. The products of the language acquisition faculty are the individual languages, or linguistic competences, which may be acquired on the basis of this faculty. The general linguist forms his conceptual representations of the language acquisition faculty on the basis of the properties of these products as they are manifested indirectly in concrete utterances and in linguistic intuitions about these utterances. In order to form his theoretical concepts, the general linguist repeatedly asks the following general question:

(51)   How must the language acquisition faculty be structured if, on the basis of it, individual human languages with the properties $P_1, P_2, P_3, \ldots,$ P_n may be acquired?

The ideas which the general linguist has in answer to this question form the content of his general linguistic conceptual representations, or concepts.

For instance, let us take the general linguistic concept 'neutral lexical entry' as a conceptual representation of an aspect of the language acquisition faculty. In §1.3 we saw that Chomsky had formed this conceptual representation on the basis of certain properties of English. These properties concern certain types of syntactic similarities – similarities such as those of (10) and (11) in §1.1 – between sentences and derived nominals. With these similarities in mind, the general question (51) may be given the specific form of (52).

(52)   How must the language acquisition faculty be structured if, on the basis of it, a language may be acquired with syntactic properties such as the relevant similarities between sentences and derived nominals in English?

If it were to be assumed that the language acquisition faculty is structured in terms of neutral lexical entries, then a language such as English could very well have the properties in question. English could then have neutral lexical entries such as "refuse" in terms of which the syntactic similarities in question could exist. 'Neutral lexical entry' is therefore a general linguistic concept which, in conceptual terms, represents an aspect of the language acquisition faculty, or language in general.

It is clear, therefore, that the general linguist forms his theoretical concepts in a way analogous to the one which was schematically represented as (21) in §6.3.3.1. Like the grammarian, the general linguist forms an "imaginary", or conceptual, representation of an underlying mechanism on the basis of properties of the products of this mechanism.

In forming his general linguistic concepts, the general linguist takes into account various criteria which these concepts must satisfy. We shall consider three of these criteria here.

6.4.3.1.1 *Explaining problematic data*
All general linguistic concepts must satisfy a certain minimal criterion.

(53)   The concepts of the general linguistic theory must play a role in explaining the problematic primary linguistic data within the grammars of all possible human languages.

This criterion for general linguistic concepts is analogous to the criterion (22) for grammatical concepts. Let us consider what the criterion (53) implies with regard to the general linguistic concept 'neutral lexical entry'. Recall that the content of this concept is, in essence, the following: "lexical entry with various fixed and a few free syntactic properties".

To adopt the criterion (53) is to insist on two things. On the one hand, the linguist who forms the general linguistic concept must show that this concept is needed for the explanation of specific problematic primary data about a given individual language. In other words, he must show that a given language contains classes of utterances of which the problematic properties may be explained grammatically with the aid of the general linguistic concept in question. Chomsky, for instance, can show that the concept 'neutral lexical entry' is needed for the grammatical explanation of properties of sentences and corresponding derived nominals in English.

On the other hand, the linguist must be able to show that the concept in question is not only a grammatical concept, but that it is in fact a general linguistic concept. There are two methods available to the general linguist to do this in practice. First, he may try to show that the concept in question is not only needed for the explanation of problematic data about one particular language, but that it is needed for the theoretical description of various languages.

The linguist would prefer these languages not to be genetically related, not to have been subject to accidental contact in the past and not to be spoken in the same geographical area. As regards the concept 'neutral lexical entry', Chomsky could try to show that this concept is needed for the description of such unrelated languages as, for instance, Eskimo, Aztec, Swahili, Russian and Walbiri.

There is a second method by which the linguist may attempt to show that a certain concept is not merely a grammatical concept, but that it is indeed a general linguistic concept. This method entails that the linguist must show that the concept represents an aspect of a language which could not have been learnt solely on the basis of contact with (some of the) utterances of the language. In other words, he tries to show that the concept represents an innate aspect of the particular language. And an innate aspect of a language is in fact an aspect of man's language acquisition faculty. A concept which represents an aspect of the language acquisition faculty, or language in general, is, by definition, a general linguistic concept.

As regards the concept 'neutral lexical entry', Chomsky could attempt to show that the concept represents an aspect of a human language which cannot be learnt solely on the basis of experience of the utterances of the language. In other words, it would have to be impossible to gain knowledge of the organization of the lexical items of a language in terms of the formal pattern of neutral lexical entries, solely on the basis of contact with these lexical items. It would have to be impossible to learn from contact with the utterances in which, for instance, *refuse(d)* and *refusal* occur, that these items are realizations of one lexical entry with various fixed and a few free syntactic properties. Should Chomsky succeed in doing this, he would satisfy the second part of the criterion (53). He would not only show that the concept 'neutral lexical entry' may be part of the grammar of English, but also that it must be part of the general linguistic theory. The general principle underlying this point will be further elaborated in §9.4.2.3.2.

6.4.3.1.2   *Expressing linguistically significant generalizations*

One of the criteria which grammatical concepts must satisfy is that they must make it possible to express the linguistically significant generalizations about the language in question. This criterion was formulated as (23) in §6.3.3.1.2. The criterion was illustrated in the same paragraph with reference to a parallelism in the structure of NPs such as *John's proof of the theorem,* VPs such as *will prove the theorem* and APs such as *even ignorant of the theorem.* This parallelism consists in the fact that constituents of all three the major classes mentioned are composed of a head preceded by a specifier and followed by a complement. According to Chomsky, this parallelism is linguistically significant and must be explicitly expressed in the grammar of English, and specifically in the base rules of this grammar.

The question arises how the base rules of grammar may be formulated and organized so as to express the kind of parallelism in question. This is a question for the general linguistic theory and, as such, it brings us to a second criterion for general linguistic concepts.

(54)   The concepts of the general linguistic theory must make it possible to express the linguistically significant generalizations about every individual language explicitly in the grammar of that language.

To satisfy this criterion Chomsky proposed the $\overline{\text{X}}$-convention. We may think of this convention as a general linguistic concept which makes it possible to formulate the base rules of a language in such a way that the linguistically significant parallelism mentioned above is explicitly expressed. How the $\overline{\text{X}}$-convention makes this possible was explained in §5.3.2.2.

There is also a negative side to the criterion (54). This criterion rules out a number of concepts as possible general linguistic concepts. More specifically, those concepts are excluded which would make it possible to express generalizations which are linguistically nonsignificant in the grammars of individual languages. Towards the end of §6.3.3.1.2 it appeared that McCawley thinks that the concept 'specifier' in the grammar of English expresses an accidental, nonsignificant similarity between constituents such as NP, VP and AP. Should McCawley's judgment be correct, it would mean that the $\overline{\text{X}}$-convention, as a general linguistic concept, fails in terms of the negative aspect of the criterion (54). This convention would then make it possible to express accidental similarities between constituent categories in the grammars of individual languages as if these similarities were linguistically significant.

The negative side of the criterion (54) also rules out a second class of concepts as possible general linguistic concepts. The concepts in question are those which, should they be included in the general linguistic theory, would make it impossible to express certain linguistically significant generalizations about human languages. In §9.4.2.2.2 this point will be illustrated with reference to a particular taxonomic phonemic concept.

6.4.3.1.3   *Restricting the power of a general linguistic theory*

A general linguistic theory has a property which may be called its FORMAL POWER. The formal power of a general linguistic theory has two aspects. One of these aspects consists in the ability of the theory to form a basis for the giving of adequate grammatical explanations for problematic primary linguistic data. The other aspect of the formal power consists in the ability of the theory to make it possible to express all linguistically relevant generalizations about individual languages.

A general linguistic theory may, as far as its formal power is concerned, be too WEAK in two respects. A first respect concerns the first aspect of the formal power. This type of "weakness" implies that the theoretical concepts of the general linguistic theory fail in terms of the criterion (53). This happens when problematic primary data about one or more individual languages exist which cannot be explained grammatically in terms of these concepts. A second respect in which a general linguistic theory may be too weak as far as its formal power is concerned has to do with the second aspect of the formal power which was mentioned above. This type of "weakness" entails that the theoretical concepts of the theory fail in terms of the criterion (54). This happens when, with respect to one or more individual languages, linguistically significant generalizations exist which cannot be explicitly expressed in grammars in terms of these concepts.

However, a general linguistic theory may also, as far as its formal power is concerned, be too STRONG. In other words, a general linguistic theory may have too much formal power. On the one hand, it may have too much formal power in the sense that its theoretical concepts make it possible to give a grammatical explanation for data which do not occur in a possible human language. In other words, the theoretical concepts create the possibility of giving solutions to problems which cannot exist in connection with possible human languages. It follows from this that such a general linguistic theory allows a description to be given of systems which do not fall within the class of possible human languages. This would constitute a failure, on the part of the theory in question, to give an adequate characterization of the content of the concept 'possible human language'. Such a general linguistic theory therefore wrongly identifies objects which are not possible human languages as possible human languages. On the other hand, a general linguistic theory may have too much formal power in that types of generalizations which never occur in human language may be formulated as being linguistically significant in terms of the theory.

On the strength of these considerations, a third criterion is adopted for general linguistic concepts.

(55)   General linguistic concepts should not confer excessive formal power upon a general linguistic theory.

The criterion (55) may be formulated differently: the concepts of a general linguistic theory must sufficiently constrain the formal power of the theory. In other words, in terms of these concepts all objects which are not possible human languages must be explicitly ruled out as potential members of the class of possible human languages. With regard to any individual general linguistic concept, the criterion (55) implies the following: the concept must represent something in terms of which a possible human language differs from an object which is not a possible human language. In his article "Some empirical issues in the theory of transformational grammar" (1972d:128–129), Chomsky argues that this is indeed the case with, for example, the general linguistic concept 'deep structure'. This concept represents a property which distinguishes a possible human language from something which is not a possible human language. In doing so, this concept places a highly desirable constraint on the formal power of the general linguistic theory of which it forms part.

SELECTED READING

Inquiry in General

Concepts, Theoretical

General Characterization

Bunge 1967a: §2.2; Caws 1966:ch.8, 9; Harré 1972:27–29; Hempel 1952:29–39; Kaplan 1964: §6.

Components of Content

Hempel 1952:39–50; 1966:91–97; Holton 1973:47–68.

Forming

Bunge 1967a: § 2.5; Hempel 1952: § III; 1966:ch.7.

Hypotheses

Barker 1957:26–30, 95–99; Bunge 1967a:ch.5; Caws 1966:ch.11; Dubin 1969: ch.9; Hanson 1969:ch.13, 20.

Theories

General Nature

Achinstein 1968:ch.4; Bunge 1967a:ch.7; Caws 1966:ch.12,36; Dubin 1969:ch.1; Hanson 1969:ch.18; 1971:45–49; Harré 1972:23–27; Hempel 1966:ch.6; Kaplan 1964:ch.34.

Axiomatizing

Achinstein 1968: 148–154; Bocheński 1965: § 13; Bunge 1967a: §8.3, 8.4; Caws 1966:ch.16; Henkin, Suppes and Tarski (eds.) 1959.

Analogies

Achinstein 1968:203–209; Hesse 1967b; Leatherdale 1974:ch.1, and the Bibliography pp.251–255.

Descriptive and Other Functions

Harré 1967:ch.1, 3; 1972:25–27; Kaplan 1964: §35.

Ontological Status

Botha 1968: §3.5.2; Braithwaite 1964:79ff.; Carnap 1952; Feigl 1950:44ff.; Feyerabend 1964; Harré 1961; Hempel 1966:80ff.; Hesse 1967a:406ff.; Maxwell 1962; Nagel 1961:ch.6; Popper 1969:ch.3; Toulmin 1965:134ff.

Structure

Hesse 1967a:406ff.; Suppe (ed.) 1974a.

Terms, Theoretical

General

Achinstein 1968:ch.5, 6; Bunge 1967a: §§2.1, 2.2; Caws 1966:ch.5, 10; Hanson 1969:34–36.

Definition

Bunge 1967a: §3.3; Caws 1966:ch.7; Hanson 1969:ch.2; Hempel 1966: 85ff.

Flight Control Mechanism of Bats

Galambos 1942; 1943; Galambos and Griffin 1942; Griffin and Galambos 1941.

Grammatical Inquiry

Axiomatizing of Grammars

Botha 1968: §3.2.3.3; Stegmüller 1969:786; Wang 1973.

Formalizing of Grammars

Bach 1964:10ff.; Koutsoudas 1966:6ff.; McCawley 1971; Robin T. Lakoff 1974: 59ff.

Intensional vs. Extensional Definitions

Bach 1964:150; Botha 1968: §3.2.4.3.

Ontological Status/Psychological Reality of Grammars

Bar-Hillel 1964; Botha 1968: § §3.5.3–3.5.5; 1971:ch.4; 1973:ch.4; 1979a, b; Chomsky 1976; Chomsky and Katz 1974:359ff.; Derwing 1973:ch.8; Derwing and Harris 1975; Fodor, Bever and Garrett 1974:ch.4; Hutchinson 1974; Jackendoff 1976:146–148; Katz 1964; 1977; Kiparsky 1968a: 171ff.; Levelt 1974:ch.17; Schwartz 1969; Steinberg 1975; Stich 1975.

Expressing Linguistically Significant Generalizations

Botha 1971:ch.3; 1973: §6.2.4.3; 1976d: §§2, 4.1–4.3; Prideaux 1971; Sadock 1976.

Technical Definition of Grammars

Bach 1964:ch.2; Chomsky 1957:ch.2; Koutsoudas 1966:1–6, 46ff.; Ruwet 1973: ch.3–4.

General Linguistic Inquiry

Technical Characterization of General Linguistic Theory

Botha 1968: §2.3; 1971: §2.2.2; Chomsky 1957:ch.6; 1965:ch.1; 1968:ch.2; Fodor, Bever and Garrett 1974:ch.3; Ruwet 1973:ch.6.

See also the items listed under the headings *Grammatical inquiry: Ontological Status* and *Expressing Linguistically Significant Generalizations*.

CHAPTER SEVEN

Giving Linguistic Explanations

7.0 PERSPECTIVE

In this chapter we shall be looking at a fifth main aspect of linguistic inquiry: the giving of linguistic explanations for problematic linguistic phenomena. Like the preceding chapters, this chapter is divided into three main sections. The first section deals with scientific explanation in general. First of all, scientific explanation is distinguished from three forms of nonscientific explanation: semantic explanation, descriptive explanation and practical explanation. We then consider the logical structure of scientific explanation and show that they have the character of arguments. The minimal formal and material criteria and the additional criteria for scientific explanations are subsequently discussed. We are also concerned with the role which theoretical descriptions play in scientific explanations. In conclusion, a summary is given of the intellectual activities involved in the giving of scientific explanations.

In the second section of this chapter, we take up two main points in connection with grammatical explanations. On the one hand, we are concerned with the general nature and special properties of grammatical explanations. On the other hand, a characterization is given of the activities involved in giving grammatical explanations. Examples are given to illustrate the function of grammatical explanations, the structure of grammatical explanations, the minimal criteria for grammatical explanations and the additional criteria by which the adequacy of grammatical explanations is judged. The differences between grammatical explanations and theoretical grammatical descriptions are then discussed in detail. In the characterization of giving grammatical explanations, it is shown how this activity is related to that of giving theoretical grammatical descriptions.

The third section of the chapter deals briefly with a number of aspects of general linguistic explanation. The discussion is based on Chomsky's distinction between three levels of success for linguistic theories: observational adequacy, descriptive adequacy and explanatory adequacy. With regard to the level of explanatory adequacy, a form of general linguistic explanation known as "internal explanation" is defined. The function, structure and properties of internal explanations are discussed with reference to examples. Subsequently, this form of explanation is compared with another form of explanation which plays a role in linguistic inquiry: external explanation. In conclusion, a problem which has cropped up in a previous chapter is taken up again, viz. the problem of determining the genuineness of linguistic intuitions. A strategy is described which may be used to solve this problem. In this strategy the concepts of grammatical explanation and explanatory adequacy of the general linguistic theory play a fundamental role.

7.1 INTRODUCTION

Consider the following two derived nominals:

(1) (a) *John's easiness to please
   (b) John's eagerness to please

We saw in § 1.4 that, for the grammarian of English, these two derived nominals are problematic. As far as their structure is concerned, they seem to be parallel, but then there is an unexpected difference in their acceptability. What is problematic in connection with (1)(a) and (b) may be formulated as the problem (2).

(2) Why is it that, whereas the derived nominal *John's easiness to please* is unacceptable, the derived nominal *John's eagerness to please* is not unacceptable?

In § 1.4 we considered the solution proposed by Chomsky for the grammatical problem (2). The gist of this solution is given below.

(3) (a) The grammar of English contains a neutral lexical entry for "easy", which specifies that this item cannot take a sentential complement. In *John's easiness to please* the item *easiness* takes a sentential complement in the surface form of *to please*. The derived nominal in question is therefore unacceptable.
   (b) The grammar of English contains a neutral lexical entry for "eager", which specifies that this item can take a sentential complement. In *John's eagerness to please* the item *eagerness* does take a sentential complement. There is therefore no structural reason why the derived nominal in question should be unacceptable.

In (3) we actually have two examples of grammatical explanations: one for the fact that *John's easiness to please* is unacceptable and one for the fact that *John's eagerness to please* is not unacceptable.

In this chapter we are concerned with the question of what is involved in giving explanations for problematic linguistic data in linguistic inquiry. Giving explanations for problematic states of affairs represents a fifth main aspect of linguistic inquiry. Linguistic inquiry has this main aspect because giving explanations is the second logical means by which grammarians pursue their ultimate objective: the search for insight into, or understanding of, a problematic linguistic reality. Schematically, the fifth aspect of linguistic inquiry may be represented as follows:

(4)

$$
\begin{array}{ccc}
\text{problematic} & & \boxed{\begin{array}{c}\text{activities of}\\ \text{fifth main}\\ \text{aspect}\end{array}} \\
\text{phenomenon} & \rightarrow & \qquad \rightarrow \qquad \text{explanation}
\end{array}
$$

This schematic representation gives rise to two problems which may be formulated as the questions (5)(a) and (b).

(5) (a)   A question concerning the output of the schema: what is a linguistic explanation?

(b)   A question concerning the content of the box: what is involved in giving linguistic explanations?

These questions will be considered from the point of view of empirical inquiry in general, of grammatical inquiry and of general linguistic inquiry.

7.2   INQUIRY IN GENERAL

Opinion is divided among scholars as to the nature and properties of scientific explanations. These differences of opinion are expressed in an extensive corpus of metascientific literature – study, for instance the subject-orientated bibliography of Nicholas Rescher's study *Scientific explanation* (1970:209–240). The disagreement among scholars is largely related to their divergent views on the nature and structure of scientific theories. As may be expected, the bounds of our study do not allow us to discuss these differences of opinion in any detail. We shall concentrate on those fundamental concepts and distinctions in the relevant literature which can contribute directly to our understanding of the explanations given in linguistic inquiry. The concepts and distinctions discussed have been taken mainly from chapter 1 of the above-mentioned study by Rescher which, because of its didactic nature, is excellently suited to our purpose.

7.2.1   Nature of Scientific Explanations

7.2.1.1   *Types of Explanation*

Scientific explanation represents one type of explanation. Let us approach our discussion of scientific explanation by comparing it with a few types of non-scientific explanation.

SEMANTIC EXPLANATION is a first general type of nonscientific explanation. The function of semantic explanation is to explicate the meaning of symbols. These include expressions of natural languages as well as symbols which are part of specially devised systems. Semantic explanations therefore provide answers to questions such as those of (6).

(6) (a) What does the expression/word A mean?
     (b) What is the value of the symbol B?
     (c) What information is conveyed by the expression/symbol C?

Semantic explanations take various conventional forms: translations, dictionary definitions, paraphrases, lists of synonyms, etc.

DESCRIPTIVE EXPLANATION represents a second form of nonscientific explanation. Descriptive explanations explain what something is like: what toothache feels like, what it feels like to miss a train, what a shooting star looks like, what anaesthetic smells like, what icecream tastes like, how a fountain-pen is constructed and how it works, and so on. The function of descriptive explanations is therefore to provide answers to questions such as those of (7).

(7) (a) What does (an) A feel like?
     (b) What does (a) B look like?
     (c) What does (a) C smell/taste like?
     (d) How is (a) D constructed?
     (e) How does (an) E work?

Note that the descriptions in question are not theoretical descriptions. They are descriptions of directly-given feelings, sensations, objects, etc.

PRACTICAL EXPLANATION represents a third general form of nonscientific explanation. Practical explanation is directed at activity in that it defines procedures, for instance, (a) *for performing certain acts:* dancing a tango, executing a backhand stroke in tennis, milking a cow, etc.; (b) *for manufacturing things:* baking bread, weaving a cloth, digging a well, etc.; (c) *for achieving certain goals:* travelling to the moon, charming ladies, passing an exam, etc. The function of practical explanation is to provide answers to questions such as those of (8).

(8) (a) How does one perform that act A?
     (b) How does one make/manufacture (a) B?
     (c) How does one achieve the goal C?

From our discussion it is clear why practical explanations are called "how to" explanations.

SCIENTIFIC EXPLANATION is directed at gaining insight or understanding.

Scientific explanation has to provide answers to "Why" questions and their variants.

(9) (a)   Why did the event A take place?
    (b)   Why does the phenomenon B have the general nature or particular properties which it has?
    (c)   Why is the object C in the state in which it is?
    (d)   Why is the state of affairs D as it is?

To ask for a scientific explanation of something is to ask for one or more reasons why it is as it is and probably cannot be different. This point may be grasped better by considering (10)–(13) below in which (b) in each case contains an explanation for the problematic state of affairs indicated in (a).

(10)(a)   Why did that fluid change into a solid, viz. ice?
    (b)   Because that fluid is water, the temperature fell below 0°C and water turns into ice at a temperature below 0°C.

(11)(a)   Why did that tree lose its leaves?
    (b)   Because that tree is an elm, it is autumn and all elms, being deciduous, lose their leaves in autumn.

(12)(a)   Why did Smith become ill?
    (b)   Because Smith is an adult male who came into contact with the virus V and 80% of all adult males who come into contact with the virus V become ill.

(13)(a)   Why don't those animals, when flying in the dark, collide with the objects in their vicinity?
    (b)   Because those animals are bats and all bats possess a flight control mechanism which works as described in (4) of §6.2.1.

Informally, scientific explanations are typically introduced by "Because" as in (b) above.

The reasons given in scientific explanations are so-called REASONS FOR BEING. These are reasons from which it is clear why things are as they are and probably cannot be otherwise. Opposed to this type of reason is another type of reason: so-called REASONS FOR KNOWING. The latter type of reason is not given when someone is asked why something is as it is. Reasons for knowing are given when someone is asked why he *says* that something is as it is. In other words, reasons for knowing are given to justify statements.

Suppose someone were to ask why he says that a fluid has turned into a solid – compare (10)(a) above. He will not give the reasons for being of (10)(b) in answer to this question. On the contrary, he will give a reason for knowing such as that he has heard from a reliable witness that the fluid has turned into a solid. Giving scientific explanations entails the giving of reasons for being. The giving of (scientific) justifications, on the other hand, involves giving reasons for knowing. We shall return to this point in §9.2.1. Note that a distinction may be drawn between grounds and reasons. GROUNDS represent the units of thought, i.e. the conceptual units, which explanations (and justifications) require. REASONS represent the linguistic forms in which these grounds are presented. It is not necessary to use such a terminological distinction in our study. We shall therefore use the term "reason" both in the sense of 'ground' as a unit of content and in the sense of 'reason' as a unit of linguistic form.

7.2.1.2   Structure of Scientific Explanations

From a logical point of view, a scientific explanation is an ordered set of propositions. Recall that we considered a PROPOSITION to be the content of a declarative sentence. The propositions of a scientific explanation may be divided into two classes. One of these classes represents the explanandum, while the other class represents the explanans. The explanandum and the explanans are related in terms of some logical relation. Let us have a closer look at the three components of a scientific explanation: the explanandum, the explanans and the connecting logical relation.

The EXPLANANDUM represents a description of whatever it is that has to be explained. We saw a number of examples of explananda above.

(14)(a) In (10)(a) the fact is described that a certain fluid has turned into a solid.

(b) In (11)(a) the fact is described that a certain tree has lost its leaves.

(c) In (12)(a) the fact is described that a certain Smith has become ill.

(d) In (13)(a) the phenomenon is described that certain animals fly in the dark without any danger of collision.

Any aspect of the world may be problematic, may call for an explanation and may therefore be mentioned in the explanandum of an explanation. Explananda do not only describe isolated facts, phenomena, events, etc. They may also describe classes of facts, phenomena, events, etc. or patterns and regularities in classes of facts, phenomena, events, etc. Moreover, generalizations, rules, laws and even entire theories that are used to explain that which is problematic may in turn call for an explanation and be mentioned in explananda.

The EXPLANANS in an explanation represents the reasons that are given to rationally comprehend the problematic phenomenon represented by the explanandum. The explanantia of a large class of scientific explanations include two types of reasons. The first type of reason given in an explanans is LAWLIKE REASONS. These reasons are normally given by way of generalizations. They may therefore be called LAWLIKE GENERALIZATIONS for short. In the explanantia of (10)–(13) we find the lawlike generalizations of (15).

(15)(a)   Water turns into ice at a temperature below 0°C.
   (b)   All elms, being deciduous, lose their leaves in autumn.
   (c)   80% of all adult males who come into contact with the virus V become ill.
   (d)   All bats possess a flight control mechanism which works as described in (4) of §6.2.1.

Such lawlike generalizations often appear in another, equivalent form: that of "If . . . then" sentences. For instance, (15)(a) has the equivalent form "If a fluid is water and the temperature falls below 0°C, then the water will turn into ice".

The fact that a lawlike generalization specifies the way things must, or at least ought to, be under certain circumstances constitutes its LAWLIKE NATURE. For instance, in autumn all elms *must* lose their leaves. A generalization which merely describes the way things in fact *are*, misses a lawlike aspect. The fact that a lawlike generalization is valid for all possible cases of a certain type constitutes its GENERALITY. All possible cases would include cases which have been subjected to inquiry, past cases, future cases, hypothetical cases, etc. A lawlike generalization therefore does not apply to a limited number of investigated cases of a particular type only. For instance, all elms of all times – past, present, future – must lose their leaves in autumn. Within the type or domain of things to which a generalization applies, its applicability may not be limited by physical, temporal, local or other factors of a random nature. For instance, it is not only the elms of the Black Forest, or the elms planted since 1930, or elms that are taller than three metres that must lose their leaves. *All* elms must lose their leaves. In short, a lawlike generalization specifies the way all things of a certain type must, or at least ought to, be under certain circumstances. The phenomena to which a lawlike generalization applies are conventionally regarded as falling within its DOMAIN.

Because they contain lawlike generalizations in their explanantia, scientific explanations have a certain modal character. Scientific explanations do not merely explain why something is as it is, but why it must of necessity be as it is or, at least, probably cannot be different. Thus, the modal nature of scientific explanations is that of necessity or, at least, of high probability. Conventionally, only those lawlike generalizations which express necessity are considered to express reasons for being. Strictly speaking, therefore, lawlike generalizations which express probability – cf. (15)(c) – do not give reasons for being.

Numerous scholars regard explanations which do not have this modal character as nonscientific. For these scholars, the giving of scientific explanations is essentially an act of showing that whatever it is that is problematic falls within the domain of a lawlike generalization. The lawlike generalizations concerned take the form of well-justified hypotheses which are integrated into scientific theories. In view of this status of lawlike generalizations, scientific explanation is commonly known as THEORETICAL EXPLANATION. Note, in conclusion, that philosophers of science, such as Peter Achinstein (1971: 94–109), argue that, in natural science, explanations may be given without *directly* appealing to laws or lawlike generalizations. The details of this point fall outside the scope of our study.

The second type of reason contained in the explanans is by nature factual. These reasons may be called FACTUAL REASONS for short. They present certain factual data about whatever it is that has to be explained. More specifically, factual data are presented from which it is clear that the lawlike generalization(s) of the explanans do in fact apply to whatever it is that is problematic. We saw examples of such factual reasons above.

(16)(a)   In (10)(b):   That fluid is water.
                          The temperature has fallen below 0°C.
   (b)   In (11)(b):   That tree is an elm.
                          It is autumn.
   (c)   In (12)(b):   Smith is an adult male.
                          Smith came into contact with the virus V.
   (d)   In (13)(b):   Those animals are bats.

It must be clear from these factual reasons that whatever it is that requires explanation does indeed fall within the domain of a lawlike generalization in the explanans. These factual reasons are therefore also known as boundary-value conditions for applying laws, or BOUNDARY CONDITIONS for short.

This brings us to the third component of scientific explanations: the LOGICAL RELATION between the explanandum and the explanans. An appropriate logical relation must exist between the explanandum and the explanans. This relation must be such that it is possible to infer the explanandum from the explanans with the aid of a known logical rule. Some scientists insist that this logical rule should be a rule of deduction. In terms of a rule of DEDUCTION, the explanandum will necessarily follow from the explanans. In other words, given the content of the explanans, the explanandum must necessarily have the content which it has. A scientific explanation in which the explanandum and the explanans are logically related in terms of a rule of deduction, is known as a DEDUCTIVE EXPLANATION.

Other scientists also accept a NONDEDUCTIVE logical relation between the explanandum and the explanans. They allow the explanandum to be inferred from the explanans in terms of a nondeductive rule. In terms of such a rule, the explanandum does not necessarily follow from the explanans. It merely follows from the explanans with a high degree of probability. A scientific explanation in which the explanandum and the explanans are logically related in terms of a nondeductive logical rule, is known as a PROBABILISTIC EXPLANATION. We shall consider examples of both a deductive explanation and a probabilistic explanation below.

7.2.1.3   *Logical Nature of Scientific Explanations*

Our discussion of the logical relation in an explanation leads us to the conclusion that a scientific explanation has the logical nature of an argument. As a logical structure, an ARGUMENT is an ordered set of propositions. Scientific explanations may be reconstructed as arguments. One of the propositions of an argument represents the conclusion. The CONCLUSION is the proposition which is advanced on the basis of, or which is inferred from, the other propositions within the same argument. If an explanation is reconstructed as an argument, the explanandum is represented by the conclusion of the argument. Those propositions in the argument on which the conclusion is based, represent the PREMISSES of the argument. If an explanation is given in the form of an argument, the explanans represents the premisses.

The premisses of an argument fall into two classes: minor premisses and major premisses. MINOR PREMISSES represent the data on which the conclusion is based. In other words, the factual reasons in the explanans of an explanation become the minor premisses of the argument. The MAJOR PREMISS of an argument authorizes the step from the minor premisses to the conclusion. In other words, the major premiss may be regarded as a warrant to draw the conclusion on the strength of the data presented in the minor premisses. The lawlike generalization in the explanans of an explanation becomes the major premiss of the argument.

The fact that a scientific explanation has the logical nature of an argument may be illustrated with reference to the explanations (10) and (12). The explanation (10) may be reconstructed in the form of an argument as follows:

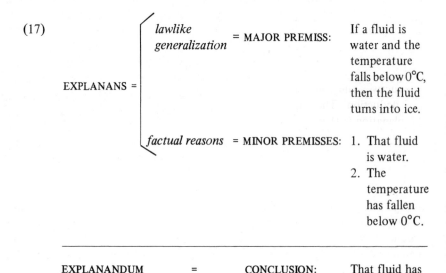

(17)

EXPLANANS =

    lawlike generalization = MAJOR PREMISS: If a fluid is water and the temperature falls below 0°C, then the fluid turns into ice.

    factual reasons = MINOR PREMISSES:
1. That fluid is water.
2. The temperature has fallen below 0°C.

EXPLANANDUM   =   CONCLUSION: That fluid has turned into ice.

The logical relation between the explanandum and the explanans in (17) is a deductive relation. In other words, the conclusion is inferred from the premises in terms of a deductive logical rule. The explanation is therefore deductive. Because its explanans contains a lawlike generalization, such an explanation is often called a DEDUCTIVE NOMOLOGICAL EXPLANATION ["nomos" is Greek for "law"]. The modal nature of this explanation is that of necessity. Given the content of the explanans, the explanandum can have no other content. In other words, the fluid could have done nothing but turn into ice. We shall return to the logical nature of the form of argument represented by (17) in §9.2.1.2.1.

As regards the explanation (12), it may be reconstructed in the form of an argument as follows:

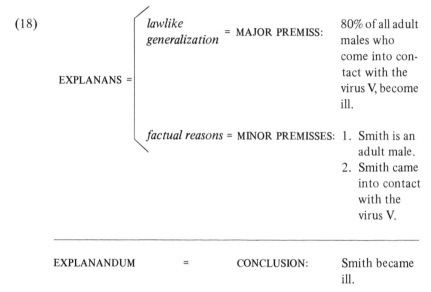

(18)

EXPLANANS =

lawlike generalization = MAJOR PREMISS: 80% of all adult males who come into contact with the virus V, become ill.

factual reasons = MINOR PREMISSES: 1. Smith is an adult male.
2. Smith came into contact with the virus V.

EXPLANANDUM = CONCLUSION: Smith became ill.

The logical relation between the explanandum and the explanans of (18) is non-deductive. The conclusion is not inferred from the premises in terms of a rule of deduction. The modal nature of the explanation is probabilistic and the explanation is therefore a "probabilistic explanation". Given the content of the explanans, the content of the explanandum does not follow necessarily, but only with a high degree of probability. In other words, Smith could be one of the 20% of adult males not affected by the virus V. His illness could therefore have another cause and need not necessarily be the result of his contact with the virus in question.

We can now return to a statement which was made in §5.2.1 about the nature of the giving of explanations as an objective of empirical inquiry. It was said that the giving of explanations is a "logical objective", but what is meant by "logical" was not made quite clear. It has now become clear that to give a scientific explanation involves the construction of a logical structure, viz. an argument.

This is the reason why the giving of explanations was presented as a "logical objective", i.e. an objective involving the construction of a logical structure.

7.2.1.4   Minimal Criteria for Scientific Explanations

Not every random collection of scientific propositions represents a scientific explanation. In order to be called a scientific explanation, a set of propositions must satisfy two types of minimal criteria: formal criteria and material criteria. We considered the minimal FORMAL CRITERIA for scientific explanations in the preceding paragraphs. These criteria apply to the form or structure of scientific explanations. The minimal formal criteria are summarized in (19) below.

(19)(a)   A scientific explanation must include a proposition which functions as the explandum.

(b)   A scientific explanation must include a set of propositions which, jointly, function as the explanans.

(c)   It must be possible to state a logical rule in terms of which the explanandum may be inferred from the explanans.

The MATERIAL CRITERIA concern the acceptability or correctness of the propositions constituting the explanans. Minimally, scientific explanations must satisfy the following two material criteria:

(20)(a)   The correctness of the data given, as factual reasons in the explanans must be beyond reasonable doubt.

(b)   The lawlike generalization given in the explanans must have been properly tested and justified.

The criterion (20)(a) entails the following: the data from which it must be clear that whatever it is that has to be explained does indeed fall in the domain of the lawlike generalization must have the status of facts. In other words, these data must represent what is actually the case. The criterion (20)(b) has two sides. On the one hand, the lawlike generalization must have withstood the confrontation with empirical data. On the other hand, this lawlike generalization may not be inconsistent with other, well-justified lawlike generalizations.

An explanation which satisfies both the minimal formal criteria and the minimal material criteria is known as an ACTUAL EXPLANATION. An explanation which satisfies the minimal formal criteria, but which has not yet been shown to satisfy the minimal material criteria as well, is known as a POSSIBLE EXPLANATION. Nicholas Rescher (1970:19) summarizes the criteria for an actual explanation as follows:

An actual explanation, therefore, must conform not only to the formal requirement that the explanatory premises, if assumed as hypotheses, will render the explanatory conclusion relatively certain or probable; it must also satisfy the material requirement that the particular premises be fact-asserting (true or highly probable) and that the general premises be law-asserting, and represent generalizations which, being well confirmed, have earned the rubric of lawfulness.

Rescher's expressions "particular premisses" and "general premisses" are equivalent to our expressions "minor premisses" and "major premisses" respectively.

7.2.1.5 *Additional Criteria for Scientific Explanations*

Not all scientific explanations which satisfy the minimal formal and material criteria are equally good. Various criteria are used to determine the relative merit of alternative explanations for the same problematic state of affairs. These criteria will be discussed in detail in the chapter of our study dealing with the justification of scientific hypotheses. For the time being, only five examples of such criteria are given below for their illustrative value.

(21)(a) *Criterion of logical power:* the stronger the logical relation between the explanans and the explanandum, the better the explanation.

(b) *Criterion of groundedness:* the stronger the justification for the lawlike generalization of the explanans, the better the explanation.

(c) *Criterion of generality:* the more general the lawlike generalization of the explanans, the better the explanation.

(d) *Criterion of lawfulness:* the stronger the modality — and, therefore, the greater the lawfulness — of the lawlike generalization of the explanans, the better the explanation.

(e) *Criterion of explanatory depth:* the deeper, or the more fundamental, the lawlike generalization of the explanans, the better the explanation.

In view of the preceding discussion, the first four criteria should present no problem. The fifth criterion will be elucidated when the explanations given in linguistic inquiry are considered.

7.2.1.6 *Theoretical Descriptions and Scientific Explanations*

There are many types of scientific explanation. These types differ from one another with regard to the types of objects which they explain, the types of reasons given in the explanans, the type of logical relation between the explanandum and the explanans, and so on. As regards the types of objects being explained, the following types of explanations may, for instance, be distinguished: explanations for individual events, phenomena, etc.; explanations of classes of events, phenomena, etc., and explanations of regularities or patterns within classes of events, phenomena, etc.

As regards the types of reasons given in the explanans, a distinction may be drawn, for example, between causal, teleological and motivational explanations. In a CAUSAL EXPLANATION one or more of the reasons given in the explanans specify the cause(s) of whatever it is that has to be explained. For instance, the coming of autumn causes elms to lose their leaves. In a TELEOLOGICAL EXPLANATION one or more of the reasons given in the explanans represent the function(s) or purpose(s) of that which has to be explained. For instance, roses are pleasantly scented so as to attract insects for pollination. In a MOTIVATIONAL EXPLANATION one or more of the reasons given in the explanans represent the motive(s) for the act or behaviour which has to be explained. For instance, Spike murdered his aunt in order to inherit her money.

As regards the type of logical relation between the explanandum and the explanans, we distinguished between two types of explanation in §§7.2.1.2 and 7.2.1.3 above: deductive explanations and probabilistic explanations.

The types of explanation which we have mentioned represent only a few of the many types of scientific explanation which exist. The nature and properties of the various types of scientific explanation fall outside the scope of our study. However, there remains one type of explanation which calls for more detailed discussion with a view to our interest in the explanations given in linguistic inquiry. This is the type of scientific explanation in which theoretical descriptions play a fundamental part.

Consider the explanation (13) for the problematic flying of bats. Notice that the essential part of this explanation is the theoretical description of the flight control mechanism of bats. The problematic flying of bats is explained in terms of the functioning of this mechanism as it was described in (4) of §6.2.1. This type of explanation explains an observable problematic phenomenon in terms of a theoretical description of an underlying mechanism.

This type of explanation is widely used in empirical inquiry. In his book *An introduction to the logic of the sciences* (1967:100), the philosopher of science Rom Harré distinguishes a subtype of this type of explanation and calls it INTERSCIENTIFIC EXPLANATION. Interscientific explanation is "interscientific" in the sense that the problematic phenomena of a given science are explained in terms of theoretical descriptions taken from another science. Harré (1967:101) argues that:

> ... the sciences can be arranged in a hierarchy such that an explanation of facts in one is given in terms of the description of facts in another, the two sets of facts being related in such a way that antecedent conditions for particular happenings in one realm are found in the other. For example certain overt pieces of behaviour in animals can be explained in terms of

motives and drives, what might be called psychological explanation, but motives and drives can themselves be given an explanation in terms of physiology, the facts of which are given a biochemical explanation, and biochemistry in common with chemistry generally is thought to be susceptible of explanation in terms of the physics of the atoms and molecules which are the units of chemistry. This is not to say that any particular piece of behaviour can be given an explanation in terms of the physics of atoms, but that the collection of more and more facts about behaviour will not provide an explanation of the piece of behaviour in question, that the mechanism of behaviour must be sought out.

Note that explanations in terms of a theoretical description need not necessarily be interscientific. Such explanations may be given in every individual science or form of inquiry which is directed at a two-levelled reality. In such a science, problematic phenomena on a (more) directly given level may be explained in terms of theoretical descriptions of objects on an underlying level.

7.2.2 Giving Scientific Explanations

This brings us to the question (5)(b): what is involved in giving scientific explanations? The answer to this question has implicitly been given in the preceding paragraphs. It remains for us to give a systematic account of what has already been said.

(22) To give a scientific explanation for a problematic phenomenon, in many cases involves
    (a) stating a descriptive proposition representing whatever it is that is problematic as precisely as possible;
    (b) presenting a well-justified lawlike generalization which states in principle what the case must/ought to be for problematic phenomena of the kind in question;
    (c) presenting accurate data about the problematic phenomenon in question from which it is clear that the phenomenon does indeed fall within the domain of the lawlike generalization; and
    (d) specifying a logical rule in terms of which the proposition describing the problematic phenomenon may be inferred from the lawlike generalization of (b) and the statements presenting the data of (c).

Finally, it must be emphasized that the lawlike generalization of (b) in many cases represents a part of a theory or of a theoretical description.

7.3 GRAMMATICAL INQUIRY

7.3.1 General

We have already considered two examples of grammatical explanations: (3)(a) and (b) in §7.1. Let us approach our study of grammatical explanations by considering another four examples of such explanations. The first three were taken from an article by Chomsky, "Problems of explanation in linguistics" (1970), which contains many typical examples of grammatical explanations.

Example 1 : Chomsky (1970:431) points out that the following sentence is ambiguous:

(23)   *I disapprove of John's drinking.*

The ambiguity of this sentence stems from the fact that the gerundive nominal *John's drinking* has two meanings. On the one hand, this nominal may have the meaning "the fact that John drinks" in (23) – the meaning that it in fact has in the following unambiguous sentence:

(24)   *I disapprove of John's drinking the beer.*

On the other hand, *John's drinking* may have the meaning "the manner in which John drinks" in (23) – the meaning that it in fact has in the following unambiguous sentence:

(25)   *I disapprove of John's excessive drinking.*

As a grammarian, Chomsky considers the ambiguity of the sentence (23) to be problematic.

(26)   Why is the English sentence *I disapprove of John's drinking* ambiguous?

Chomsky offers the grammatical explantion (27) as a solution to the problem formulated in (26).

(27)   Sentences have at least as many semantic interpretations as they have distinct deep structures. In the grammar of English the sentence *I disapprove of John's drinking* is assigned two different deep structures: one of these determines a "fact that" interpretation, while the other determines a "manner in which" interpretation. [The transformations deriving from these two deep structures one and the same surface structure obliterate the differences between these deep structures.] Thus, the sentence in question is ambiguous.

Example 2 : In addition to the sentences (23)–(25), Chomsky (1970:431) also gives the following sentence:

(28)   **I disapprove of John's excessive drinking the beer.*

As a grammarian, Chomsky considers (28) to be problematic.

(29)   Why is the sentence *I disapprove of John's excessive drinking the beer* unacceptable?

The grammatical explanation which Chomsky gives in answer to this question is parallel to that of (27).

(30)   Alternative deep structures of sentences may be extended in one, but not both, of two ways. The grammar of English assigns two alternative deep structures to the sentence *I disapprove of John's drinking.* The sentence (28) was formed by extending a single deep structure in both of two alternative manners: the manner of the sentence (24) and the manner of the sentence (25). Thus, the sentence (28) is unacceptable.

Example 3 : Chomsky (1970:432) claims that English has very general transformations which operate on the structure underlying the sentence (31) to derive the sentence (32).

(31)   *I don't like John's cooking any more than I like Bill's cooking.*

(32)   *I don't like John's cooking any more than Bill's.*

He points out that the sentence (31) is ambiguous. It allows of a "fact" interpretation: 'I don't like the fact that John cooks any more than the fact that Bill cooks'. Or, it also allows of a "quality" interpretation: 'I don't like the quality of John's cooking any more than the quality of Bill's cooking'. However, the sentence (32) cannot have a mixed "fact/quality" interpretation. It cannot, for example, mean: 'I don't like the quality of John's cooking any more than I do the fact that Bill cooks'. Neither can it have the opposite meaning: 'I don't like the fact that John cooks any more than I like the quality of Bill's cooking'. For the grammarian of English this is a problematic state of affairs which may be formulated as the problem (33).

(33)   Why doesn't the sentence *I don't like John's cooking any more than Bill's* have a mixed "fact/quality" interpretation?

Chomsky offers the following grammatical explanation as a solution to this problem:

(34)   There is a general linguistic condition on the applicability of deletion
transformations: an element may be deleted only if (a) the element
to be deleted is identical to some other element in the P-marker, or
(b) the element to be deleted is a constant single element. The sentence
(32) is derived by applying a deletion transformation to the structure
underlying (31). In order to derive the former sentence in such a way
that it has a mixed "fact/quality" interpretation, this deletion transformation must violate part (a) of the general linguistic condition
stated above. Consequently the sentence (32) cannot have a mixed
"fact/quality" interpretation.

The general linguistic condition referred to in (34) is known as the RECOVER-
ABILITY CONDITION. Its function is to ensure that we can always recover a
unique deep structure for a given surface structure. This implies that we should
always be able to recover, in the deep structure, constituents which have been
deleted in the surface structure. Part (b) of the recoverability condition – which
is illustrated by Emmon Bach in his *Syntactic theory* (1974a: 100–101) – does
not concern us here.

Example 4 : The substance of the fourth example of a grammatical explanation was taken from the above-mentioned work by Emmon Bach (pp.210–211).
Consider the following sentences:

(35)   *Mary lives in New York and Chicago.*

(36)   *Where does Mary live?*

(37)   **Where does Mary live in New York and?*

The two interrogative sentences (36) and (37) were derived by applying, among
other things, the *wh*-movement transformation. The *wh*-movement transformation moves an NP with the feature [+ wh] to the beginning of the sentence. In
the derivation of (37), this transformation was applied to a structure similar to
that underlying the declarative sentence (35).

Note that a problematic discrepancy exists between the interrogative sentences
(36) and (37).

(38)   Why is it that, whereas the interrogative sentence *Where does Mary
live in New York and?* is unacceptable, the interrogative sentence
Where does Mary live? is not unacceptable?

The conventional answer given by generative grammarians to this question takes
the form of grammatical explanations such as that of (39).

(39)(a)   There is a general linguistic condition which restricts the applicability of movement transformations in the case of coordinate structures: no transformation may (a) move a conjunct that is part of a coordinate structure out of this structure, or (b) move an element that is part of a conjunct out of this conjunct. In the derivation of the sentence *Where does Mary live in New York and?* the *wh*-movement transformation, among other things, was applied. Contrary to part (a) of the general linguistic condition mentioned above, this transformation has moved the NP with the feature [+ wh] out of the coordinate structure *New York and* [+ wh]$_{NP}$ and placed it at the beginning of the sentence (where it is phonologically realized by the interrogative *where*). Thus, the interrogative sentence in question is unacceptable.

(b)   The *wh*-movement transformation, among other things, was applied in the derivation of the interrogative sentence *Where does Mary live?* as well. The rule moved an NP with the feature [+ wh] to the beginning of the sentence. This NP is not a conjunct that is part of a coordinate structure. The movement therefore does not violate the general linguistic condition mentioned above. Consequently, the interrogative sentence in question is not unacceptable.

The general linguistic condition referred to in (39) is known in the literature as the COORDINATE STRUCTURE CONSTRAINT. The Coordinate Structure Constraint was proposed by John Ross in his dissertation *Constraints on variables in syntax* (1967: §4.2).

Two main points in connection with grammatical explanations such as the four given above will be considered below. First, we shall concentrate on the general nature and particular properties of grammatical explanations. Then we shall discuss the nature of the intellectual activities involved in giving grammatical explanations.

7.3.2   Nature of Grammatical Explanations

7.3.2.1   *Function of Grammatical Explanations*

Consider the formulation of the grammatical problems (2), (26), (29), (33) and (38) above for which solutions are offered in the form of grammatical explanations. Notice that all these problems are formulated as "Why" questions.

(40)(a)   Why is it that, whereas the derived nominal *John's easiness to please* is unacceptable, the derived nominal *John's eagerness to please* is not unacceptable? (= (2))

(b)   Why is the English sentence *I disapprove of John's drinking* ambiguous? (= (26))

(c)   Why doesn't the sentence *I don't like John's cooking anymore than Bill's* have a mixed "fact/quality" interpretation? (= (33))

By asking such "Why" questions the grammarian is asking for reasons from which it will be clear that whatever it is that is problematic probably cannot be different.

Recall that the problematic phenomenon exists on the directly given level of products of linguistic performance: properties of classes of utterances, or sentences, as these properties are intuitively experienced by native speakers of the language. The general function of a GRAMMATICAL EXPLANATION is to give the reason(s) why certain classes of utterances, or sentences, probably must have the intuitive properties which they have. In other words, grammatical explanations account for the grammarian's primary linguistic data about the sentences of his language. Grammatical explanations therefore offer solutions to the fundamental types of grammatical problems which are formulated as follows in (4) of §4.3.1.1:

(41)(a)   How should the property P of the class of utterances U be explained?
   (b)   How should the similarity S between utterances of the class C_1 and utterances of the class C_2 be explained?
   (c)   How should the difference D between utterances of the class C_1 and utterances of the class C_2 be explained?

The grammatical explanations which account for the problematic properties of a class of utterances contribute to the grammarian's insight into (a) the way in which native speakers produce the utterances, (b) the way in which native speakers interpret the utterances and (c) the intuitive judgments which native speakers have about the utterances. It is against this background that Chomsky (1970:428) characterizes the function of a grammatical explanation as follows:

> . . . it suggests an explanation for the fact that (under the idealization mentioned) a speaker of the language in question will perceive, interpret, form or use an utterance in certain ways and not in other ways.

Here "the idealization mentioned" refers to that of the ideal speaker-hearer.

In recapitulation, a grammatical explanation may be characterized as follows in terms of its function: a grammatical explanation furnishes the reason(s) why sentences, or classes of utterances, of a particular human language must have the properties intuitively assigned to them by native speakers of the language. Recall that a class of utterances includes all those utterances which, for native speakers, are repetitions of one another.

7.3.2.2   *Structure of Grammatical Explanations*

Grammatical explanations have the logical structure of arguments. For instance, the grammatical explanation (3)(a) may be reconstructed as follows in the typical format of an argument:

(42)

EXPLANANS =

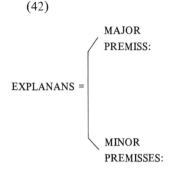

MAJOR PREMISS: If it is specified in the neutral lexical entry for a lexical item that this item may not take a sentential complement and if in a particular expression this item does take a sentential complement, then this expression is unacceptable.

MINOR PREMISSES:
1. In the neutral lexical entry for "easy" it is specified that "easy" may not take a sentential complement.
2. In the derived nominal *John's easiness to please* "easy", in the form of *easiness*, does occur with a sentential complement, viz. *to please*.

EXPLANANDUM = CONCLUSION: The derived nominal *John's easiness to please* is unacceptable.

It is clear from (42) that a grammatical explanation, too, may be analyzed as consisting of three main components: an explanans, an explanandum and a logical relation between the explanans and the explanandum. We shall consider these three structural components of grammatical explanations individually.

7.3.2.2.1   *The explanandum*

The explanandum of a grammatical explanation is a proposition which represents a problematic grammatical phenomenon such as

(43)(a)   the phenomenon that native speakers of English find *John's easiness to please* unacceptable – cf. (3)(a) above;

(b)   the phenomenon that native speakers of English find *I disapprove of John's drinking* ambiguous – cf. (27) above;

(c)   the phenomenon that native speakers of English find *I disapprove of John's excessive drinking the beer* unacceptable – cf. (30) above;

(d)   the phenomenon that native speakers of English find that *I don't like John's cooking any more than Bill's* cannot have a mixed "fact/quality" interpretation – cf. (34) above;

(e)   the phenomenon that native speakers of English find *Where does Mary live in New York and?* unacceptable – cf. (39)(a) above.

The explananda of (43) bring to the surface a certain problem which the grammarian encounters in his inquiry. This is the problem of the familiarity, the obviousness of problematic grammatical phenomena. Every native speaker makes intuitive linguistic judgments such as those given in (43)(a)–(e). He practically lives with such intuitive linguistic judgments from day to day. For this very reason he does not find these judgments "strange", "extraordinary", "abnormal", etc. The same applies to the grammarian as native speaker of the language he is investigating. At a first glance he does not find these judgments "strange", "extraordinary" or "abnormal" either. Grammarians – or, for that matter, people in general – find it difficult to perceive that familiar, obvious, ordinary phenomena can be problematic and call for an explanation. The familiarity of a phenomenon can effectively conceal its problematic nature. In his inquiry, the grammarian first has to overcome his familiarity with grammatical phenomena. As grammarian of the language in question he mentally has to place himself at a distance from the data about the language. He must consider them afresh, penetrate beneath their shell of familiarity and obviousness and discover their hidden problematic nature. Chomsky (1970:425) strikingly illustrates the familiarity of grammatical phenomena by means of the following analogy:

> The familiarity of phenomena can be so great that we really do not see them at all, a matter that has been much discussed by literary theorists and philosophers. For example, Viktor Shklovskij, in the early 1920s developed the idea that the function of poetic art is that of 'making strange' the object depicted. 'People living at the seashore grow so accustomed to the murmur of the waves that they never hear it. By the same token, we scarcely ever hear the words which we utter – We look at each other, but we do not see each other any more. Our perception of the world has withered away; what has remained is mere recognition.' Thus the goal of the artist is to transfer what is depicted to the 'sphere of new perception'; as an example, he cites a story by Tolstoy in which social customs and institutions are 'made strange' by the device of presenting them from the viewpoint of a narrator who happens to be a horse.

To be able to operate effectively, the grammarian therefore has to be continuously aware of the misleading familiarity of primary linguistic data.

Recall, in conclusion, that not every intuitive linguistic judgment may be assigned the status of a problematic grammatical phenomenon. It should be clear from the discussion in §4.3.2.2.2.2 that genuine linguistic intuitions alone fall within the domain of problematic data to be accounted for by grammatical explanations. In §7.4.6 we shall consider a strategy for determining whether or not a given intuitive linguistic judgment represents a genuine linguistic intuition. Employment of this strategy by the linguist has the effect of delimiting the explanatory domain of generative grammars.

7.3.2.2.2   *The explanans*
The explanans of a grammatical explanation gives the reasons for being of the

problematic phenomenon. It must be clear from these reasons why the sentences in question cannot have properties other than those which they in fact have. These reasons fall into the two classes which we discussed in §7.2.1.2: lawlike reasons and factual reasons.

7.3.2.2.2.1 *Lawlike reasons*   The lawlike reasons of grammatical explanations take the form of generalizations. We may therefore call them "lawlike generalizations". Such lawlike generalizations can take the form of "If . . . then" statements.

(44)(a) If it is specified in the neutral lexical entry for a lexical item that it may not take a sentential complement and if in a particular expression this item does take a sentential complement, then this expression is unacceptable – cf. (3)(a) and (42) above.

(b) If the grammatical rules of English assign more than one alternative deep structure to a sentence, then this sentence is ambiguous – cf. (27) above.

(c) If the grammatical rules of English generate two deep structures as alternatives, then they cannot undergo the same extensions – cf. (30) above.

(d) If the deletion transformation T_x violates the recoverability condition in the derivation of a given sentence, then this sentence is unacceptable in a given interpretation – cf. (34) above.

(e) If the movement transformation T_y violates the Coordinate Structure Constraint in the derivation of a given sentence, then this sentence is unacceptable – cf. (39)(a) above.

The "If" part of lawlike generalizations like those of (44) is known as the ANTECEDENT. The "then" part is known as the CONSEQUENT.

The first question which arises is: how does the grammarian come by the lawlike generalizations which he uses in his grammatical explanations? Looking at the generalizations of (44) it is clear that they are based on the content of grammars, or theoretical grammatical descriptions, and on the content of the general linguistic theory.

Consider the lawlike generalizations (44)(a)–(c). These three generalizations are based directly on the grammar of English. In (44)(a) the grammarian appeals to the content of particular lexical entries in the grammar of English. In (44)(b) and (c) the grammarian appeals to certain base rules of English. In these three lawlike generalizations language-particular laws are invoked in order to explain the problematic phenomena in question.

The lawlike generalizations (44)(d) and (e) are more complex. They are based both on the content of a (possible) language-particular rule and on the content of a principle contained in the general linguistic theory. The generalization (44)(d) is based on a language-particular deletion transformation T_x and the recoverability condition as substantive universal. The lawlike generalization

(44)(e), likewise, is based on a possible language-particular rule, the movement transformation T_y and a general linguistic principle, the Coordinate Structure Constraint. In these two lawlike generalizations an appeal is therefore made to both language-particular and universal laws to explain the problematic grammatical phenomena in question.

At this point we should note that a distinction is drawn between two types of grammatical explanations. A first type of grammatical explanation uses *mainly* language-particular laws to explain problematic grammatical phenomena. The grammatical explanations (3)(a), (3)(b), (27) and (30) are examples of this first type. The lawlike generalizations in these explanations are formulated in terms of language-particular rules and lexical entries. Grammatical explanations of this type explain the problematic properties of sentences by showing that the sentences must necessarily have these properties because the particular language in question is as it is.

Note that we say that grammatical explanations of the first type use *mainly* language-particular laws. The qualification "mainly" is used for a very particular reason. Recall that the general linguistic theory stipulates the type, form and organization of the rules and lexical entries in the grammars of the individual languages. In this way the general linguistic theory determines not only the possible types of language-particular laws, but also the form and organization of these laws. It then follows that the laws embodied in the formal and organizational universals play an indirect role in grammatical explanations of the first type. Such laws are by nature general linguistic or universal laws. To summarize: grammatical explanations of the first type appeal directly to language-particular laws. In addition, however, they appeal indirectly to universal laws as well. Therefore every grammatical explanation of the first type also has a general linguistic aspect. That is the reason for using the qualification "mainly" above.

The second type of grammatical explanation makes direct use not only of language-particular laws, but also of universal laws. The explanations (34), (39)(a) and (39)(b) belong to this type. For example, in (34) a direct appeal is made to the universal recoverability condition on deletion transformations. In (39)(a) and (b) a direct appeal is made to the universal Coordinate Structure Constraint. To summarize: grammatical explanations of the second type explain the problematic properties of sentences by asserting that part of the reason why sentences must have these properties is that language in general is as it is. In addition they appeal to language-particular laws, as appeared from our discussion of the structure of the lawlike generalizations (44)(d) and (e).

This brings us to a second question which arises in connection with the lawlike generalizations of grammatical explanations: in what respect are these generalizations lawlike? Language-particular lawlike generalizations are lawlike in that they specify what properties the sentences of individual human languages must of necessity have. For example, the base rules of English specify that the sentence *I disapprove of John's excessive drinking the beer* can but be ungrammatical. Thus language-particular laws do not merely represent summaries of the properties of a corpus of investigated utterances. They specify what must of necessity be the case with the sentences of individual languages.

Universal lawlike generalizations are lawlike in that they specify what properties individual human languages must have as manifestations of human language in general. For instance, the Coordinate Structure Constraint specifies that English, as a typical human language, cannot have a movement transformation which derives the sentence *Where does Mary live in New York and?*. By implication this universal law specifies that the interrogative sentence in question can but be ungrammatical.

A third question which arises in connection with the lawlike generalizations of grammatical explanations concerns the factors which contribute to the generality of these lawlike generalizations. Let us first look at universal lawlike generalizations such as those formulated in terms of the recoverability condition and the Coordinate Structure Constraint. Two factors contribute to the generality of these generalizations. The first factor is their universality. Universal lawlike generalizations never apply only to some subset of individual languages. The two general linguistic conditions concerned apply to all human languages. The second factor which contributes to the generality of such general linguistic conditions is their applicability to classes of grammatical rules. For example, the recoverability condition applies to all deletion transformations, not only to the one which operates in the derivation of sentences such as *I don't like John's cooking any more than Bill's*. And the Coordinate Structure Constraint applies to all transformations which move NPs, not only to *wh*-movement in English.

This brings us to the generality of language-particular lawlike generalizations. Once again there are two factors which contribute to the generality of these generalizations. The first is the factor of the comprehensiveness of the class of linguistic data about the language in question which fall within the domain of the generalization. The larger this class, the more general the generalization. Language-particular lawlike generalizations which are expressed in terms of grammatical rules are more general as a class than those which are expressed in terms of lexical entries. A lexical entry is, by its very nature, applicable to a smaller class of linguistic data than a grammatical rule.

The second factor contributing to the generality of language-particular lawlike generalizations is that of the systematic content of the grammatical concepts in terms of which the generalization is expressed. In § §6.3.2.2 and 6.3.3.1.3 the nature of the systematic content, or the systematic component in the content, of grammatical concepts was discussed. The larger the systematic content of the grammatical concepts in a language-particular lawlike generalization, the more general is this generalization. This implies, on the one hand, that it is possible for a given language-particular lawlike generalization as a whole to apply to a relatively small class of linguistic data, but at the same time to be quite general in that it is expressed in terms of grammatical concepts with considerable systematic content. The fact that a grammatical concept has a large systematic content indicates that it can be used to express a variety of language-particular lawlike generalizations. On the other hand, however, a language-particular lawlike generalization expressed in terms of one or more *ad hoc* grammatical concepts will be of limited generality.

7.3.2.2.2.2   *Factual reasons*   Factual reasons represent the second type of reasons contained in the explanans of a grammatical explanation. Let us consider a few examples of such reasons.

(45)(a)   (i)   In the neutral lexical entry for "easy" it is specified that "easy" may not take a sentential complement.

        (ii)   In the derived nominal *John's easiness to please* "easy", in the form of *easiness*, does take a sentential complement, *to please* – cf. (3)(a) and (42) above.

   (b)   (i)   In the grammar of English two alternative deep structures are assigned to the sentence *I disapprove of John's drinking.*

        (ii)   One of these determines a "fact that" interpretation, the other a "manner in which" interpretation – cf. (27) above.

   (c)   (i)   The grammar of English assigns two alternative deep structures to the sentence *I disapprove of John's drinking* – cf. (30) above.

        (ii)   The sentence **I disapprove of John's excessive drinking the beer* is derived by extending one of the deep structures in both of two alternative manners: the manner of the sentence *I disapprove of John's drinking the beer* and the manner of *I disapprove of John's excessive drinking* – cf. (30) above.

   (d)   (i)   The sentence *I don't like John's cooking any more than Bill's* is derived by applying a deletion transformation to the structure underlying the sentence *I don't like John's cooking any more than Bill's cooking* – cf. (34) above.

        (ii)   To be able to derive this sentence in such a way that it has a mixed "fact/quality" interpretation, this deletion transformation must violate the recoverability condition – cf. (34) above.

   (e)   (i)   In the derivation of the sentence **Where does Mary live in New York and?*, *wh*-movement, among other transformations, was applied – cf. (39)(a) above.

        (ii)   This transformation violates part (a) of the Coordinate Structure Constraint in that it moves an NP with the feature [+wh] out of the coordinate structure to the beginning of the sentence (where it is realized phonologically as the interrogative form *where*) – cf. (39)(a) above.

As part of the explanans of grammatical explanations, factual reasons such as the nine above operate as boundary conditions. These factual reasons contain data about the problematic phenomenon of the explanandum from which it must be clear that this phenomenon does indeed fall within the domain of the lawlike generalization of the explanans. Factual reasons are therefore reasons for applying a lawlike linguistic generalization to a problematic grammatical phenomenon.

We have seen that the problematic phenomenon of the explanandum is a sentence, or a class of utterances, which has some property or other which cannot be directly understood. Thus the data contained in the factual reasons of the explanans are data about sentences: data about structural properties (cf. (45)(a), (b), (c)(i)); data about the grammatical rules (cf. (c)(ii), (d)(i), (e)(i)) and general linguistic conditions (cf. (d)(ii), (e)(ii)) which are operative in the derivation of the sentences; etc. A factual reason may contain any datum which shows clearly that a problematic sentence falls within the domain of a lawlike generalization, be it a language-particular lawlike generalization, or a universal one.

7.3.2.2.2.3 *The logical relation*   Let us return to the grammatical explanation which was reconstructed in the form of the argument (42) above. Note that the argument is a deductive one: the conclusion is inferred from the premises by means of a logical rule of deduction. Given the content of the premises, the content of the explanandum necessarily follows. For instance, given that the interrogative sentence *Where does Mary live in New York and?* is derived with the aid of the *wh*-movement transformation and given that in the derivation of this interrogative sentence this transformation violates the Coordinate Structure Constraint, then it cannot but be concluded that this interrogative sentence must be unacceptable. The expression "follows" – cf. (26)(c) in §1.5 – is used to indicate a deductive relationship between two or more propositions.

The fact that the grammatical explanation in question may be reconstructed in the form of a deductive argument makes it a deductive explanation. The grammatical explanations given in linguistic inquiry are typically deductive explanations. Probabilistic explanations play no role in Chomskyan generative grammar. This implies, among other things, that statistical generalizations cannot be used as lawlike generalizations in grammatical explanations. For a typical example of a statistical generalization, compare (15)(c) in §7.2.1.2. It is Chomsky's point of view (1957:16ff.) that insight into the structure of human language(s) cannot be gained in statistical terms.

At this point a possible misunderstanding must be cleared up. In claiming that an explanandum necessarily follows from an explanans, two things are *not* being claimed. Firstly, it is not claimed that the propositions contained in the explanans are true. The nature of the logical relation between the explanandum and the explanans does not guarantee the correctness of these propositions. For instance, given the fact that the Coordinate Structure Constraint forms part of the explanans of the deductive explanations (39)(a) and (b), it does not follow that this general linguistic principle is correct. Propositions may also necessarily follow from false propositions. Secondly, it is not claimed that another, better explanation for the problematic phenomenon cannot be given. Should one or more of the propositions in the explanans of a deductive explanation be false, then this explanation – despite its deductive character – would be unacceptable. Even if all the propositions in the explanans of a deductive explanation were true, then it would still be possible to find better alternatives for this explanation. This brings us to the minimal and additional criteria for grammatical explanations.

7.3.2.3   *Minimal Criteria for Grammatical Explanations*

The grammatical explanations of linguistic inquiry must satisfy the minimal criteria for scientific explanations in general. On the one hand, there are the minimal formal criteria. A set of propositions about an individual human language represents a grammatical explanation only if it satisfies the formal criteria of (46).

(46)(a)   One (or more) of the propositions must function as the explanandum.
   (b)   The other propositions must jointly function as the explanans.
   (c)   It must be possible to state a logical rule in terms of which the explanandum may be inferred from the explanans.

On the other hand, there are the minimal material criteria. Two of these apply to the lawlike generalizations of the explanans.

(47)(a)   Thorough testing may not have shown the lawlike generalization in question to be (probably) false.
   (b)   It must be possible to furnish reasons why the lawlike generalization in question is probably true.

The nature of the testing referred to in (47)(a) is dealt with in chapter 10. What is involved in furnishing the reasons of (47)(b) will be discussed in chapter 9.

The material criteria of (47) imply that grammatical and general linguistic principles that are used in lawlike generalizations must be psychologically real. This point is formulated by Chomsky and Katz (1974:365) with the aid of an analogy:

> . . . to explain observable effects like the change of the color of water when dye is put in it in terms of the migration of dye molecules commits scientists to the reality of the unobserved causal conditions, since such explanations make sense only if we adopt the realistic assumption that the theoretical terms in which they are couched actually refer to things in nature. If one were to say that the term 'molecule' in the foregoing explanation is a mere *façon de parler*, that it denotes nothing real, the 'explanation' would become nonsense. These considerations are quite general, applying to linguistic explanations as much as to explanations in physics. We postulate certain properties of the brain, e.g., that it must contain some neural mechanisms that store the

information in the grammar, on the grounds that properties of linguistic behaviour can be explained by assuming them to be causal consequences of brain mechanisms with access to such infomation. To explain the grammatical judgments of speakers on the basis of such a hypothesized causal chain while denying the existence of essential links in the chain makes no more sense than to explain diffusion while denying the existence of molecules.

Recall Rescher's distinction between actual and possible explanations, which was mentioned in §7.2.1.4. This distinction may be applied as follows to the point of view of Chomsky and Katz cited above: a grammatical explanation which is based on a linguistic principle which may be assumed to be psychologically real, represents an ACTUAL GRAMMATICAL EXPLANATION; a grammatical explanation which is based on a linguistic principle of which it is unclear whether it is psychologically real or not, represents a POSSIBLE GRAMMATICAL EXPLANATION. Note also that it is quite clear from the quotation above that for Chomsky and Katz linguistic explanations in general, and grammatical explanations in particular, are CAUSAL EXPLANATIONS.

A third material criterion applies to the factual reasons in the explanans of grammatical explanations.

(48)   The accuracy of the data contained in the factual reasons must be beyond reasonable doubt.

This criterion implies that the data in question must have the status of facts.

7.3.2.4   *Additional Criteria for Grammatical Explanations*

As may be expected, linguistic inquiry is not primarily interested in giving minimally adequate explanations. Grammarians want to give the most adequate explanations possible. To ensure that their explanations are as adequate as possible, grammarians adopt a number of additional criteria for these explanations. We shall consider two of these at this point in our study.

The first additional criterion for grammatical explanations is a criterion of generality.

(49)   The greater the generality of the lawlike generalization in the explanans, the better the grammatical explanation.

Understanding of a problematic phenomenon involves, among other things, insight into its relationship with other, seemingly unrelated phenomena. To show that a problematic phenomenon falls within the domain of a lawlike generalization is to show not only that, but also how this phenomenon is related to other phenomena. Therefore, the more general a lawlike generalization, the larger the class of phenomena for which it specifies mutual relationships. This explains why grammarians continuously strive to find the most general lawlike generalizations possible for their grammatical explanations. For example, Chomsky (1970: 431–432) argues that the processes, i.e. the grammatical rules, in terms of which the ambiguity of *I disapprove of John's drinking* may be explained are quite general:

> The processes that are involved in examples (4)–(6) [our (23)–(25) above – R.P.B.] are quite general in English. Thus the sentence 'I disapprove of John's cooking' may be understood as indicating either that I think his wife should cook or that I think he uses too much garlic, and so on. Again the ambiguity is resolved if we extend the sentence in the manner indicated in (5) and (6).

Chomsky uses this argumentation in an effect to show that his grammatical explanation (27) must be judged favourably in terms of the criterion of generality stated above.

Chomsky (1970:433ff.) uses a similar argument in relation to the grammatical explanation (34). More specifically, he attempts to show that the recoverability condition represents a rather general principle. The same condition may be invoked to explain, for instance, the limited ambiguity of a sentence such as *I know a taller man than Bill, and so does John*. Recall, in conclusion, that we considered three factors which contribute to the generality of the lawlike generalizations of grammatical explanations in §7.3.2.2.2.1.

The second additional criterion for grammatical explanations is a criterion of depth.

(50)   The deeper a grammatical explanation, the better the explanation.

But what is to be understood under "the depth of a grammatical explanation"? The DEPTH of a grammatical explanation is determined by the degree of fundamentality of the lawlike generalization(s) in the explanans. In linguistic inquiry a lawlike generalization which holds for human language in general is more fundamental than one which is valid for one or a few individual languages only. For instance, a lawlike generalization which is formulated in terms of the Co-ordinate Structure Constraint is more fundamental than one which is formulated in terms of only one rule from the grammar of English.

Suppose that two alternative grammatical explanations, Explanation A and Explanation B, could be given for a certain problematic grammatical phenomenon, say, the unacceptability of a given sentence. Explanation A accounts for the phenomenon in question with the aid of a lawlike generalization formulated in terms of a rule of the language in question. Explanation B, on the other hand, explains the phenomenon in question with the aid of a lawlike generalization formulated in terms of a general linguistic principle as well. In terms of the crition (50), Explanation B is a better explanation than Explanation A. The former explanation has greater depth than the latter. Explanation A shows that the grammatical phenomenon in question must be as it is because one individual language is as it is. Explanation B, on the other hand, shows that the grammatical phenomenon in question must be as it is because human language in general is as it is.

7.3.2.5   *Theoretical Descriptions and Grammatical Explanations*

We have seen that grammatical explanations account for problematic grammatical phenomena in terms of both language-particular rules and lexical entries and general linguistic principles. On the one hand, these rules, lexical entries and principles function as laws in the lawlike generalization of such explanations. On the other hand, the factual reasons given in such explanations may also refer to these rules, lexical entries and principles. In chapter 6 we saw that theoretical grammatical descriptions are composed of language-particular rules and lexical entries and that theoretical general linguistic descriptions are composed of general linguistic principles or linguistic universals. This poses the question of the relationship between theoretical linguistic — grammatical and general linguistic — descriptions and grammatical explanations. In what ways do these descriptions and explanations differ?

Let us approach this question by looking at a concrete example. In §6.1 we considered an example of a (fragment of) a theoretical grammatical description which is repeated as (51) below.

(51)   The lexicon contains a single lexical entry for "refuse". In this single lexical entry are specified the fixed syntactic properties of "refuse", viz. those selectional and subcategorization features which "refuse" manifests in all expressions in which it occurs. What is not specified in this single lexical entry for "refuse", however, is whether "refuse" is a verb or a noun. The lexical entry is neutral in that "refuse" is unspecified in terms of those syntactic properties which distinguish verbs from nouns. This entails that the lexical item "refuse" can be inserted in deep structures both under the node V and the node N. When "refuse" is inserted under the node V in a deep structure, it has the phonological form *refuse.* If, on the other hand, "refuse" is inserted under the node N, it will have the phonological form *refusal.* Morphological rules specify the appropriate phonological form of "refuse".

Chomsky offered this fragment of a theoretical grammatical description as part of a grammatical explanation, viz. his grammatical explanation for the existence of certain syntactic similarities between the sentence *John has refused the offer* and the derived nominal *John's refusal of the offer.* The syntactic similarities in question were given as (10) and (11) in §1.1. The grammatical explanation with which we are concerned may be reconstructed as (52).

(52)   MaP : If a verb and a noun are specified in the grammar of English in terms of a neutral lexical entry, then sentences containing this verb and nominal expressions containing this noun exhibit syntactic similarities of the type S.

MiP : 1. In the grammar of English the lexical entry of (51) is assigned to the verb *refuse* and the noun *refusal.*

2. The derived nominal *John's refusal of the offer*, in which *refusal* appears as noun, corresponds to the sentence *John has refused the offer*, in which *refuse* appears as verb.

C   : The sentence *John has refused the offer* and the derived nominal *John's refusal of the offer* exhibit syntactic similarities of the type S.

In (52) and other similar reconstructions of arguments, the symbols "MaP", "MiP" and "C" refer to the major premiss(es), minor premiss(es) and conclusion respectively. "Syntactic similarities of the type S" in (52) denotes the selectional features illustrated by (10) and (11) in §1.1.

But let is compare the theoretical grammatical description (51) with the grammatical explanation (52). It is obvious that the description and the explanation in question are not identical. A first difference relates to their function. The grammatical explanation gives an answer to a "Why" question: Why do the sentence *John has refused the offer* and the derived nominal *John's refusal of the offer* exhibit syntactic similarities of the type S? In answer to this question, the grammatical explanation (52) furnishes three interrelated reasons: one lawlike reason and two factual reasons. The theoretical grammatical description, on the other hand, does not answer such a "Why" question. Consequently, this description is not composed of reasons. It then follows that theoretical grammatical descriptions lack the lawlike aspect which is characteristic of grammatical explanations. It is not clear from these descriptions why the linguistic competence must have the structure which it in fact has, whereas it is quite clear from grammatical explanations why sentences or classes of utterances must necessarily have the properties which they have.

A second difference relates to the object at which the theoretical grammatical description (51) is directed, as opposed to the object at which the grammatical description (52) is directed. The explanation is directed at a problematic phenomenon on the directly-given level of the grammarian's linguistic reality. It is concerned with the explanation of problematic properties of sentences as these are manifested in (classes of) products of linguistic performance. The description, on the other hand, is directed at the linguistic competence on the underlying level of the grammarian's linguistic reality. The description gives a conceptual representation of the content and structure of a small part of this mental capacity.

A third difference relates to the structure of the theoretical grammatical description (51) and that of the grammatical explanation (52) respectively. The grammatical explanation is composed of an explanandum and an explanans which are related in terms of a deductive logical relation. The theoretical grammatical description is not structured in the same way. Notice that the theoretical grammatical description forms part of the antecedent of the lawlike generalization in the grammatical explanation. Thus, the grammatical explanation accounts for the problematic phenomenon in terms of, among other things, a theoretical description of an aspect of an underlying mental capacity. The grammatical explanation shows how something which is problematic at the level of (classes of) products of linguistic performance may be understood in terms of the content and structure of a mental capacity which plays a central role in their production. Generative grammarians such as Chomsky and Katz (1974:365) therefore regard products of linguistic performance as "effects". The linguistic competence is accordingly represented as a mechanism which has a causal function with regard to these "effects". We have already seen that to explain a problematic phenomenon in terms of a possible cause is to give a causal explanation for this phenomenon. Moreover, it is by this time quite clear that grammatical explanations belong to the type of explanations which relate two levels of a complex reality. §7.2.1.6 above may be reread against this background.

A fourth difference between the theoretical grammatical description (51) and the grammatical explanation (52) relates to their finer logical organization. The grammatical explanation is a set of propositions arranged in terms of a major premiss, minor premisses and a conclusion. The conclusion follows from the major and minor premisses in terms of a logical rule of deduction. The theoretical grammatical description, on the other hand, does not display the same finer logical organization. It is merely a set of propositions which are mutually related in terms of the logical relation of conjunction: "and"/"as well . . . as".

In linguistic inquiry these four differences serve to distinguish between theoretical grammatical descriptions and grammatical explanations. Having thus clearly drawn this distinction, it is obviously misleading to say that a generative grammar explains problematic grammatical phenomena. A generative grammar is nothing but a theoretical grammatical description and as such cannot explain problematic grammatical phenomena. It is possible though, that a grammarian may use fragments of generative grammars in his grammatical explanations. In particular, a fragment of a generative grammar may form the core of the lawlike generalization in the explanans. But then it would still be only one part of the grammatical explanation. In short, a generative grammar as such explains nothing. However, a grammarian may use fragments of such a grammar as parts of his grammatical explanations. Chomsky (1970:464) agrees with this point of view:

I would be prepared to accept Professor Black's argument that a grammar, like

Kepler's laws, provides a codification of certain facts. Like Kepler's laws, this codification can play a role in explanation of phenomena. We can use Kepler's laws to explain why a planet occupies a certain position (given an earlier state of the system), and we can use the rules of English grammar to explain why a person understands a certain sentence to be ambiguous.

The expression "codification" is used here in the same sense as our expression "theoretical description".

7.3.3   Giving Grammatical Explanations

We have not yet said anything about the second main point in connection with grammatical explanations. This second point relates to the question of the intellectual activities involved in giving grammatical explanations. Generally speaking, to give a grammatical explanation is to argue or to reason. The giving of grammatical explanations may be described as follows in terms of the various activities involved:

(53)   The grammarian gives a grammatical explanation by
    (a)   presenting an explanandum containing one or more sentences and one or more problematic properties of each of these sentences;
    (b)   presenting an explanans containing
        (i)   a lawlike reason, formulated in terms of a fragment of a grammar (and in certain cases a fragment of the general linguistic theory), in terms of which the aforementioned sentences must necessarily have the properties which they have; and
        (ii)   one or more factual reasons – data about structural properties of the sentences involved – from which it must be clear that these sentences do indeed fall within the domain of the lawlike reason of (b);
    (c)   indicating the logical rule in terms of which the explanandum may be inferred from the explanans.

Note that in (53) the expression "sentences" is used as a synonym for "sentences or constituents of sentences".

It should be quite clear from our discussion of the nature of grammatical explanations, what is involved in each of the activities mentioned in (53). We shall therefore not illustrate these activities by giving more examples.

A topic which does deserve some attention, though, is that of the relationship between giving theoretical grammatical descriptions and giving grammatical explanations. In linguistic inquiry these two activities are tightly interwoven. On the one hand, giving grammatical explanations involves working with the products of both grammatical and general linguistic description. This point was discussed in some detail when we considered the source of the lawlike generalizations used in grammatical explanations.

On the other hand, in constructing a grammatical description, the grammarian is constantly aware of the fact that it must be possible to use the product of his description in the giving of grammatical explanations. In other words, in constructing theoretical grammatical descriptions, the grammarian takes into account the criterion that these descriptions must have explanatory power. This criterion is taken into account when the grammarian forms the grammatical concepts of which theoretical grammatical descriptions are composed. As we saw in the previous chapter, grammatical concepts must satisfy the criteria repeated here as (54).

(54)(a) Grammatical concepts must make it possible to explain the problematic primary linguistic data about the language with the aid of the grammar of that language (= (22) in §6.3.3.1.1).

(b) Grammatical concepts must make it possible to express the linguistically significant generalizations about a language (= (23) in §6.3.3.1.1).

(c) The language-specific content of grammatical concepts must as far as possible be systematic (= (25) in §6.3.3.1.1).

(d) The general linguistic content of grammatical concepts must be as large as possible (= 27) in §6.3.3.1.1).

Each of these four criteria contributes to the explanatory power of theoretical grammatical descriptions. The first criterion ensures that fragments of these descriptions may be used as lawlike reasons in the explanans of grammatical explanations. The second, third and fourth criteria ensure that these lawlike reasons will have the desired generality. Finally, the fourth criterion has an additional function: it contributes to the depth of grammatical explanations.

7.4 GENERAL LINGUISTIC INQUIRY

7.4.1 General

Recall that grammatical explanations provide answers to questions of the following general type:

(55) Why does the sentence S in the particular language L have the property P?

The problematic phenomena at which grammatical explanations are directed are the sentences, or classes of utterances, of a particular human language. GENERAL LINGUISTIC EXPLANATIONS, on the other hand, are directed at the problematic properties of (the grammars of) individual languages. They provide answers to questions of the following general type:

(56)   Why does the language L, as it is described in the grammar G, have the property P?

We shall refer to general linguistic explanations which provide answers to questions of the general form (56) by the expression "internal explanations". The reason for using this expression will become clear in §7.4.4.

7.4.2   Levels of Adequacy of Linguistic Theories

The nature of internal explanations is determined by a distinction which was initially drawn by Chomsky. Chomsky distinguishes three levels of success or adequacy for linguistic theories: observational, descriptive and explanatory adequacy.

7.4.2.1   *Observational Adequacy*

OBSERVATIONAL ADEQUACY represents the lowest level of adequacy which a grammar can attain.

(57)   A grammar is observationally adequate if it presents the observed primary data correctly. (Chomsky 1964:28)

Suppose that the primary linguistic data comprised the set of utterances (58) and the associated intuitive judgments about them.

(58)(a)   *John is easy to please.*
  (b)   *John's being easy to please*
  (c)   **John's easiness to please*

What would an observationally adequate grammar of (58) look like? In order to be observationally adequate a grammar need only specify — for instance in the form of a list — that (58)(a) is an acceptable utterance in English, that (58)(b) is an acceptable utterance in English and that (58)(c) is an unacceptable utterance in English.

7.4.2.2   *Descriptive Adequacy*

DESCRIPTIVE ADEQUACY is a higher level of adequacy for grammars. As, among others, Bach (1974a:238) and Peters (1970) have shown, Chomsky gives various definitions of the content of the concept 'descriptive adequacy'. We have chosen the one which fits in best with his mentalistic view of a grammar.

(59)   A grammar is descriptively adequate to the extent that it is psycho-logically real, i.e. to the extent that it correctly describes the intrinsic competence of the idealized native speaker (Chomsky 1965:24).

The criterion (59) entails among other things, that the grammar may not merely present a limited corpus of primary data about the language. According to (59), it must generate all the sentences of the language in terms of psychologically real rules (and lexical entries). In order to be psychologically real, these rules must – as we have seen in §6.3.2.3.2 – in some way or other represent elements of the structure of the linguistic competence. According to Chomsky, a grammar's success in expressing linguistically significant generalizations gives an indication of its descriptive adequacy. Therefore, a grammar which does not succeed in expressing the linguistically significant generalizations about the language, does not attain the level of descriptive adequacy.

7.4.2.3   *Explanatory Adequacy*

Observational and descriptive adequacy apply primarily to grammars. EXPLA-NATORY ADEQUACY, on the other hand, respresents a level of success for a general linguistic theory.

(60)   A general linguistic theory is explanatorily adequate if it provides some principled basis for selecting among all the grammars of a given language which are consistent with the available data about the language, the descriptively adequate grammar for that language (Chomsky 1964:28).

Both a grammarian investigating a language and a child acquiring a language can construct alternative grammars for the language on the basis of the available data about the language. The alternative grammars constructed by the grammarian take the form of alternative theoretical descriptions of the language. The alternative grammars constructed by the child, on the other hand, take the form of alternative linguistic competences or internalized grammars of the language. But there is but one psychologically real grammar of the language and the child can have but one internalized grammar of the language. Therefore, both the grammarian and the child who is acquiring a language must select "the grammar" of the language from among the alternative grammars. A general linguistic theory has attained the level of explanatory adequacy (a) if it provides the grammarian with a principled basis for selecting the psychologically real, or descriptively adequate, grammar for the language and (b) if this principled basis also gives an accurate representation of the way in which the child actually selects "the internalized grammar" from among the various alternatives that are consistent with his linguistic experience.

In order to be explanatorily adequate, the general linguistic theory must therefore provide an answer to the general question formulated as follows by Emmon Bach (1974a:239):

(61)   Why do speakers of a language have the grammars that they have?

In our discussion below, we shall more or less adhere to Bach's (1974a:240ff.; 1974b:156ff.) method of dealing with the nature of internal explanations.

To enable him to develop a general linguistic theory which is explanatorily adequate, Chomsky breaks down the problem (61) into two subquestions.

(62)(a)   What is the class of grammars from which the child chooses the grammar of his language?

(b)   How does the child select from this class the correct grammar for his language?

The general linguist attempts to answer the question (62)(a) by developing a general linguistic theory which includes a rich set of linguistic universals. Each universal restricts the class of grammars from which the child selects the grammar of his language. For instance, the recoverability condition of (34) above excludes from this class all grammars containing deletion transformations which violate this condition. The richer the set of linguistic universals, the smaller the class of grammars from which the child has to select the grammar of his language. In answer to the question (62)(b), the general linguist develops an EVALUATION PROCEDURE as part of the general linguistic theory. This evaluation procedure must provide the grammarian and the child with a basis for selecting the correct grammar for the language from the limited class of possible grammars. The evaluation procedure is designed so as to make it possible to choose as the descriptively adequate grammar of the language, the linguistic grammar which is most successful in expressing linguistically significant generalizations. For the grammarian, therefore, "descriptively adequate" in practice means "most highly valued in terms of the ability to express linguistically significant generalizations". A discussion of the technical content of the evaluation procedure falls outside the scope of our study.

What is involved in giving an internal explanation for a particular problematic property of (the grammar of) a language? There are two complementary ways –

corresponding to the questions (62)(a) and (b) – in which an internal explanation may be given for such a property. On the one hand, the property may be explained by showing that there is a linguistic universal which specifies that human language in general should have this property. The individual language in question then has the property in question, because this language is a realization of human language in general. On the other hand, the problematic property may be accounted for by showing that it is highly valued by the evaluation procedure as a property of human language in general.

7.4.3 Sample of an Internal Explanation

Let us consider an example of a general linguistic explanation given in the first of the two ways mentioned above. Central to Chomsky's lexicalist grammar of English is the claim that English lacks a particular grammatical rule, viz. a nominalization transformation which would produce derived nominals on the basis of roughly the same deep structure as that from which corresponding sentences are derived. In §1.2 we saw how such a rule operated in Lees's grammar of English nominalizations. The general linguist may find the absence of the transformation in question from the grammar of English problematic. English does, after all, contain a transformation of gerundive nominalization. Is the absence of a transformation of derived nominalization to be regarded as an idiosyncratic property of English? Or could the absence of this transformation from the grammar of English perhaps be understood in terms of a principle which applies to human language in general? These questions give rise to the following general linguistic problem:

(63) Why doesn't (the [child's] grammar of) English contain a transformation of derived nominalization?

The answer to this question may take the form of an internal explanation.

It is of course possible, in principle, to conceive of a number of alternative explanations in answer to the question (63). One such explanation might very well be that of (64).

(64) The recoverability condition rules out as impossible in human language all deletion transformations which delete elements from an underlying P-marker so that these elements are no longer recoverable on the basis of the correlating more superficial P-marker. Formulated as a general rule, a transformation of nominalization in English would have to delete elements in the derivation of (many) derived nominals. These deletions are such that the deleted element is no longer recoverable. For this reason there is no transformation of derivative nominalization in the most highly valued grammar of English.

The general linguistic explanation (64) is presented, not as an actual or a good explanation for the problematic property of English in question, but as a typical example of an internal explanation.

One aspect of the explanation (64) needs to be elucidated: the fact that a transformation of derivative nominalization in English would have to perform inadmissible deletions. This particular property of the transformation in question is related to the fact that a large number of derived nominals are both syntactically and semantically irregular. The implications of this point were discussed in detail in §§1.4 and 4.3.2.1.2. Recall, for instance, that the derived nominal (65)(a) does not have the meaning of (65)(b), but that of (65)(c).

(65)(a)   *John's deeds*
   (b)   *things which John did*
   (c)   *fairly significant things which John did*

Given the assumption that transformations are meaning-preserving, the derived nominal (65)(a) cannot be derived from a structure underlying (65)(b). On the contrary, under this assumption a transformation should exist which must derive this nominal from a structure such as that underlying (65)(c). Note that the transformation which does this must, among other things, delete the underlying element "fairly significant". And the structure of *John's deeds* offers no basis on which this deleted element may be recovered. The deletion therefore violates the recoverability condition. Chomsky (1972b:19–20, n.10) discuss numerous similar cases in which this particular condition is violated. In (72) of §9.3.2.3.2 it will be shown that the syntactic irregularity of derived nominals poses a similar problem for the recoverability condition. More examples of internal explanations are given by Emmon Bach in his article "Explanatory inadequacy" (1974b: 158ff.). Bach's examples are more authentic from a purely linguistic point of view than the one discussed above. But they are, at the same time, far more complicated and therefore require more knowledge of general linguistics than is required for purposes of our study.

7.4.4   Structure of Internal Explanations

The structure of internal explanations such as that of (64) is similar to that of the grammatical explanations which we considered in §7.3. This becomes quite clear if we reconstruct the internal explanation (64) as follows:

(66)

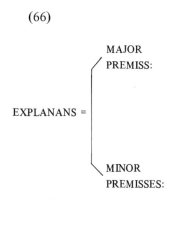

EXPLANANS =

MAJOR PREMISS:

If a deletion transformation deletes elements from an underlying P-marker so as to make it impossible to recover these elements on the basis of a corresponding more superficial structure, then this transformation does not occur in any human language.

MINOR PREMISSES:

1. A transformation of nominalization would, in the case of many derived nominals in English, have to perform deletions.
2. The deletions which the nominalization transformation would have to perform would be such that the deleted elements would not be recoverable.

EXPLANDUM = CONCLUSION: A transformation of derived nominalization does not occur in English.

In the explanandum of a typical internal explanation, a problematic property of the (grammar of) an individual human language is stated. The explanans presents reasons in terms of which this problematic property may be understood. One of these reasons takes the form of a lawlike generalization. In (66) above the lawlike generalization is formulated in terms of the recoverability condition on deletion transformations. To use linguistic universals in such lawlike generalizations, is typical of internal explanations. This typical characteristic accounts for our calling general linguistic explanations INTERNAL EXPLANATIONS. The lawlike generalizations used in these explanations are internal to, or derived from, a general linguistic theory. In other words, the lawlike generalizations of these explanations are linguistic generalizations.

Let us take a look at the criteria for the lawlike generalizations which are used in general linguistic explanations. In his recent paper "A theory of core grammar" (1978:16), Chomsky stresses the point that these generalizations may not represent mere "descriptive catalogues". A descriptive catalogue expresses "a certain empirical generalization over observed structures". For Chomsky (1978:23), Ross's Complex Noun Phrase Constraint and Wh-Island-Constraint represent typical cases of such descriptive catalogues:

They merely say that constructions of this or that type are ungrammatical . . . generalizations of that sort do not enter into explanations. They leave open the question why this or that should be so.

Chomsky (1978:16) explicitly formulates two criteria which the principles expressed in the lawlike generalizations required in general linguistic explanations should meet:

a. they ought to be natural as principles of mental computation, b. they ought to be genuinely explanatory in that they unify a variety of such [i.e., descriptive – R.P.B.] generalizations and ground them in a system that has a certain degree of deductive structure.

Chomsky's first criterion expresses the requirement that the principles in question should be psychologically real. In §7.3.2.3 we saw that this criterion holds for the principles involved in grammatical explanations as well. The second criterion formulated by Chomsky is complex in the sense that it can be broken down into several more elementary criteria, including those relating to the generality and modal character of the lawlike generalizations under consideration. These more elementary criteria were considered in §7.2.1.2 in the context of empirical inquiry in general. Notice, incidentally, that Chomsky (1978:17–18) claims that his principle of subjacency satisfies both these criteria:

Thus the principle meets the condition of being a genuine unifying principle (condition b), that is, a number of island constraints can be deduced from it. It is furthermore a natural principle (condition a), that is, it makes sense to suppose that mental computation is restricted by principles that limit the range over which such calculation applies.

The aforementioned article by Chomsky may be consulted for his principle of subjacency as well as for Ross's Complex Noun Phrase Constraint and Island-Constraints.

In addition to the lawlike reason, the explanans contains one or more factual reasons. The function of these factual reasons is to present data about the problematic phenomenon in question from which it must be clear that this phenomenon does indeed fall within the domain of the lawlike generalization. Note also that, in the case of the internal explanation (66), the explanandum is deductively inferred from the explanans. Internal explanations, too, are deductive explanations.

In an internal explanation a problematic property of one mental capacity – an internalized grammar, or linguistic competence – is explained in terms of properties of another, more fundamental mental capacity – the language acquisition faculty. In these internal explanations the function of the lawlike generalizations – as part of the general linguistic theory – is primarily to describe the structure and content of man's language acquisition faculty. Internal explanations therefore have the following general tenet: that a particular (internalized) grammar should have the properties that it has is necessary, because man's language acquisition faculty has the properties which it has.

7.4.5   External Explanations

We have seen that general linguistic explanations, as internal explanations, are explanations on a deeper level than grammatical explanations. Grammatical explanations, with the aid especially of grammars, account for the problematic properties of sentences of an individual language. Internal explanations penetrate to a deeper level. With the aid of lawlike generalizations about language in general, they account for the problematic properties of grammars. It is possible to penetrate to a still deeper level and to consider the properties of human language in general as problematic. Why, for example, does human language in general have a structural element known as "the recoverability condition"? To answer such questions the linguist has to give an explanation of a problematic linguistic phenomenon at an even deeper level. For reasons which will soon be clear, explanations at this even deeper level are called "external explanations" in linguistic inquiry.

External explanations provide answers to questions of the following general type:

(67)   Why does human language in general, as it is described in the general linguistic theory T, have the property P?

EXTERNAL EXPLANATIONS are therefore explanations of general linguistic principles, or linguistic universals. We may also say that external explanations are explanations of problematic aspects of the content of general linguistic theories. In other words, external explanations attempt to show why man's language faculty must of necessity have the properties which it has. The three levels at which linguistic phenomena can be explained may be schematically represented as follows:

(68)   LEVELS OF EXPLANATION

level	explained phenomenon	explanatory mechanism
grammatical explanation	properties of sentences	lawlike generalizations about linguistic competence
internal (general linguistic) explanation	properties of linguistic competence	lawlike generalizations about language acquisition faculty
external explanation	properties of language acquisition faculty	lawlike generalizations about ???

This schema has been oversimplified in various ways. The most obvious over-simplification is the fact that in the topmost square of the righthand column no mention is made of the role of general linguistic principles in grammatical explanation.

The most interesting part of this schema is the last square in the righthand column, i.e. the one with the three question marks. The question is this: in terms of what type(s) of lawlike generalizations can the problematic properties of the language acquisition faculty or the general linguistic theory be explained? For instance, in terms of what considerations can an explanation be given of the fact that the recoverability condition is part of the general linguistic theory? It goes without saying that the general linguist cannot explain such general linguistic principles in terms of other general linguistic principles. He cannot account for certain problematic properties of the language acquisition faculty in terms of other problematic properties of the language acquisition faculty. To explain these problematic properties, the general linguist has to look beyond his two-levelled linguistic reality in an attempt to find explanatory principles.

This general linguists in fact often do. They turn to anatomy, physiology, neurology, perception psychology, cognitive psychology, and so on in their quest for lawlike generalizations in terms of which the problematic properties of the language acquisition faculty may be explained. These lawlike generalizations are, strictly speaking, nonlinguistic. They are external to the linguistic reality and linguistic theories of the generative grammarian. It is for this reason that the explanations given in terms of these lawlike generalizations are known as "external explanations".

In a certain sense it is quite natural to seek an external explanation of problematic aspects of the language acquisition faculty, or human language in general. Human language is not an isolated system, but interacts with a large number of other, nonlinguistic systems. In other words, the linguistic reality of the generative grammarian is integrated with a number of other realities in a larger reality. It is to be expected that these realities will influence one another and, therefore, that properties of the one may be understood in terms of properties of the other. For instance, a certain anatomical mechanism — the vocal tract — is needed in oral language use. It is quite conceivable that certain properties of human language should be as they are because this vocal tract has definite possibilities and definite limitations. In other words, there may be anatomical explanations for certain properties of human language in general. These constitute external explanations in terms of anatomical principles.

Successful oral use of human language also requires the processing of utterances with the aid of the human perception mechanisms. Once again, it is quite conceivable that certain properties of human language in general must be as they are because man's perception mechanisms have the possibilities and limitations which they have. This opens up the possibility of giving perceptual explanations for problematic properties of human language in general. These would constitute external explanations in terms of perceptual principles. Neurological, cognitive and various other kinds of nonlinguistic principles may be used in an analogous way in lawlike generalizations of the explanantia of external explanations of problematic properties of language in general.

Let us consider a simple example of a possible external explanation. Our problem is the following:

(69)   Why does human language in general have a structural element known as "the recoverability condition"?

An external explanation such as that of (70) may be offered in answer to this question.

(70)   For purposes of the perceptual processing of speech it is desirable that there be as little difference as possible between the surface structure and the deep structure of a sentence. The function of the recoverability condition is to limit the possible differences between the surface and deep structure of sentences. For this reason human language in general has a structural element known as "the recoverability condition".

Notice that the explanation (70) is a perceptual explanation. It makes use of a lawlike generalization incorporating a perceptual principle to account for an aspect of human language in general.

Note that the external explanation (70) makes use of the expressions "purposes" and "function". The use of these expressions gives an indication of the general form of explanation with which we are dealing here, viz. TELEOLOGICAL or FUNCTIONAL EXPLANATION. In explanations of this form, something is explained in terms of its purpose or function. The existence of the recoverability condition is explained, in the example above, in terms of its supposed function in speech perception. Whether this explanation has substantive merit does not concern us here. It is given merely to illustrate a particular form of explanation. In his article "Explanation in phonology" (1972), Paul Kiparsky argues that in linguistic inquiry functional explanations are relevant at the level of grammatical explanation as well. We cannot discuss Kiparsky's argument here, as it requires a considerable amount of knowledge of generative phonology. A similar consideration makes it impossible here to outline Chomsky's view of the status of functional explanations. This view is explicated in the article "Filters and control" (1977:436–438) authored jointly by Chomsky and Lasnik. Finally, the Chicago Linguistic Society's volume *Functionalism* (= Grossman, San and Vance (eds.) 1975), contains numerous examples of linguistic explanations which could be called "functional".

7.4.6   A Strategy for Assessing the Genuineness of Linguistic Intuitions

We saw in §4.3.2.2.2.2 that not all intuitive linguistic judgments of native speakers represent genuine linguistic intuitions. Only those intuitive linguistic judgments that reflect an aspect of the content and structure of native speakers' linguistic competence represent genuine linguistic intuitions. Intuitive linguistic judgments which are the result of nonlinguistic factors operating in linguistic performance do not represent genuine linguistic intuitions. These nonlinguistic factors which are at the root of spurious linguistic intuitions include, among others, the factors of perceptual complexity, perceptual contrast, articulatory complexity, context/situation and knowledge of the world. As spurious linguistic intuitions shed no light on the native speaker's linguistic competence, generative grammarians are forced to exclude them from their corpus of primary linguistic data.

We saw in §4.3.2.2.2.2 that the grammarian is faced with a problem of evaluation. He must decide, in principle, for every intuitive linguistic judgment which he comes across in his investigation, whether or not it represents a genuine linguistic intuition. In other words, to be able to include an intuitive linguistic judgment J in his corpus of primary data, the grammarian must be able to answer the question (71).

(71)   Does the intuitive linguistic judgment J represent a genuine linguistic intuition or not?

In §4.3.2.2.2.2 we also saw that it can be very difficult to answer this question and that grammarians often have to resort to an intricate strategy in order to form judgments about genuineness. We are now better equipped to look at this strategy in more detail. We shall do so mainly with reference to an article by Thomas Bever, "The ascent of the specious or, there's a lot we don't know about mirrors" (1974).

7.4.6.1   *An Application of the Strategy*

Let us look at the concrete case in which Bever applies the strategy. Suppose a grammarian were to be confronted in his investigation of a given aspect of English syntax with the following four intuitive linguistic judgments:

(72)(a)   The utterance *The horse that was ridden past the barn fell* is acceptable.

(b)   The utterance *The horse ridden past the barn fell* is acceptable.

(c)   The utterance *The horse that was raced past the barn fell* is acceptable.

(d)   The utterance *The horse raced past the barn fell* is unacceptable.

Suppose, moreover, that the grammarian were not sure that the judgment (72)(d) is genuine. He judges that the utterance *The horse raced past the barn fell* is related to the utterance *The horse that was raced past the barn fell* in exactly the same way that the utterance *The horse ridden past the barn fell* is related to the utterance *The horse that was ridden past the barn fell.* However, whereas the utterance *The horse ridden past the barn fell* is judged to be acceptable, the utterance *The horse raced past the barn fell*, against all expectation, is considered to be unacceptable. The unexpectedness of the judgment (72)(d) may cause the grammarian to doubt the genuineness of the linguistic intuition it represents. But the grammarian is aware of no obvious nongrammatical factor which could be responsible for the spuriousness of the intuition. What should he do to form a judgment as to the genuineness of (72)(d)?

The strategy he could follow to reach such a judgment is at once complex and indirect. The first step is to try and give a grammatical explanation for the unacceptability of the utterance *The horse raced past the barn fell.* According to Bever (1974:182) there is an obvious grammatical explanation for the unacceptability of this utterance. The essence of this explanation may be reconstructed as in (73).

(73)   If the relative clause on an initial noun is passivized and the past participle of the verb in that clause is homonomous with the simple past, then the relative pronoun and the form of "be" may not be deleted from the relative clause. In the utterance *The horse raced past the barn fell* the relative clause – "Someone raced the horse" – on the initial noun *horse* has been passivized. In the passivized relative clause the past participle *raced* is homonomous with the simple past *raced.* In addition, in the passivized relative clause the relative pronoun *that* and the form *was* of the copula *be* have been deleted. Consequently, the utterance *The horse raced past the barn fell* is unacceptable.

Note, in passing, that the content of the intuitive judgments of (72)(b) and (c) can be explained in terms of the lawlike generalization of (73) as well. The utterance *The horse ridden past the barn fell* is not unacceptable because *ridden* is not homonomous with *rode.* The utterance *The horse that was raced past the barn fell* is not unacceptable because *that was* has not been deleted.

The second step in the strategy is to appraise the grammatical explanation given to account for the dubious intuitive judgment on the basis of the following two questions:

(74)(a)   Can the language-specific generalization used in the explanation be formulated within the framework of a general linguistic theory aiming at explanatory adequacy?

(b)   Is the explanation a "genuine" explanation or does it merely describe the problematic data?

Let us consider the grammatical explanation (73) from the point of view of the first question. Seen from this point of view, Bever (1974:182) finds a certain aspect of the lawlike generalization in the grammatical explanation (73) unacceptable. He points out that in order to formulate this generalization, the transformational rules applying in a derivation must be made sensitive to potential derivations that the relative clause verb might have entered into. Thus the transformation deleting the relative pronoun and the relevant form of "be" must do something else before performing the deletion: it must determine whether or not the past participle and the simple past of the relative clause verb are homonomous.

Within the standard approach to generative grammar, transformations do not have the power to do this. Therefore, in order to formulate the lawlike generalization in question, the general linguistic theory has to be revised to make provision for transformational rules that do have this power. The general linguistic theory will then allow a new type of transformational rule: one which is sensitive to potential derivations. By allowing this new type of transformational rule, the general linguistic theory weakens its restrictions on the class of grammars which are possible in human language. To this class are now added grammars containing transformational rules of the new type. By weakening its restrictions on the class of possible grammars, the general linguistic theory becomes explanatorily less adequate – cf. §7.4.2.3. From the point of view of the question (74)(a), therefore, the grammatical explanation is unacceptable. To make provision for such an explanation the general linguistic theory has to be made explanatorily less adequate.

But the explanation (73) must also be considered from the point of view of the question (74)(b). Bever (1974:182) judges that, seen from this point of view, the grammatical explanation in question is not a "genuine" explanation either. According to him, it fails in that it does not indicate why the lawlike generalization is as it is. This explanation does not in fact make clear what exactly the homonymy of the past participle and the simple past of the verb has to do with the unacceptability of *The horse raced past the barn fell.* Bever then argues that (73) does not really explain the problematic phenomenon in question, but merely describes it. From the point of view of the questions (74)(a) and (b), therefore, one can but conclude that the most obvious grammatical explanation for the phenomenon in question is unacceptable.

The third step in the strategy under consideration entails that the grammarian seeks a nonlinguistic explanation for the problematic intuitive linguistic judgment. Bever (1974:181–182) claims that the unacceptability of the utterance *The horse raced past the barn fell* may be explained in terms of his theory of speech perception. This theory describes, among other things, the perceptual strategies the hearer uses in speech perception. According to Bever (1974:180), the function of these perceptual strategies is "to take an external sequence of lexical classes as input and map it onto a possible internal form". In this internal form the functional relationships existing in the sentence must be expressed. The following are two examples of Bever's perceptual strategies (1974:180):

(75)(a) N_1 at clause beginning $\longrightarrow N_1$ = actor of next inflected verb
  (b) N_2 following verb $\longrightarrow N_2$ = object of verb

The first perceptual strategy above specifies that a noun occurring at the beginning of a sentence in its external form, in the internal form denotes the perpetrator of the act expressed by the first inflected verb following the noun. The second perceptual strategy specifies that a noun following the verb in the external form of a sentence, in the internal form denotes the object of the act expressed by this verb.

An utterance may be perceptually complex in various respects. For instance, the external form of the utterance may be such that the hearer starts processing it perceptually in terms of perceptual strategies that are applicable but inappropriate. Having applied an inappropriate perceptual strategy, the speaker realizes that his perceptual processing of the sentence has gone wrong somewhere. The result is that he regards the utterance as unacceptable. Perceptual complexity is therefore one of the causes of unacceptability.

Against this background Bever proposes the perceptual explanation (76) for the unacceptability of *The horse raced past the barn fell.*

(76)   If the external form of an utterance is such that the hearer can start processing it in terms of one or more inappropriate perceptual strategies, then the hearer intuitively judges the utterance to be unacceptable. The external form of the utterance *The horse raced past the barn fell* is such that a hearer can start processing it perceptually in terms of two inappropriate perceptual strategies, viz. (75)(a) and (b). In terms of these two strategies the hearer can process the first NVN series perceptually as a plausible clause. This leaves him bewildered as to how to deal with the remaining word *fell*. Consequently, the hearer intuitively judges that the utterance *The horse raced past the barn fell* is unacceptable.

Note that the external form of the utterances *The horse that was raced past the barn fell* and *The horse ridden past the barn fell* are not such that they allow processing by application of the inappropriate perceptual strategies (75)(a) and (b). Thus the lawlike generalization of (76) can serve as a basis for a perceptual explanation of the contrast in acceptability between the utterances in question.

The fourth step in the strategy entails that the grammarian critically evaluates the nonlinguistic explanation of the problematic intuitive linguistic judgment. This he does on the basis of two questions.

(77)(a)   Is the lawlike generalization of the nonlinguistic explanation for the problematic phenomenon independently motivated?
  (b)   Is the nonlinguistic explanation a "genuine" explanation or does it merely describe the problematic data?

Bever judges the perceptual explanation (76) to be acceptable from the point of view of both these questions.

As regards the question (77)(a), he points out that the lawlike generalization in question – and particularly the two perceptual strategies (75)(a) and (b) – already form part of his theory of speech perception. In other words, it was not necessary for him to postulate this generalization and these perceptual strategies specially for the purpose of explaining the unacceptability of the utterance in question. They are therefore not *ad hoc*. Moreover, as regards the question (77)(b), Bever argues that (76) represents a "genuine" explanation. It is quite clear from this explanation why the homonymy of the past participle and the simple past is an important factor in the unacceptability of the utterance concerned. Only if the past participle is homonomous with – and therefore easily confused with – the simple past, can the external form of an utterance be such that it allows processing by the inappropriate application of the perceptual strategies (75)(a) and (b).

The preceding discussion may be summarized as follows:

(78)(a) A grammatical explanation of the intuitive linguistic judgment (72)(d)
  (i) requires the general linguistic theory to be revised in such a way that it becomes explanatorily less adequate and
  (ii) is in fact not a "genuine" explanation, but a "mere" description of the problematic data.

(b) A nonlinguistic, perceptual explanation for the intuitive linguistic judgment (72)(d)
  (i) may be given in terms of an independently motivated lawlike generalization and
  (ii) is a "genuine" explanation and not a "mere" description of the problematic data.

On the basis of (78) the grammarian now forms the following judgment about the problematic intuitive linguistic judgment:

(79) The intuitive linguistic judgment that the utterance *The horse raced past the barn fell* is unacceptable, does not represent a genuine linguistic intuition. The judgment is based on perception and as such is not a problematic datum within the domain of grammatical inquiry.

7.4.6.2 *Complexity of the Strategy*

Notice that the judgment (79) was reached by way of an extremely complex strategy. It is complex, firstly, in that it involves four highly technical steps. The first step requires the construction of a grammatical explanation for the problematic intuitive judgment. The second step requires the critical appraisal of this explanation from two points of view: that of the explanatory adequacy of the general linguistic theory and that of the distinction between a "genuine" grammatical explanation and a "mere" description. The third step requires the construction of a nonlinguistic explanation for the problematic intuitive judgment. The fourth and last step requires the critical evaluation of this explanation from two points of view: that of the independent motivation for the lawlike generalization in question and that of the distinction between a "genuine" explanation and a "mere" description.

This strategy is complex not only because it involves four highly sophisticated steps, but also because, in the third step, the extreme complexity of linguistic performance has to be taken into account. What does this imply?

In §3.3.1.2 we saw that linguistic performance is the result of the interaction of a number of factors: the grammatical factor of linguistic competence, the factor of speech production, the factor of speech perception, the nonlinguistic psychological factor of restrictions on the human memory, concentration, attention, etc., the factor of social environment and status, the factor of dialectal variation, the factor of idiolectal variation, the pragmatic factor of physical and perceptual context, the pragmatic factor of the language user's knowledge and view of the world, and so on. Each of these factors could be at the root of an intuitive linguistic judgment − a nongenuine linguistic intuition − of the language user. Compare §4.3.2.2.2.2 for details on this point.

It therefore follows that the evaluation of the genuineness of a particular intuitive linguistic judgment is in fact even more complex than it seemed in §7.4.6.1 above. In carrying out the third step of the evaluation of the genuineness of the intuitive linguistic judgment (72)(d) − i.e. the giving of an alternative, nonlinguistic explanation − only one nonlinguistic factor was investigated: that of the role of the hearer's perceptual strategies. In practice, however, it may be necessary to establish, for a large number of the nonlinguistic factors mentioned above, whether or not they play a role in the forming of a particular intuitive linguistic judgment. This implies that in order to evaluate the genuineness of this intuitive linguistic judgment a number of alternative nonlinguistic explanations would have to be given and evaluated. It is a mere piece of good luck if the first type of nonlinguistic explanation which is considered emerges as being the most adequate explanation.

This last point may be illustrated by an example. Consider the following intuitive linguistic judgment:

(80)   The utterance *I hope it for to be stopping raining when I am having leaving* is unacceptable.

The grammarian of English cannot simply assume that the unacceptability of the utterance (80) must be ascribed to the grammatical factor of linguistic competence. In principle, any of the nonlinguistic factors mentioned above could be responsible for the unacceptability of this utterance. Which of these factors is in fact responsible can only be determined by trying to give an explanation for the unacceptability of this utterance in terms of each of the nonlinguistic factors in turn. The grammarian must therefore attempt to find a grammatical explanation, a perceptual explanation, a pragmatic explanation, and so on. He then has to decide which of these alternative explanations is the most acceptable from the point of view of the questions (74)(a) and (b) and (77)(a) and (b). Only then can he judge whether the intuitive linguistic judgment (80) represents a genuine linguistic intuition.

According to Bever (1974:192), it is impossible to give a satisfactory non-linguistic explanation for the intuitive linguistic judgment in question in terms of any of the nonlinguistic factors mentioned above. He therefore assumes that the intuitive linguistic judgment does indeed represent a genuine linguistic intuition. By implication, the intuitive linguistic judgment (80) falls within the domain of problematic data of grammatical inquiry. But to establish this, the grammarian has had to perform a complex investigation. Because of its complexity, this type of investigation is often neglected by generative grammarians when they have to assess the genuineness of dubious linguistic intuitions. They then exclude or include such intuitions in their corpus of problematic linguistic data on completely arbitrary grounds.

7.4.6.3   *Philosophical Basis of the Strategy*

The strategy to determine the status of intuitive linguistic judgments outlined above is based on a number of general philosophical assumptions. Bever (1974: 178) formulates these assumptions as follows:

(81)(a)   Specific factual phenomena are often the result of interactions among different (physical, psychological biological) systems.

    (b)   The formal theory in each system should be as limited as possible to be as testable as possible.

    (c)   When a new fact can be described by two existing systems, but would require elaboration of one of them and not the other, the fact is interpreted as due to the system not requiring elaboration for its description.

To (b) above the following should be added " . . . and as explanatorily adequate as possible".

The methodological assumptions of (81) are part of a comprehensive general philosophical position called RATIONALISM by generative grammarians such as Chomsky. The essence of the rationalist point of view with regard to the facts or data of grammatical inquiry may be formulated as in (82).

(82)   Intuitive linguistic judgments result from the working of a number of factors. Only those intuitive judgments which result from the grammatical factor of linguistic competence fall within the domain of grammatical inquiry.

The most explicit formulation of this rationalist point of view with regard to the data of grammatical inquiry was given by Bever (1974) and by Katz and Bever (1974) jointly.

Other linguists – who also profess to be generative grammarians – take another view of the data of grammatical inquiry. Their point of view forms part of the comprehensive general philosophical position known as EMPIRICISM. The essence of this view may be formulated as in (83).

(83)   *All* intuitive linguistic judgments which can be studied systematically fall within the domain of grammatical inquiry.

James McCawley (1974) and George Lakoff (1974a, 1974b) are the two leading exponents of the empiricist point of view. Their views about the domain of linguistic inquiry are neatly summarized in the following statement by Lakoff (1974a:151):

> I take linguistics to be the study of natural language in *all* of its manifestations. This is a broad conception of the field, and I think it is an appropriately broad one. It includes not just syntax-semantics, phonetics-phonology, historical linguistics, anthropological linguistics, etc., which form the core of most academic programs in this country, but also the role of language in social interaction, in literature, in ritual, and in propaganda, and as well the study of the relationship between language and thought, speech production and perception, linguistic disorders, etc.

In the kind of linguistic inquiry practised by Lakoff, McCawley and others, no distinction is drawn between genuine and nongenuine intuitions. A grammarian must be able to give explanations for all systematic intuitive judgments the native speaker has about the utterances of his language. Within the empiricist approach to linguistic inquiry, a grammar must have the same function as the one which is assigned, jointly, to a grammar, a theory of speech perception, a pragmatic theory of context and speech acts, a theory of dialectal variation, a theory of social variation, and so on within the rationalist approach. An empiricist grammar can obviously no longer be a description of the linguistic competence of the ideal speaker. Within the empiricist approach this idealization is not made.

Rationalists such as Chomsky, Katz and Bever raise two main objections to the empiricist point of view of (83). On the one hand, this view makes it completely impossible for the general linguistic theory to attain the level of explanatory adequacy. The formal power of the general linguistic theory has to be greatly extended in order to allow grammars which can account for all systematic intuitive linguistic judgments. This theory can therefore no longer give a restrictive characterization of the class of possible grammars for human language. Consequently, this theory can no longer offer a solution for the fundamental problem (61). On the other hand, the empiricist point of view precludes the possibility of constructing grammars which may be used to give "genuine" grammatical explanations. According to Chomsky and his followers, empiricist grammars are mere mechanisms for enumerating problematic linguistic data. As Chomsky (1978:10) puts it, a non-rationalist approach boils down to " . . . a kind of butterfly collecting or elaborate taxonomies of sensations and observations". Both these objections to the empiricist point of view (83) were in fact illustrated in §7.4.6.1 where Bever's reasons for the unacceptability of the grammatical explanation (73) were discussed. In retrospect, this grammatical explanation appears to be an empiricist one.

7.4.7   Giving General Linguistic Explanations

We have now reached a point at which it has become possible to give a general characterization of the giving of general linguistic explanations. The characterization (84) below applies only to internal explanations. Most generative grammarians apparently do not regard the giving of external explanations as being one of the activities involved in linguistic inquiry.

(84)   The general linguist provides an INTERNAL EXPLANATION by
    (a)   presenting an explanandum stating one or more problematic properties of the (internalized) grammar of a particular language;
    (b)   presenting an explanans containing
        (i)   a lawlike reason, formulated in terms of one or more linguistic universals, in terms of which the language in question probably must have the given property/ies; and
        (ii)   one or more factual reasons – data about the property/ies mentioned and about the larger grammar of the language – from which it must be clear that whatever it is that is problematic does indeed fall within the domain of the lawlike generalization of (b)(i);
    (c)   indicating the logical rule by which the explanandum (a) may be inferred from the explanans (b).

It is clear that internal general linguistic explanation is similar to grammatical explanation – see (53) above – in that it represents a form of reasoning.

SELECTED READING

Inquiry in General

Structure of Scientific Explanations

Bunge 1967b:3–7; Hempel 1965:331–496; 1966:49–69; Hempel and Oppenheim 1953; Rescher 1970:Part II.

Deductive Nomological Explanations

Achinstein 1971:99–109; Hempel 1962; 1965:331–496; 1966:49–54; Nagel 1971:ch.3.

Interscientific Explanation

Bunge 1967b:34–42; Harré 1967:100ff.

Logical Structure of Arguments

Alexander 1969:4ff.; Botha 1973:23–28; Copi 1965:3ff.; Salmon 1963:2–3.

Criteria for Scientific Explanations

Achinstein 1971:78–84; Hempel 1966:47–49.

Probabilistic Explanations

Hempel 1965: 331–496; 1966:58–69; Salmon 1965: Rescher 1970:37ff.

Types of Scientific Explanation

Broad 1919; Cohen 1950/51; Fain 1963; Kaplan 1964:ch. 38, 39; Nagel 1961:ch.2.

Explanation vs. Description

Botha 1973:170–172; Harré 1967.

Lawlike Generalizations/Laws

Achinstein 1971:ch.I–III, V; Bunge 1967a:ch.6; Hempel 1966:54–58, 59–67; Kaplan 1964:ch.11–14; Nagel 1961:47–48, 79–105; Rescher 1970:10ff., 97ff. Rescher 1970 (209–240) contains an exhaustive systematic bibliography of publications dealing with scientific explanation and related subjects which appeared up to 1970.

Linguistic Inquiry

Few systematic studies have been made of the nature and properties of the explanations given in linguistic inquiry. The studies that do exist generally do not systematically distinguish between grammatical and internal (general linguistic) explanation. As a result it is not possible to give a bibliography which takes into account the various finer distinctions we have made in our study.

General Discussions

Chomsky 1978:13ff.; Dougherty 1974; Dretske 1974; Sampson 1976; Sanders 1974.

External Explanations

Bach 1974a:251–252; 1974b:167–170; Chomsky and Lasnik 1977:436–438; Clark and Haviland 1974; Kiparsky 1972; O'Hala 1974; Schane 1972; Whitaker 1974.

Grammatical and Internal (General Linguistic) Explanation

Bach 1974a:240–251; 1974b:153–167; Black 1970:452–461; Chomsky 1962a; 1968:23ff.; 1970; Jackendoff 1976; Katz 1977:561, n.2; Perlmutter and Oreznik 1973; Vennemann 1973.

Levels of Adequacy for Linguistic Theories

Descriptive Adequacy

Bach 1974a:238–240; Chomsky 1964:ch.2; 1965:24–25, 30–47; Fodor, Bever and Garrett 1974:81–82, 85–92, 92–95.

Explanatory Adequacy

Bach 1974a:240–251; 1974b:156–166; Chomsky 1964:ch.2; 1965:25–27, 30–47; Peters 1970; 1972b.

Observational Adequacy

Bach 1974a:236–237; Chomsky 1964:ch.2; Fodor and Garrett 1974:81–82, 85–92.

Rationalism (vs. Empiricism) in Delimiting the Explanatory Domain of Generative Grammars

The volume *An integrated theory of linguistic ability*, edited by Bever, Katz and Langendoen (1977), contains various contributions explicating and/or applying the rationalist approach in delimiting the explanatory domain of generative grammars. Cf. also Katz 1977:571ff. for a discussion of the role which generative grammarians' pretheoretic intuitions play in the *initial* delimitation of the explanatory domain of generative grammars.

CHAPTER EIGHT

Making Linguistic Projections

8.0 PERSPECTIVE

Making linguistic projections – predictions and postdictions – represents a sixth main aspect of linguistic inquiry. Chapter 8 of our study deals with this main aspect from three different angles. In the first section of the chapter we shall look at what is involved in making scientific projections in empirical inquiry in general. Four forms of nonscientific projection are distinguished first. Against this background a characterization is then given of the general nature of the scientific form of projection. The discussion of the structure of scientific projections will show it to be analogous to that of scientific explanations. At this point a distinction is drawn between various principal forms of scientific projection: deductive projection vs. nondeductive projection, strict scientific projection vs. lax scientific projection and extrapolation vs. intrapolation. This is followed by a discussion of the differences between scientific projections and scientific explanations. The criteria for and functions of scientific projections are subsequently considered and finally a characterization is given of the intellectual activities involved in making scientific projections. It will emerge that, in essence, scientific projection represents the same type of argumentation as scientific explanation.

The second section of the chapter deals with the projections made in grammatical inquiry. On the one hand, they are discussed with reference to their general nature and particular properties. On the other hand they are considered in terms of the activities involved in making grammatical projections. As regards the first point, examples are given on the basis of which the principal forms of grammatical projection, the atemporal nature of grammatical predictions, the distinction between direct and indirect grammatical predictions, the structure of direct grammatical predictions and the functions of grammatical projections can be discussed. Finally, a brief characterization is given of direct grammatical prediction as an intellectual activity and of the process of indirect grammatical prediction.

In the third section of the chapter we take a look at the projections made in general linguistic inquiry. This is done against the background of a distinction between internal general linguistic predictions and external general linguistic projections. The general nature and structure of both are discussed. In the discussion of external general linguistic projections we take a look at how a general linguistic theory can be used in conjunction with a theory of linguistic change to make projections about possible linguistic changes. The chapter is concluded with a characterization of the making of general linguistic projections as an intellectual activity.

8.1   INTRODUCTION

The following is a reconstruction of a fragment of the argumentation in Chomsky's article "Remarks on nominalization" (p.27):

(1) (a)   The expression *his criticism of the book before he read it* will be unacceptable. This expression is a derived nominal containing a *before*-clause as a constituent. In the deep structure, a *before*-clause is an adjunct of a VP, not of an NP. All derived nominals have the deep structure of NPs.

   (b)   The expression *his criticizing the book before he read it* will not be unacceptable. This expression is a gerundive nominal which contains a *before*-clause as a constituent. In the deep structure, a *before*-clause is an adjunct of a VP. All gerundive nominals have the deep structure of sentences and may therefore contain VPs as constituents.

In (1)(a) and (b) we see two examples of grammatical predictions which may be made on the basis of Chomsky's lexicalist hypothesis. We saw in §3.3.1.3 that a grammatical investigation of nominalization in English does indeed have the making of such predictions as an objective. McCawley (1973:9) formulated this point as follows:

. . . an analysis of nominalizations would be required not merely to provide dictionary entries for all existing nominalizations but to correctly predict which non-occurring ones are accidentally excluded and which ones systematically excluded.

In (1)(a) above it is predicted on systematic syntactic grounds that the derived nominal *his criticism of the book before he read it* will not occur in English. The making of such predictions and related postdictions represents a sixth main aspect of linguistic inquiry. In the paragraphs which follow, this aspect of linguistic inquiry will be dealt with in detail.

But let us simplify our task by agreeing that, whenever possible, the expression "scientific projections" will be used as a synonym for the rather unwieldy expression "scientific predictions and scientific postdictions". In the two preceding chapters we became acquainted with two of the logical ways in which scientists pursue their ultimate objective of gaining insight into the problematic reality. These two logical ways were the giving of theoretical descriptions and the giving of scientific explanations. The making of scientific projections represents a third logical way pursued in this search for insight.

Schematically, the making of scientific projections as a main aspect of linguistic inquiry may be represented as follows:

(2)

| knowledge of aspects of a known reality | → | activities of sixth main aspect | → | projections about aspects of an unknown reality |

In terms of the diagram (2), making linguistic projections involves the following: on the strength of what is known, claims are made about the unknown. However, this is an extremely vague characterization of linguistic projection. We will attempt to give a more precise characterization of the nature of linguistic projection by asking ourselves two fundamental questions.

(3) (a) What are the general nature and particular properties of linguistic projections?

(b) What intellectual activities are involved in making linguistic projections?

These two questions will be considered, first from the angle of inquiry in general, and then from the angle of grammatical inquiry and general linguistic inquiry. As regards inquiry in general, we will be guided in our discussion by the characterization of the nature and properties of scientific projection as given by Mario Bunge (1967b:ch.10).

8.2   INQUIRY IN GENERAL

8.2.1   Nature of Scientific Projections

8.2.1.1   *Forms of Nonscientific Projection*

Scientific projection is but one of the forms which anticipation of the future and retrospection over the past may take. Let us consider a number of forms of nonscientific projection.

A first form of nonscientific projection may be called EXPECTATION for short. Expectation is an involuntary, spontaneous form of projection found in all higher animals. For instance, think of a dog who becomes excited when shown his leash. The view of his leash spontaneously aroused the following expectation in the dog:

(4)   A walk will soon follow.

Higher animals possess the ability to have such expectations about the future on the strength of their past experience. However, it is important to note that these expectations originate in an unreasoned and spontaneous way. Bunge (1967b:66) accordingly characterizes expectation as "an automatic attitude of anticipation".

A second form of nonscientific projection is GUESSING. Someone who knows next to nothing of British politics ventures a guess when he claims the following:

(5)   The Liberal Party will win the 1979 general election in the United Kingdom.

Guessing, unlike expectation, is (almost) completely unfounded. Whereas expectation is at least based on experience, guesswork lacks this basis. As guesses are not based on knowledge of a past or present, they represent a nonreasoned form of projection. However, unlike expectations, guesses are made consciously. Thus, guessing, according to Bunge (1967b:66), is "a conscious but nonrational attempt to figure out what is, was or will be the case without any ground whatever".

A third form of nonscientific projection may be called PROPHESYING, through lack of a better name. Prophecies, such as those made by religious freaks, political prophets of doom, soothsayers, gypsies, and so on, are as unfounded as guesses. But prophecies are far less specific, far more vague and ambiguous than guesses, as is clear from the following examples of prophecies:

(6) (a)   The world will come to an end.
    (b)   The East and the West will be involved in a death-struggle.
    (c)   You will undertake a voyage.
    (d)   Great happiness/sadness awaits you.

The ambiguity which is so characteristic of many prophecies is beautifully illustrated by the prophecies of the oracles. When Croesus asked the oracle of Delphi what would happen if he attacked the Persians, the oracle answered: "A great kingdom will be destroyed.". Croesus did not perceive the ambiguity of this prophecy and launched his attack. The result was that a mighty kingdom was destroyed – his own. The essence of prophesying, then, is characterized by Bunge (1967b:66) as

large scale guessing on the alleged ground of revelation or other esoteric source (occult 'science', untested 'laws' of history, special powers of the leader, etc.).

The last form of nonscientific projection which we will consider is that of PROGNOSIS or COMMON SENSE PREDICTION. Typical examples of this form of projection are the weather forecast (7)(a) given by the seasoned fisherman, the forecast (7)(b) made by the punter and the prediction (7)(c) made by the amateur seismologist.

(7) (a) If the herring are out tonight, it will rain tomorrow.
    (b) If the track is heavy, Red Rum — and not Black Beauty — will win Saturday's race.
    (c) As the snakes have interrupted their hibernation and are fleeing from their holes, I expect an earthquake within the next few days.

Unlike guesses, prognoses are grounded. They are based on accidental generalizations. ACCIDENTAL GENERALIZATIONS usually deal with the repeated co-occurrence or repeated succession of two (types of) events or phenomena. This type of generalization lacks a lawlike aspect. It states what is generally the case — not what should generally of necessity be the case.

Prognoses are typically conditional. Their conditional nature is reflected linguistically in expressions such as "if . . . then", "as", "because". Guesses and prophecies, on the other hand, are typically offered as unconditional statements. This can be seen from the guess (5) and the prophecy (6) above. Prognosis is characterized by Bunge (1967b:66) as "forecast with the help of more or less tacit empirical generalizations". Having had a brief look at four forms of non-scientific projection, we can now turn to scientific projection.

8.2.1.2 *Scientific Projection*

Recall that we have included both the making of predictions and the making of postdictions in the expression "scientific projection". Scientific predictions are made in answer to questions of the following types:

(8) (a) When will the event E occur?
    (b) What would the properties of the phenomenon P be if it should occur?
    (c) What would the nature of the state of affairs S be under the circumstances C?
    (d) What would happen to the object O if X were to be the case?

From these questions it is clear that SCIENTIFIC PREDICTIONS make claims about events, phenomena, states of affairs, and so on, in an unknown future reality.

SCIENTIFIC POSTDICTIONS or RETRODICTIONS, by contrast, make claims about events, phenomena, states of affairs, and so on, in an unknown reality of the past. The following questions are typical of those for which scientific postdictions provide answers:

(9) (a) When did the event E occur?
    (b) What were the properties of the phenomenon P when it occurred?

(c)   What was the nature of the state of affairs S under the circumstances C?

(d)   What happened to the object O when X occurred?

Note that the making of scientific predictions and the making of scientific postdictions involve essentially the same activity, that of knowledge or experience
of a known reality being projected onto an unknown reality. According to the
conventional metascientific view, the unknown reality is a future reality in the
case of scientific predictions and a past reality in the case of scientific postdictions. The fundamental difference between scientific predictions and scientific
postdictions is therefore a temporal one.

Let us now consider the properties of scientific projections with reference to
two simple examples: the prediction of (10) and the corresponding postdiction
of (11).

(10)(a)   *Question* : What will happen to that fluid if the temperature falls
below 0°C tonight?

(b)   *Prediction* : The fluid will turn into ice (if the temperature falls
below 0°C tonight). The fluid is water, and water turns into ice at
a temperature lower than 0°C.

(11)(a)   *Question* : What happened to that fluid when the temperature fell
below 0°C last night?

(b)   *Postdiction* : The fluid turned into ice (when the temperature fell
below 0°C last night). The fluid is water, and water turns into ice
at a temperature lower than 0°C.

The prediction (10)(b) and the postdiction (11)(b) are extremely, probably even
untypically, simple examples of scientific projections. But still, they serve to
illustrate the salient features of scientific projections quite well.

Before discussing these features, let us point out an ambiguity in the use of
the expressions "prediction", "postdiction" and "projection". On the one hand,
these expressions are used to denote the whole of an argument such as (10)(b)
and/or (11)(b). On the other hand, these terms are used to denote the first claim
in an argument such as (10)(b) and/or (11)(b). To avoid confusion we will agree
that in *this* chapter

(12)(a)   the term "prediction" is used to denote an argument such as
(10)(b) as a whole;

(b)   the term "predictive claim" is used to denote the first claim in an
argument such as (10)(b);

(c)   the term "postdiction" is used to denote an argument such as
(11)(b) as a whole;

(d)   the term "postdictive claim" is used to denote the first claim in an argument such as (11)(b);

(e)   the term "projection" is used to denote both a prediction in the sense of (a) and a postdiction in the sense of (c);

(f)   the term "projective claim" is used to denote both a predictive claim in the sense of (b) and a postdictive claim in the sense of (d).

A first important feature of scientific projections is that they are reasoned. If the projections (10)(b) and (11)(b) had not been reasoned, they would have taken the following form:

(13)(a)   The fluid will turn into ice (if the temperature falls below 0°C tonight).

(b)   The fluid turned into ice (when the temperature fell below 0°C last night).

In a nonreasoned form the projections in question are therefore the same as projective claims.

Notice in what way the projections (10)(b) and (11)(b) are reasoned. Two types of reasons are given for the expectation expressed in the projective claim. Firstly, a FACTUAL DATUM is given about the object with which the projective claim deals. In both the prediction (10)(b) and the postdiction (11)(b) this datum is the same.

(14)   The fluid is water.

Secondly, a LAWLIKE GENERALIZATION is given which, on the strength of the factual datum mentioned above, applies to the object with which the projective claim deals. In both the prediction (10)(b) and the postdiction (11)(b) this lawlike generalization is the same.

(15)   Water turns into ice at a temperature lower than 0°C.

Thus, the claims made about an unknown reality by scientific projections are explicitly based on factual data and lawlike generalizations about a known reality. Guesses and prophecies, by contrast, are ungrounded. Expectations such as that of (4) are based on experience, but are unreasoned. Prognoses may be reasoned in terms of factual data and accidental generalizations, but they often lack explicit reasoning.

A second important feature of scientific projections is that they are conditional. This is the result of their being grounded. Scientific projections are conditional in the following respect: the projective claim is made on condition that the lawlike generalization and factual data on which it is based are beyond reasonable doubt. The conditional nature of scientific projections need not be reflected linguistically in the use of expressions such as "if . . . then", "as", "because", and so on. By giving the factual and lawlike grounds for the projective statement, its conditional nature is stated automatically.

A third central feature of scientific projections is the lawlike nature of the generalizations on which the projective claim is based. These generalizations specify the way things must necessarily be under certain circumstances. The accidental generalizations used in prognoses, by contrast, are not lawlike. They merely describe things as they generally are, but fail to state the necessary relationships between them in any lawlike fashion. In §7.2.1 we saw that the scientist's theoretical descriptions are the source of his lawlike generalizations. In terms of the source of their lawlike generalizations, scientific projections are therefore THEORETICAL PROJECTIONS.

A fourth central feature of scientific projections, which is related to the three features already mentioned, is that their accuracy may be improved. Bunge (1967b:69) formulates this point as follows:

[Scientific projection] can be as *accurate* as our knowledge about laws and circumstances, whereas prophecies are inherently indefinite and prognoses can be accurate but there is no means of improving their accuracy – except to replace them by scientific predictions made with corrigible law statements and data. Improvable accuracy, rather than accuracy, is a hallmark of scientific prediction: it can be accurate as in astronomy or it can consist of rough estimates like those of the behavioral sciences. The point is not that scientific prediction is accurate in an absolute sense but that it is founded and, for this reason, it can be improved.

The essence of scientific projection, as described by Bunge (1967b:66), is that it is "forecast (or aftercast) with the help of scientific (or technological) theories and data". The distinctive features of scientific projections may be said to be their reasoned, conditional and lawlike nature and their improvable accuracy.

8.2.1.3   *Structure of Scientific Projections*

We have repeatedly referred to the argumentative or reasoned nature of scientific projections. From a logical point of view, therefore, a scientific projection may be seen as a set of mutually related propositions which are structured in the form of an argument. The prediction (10)(b), for instance, may be reconstructed as follows in the form of an argument:

(16)   MAJOR PREMISS   : If a fluid is water and the temperature falls below
                                        0°C, then the fluid will turn into ice.
          MINOR PREMISSES : The fluid is water.
                                        Suppose the temperature fell below 0°C tonight.

          CONCLUSION   : The fluid will turn into ice tonight.

Notice that the logical structure of a scientific projection is parallel to that of a scientific explanation. The logical structure of scientific projections and explanations contains the same components. Firstly, scientific projections contain a proposition describing the predicted or postdicted phenomenon, event or object. This proposition is called the PROJECTANDUM and it constitutes the conclusion of the projective argument. We used the expression "projective claim" as an informal synonym for "projectandum". Secondly, a scientific projection contains a number of propositions on which the projectandum is based. These propositions represent the PROJECTANS and they constitute the premisses of the projective argument. These premisses are divided into a major premiss and one or more minor premisses. The major premiss contains the lawlike generalization in terms of which the projection is reasoned. In the minor premiss(es) data and/or circumstances are specified from which it is clear that the lawlike generalization does indeed apply to the projected phenomenon, event or object. Finally, in scientific projection, it must be possible to indicate the logical rule in terms of which the projectandum may be inferred from the projectans. In the reconstructed argument (16), this logical rule is a rule of deduction. The general nature of logical rules of deduction was indicated in a preliminary fashion in §§7.2.1.2 and 7.3.2.2.3.

According to what has been said so far – and this reflects the conventional opinion – there is no essential difference, as far as logical structure is concerned, between scientific projections and scientific explanations. [Rom Harré (1967: 79–80) is a philosopher of science who does not subscribe to this view]. However, there are also some important nonlogical differences between scientific projections and scientific explanations. A few of these differences will be discussed in §8.2.1.5 below. But first we have to point out an important oversimplification which was made in our discussion of the logical structure of scientific projections.

8.2.1.4   *Types of Scientific Projection*

Our discussion so far is oversimplified in that it does not explicitly show that there are various forms of scientific projection. This applies to both prediction and postdiction. The various main types of scientific projection are discussed by Bunge (1967b:74–94) in some detail. We shall merely indicate a few of these types.

A first distinction that has to be drawn is between DEDUCTIVE and NON-

DEDUCTIVE PROJECTION. In the case of deductive — that is, deterministic — projection, the projectandum necessarily follows from the projectans. The prediction (10)(b) and the postdiction (11)(b) are deductive projections. In the case of nondeductive — or stochastic — projection, by contrast, the projectandum can be inferred from the projectans only with a certain degree of probability. The lawlike generalization of a large class of nondeductive projections is a statistic generalization. A simple type of statistical projection is the prediction of the voting behaviour of a stable society on the strength of a statistical generalization about the voting behaviour of part of the society.

A second distinction which has to be drawn is between STRICT and LAX SCIENTIFIC PROJECTION. In the case of strict scientific projections, the projectans only contains generalizations from scientific theories and factual data. The prediction (10)(b) and the postdiction (11)(b) are strict scientific projections in this sense. Lax scientific projections also contain such generalizations and data in their projectans. But, in addition to these, the projectantia of lax scientific projections contain assumptions and patterns which cannot be regarded as proper scientific laws. Many of the predictions and postdictions made by historians are the result of lax scientific projection. For example, in 1835 De Tocqueville predicted that, given time, the U.S.A. and Russia would rule the destiny of more than a quarter of the world's population. He made this prediction by projecting onto the future an observed trend: the major territorial expansion and fast development of both the U.S.A. and Russia at that time. This trend gives the prediction in question its "lax" character, as it cannot be regarded as a scientific law.

A third distinction which has to be drawn, is between EXTRAPOLATION and INTERPOLATION. Extrapolation involves the projection of what is known onto a reality which is completely unknown. Postdictions about the origin of social institutions are examples of extrapolations. Interpolation, by contrast, involves the projection of what is known onto a reality which is not completely unknown. Roughly, interpolation involves determining an unknown point between two (or more) known points. The hypothetical reconstruction of a missing link in, for instance, man's evolution is an example of an interpolation.

8.2.1.5   *Differences between Scientific Projection and Explanation*

Philosophers of science such as Bunge (1967b:69–70, 116–117), Kaplan (1964: 349–351) and Toulmin (1961:ch.2) draw the attention to various differences between scientific projection and scientific explanation. It is impossible to discuss all of them here. We shall briefly look at six of these differences, mainly for their illustrative value.

A first difference concerns the temporal factor. An important feature of scientific projections is the difference in time between the projectandum and the projectans. The point in time at which that which is described in the projectandum occurs/(would have) occurred, precedes or follows that at which the projectans is presented. This temporal difference is not to be found in explanations.

A second difference, closely related to the first, concerns the actuality of what is being projected or explained. Explanations are always directed at an actuality — something which really is. Scientists may of course be mistaken as to the nature of this actuality. In this case, their explanations are unsuccessful. Scientific projections, on the contrary, are not directed at an analogous actuality at the point in time when they are made. The conclusion of a projective argument states a potentiality. In other words, it expresses an expectation about a potential reality.

A third difference, which is in turn related to the second, concerns the direction of the argumentation. In an explanation, the conclusion of the argument is given. It remains to find the premisses of the argument. In projections, however, the premisses of the argument are given and it is the conclusion that has to be determined.

A fourth difference concerns the nature of the projectandum. The explanandum of a scientific explanation may take various forms. It could be a single proposition mentioning a specific individual phenomenon or event, or it could be a generalization expressing a law. The projectandum of a scientific projection does not take the form of a lawlike generalization. In other words, the existence of lawlike generalizations is not scientifically predicted. Once the existence of a lawlike generalization has been established, however, its nature or occurrence may be explained scientifically.

A fifth difference concerns the depth of scientific explanations as opposed to the "depth" of scientific projections. In §7.2.1.5 we saw that it is possible to talk of the depth of alternative scientific explanations. It does not seem to make sense, however, to talk of the "depth" of scientific projections. In short, a useful concept "explanatory depth" does exist, but there is no analogous concept such as "projective depth".

A sixth and last difference which will be mentioned here may be formulated as follows: not every scientific explanation has a corresponding scientific projection and not every scientific projection has a corresponding scientific explanation. On the one hand, for example, Aristotle's natural science and psychology could explain certain physical and mental phenomena, but no accurate projections could be made about these phenomena on the basis of his natural science and psychology. On the other hand, to take another example, accurate projections can be made about the voting behaviour in a particular election involving the entire population of the U.S.A., on the strength of certain trends in the electoral behaviour of the inhabitants of individual states of the U.S.A. However, despite their accuracy, these projections provide no basis on which the electoral behaviour in question may be scientifically explained.

A further striking illustration of the asymmetry between explanatory success and projective success is to be found in Stephen Toulmin's discussion (1961: 27ff.) of the differences between the Babilonian and the Ionic astronomy.

8.2.1.6   *Minimal Criteria for Scientific Projections*

Scientific projections must satisfy certain minimal criteria. A first class of criteria applies to the projection – prediction or postdiction – as a whole. In §8.2.1.3 we saw that scientific projections and scientific explanations have basically the same logical structure. As a result of this similarity in logical structure, the minimal formal and material criteria for scientific explanations apply to scientific projections as well. These criteria were discussed in §7.2.1.4. They are repeated here with the necessary adjustments and without further discussion.

(17)(a)   *Formal criteria*
   (i)   A scientific projection must contain a proposition which functions as the projectandum.
   (ii)   A scientific projection must contain a set of propositions which, as a whole, functions as the projectans.
   (iii) It must be possible to indicate the logical rule by which the projectandum may be inferred from the projectans.
 (b)   *Material criteria*
   (i)   The lawlike generalization given in the projectans must have been properly tested and well justified.
   (ii)   The accuracy of the data given in the projectans must be beyond reasonable doubt.

A second class of criteria applies to the projective claim or projectandum. Among these criteria the following two are fundamental.

(18)(a)   The projectandum must be informative, i.e. synthetic.
 (b)   The projectandum must be testable.

In terms of the criterion (18)(a) the projectandum must state something which is not merely formally correct. The accuracy of the statement made in the projectandum must be testable only on the strength of empirical data about reality. The following two projectanda do not satisfy the criterion (18)(a):

(19)(a)   Tom will win or lose the American presidential election.
 (b)   Tom may win the American presidential election.

The statement (19)(a) has no informative content. It is consistent with two mutually exclusive states of affairs. As regards the statement (19)(b), the use of the modal "may" strips it of all informative content. As far as the information it offers is concerned, this statement could just as well have read as follows:

(20)   Tom may *not* win the American presidential election.

A statement with exactly the same content as its negation has no informative content. Such statements cannot play the role of projectanda.

This brings us to the criterion (18)(b). A statement may have a definite, precise content and still be unacceptable as a projectandum. This is the case when it is in principle impossible to check the accuracy of the statement. Compare, for instance, the following statement:

(21)   Not six, but seven angels at a time can dance on the head of that pin.

As far as preciseness and definiteness are concerned, the content of this statement is unobjectionable, and yet it is, in principle, impossible to find empirical data against which to check it. It therefore does not satisfy the criterion (18) (b) for projectanda. Bunge (1967b:97) formulates the criteria (18)(a) and (b) for projectanda as follows:

> . . . a projective proposition must have both a high information content and a high degree of testability. Or, as we may also say, a projection must be both referentially and evidentially definite if it is to count as a test of the body of hypotheses from which it derives.

We shall return to both these criteria in chapters 9 and 10.

8.2.1.7   *Functions of Scientific Projection*

Now that we have some idea of what is involved in scientific projection, it remains to determine the functions of scientific projection in empirical inquiry. Three functions may be distinguished: an epistemological, a methodological and a pragmatic function.

The EPISTEMOLOGICAL FUNCTION of scientific projection is that it yields potential knowledge about an unknown reality. New knowledge may therefore be anticipated on a rational basis by means of scientific projections.

The METHODOLOGICAL FUNCTION of scientific projection is that it offers a method of testing and justifying theoretical descriptions. We have seen that scientific projections are made on the strength of, among other things, lawlike generalizations. These lawlike generalizations are taken from theoretical descriptions. Thus the ultimate basis of scientific projections is theoretical description. If a theoretical description forms the basis of accurate projections, there is reason to suspect that this description is probably correct. A theoretical description on the basis of which incorrect projections are made cannot itself be correct. In chapters 9 and 10 we shall consider in greater detail the role of scientific projection in the justification and testing of scientific theories.

The PRAGMATIC FUNCTION of scientific projection is, strictly speaking, an extrascientific function. The pragmatic function of scientific projections is to provide guidelines for practical action. If a certain event or phenomenon is predictable, measures may be taken to ensure reasonable action in anticipation of, or in reaction to this event or phenomenon. Think of the reasonable action made possible by predictions of natural catastrophes such as earthquakes, volcanic eruptions, tidal waves, storms, droughts, etc. Philosophers of science agree that scientific prediction grants man a degree of control over his future. It is clear that this pragmatic function of scientific prediction is not part of the conduct of scientific inquiry. That is why we characterized it above as extrascientific.

8.2.2   Making Scientific Projections

Our second fundamental question, (3)(b), concerned the activities involved in the making of scientific projections. What activities does a scientist carry out in making a scientific projection? From the preceding discussion it is clear that the scientist making a projection is in fact reasoning.

(22)   To make a scientific projection involves
   (a)   stating a conditional proposition about a phenomenon, event, object or state of affairs in an unknown nonpresent reality;
   (b)   providing factual data about a known reality on which the conditional proposition of (a) is based;
   (c)   offering a generalization in which a lawlike relation is stated between the phenomenon, etc. of (a), on the one hand, and the phenomenon, etc. about which the factual data of (b) exist, on the other hand; and
   (d)   indicating the logical rule by which the conditional proposition of (a) may be inferred from the propositions in terms of which the factual data of (b) and the lawlike generalization of (c) are presented.

Note, in conclusion, that there is a clear relationship between scientific projection on the one hand and theoretical description and scientific explanation on the other hand. The lawlike generalizations used in the projectantia of scientific projections are the products of theoretical description. From a strict logical point of view, scientific explanation and scientific projection represent the same type of argumentation.

8.3   GRAMMATICAL INQUIRY

8.3.1   General

In §8.1 two examples of grammatical projections – and specifically of grammatical predictions – were given as (1)(a) and (b). To get a better idea of what is involved in the making of grammatical projections we need to look at more examples of such projections. Consider the four examples below.

(23)(a) The derived nominal *John's easiness to succeed* will be unacceptable. In this nominal *easiness* has a sentential complement with the surface form *to succeed*. The grammar of English contains a neutral lexical entry for "easy" in which it is specified that this item may not take a sentential complement.

   (b) The sentence *I dislike John's complaining* will be ambiguous. In the grammar of English this sentence is assigned two different deep structures. Sentences to which the grammar of English assigns two deep structures must be ambiguous.

   (c) The sentence *I dislike John's complaining more than Bill's* will not have a mixed "fact/manner" interpretation. To have such an interpretation this sentence must be derived by means of, among other things, a deletion transformation from either the deep structure underlying (24), or the deep structure underlying (25):

   (24) *I dislike the fact of John's complaining more than I dislike the manner of Bill's complaining.*

   (25) *I dislike the manner of John's complaining more than I dislike the fact of Bill's complaining.*

   The deletion transformation T_x which derives *I dislike John's complaining more than Bill's* from the deep structure underlying (24) or (25) deletes an element which is not identical to another element in the same P-marker. There is a general linguistic condition on the applicability of deletion transformations which states that an element may be deleted only if it is
   (α) identical to another element in the P-marker, or
   (β) a constant single element.

   (d) The interrogative sentence *Who does John love Mary and?* will be unacceptable. To derive this sentence the *wh*-movement transformation has to be applied to a deep structure such as that underlying the sentence

   (26) *John loves Mary and Sue.*

   In the derivation of *Who does John love Mary and?* the transformation in question, T_y, moves a conjunct, viz. the NP with the feature [+ wh], of a coordinate structure, viz. *Mary and* [+ wh]$_{NP}$, out of this structure and places it at the beginning of the sentence (where it is realized phonologically by the interrogative form *who*). There is a general linguistic condition, the Coordinate Structure Constraint, which restricts the applicability of movement transformations to coordinate structures: no transformation may

(α) move a conjunct of a coordinate structure out of this structure, or

(β) move an element of a conjunct out of this conjunct.

The linguistic background to the four grammatical predictions given above was discussed in chapter 7. In §7.1.1 we considered the grammatical explanation (3)(a) and in §7.2.1 the grammatical explanations (27), (34) and (39)(a). These grammatical explanations correspond to the four grammatical predictions of (23).

Recall that we are interested in two main points in connection with grammatical projection(s). Firstly, we want to know what the general nature and particular properties of grammatical projections are. Secondly, we are interested in the activities the generative grammarian has to carry out in making grammatical projections.

8.3.2   Nature of Grammatical Projections

8.3.2.1   *Four General Points*

GRAMMATICAL PROJECTIONS are grammatical in that their projective claims deal with the properties of sentences – underlying classes of utterances that are repetitions of one another – of a particular language. Four general points need to be made about the nature of grammatical projections.

8.3.2.1.1   *Main types of grammatical projection*

A first general point concerns the main types of grammatical projection that are found. In §8.2.1.2 it was shown that the scientific projections of empirical inquiry generally take two main forms: that of predictions and that of post-dictions. The examples (1)(a) and (b) and (23)(a)–(d) show that grammatical projections may take the form of predictions.

However, generative grammarians do not on a systematic basis and on an extensive scale make grammatical postdictions about the history of a particular language. A synchronic grammar of a language does not reconstruct or reca-pitulate the historical development of the language in addition to giving a theoretical description of the language. The reasons why a generative grammar does not give such a reconstruction or recapitulation are discussed at length by Robert King in his book *Historical linguistics and generative grammar* (1969: §4.6). The reconstruction of the history of a language is regarded as the task of the historical grammarian. The two main methods of reconstruction – internal reconstruction and comparative reconstruction – are discussed in the aforementioned book by King (1969:ch.7) as well as in numerous introductions to general and historical linguistics. To return to the main point: in view of the fact that grammatical postdictions are not made in any systematic or extensive way, we shall be concerned mainly with grammatical predictions. However, in §8.4.3.4 we shall consider a type of grammatical projection which may be regarded as postdiction.

8.3.2.1.2   *The atemporal nature of grammatical predictions*

A second general point concerns the atemporal nature of grammatical predictions. In the conventional type of metascientific characterization of scientific predictions, the temporal aspect of such predictions is stressed. Scientific prediction is typically regarded as the projection of experience or knowledge of a known reality in the past or present onto an unknown future reality.

Grammatical prediction in fact involves the projection of experience or knowledge of a known linguistic reality onto an unknown reality. But in the case of grammatical prediction, these two realities need not be separated by a temporal difference. The unknown linguistic reality about which the grammatical predictions are made need not be a future reality. Grammatical prediction in fact involves the projection of experience or knowledge of a known part of reality onto an unknown part of the same reality. Schematically this point may be represented as follows:

```
(27)  ┌─────────┬─────────┐              ┌─────────┬─────────┐
      │    s    │    s    │              │    s    │    s    │
      │  u e    │    e    │              │  u e    │    e    │
      │  n n  k n │ grammatical │        │  n n  k n │
      │  k t  n t │            │         │  k t  n t │
      │  n e  o e ├──────────────→       │  n e  o e │
      │  o n  w n │ prediction │         │  o n  w n │
      │  w c  n c │            │         │  w c  n c │
      │  n e    e │              │       │  n e    e │
      │    s    s │              │       │    s    s │
      └─────────┴─────────┘              └─────────┴─────────┘
```

In the diagram (27) "unknown" and "known" are used in the sense of "scientifically unknown" and "scientifically known" respectively.

The atemporal nature of grammatical predictions must be seen against the background of two of the criteria adopted for generative grammars. These two criteria were formulated as (11)(d) and (e) in §6.3.2.1. They are repeated here for ease of reference.

(28)(a)   The rules (of the grammar) must enumerate all the grammatical sentences of the language and no ungrammatical sentences.

   (b)   The rules must assign an appropriate structural description to each enumerated sentence.

The grammar must enumerate and assign structural descriptions to an infinite number of sentences. But the grammarian constructs his grammar on the basis of his knowledge of the properties of a limited number of sentences. As a result, in a generative grammar, knowledge about a known part of a linguistic reality must necessarily be projected onto the remaining unknown part of this reality. Generative grammarians typically formulate this point as follows: "A grammar must be a predictive theory which will project an unlimited number of new sentences not in the original corpus." This formulation is given by Emmon Bach in his book *An introduction to transformational grammars* (1964:186).

An obvious question now arises: why do generative grammarians call grammatical projections "predictions" if they do not actually refer to a future reality? The typical reply to this question is formulated as follows by Chen (1973:176, n.3):

'Predictions' . . . are used in the sense of hypotheses testable against data unknown at the time of the formulation of the hypotheses.

Thus, grammatical predictions are "predictions" in that they represent hypothetical statements which have to be tested in the future.

The preceding discussion forms the basis for the characterization (29) of the general nature of grammatical predictions.

(29)   GRAMMATICAL PREDICTIONS are
   (a)   "grammatical" in that they represent claims about the properties of sentences in a particular human language;
   (b)   "predictions" in that they represent claims about the properties of noninvestigated sentences and are testable against data which are unknown at the time of their formulation.

The (a) and (b) parts of this characterization will be further refined in §§8.3.2.1.4 and 8.3.2.2.1 respectively.

8.3.2.1.3   *Direct vs. indirect grammatical predictions*

A third general point concerns the distinction between DIRECT and INDIRECT GRAMMATICAL PREDICTIONS. A generative grammar that satisfies the criteria (28)(a) and (b) makes an infinite number of indirect predictions. As regards (28)(a), the grammar of a particular language indirectly predicts that the sentences it generates are grammatical in that language. The same grammar indirectly predicts that the strings it does not generate are ungrammatical in that language. As regards (28)(b), by assigning structural descriptions to the sentences it generates, the grammar indirectly predicts that these sentences will have certain properties. These predictions are indirect in two respects. On the one hand, they are made about the unlimited class of sentences of the language in question. These predictions are not directed at specific individual sentences of the language.

On the other hand, these predictions do not take the form of an argument as scientific predictions typically do.

In this characterization of indirect grammatical predictions, we have also, by implication, characterized direct grammatical predictions. The grammatical predictions (1)(a) and (b) and (23)(a)—(d) are examples of direct grammatical predictions. Their directness is two-sided. On the one hand, they are directed at specific individual sentences and other units of the language in question. On the other hand, these predictions take the form of an argument as scientific predictions typically do. Cryptically, the distinction between indirect and direct grammatical predictions may be formulated as follows: indirect grammatical predictions are made by the *grammar* of a particular language, whereas direct grammatical predictions are made by the *grammarian* of the language on the basis of this grammar. Our main concern in the paragraphs below will be with direct grammatical predictions.

8.3.2.1.4 *Grammatical predictions vs. calculations*

A fourth general point involves a distinction between GRAMMATICAL PREDIC-TIONS and CALCULATIONS. In terms of this distinction, as drawn by Katz (1977:571), grammatical predictions can be made only about those properties and relations of sentences defined by the general linguistic theory as constitutive of some level of linguistic structure. Thus, on the basis of the P-markers assigned to two sentences S_1 and S_2 grammatical predictions such as the following may be made: "(a) S_1 will be grammatical, S_2 ungrammatical; (b) S_1 and S_2 will have different subjects; (c) S_1 will be an interrogative, S_2 an imperative". It is possible to make these grammatical predictions because the properties about which they express claims are defined in the general linguistic theory as grammatical pro-perties constitutive of syntactic (phrase) structure. These, of course, are the properties denoted by the expressions "grammatical", "ungrammatical", "subject", "interrogative" and "imperative".

The structural representations assigned to sentences, however, may exhibit properties and relations of an accidental or nonessential sort. These are the properties and relations not defined in the general linguistic theory as consti-tutive of some level of linguistic structure. Claims about such nonessential properties and relations that may be exhibited by sentences represent, in the terminology of Katz (1977:571), "calculations" about sentences. Thus, on the basis of the P-markers assigned to the sentences S_1 and S_2, calculations such as the following may be made: "(a) S_1 contains exactly 17,375,031 morphemes more than S_2; (b) The ratio of phrases to clauses in S_1 is the same as the ratio of the occurrences of *fudge* in S_1 to the occurrences of *jelly-beans* in S_2". The number of morphemes per sentence, the ratio of phrases to clauses, and the ratio of the occurrence of certain lexical items to the occurrence of certain other lexical items are not defined in the general linguistic theory as properties constitutive of some level of linguistic structure. Therefore, no grammatical predictions are made about these and similar other accidental properties of sentences.

The (a) part of the characterization (29) of grammatical predictions may now be refined as follows: grammatical predictions are (a) "grammatical" in that they represent claims about *definitional or constitutive* properties of sentences in a particular human language. It is against this background that Katz (1977:562, n.2) uses the expression "predict" in the following sense:

> a grammar G predicts that a sentence S has the property or relation R just in case linguistic theory defines R as a grammatical property or relation and the structural description of S in G together with the definition of R implies that S has R.

8.3.2.2   Structure of Direct Grammatical Predictions

Let us consider the logical structure of direct grammatical predictions. Their logical structure is analogous to that of grammatical explanations. Direct grammatical predictions are logically composed of three main components: a projectandum, a projectans and a logical relation between the projectandum and the projectans. This is illustrated by the reconstruction (30) of the direct grammatical prediction (1)(a).

(30)

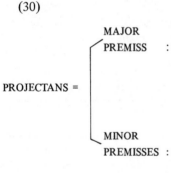

PROJECTANS =

MAJOR PREMISS :   If the grammar of English specifies that derived nominals have the internal structure of NPs and the internal structure of a given derived nominal differs from that of an NP, then this derived nominal will be unacceptable.

MINOR PREMISSES :   1. The grammar of English specifies that derived nominals have the internal structure of NPs.
2. The expression *his criticism of the book before he read it* is a derived nominal which contains a structural element of a VP in the form of the *before* clause.

PROJECTANDUM = CONCLUSION: The expression *his criticism of the book before he read it* will be unacceptable.

We shall discuss each of the three main components of a direct grammatical prediction individually.

8.3.2.2.1   The projectandum

The projectandum of a direct grammatical prediction is a proposition in which a particular grammatical property is ascribed to one or more sentences or other linguistic units. In other words, the projectandum expresses the grammarian's expectation that one or more sentences or other linguistic units will have a particular grammatical property. For instance:

(31)(a)   in the projectandum of (30) the property of unacceptability is ascribed to *his criticism of the book before he read it*;

(b)   in the projectandum of (23)(b) the property of ambiguity is ascribed to *I dislike John's complaining*;

(c)   in the projectandum of (23)(c) the impossibility of a particular interpretation is indicated for *I dislike John's complaining more than Bill's*; etc.

The grammatical properties ascribed to the linguistic units in the projectanda of (31)(a)–(c) are properties about which native speakers of English have linguistic intuitions. It seems, therefore, that direct grammatical predictions are predictions of linguistic intuitions as judgments about the utterances in which the linguistic units in question are realized.

This impression is essentially correct, but should be refined. Some direct grammatical predictions make predictions about properties of sentences about which native speakers of the language in question cannot have linguistic intuitions. However, these properties may then be reduced to properties about which native speakers can have linguistic intuitions. Our first impression must therefore be refined as follows: direct grammatical predictions make predictions about (a) properties of sentences about which native speakers can have linguistic intuitions or (b) properties of sentences which may be reduced to properties about which native speakers can have linguistic intuitions. Ultimately, then, direct grammatical predictions are predictions about the properties of products of linguistic performance.

Point (b) above may be illustrated with reference to an example taken from Chomsky's work. Consider the following English expressions:

(32)(a)   *The book is readable.*   (= (53)a.)
(b)   *the book's readability*   (= (53)b.)
(c)   *John is self-indulgent.*   (= (53)c.)
(d)   *John's self-indulgence*   (= (53)d.)

The numbers on the righthand side are Chomsky's. With reference to these expressions Chomsky (1972b:55) argues as follows:

If the lexicalist hypothesis is accepted for the full range of derived nominals, then (53b) and (53d) must be analyzed in terms of base structures such as (51). Since *readability* and *self-indulgence* are obviously derived from *readable* and *self-indulgent*, it follows that (53a) and (53c) must in effect also be base structures rather than transforms from other structures such as, perhaps (54):

(54)a.   the book is able [s for the book to be read] s
   b.   John in indulgent to John.

The base structure (51) to which Chomsky refers is represented here as (33).

(33)

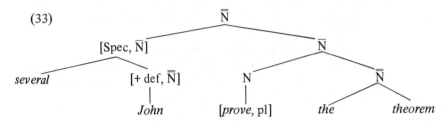

(several of John's proofs of the theorem)

In reasoning thus, Chomsky in fact makes two direct grammatical predictions. These may be reconstructed as (34)(a) and (b) respectively.

(34)(a)   The expressions *the book's readability* and *John's self-indulgence* will have base structures such as (33). These two expressions are derived nominals. All derived nominals have base structures of the general form of (33).

   (b)   The expressions *The book is readable* and *John is self-indulgent* will be base structures rather than transforms. In the grammar of English, *readability* and *self-indulgence* are analyzed as base structures. In particular, they are derived from *readable* and *self-indulgent* respectively. Structures from which base structures are derived cannot be transforms, but must be base structures themselves.

Note that the predictions made in (34)(a) and (b) concern the base structure of linguistic units. Native speakers of a language cannot have linguistic intuitions about base structures. However, properties of base structures may be related to properties of utterances about which native speakers can have linguistic intuitions.
   The latter point may be illustrated with reference to the direct grammatical prediction (34)(b). It is specified in the projectandum of this prediction that the expression *The book is readable,* among others, will not be a transform, but a base structure. If the expression *The book is readable* were a transform, *readable* would have to be the transform of *able to be read,* and if *readable* were the transform of *able to be read,* these two expressions would have to have the same meaning. Although native speakers of English can have no intuitions about base structures and transforms, they can have intuitions about the similarity or difference in meaning between two expressions. According to Chomsky (1972b: 55), their intuition is that *readable* and *able to be read* do not have the same

meaning. The meaning of *readable* is far more limited than that of *able to be read*. This example serves to illustrate how a property of sentences or linguistic units about which native speakers can have no linguistic intuitions may be reduced to properties of utterances about which native speakers can have linguistic intuitions.

Consider once again the characterization (29) of the general nature of direct grammatical predictions. In the (b) part of this characterization it is said, among other things, that in direct grammatical predictions claims are made about the properties of unknown sentences on the basis of the properties of other, investigated sentences. Looking at the grammatical predictions (34)(a) and (b), however, we find that this point has to be refined. Note the general form of these two predictions: on the basis of a known property of a sentence (or a constituent of a sentence) – and in accordance with a lawlike linguistic generalization – a claim is made about another, unknown property of *the same* sentence (or a constituent of the sentence). Thus, direct grammatical predictions do not make claims solely about the properties of unknown sentences. They may also make claims about unknown properties of otherwise known sentences.

8.3.2.2.2   *The projectans*
The projectans of a direct grammatical prediction has the same components as the explanans of a grammatical explanation. A projectans is composed of two parts: a lawlike generalization and propositions presenting factual linguistic data. In the generalization, a lawlike reason is given for the expectation expressed in the prediction. The factual reasons for this expectation are given in the latter propositions.

8.3.2.2.2.1   *The lawlike generalization*   The projectantia of the direct grammatical predictions which we considered above contain lawlike generalizations which may be reconstructed as in (35)(a)–(d).

(35)(a)   If it is specified in the neutral lexical entry for a lexical item that it may not take a sentential complement and if in a particular expression this item does take a sentential complement, then this expression will be unacceptable – cf. (23)(a) above.

(b)   If the grammatical rules of English assign more than one alternative deep structure to a sentence, then this sentence will be ambiguous – cf. (23)(b) above.

(c)   If the deletion transformation T_x violates the recoverability condition in the derivation of a given sentence, then this sentence will be unacceptable in a given interpretation – cf. (23)(c) above.

(d)   If the movement transformation T_y violates the Coordinate Structure Constraint in the derivation of a given sentence, then this sentence will be unacceptable – cf. (23)(d) above.

Notice that these four lawlike generalizations occur in exactly the same form in grammatical explanations. To see this, have another look at (44)(a), (b), (d) and (e) in §7.3.2.2.2.1.

The lawlike generalizations which occur in projectantia belong to the same two types as the lawlike generalizations occurring in explanantia. The first type of lawlike generalization is based primarily on the grammar or theoretical grammatical description of the language in question. The lawlike generalizations (35)(a) and (b) belong to this type. These two lawlike generalizations are based on a neutral lexical entry and the base rules of a particular language respectively. Such lawlike generalizations are by nature language-specific. A grammarian who bases a direct grammatical prediction on a language-specific generalization is, in general terms, saying the following: I have the expectation E about the property/ ies P of the sentence(s) S because the language in question is as it is. How the language in question "is", is described in its grammar. Therefore, a first type of direct grammatical prediction is based on a theoretical description of the language in question, or of the linguistic competence of the users of this language.

The second type of lawlike generalization is based both on the content of a (possible) part of a grammar and on a principle of the general linguistic theory. The lawlike generalizations (35)(c) and (d) above belong to this type. These law-like generalizations are based on (possible) rules, T_x and T_y, in the grammar of English and on general linguistic conditions — such as the recoverability condition and the Coordinate Structure Constraint — on the applicability of transformations. Lawlike generalizations of this type therefore have both a language-specific and a language-independent, or universal, aspect. To base a grammatical prediction on such a lawlike generalization is, in general terms, for the grammarian to say the following: I have the expectation E about the property/ies P of the sentence(s) S of the language L, on the one hand, because L is as it is and, on the other hand, because human language in general is as it is.

8.3.2.2.2.2   *The factual reasons*   Consider the following examples of the types of factual reasons that are offered in the projectantia of direct grammatical predictions.

(36)(a)   In the derived nominal *John's easiness to succeed* "easy" has a sentential complement with the surface form *to succeed* – cf. (23)(a) above.

   (b)   In the grammar of English two alternative deep structures are assigned to the sentence *I dislike John's complaining* – cf. (23)(b) above.

   (c)   (i)   The interrogative sentence *Who does John love Mary and?* is derived by applying the *wh*-movement transformation to a deep structure such as that underlying the sentence *John loves Mary and Sue.*

(ii) In the derivation of *Who does John love Mary and?* the transformation in question moves a conjunct, viz. the NP with the feature [+ wh], of a coordinate structure, *Mary and* [+ wh]$_{NP}$, out of this structure, and places it at the beginning of the sentence (where it is realized phonologically by the interrogative form *who*) – cf. (23)(d) above.

Note that the types of data given in the factual reasons of the projectantia of direct grammatical predictions are the same as those given in the explanantia of grammatical explanations. Compare (45)(a), (b) and (e) in §7.3.2.2.2.2 on this point. These factual data are data about sentences: data about structural properties of sentences (cf. (36)(a) and (b)), data about grammatical rules that play a role in the derivation of sentences (cf. (36)(c)(i) and (ii)), and so on. The factual data of the projectans may include any datum about a sentence on which – with the aid of the lawlike generalization – an expectation about an unknown grammatical property of the same or another sentence may be based.

8.3.2.2.3   *The logical relation*
The argument (30) above is a deductive argument. Given the content of the premisses, the content of the conclusion necessarily follows. Or, in concrete terms, given the content of the premisses, it can but be concluded that the expression *his criticism of the book before he read it* will be unacceptable. Thus, the logical relation between the projectandum and the projectans is a deductive relation. This is typically the case with direct grammatical predictions. The expectation expressed in the projectandum necessarily follows from the lawlike generalization and factual reasons of the projectans. Direct grammatical predictions therefore represent DEDUCTIVE PROJECTIONS. Grammatical predictions of a nondeductive or stochastic nature are not made in linguistic inquiry.

8.3.2.3   *Other Characteristics of Grammatical Projections*

Before concluding our discussion of the nature of grammatical projections, three points remain to be dealt with.
The first point concerns the functions of grammatical predictions. These predictions have both the epistemological and the methodological functions of scientific projections in general. On the one hand, grammatical predictions yield potential knowledge about unknown parts of a language-specific reality. On the other hand, grammatical predictions play an important role in the justification and testing of linguistic theories. This latter function will be discussed in chapters 9 and 10. Note, however, that grammatical predictions are not made to serve as guidelines for practical action in linguistic inquiry. In other words, grammatical predictions do not have the pragmatic function which scientific predictions generally have. In making predictions the grammarian does not attempt to gain

control over the linguistic performance of the users of the language in question.
The second point relates to the minimal criteria for grammatical predictions.
These are the same as the minimal criteria for scientific projections in general.
These criteria, both formal and material, were discussed in §8.2.1.6.

The third point relates to the type to which the grammatical predictions of
the preceding paragraphs belong. In §8.4.3.4 it will be shown that these grammatical predictions represent internal grammatical projections as distinguished
from a second type of grammatical projection, viz. external grammatical projections.

8.3.3   Making Grammatical Predictions

The second question which may be raised in connection with grammatical
projection(s) is the following: what intellectual activities are involved in the
making of grammatical predictions in linguistic inquiry? This question must be
answered against the background of our distinction between direct and indirect
grammatical predictions.

The main activities involved in the making of direct grammatical predictions
are characterized as follows:

(37)   A grammarian makes a direct grammatical prediction by
    (a)   stating a proposition about an unknown but essential property
        of one or more sentences or classes of utterances;
    (b)   presenting a factual basis for the proposition of (a) in the form
        of linguistic data about the sentence(s) in question or about
        other, related sentences;
    (c)   presenting a lawlike basis for the proposition of (a) in the form
        of a theoretical linguistic generalization in which the relatedness
        of the property of (a) and the linguistic data of (b) is specified;
    (d)   indicating the logical relation between the proposition of (a)
        and the propositions by which the linguistic data of (b) and the
        linguistic generalization of (c) are presented.

In this characterization, the expression "sentences" is used as a shorter synonym
for "sentences or constituents of sentences".

In order to make a direct grammatical prediction, it is therefore necessary to
construct an argument. In §8.4.3.4 it will be shown that (37) gives a characterization of the activities involved in making the type of prediction that represents
internal grammatical projections. In the same paragraph it will become clear that
generative grammarians make another type of grammatical projection as well,
viz. external grammatical projections.

Recall that, in terms of §8.3.2.1.3, indirect grammatical predictions are made by a generative grammar. The process by which these predictions are made is the process of mechanically generating sentences.

(38) A grammar makes indirect grammatical predictions about sentences which are not included in the original corpus by
  (a) enumerating these sentences, and thus ascribing to them the property of grammaticality, or by not enumerating them, and thus ascribing to them the property of ungrammaticality, and
  (b) assigning structural descriptions to the enumerated sentences.

Notice that in (38) it is not an activity that is being described, but a process. It is clear that there is a difference in character between the mechanical process of generating sentences and the construction of arguments in order to make direct grammatical predictions.

8.4 GENERAL LINGUISTIC INQUIRY

8.4.1 General

Consider the following two fragments of linguistic argumentation:

(39)(a) Dutch will not have a nominalization transformation for the derivation of derived nominals. Such a nominalization transformation would have to perform deletions in the derivation of many derived nominals in Dutch. In many cases these deletions are such that the deleted elements are irrecoverable. The recoverability condition on deletion rules out as impossible in human language, all deletion transformations that delete elements in an underlying P-marker so that these elements cannot be recovered.
  (b) The syntactic component of Walbiri will include transformational rules. Walbiri is a typical human language. The syntactic component of all possible human languages includes, among other things, transformational rules.

In (39)(a) and (b) we have typical examples of general linguistic projections. In particular, they represent internal general linguistic predictions. In the paragraphs below we shall discuss the nature and properties of internal general linguistic predictions, the nature and properties of the corresponding external general linguistic projections and the activities involved in the making of general linguistic projections.

8.4.2   Nature of Internal General Linguistic Predictions

8.4.2.1   *"Possible Human Language"*

In the preceding paragraphs we saw that grammatical predictions express reasoned expectations about unknown properties of sentences in individual human languages. INTERNAL GENERAL LINGUISTIC PREDICTIONS, by contrast, are directed at the properties of the (internalized) grammars of the individual human languages. In other words, internal general linguistic predictions express reasoned expectations about the properties that the linguistic competence of speakers of human languages ought or ought not to have. For instance, in (39)(a) the expectation is expressed that Dutch will not have a transformation of derivative nominalization. In (39)(b) the expectation is expressed that transformational rules will be a structural element of the syntax of Walbiri.

The universals of the general linguistic theory form the basis for internal general linguistic predictions. Recall that, in technical terms, this theory has to give a characterization of a possible human language. The general linguist constructs this theory on the basis of his knowledge of the properties of a limited number of individual human languages. By means of the general linguistic theory, the general linguist is therefore in fact projecting knowledge about a limited part of a linguistic reality onto the remaining, unknown part of this reality. Schematically this point may be illustrated as follows:

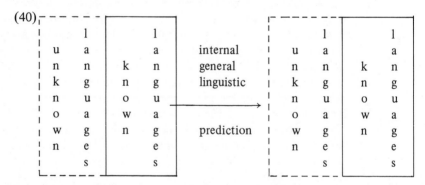

In the diagram (40) "known" and "unknown" are used in the sense of "scientifically known" and "scientifically unknown" respectively.

The diagram (40) also illustrates a further characteristic of internal general linguistic predictions. As with grammatical predictions, internal general linguistic predictions are atemporal. In internal general linguistic predictions the known linguistic reality and the unknown linguistic reality exist at the same point in time. Internal general linguistic predictions such as (39)(a) and (b) do not in essence express expectations about a future linguistic reality. The qualification "in essence" is used for a particular reason. It is the aim of the general linguistic theory to give a characterization of *all* possible human languages. All possible human languages need not, of course, actually be in current use. Human languages used in the past and those that will be used in the future are also members of the class of possible human languages. Therefore, in terms of its aim, the general linguistic theory should also be able to serve as a basis for internal general linguistic postdictions about a linguistic reality of the past and for internal general linguistic predictions about a linguistic reality of the future.

In preceding chapters we saw that the general linguistic theory is composed of linguistic universals. Each linguistic universal specifies a property of human language in general. By implication, therefore, every linguistic universal expresses a restriction on the class of possible human languages. As such, every linguistic universal may serve as a basis for a class of internal general linguistic predictions about noninvestigated individual human languages. Substantive universals serve as a basis for predictions about the linguistic units and grammatical rules that will occur in individual human languages. The term "linguistic units" is used here in a broad sense to denote linguistic properties, items, constituents, categories, and so on. For example, the universal inventory of phonetic features serves as a basis for predictions about the components of the phonetic segments of individual languages. Formal universals serve as a basis for predictions about the various forms the grammatical rules and lexical entries of the individual languages will take. In (39)(b), for example, a prediction is made about the form that one of the types of rules of the syntax of Walbiri will take: the form of transformational rules. Finally, organizational universals serve as a basis for predictions about the ways in which the rules and lexical entries of individual languages will be organized (into components).

Consider the following two points about internal general linguistic predictions:

(41)(a)   Internal general linguistic predictions express, among other things, expectations about the presence/absence of certain rules in individual human languages.

(b)   Internal general linguistic predictions express, among other things, expectations about the form that all grammatical rules will take in individual languages.

These two statements are interesting from a metascientific point of view. Grammatical rules represent lawlike generalizations. It thus appears from (41)(a) and (b) that internal general linguistic predictions express claims about, among other things, the existence and form of lawlike generalizations. But, as we saw in §8.2.1.5 above, a philosopher of science such as Bunge (1967b:69, 116) holds that scientific predictions do not express expectations about laws: " . . . we make no nomological prediction of laws although we do sometimes anticipate or prognose in outline their discovery" (p.116). Internal general linguistic predictions express expectations about lawlike generalizations. Within the broader context of empirical inquiry in general, therefore, they seem to represent a special form of scientific prediction.

8.4.2.2   Structure of Internal General Linguistic Predictions

The logical structure of internal general linguistic predictions may be illustrated
with reference to the following reconstruction of the prediction (39)(b):

(42)

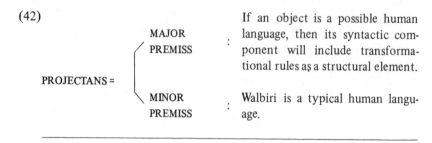

PROJECTANS =

MAJOR PREMISS : If an object is a possible human language, then its syntactic component will include transformational rules aş a structural element.

MINOR PREMISS : Walbiri is a typical human language.

PROJECTANDUM = CONCLUSION : The syntax of Walbiri will include
transformational rules as a structural element.

The first main component of an internal general linguistic prediction is a projectandum. The projectandum is a proposition which expresses an expectation about
a property of an individual language.

The second main component, the projectans, contains the linguistic reasons
or grounds for the expectation expressed by the projectans. 'One of these reasons
– viz. the one contained in the major premiss – is a lawlike generalization. It is
formulated in terms of some linguistic universal or other. In (42) above, it is a
universal which specifies that the syntax of all human languages is constructed
in terms of a certain type of rule – transformational rules. The other reason(s)
given in the projectans is/are of a factual nature. In (42) this factual reason takes
the simplest possible form: that of a statement that a particular object, Walbiri,
is indeed a typical human language. In some internal general linguistic predictions – for instance (39)(a) above – these factual reasons are more complex. In
such predictions more detailed factual particulars are given about the language in
question.

The last main component of an internal general linguistic prediction is the
logical relation between the projectandum and the projectans. As is typically
the case, this logical relation is a deductive relation in (42). Given the content
of the projectans, the projectandum must necessarily have the content that it
in fact has. In general linguistic inquiry, as in grammatical inquiry, predictions of
a nondeductive nature are not made.

At this point we can answer an obvious question about general linguistic
predictions: in what way are general linguistic predictions "internal"? They are
internal in the sense that they contain no element which relates to something
outside the linguistic reality of the general linguist. This characterization holds
for both the projectandum and the projectans. The projectandum of internal

general linguistic predictions refers to properties of the (internalized) grammar of an individual language. Should the projectandum refer to anything other than such a property, it would be referring to something outside the directly given level of the general linguist's linguistic reality. Thus, the projectandum of an internal general linguistic prediction cannot express an expectation about anything other than a property of an (internalized) grammar. The lawlike generalization of the projectans concerns language in general or man's language acquisition faculty. Should it represent a generalization about anything else, then it would concern something outside the underlying level of the general linguist's linguistic reality. In other words, the projectans of an internal general linguistic prediction cannot contain a lawlike generalization which, as a whole, does not form part of the general linguistic theory.

By implication we have already given a characterization of noninternal, or EXTERNAL GENERAL LINGUISTIC PROJECTIONS. These are general linguistic projections of which either the projectandum, or the projectans, or both the projectandum and the projectans refer to objects outside the linguistic reality of the general linguist. Let us consider the nature of external general linguistic projections in more detail.

8.4.3   Nature of External General Linguistic Projections

8.4.3.1   *"Possible Linguistic Change"*

A distinction may be drawn between a more limited and a broader view of what, in technical terms, the task is of a general linguistic theory. The more limited, standard view is the one we considered above.

(43)   It is the task of a general linguistic theory to give a characterization of a possible human language.

The broader view of the task of a general linguistic theory includes this more limited view. However, within this broader view one or more additional tasks are assigned to a general linguistic theory. In the literature on the subject various additional tasks have been proposed for a general linguistic theory. Among these, that of (44) is central.

(44)   A general linguistic theory, in conjunction with a theory of linguistic change, has the additional task of giving a characterization of a possible linguistic change.

The general linguistic theory is assigned this additional task by generative grammarians such as Paul Kiparsky (1968a; 1968b) and David Lightfoot (1976a;

1976b; in press). These linguists differ about various aspects of the afore-mentioned additional task of a general linguistic theory. Their differences of opinion, however, fall outside the scope of our study. In our discussion we shall limit ourselves to those aspects on which they more or less agree.

Let us start by determining how a general linguistic theory and a theory of linguistic change would have to be used in conjunction in order to give a characterization of what is and what is not a possible linguistic change. The function of the general linguistic theory is as follows: it must specify the upper limit to the class of possible linguistic changes. In other words, a general linguistic theory must specify what linguistic changes are possible in an absolute sense, and what linguistic changes are impossible in an absolute sense. Those linguistic changes which can be described in terms of the linguistic universals of the general linguistic theory are possible in an absolute sense. Those linguistic changes, on the contrary, which cannot be described in terms of these universals are impossible in an absolute sense. Every linguistic universal therefore admits certain linguistic changes to the class of possible linguistic changes and excludes others from this class. In his book *Principles of diachronic syntax* (in press: 142), Lightfoot goes to the heart of the matter:

> If one takes a theory of grammar to specify what counts as a possible grammar of a natural language, this will provide the upper boundary to possible diachronic changes: no grammar can change historically into something which is not a possible grammar of a natural language.

It follows that the linguistic universals specify what differences between two successive stages of a particular language cannot exist in an absolute sense. Likewise, the general linguistic theory by implication specifies what differences between two successive stages of a language could exist, viz. those differences that can be described in terms of linguistic universals However, the differences which do in fact exist between two successive stages of a language are but a limited subclass of the differences which are admitted as possible in an absolute sense by the general linguistic theory. This brings us to the part that a theory of linguistic change may play in specifying what are and what are not possible linguistic changes. A theory of linguistic change may specify, among other things, the lower boundary to the class of possible linguistic changes. This implies that a theory of linguistic change may specify what the (types of) linguistic changes are by which one stage of a language can change into a successive stage. In other words, a theory of linguistic change may specify, among other things, what types of differences can and what types of differences cannot exist between two successive stages of a language. Lightfoot (in press: 142) illustrates this point as follows:

> If there are lower bounds, these will presumably be a function of a theory of change. There clearly are lower bounds, since grammars do not change in

wholesale fashion, for example changing all lexical entries from one genera-
tion to the next.

Schematically the way in which a general linguistic theory and a theory of
linguistic change collaborate in specifying a possible linguistic change may be
represented as follows:

(45)

A = class of possible linguistic changes which, according to general
  linguistic theory, are possible in an absolute sense.
B = class of changes in terms of which one stage of a language may
  change into a subsequent stage according to a theory of linguistic
  change.

Note in passing that, conventionally, a comprehensive theory of linguistic change
is required to do more than give a mere characterization of the individual types
of linguistic change of B in (45). It is expected that such a theory should, for
instance, also specify what the types of linguistic change of B have in common,
what the possible causes of these types of linguistic change are, and so on.

To give a characterization of a possible linguistic change involves making
three kinds of general linguistic projections. The first kind is postdictions:
claims about the linguistic changes that have (have not) occurred in the history
of human languages. The second kind is projections about a linguistic reality
of the present: claims about the linguistic changes which may (not) be occurring
in human languages at present. The third kind is literally predictions: claims
about which linguistic changes will (not) occur in human languages in the future.
Historical data are the most readily available data concerning linguistic change.
These are data concerning linguistic changes which did (not) occur in the history
of human languages. For this reason generative grammarians such as Lightfoot
and Kiparsky regard the general linguistic projections about possible linguistic
changes as postdictions. Paradoxically, however, they call these postdictions
"predictions". Recall that these postdictions regarding which linguistic changes
could or could not have occurred in the history of human languages are made
on the basis of, among other things, the general linguistic theory. For this reason
these postdictions are called "general linguistic projections". These projections
should be regarded as "external" for various reasons which we will consider
below. We shall discuss these reasons with reference to an example of the type
of projection about the possible linguistic changes in question.

8.4.3.2   *A Sample Projection about Possible Linguistic Changes*

One of the principles of Chomsky's general linguistic theory which we have considered is the $\overline{X}$-convention. Let us look at a sample projection concerning a possible linguistic change which may be made on the basis of, among other things, this linguistic universal.

In §5.3.2.2 we saw that for Chomsky there is a linguistically significant similarity between, among other things, the following base rules of English:

(46)(a) $\overline{N} \longrightarrow N$ ——— $Comp_N$
   (b) $\overline{V} \longrightarrow V$ ——— $Comp_V$
   (c) $\overline{A} \longrightarrow A$ ——— $Comp_A$

With the aid of the $\overline{X}$-convention it becomes possible to collapse these three rules into a single rule schema (47).

(47) $\overline{X} \longrightarrow X$ ——— $Comp_X$

By allowing the collapsing or abbreviation of the rules of (46) to the rule schema (47), the $\overline{X}$-convention implies that, from a general linguistic point of view, these three rules form a unit.

The $\overline{X}$-convention, in conjunction with the theory of linguistic change proposed by Kiparsky, can now serve as a basis for the following projection about an (im)possible linguistic change:

(48)   In English every linguistic change which changes (simplifies) one of the three rules of (46) without changing (simplifying) the other two rules of (46) in a parallel way is impossible. In the grammar the rules of (46) are collapsed into a single rule schema in terms of the $\overline{X}$-convention. Rules which can be collapsed into a single rule schema in terms of the $\overline{X}$-convention cannot be changed (simplified) individually in a nonparallel way by a linguistic change.

An example of a linguistic change which is ruled out in (48) is one which would change the order of N and $Comp_N$ within $\overline{N}$ – – N – $Comp_N$ > $Comp_N$ – N – – without making a parallel change within $\overline{V}$ and $\overline{A}$. The projection of (48) can be made with the necessary modifications, for every individual language of which the grammar includes the $\overline{X}$-convention. The gist of this projection is simply that if a conceivable linguistic change treats base rules which are related in terms of the $\overline{X}$-convention as unrelated, then this conceivable linguistic change is not a possible linguistic change. What would be the consequences if instances of such, presumably "impossible" linguistic changes were to be found? This question will be discussed in §10.4.2.3.1.

The general linguistic projection (48) is an external projection. It goes beyond the linguistic reality of the conventional general linguist in two senses. On the one hand, the projectandum does not express a claim about one or more properties of the grammar of an individual language. A claim is made about a change in an individual human language: a difference in the properties of the grammars of two successive stages of the language. On the other hand, the lawlike generalization of the projectans contains assumptions that are not part of the general linguistic theory. These assumptions represent principles of the theory of linguistic change which is supported by Kiparsky, among others.

> (49)(a) Linguistic change is a change, particularly, in the rules of the grammar of a language.
>
> (b) Linguistic change ultimately involves a simplification of the rules mentioned in (a).

These assumptions are external to the general linguist's linguistic reality. They do not deal with the content or form of man's language faculty. Kiparsky's article, "Linguistic universals and linguistic change" (1968a:179–181), and chapters 1, 3 and 7 of Lightfoot's book, *Principles of diachronic syntax*, may be studied for further examples of general linguistic projections about possible linguistic changes.

Note, finally, that it is not claimed here that the assumptions of (49) are correct. They are presented merely for their illustrative value as principles which may be incorporated in a theory of linguistic change. Lightfoot (to appear) recently even argued that there is *no* theory of linguistic change. He claims (to appear: 1) that on the basis of

> a restrictive theory of grammar and some simple statements about the nature of language acquisition, one can distinguish between possible and impossible changes and obtain an adequately predictive system about when changes will occur and what they would be. When the proper distinctions are drawn, it turns out that for the usual goals, there is no need to invoke 'historical principles' of any kind, or any theory of change.

Even if Lightfoot's argument is sound, projections about possible linguistic changes will still be external. On the one hand, these projections will still concern phenomena outside the narrow linguistic reality of the conventional general linguist. On the other hand, these projections will still be based, in part, on lawlike generalizations which are not part of the general linguistic theory. These are the "simple statements about the nature of language acquisition" which would be part of a theory of language acquisition.

8.4.3.3 *Structure of Projections about Possible Linguistic Changes*

Let us consider in more detail the nature and components of projections about possible linguistic changes. Looking again at the sample projection (48), we see that, as expected, it is composed of three parts: a projectandum, a projectans and a logical relation between the two.

The projectandum expresses a proposition, or expectation, of the general form of (50).

(50)   In the language(s) L, C is an (im)possible linguistic change.

The projectans contains the usual factual data and lawlike generalization. The factual data deal with one or more properties of the grammar of the language(s) L mentioned in the projectandum. These factual data take the general form of (51).

(51)   The rule(s) R of the language(s) L has/have the property P.

The factual data of (51) could also deal with lexical entries. This is the case when the linguistic change in question involves not rule change, but restructuring of the lexicon. The lawlike generalization of the projectans is composed in terms of both concepts and/or assumptions that are part of the general linguistic theory and concepts and/or assumptions that are part of the theory of linguistic change. This lawlike generalization takes the general form of (52).

(52)   If grammatical rules or lexical entries have the general linguistic property P, then they can(not) be changed in the manner M by a linguistic change.

One general point has to be stressed. External general linguistic projections do not deal exclusively with possible linguistic changes. Such projections may be made about various types of linguistic phenomena which fall outside the linguistic reality of the general linguist, but which are systematically related to phenomena within this reality. External general linguistic projections may be made about (im)possible (types of) differences between the horizontal (social) dialects of a language, about (im)possible steps or phases in the nonidealized process of language acquisition, and so on. In each case, an auxiliary theory is needed, in addition to the general linguistic theory, as a basis for such a projection. In the case of the historical projections mentioned above, this auxiliary theory was a theory of linguistic change. In the case of projections about social differences in a language, the auxiliary theory would be a sociolinguistic one. For external general linguistic projections about the nonidealized process of language acquisition, a psychological auxiliary theory would be needed. The nature and function(s) of such auxiliary theories will be discussed in detail in chapters 9 and 10.

8.4.3.4   *Retrospect: External Grammatical Projections*

Against this background, we can elaborate somewhat on the impression given of grammatical projections in §8.3.2. Recall that the grammatical projections with which we were concerned in that paragraph were predictions about the properties of the sentences of a language. These projections were therefore concerned with objects within the grammarian's linguistic reality. For this very reason they were called INTERNAL GRAMMATICAL PROJECTIONS.

However, grammatical hypotheses may also be used as part of the basis for EXTERNAL GRAMMATICAL PROJECTIONS, i.e. projections about objects outside the grammarian's linguistic reality. As in the case of external general linguistic projections, additional assumptions are needed to make external grammatical projections. These additional assumptions are not part of the grammar, but of the theory which relates the linguistic competence to the external grammatical objects about which the external grammatical projections are to be made. Examples of external grammatical projections are given in §§9.3.2.4.2 and 10.3.2.3.3, which is a more natural context in which to discuss them. It will also be shown then how such projections may be used to justify and to test grammatical hypotheses.

8.4.4   Making General Linguistic Projections

We have not yet established what is involved in making general linguistic projections. In discussing this, the distinction between internal and external general linguistic projection should be kept in mind. Let us first take a look at internal general linguistic projection.

(53)   The general linguist makes an internal general linguistic prediction by
   (a)   stating a proposition about an unknown property of one or more grammars of individual human languages;
   (b)   presenting a factual basis for the proposition of (a) in the form of one or more linguistic data about the grammar(s) of (a);
   (c)   presenting a lawlike basis for the proposition of (a) in the form of a linguistic universal in which the property of (a) is related to the data of (b);
   (d)   stating the logical relationship between the proposition of (a) and the linguistic data of (b) and the linguistic universal of (c).

This brings us to the making of external general linguistic projections, and particularly the making of projections about possible linguistic changes.

(54)   The general linguist makes a projection about a possible linguistic change by

(a)   stating a proposition to the effect that a given conceivable linguistic change in one or more individual languages is, or is not, possible;

(b)   presenting a factual basis for the proposition of (a) in the form of data about the properties of the grammar(s) of the language(s) in question;

(c)   presenting a lawlike basis for the proposition of (a) in the form of one or more generalizations in terms of which the properties of (the grammar(s) of) the language(s) of (b) are related to a particular form of linguistic change;

(d)   stating the logical relation between the proposition of (a) and the propostions in terms of which the data of (b) and the generalization of (c) are presented.

It is clear from (53) and (54) above that making general linguistic projections — both internal and external — is a form of argumentation. Note in conclusion that a growing number of generative grammarians regard the making of external general linguistic projections as a normal part of linguistic inquiry. In chapters 9 and 10 it will be shown that such projections play an important role in the justification and criticism of general linguistic hypotheses. By contrast, only a few generative grammarians regard the giving of external general linguistic explanations as an essential part of linguistic inquiry.

SELECTED READING

Inquiry in General

Structure of Scientific Projections

Bunge 1967b:69–70; Harré 1967:79–80; Rudner 1966:63–67; as well as the items listed under the heading "Structure of scientific explanations" on p. 237.

Types of Nonscientific Projection

Bunge 1967b:65–68.

Types of Scientific Projection

Bunge 1967b:74–107.

Scientific Projection vs. Scientific Explanation

Bunge 1967b:69–70, 116–117; Hanson 1959; Kaplan 1964:349–351; Rescher 1958; Scriven 1963; Toulmin 1961:ch.1; as well as the bibliography in Rescher 1970:234–236.

Linguistic Inquiry

Even less has been written about the nature and properties of linguistic projections than about linguistic explanations. For (loose) remarks on linguistic projection, the following works may be considered: Bach 1964:5–6, 93, 176, 186; Chen 1973; Kiparsky 1968a: 179ff.; Lightfoot 1976b; in press: ch.1, 3; Wirth 1975:212–214; as well as the items listed under the following headings: Grammatical inquiry, objectives of inquiry, projection p. 49; General linguistic inquiry, objectives of inquiry, postdictions p. 50.

CHAPTER NINE

Justifying Linguistic Hypotheses

9.0 PERSPECTIVE

In this chapter we shall be looking at the justification of linguistic hypotheses as a seventh main aspect of linguistic inquiry. The first section of the chapter deals with the justification of scientific hypotheses in general. First of all, it is shown how the justification of scientific hypotheses is related to the criteria adopted for scientific knowledge. Scientific justification is characterized in general terms by the giving of "reasons of knowing". A scientific justification is then shown to be made up of three components: a factual, a systematic and a nonobjective component. The nature and logical structure of each of these three components are subsequently discussed in more detail. The first section is concluded with a characterization of the intellectual activities involved in the justification of scientific hypotheses.

The second section of the chapter deals with the justification of grammatical hypotheses and theories in linguistic inquiry. These justifications are made up of three objective components — a factual, a systematic and an external component — and one nonobjective component. First of all, the factual component is shown to be composed of reductive forms of argument, various types of linguistic evidence, certain minimal criteria for linguistic evidence and additional criteria for such evidence. It is then explained how the systematic component is related to the factual component and how it uses systematic considerations or standards of acceptability. This is followed by a discussion of the role of external evidence in the justification of the psychological reality of grammatical hypotheses. In conclusion, a characterization is given of the intellectual activities involved in justifying grammatical hypotheses.

The topic of the third section of this chapter is the justification of general linguistic hypotheses and theories. The discussion follows the same lines as that of the justification of grammatical hypotheses. The internal structure of the factual, the systematic and the external components of general linguistic justifications are discussed in this order. This entails an examination of the forms of argument and the types of linguistic evidence employed, as well as of the minimal and additional criteria adopted for this evidence. As regards the external component, it is shown how the universality, psychological reality and genuineness of linguistic universals may be justified on the basis of external evidence. Subsequently, the nature of and mechanisms within the nonobjective component of both grammatical and general linguistic justifications are discussed. This section is concluded by indicating the similarities which exist between the intellectual activities involved in justifying grammatical hypotheses and those involved in justifying general linguistic hypotheses.

9.1   INTRODUCTION

Let us return once more to §1.4 in which it was explained how Chomsky uses the difference in productivity between gerundive and derivative nominalization as a basis for his choice of the lexicalist hypothesis over the transformationalist hypothesis. The part of Chomsky's argument (1972b:26) with which we are concerned is the following:

(1)   Summarizing these observations, we see that the lexicalist hypothesis explains a variety of facts of the sort illustrated by examples [(19)] through [(21)] ... The transformationalist hypothesis is no doubt consistent with these facts, but it derives no support from them, since it would also be consistent with the discovery, were it a fact, that derived nominals exist in all cases in which we have gerundive nominals. Hence the facts that have been cited give strong empirical support to the lexicalist hypothesis and no support to the transformationalist hypothesis. Other things being equal, then, they would lead us to accept the lexicalist hypothesis from which these facts follow.

This is a typical example of a fragment of a justification of a linguistic hypothesis. The lexicalist hypothesis is justified by comparing its metascientific properties to those of the transformationalist hypothesis. The justification of linguistic hypotheses constitutes a seventh main aspect of linguistic inquiry.

Schematically this seventh main aspect of linguistic inquiry may be represented as follows:

(2)

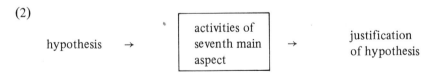

hypothesis   →   [activities of seventh main aspect]   →   justification of hypothesis

As in the case of the other main aspects of linguistic inquiry, two fundamental questions arise in connection with the justification of linguistic hypotheses.

(3) (a)   What is the general nature of the justification of a linguistic hypothesis?

(b)   What are the intellectual activities involved in justifying linguistic hypotheses?

We shall consider these questions from the by now familiar three general angles. As regards empirical inquiry in general, only the outline of the answers to these questions will be given. The details will be filled in when we consider the justifications given in linguistic inquiry.

9.2   INQUIRY IN GENERAL

9.2.1   Nature of Scientific Justifications

9.2.1.1   *General*

For the sake of convenience, the expression SCIENTIFIC JUSTIFICATIONS will be used to denote the justifications given for scientific hypotheses and theories in empirical inquiry. The reason for requiring that scientific hypotheses and theories be justified, stems from the fact that scientists adopt certain criteria for scientific knowledge. Recall that scientists seek scientific knowledge by constructing hypotheses and theories (= theoretical descriptions). Bearing in mind this general point, the criteria mentioned above may be formulated as in (4)(a) and (b).

(4) (a)   Scientific hypotheses and theories must be testable and their accuracy must in fact be tested.

(b)   Scientific hypotheses and theories must be grounded.

Both these criteria require that scientific hypotheses and theories be justified. The criterion (4)(a) implicitly requires an initial measure of justification, whilst the criterion (4)(b) explicitly requires as large a measure of justification as possible. Before discussing these points any further, there is a matter of terminology to be cleared up. Empirical inquiry is concerned with both individual hypotheses and sets of hypotheses which have been integrated into theories. To simplify matters we shall be using the expression "hypothesis/es" as an abbreviation for "individual hypothesis/es and theory/ies", except where otherwise indicated.

As regards the first criterion, (4)(a), scientists do not test every random conjecture. An infinite number of random conjectures can be made which cannot in principle contribute to the expansion of the existing scientific knowledge. Only those conjectures or hypotheses which do have the potential of increasing this knowledge are tested. In other words, only hypotheses which could probably be correct are subjected to testing. Therefore, in order to qualify for testing, an initial measure of justification for a hypothesis should already exist.

However, to be assimilated in the existing corpus of scientific knowledge, a hypothesis must have more than an initial measure of justification. Hence the second criterion, (4)(b), which explicitly requires a maximal measure of justification for scientific hypotheses. A hypothesis is grounded, or maximally justified, if everything points to its being probably correct and if there is no clear indication to the contrary. It will be shown below that it is impossible to demonstrate logically that a hypothesis is beyond all doubt true. To show that a hypothesis is grounded or maximally justified is to show that its correctness is beyond *reasonable* doubt.

From what has been said above about scientific justifications, it follows that a scientific justification for a hypothesis H represents an answer to a certain question about H.

(5)   Why should the hypothesis H be regarded as probably correct?

This question demands reasons. The scientific justification of a hypothesis H therefore takes the form of an argument in which reasons why H should be regarded as being probably correct are given in a coherent way.

In §7.2.1.1 we saw that reasons are also an essential component of scientific explanations. The reasons given in scientific justifications, however, are not of the same kind as those in terms of which scientific explanations are given. The latter are known as "reasons for being": reasons from which it is clear why a (problematic) state of affairs is as it is and (probably) cannot be different. The former kind of reasons is known as "reasons for knowing": reasons someone gives to show why he *claims* that something is as it is and (probably) cannot be any different.

The reasons constituting a scientific justification fall into two basic classes, viz. objective and nonobjective reasons. Objective reasons include two main types of reason, viz. factual and systematic. On the basis of this distinction a scientific justification may be broken down into three components: a factual, a systematic and a nonobjective component. In our discussion of the nature of each of these three components of a scientific justification, we shall refer once more to the biological theory formulated as (4) in §6.2.1. Recall that the theory in question dealt with the nature of the flight control mechanism with which bats are endowed. To facilitate the discussion, we here quote Hartridge's (1920: 56) original formulation of this theory.

(6)   I suggest then that bats during flight emit a short wave-length note and that this sound is reflected from objects in the vicinity. The reflected sound gives the bat information concerning its surroundings. If the path ahead is clear of obstacles, no sound waves are reflected back to the listener. If there are obstacles then these will reflect the sound and the bat will receive an audible warning.

Our exposition of the nature and components of a scientific justification follows roughly the same lines as that given in *The justification of linguistic hypotheses: a study of nondemonstrative inference in transformational grammar* (Botha 1973: (especially) ch.2).

9.2.1.2   *The Factual Component*

The FACTUAL REASONS in the justification of a hypothesis have two sources. On the one hand, a hypothesis derives a certain measure of FACTUAL JUSTIFICA-TION from the problematic data which it serves to explain. On the other hand, a hypothesis derives additional factual justification from data which show that the projections which may be made on the basis of this hypothesis are in fact correct. Recall that we distinguished between two basic types of scientific projection: predictions and postdictions.

9.2.1.2.1   *Justification on the basis of explained data*
The problematic data about the way bats control their flight in the dark include the following:

(7) (a)   Bats have the ability to fly collision-free in the dark.
   (b)   A bat's sight, touch, smell or taste plays no role in controlling its flight in the dark.

These problematic data may be explained in terms of the biological theory — or "hypothesis", as Hartridge calls it — which was quoted as (6) above. Scientists use the fact that this theory forms a basis for the explanation of the data in question in order to justify the theory. This fact is used as follows within the framework of the argument (8).

(8)   MaP : If bats have the flight control mechanism of (6), then they should be able to fly collision-free in the dark without their flight being controlled by their sight, touch, smell or taste.
   MiP : 1. Bats have the ability to fly collision-free in the dark.
        2. A bat's sight, touch, smell or taste plays no role in controlling its flight in the dark.

   C   : Bats probably possess the flight control mechanism of (6).

[MaP = "major premiss", MiP = "minor premisses", C = "conclusion"]

Recall that the "If . . . then" statement of the major premiss represents a conditional statement. The "If" part is the antecedent and the "then" part the consequent of this conditional statement.

Let us consider the argument (8) — which may be called a "supporting argument" — in more detail. As far as its logical form is concerned, (8) is not a deductive argument. The logical form of deductive arguments, such as those which we considered in preceding chapters, may be symbolically represented as follows:

(9) MaP : If p, then q
MiP : p

_____

C   : Therefore q

In deductive arguments of the form symbolized in (9), a logical rule of DEDUCTION is used to do the following: from a conditional statement ("If p, then q") and a proposition constituting its antecedent ("p") the consequent ("Therefore q") is inferred. We shall return to the form of argument (9) in §10.2.1.2.1.

The supporting argument (8) does not have the logical form of (9), but that of (10).

(10)   MaP : If p, then q
MiP : q

_____

C   : Therefore p

An argument with the logical form symbolized in (10) is called a REDUCTIVE ARGUMENT. In reductive arguments a logical rule of REDUCTION is used to do the following: from a conditional statement ("If p, then q") and a proposition constituting its consequent ("q") the antecedent ("Therefore p") is inferred.

We saw in §§7.2.1.2 and 7.2.1.3 that a large class of scientific explanations have the logical form of deductive arguments. By contrast, a factual justification of the type in question has the logical form of a reductive argument. By drastically oversimplifying this difference, it may also be formulated in the following, far less precise way: in a deductive explanation a description of the problematic data is inferred from, among other things, a hypothesis. In a reductive (or factual) justification, on the other hand, the (accuracy of the) hypothesis is inferred from, among other things, a description of the problematic data. "Inferred" in this context does not mean "discovered" or "thought out". It means "related, in terms of a logical rule, to".

Reductive arguments differ from deductive arguments in an important logical respect. Deductive arguments have the logical property of being DEMONSTRATIVE or FORMALLY VALID. If the premises of a deductive argument are true, the conclusion must necessarily be true. Therefore, to say that a form of argument is demonstrative is to say that it is truth-preserving. Deductive arguments are truth-preserving because they are nonampliative or not content-extending. In other words, the conclusion of a deductive argument contains no information that is not already present in the premises. Nothing is stated in the conclusion that is not already stated in the premises. In view of these considerations, deductive arguments are called DEMONSTRATIVE ARGUMENTS.

Reductive arguments, on the other hand, have the property of being NON-DEMONSTRATIVE or FORMALLY INVALID. If the premisses of a reductive argument are true, it does not necessarily follow that the conclusion is true. Therefore reductive arguments do not have the property of being truth-preserving. The reason for this is that they are ampliative or content-extending. In reductive arguments the conclusion includes elements of content that are not present in the premisses. The conclusion goes beyond what is stated in the premisses. In view of these considerations, reductive arguments are known as NONDEMONSTRATIVE ARGUMENTS.

To call a supporting argument such as (8) nondemonstrative is to imply the following: the fact that the problematic data presented in the minor premisses may be explained on the basis of the theory mentioned in the conclusion does not imply that this theory is necessarily true. It is always logically possible that these data may be explained on the basis of an alternative theory or hypotheses such as, for instance, the theory formulated in (11).

(11)   Bats control their flight in the dark by means of a sixth sense which they uniquely possess.

In his book *The philosophy of science: a systematic account* (1966:11), Peter Caws uses a striking example to illustrate the nondemonstrative nature of reductive arguments:

A sentence which is a consequence of one hypothesis may also be the consequence of another hypothesis, and if all we have is the consequence we do not know which hypothesis to choose. The sentence 'If a man takes arsenic, he will die' while certainly true of most people, does not allow us to conclude that if any one of them dies he must have taken arsenic. There are many ways of dying. One of them must have occurred, but which, without further inquiry, we cannot say.

Data that can be explained on the basis of a hypothesis therefore do not prove or demonstrate the truth of the hypothesis. However, the data explained by a hypothesis may be regarded as evidence for the hypothesis. Data constitute EVIDENCE for a hypothesis if these data — as presented in the minor premiss(es) of one or more arguments — indicate inconclusively that the hypothesis could possibly be true. If the data in question can be explained on the basis of the hypothesis, they constitute SUPPORTING EVIDENCE for the hypothesis. The kind of factual justification which a hypothesis derives from the data it serves to explain is therefore known as (FACTUAL/EMPIRICAL) SUPPORTING EVIDENCE FOR THE HYPOTHESIS. The form of reductive argument in which supporting evidence is presented for a hypothesis is known as a SUPPORTING ARGUMENT. Notice that the argument (8) above was called a "supporting argument" in accordance with this terminology. In §9.2.1.2.2 below we shall consider a second type of factual justification for a hypothesis, a second type of evidence and a second, associated form of reductive argument.

In a previous section of our study we did in fact briefly look at supporting arguments such as that of (8). This was in §5.2.2.2 when we considered Hanson's logical rule of retroduction as a possible logical rule for discovery. This rule of retroduction is identical to the one discussed above. In empirical inquiry Hanson's logical rule of retroduction therefore plays a role in the context of justification and not in the context of discovery.

Before considering the second source of factual justification, one more general distinction should be noted. We have consistently distinguished between an argument and a form of argument. For instance, the supporting argument (8) is an (individual) argument. It represents a concrete case or instance of the (general) form of argument known as "supporting arguments". As a form of argument, supporting arguments represent a subform of an even more general form of argument, viz. reductive arguments. The form of argument of which an individual argument is a concrete instance becomes clear when the argument is symbolically reconstructed as in (9) and (10) above. In such a reconstruction 'p' is conventionally used to symbolize the antededent of a conditional statement, whereas 'q' is used to symbolize its consequent.

9.2.1.2.2   *Justification on the basis of projected data*

For the purpose of the discussion in the remaining part of our study, we shall be using the expressions "projection", "prediction" and "postdiction" in the narrower sense of "projective statement", "predictive statement" and "post-dictive statement" respectively. This use of the terms in question was elucidated in (12) of §8.2.1.2. In addition, for the sake of brevity, we shall be using the expression PROJECTED DATA in the sense of "data which might bear out the accuracy of projective statements". To take an example: the predictions of (12), among others, could be made on the basis of the biological theory (6).

(12)(a)   Bats that have lost the ability to produce supersonic cries will no longer be able to fly collision-free in the dark.

  (b)   Bats that have lost the ability to register the echoes of their super-sonic cries will no longer be able to fly collision-free in the dark.

Biologists such as Griffin and Galambos were able to produce experimental data from which it is clear that both these predictions are correct. It emerges from these data that neither "mute" ((12)(a)) nor "deaf" ((12)(b)) bats have the ability to fly collision-free in the dark.

Data which bear out the projections which may be made on the basis of a hypothesis constitute the second source of factual justification for such a hypothesis. The measure of factual justification which the hypothesis derives from projected data is known as THE CONFIRMATION OF THE HYPOTHESIS. The data in question are known as CONFIRMING EVIDENCE for the hypothesis.

Confirming evidence is obtained by testing the hypothesis, as we shall see in chapter 10.

The argument within the framework of which the data referred to above constitute confirming evidence for the biological theory (6) may be reconstructed as follows:

(13)   MaP : If bats possess the flight control mechanism of (6), then "mute" and "deaf" bats should not be able to fly collision-free in the dark.

MiP : 1. "Mute" bats cannot fly collision-free in the dark (any more).
2. "Deaf" bats cannot fly collision-free in the dark (any more).

C   : Bats probably possess the flight control mechanism of (6).

For obvious reasons, the argument (13) may be called a CONFIRMING ARGUMENT.

Confirming arguments such as (13) represent a subform of reductive arguments as well. Symbolically the logical form of confirming arguments may be represented as follows:

(14)   MaP : If p, then q
MiP : q

C   : Therefore p

At a first glance there seems to be no logical difference between confirming arguments such as (14) and supporting arguments such as (10). This impression is correct in the sense that both these forms of argument make use of the logical rule of reduction. However, they do not use this rule in the same way. In supporting arguments the reduction is carried out REGRESSIVELY. This means that the known consequent, i.e. the description of the problematic data, is taken as the starting-point of the inference. In confirming arguments, on the other hand, the reduction is carried out PROGRESSIVELY. In other words, the known antecedent, i.e. the hypothesis, is taken as the starting-point of the inference. This distinction between regressive and progressive reduction is discussed by the logician Bocheński in his book *The methods of contemporary thought* (1965:92). In view of this distinction, we shall refer to supporting and confirming arguments as REGRESSIVELY REDUCTIVE ARGUMENTS and PROGRESSIVELY REDUCTIVE ARGUMENTS respectively.

As typical reductive arguments, confirming arguments are nondemonstrative as well. In other words, the data forming confirming evidence for a hypothesis merely serve to indicate inconclusively that the hypothesis may be true. It is still logically possible to derive the projections in question from an alternative hypothesis. For instance, as an alternative to the theory (6), the hypothesis (15) could equally well serve as a basis for the prediction that "deaf" bats should not be able to fly collison-free in the dark.

(15)   Destruction of a bat's auditory sense disturbs its sense of balance: a bat whose balance has been disturbed is unable to fly collision-free in the dark.

What is important is that confirming evidence cannot be used to show conclusively that a hypothesis is true either. Our discussion up to this point may be summarized as follows:

(16)   The factual justification of a hypothesis comprises
    (a)   the support which the hypothesis derives from the data which it helps to explain and
    (b)   the confirmation which the hypothesis derives from data from which it is clear that projections of the hypothesis are correct.

In (16)(b) one aspect of the epistemological function of scientific projections is instantiated: scientific projections play an important role in the justification of scientific hypotheses. In §10.2.1 it will be shown how the factual justification for a hypothesis is related to a certain general philosophical truth criterion.

9.2.1.2.3   *Minimal criteria for evidence*

In order to qualify as evidence for a hypothesis, data must satisfy a number of minimal criteria.

(17)(a)   The data must be logically relevant to the hypothesis.
    (b)   The data must be qualitatively relevant to the hypothesis.
    (c)   The accuracy of the data must be beyond reasonable doubt.

Each one of these criteria will be discussed individually.

We have in fact already considered the criterion of logical relevance (17)(a). In terms of this criterion, the data under consideration qualify as evidence for the hypothesis in question only if these data can appear in the minor premiss(es) of an argument of which the hypothesis is the conclusion. In negative terms this implies that the data under consideration do not qualify as evidence for the hypothesis in question if these data cannot be related to the hypothesis in terms of a logical rule. Therefore, the data may be said to be LOGICALLY RELEVANT to the hypothesis if it is possible to relate them to the hypothesis by means of a logical rule.

In terms of the criterion of qualitative relevance (17)(b), it must be possible to indicate an inherent substantive connection between the phenomena on which the data have a bearing and the phenomena with which the hypothesis deals. An example will serve to illustrate this point. Suppose somebody presented the datum of (18)(b) as evidence for the hypothesis (18)(a).

(18)(a)   Bats possess the flight control mechanism of (6).
    (b)   Bats are mammals.

One could reasonably demand to know what the fact that bats are mammals has to do with their ability to fly collision-free in the dark. To demand this is to voice doubts as to the qualitative relevance of the datum (18)(b) to the hypothesis (18)(a). It is not at all obvious that one should be able to justify a hypothesis about the flying ability of animals by referring to the way in which they feed their young. The data under consideration are QUALITATIVELY RELEVANT to the hypothesis in question if the data and the hypothesis have a bearing on objects or states of affairs which exhibit an apparent material similarity.

The criterion of accuracy, (17)(c), is self-evident. Incorrect data cannot constitute evidence for a hypothesis. Suppose that "deaf" bats did not in fact lose the ability to fly collision-free in the dark. Then the datum contained in the second minor premiss of the confirming argument (13) would be inaccurate and would not count as evidence for the theory (6). The criterion (17)(c) requires data to be factual, i.e. to represent what is indeed the case with that part of reality with which the scientist is concerned. This criterion enables us to call the justification which a hypothesis derives from explained and projected data, "factual" justification.

9.2.1.2.4   *Additional criteria for evidence*
A fundamental property of the factual justification for a hypothesis is that it is inconclusive. The factual justification for a hypothesis does not constitute logical or mathematical proof that the hypothesis is undoubtedly true. The inconclusive nature of factual justification has a number of important consequences. A first consequence is that scientists adopt certain criteria for evidence to ensure that the evidence provides as large a measure of justification for a hypothesis as possible. On the basis of the minimal criteria for evidence, the scientist determines *whether or not* there is any factual justification for the hypothesis in question. If it appears that factual justification for the hypothesis does exist, he lays on additional criteria to determine *the extent of* the justification. Two of these additional criteria for evidence are fundamental. Before considering these criteria, there is a matter of terminology to be cleared up. The expression POSITIVE INSTANCE OF A HYPOTHESIS will be used to refer to the following two kinds of data: a datum which is explained by the hypothesis, on the one hand, and a datum from which it is clear that some of the projections of a hypothesis are correct, on the other hand.

A first fundamental criterion for evidence is that of EVIDENTIAL COMPRE-HENSIVENESS.

(19)   The larger the number of positive instances of a hypothesis, the greater the extent of the factual justification for the hypothesis.

In terms of the criterion (19), the extent of the factual justification for a hypothesis is related to the size of the corpus of evidence for the hypothesis. This corpus includes both supporting and confirming evidence.

A second fundamental criterion for evidence is that of EVIDENTIAL INDEPENDENCE.

(20)   The larger the variety of mutually independent types of data to which the positive instances of a hypothesis belong, the greater the extent of the factual justification for the hypothesis.

This criterion of evidential independence is also known as "the principle of converging evidence" or "the principle of independent motivation/justification".

In his book *The foundations of scientific inference* (1970:130), the philosopher of science and logician Wesley Salmon elucidates the content of the criterion of evidential independence with reference to Newton's theory of gravity.

It is universally recognized that the degree to which a hypothesis is confirmed depends not only upon the number of confirming instances, but also upon their variety. For instance, observations of the position of Mars confirm Newton's theory, but after a certain number of these observations each new one contributes very little to the confirmation of the theory. We want some observations of falling bodies, some observations of the tides, and a good torsion balance experiment. Any confirming instances of one of the subsequent sorts would contribute far more to the confirmation of the theory than would another observation of Mars.

[The theory under consideration states that any two bodies attract each other with a force which is proportional to the product of their masses and inversely proportional to the square of the distance between their centres.]

In the quotation above, Salmon mentions data belonging to four apparently independent types: data about Mars, i.e. data about the gravitation between astronomically large bodies that are situated at astronomical distances from one another; data about the tides, i.e. data about the gravitation between an astronomically large body (the earth) and its smaller satellite (the moon); data about falling bodies, i.e. data about the gravitation between an astronomically large body (the earth) and much smaller bodies (such as apples or projectiles); data about a torsion balance experiment. i.e. data about the gravitation between two bodies of a subastronomical size. The larger the number of apparently independent data that converge upon Newton's theory – i.e. that are positive instances of this theory – the larger the extent of the factual justification for the theory.

It is clear from the quotation above that the criterion of evidential independence plays a role in all forms of empirical inquiry.

In §7.2.1.5 we saw that one of the criteria for scientific explanations is the criterion of generality. We have just elucidated the factual aspect of this criterion. The factual aspect of the generality of a hypothesis/law/theory is a function of two factors.

(21)   The generality of a hypothesis, law or theory is determined by the comprehensiveness of each of the various kinds of positive instances of the hypothesis, law or theory, on the one hand, and by the variety in the kinds of positive instances of the hypothesis, law or theory, on the other hand.

In (21) a relationship is shown to exist between three criteria: on the one hand, the criterion of generality as it applies to scientific explanations and, on the other hand, the criteria of evidential comprehensiveness and evidential independence as they apply in the justification of scientific hypotheses.

One general point in connection with criteria for evidence remains to be considered, viz. that of the logical status of these criteria in the justification of a hypothesis. In a field of inquiry with precise criteria for evidence, these criteria are used in the justification of hypotheses by employing them as major premises of deductive arguments. By reformulating the criterion of comprehensiveness as an "If . . . then" statement, it may be employed as follows in the deductive argument (22):

(22)   MaP : If the corpus of positive instances of a hypothesis H is of the extent E, then the hypothesis derives the measure M of factual justification from this corpus.

MiP : The corpus of positive instances of the hypothesis h is of the extent E.

C   : The hypothesis h derives the measure M of factual justification from this corpus of positive instances.

In the argument (22) E symbolizes a numerical value on a scale of evidential comprehensiveness and M symbolizes a numerical value on a scale of measures of factual justification. Reconstructed symbolically the argument (22) is clearly a concrete instance of the demonstrative form of argument which was presented as (9) in §9.2.1.2.1. The criterion of evidential independence has the same logical status in the justification of a hypothesis as the criterion of evidential comprehensiveness, viz. that of major premise in a demonstrative argument.

9.2.1.3   *The Systematic Component*

Recall that a hypothesis represents a possible solution to a problem. Not all hypotheses are equally acceptable as solutions to problems. The greater the degree of factual justification for a hypothesis, the more acceptable it is as a solution to a problem. However, we have seen that the factual justification for a hypothesis is, in principle, inconclusive. This has a second important consequence – the first was discussed in §9.2.1.2.4 above – viz. that scientists attempt to increase the ACCEPTABILITY of their hypotheses by presenting additional justification for these hypotheses. This additional justification is not given in terms of the positive instances of the hypothesis, but mainly in terms of SYSTEMATIC CONSIDERATIONS or REASONS. The additional justification for a hypothesis, as distinguished from the factual justification, is therefore commonly known as THE SYSTEMATIC JUSTIFICATION FOR A HYPOTHESIS.

First let us look at a typical case in which systematic justification is given for a hypothesis. Hartridge (1920:57) points out that the following facts also fit in with the biological theory (6):

(23)(a)   It is a known fact that bats emit cries which have a short wavelength – close to the auditory limit of most people and beyond that of others.

(b)   The bat's external ear (pinna) is large and well developed; numerous scientists have observed that bats have an acutely developed sense of hearing.

(c)   Bats are not disturbed by human speech, but are strongly disturbed by a clapping of hands or the sound of paper being torn.

These facts are neither directly explained, nor directly predicted by the theory (6). Yet they fit in with the theory, thereby according a degree of systematic justification to this theory. This, in turn, increases the acceptability of the theory. Underlying this view is the following systematic consideration:

(24)   The better a hypothesis fits in with existing facts/knowledge, the larger the extent of the systematic justification and the greater the acceptability of the hypothesis.

A systematic consideration such as (24) is also known as an ACCEPTABILITY STANDARD by virtue of the fact that it may be used to judge the acceptability of a hypothesis.

It appears from the work of Bunge (1967b:§15.7), for example, that, in addition to (24), a large number of other systematic considerations play a role in the justification of hypotheses. The following systematic considerations, for example, are widely used:

(25)(a)   The better a hypothesis can be integrated into an existing, well-justified theory, the larger the extent of the systematic justification and the greater the acceptability of the hypothesis.

(b)   The more fruitful a hypothesis is in a heuristic sense, the larger the extent of the systematic justification and the greater the acceptability of the hypothesis.

(c)   The greater the conceptual simplicity of a hypothesis, the larger the extent of the systematic justification and the greater the acceptability of the hypothesis.

[As regards (25)(b), a hypothesis is HEURISTICALLY FRUITFUL if it leads scientists to the making of new discoveries.] However, the most fundamental acceptability standard for a hypothesis is and remains the one mentioned at the beginning of this paragraph.

(26)   The larger the extent of the factual justification for a hypothesis, the more acceptable the hypothesis.

This brings us to the systematic nature of the considerations (24) and (25)(a) −(c). These considerations are called "systematic" in virtue of the fact that they deal, more or less directly, with the relatedness of a hypothesis to existing facts, knowledge, hypotheses, theories or theoretical concepts. All these considerations are concerned with the extent to which a hypothesis fits in with or may be linked to one of these classes of metascientific objects.

Let us finally consider the logical status of systematic considerations/acceptability standards in the justification of a hypothesis. The consideration/standard (24), for instance, may be reformulated as follows:

(27)   If a hypothesis H is consistent with all the existing facts, then it has the measure M of systematic justification/acceptability.

In (27) M symbolizes a numerical value on a scale of systematic justification/acceptability. In the form of (27), a systematic consideration/acceptability standard is employed in the justification of a hypothesis as the major premiss of a deductive argument of the form (28).

(28)   MaP : If a hypothesis H is consistent with all the existing facts, then it has the measure M of systematic justification/acceptability.
MiP : The hypothesis h is consistent with all the existing facts.

C   : The hypothesis h has the measure M of systematic justification/acceptability.

It is clear, therefore, that the logical status of systematic considerations/accept-ability standards is analogous to that of criteria for evidence. In both cases the logical status is that of major premiss of a deductive (demonstrative) argument.

To establish the measure of systematic justification for the acceptability of a hypothesis in a nonarbitrary way, is no simple task. In order to do so two requirements have to be met. On the one hand, the relative weight of the various systematic considerations/acceptability standards must be established. On the other hand, an adequate scale of systematic justification/acceptability must be available. Few fields of inquiry can claim to satisfy these two requirements. In general, therefore, the measure of systematic justification/acceptability accorded to hypotheses cannot be said to represent more than the approximate judgments of scientists. Consequently, the systematic justification for a hypothesis is also inconclusive. Together, the factual and systematic justification for a hypothesis can do no more than establish a high measure of probability for the hypothesis. It will be shown in §10.2.1 that the systematic justification for a hypothesis is related to a specific general philosophical truth criterion as well.

9.2.1.4   *The Nonobjective Component*

In the factual and systematic justification of a hypothesis, objective considera-tions, or objective reasons, are adduced to show that a hypothesis is probably true. These considerations are objective in that they relate to data, facts, know-ledge, hypotheses or theories about the reality at which the inquiry is directed. The larger the extent of the objective justification for a hypothesis, the more convinced scientists will be of its probable correctness. Seeing that this justifica-tion is essentially inconclusive, however, it cannot compel the scientist to accept the hypothesis as true.

This brings us to the third consequence of the inconclusive nature of the justification for a hypothesis, viz. the possibility that NONOBJECTIVE CON-SIDERATIONS may play a role in the justification of a hypothesis. Scientists may use nonobjective considerations or reasons in an attempt to heighten the persuasive power of the justification presented for a hypothesis. These considera-tions, of which a few examples will be given below, are nonobjective because they do not take the form of data, facts, knowledge, hypotheses or theories about the reality at which the inquiry is directed. There are various nonobjective considerations which may play a role in the justification of hypotheses, but we shall only consider three classes.

A first class of nonobjective considerations concern the way in which the justification for a hypothesis is structured and presented. The more skillfully this is done, the bigger the "impact" of the justification. Among these considerations those of (29) are central.

(29)(a)   The more transparent the interrelatedness of the individual argu-

ments for a hypothesis, the greater is their persuasive power.
(b)　The more transparent the internal structure of the individual arguments for a hypothesis and the simpler the steps in which these arguments are presented, the greater is their persuasive power.
(c)　The more readily understandable, nonambiguous and "striking" (in terms of analogies, comparisons, images, etc.) the sentences in terms of which the arguments for a hypothesis are linguistically expressed, the greater is the persuasive power of these arguments.

Technical considerations such as these are often called RHETORICAL CONSIDERATIONS.

A second class of nonobjective considerations are by nature psychological. These considerations relate to the scientist in his personal capacity. We only mention two of these psychological considerations.

(30)(a)　The higher the scientific standing of a scientist, the greater is the persuasive power of his arguments.
(b)　The more strongly an argument suggests that dissenters who refuse to accpet it are irrational, narrow-minded or behind the times, the greater is the persuasive power of the argument.

The psychological consideration (30)(a) relates to the personal qualities of the scientist attempting to justify a hypothesis. It implies that arguments of well-known and respected scholars in a field will be more persuasive than the arguments of their less well-known colleagues. For instance, a famous medical researcher will have less trouble than an unknown herbalist to persuade his colleagues that he has discovered a cause of cancer. The psychological consideration (30)(b) relates to the personal qualities of the scientist at whom an argument is directed. This consideration is based on man's fear of belonging to an unappreciated (minority) group.

A third class of nonobjective considerations may be termed socio-cultural. These considerations relate to the nature and values of the society and culture within which a scientist conducts his research. The consideration (31) is a typical example.

(31)　The less compatible the content of a hypothesis is with the prevailing *Zeitgeist*, intellectual trend or climate, cultural mood or social values, the less persuasive are the argument(s) presented in justification of the hypothesis.

For instance, in his book *Beyond freedom and dignity* (1972), the psychologist B.F. Skinner propounds a theory to the effect that human behaviour should be controlled by technology. However, the technological control of human behaviour clashes with the prevailing intellectual mood about the freedom of the individual to work out his own destiny. In terms of the consideration (31), the fact that Skinner's theory clashes with the prevailing intellectual mood may weaken the persuasive power of the objective justification he may be able to furnish for it.

It is most important that objective and nonobjective considerations should be clearly distinguished in the appraisal of the justification for a hypothesis. A scientific justification may not be judged strong or weak on the strength of non-objective considerations. Such considerations do not reflect the true objective power of the justification.

Moreover, nonobjective considerations may never be consciously used to bring other scientists under a false impression as to the merit of a hypothesis. A scientist who does so is guilty of employing NONREASONABLE STRATEGIES OF PERSUASION. However, it is important that the way in which a good justification is presented should not detract from its merit. To prevent this, the scientist who puts forward a justification for a hypothesis should take into account the rhetorical considerations mentioned above. But he may not consciously use these considerations to give a poor justification the appearance of having great merit.

9.2.2   Giving Scientific Justifications

This brings us to the question, (3)(b), concerning the intellectual activities involved in giving a scientific justification. The giving of scientific justifications essentially involves reasoning or the propounding of arguments.

(32)   To justify a scientific hypothesis H involves
  - (a)   presenting, within the framework of one or more reductive arguments, supporting evidence for H, i.e. factual data which may be explained on the basis of H;
  - (b)   presenting, within the framework of one or more reductive arguments, confirming evidence for H, i.e. factual data from which it is clear that H makes accurate projections;
  - (c)   demonstrating, within the framework of one or more deductive arguments, that the supporting evidence of (a) and the confirming evidence of (b)
      (i) is sufficiently comprehensive and
      (ii) belongs to mutually independent kinds;
  - (d)   demonstrating, within the framework of one or more deductive arguments, that there is a measure of systematic justification for H, i.e. that H is consistent with existing, accepted facts, knowledge, hypotheses, theories, and so on;
  - (e)   comparing the measure of justification which H derives from

(a)−(d) with the measure of justification which there is for alternative hypothesis h, . . . , h_n; and

(f)   presenting the arguments of (a)−(d) and the result of (e) as a well-integrated, clear and coherent case for H.

The basis for and nature of (32)(a)−(d) and (f) should be clear from the preceding discussion. Only (32)(e) requires elucidation.

The basis for the "comparative" part, (32)(e), of the giving of scientific justifications was implicitly established in the preceding paragraphs. We saw that it is a fundamental property of the justification for a hypothesis that it is inconclusive. This leaves the logical possibility of proposing alternatives for the hypothesis. In practice, more than one alternative hypothesis is often proposed as a solution to a particular nontrivial problem. This is the reason for including (32)(e) as part of the giving of scientific justifications. Having compared the relative merit of the various alternative, inconclusively justified hypotheses, the scientist chooses the hypothesis with the largest measure of justification.

9.3   GRAMMATICAL INQUIRY

9.3.1   General

The linguistic justification presented as (1) in §9.1 represents a fragment of a justification for a grammatical hypothesis. This justification may therefore be called a GRAMMATICAL JUSTIFICATION for short. In (33) another example of a fragment of a grammatical justification is given. The fragment comes from Chomsky's "Remarks on nominalization" (1972b:54).

(33)   The strongest and most interesting conclusion that follows from the lexicalist hypothesis is that derived nominals should have the form of base sentences, whereas gerundive nominals may in general have the form of transforms. We have indicated that in many cases this conclusion is confirmed, and that at least some apparent counterexamples (e.g., *the city's destruction by the enemy*) can be satisfactorily explained in terms of independently motivated rules.

Recall that a number of properties of the internal structure of derived and gerundive nominals were noted in §4.3.2.1.2.

We shall consider two main points in connection with (fragments of) grammatical justifications such as (1) and (33). On the one hand, we must determine the general nature and particular properties of such justifications. On the other hand, we must try to establish what is involved in the giving of such justifications.

9.3.2   Nature of Grammatical Justifications

9.3.2.1   *Fragmentary Nature and Complexity*

As we saw in §§3.3.1.3 and 6.3.2.1, grammatical inquiry has the technical objective of constructing a complete generative grammar for the language in question. Such a grammar must satisfy the criteria of adequacy presented as (11)(a)–(f) in §6.3.2.1. To justify a proposed grammar for a language as being complete, naturally involves showing that the grammar is indeed reasonably successful in terms of these criteria. However, so far there is not a single human language for which a grammar has been constructed which could be called a "complete grammar". Human languages are simply far too complex and their structure is far too poorly understood by grammarians. To practise grammatical inquiry is in fact to construct small fragments of grammars. These fragments are composed of individual grammatical hypotheses. Consequently, justification in the context of grammatical inquiry generally implies the justification of individual grammatical hypotheses and the fragmentary grammars into which these hypotheses are integrated. Compared with the justification for a complete grammar, then, these justifications are by nature fragmentary. However, when giving such fragmentary grammatical justifications, the grammarian naturally has to take into account the above-mentioned criteria for complete grammars. In general terms, therefore, a grammatical hypothesis may be said to be well-justified if it can form part of a complete grammar which would satisfy these criteria.

When we say that the justifications given in grammatical inquiry are by nature fragmentary, we are not implying that these justifications are in any way uncomplicated. On the contrary, the justification of a grammatical hypothesis is in fact highly complex. The complexity of a grammatical justification is codetermined by the fact that the linguistic reality at which the grammatical hypothesis is directed is a complex reality. The grammarian's reality is complex in the sense that it has two levels. In §3.3.1.1 we saw that this reality includes both a directly-given level of products of linguistic performance and an underlying level which takes the form of an abstract mental capacity, the linguistic competence. It was further shown in preceding paragraphs that a grammatical hypothesis has a function with regard to each of these levels. With regard to the directly-given level of products of linguistic performance it has an explanatory function: a grammatical hypothesis must serve as a basis for the explanation of the problematic properties of sentences or classes of utterances which are repetitions of one another. [For the purpose of the discussion in this paragraph, we shall consider the projective function of a grammatical hypothesis to be part of its explanatory function.] With regard to the underlying level of linguistic competence, a grammatical hypothesis has a descriptive function: it must characterize an aspect of the form of the linguistic competence. This dual function of grammatical hypotheses entails that their justification must have two major aspects. First, a grammatical justification must have an aspect from which it is clear that the hypothesis in question can, in an illuminating way, serve as a basis for grammatical explanations. Second, a grammatical justification must have an aspect from which it is clear that the hypothesis in question probably correctly describes a part of the form of the linguistic competence.

These two aspects of the justification of a grammatical hypothesis are closely related. The exact nature of this relatedness will become clear as we progress. Let us start by considering the various components of a grammatical justification individually.

9.3.2.2   *The Factual Component*

The first component of a grammatical justification is a factual one. In this component factual data are presented as the basis for reasons why a grammatical hypothesis could be true. These factual data are derived from two sources. On the one hand, they represent data that can be explained on the basis of the hypothesis. On the other hand, they represent data from which it is clear that projections that can be made on the basis of the hypothesis are correct.

9.3.2.2.1   *Justification on the basis of explained data*
Let us once again consider the fragment of justification presented in (1). This justification is composed, among other things, of an argument which may be reconstructed as follows:

(34)   MaP : If the lexicalist hypothesis is true, then the gerundive nominals
of (35) should be acceptable, whereas the derived nominals of
(36) should be unacceptable.
MiP : 1. The gerundive nominals of (35) are acceptable.
2. The derived nominals of (36) are unacceptable.

C   : The lexicalist hypothesis is true.

(35)(a)   *John's being easy (difficult) to please*
(b)   *John's being certain (likely) to win the prize*
(c)   *John's amusing (interesting) the children with his stories*

(36)(a)   **John's easiness (difficulty) to please*
(b)   **John's certainty (likelihood) to win the prize*
(c)   **John's amusement (interest) of the children with his stories*

The linguistic background for the argument (34) was discussed in some detail in §1.4.

A symbolic reconstruction of the argument (34) clearly brings out its reductive nature.

(37)   MaP : If p, then q
       MiP : q

       _____

       C   : Therefore p

In the argument (34) the reduction is carried out regressively. The starting-point of the reduction is a (pretheoretical) description of the problematic data presented in the minor premisses, viz. the acceptability of the gerundive nominals of (35) as opposed to the unacceptability of the derived nominals of (36). From this description, the inference proceeds to the conclusion that the lexicalist hypothesis is true, since this hypothesis serves as the basis for explaining the data in question. As a regressively reductive argument, (34) therefore represents a supporting argument. The data presented in the minor premisses of the argument constitute supporting evidence for the lexicalist hypothesis. This supporting evidence is inconclusive, because, as a reductive argument (34) is nondemonstrative. Nothing in this argument precludes the possibility of explaining the problematic data on the strength of an alternative hypothesis.

Grammarians put forward supporting arguments to justify their grammatical hypotheses on the strength of two considerations. One of these, a general consideration, is of a metascientific nature and implies that grammarians subscribe to the principle (38).

(38)   The fact that a hypothesis has explanatory power indicates that the hypothesis could be true.

Note the cautious formulation of this principle: it does *not* go as far as claiming that a hypothesis with explanatory power is in fact true.

The other, more specific, consideration is related to a criterion which a complete grammar must satisfy. This is the criterion that a grammar should assign appropriate structural descriptions to the sentences of a language – cf. (11)(e) in §6.3.2.1 or (28)(b) in §8.3.2.1.2. A structural description of a sentence is appropriate if it can serve as a basis for explaining the problematic properties of the sentence. The second reason why grammarians put forward supporting arguments to justify their grammatical hypotheses may therefore be formulated as follows:

(39)   The fact that a hypothesis has explanatory power makes it a potential part of a complete grammar which assigns appropriate structural descriptions to the sentences of the language in question.

A grammatical hypothesis without explanatory power cannot be used in such a grammar. We have more than once used the expression "explanatory power". To say that a hypothesis has EXPLANATORY POWER is a short way of saying that the hypothesis may be used as (part of a) lawlike generalization in an explanation.

9.3.2.2.2   *Justification on the basis of projected data*
In terms of the lexicalist hypothesis, the derived nominal *several of John's proofs of the theorem* is assigned the following deep structure:

(40)

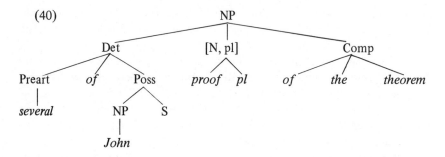

One aspect of this deep structure should be specially noted: the structure of the possessive construction *John's proofs* has the form NPs – N and the rules assigning this structure are base rules. Traditionally, however, such possessive constructions were transformationally derived from a deep structure of the form *N that NP has* (in the present case, therefore, something like *proofs that John has*).

Chomsky (1972:37–38) puts forward the following arguments in justification of the structure NPs – N for *John's proofs*:

(41)   If this approach is correct, we would expect to find structures of the form NPs – N even where the N is not a derived nominal, and where the possessive construction in question does not derive from the corresponding structure: *N that NP has*. In fact, there is some evidence in support of this expectation. A number of people have noted that the distinction between alienable and inalienable possession, formally marked in certain languages, has a certain status in English as well. Thus the phrase *John's leg* is ambiguous: it can be used to refer either to the leg that John happens to have in his possession (alienable possession), that he is, say, holding under his arm; or to the leg that is, in fact, part of John's body (inalienable possession). But the phrase *the leg that John has* has only the sense of alienable possession. We cannot say that the leg that John has hurts or that it is weak from the climb, though we can make this statement of John's leg, in the inalienable sense of the phrase *John's leg*. These observations lend plausibility to the view that *John's leg* has another source in addition to the structure underlying *the leg that John has*, from

which it can be derived (in the alienable sense) along the same lines as *John's table* from the structure underlying *the table that John has.*

Central to Chomsky's reasoning above is the argument which may be reconstructed as follows:

(42)   MaP : If the lexicalist hypothesis is true, then it may be expected that English will have possessive constructions of the form NPs – N in which the N is not a derived nominal and which cannot be derived from the structure *N that NP has.*

       MiP : 1. In the sense of inalienable possession, *John's leg* is a possessive construction of the form NPs – N in which the N is not a derived nominal.

           2. In the sense of inalienable possession, *John's leg* cannot be derived from the structure *N that NP has.*

    C   : The lexicalist hypothesis is true.

The argument (42) is a reductive argument of the form symbolized in (37). The difference between (42) and the supporting argument (34) is that in the former the reduction is carried out progressively. The starting-point of the inference is not the description of the data in the minor premisses, but the lexicalist hypothesis. The conclusion, that this hypothesis is true, is reached on the strength of the fact that a prediction which can be made on the basis of the hypothesis is correct. The linguistic data which bear out the accuracy of the prediction constitute confirming evidence for the lexicalist hypothesis. The argument (42) is a confirming argument and, as a typical reductive argument, it is nondemonstrative. The logical possibility exists that the prediction in question may be made on the basis of an alternative hypothesis.

Grammarians use confirming arguments to justify grammatical hypotheses on the strength of two considerations: a general metascientific consideration and a more specific linguistic one. The general consideration implies that grammarians subscribe to the metascientific principle (43).

(43)   The fact that a hypothesis serves as a basis for correct projections indicates that the hypothesis could be true.

Notice the cautious formulation of this principle. It does *not* claim that hypotheses which serve as a basis for correct projections are in fact true.

The more specific consideration is related to a linguistic criterion adopted for a complete grammar, viz. the so-called ALL-AND-ONLY criterion which was formulated as (11)(d) in §6.3.2.1 and as (28)(a) in §8.3.2.1.2. In terms of this criterion, the grammar of a particular language must generate all the grammatical sentences and only the grammatical sentences of the language. A language consists of an infinite number of sentences. A grammarian, however, can only examine a limited number of these sentences when constructing his grammar. Therefore, in order to satisfy the all-and-only criterion, the grammar has to make predictions about those sentences that have not been examined. Against this background the second reason why grammarians make use of confirming arguments may be formulated as (44).

(44)   The fact that the projections which can be made on the basis of a grammatical hypothesis are correct, makes it a potential part of a complete grammar which satisfies the all-and-only criterion.

It is obvious that a grammatical hypothesis that makes incorrect projections cannot form part of a complete grammar which satisfies the all-and-only criterion.

At this point it could be useful to explain how the metascientific expressions "(factual/empirical) support" and "follow from" are used in linguistic inquiry. In preceding paragraphs we consistently used the expression "support" to denote the factual justification which a hypothesis derives from the data that it explains. Generative grammarians also use the expression (FACTUAL/EMPIRICAL) SUPPORT in this sense. In addition, however, they use it to denote the factual justification which a hypothesis derives from the data which bear out the correctness of the projections that can be made on the basis of the hypothesis. In other words, generative grammarians do not draw such a sharp terminological distinction between support and confirmation for a hypothesis as we did in §9.2.1.2.

As regards the expression FOLLOW FROM, generative grammarians use this term in two senses. On the one hand, they use it in the sense of "explained by" – as Chomsky does in (1) above. On the other hand, they use it in the sense of "predicted by". Underlying both these senses is the fundamental logical notion 'inferred in terms of a rule of deduction'.

9.3.2.2.3   *Types of linguistic evidence*

Various types of evidence are used in linguistic inquiry to justify grammatical hypotheses. A first distinction that can be drawn between the various types is that between internal linguistic evidence, or internal evidence for short, and external linguistic evidence, or external evidence for short. INTERNAL EVIDENCE consists of linguistic data about objects within the grammarian's linguistic reality. These linguistic data concern the utterances of a language and the linguistic competence underlying these utterances. EXTERNAL EVIDENCE, by contrast, consists of data about objects and phenomena outside the grammarian's linguistic reality. We shall consider the nature of three types of internal evidence below. The nature and role of external evidence will be the topic of §9.3.2.4.1.

The primary source of internal evidence is the linguistic intuitions which native speakers of a language have about the properties of utterances of the language. In the minor premise of the argument (34), linguistic intuitions are cited as supporting evidence for the lexicalist hypothesis. The two statements in terms of which this evidence is presented may be called EVIDENTIAL STATEMENTS.

(45)(a)   The gerundive nominals of (35) are acceptable.
(b)   The derived nominals of (36) are unacceptable.

To simplify matters, we shall use the expression INTUITIVE EVIDENCE to denote linguistic intuitions which are used as evidence for grammatical hypotheses.

Consider the evidence presented in the minor premisses of the argument (42) as confirming evidence for the lexicalist hypothesis.

(46)(a)   In the sense of inalienable possession, *John's leg* is a possessive construction of the form NPs – N in which the N is not a derived nominal.
(b)   In the sense of inalienable possession, *John's leg* cannot be derived from the structure *N that NP has.*

It is obvious that the evidential statements (46)(a) and (b) do not present intuitive evidence. Native speakers of English do not have linguistic intuitions about either what is and what is not a derived nominal, or the structure from which possessive constructions are derived. These two evidential statements in fact express grammatical hypotheses of the linguist himself. Thus, in this case, the evidence for the grammatical hypothesis in turn takes the form of (other) grammatical hypotheses. If the evidence for a grammatical hypothesis takes the form of (other) grammatical hypotheses, we call it HYPOTHETICAL EVIDENCE. This constitutes the second type of internal evidence that generative grammarians use in the justification of grammatical hypotheses.

The third type of internal evidence for grammatical hypotheses takes the form of theoretical intuitions of skilled grammarians about the rules and structures of a language. Recall that we considered one of Chomsky's theoretical intuitions in §§5.3.2.2 and 6.3.3.1.2. It is repeated here as (47).

(47)   There is a linguistically significant parallelism in the structure of NPs such as *John's proofs of the theorem*, VPs such as *will prove the theorem* and APs such as *even ignorant of the theorem.*

The rules and structural descriptions of a grammar which make it possible to express such theoretical intuitions derive a measure of support from these intuitions. We may say that these theoretical intuitions provide THEORETICAL INTUITIVE EVIDENCE for the grammatical hypotheses in terms of which the rules and structures in question are formulated.

It is by no means accidental that grammarians use this type of evidence in the justification of grammatical hypotheses. One of the criteria for a complete grammar is that it should explicitly express the linguistically significant generalizations about the language. To justify an individual grammatical hypothesis by presenting theoretical intuitive evidence is to show that this hypothesis can be a potential part of a complete grammar which satisfies this criterion. The criterion in question was formulated as (11)(f) in §6.3.2.1.

9.3.2.2.4   *Minimal criteria for linguistic evidence*
In order to constitute supporting or confirming evidence for grammatical hypotheses, linguistic data must satisfy the three minimal criteria of (17)(a)–(c), viz. the criteria of logical relevance, qualitative relevance and accuracy of factualness.

The implication of the criterion of logical relevance is clear: the evidential statement in which the linguistic data are presented must be related to the grammatical hypothesis in question in terms of an appropriate, specifiable logical rule. It therefore follows that it should be possible in grammatical justification to present the data in the minor premiss(es) of an argument of which the grammatical hypothesis in question is the conclusion.

Recall that, in terms of the criterion of qualitative relevance, it must be possible to indicate an inherent substantive connection between the phenomena on which the data have a bearing and the phenomena with which the hypothesis in question deals. This criterion is especially important in the case of intuitive evidence. The reason for its importance is to be found in the distinction between genuine and spurious linguistic intuitions. Spurious linguistic intuitions – of which some examples were given in §4.3.2.2.2.2 – do not have the linguistic competence as source. Consequently, they do not represent data about the linguistic competence. In terms of the criterion of qualitative relevance, therefore, such spurious linguistic intuitions are qualitatively irrelevant with regard to a grammatical hypothesis about the linguistic competence. Spurious linguistic intuitions represent data about objects or phenomena outside the grammarian's linguistic reality. If it were possible, however, to establish some kind of relationship between these data and properties of the linguistic competence, such spurious linguistic intuitions could constitute external evidence for grammatical hypotheses. How such a relationship may be established will be seen in §9.3.2.4.3.

We have already considered the criterion of factualness or accuracy in connection with intuitive evidence. That was in §4.3.2.2.2.2 where the point was made that linguistic intuitions, as primary linguistic data, must be accurate. We shall now consider the implications of this criterion for the hypothetical evidence presented for the justification of grammatical hypotheses in evidential statements such as (46)(a) and (b). We saw that hypothetical evidence takes the form of grammatical hypotheses. To require hypothetical evidence to be accurate is therefore to require that the grammatical hypotheses expressing this evidence be justified as well. In (41) above, Chomsky does in fact offer a justification for the grammatical hypotheses which constitute the evidential statements (46)(a) and (b). Let us try to establish how Chomsky justifies the hypothesis (46)(b), that in the sense of inalienable possession, *John's leg* cannot be derived from the structure *N that NP has*. The argument which Chomsky puts forward to justify this hypothesis may be reconstructed as follows:

(48)   MaP : If *John's leg* should be transformationally derived from a structure of the form *N that NP has,* then the expression *leg that
John has* would have to have the sense of inalienable possession
as well.

       MiP : The expression *leg that John has* does not have the sense of
inalienable possession.

       C   : *John's leg* must not be transformationally derived from a struc-
ture of the form *N that NP has.*

Certain linguistic assumptions underlie the major premise of the argument (48).
One such assumption is the grammatical assumption that the expression *leg that
John has* is transformationally derived from a structure of the form *N that NP
has.* A second assumption is the general linguistic assumption that two expressions that are derived from the same deep structure must have basically the
same (set of) meaning(s). According to this assumption, *John's leg* and *leg that
John has* would have to have the same meanings if they were both to be derived
from a structure of the form *N that NP has.* However, as is clear from the linguistic datum presented in the minor premiss of the argument (48), this is not the
case: the two expressions have quite different meanings.

Let us consider more closely the linguistic datum in the minor premiss of the
argument (48). Note that this datum does not represent a linguistic intuition.
Consequently, it does not constitute intuitive evidence for the hypothesis in
question. Native speakers of English do not have linguistic intuitions about
abstract linguistic properties such as (in)alienable possession. Thus, the linguistic
datum presented in the minor premiss has the status of a grammatical hypothesis
as well. In terms of the criterion of factualness, Chomsky may consequently be
required to justify this hypothesis too. This he does in fact do in (41). The argument he puts forward in justification of this hypothesis may be reconstructed
as follows:

(49)   MaP : If it were to be possible to interpret the expression *leg that John
has* in the sense of inalienable possession, then it should be
possible in English to say the following: "The leg that John has
hurts", "The leg that John has is weak from the climb".

       MiP : It is not possible in English to say either "The leg that John has
hurts", or "The leg that John has is weak from the climb".

       C   : The expression *leg that John has* cannot be interpreted in the
sense of inalienable possession.

Notice that the linguistic data presented in the minor premiss of (49) as evidence for the hypothesis contained in the conclusion represent linguistic intuitions. Native speakers of English do have intuitions about what can and what cannot be said in English. If there is no immediately apparent reason to doubt the genuineness or accuracy of a given linguistic intuition, it need not be justified by the grammarian of English. Chomsky therefore does not justify the content of this intuition.

A number of general points about the nature and structure of justifications for grammatical hypotheses have emerged from the preceding discussion. Let us consider three of them.

(50)(a)   Evidence for a given grammatical hypothesis may take the form of other grammatical hypotheses.

(b)   The grammatical hypotheses presented as evidence for other grammatical hypotheses must, in turn, be justified.

(c)   The factual justification for a grammatical hypothesis must ultimately — directly or indirectly — be given in terms of intuitive evidence.

The third point above implies that intuitive evidence may be regarded as THE ULTIMATE EVIDENCE FOR GRAMMATICAL HYPOTHESES. Thus, linguistic intuitions may be said to form the hard bedrock of the factual foundation on which linguistic justifications rest.

Note also that (50)(c) ties in with what was said in §8.3.2.2.1 about the nature of the projectandum of grammatical predictions. This projectandum deals either with properties of sentences about which native speakers can have linguistic intuitions, or with properties of sentences about which native speakers cannot have linguistic intuitions, but which may be reduced to certain other properties of sentences about which native speakers can have linguistic intuitions.

A fourth general point concerns the structure of grammatical justifications or, more specifically, the way in which the arguments constituting a justification are interrelated.

(51)   A first kind of relationship in terms of which arguments in a grammatical justification may be interrelated is that of SUPPLEMENTATION.

What is meant by saying that two arguments A_1 and A_2 are interrelated in terms of the relationship of supplementation is this: the argument A_2 SUPPLEMENTS the argument A_1 if A_2 is presented in justification of a premiss of A_1. In terms of the relation of supplementation, the relevant premiss of A_1 represents the conclusion of A_2. We can say, for instance, that the argument (48) above supplements the argument (42) in this sense: the second minor premiss of (42) constitutes the conclusion of (48). The argument (48), in turn, is supplemented by the argument (49): the minor premiss of (48) is the conclusion of (49). GRAMMATICAL

ARGUMENTS, i.e. arguments presented in the justification of grammatical hypotheses, which are interrelated in terms of the relation of supplementation, form a logical chain. Schematically the structure of such a logical chain may be represented as follows:

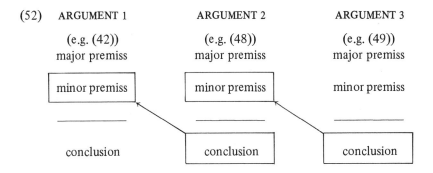

(52) ARGUMENT 1 ARGUMENT 2 ARGUMENT 3

(e.g. (42)) (e.g. (48)) (e.g. (49))

major premiss major premiss major premiss

minor premiss minor premiss minor premiss

conclusion conclusion conclusion

9.3.2.2.5 *Additional criteria for linguistic evidence*

A grammatical hypothesis cannot be justified conclusively by means of either supporting or confirming evidence. To ensure that a grammatical hypothesis derives as large a measure of justification from such evidence as possible, generative grammarians adopt additional criteria for evidence. In grammatical inquiry, as in empirical inquiry in general, the criteria of evidential comprehensiveness and evidential independence play an important role.

9.3.2.2.5.1 *Criterion of evidential comprehensiveness*

Recall that in (19) of §9.2.1.2.4 the criterion of evidential comprehensiveness was formulated in the following general terms: the larger the number of positive instances of a hypothesis, the greater the extent of the factual justification for the hypothesis. The role of this criterion in linguistic inquiry may be illustrated with reference to two pieces of critical comment by McCawley on parts of Chomsky's argumentation in favour of the lexicalist hypothesis.

McCawley's (1973:9) first piece of critical comment, (53) below, deals with Chomsky's view that derived nominals are generally semantically irregular.

(53) Either treatment [= the lexicalist and the transformationalist – R.P.B.] says that the relationship between nominalizations [= derived nominals – R.P.B.] and their meanings is pure chaos. Perhaps nothing is really systematic, as Chomsky seems to suggest; however, it takes more to establish that than a list of 14 words and a comment that their meanings are wildly diverse.

The fourteen derived nominals which Chomsky (1972b:19) cites in justification of the hypothesis in question are *laughter, marriage, construction, actions, activities, revolution, belief, doubt, conversion, permutation, trial, residence, qualifications* and *specifications.* In (53) McCawley is in fact saying that a corpus of evidence comprising only fourteen derived nominals is insufficiently comprehensive to form a basis for the factual justification of the grammatical hypothesis in question.

In his second piece of critical comment, McCawley (1973:9–10) makes a similar claim about the justification for Chomsky's use of neutral lexical entries in the grammar of English.

(54)   The only kinds of nominalizations [= derived nominals – R.P.B.] which Chomsky explicitly discusses are action and property nominalizations, which normally take exactly the same NPs as do corresponding verbs or adjectives and for which a single dictionary entry giving the nominalization and the related verb or adjective, with a single statement of selectional and strict subcategorization properties, has at least some plausibility. However, it would take great ingenuity in the employment of curly and angular brackets (though nothing in the way of linguistic insight) to combine action, agent and object nominalizations and a related verb into a single dictionary entry that gives the strict subcategorization properties of all.

The expressions *their refusal of my offer, John's honesty, the discoverer of radium* and *Dostoevski's writings* are examples of action, property, agent and object nominals respectively. Note, further, that McCawley's "single dictionary entry" is the equivalent of what we have been calling a "single lexical entry".

In his critical comment (54), McCawley uses an argument which may be reconstructed as follows:

(55)   MaP : If a corpus of evidence contains no examples of neutral lexical entries in which action, agent and object nominals are combined with a related verb, then this corpus of evidence is insufficiently comprehensive as a basis for the factual justification of a hypothesis about the role of neutral lexical entries in the grammar of English.

MiP : Chomsky's corpus of evidence contains no examples of lexical entries in which action, agent and object nominals are combined with a related verb.

C   : Chomsky's corpus of evidence is insufficiently comprehensive as a basis for the factual justification of his hypothesis about the role of neutral lexical entries in the grammar of English.

The reconstructed argument (55) clearly illustrates the logical status of the criterion of evidential comprehensiveness in the justification of a grammatical hypothesis. The argument (55) is a demonstrative argument of the following form:

(56)   MaP : If p, then q
        MiP : p

      C   : Therefore q

Within this demonstrative form of argument the criterion of evidential comprehensiveness has the status of major premiss. This is in fact true of all criteria of evidence used in the justification of grammatical hypotheses.

The crucial concept in the criterion of evidential comprehensiveness is '(in)-sufficiently comprehensive'. The question is: how comprehensive should a corpus of evidence be in order to be (in)sufficiently comprehensive? Linguistic inquiry lacks explicit and precise criteria for (in)sufficient comprehensiveness on the basis of which a nonarbitrary judgment of the (in)sufficient comprehensiveness of a given corpus of evidence may be made. A generative grammarian's judgments about the (in)sufficient comprehensiveness of corpora of evidence therefore have the status of educated estimates. These estimates are based on the grammarian's experience in the conduct of linguistic inquiry.

The criterion of evidential comprehensiveness too is related to the all-and-only criterion and the criterion of appropriate structural descriptions which complete grammars must satisfy. This relatedness may be formulated as (57).

(57)   The more comprehensive the evidence for a grammatical hypothesis, the more suitable it is as a potential part of a grammar which has to satisfy the all-and-only criterion and the criterion of appropriate structural descriptions.

Viewed against the background of the discussion which gave rise to the points (39) and (44) above, (57) requires no further elaboration.

9.3.2.2.5.2   *Criterion of evidential independence*   In §9.2.1.2.4 the second important criterion for evidence, the criterion of evidential independence, was formulated as (20): the larger the variety of mutually independent types of data to which the positive instances of a hypothesis belong, the greater the extent of the factual justification for the hypothesis. Chomsky makes frequent use of this criterion in his justification of the lexicalist hypothesis. Let us consider a typical instance.

In order for derived nominals to be generated as base structures, they must be assigned a structure of the general form determiner/specifier-noun-complement. Compare, for instance, the structure (40) assigned to *several of John's proofs of the theorem*. But what additional justification can be given for the structure determiner-noun-complement as a base structure? Chomsky's (1972b:34) answer to this question is as follows:

(58)   The structures [22], and others like them, raise many problems; they do, however, suggest quite strongly that there are base noun phrases of the form determiner-noun-complement, quite apart from nominalizations. In fact, the range of noun complements seems almost as great as the range of verb complements, and the two sets are remarkably similar. There is also a wide range of adjective complements (*eager (for Bill) to leave, proud of John,* etc.). Therefore, it is quite natural to suppose that the categorial component of the base contains rules with the effect of [20], [21], a conclusion which lends further support to the lexicalist assumption.

In (58), [22] refers to NPs such as *the WEATHER in England, the STORY of Bill's exploits, his ADVANTAGE over his rivals, a MAN to do the job* and *my CANDIDATE for a trip to the moon.* According to Chomsky, these NPs have a base structure of the form determiner-noun-complement. The noun, as head of the NP, is printed in bold type in the examples just quoted. The numbers [20] and [21] in (58) refer to Chomsky's base rules, which are given below as (59) and (60) respectively.

(59)(a)   NP $\longrightarrow$ N Comp
   (b)   VP $\longrightarrow$ V Comp
   (c)   AP $\longrightarrow$ A Comp

(60)   Comp $\longrightarrow$ NP, S, NP S, NP Prep-P, Prep-P Prep-P, etc.

Central to (58) is an argument that may be reconstructed as follows:

(61)   MaP : If the base structure determiner-noun-complement must be assigned independently to NPs other than derived nominals as well, then the extent of the factual justification for the lexicalist hypothesis is increased.
   MiP : The base structure determiner-noun-complement must be assigned independently to the NPs of [22] — which are not derived nominals.

   C   : The extent of the factual justification for the lexicalist hypothesis is increased.

The criterion of evidential independence is used in the major premiss of this demonstrative argument.

The argument (61) presupposes that two other supporting arguments have been given for the hypothesis that determiner-noun-complement represents a base structure of English. The hypothesis derives a measure of justification from the first of these supporting arguments on the strength of the fact that it offers an explanation of problematic properties of derived nominals. The hypothesis in question derives a measure of justification from the second supporting argument on the strength of the fact that it offers an explanation of problematic NPs such as [22].

Notice that this is a case where two arguments – say Argument 1 and Argument 2 – present evidence for one and the same grammatical hypothesis. This brings us to a second type of interrelatedness which may exist between the arguments in a justification.

(62)   A second kind of relation in terms of which arguments in a grammatical justification may be interrelated is that of COMPLEMENTATION.

[For details of the first kind of relation, that of supplementation, refer to (52) above.] Two arguments COMPLEMENT one another if they have thè same hypothesis as their conclusion.

Schematically the complementary relation between arguments within a grammatical justification may be represented as follows:

(63)   HYPOTHESIS

(Determiner-noun-specifier is a base structure of English.)

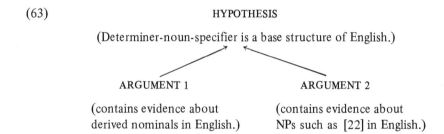

ARGUMENT 1   ARGUMENT 2

(contains evidence about   (contains evidence about
derived nominals in English.)   NPs such as [22] in English.)

In (63) ARGUMENT 1 and ARGUMENT 2 – which present independent evidence for the HYPOTHESIS – complement one another. Independent evidence is not limited to complementing supporting arguments, but may also be presented within the framework of confirming arguments.

An important question arises in connection with the criterion of independent evidence, viz. what does "independent" mean? In other words, what criteria must two (sets of) linguistic data satisfy in order to be mutually independent? This is a complex question to which no clear, well-motivated answer has as yet been given by generative grammarians. The general principle of independence (64) may be used as a rule of thumb.

(64)   Two (sets of) linguistic data are mutually independent if they deal with

(a)   different types of linguistic units, such as sentences as opposed to nonsentence-like syntactic constituents, derived nominals as opposed to nonderived nouns, etc.;

(b)   different grammatical classes or subclasses of linguistic units, such as NPs as opposed to APs or VPs, nouns as opposed to verbs, etc.;

(c)   different linguistic units of a particular type or class, such as *John's easiness to please* as opposed to *John's eagerness to please* within the class of derived nominals, *upon* as opposed to *back* within the class of prepositions, etc.;

(d)   different linguistic aspects or subaspects of the same (type/class of) linguistic units, such as the syntactic as opposed to the phonological as opposed to the semantic aspect of the same (type/class of) lexical items, the constituent structure as opposed to the lexical aspect of the same (type/class of) sentences, etc.;

(e)   different linguistic properties of the same aspect, such as the semantic property of synonymy as opposed to that of ambiguity, the semantic property of meaninglessness as opposed to that of semantic anomaly, etc.

On an informal, intuitive basis distinctions may be drawn between various degrees of independence. For instance, linguists intuitively "feel" that two (sets of) data about different grammatical classes are mutually more independent than two (sets of) data about different members of the same grammatical class. However, such intuitions about degrees of independence have not acquired the objective status of precise, nonarbitrary criteria for evidential independence in linguistic inquiry. Generative grammarians' judgments as regards the independence of linguistic evidence therefore represent educated estimates rather than precise, well-motivated statements.

Finally, the criterion of evidential independence is related to two criteria that we have already considered, viz. a criterion for grammatical concepts and a criterion for grammatical explanations. The criterion for grammatical concepts is that of (25) in §6.3.3.1.3: the language-specific content of grammatical concepts must be as systematic as possible. In this criterion, the criterion of evidential independence is anticipated. If the grammatical concepts constituting a given grammatical hypothesis were to be without systematic content, it would be almost impossible to put forward independent evidence for this hypothesis.

The criterion for grammatical explanations to which that of evidential independence is related was formulated as (49) in §7.3.2.4: the more general the lawlike generalization in the explanans, the better the grammatical explanation. The criterion of evidential independence logically instantiates one aspect of this criterion of generality. It is clear that the variety of the independent types of evidence for a hypothesis is indicative of the generality of this hypothesis in its capacity as lawlike generalization in a grammatical explanation. Another aspect of the criterion of generality is logically instantiated in the criterion of evidential comprehensiveness. The more comprehensive the evidence for a hypothesis, the greater the generality of the hypothesis in its capacity as lawlike generalization.

9.3.2.3   *The Systematic Component*

9.3.2.3.1   *The acceptability of grammatical hypotheses*
Consider once again Chomsky's case for the lexicalist hypothesis, which was presented in §9.1 above. Particularly note its final statement.

(65)   Other things being equal, then, they [= the facts] would lead us to ACCEPT the lexicalist hypothesis from which these facts follow.

The statement (65) – with ACCEPT the key expression – is revealing in two respects.

First, it appears from this statement that generative grammarians work with the notion of the acceptability of a grammatical hypothesis. We saw in §9.2.1.3 that, in empirical inquiry, the acceptability of a hypothesis reflects the extent to which the hypothesis is acceptable as a solution to a problem. Second, it appears from the statement (65) and the statements preceding it, that the fundamental criterion for the acceptability of a hypothesis is the extent of the factual justification for the hypothesis. This has the following implications:

(66)   The measure of acceptability of a grammatical hypothesis is, in the first instance, determined by the following four factors:
  (a)   the availability of supporting evidence for the hypothesis;
  (b)   the availability of confirming evidence for the hypothesis;
  (c)   the comprehensiveness of the supporting and confirming evidence for the hypothesis; and
  (d)   the extent to which the supporting and confirming evidence for the hypothesis belong to mutually independent types.

Thus, the degree of acceptability of a grammatical hypothesis is primarily determined by the factual justification for the hypothesis.

However, we have seen that the factual justification for a grammatical hypothesis is, in principle, inconclusive. On the one hand, this justification is given within the framework of nondemonstrative – supporting and confirming – arguments. On the other hand, generative grammarians' judgments about the comprehensiveness and independence of the evidence for a hypothesis do not have the status of precise and reasoned statements. It is therefore to be expected that grammarians will attempt to increase the acceptability of their grammatical hypotheses by presenting systematic justification – in addition to factual justification – for these hypotheses. The function of systematic justification is to limit the inconclusiveness of the total justification for a hypothesis.

Before continuing, however, a possible misunderstanding has to be prevented. To accept a grammatical hypothesis does not mean that it is accorded the status of being "undoubtedly true" or "the ultimate solution to the problem". In grammatical inquiry, as in empirical inquiry in general, there are no "final truths" or "ultimate solutions".

9.3.2.3.2   *Acceptability standards for grammatical hypotheses*
We come now to the considerations in terms of which generative grammarians present systematic justification for grammatical hypotheses. These considerations determine the measure of acceptability of a hypothesis. Accordingly, they are known as ACCEPTABILITY STANDARDS.

A first acceptability standard for grammatical hypotheses is the one adopted by Chomsky in the argument (1). This standard may be reconstructed as follows:

(67)   Given a corpus of linguistic data and given two alternative hypotheses H_1 and H_2, then H_1 is more acceptable than H_2 if it is the case that whereas
   (a)   the data in C can be explained on the basis of H_1,
   (b) H_2 is merely consistent with the data in C, but does not explain them.

It is on this standard that Chomsky bases his choice of the lexicalist hypothesis and his rejection of the transformationalist hypothesis in (1). The lexicalist hypothesis may be substituted for H_1 in (67), whereas the transformationalist hypothesis must be substituted for H_2.

What does Chomsky mean when he argues that the transformationalist hypothesis would be consistent with two contradictory and therefore mutually exclusive sets of facts? He could imply that the transformationalist hypothesis does not in fact make any (precise) claims about either of these two contradictory sets of facts. If this were so, then the transformationalist hypothesis could be consistent with both sets of facts. He further implies that neither of these sets of facts can support the transformationalist hypothesis, nor can they be used to show that this hypothesis is false. Moreover, it is clear that the acceptability standard (67) is related to the requirement that a complete grammar must assign appropriate structural descriptions to the sentences of a language. A complete grammar cannot satisfy this requirement if the individual grammatical hypotheses constituting the grammar lack the explanatory power at which the standard (67) is directed.

The acceptability standard (68) is related to that of (67).

(68)   The richer and the more precise the content of a grammatical hypothesis, the more acceptable the hypothesis.

In terms of the standard (68), a grammatical hypothesis must assert as much as possible, with as few *ad hoc* qualifications as possible, about the phenomena on which it has a bearing. In addition, the content of the assertion must be maximally explicit. A grammatical hypothesis which is assigned a large measure of merit in terms of the standard (68) is known as a STRONG or a POWERFUL HYPOTHESIS.

Strong hypotheses are highly valued for two reasons. The first is that a strong hypothesis has greater potential for making a significant contribution to the expansion of existing knowledge than a weak(er) hypothesis. In the quote (1), Chomsky in fact implies that the transformationalist hypothesis is a weak hypothesis.

The second reason for according greater merit to strong hypotheses in linguistic inquiry is related to another acceptability standard.

(69)   The greater the refutability of a grammatical hypothesis, the more acceptable the hypothesis.

The refutability, or disconfirmability, of scientific hypotheses will be discussed in detail in chapter 10. All we are going to say at this point is that the refutability of a scientific hypothesis is its potential for being proven false. In view of the criterion of reliability adopted for scientific knowledge, it is clear why the standard (69) is important. If a hypothesis is not refutable, it is impossible to determine whether or not the potential knowledge it contains is reliable. The richer in content a hypothesis, and the more precise this content, the greater the refutability of the hypothesis, and with that, it has also become clear how the standards (68) and (69) are interrelated. In the quote presented as (1) above, Chomsky claims that the transformationalist hypothesis is less refutable than the lexicalist hypothesis.

Generative grammarians use another acceptability standard which is related to that of (67).

(70)   Given a corpus C of linguistic data and given two alternative grammatical hypotheses H_1 and H_2, then H_1 is more acceptable than H_2 if it is the case that whereas
(a)   the data of C can be explained by H_1,
(b)   these data can merely be described or represented, but not explained, by H_2.

This acceptability standard is not entirely new to us as we saw in §7.4.6 that it plays a role in Bever's strategy for establishing the genuineness of linguistic intuitions.

The question is: what does the distinction between an explanation and a description or representation invoked in the standard (70) entail? This distinction entails the following: in an explanation of data one or more reasons are given why the data are as they are and (probably) cannot be any different. In a representation or description of data, on the other hand, the data are merely presented without any reasons of the kind in question being furnished. In other words, an explanation has a lawlike aspect which a description or representation lacks. And with that we have shown how the standards (70) and (67) are related. In both these standards the principle of lawlikeness plays an important role. As regards (70), a hypothesis that is merely consistent with a particular corpus of data lacks a lawlike aspect with regard to these data. Therefore, the two acceptability standards (67) and (70) instantiate a fundamental criterion which is used to establish the merit of grammatical explanations, viz. the criterion of lawlikeness.

Generative grammarians also use a number of acceptability standards in which some notion of generality or other is central. A first example of such a standard is that of non-*ad hoc*ness in a language-specific sense.

(71)   The less *ad hoc* a grammatical hypothesis is in a language-specific sense, the more acceptable the hypothesis.

The expression *ad hoc* in (71) may be interpreted in two different ways.

A first sense in which *ad hoc* is used in this context is that of "without independent motivation/evidence". If *ad hoc* is interpreted in this sense, the standard (71) corresponds to the criterion of evidential independence. What has been said about the latter criterion, then, applies to the standard (71) as well.

A second sense in which *ad hoc* is used in the context of (71) is the following: a grammatical hypothesis is *ad hoc* if it postulates a grammatical entity which is UNIQUE or IDIOSYNCRATIC in the language concerned. The terms "unique" and "idiosyncratic" may be interpreted in two ways. On the one hand, if the grammatical entity in question is a linguistic unit, structural element or property, then "unique" or "idiosyncratic" has the sense of nonexplicable on the basis of a general grammatical principle of the language in question. It is in this sense that derived nominals such as *deeds, marriage,* etc. are idiosyncratic with regard to elements of their meaning. On the other hand, if the grammatical entity concerned is a rule, then "unique" or "idiosyncratic" has the meaning of limited generality. Jackendoff uses the expression "idiosyncratic" in this sense in an argument against the transformationalist hypothesis.

Jackendoff (1974a:3—4) argues that the transformationalist hypothesis requires the postulation of a large number of idiosyncratic transformational rules for English. These transformations are needed to generate syntactically and/or semantically irregular derived nominals. With regard to syntactically irregular derived nominals he argues as follows:

(72)   . . . many derived nominals do not correspond precisely to well-formed sentences:

[14]   **John doubted about their proposal*

> **It is probable John's leaving*
> **John advised to Bill*

[15] **John's doubting about their proposal*
      *Its being probable John's leaving
      *John's advising to Bill

[16] *John's doubts about their proposal*
      the probability of John's leaving
      John's advice to Bill

Transformations which perform all the minor syntactic adjustments necessary to produce [16] from well-formed sentences will be numerous and highly idiosyncratic, if at all statable.

As the transformationalist hypothesis requires the postulation of such idiosyncratic transformations, it is relatively unacceptable in terms of the acceptability standard (71).

In empirical inquiry the postulation of unique or idiosyncratic entities is avoided as far as possible. A reality containing numerous unique or idiosyncratic entities would be chaotic and devoid of any regularity. It is the aim of empirical inquiry to show that, underneath what appears to be chaotic, there are laws, systems and regularity. It is therefore easy to see why generative grammarians use the acceptability standard (71). With *ad hoc* used in this sense, the standard (71) instantiates a criterion adopted for grammatical knowledge, viz. the criterion of lawlikeness which was discussed in §3.3.1.4.

This brings us to a second acceptability standard which is based on some notion of generality.

(73) The less *ad hoc* a grammatical hypothesis is in a general linguistic sense, the more acceptable the hypothesis.

A grammatical hypothesis is *ad hoc* in a general linguistic sense if it postulates a *kind* of grammatical entity which does not typically occur in human languages. Such a grammatical hypothesis would imply that the language in question is, in a certain sense, unique within the class of human languages. The larger the contribution which linguistic universals make to the content of a grammatical hypothesis, the less *ad hoc* this hypothesis is in a general linguistic sense. Suppose that, as a distinct type of lexical entry, neutral lexical entries were limited to the grammar of English. They would then represent a unique or idiosyncratic aspect of English. For this reason the lexicalist hypothesis, which assumes the existence of such lexical entries, would not be accorded a large measure of merit in terms of the acceptability standard (73).

Let us consider another example of the function of the acceptability standard (73). Suppose that the transformationalist hypothesis did in fact require that the grammar of English incorporate a transformation of derivative nominalization which violates the recoverability condition on deletion transformations. If the recoverability condition is a well-justified universal, then such a transformation will be *ad hoc* from a general linguistic point of view. It will be a unique entity, the existence of which is assumed by the transformationalist hypothesis. In view of this fact, the transformationalist hypothesis will be without merit in terms of the standard of acceptability (73).

In the context of justification, the acceptability standard (73) logically instantiates an aspect of a criterion for grammatical explanations, viz. the criterion of explanatory depth which was formulated as (50) in §7.3.2.4. The less *ad hoc* a grammatical hypothesis is in a general linguistic sense, the deeper the grammatical explanation(s) which can be given on the basis of this hypothesis. Note further that the acceptability standard (73) is anticipated in one of the criteria for grammatical concepts which was formulated as (27) in §6.3.3.1.4, viz. the general linguistic content of grammatical concepts must be as large as possible. It is clearly impossible for grammatical hypotheses to be non-*ad hoc* in a general linguistic sense if they are composed of grammatical concepts without a grain of general linguistic content.

A variant of the acceptability standard (73), which is widely used in the justification of grammatical hypotheses, is the standard of restricted formal/descriptive power.

(74)   The greater the additional formal power which the formulation of a grammatical hypothesis requires from the general linguistic theory, the less acceptable the hypothesis.

A grammatical hypothesis which can be formulated in terms of the available general linguistic concepts and principles requires no additional formal power of the general linguistic theory. By contrast, a grammatical hypothesis that cannot be formulated in terms of the available general linguistic principles or concepts, could require an extension of the formal power of the general linguistic theory. Suppose, for instance, that, in order to formulate a grammatical hypothesis, certain new general linguistic concepts or principles were in fact formed. By including these new concepts or principles in the general linguistic theory, its characterization of the concept 'possible human language' could be made less restrictive. The formation of the general linguistic concept 'syntactic transformation' had such a negative effect on the formal power of the general linguistic theory. The general linguistic concepts or principles in question include more than just new types of rules. Also, new kinds of linguistic units, categories, levels of structure, and so on may result in an extension of the formal power of the general linguistic theory.

The reasons why a nonessential extension of the formal power of the general linguistic theory is undesirable, were discussed in detail in §6.4.3.1.3. Only the essence of these reasons will be repeated here. The general linguistic theory must give a restrictive characterization of the concept 'possible human language'. This implies that the class of possible grammars that may be constructed in terms of the general linguistic theory must be as small as possible. With every additional kind of general linguistic entity – i.e. kind of linguistic unit, kind of structure, kind of rule, etc. – postulated by the general linguistic theory, the possibility arises that this class of grammars may be extended. With every new general linguistic entity, a new class of possible grammatical solutions are offered for a set of problematic data. This could cause the general linguistic theory to become less restrictive in its characterization of the content of the concept 'possible human language'. New kinds of general linguistic entities may therefore be formed only if it would be impossible to construct descriptively adequate grammars for individual languages without them.

The acceptability standards (71), (73) and (74) deal with the relatedness of grammatical hypotheses to other linguistic hypotheses, i.e. grammatical hypotheses and general linguistic hypotheses. Therefore, these standards are specific instances of the general criterion of theoretical fit or systematic interrelatedness which was formulated as (25)(a) in §9.2.1.3. A grammatical hypothesis must also fit in, or be consistent, with the existing linguistic facts. Thus, the general criterion (24) in §9.2.1.3 applies to grammatical inquiry as well. A third general acceptability standard which applies to grammatical inquiry is that of heuristic fruitfulness, formulated as (25)(b) in §9.2.1.3: the more fruitful a hypothesis is in a heuristic sense, the higher the degree of systematic justification and the greater the acceptability of the hypothesis. Let us consider an example of the way in which this criterion could be used in the justification of the lexicalist hypothesis.

Recall that a hypothesis is heuristically fruitful if it induces the scientist, via the formulation of further hypotheses, to make new discoveries. The lexicalist hypothesis is potentially fruitful from this heuristic point of view. To begin with, it induced Chomsky to formulate a variety of new grammatical hypotheses about English. Among these are the three of (75).

(75)(a) English does not in fact have a passive transformation; the two most important operations carried out by this supposed "transformation" are in fact carried out by two separate transformations, viz. Agent Postposing and NP Preposing.

(b) The base rules for NPs, VPs and APs are parallel in structure.

(c) Possessive constructions such as *John's leg* are generated directly by the base rules.

The lexicalist hypothesis also induced Chomsky to formulate various new hypotheses about language in general. Among these are the four general linguistic hypotheses of (76).

(76)(a)   Generalizations about the base rules of languages may be expressed in terms of the $\overline{\text{X}}$-convention.

(b)   In addition to S, cyclic-transformations can also have NP as their domain.

(c)   Neutral lexical entries are a structural element of the lexicon.

(d)   Nonlexical syntactic categories too are combinations of syntactic features.

For a (further) illustration of the content of the grammatical and general linguistic hypotheses mentioned above, technical works on generative grammar may be consulted.

Suppose that it were to appear in future that the hypotheses (75) and (76) are well-justified and that they can survive thorough testing. Then the lexicalist hypothesis would have been found to be actually — and not only potentially — fruitful. In these circumstances the lexicalist hypothesis would be highly acceptable in terms of the standard of heuristic fruitfulness.

In conclusion, it has to be noted that the preceding discussion does not represent an attempt at giving a comprehensive survey of the acceptability standards involved in linguistic inquiry. Only those standards that are used fairly widely have been mentioned. A more comprehensive survey may be found in *The justification of linguistic hypotheses* (= Botha 1973: §6.2).

9.3.2.3.3   *Logical status of grammatical acceptability standards*

Let us consider the logical status of the acceptability standard (67) within Chomsky's justification (1). The argument in which Chomsky uses this standard within the framework of (1) may be reconstructed as follows:

(77)   MaP : If a grammatical hypothesis H_1 can serve as a basis for the explanation of a given corpus of linguistic data, whereas an alternative hypothesis H_2 is at best consistent with these data, then H_1 is more acceptable than H_2.

MiP : 1. The lexicalist hypothesis serves as a basis for the explanation of the acceptability of the gerundive nominals (35) and the unacceptability of the derived nominals (36).

2. The transformationalist hypothesis is at best consistent with these data.

C   : The lexicalist hypothesis is more acceptable than the transformationalist hypothesis.

It is clear from (77) that, in the context of grammatical justifications, standards of acceptability have the logical status of the major premiss of demonstrative arguments.

But let us focus our attention on the minor premisses of the argument (77). Notice that in these minor premisses metascientific data are presented about grammatical hypotheses: data about the explanatory power of the lexicalist hypothesis and data about a logical property (consistency) of the transformationalist hypothesis. Since these data are presented in justification of a claim, viz. the conclusion of (77), they constitute evidence for this claim. On account of the fact that this evidence deals with metascientific objects, it may be called META-SCIENTIFIC EVIDENCE.

Metascientific evidence is also used in another component of grammatical justifications, viz. in those demonstrative arguments that are put forward to justify judgments about the extent of the factual justification for grammatical hypotheses. An example of such an argument was presented as (55) in §9.3.2.2.5. Within the framework of such arguments, metascientific evidence takes the form of data about the comprehensiveness and independence of evidential statements/ corpora. For example, in the argument (55), data about the insufficient comprehensiveness of the evidence about the role of neutral lexical entries in the grammar of English represent the metascientific evidence.

The argument (77) illustrates another general property of grammatical justifications, viz. their comparative nature. In linguistic inquiry, the justification of a grammatical hypothesis commonly involves comparing its merit to the merit of an alternative hyothesis. Chomsky's weighing up of the lexicalist hypothesis against the transformationalist hypothesis illustrates this point rather well. Comparison is an essential part of grammatical justificatin in cases where alternative hypotheses have been/are being proposed as solutions for a particular problem. If only one hypothesis has been proposed as the solution to a grammatical problem, no such comparison can of course be made. Consequently, there can be no principle that decrees that the justification of a grammatical hypothesis *must* include comparison with an alternative.

9.3.2.4   The External Component

9.3.2.4.1   *Psychological reality of grammatical hypotheses*
Having justified a grammatical hypothesis, such as the lexicalist hypothesis, with the aid of the factual means of §9.3.2.2 and the systematic means of §9.3.2.3, one question remains: in what function has this hypothesis been justified? This question is related to the distinction drawn in §9.3.2.1 between the descriptive and the explanatory function of a grammatical hypothesis. The answer given to this question by generative grammarians such as Bresnan (1976), Hastings and Koutsoudas (1976), Hutchinson (1974) and Kiparsky (1968a) is the following: with the aid of the means in question the grammatical hypothesis can be partly justified in its explanatory function, but not in its descriptive function. To justify a grammatical hypothesis in its explanatory function is to show that it has a measure of merit as a basis for the explanation of problematic properties of

utterances. To justify such a hypothesis in its descriptive function is to show that it possibly gives an accurate representation of an aspect of the form of the linguistic competence. A grammatical hypothesis which represents or describes an aspect of the form of the linguistic competence is psychologically real.

These linguists' answer to the question posed above is based on the following principle:

(78)   The fact that certain data about utterances can be explained on the basis of a grammatical hypothesis does not necessarily imply that the hypothesis gives an accurate representation of an aspect of the form of the linguistic competence underlying these utterances.

The point is that the same set of linguistic data may be explained on the basis of alternative hypotheses. Two alternative hypotheses make two different claims about the underlying linguistic competence which, in principle, cannot both be true. Generative grammarians, therefore, judge that additional means are needed to justify a grammatical hypothesis in its descriptive function: means that can supplement the factual and systematic means discussed above.

Moreover, the factual and systematic means at the grammarian's disposal are not sufficient for the justification of a grammatical hypothesis in its explanatory function. Recall that the grammarian using a grammatical hypothesis in its explanatory function attempts to account for one or more problematic properties of utterances in terms of the properties of the underlying linguistic competence. Such an explanation cannot be well-justified if it is not sufficiently clear that the grammatical hypothesis concerned gives a correct representation or description of the properties of the linguistic competence. It is on the strength of these considerations that Chomsky and Katz (1974:365) adopt the criterion formulated in §7.3.2.3, viz. that the grammatical and general linguistic principles used in the lawlike generalizations of linguistic explanations should be psychologically real. The factual and systematic means of justification discussed above do not in fact provide sufficient grounds for assuming that the linguistic principles in question are psychologically real. The result is that to justify grammatical hypotheses in their explanatory function, these factual and systematic means need to be supplemented by other additional means.

The distinction that has been drawn between the justification of a grammatical hypothesis in its explanatory function and the justification of such a hypothesis in its descriptive function may be illuminated with reference to a parallel distinction made by Joan Bresnan. In her article "Toward a realistic model of transformational grammar" (1976:1), Bresnan differentiates between two fundamental problems at which grammatical inquiry has been directed during the past ten or more years, viz. the grammatical characterization problem vs. the grammatical realization problem. As a basis for this distinction she quotes Chomsky's fundamental assumption that "a reasonable model of language use will incorporate as a basic component, the generative grammar that expresses the speaker-hearer's knowledge of the language".

The GRAMMATICAL CHARACTERIZATION PROBLEM is the problem of giving an adequate characterization of the speaker's unconscious knowledge of his native language. In our terminology, therefore, it is the problem of giving a description of the content of the ideal speaker's linguistic competence. The GRAMMATICAL REALIZATION PROBLEM, by contrast, is the problem of specifying the psychological mechanisms in which the structural parts of a grammar are realized. In other words, it is the problem of specifying the relation between a grammar and a model of language use: a model of language use of which, according to Chomsky, this grammar forms a basic part. In our terminology, therefore, the grammatical realization problem is the problem of specifying the structure or form of the ideal speaker's linguistic competence.

The solution to both the grammatical characterization problem and the grammatical realization problem is sought in terms of grammatical hypotheses. These grammatical hypotheses can be partly justified, with the aid of factual and systematic means, as solutions to the grammatical characterization problem. Insofar as a given grammatical hypothesis has been justified as part of such a solution, it has been justified in its explanatory function. However, the factual and systematic means at the grammarian's disposal are completely inadequate for the justification of a grammatical hypothesis as part of the solution to the grammatical realization problem. In other words, these means are not sufficient to justify a grammatical hypothesis in its descriptive function.

What additional means are available for the justification of grammatical hypotheses in their explanatory and descriptive function? These additional means must, of course, be independent of the factual and systematic means which we have discussed. What has to be shown by these additional means is that the content of a given grammatical hypothesis probably correctly represents an aspect of the form of the linguistic competence.

Generative grammarians have tried various means of justifying grammatical hypotheses in their descriptive function. However, it has been shown by for instance, Botha (1968:§3.5.4; 1971:ch.4; 1973:ch.4) and Hutchinson (1974) that a number of these means are not at all adequate for the purpose. Details of the nature and defects of these means fall outside the scope of our study. We shall limit our discussion to those means that are not obviously inadequate. One of these means will be discussed in some detail below, viz. the giving of an external linguistic justification for a grammatical hypothesis in its descriptive function.

First we have to establish what an external linguistic justification is. In the factual justifications which we considered in §9.3.2.2, internal linguistic evidence is presented for grammatical hypotheses. Therefore, these justifications represent INTERNAL LINGUISTIC JUSTIFICATIONS. Generative grammarians attempt to justify grammatical hypotheses in their descriptive function by adducing external linguistic evidence, or external evidence for short, for these hypotheses. EXTERNAL EVIDENCE takes the form of data about objects or phenomena outside the grammarian's linguistic reality. An EXTERNAL LINGUISTIC JUSTIFICATION for a grammatical hypothesis, therefore, is a justification in which such external evidence is presented for the hypothesis.

9.3.2.4.2   *A neuropsychological justification of the lexicalist hypothesis*
Let us consider an example of an external linguistic justification: a neuropsychological justification of the lexicalist hypothesis. In his article "Unsolicited nominalizations by aphasics: the plausibility of the lexicalist model" (1972), Harry Whitaker presents data about the linguistic performance of aphasics in justification of the lexicalist hypothesis. We shall call these data NEUROPSYCHO-LOGICAL EVIDENCE. Whitaker uses the expression "lexicalist hypothesis", to refer to the content of (79).

(79)   A verb and its corresponding derived nominal are specified in the lexicon in a single (neutral) lexical entry.

Where he uses the expression "transformationalist hypothesis", he refers to the content of (80).

(80)   Only verbs are specified in the lexicon; the corresponding derived nominals are generated transformationally.

Whitaker (1972:64) further regards aphasia as "impaired adult language ability due to brain damage".

In his article, Whitaker presents data about dynamic aphasia to confirm the lexicalist hypothesis. In DYNAMIC APHASIA a person's ability to use verbs and his ability to use nouns are not impaired in the same way or to the same extent. For Whitaker it is particularly significant that aphasics who experience difficulties in using a given verb quite often are able to use the corresponding derived nominal with relative ease. It even happens that instead of using the required verb, the aphasic uses the corresponding derived nominal. Whitaker (1972:69) formulates the essence of this phenomenon and his conclusions as follows:

> . . . in certain cases of aphasic impairment nouns seem to be available to a significantly greater degree than verbs as the above data show. What is striking is that under such conditions verbs are generally nominalized, rather than being blocked altogether which one might reasonably have predicted. This phenomenon strongly suggests that the lexical entry is coded in the brain in both its verbal and nominal forms and under the noun-facilitation circumstances, the nominal is retrievable.

The last statement in the passage quoted above fits in with the lexicalist hypothesis. But what does "fits in" mean in this context? According to Whitaker, the lexicalist hypothesis suggests that, in order to use a verb or its corresponding derived nominal, a speaker merely has to retrieve them from the brain, ready for use. According to the lexicalist hypothesis, both the verb and the derived nominal are stored in the brain as lexical items. This has an important implication: even if a speaker's ability to use verbs is impaired, he should still be able to use the corresponding derived nominals.

According to Whitaker, the transformationalist hypothesis suggests that only verbs are stored in the brain as lexical items. Before derived nominals can be used, they have to be transformationally derived from a structure in which the corresponding verbs occur. Whitaker judges this implication of the transformationalist hypothesis to be inconsistent with the neuropsychological data mentioned above. It is not at all clear how a speaker should be able to produce a derived nominal transformationally when he has lost the ability to use the verb from which the nominal is derived. The transformationalist hypothesis suggests that, if a speaker loses the ability to use a verb, he should at the same time lose the ability to use the corresponding derived nominal.

It further appears that the aphasics on whom the neuropsychological data in question have a bearing did not retain normal control over basic transformational processes such as question formation, negation, complementation and passive formation. However, to be able, in terms of the transformationalist hypothesis, to use the derived nominals as they do, aphasics must have retained control over the highly complex transformational process(es) of derivative nominalization. This is quite incompatible with their loss of control over the more basic processes mentioned above.

Whitaker therefore finds the transformationalist hypothesis highly implausible in its descriptive function:

> If we are to maintain that derived nominals are transformationally related to their source verbs, it is clear that such a model would account for the verbal behaviour in question only by a complicated and rather suspect set of principles of brain function. In spite of serious impairments in the use of very general features and rules in the grammar, one would have to argue that these patients were able to make use of a transformational rule which, on good theoretical evidence, must keep track of highly idiosyncratic semantic and syntactic properties. It is even possible to imagine such a model requiring us to assume that brain damage adds functions rather than or in addition to impairing them, certainly an untenable consequence. If, on the other hand, we maintain that verbs and their associated derived nominals are both listed in the lexical entry or coded together we have no additional linguistic or performance variables to account for except the aphasic impairment itself that hierarchizes nouns and verbs in the process of lexical retrieval.

In §9.3.2.4.3 below we shall return to an important assumption which implicitly underlies Whitaker's conclusion.

First note that Whitaker uses two basic arguments: one in favour of the lexicalist hypothesis and one against the transformationalist hypothesis. The former argument may be reconstructed as follows:

(81)   MaP : If the lexicalist hypothesis is psychologically real, then dynamic aphasia will affect a person's ability to use verbs and corresponding derived nominals in a nonparallel way.

MiP : Persons A, B and C are affected by dynamic aphasia in such a way that, whereas their ability to use verbs is impaired, their ability to use the corresponding nominals has remained unimpaired or has even increased.

C   : The lexicalist hypothesis is psychologically real.

The argument (81) is a reductive argument in which confirming evidence is presented for the lexicalist hypothesis.

Whitaker's argument against the transformationalist hypothesis may be reconstructed as follows:

(82)   MaP : If the transformationalist hypothesis is psychologically real, then dynamic aphasia will not affect a person's ability to use verbs and corresponding nominals in a nonparallel way.

MiP : Persons A, B and C are affected by dynamic aphasia in such a way that, whereas their ability to use verbs is impaired, their ability to use the corresponding nominals has remained unimpaired or has even increased.

C   : The transformationalist hypothesis is not psychologically real.

The argument (82) is a demonstrative argument representative of a form which we shall look at in closer detail in §§10.2.2.1 and 10.3.2.3.2.

9.3.2.4.3   *Nature of external linguistic justifications*
We can now have a closer look at the nature of external linguistic justifications, with reference to Whitaker's neuropsychological justification of the lexicalist hypothesis. External evidence, such as the neuropsychological evidence in Whitaker's argument (81), represents data about objects or phenomena outside the grammarian's two-levelled linguistic reality. By his choice of a particular aim of inquiry and, more specifically, by his creation of an ideal speaker, the grammarian consciously excludes these objects or phenomena from the domain of a grammar. For instance, in terms of its objectives, a grammar need not explain the properties of the products of the linguistic performance of dynamic aphasics. The ideal speaker's linguistic performance is perfect and unimpaired by, for

instance, dynamic aphasia. Data about products of the linguistic performance of aphasics are therefore, strictly speaking, qualitatively irrelevant with regard to hypotheses about the form of an ideal speaker's linguistic competence.

How is it possible, then, for linguists — such as Whitaker and many others — to use external evidence in the justification of grammatical hypotheses? The gist of the answer to this question is that these linguists use additional assumptions, an AUXILIARY or BRIDGE THEORY, to try and relate the form of the ideal speaker's linguistic competence to the external linguistic objects or phenomena from which the external evidence is derived. In other words, they try to show that there is a systematic correspondence or interaction between the properties of the linguistic competence and the properties of these objects or phenomena. If such a correspondence or interaction does indeed exist, grammatical hypotheses about the form of the linguistic competence, *by implication*, also express claims about the properties of these objects or phenomena. Under these circumstances, data about external linguistic objects or phenomena do become qualitatively relevant to the justification of grammatical hypotheses.

The bridge theory mentioned above is a central component of an external linguistic justification. We have in fact already seen how such a bridge theory is used. In §8.4.3.2 we saw how external linguistic projections about possible linguistic changes may be made by means of the general linguistic theory. There the bridge theory was a theory of linguistic change of which the major assumptions were given as (49). In the case of Whitaker's neuropsychological justification of the lexicalist hypothesis, the bridge theory deals with the relatedness between a speaker's linguistic competence and the structure and functioning of his brain.

The principal assumption of Whitaker's bridge theory (1972:64) is the following:

> Although it may be the case that the relation between mind and brain is not one of identity but one of complicated, intricate and perhaps even inconsistent principles, there is no *a priori* reason to accept this view ... .

In the absence of these assumptions, performance data about the brain functioning of aphasics, are qualitatively irrelevant with regard to grammatical hypotheses about the form of the ideal speaker's linguistic competence. Without this assumption, such hypotheses can express no claims about the products of linguistic performance that result from the brain functioning of aphasics.

The problem with external linguistic justifications, then, is the bridge theory. If this theory is not itself well-justified, the external data in question do not constitute evidence for the grammatical hypothesis in question. If, on the other hand, this theory is well-justified, the external data in question can constitute either supporting or confirming evidence for the grammatical hypothesis. If projections made by the grammatical hypothesis — in conjunction with the bridge theory — are borne out by the external data, then these constitute confirming evidence for the hypothesis. If the grammatical hypothesis — in conjunction with the bridge theory — forms a basis for explaining the external data, then these constitute supporting evidence for the hypothesis.

Note that the criterion of evidential independence plays an important role in the use of external evidence for grammatical hypotheses. Evidence from outside the grammarian's linguistic reality is, obviously quite independent of evidence from inside this reality. What we have here is in fact an extreme case of independence. The degree of independence of external evidence is such that, as we have seen, its qualitative relevance first has to be established.

Generative grammarians use various types of external evidence in the justification of grammatical hypotheses: data about linguistic changes, dialectal variation, idiodialectal variation, sociolinguistic phenomena such as borrowing, creolization and pidginization, language acquisition and child language, speech errors that are not the result of aphasia, etc. The use of each of these types of external evidence presupposes the existence of an appropriate and adequate bridge theory of the type considered above.

In practice, this bridge theory is often poorly articulated and even more poorly justified. As a result, many generative grammarians are highly sceptical about external linguistic justification for grammatical hypotheses. Such grammarians are generally reluctant to abandon a grammatical hypothesis for the mere reason that no external linguistic justification can be given for the hypothesis. Whitaker (1972:62) summarizes the situation with regard to (neuro)-psychological evidence as follows:

> Being unable to find psychological evidence for a rule or feature is not in itself considered sufficient reason to warrant changing theoretical linguistic constructs. As in the previous case, such studies have had predictably little impact on linguistics. In most cases the grammar is assumed, and the question is not whether the linguistic hypotheses are valid but whether they can be applied successfully as parameters of verbal behaviour.

In informal terms, as far as external linguistic justification is concerned, many generative grammarians are of the opinion that it is fine to be able to give an external linguistic justification for a grammatical hypothesis, but that it is no catastrophe if no such justification can be given. The reasons why this rather superficial view is untenable have recently been spelled out by various scholars, e.g. by Botha (1979 a, b).

What is Chomsky's view of the status of external linguistic justifications? In principle, he explicitly provides for such justifications. That this is indeed the case, is clear from the article "What the linguist is talking about" (1974:359—360), written in collaboration with Katz:

> Thus suppose it were discovered, say, by neurophysiological investigation or by psycholinguistic study, that all the linguist's data (and more) can be better explained by assuming that the organism has a system of perceptual strategies

not involving the principles of generative grammar in any manner. The linguist who postulates a *dag* as "true of" the organism will be unperturbed. Linguists who take the realist position, claiming that a *dag* actually describes the speech mechanisms at work, might well abandon their formerly held comprehensive performance theory, with its idealized components and its specific principles and properties.

The passage quoted leaves no doubt about Chomsky's (and Katz's) willingness to accept external linguistic evidence — such as neuropsychological and psycho-linguistic evidence — in the justification of grammatical hypotheses. In practice, however, Chomsky, as a grammarian of English, very rarely uses such evidence himself. A more penetrating analysis of Chomsky's position on the status of external linguistic justifications is presented in (Botha 1979a, b).

The passage quoted above offers a further interesting insight. It shows, as was implied in §6.3.2.3.2, that Chomsky advocates a reasonably strong form of psychological reality for grammars. If this were not the case, there would be no reason for him to accept neurophysiological and psycholinguistic evidence in the justification of grammatical hypotheses. The greater the degree of psychological reality a grammarian requires of a grammar, the greater the weight which has to be accorded to external linguistic evidence in grammatical justifications.

In conclusion, notice that we have discussed the role of external linguistic evidence in the justification of grammatical hypotheses only with regard to their descriptive function. Some generative grammarians use such evidence for another purpose. These are the grammarians who, although they do not require a grammatical hypothesis to be psychologically real, provide external evidence for their hypotheses. They use external evidence to justify grammatical hypotheses in their explanatory function. This they do within the framework of the criteria of evidential comprehensiveness and evidential independence.

9.3.2.5 *Retrospect*

Three general points in connection with the preceding discussion of the nature of grammatical justifications have to be stressed. First, the picture that has been given of the structure of a grammatical justification is an optimal picture. In other words, not every grammatical justification given by generative grammar-rians in fact contains each of the structural components discussed above. Every justification must, however, include supporting and confirming arguments as minimal structural components. Every additional component that such a justi-fication has, enhances its power as a grammatical justification.

Second, to call the external component of a grammatical justification "exter-nal", is *not* to imply two things. On the one hand, it is not implied that factual data play no role in the structure of the external component. On the other hand, it is not implied that systematic considerations play no role in the structure of the external component. On the contrary, it is quite clear that the external component of a grammatical justification is composed of, among other things, both factual data and systematic considerations. The factual data are external linguistic data. The systematic considerations concern the relatedness of the justified grammatical hypothesis to a bridge theory of the type described above. These points should be kept in mind when we discuss the external components of general linguistic justifications (§9.4.2.3) of grammatical criticism (§10.3.2.3) and of general linguistic criticism (§10.4.2.3).

Third, nothing has been said about the nonobjective component of grammatical justifications. In all essential respects, this component is the same as that of general linguistic justifications. We therefore postpone its discussion to §9.4.2.4 where general linguistic justification will be considered.

9.3.3   Giving Grammatical Justifications

In our preceding, reasonably comprehensive discussion of the various parts constituting a justification for a grammatical hypothesis, an indirect characterization of the intellectual activities involved in the justification of hypotheses in grammatical inquiry was in fact given. This characterization can now be explicitly formulated as (83).

(83)(a)   To justify a grammatical hypothesis H in its *explanatory function* involves

    (i)   presenting, within the framework of one or more regressively reductive arguments, internal evidence which supports H — i.e. data about the grammarians linguistic reality which may be explained on the basis of H;

    (ii)   presenting, within the framework of one or more progressively reductive arguments, internal evidence which confirms H — i.e. data about the grammarian's linguistic reality which show that H makes certain accurate projections;

    (iii)   appraising the intuitive evidence provided for H within the arguments of (i) and (ii) to establish its

        (α) accuracy, i.e. factualness, and

        (β) qualitative relevance, i.e. genuineness;

    (iv)   in the case where one or more of the arguments of (i) and (ii) contain hypothetical evidence for H, justifying the grammatical hypotheses concerned — ultimately by means of the aid of intuitive evidence;

    (v)   demonstrating, within the framework of one or more deductive arguments, that the supporting evidence of (i) and the confirming evidence of (ii)

(α) are sufficiently comprehensive, and

(β) belong to mutually independent kinds;

(vi)   demonstrating, within the framework of one or more deductive arguments, that there is a measure of systematic justification for H, i.e. that H is acceptable within the framework of the standards discussed in §9.3.2.3.2;

(vii) comparing the measure of internal linguistic justification for H with the measure of justification for alternative grammatical hypotheses;

(viii) presenting the arguments of (i)–(vi) (and the finding of (vii)) in the form of a well-integrated, coherent case for H so that it is clear

(α) which arguments are major arguments,

(β) which arguments supplement other arguments, and

(γ) which arguments complement one another.

(b)   To justify a grammatical hypothesis H in its *descriptive function*, thereby further justifying it in its explanatory function, involves, in addition to (a) above,

(i)   presenting external linguistic data as supporting and/or confirming evidence for H;

(ii)   showing that the bridge theory by which these data are made qualitatively relevant to H is itself well-justified; and

(iii) comparing the measure of external linguistic justification for H with the measure of external linguistic justification for alternative grammatical hypotheses.

(c)   To provide internal and external linguistic justification for the grammatical hypothesis H does NOT involve the use of misleading strategies of persuasion in a conscious attempt to create an inaccurate impression of the merit of H.

It is clear from this characterization that the giving of grammatical justifications is a type of reasoning. It is also quite obvious that it is an intellectual activity which requires considerable skill in the use of forms of argument, evidential criteria and acceptability standards. Finally, to be able to present the arguments resulting from the use of these forms, criteria and standards in a clear, coherent manner, considerable rhetorical skills are required.

9.4   GENERAL LINGUISTIC INQUIRY

9.4.1   General

The five assertions below express typical general linguistic hypotheses.

(84)(a)   The base rules for the major category constituents of human languages exhibit a significant parallelism which can be expressed in terms of the concepts 'specifier', 'head' and 'complement'.

(b)   The lexicon of any human language is composed of, among other things, neutral lexical entries.

(c)   Nonlexical syntactic categories are complexes of syntactic features.

(d)   In addition to S, cyclic transformations have NP as their domain.

(e)   Deletion transformations can delete a syntactic element E only if (a) E is identical to another element in the P-marker, or (b) E is a constant single element.

The justifications given for such general linguistic hypotheses and the theories into which they are integrated may conveniently be called GENERAL LINGUISTIC JUSTIFICATIONS. We shall first consider the nature and components of such justifications and then attempt to establish precisely what is involved in the giving of general linguistic justifications.

Before entering into details, however, a word or two about the by now well-known distinction between the descriptive and the explanatory function of a linguistic hypothesis. This distinction applies to general linguistic hypotheses as well. A general linguistic hypothesis performs its explanatory function at the more directly given level of the general linguist's linguistic reality, viz. the level of properties of the grammars of individual languages. It performs its descriptive function at the underlying level of the general linguist's· linguistic reality, viz. the level of man's language acquisition faculty. A general linguistic hypothesis must be justified in both these functions.

9.4.2   Nature of General Linguistic Justifications

9.4.2.1   *The Factual Component*

The first, factual component of a general linguistic justification has two aspects. On the one hand, a general linguistic hypothesis derives a first measure of factual justification from the linguistic data which it explains. On the other hand, the hypothesis derives a further measure of factual justification from the linguistic data which show the projections made on the basis of the hypothesis to be correct.

9.4.2.1.1   *Justification on the basis of explained data*
We saw in §7.4.1 that internal general linguistic explanations are explanations of problematic properties of the grammars of individual languages. In these explanations general linguistic hypotheses play the role of lawlike generalizations. The data which have a bearing on the aforementioned properties and which may be

explained with the aid of a general linguistic hypothesis support the hypothesis. This point is best illustrated by an example.

In the internal general linguistic explanation presented as (66) in §7.4.4, the recoverability condition on deletion transformations plays the role of lawlike generalization. In (66) problematic properties of the grammar of English are explained in terms of this general linguistic hypothesis. The linguistic data about these properties may be used to justify this hypothesis by presenting them in the minor premisses of the following argument:

(85)   MaP : If the recoverability condition is correct, then human languages will not have deletion transformations of the type T.

MiP : 1. In English the transformation of derivative nominalization will be a transformation of the type T.

2. (The descriptively adequate grammar of) English does not in fact include a transformation of derivative nominalization.

C   : The recoverability condition is correct.

[A deletion transformation of the type T is one which deletes an element in a nonrecoverable way.]

The argument (85) is regressively reductive and therefore nondemonstrative. In this argument linguistic data about the properties of the grammar of a particular language are presented as supporting evidence for the recoverability condition. It is important that it should be possible to present this kind of supporting evidence for a general linguistic hypothesis. If it is indeed possible, it shows that the general linguistic hypothesis in question can form part of a general linguistic theory which satisfies Chomsky's criterion of explanatory adequacy. This criterion, which was discussed in §7.4.2.3, involves roughly the following: it must be clear from the general linguistic theory why speakers of a language have the grammar which they have. It should, for instance, be clear from this theory why speakers of English do not have a transformation of derivative nominalization in their grammar.

In chapter 7 it was also shown that general linguistic hypotheses in conjunction with grammatical hypotheses, may be used as lawlike generalizations in grammatical explanations. In the grammatical explanations (34) and (39)(a)−(b) of §7.3.1, the recoverability condition and the Coordinate Structure Constraint, respectively, play the role of lawlike generalizations. The problematic data that are explained in grammatical explanations are data about properties of the sentences of individual languages. However, these data do not directly support the general linguistic hypotheses invoked in grammatical explanations. The main point is that general linguistic hypotheses make no direct assertions about the properties of sentences of individual languages. Such hypotheses express claims about the properties of grammars. Via these properties of grammars, general linguistic hypotheses make indirect assertions about the properties of sentences. In other words, general linguistic hypotheses make claims about the sentences of individual languages via grammatical hypotheses. This point is illustrated by the grammatical explanation (34) in §7.3.1. In this explanation the recoverability condition asserts a claim about the interpretation of the sentence *I don't like John's cooking any more than Bill's* via a grammatical hypothesis about a possible deletion rule in the grammar of English.

A general linguistic hypothesis therefore derives no direct factual justification from the fact that it is used in conjunction with one or more grammatical hypotheses in grammatical explanations. This fact does, however, provide a different kind of justification, viz. a measure of systematic justification, for the hypothesis, as we shall see in §9.4.2.2.2 below.

9.4.2.1.2 *Justification on the basis of projected data*

It was shown in chapter 8 that general linguistic hypotheses can serve as a basis for general linguistic projections, i.e. projections about the properties of grammars of possible human languages. Linguistic data about these properties, from which it is clear that the projections in question are correct, form the second source of factual justification for general linguistic hypotheses.

To see this, let us look again at the general linguistic prediction (39)(a) in §8.4.1. Notice that the recoverability condition forms the basis of the lawlike generalization in terms of which this prediction is made. The following argument may therefore be constructed in justification of the recoverability condition:

(86)   MaP : If the recoverability condition is correct, then human languages will not have deletion transformations of the type T.

MiP : 1. In Dutch a transformation of derivative nominalization will be a transformation of the type T.

2. (The descriptively adequate grammar of) Dutch does not in fact include a transformation of derivative nominalization.

C   : The recoverability condition is correct.

[In (86) too, a transformation of the type T is a transformation which deletes an element in a nonrecoverable way.]

The argument (86) is progressively reductive and therefore nondemonstrative. In this argument, data about properties of (the grammar of) a particular language are presented as confirming evidence for the recoverability condition. Generative grammarians place a high premium on such evidence from which it appears that general linguistic hypotheses make accurate predictions. A general linguistic hypothesis that makes inaccurate predictions cannot form part of a general linguistic theory which gives a characterization of the concept 'possible human language'. We saw in §8.4.2.1 that in order to give such a characterization, accurate predictions have to be made about noninvestigated human languages.

Note that general linguistic hypotheses, in conjunction with grammatical hypotheses, may serve as a basis for grammatical projections as well. The recoverability condition and the Coordinate Structure Constraint are used for this purpose in the grammatical predictions (23)(c) and (d) of §8.3.1 respectively. The linguistic data from which it appears that these grammatical predictions are (in)correct are data about the sentences of individual languages. For reasons that were discussed in §9.4.2.1.1 such data do not provide direct factual justification for the general linguistic hypotheses concerned. A general linguistic hypothesis does, however, derive a measure of systematic justification from the fact that, in conjunction with one or more grammatical hypotheses, it may be used as a basis for accurate grammatical projections. This point will be discussed in more detail in §9.4.2.2.2 below.

9.4.2.1.3   *Types and criteria of evidence*

It must be emphasized that the data presented as evidence for general linguistic hypotheses are not intuitive linguistic data about the properties of sentences of individual languages. These data are linguistic data about the properties of grammars of individual human languages. For instance, compare the following two assertions in which evidence is presented for the recoverability condition as a general linguistic hypothesis.

(87)(a)   (The descriptively adequate grammar of) English does not include a transformation of derivative nominalization (cf. (85) above).

   (b)   (The descriptively adequate grammar of) Dutch does not include a transformation of derivative nominalization (cf. (86) above).

The data of (87) constitute hypothetical evidence for the general linguistic hypothesis in question. The grammatical hypotheses constituting this evidence must therefore be justified by means of supplementary arguments. It is important that such grammatical hypotheses should form part of descriptively adequate grammars of individual languages. Hypotheses that are part of descriptively inadequate grammars cannot be used as evidence for general linguistic hypotheses. We shall return to this point in §10.4.2.1.2 below.

Hypothetical evidence for general linguistic hypotheses is by nature internal evidence, i.e. it takes the form of data about objects within the generative grammarian's linguistic reality. We shall see in §9.4.2.3 below that external evidence may be used for the justification of general linguistic hypotheses as well.

In order to be suitable for use as evidence for general linguistic hypotheses, linguistic data must satisfy the usual three minimal criteria, viz. the criteria of logical relevance, qualitative relevance and accuracy. What was said about these criteria in §9.3.2.2.4 applies here as well. In addition, both the criterion of evidential independence and the criterion of evidential comprehensiveness play an important role in the justification of general linguistic hypotheses. In the context of general linguistic inquiry, the criterion of evidential comprehensiveness, in general terms, involves the following:

(88)   The greater the number of positive instances a general linguistic hypothesis has at the level of properties of the grammars of individual languages, the larger the extent of the factual justification for the hypothesis.

The content of the criterion of evidential independence is parallel to that of (88).

(89)   The larger the variety of mutually independent types of data – about the properties of the grammars of individual languages – which constitute the positive instances of a general linguistic hypothesis, the larger the extent of the factual justification for the hypothesis.

We shall consider two specific applications of the criteria (88) and (89) below.

9.4.2.2   The Systematic Component

9.4.2.2.1   Importance of the systematic component
The systematic component is, for two reasons, of the utmost importance in a general linguistic justification. The first is a general metascientific reason: the factual justification of a general linguistic hypothesis is essentially inconclusive. It therefore needs to be supplemented on the basis of systematic considerations, or acceptability standards. The second is a specific linguistic reason: a general linguistic theory is a theory about other theories, viz. grammars. In other words, the general linguistic theory deals with an object, the human language faculty, which manifests itself in other objects, linguistic competences. Linguistic competences can be studied only by means of further theories, viz. grammars. It is clear, therefore, that there is a close, systematic relatedness between general linguistic hypotheses and grammatical hypotheses. This systematic relatedness plays an important role in the justification of general linguistic hypotheses. Bearing this in mind, we shall now consider a number of the systematic considerations, or acceptability standards, which are used in general linguistic justifications.

9.4.2.2.2   Acceptability standards for general linguistic hypotheses
One of the most fundamental acceptability standards for general linguistic hypotheses is that of (90).

(90)   The greater the role that a general linguistic hypothesis plays in the giving of grammatical explanations, the more acceptable the hypothesis.

General linguistic hypotheses may play a more or less direct role in grammatical explanations. This point may be elucidated with reference to the grammatical explanations which we considered in chapter 7.

Of the various types of general linguistic hypotheses, substantive universals play the most direct role in grammatical explanations. These universals can be directly used in conjunction with grammatical hypotheses to construct lawlike generalizations on the basis of which grammatical explanations may be given. This point is illustrated by the grammatical explanations (34) and (39)(a)–(b) in §7.3.1. In the grammatical explanation (34), the recoverability condition is used in conjunction with a grammatical hypothesis about a possible deletion rule in English to construct the following lawlike generalization:

(91)   If the deletion transformation T_x violates the recoverability condition in the derivation of a given sentence, then this sentence will be unacceptable in a given interpretation.

In the grammatical explanation (39)(a), the Coordinate Structure Constraint, in conjunction with a grammatical hypothesis about a possible movement rule of English, is used in an analogous way to construct the following lawlike generalization:

(92)   If the movement transformation T_y violates the Coordinate Structure Constraint in the derivation of a given sentence, then this sentence will be unacceptable.

The recoverability condition and the Coordinate Structure Constraint are positively valued in terms of the acceptability standard (90) in view of the role which they play in (91) and (92) respectively.

Formal universals also play a role in grammatical explanations, although their role is less direct than that of substantive universals. Formal universals specify the *types* of rules, structures, categories, linguistic units, features, etc. in terms of which grammatical hypotheses are formulated. In chapter 7 we looked at a number of examples of grammatical explanations in which general linguistic hypotheses postulating formal universals play this less direct role. In the explanations (3)(a) and (b) in §7.1, the hypothesis about neutral lexical entries plays such a role. The result is that it becomes possible to formulate the lawlike generalization (93).

(93)   If it is specified in the neutral lexical entry for a lexical item that this item may not take a sentential complement and if in a given expression this item does take a sentential complement, then this expression is unacceptable.

The deep structure hypothesis plays an analogous role in the grammatical explanations (27) and (30) in §7.3.1. A general linguistic hypothesis which plays neither an indirect nor a direct role in the giving of grammatical explanations is completely unacceptable in terms of the criterion (90).

The acceptability standard of projective adequacy is analogous to that of explanatory adequacy.

(94)   The greater the role that a general linguistic hypothesis plays in the making of correct grammatical predictions, the more acceptable the hypothesis.

The interpretation of this standard is parallel to that of the standard (90) of explanatory adequacy. In grammatical predictions such as (23)(c) and (d) in §8.3.1, substantive universals are used in a direct way, in conjunction with grammatical hypotheses, as the lawlike basis for grammatical predictions. In the grammatical predictions (1)(a) and (b) in §8.1 and (23)(a) and (b) in §8.3.1, formal universals play a less direct role in the formulation of the lawlike generalization. Both the former substantive universals and the latter formal universals are positively valued for their projective power in terms of the acceptability standard (94).

A third acceptability standard, which concerns the interrelatedness of the general linguistic theory and individual grammars, hinges on the concept 'linguistically significant generalization'.

(95)   The greater the role that a general linguistic hypothesis plays in the expression of linguistically significant generalizations, the more acceptable the hypothesis.

This standard was anticipated in the criterion for the formation of general linguistic concepts, which was formulated as (54) in §6.4.3.1.2. In terms of its rules and lexical entries a grammar must express all the linguistically significant generalizations about a language. Various formal universals are needed in order to formulate these rules and lexical entries. The general linguistic hypotheses which postulate these formal univerals are accorded a measure of merit in terms of the standard (95). For example, in terms of this standard a certain measure of merit is accorded to the general linguistic hypothesis which postulates the $\overline{X}$-convention. It was shown in §5.3.2.2 how this convention and certain base rules governed by it make it possible to express linguistically significant generalizations about the parallelism in the structure of NPs, VPs and APs in the grammar of English.

The acceptability standard (95) has two variants which are formulated in negative terms. The first is presented here as (96).

(96)   A general linguistic hypothesis which makes it possible to express linguistically nonsignificant generalizations is unacceptable.

Apart from other considerations, McCawley bases his judgment that the X̄-convention is unacceptable on this standard. The X̄-convention is formulated in terms of, among other things, the concept 'specifier'. According to McCawley, 'specifier' is a linguistically nonsignificant category in the grammar of English. This point was discussed in more detail in §6.3.3.1.2. The second negative variant of the standard (95) is the following:

(97)   If a linguistically significant generalization S about a particular language L cannot be expressed in the grammar G or L as a result of the occurrence of the general linguistic hypothesis H in the general linguistic theory within the framework of which G must be constructed, then H is unacceptable.

In short, a general linguistic hypothesis which makes it impossible to express known linguistically significant generalizations about individual languages is unacceptable. The standard (97) is an important one in linguistic inquiry. It was first used by Morris Halle in his book *The sound pattern of Russian* (1959) to show that a particular general linguistic hypothesis of taxonomic phonology is unacceptable.

The form of argument within which the standard (97) is used may be reconstructed as follows:

(98)   MaP : If a linguistically significant generalization S about a particular language L cannot be formulated in the grammar G of L as a result of the occurrence of the general linguistic hypothesis H in the general linguistic theory within the framework of which G must be constructed, then H is unacceptable.

        MiP : There is a linguistically significant generalization s about the language l which cannot be formulated in the grammar g of t as a result of the general linguistic hypothesis h in the general linguistic theory within the framework of which g must be constructed.

_____

        C   : The general linguistic hypothesis h is unacceptable.

Arguments that are concrete instances of this form of argument are known as HALLEAN ARGUMENTS. The properties and limitations of this form of argument are discussed in detail by Jerrold Sadock in his article "On significant generalizations: notes on the Hallean syllogism" (1976).

The form of argument (98) illustrates the status of acceptability standards in general linguistic justifications. In these justifications, acceptability standards have the status of the major premiss of demonstrative arguments.

Another acceptability standard which is used in addition to those already discussed is one which is concerned with the relation between a new general linguistic hypothesis and the general linguistic theory of which it must form a part. This is the standard of restricted formal/descriptive power.

(99)   The more a general linguistic hypothesis contributes to restricting the formal/descriptive power of the general linguistic theory, the more acceptable the hypothesis.

The standard (99) is the general linguistic correlate of the grammatical acceptability standard (74). It is anticipated in the criterion for general linguistic concepts that are to be used in the construction of general linguistic hypotheses. This criterion was formulated as (55) in §6.4.3.1.3. This standard also instantiates one of the objectives of the general linguistic theory, viz. that it must give a restrictive characterization of the content of the concept 'possible human language'. It is sufficient to point out that a general linguistic hypothesis is positively valued in terms of (99) if it contributes to the restriction of the class of possible human languages.

Chomsky (1972d:128—129), for instance, bases one of his arguments for the deep structure hypothesis on this standard of restricted formal/descriptive power. The hypothesis in question restricts the class of possible human languages in the following way: it excludes, as being impossible, any language that does not include a level of deep structure as a structural element. The standard of restricted formal/descriptive power is therefore responsible for ensuring that the general linguistic theory is not overly powerful, i.e. that it does not have excessive formal/descriptive power. The standards (90), (94) and (95), by contrast, have to ensure that the general linguistic theory is not too weak, i.e. that it does not have too little formal/descriptive power. The expressions "strong" and "weak" are used in the same sense in the discussion in §6.4.3.1.3.

The six acceptability standards discussed above are characteristic of generative grammar. In addition to these, generative grammarians use a number of general metascientific standards in the justification of general linguistic hypotheses, such as the standard of maximal content, the standard of refutability, and the standard of heuristic fruitfulness. These standards were discussed and illustrated in §9.3.2.3.2. What was said about the role of these standards in grammatical justification applies, with certain minor adjustments, to their role in general linguistic justification.

9.4.2.3   *The External Component*

9.4.2.3.1   *Universality, psychological reality, genuineness*
Suppose that it were possible to justify the $\bar{X}$-convention with the aid of (some of) the factual means of §9.4.2.2. Then some generative grammarians would insist on presenting additional justification for this general linguistic hypothesis.

This additional justification would have to present satisfactory answers to one or more of the following three questions:

(100) (a)   Does the $\overline{\text{X}}$ - convention indeed represent a nonaccidental property of human language in general?
(b)   Is the $\overline{\text{X}}$-convention psychologically real?
(c)   Doesn't the $\overline{\text{X}}$-convention perhaps represent a component of a nonlinguistic psychological mechanism or system?

A positive answer to the question (100)(a) would constitute additional justification for the universality or language-independence of the $\overline{\text{X}}$-convention. A positive answer to (100)(b) would constitute additional justification for the $\overline{\text{X}}$-convention in its descriptive function. A negative answer to (100)(c) would constitute additional justification for the genuineness of the $\overline{\text{X}}$-convention as a linguistic principle.

Note that the three questions formulated in (100) could apply to every general linguistic hypothesis. Generative grammarians have reacted to these questions by developing various kinds of additional justification for general linguistic hypotheses. We shall consider one of these, viz. external linguistic justification. In the context of general linguistic inquiry, as in the context of grammatical inquiry, an external linguistic justification is one in which data from outside the generative grammarian's linguistic reality are presented as supporting or confirming evidence for a hypothesis. Let us therefore try to establish how the questions in (100) could be answered with reference to such external linguistic justifications.

9.4.2.3.2   *External justification of universality*

Consider the question (100)(a). It is based on a certain distinction: the distinction between ESSENTIAL and ACCIDENTAL LINGUISTIC UNIVERSALS. In their book *The sound pattern of English* (1968:4), Chomsky and Halle illustrate this distinction by sketching an imaginary situation in which only the inhabitants of Tasmania survive a future war. Every principle of the Tasmanian grammar would then apply to all human languages, since there would be only one. Every principle of Tasmanian would have become an accidental universal. By contrast, essential universals are those linguistic principles which must be assumed to be innate in the form of the language acquisition faculty. Accidental universals do not define the class of possible human languages, whereas essential universals do.

Suppose that, as a result of some catastrophe or other, English were to survive as the only human language. How would it then be possible to establish whether, for instance, the $\overline{\text{X}}$-convention — which plays a role in the grammar of English — is an essential universal? The typical kind of argument given by generative grammarians in justification of the hypothesis that a given linguistic principle is in fact language-independent could then no longer be given. This is the kind of argument in which CROSS-LINGUISTIC EVIDENCE is used, i.e. data about a variety of genetically unrelated languages from which it appears that the linguistic principle in question is a property of the grammar of each one of these languages. However, in our imaginary situation only one language, English, exists. The question which arises is this: how can a general linguistic hypothesis be justified in the absence of cross-linguistic evidence?

The essence of one of the possible answers to this question was formulated as follows by Chomsky and Halle (1968:43):

> It is reasonable to suppose that the principle of the transformational cycle and the principles of organization of grammar that we have formulated in terms of certain notational conventions are, if correct, a part of universal grammar rather than of the particular grammar of English. Specifically, it is difficult to imagine how such principles could be 'learned' or 'invented' in some way by each speaker of the language, on the basis of the data available to him. It therefore seems necessary to assume that these principles constitute a part of the schema that serves as a precondition for language acquisition and that determines the general character of what is acquired.

In the passage quoted above the part following the word "Specifically" is particularly important. It leads us to the heart of the matter, viz. that a general linguistic hypothesis can be justified as an essential universal by arguing that it is so abstract that it cannot be learned on the basis of the utterances with which a child comes into contact during the period of language acquisition. In his *Reflections on language* (1975c:91), Chomsky puts the matter in a nutshell:

> Noting that the mechanisms [= possible linguistic universals − R.P.B.] appear to function in the absence of relevant experience, we draw the natural conclusion that they are not learned, but are part of the system that makes learning possible.

Within this framework, the following argument could be given for the status of the $\overline{\text{X}}$-convention as an essential universal:

(101)   MaP : If a linguistic principle cannot be learned on the basis of data about the properties of utterances, then this principle is an essential universal.

   MiP : The data $D_1, D_2, \ldots, D_n$ indicate that the $\overline{\text{X}}$-convention cannot be learned on the basis of data about the properties of utterances.

   C   : The $\overline{\text{X}}$-convention is an essential universal.

The justification given in terms of the argument (101) for the $\bar{X}$-convention has two interesting aspects.

The first interesting aspect of (101) is the fact that the data about the possibility of the $\bar{X}$-convention being learned, to which reference is made in the minor premiss of (101), are not internal linguistic data. Data about the learnability of any principle must be psychological data. The second interesting aspect of the justification is that it presupposes the existence of a certain psychological theory, viz. a theory of learning in which a clear distinction is drawn between what can and what cannot be learned on the basis of certain presented data. If no such well-justified theory exists, the argument (101) has little force. Chomsky illustrates the use of the form of argument underlying (101) with reference to a variety of examples in his article "On cognitive structures and their development" (1975e:7ff.). For an interesting line of argument for the language-independence of a linguistic principle in which no reference is made either to cross-linguistic evidence or to external linguistic data, Emmon Bach's article "Explanatory inadequacy" (1974b:165–166) may be consulted.

9.4.2.3.3 *External justification of psychological reality*
This brings us to (100)(b), the question relating to the psychological reality of the $\bar{X}$-convention. This question asks for an (additional) indication that the $\bar{X}$-convention represents an aspect of the form of the language acquisition faculty. The question (100)(b) could interest two classes of generative grammarians. On the one hand, there are those generative grammarians for whom the nonaccidental universality of a general linguistic principle is not a sufficient indication of the psychological reality of the principle. On the other hand, there is the class of generative grammarians for whom this *kind* of indication is sufficient, but who consider the psychological justification discussed in the previous paragraph to be inadequate as a type of justification for the nonaccidental universality of a general linguistic principle. They could, for instance, point out the nonavailability of the well-justified theory of learning which the psychological justification in question presupposes.

The (additional) justification of the psychological reality of the $\bar{X}$-convention could be given in the form of an external linguistic justification in which diachronic evidence is presented for the $\bar{X}$-convention. For an example of a potential diachronic justification of the $\bar{X}$-convention, take another look at §8.4.3.2 where it is explained how general linguistic principles, and particularly the $\bar{X}$-convention, may be used in conjunction with a theory of linguistic change to make projections about possible linguistic changes. Data about linguistic changes which did in fact occur, or that are in the process of occurring, should show whether these projections are correct. Should the projections appear to be correct, then these data would represent diachronic evidence from which the $\bar{X}$-convention derives a measure of confirmation. The general form of the argument in which the confirming evidence is presented is as follows:

(102) MaP : If the $\bar{X}$-convention is psychologically real, then linguistic changes should change/simplify base rules that are abbreviated in terms of the $\bar{X}$-convention in a parallel way.

MiP : 1. The base rules for NP, VP and AP in English are abbreviated in terms of the $\bar{X}$-convention.

2. It appears from the historical data D that the linguistic change C changed/simplified the base rules for NP, VP and AP in English in a parallel way.

C   : The $\bar{X}$-convention is psychologically real.

The form of argument (102) is reductive and the reduction is carried out progressively. The reduction in this form of argument could also be carried out regressively. This would be the case if the historical data D about the linguistic change C had the status of problematic data. The $\bar{X}$-convention, in conjunction with a theory of linguistic change, could then be used as a basis for the explanation of these data. The historical data in question would then constitute supporting evidence for the $\bar{X}$-convention. In his article, "Linguistic universals and linguistic change" (1968a), Paul Kiparsky cites a variety of cases in which historical data about linguistic change are used as supporting and confirming evidence for general linguistic hypotheses.

The general nature of the external linguistic justifications given for general linguistic hypotheses is analogous to that of the external linguistic justifications given for grammatical hypotheses. In both cases, therefore, a bridge theory is needed to make the external data qualitatively relevant to the hypothesis. In the case of the potential psychological justification of §9.4.2.3.2, the bridge theory is a psychological theory of learning. In the potential diachronic justification which we have just considered, the assumed bridge theory is a theory of linguistic change. Two of the fundamental assumptions of the latter theory were given as (49) in §8.4.3.2. The force of an external linguistic justification covaries with the measure of justification which exists for the bridge theory.

9.4.2.3.4 *External justification of genuineness*

The question (100)(c) about the genuineness of the $\bar{X}$-convention as a linguistic principle remains to be discussed. The question implies that a distinction can be drawn between genuine and spurious linguistic universals. That such a distinction can and should indeed be drawn is made abundantly clear in the work of Thomas Bever (1974:197–199; 1975:596ff.). Let us consider this distinction with reference to an example.

In his article, "Upstairs primacy" (1972), John Ross proposed the principle (103) as a linguistic universal.

(103)   Transformational rules which optionally reorder constituents within

clauses apply more freely in matrix sentences than in embedded sentences.

On the basis of this principle an explanation may be given for the fact that, whereas the sentence (104)(b) is unacceptable, the sentence (104)(d) is acceptable.

(104)(a)   *After John hurriedly ate his sandwich Bill left.*
   (b)   **After hurriedly John ate his sandwich Bill left.*
   (c)   *Bill hurriedly left after John ate his sandwich.*
   (d)   *Hurriedly Bill left after John ate his sandwich.*

Both (104)(b) and (104)(d) are derived by means of a transformation which moves a modal adverb, *hurriedly*, to the beginning of the clause. This fact can be established by comparing (104)(b) with (104)(a) and (104)(d) with (104)(c). In the case of (104)(d) this movement took place in the main clause, *Bill hurriedly left*, resulting in an acceptable sentence. In the case of (104)(b), on the other hand, the movement took place in an embedded clause, *After John hurriedly ate his sandwich*, resulting in an unacceptable sentence. This restriction on the applicability of the transformation in question can be explained on the basis of the principle (103). Ross found that the principle applies to a number of languages and proposed it as a linguistic universal, calling it THE PENTHOUSE PRINCIPLE: "more goes on upstairs than downstairs".

Bever, however, argues that the Penthouse Principle has a perceptual basis. He bases his argument on what is known about the way in which material is stored in man's perceptual memory. The gist of Bever's argument (1974:198) is as follows:

(105)   . . . I found that immediate memory for material in subordinate clauses is searched from left to right. However, immediate memory for material in main clauses shows no left-right pattern. Our interpretation is that information in a main clause can be accessed in parallel while information in the subordinate clause is accessed serially. The reason for this difference may be that the clause is primary in perception and accordingly listeners store it in the most flexible manner possible. Since subordinate clauses are constituents by definition they are stored as units: to access their internal content requires starting at their beginning and searching left to right. The perceptual differentiation of main and subordinate clauses predicts the Penthouse Principle. The goal of a perceptual mechanism is to isolate the major grammatical relations: a clause in which the constituents are in a non-canonical order will be more complex than a clause in which they are in a canonical order . . . In a main clause, this effect should be relatively slight since constituents are accessed perceptually in parallel: if they are out of the canonical

order they can be reordered directly. However, in a subordinate clause, constituents in a noncanonical order should produce much greater perceptual difficulty: if the subordinate clause is accessed from left to right any constituent which is out of canonical order must be stored until its appropriate "slot" is found. This explains why more reordering transformations can apply to main clauses than to subordinate ones.

Bever emphasizes that the perceptual theory involved in (105) is independently motivated, i.e. it is justified independently of the Penthouse Principle. This is the background against which a distinction can be drawn between genuine and spurious linguistic universals.

Bever regards the Penthouse Principle as an example of a SPURIOUS LINGUIS-TIC UNIVERSAL. It is in fact a special manifestation of a general perceptual principle and a general perceptual principle cannot be a linguistic principle. A GENUINE LINGUISTIC UNIVERSAL is never the manifestation of a nonlinguistic principle. Bever (1975: 596ff.) shows that a number of linguistic universals that were proposed recently have the same status as the Penthouse Principle, i.e. that of a manifestation of a perceptual principle. He further argues that, in addition to perceptual principles, other nonlinguistic principles too may pose as linguistic universals.

It is against this background that the question (100)(c) about the genuineness of the $\bar{X}$-convention arises. Suppose that this convention were psychologically real in the sense that it represents an aspect of the human mind. Then there could still be doubts as to whether this aspect is an aspect of man's language acquisition faculty or of a nonlinguistic mental capacity. How, then, is it possible to justify the $\bar{X}$-convention — or any other general linguistic principle — as being a genuine linguistic universal?

For the purpose of answering this question, we shall call a theory about a non-linguistic mental capacity, or system which plays a role in linguistic performance, a "theory T" for short. The general nature of the justification of a general linguistic principle as a genuine linguistic universal may then be characterized as follows:

(106) (a)   It must be shown that no proposed theory T includes the general linguistic principle in question in a general form.

(b)   If a proposed theory T does include the general linguistic principle concerned, it must be shown that this theory is not independently motivated.

It is impossible, in the context of (106), to argue conclusively that a given general linguistic principle is a genuine universal. The justification that can be given within this framework exists only in relation to certain theories T that have been proposed at a given moment. Moreover, the justification is by nature external, i.e. it is not given in terms of linguistic data or theories which have a bearing on the general linguist's linguistic reality. It is given with reference to theories about objects outside this linguistic reality, such as the human perceptual system.

9.4.2.4   *The Nonobjective Component*

The considerations which play a role in the factual, systematic and external components of linguistic – grammatical and general linguistic – justifications are by nature objective. They are objective in the sense that they take the form of data, facts, knowledge, hypotheses or theories about an objective linguistic and extra-linguistic reality. Jointly, these three components constitute the OBJECTIVE COMPONENT of linguistic justifications. A justification derives a certain measure of persuasive power from the objective component. However, since the justification which a linguistic hypothesis derives from its objective component is essentially inconclusive, this persuasive power is less than compelling. This opens up the way for nonobjective considerations to play a role in linguistic justification. The function of such nonobjective considerations is to increase the persuasive power of linguistic justifications. Jointly, these nonobjective considerations constitute the NONOBJECTIVE COMPONENT of such justifications.

Various nonobjective considerations may contribute to the persuasive power of linguistic justifications. Among these are rhetorical considerations such as those of (29), psychological considerations such as those of (30) and socio-cultural considerations such as that of (31) in §9.2.1.4 above. It goes without saying that the nonobjective considerations which play a role in the justification of a linguistic hypothesis have no bearing whatsoever on its scientific merit. For instance, a linguistic hypothesis derives no merit from the mere fact that it is proposed by, say, Noam Chomsky. Nor does a linguistic hypothesis derive any merit from the fact that its advocate calls the arguments in favour of the hypothesis "strong", "powerful" or "compelling".

Nonobjective considerations such as those mentioned above are easily recognizable as such. However, there are a number of nonobjective considerations that are not as easily recognized. These are nonobjective considerations that are the result of the misuse of objective considerations. A grammarian who consciously misuses an objective consideration in order to heighten the persuasive power of the justification for a linguistic hypothesis is guilty of practising deception. He employs a nonreasonable strategy of persuasion. Such strategies are unfortunately used in the justification of linguistic hypotheses. Let us consider three of these nonreasonable strategies of persuasion for their illustrative value.

A first example of a nonreasonable strategy of persuasion is based on the distinction between the explanatory and predictive power of a linguistic hypothesis. Many generative grammarians accord a higher measure of merit to a linguistic hypothesis if, in addition to explanatory success, the hypothesis *unexpectedly* appears to have predictive success as well. This creates the possibility of using the following nonreasonable strategy of persuasion:

(107) (a)   A grammarian G who justifies a linguistic hypothesis H knows in advance that there are, say, four linguistic facts F_1, F_2, F_3, and F_4 which follow from H.

(b)   In the justification of H, G first presents F_1 and F_2 as facts that are explained by H.

(c)   G subsequently presents F_3 and F_4 as facts that are, *unexpectedly*, correctly predicted by H and commends H on the strength of its *unexpected* predictive success.

A second example of a nonreasonable strategy of persuasion is the result of the misuse of the criterion of evidential independence. We have seen that no precise criterion exists on the basis of which a decision may be made as to whether or not two linguistic data are mutually independent. This enables grammarians to use the following nonreasonable strategy of persuasion:

(108) (a)   A grammarian G can present, say, two linguistic data D_1 and D_2, that can be explained on the basis of a linguistic hypothesis H, as supporting evidence for H.

(b)   In presenting D_1 and D_2, G points out an arbitrary difference between D_1 and D_2.

(c)   On the basis of this arbitrary difference between D_1 and D_2, G argues that D_1 and D_2 represent independent evidence for H.

As regards (108)(b), the grammarian in question naturally neglects to mention the fact that the difference between the two data in question is an arbitrary one.

A third and last example of a nonreasonable strategy of persuasion is based on the comparative aspect of linguistic justifications. Many generative grammarians are prepared to accord a higher measure of merit to a linguistic hypothesis if it appears on comparison to be the best of a number of alternatives. This fact may be misused within the framework of the following nonreasonable strategy of persuasion:

(109) (a)   A grammarian G wants to justify a linguistic hypothesis H, for which no good alternative in fact exists.

(b)   When presenting the justification for H_1, G chooses or invents an alternative, H_2, which he knows in advance to have far less merit than H_1.

(c)   G presents H_2 as a genuine alternative for H_1 and strongly commends H_1 if it appears on comparison to be a far better hypothesis than H_2.

The justification of linguistic hypotheses (Botha 1973:Appendix 7) and *On the logic of linguistic research* (Botha 1977: §7) may be consulted for more examples of such nonreasonable strategies of persuasion that have in fact been used in the justification of linguistic hypotheses.

The conscious use of strategies of persuasion such as the three mentioned above is objectionable in two respects. On the one hand, as strategies of deception they are a manifestation of intellectual dishonesty. On the other hand, they are stumbling-blocks along the way to the achievement of the ultimate objective of linguistic inquiry. Grammarians can never gain the desired insight into the nature of human language(s) by employing these strategies.

9.4.3   Giving General Linguistic Justifications

The giving of general linguistic justifications does not differ in any essential respect from the giving of grammatical justifications. The giving of general linguistic justifications also involves argumentation. Moreover, as an intellectual enterprise, it is composed of the same main parts as the giving of grammatical justifications. These parts were systematically enumerated in (83) of §9.3.3 and will not be repeated here. The characterization given in (83) may therefore be applied to the giving of general linguistic justifications with only a few minor adjustments.

SELECTED READING

Inquiry in General

General Discussions of Scientific Justifications

Achinstein 1971:ch.vi; Barker 1957; Blackburn 1973; Bocheński 1965:ch.v; Bunge 1967b:§15.1; Caws 1966:ch.24–35; Cohen 1970; Hanson 1971:73–76; Harré 1967:ch.5–7; 1972:ch.2; Hempel 1966:ch.4; Hesse 1974; Laudan 1977: 106ff.; Salmon 1967.

Factual Component of Scientific Justifications

Botha 1973: §§2.1–2.4, 2.5.1–2.5.3, 3.1–3.3.1, 4.1 and particularly the literature to which reference is made in these paragraphs.

Systematic Component of Scientific Justifications

Botha 1973:§§2.5.1, 2.5.2, 2.5.4, Appendix 2.5, 6.1 and particularly the literature to which reference is made in these paragraphs; Harré 1967:ch.7; Bunge 1967b:§15.7.

Nonobjective Component of Scientific Justifications

Botha 1973: § §2.5.1, 2.5.2, 2.5.5 and particularly the literature to which reference is made in these paragraphs; 1977: §2.3.1.2.6; Laudan 1977:ch.4; Ziman 1968: 31–32.

Linguistic Inquiry

Publications dealing with linguistic justification don't normally differentiate between grammatical and general linguistic justifications. No distinction will therefore be made between literature on grammatical justification and literature on general linguistic justification below.

General Discussions of Linguistic Justifications

Botha 1976a; 1976b; 1976c; Dougherty 1975; 1976; Sampson 1975a; Stich 1975; Wirth (ed.) 1976.

Factual Component

Forms of Argument

Botha 1973:ch.3, §4.1; 1976b: §§2, 3.

Criteria for Evidence

Evidential comprehensiveness: Botha 1973: §5.6.
Evidential independence: Botha 1973: §§5.7, 6.2.4; Perlmutter and Oreznik 1973; Perloff and Wirth 1976.
Problems in connection with intuitive evidence: See the rubric "Empirical status of intuitive data" on p. 404.

Systematic Component

Acceptability of Linguistic Hypotheses

Botha 1973: §6.1.

Function of Standards of Acceptability

Botha 1973: §6.3.

Logical Status of Standards of Acceptability

Botha 1973: §6.4.

Problems in Connection with Standards of Acceptability

Botha 1973: §6.5.

Variety of Standards of Acceptability

General survey: Botha 1973: §6.2 and the literature referred to in this paragraph

Limited descriptive/formal power: Bach 1974a:173–176, 206–214; Botha 1973: §6.2.7.2; Chomsky 1972d:125–129; 1974:47–49; Zwicky 1975: §25.

Heuristic fruitfulness: Botha 1973: §6.2.9; Evers 1976.

Expression of linguistically significant generalizations: Botha 1971:ch.3; 1973: §6.2.4.3; Prideaux 1971; Sadock 1976.

Nonobjective Component

Botha 1973: §7.1, Appendix 7; 1976d; 1977: §§2.3.1.2.6, 7.

External Linguistic Justification

General Nature

Bach 1974b:167–168; Botha 1971: §§4.1, 4.2, 4.3.1, 4.3.2, 4.3.3.4, 4.3.3.5; 1973: §4.2.1; Hutchinson 1974:59–73; Kiparsky 1968a:171–174.

Problems in Connection with External Linguistic Justifications

Botha 1971: §4.3.3.5.1–4.3.3.5.7; 1973:ch.4; 1979 a and b.

Examples of External Linguistic Justifications in Terms of

Diachronic evidence: Kiparsky 1968a; 1968b; 1975: §4; Schane 1976;

Dialectal/idiolectal evidence: Carden 1970; Elliot, Legum and Thompson 1969;

Neurolinguistic evidence: Stich 1975:101ff.; Weigl and Bierwisch 1970; Whitaker 1970; 1972;

Psycholinguistic evidence: Crothers 1971; Ferguson 1971; Foss and Fay 1975; Fromkin 1975;   Hastings and Koutsoudas 1976; Wirth 1975;

Sociolinguistic evidence: Hyman 1970; Ferguson 1971:141ff.; Vanek 1971:379.

For further examples of external linguistic justifications, see Botha 1973:134 n.11–16.

CHAPTER TEN

Criticizing Linguistic Hypotheses

10.0 PERSPECTIVE

This chapter deals with an eighth main aspect of linguistic inquiry, viz. the criticizing of linguistic hypotheses. The first section of the chapter deals with the criticism levelled at scientific hypotheses in general. The discussion is presented against the background of a distinction between two concepts of truth: a correspondence and a coherence concept of truth. Subsequently, three major components are distinguished within the criticism of scientific hypotheses: a factual, a systematic and a nonobjective component. As regards the factual component, the internal structure and inconclusive nature of a fragment of factual criticism of a scientific hypothesis are discussed in detail. As regards the systematic component, the most important points of the systematic criticism of a scientific hypothesis are briefly noted. A number of the most important considerations which play a role in the nonobjective component of the criticism of such hypotheses are then presented. The first section ends with a brief characterization of the intellectual activities involved in the criticizing of scientific hypotheses.

The first section forms the background for the discussion of the criticism of grammatical hypotheses in the second section of the chapter. The nature and properties of the factual, systematic and external criticism of grammatical hypotheses are discussed in this order. This is followed by a detailed discussion of the intellectual activities involved in criticizing grammatical hypotheses. In this discussion, we concentrate on the factual criticism – or testing – of grammatical hypotheses. The activities involved in the testing of grammatical hypotheses include assessing the testability of grammatical hypotheses, deriving test implications, collecting raw linguistic data, processing the raw linguistic data, confronting the derived test implications with idealized linguistic data and interpreting the disconfirming evidence resulting from this confrontation.

The third section of the chapter deals with the criticism of general linguistic hypotheses. The source, logical form and distinctive features of the factual, systematic and external components of this criticism are considered in some detail. The reasons why both factual and external criticism are inconclusive are discussed in depth. In conclusion, the intellectual activities involved in criticizing general linguistic hypotheses are discussed. It is shown how the distinction between an absolute and a relative view of linguistic universals complicates the refutation of the hypotheses postulating these universals.

10.1   INTRODUCTION

Among the examples of linguistic projections which we considered in chapter 8 was Chomsky's grammatical prediction about the acceptability of the expression *his criticism of the book before he read it.* According to this prediction – as it was presented in (1)(a) of §8.1 and (30) of §8.3.2.2 – the expression will be unacceptable. However, Chomsky (1972b:27) points out that some speakers of English do find this expression acceptable. This acceptability judgment can be related as follows to the merit of the lexicalist hypothesis:

(1)   If the lexicalist hypothesis is correct, then, at the level of deep structure, all derived nominals should have the internal structure of NPs. Therefore, derived nominals which do not have the deep structure of an NP should be unacceptable. The expression *his criticism of the book before he read it* is a derived nominal which, in the form of a *before* clause, includes a structural element of a VP. As a result, this expression should be unacceptable. However, certain native speakers of English do find it acceptable. It is clear, therefore, that derived nominals do exist which, despite the fact that they do not have the deep structure of NPs, are still acceptable. It would follow from this that the lexicalist hypothesis, which claims the contrary, is incorrect.

The argument (1) represents a fragment of the criticism which could be levelled at the lexicalist hypothesis. It also indicates the existence of an eighth main aspect of linguistic inquiry, viz. the criticizing of the hypotheses constituting theoretical linguistic descriptions, or linguistic theories.

Insofar as linguistic inquiry does have this main aspect, it is a typical form of empirical inquiry. Recall that the principal criteria adopted for scientific knowledge in empirical inquiry are that such knowledge must be testable and must in fact have been tested. Information of which the accuracy cannot be tested cannot be granted the status of scientific knowledge. Only testable information which successfully survives thorough testing is admitted to the corpus of scientific knowledge. The criticism levelled at scientific hypotheses by scientists originates from this testing.

Schematically the main aspect of linguistic inquiry under consideration may be represented as follows:

(2)

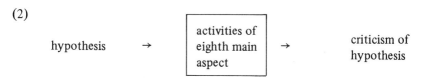

For a better comprehension of what is involved in criticizing linguistic hypotheses, two general questions in connection with this diagram have to be answered.

(3) (a)   What is the nature of the criticism levelled at linguistic hypotheses?
(b)   What is involved in criticizing linguistic hypotheses?

These two questions will first be considered from the angle of empirical inquiry in general. The findings will then be further elaborated with reference to the criticism of grammatical and general linguistic hypotheses in linguistic inquiry. As in previous chapters, the expression "hypothesis/es" will be used as an abbreviation for "individual hypothesis/es and theory/ies", except where the contrary is indicated.

10.2   INQUIRY IN GENERAL

10.2.1   Nature of Criticism of Scientific Hypotheses

10.2.1.1   *General*

In the justification of a scientific hypothesis the merits of the hypothesis are indicated. In the criticism of a scientific hypothesis, by contrast, the defects or limitations of the hypothesis are pointed out. Criticism of a scientific hypothesis H, therefore, provides an answer to the general question (4).

(4)   What defects or limitations does the hypothesis H have?

The most serious defect a scientific hypothesis can have is that it is false or incorrect. The scientist's ultimate purpose in criticizing a scientific hypothesis is therefore to provide reasons why the hypothesis should be regarded as probably incorrect.

In previous chapters we have repeatedly used a concept TRUTH. This concept was implied in the use of sets of synonymous expressions such as "true", "accurate", "correct" and "untrue/false", "inaccurate", "incorrect". Let us have a closer look at the content of the concept 'truth' with reference to the following question:

(5)   What criteria must a proposition, such as a scientific hypothesis, satisfy in order to be true?

The question (5) is an exceptionally intricate philosophical one. In fact, supplying an answer to this question is one of the primary objectives of an entire philosophical subdiscipline, viz. epistemology. Over the centuries various epistemological theories have been developed in an attempt to answer this question. A discussion of the content, merits and defects of the various theories of truth falls outside the scope of our study. The most we can do is briefly to note the central assumptions of two important present-day theories of truth.

The first theory is known as the CORRESPONDENCE THEORY OF TRUTH. Its central assumption, as indicated by, for instance, Peter Caws (1966:15), is the following:

(6)   The truth of a proposition depends on the answer to the question whether the actual state of affairs to which the proposition refers corresponds to what the proposition asserts about it.

A proposition is true if the state of affairs in question is as the proposition represents it. If the state of affairs does not correspond to what the proposition asserts about it, the proposition is false. The concept EXPERIENCE plays an important role in the correspondence theory. Whether or not a correspondence exists between what a proposition asserts about a given state of affairs and this state of affairs as it actually is, is determined by way of scientists' experience of reality. The correspondence theory provides for a kind of truth known as EMPIRICAL TRUTH.

The second theory is known as the COHERENCE THEORY OF TRUTH. According to Abraham Kaplan (1964:314), this theory is based on the following central assumption:

(7)   The truth of a proposition depends on the answer to the question of whether the proposition fits in, i.e. is consistent, with a system of other propositions which are accepted.

Within the framework of this theory a proposition is true if it fits in with such a system of propositions. The proposition is false if it cannot be fitted into such a system, for instance if the proposition is inconsistent with one or more of the other propositions within the system. The kind of truth for which the coherence theory provides is known as SYSTEMATIC TRUTH.

From the point of view of empirical inquiry, the correspondence theory is more fundamental than the coherence theory. The more fundamental status of the correspondence theory is the result of the fact that empirical inquiry is regulated by the REALITY PRINCIPLE. According to Kaplan, this principle implies that scientists' thoughts are subject to control by the properties of the objects about which they are thinking. It is clear, therefore, that the factual component in the justification of scientific hypotheses can be traced back to a concept of empirical truth. However, in addition to this concept of truth, a concept of systematic truth plays a role in empirical inquiry as well. The systematic component of scientific justifications is based on a concept of systematic truth.

In view of what has been said, it is to be expected that both empirical and systematic criteria of truth will play a role in the criticism of scientific hypotheses. We shall see below that the criticism levelled at scientific hypotheses has both a factual (= "empirical") and a systematic component. In addition to these two objective components, the criticism in question may have a nonobjective component as well. It will appear, however, that for nonincidental reasons non-objective considerations play a much more limited role in the criticism of scientific hypotheses than in the justification of these hypotheses. But let us consider the three components of the criticism of scientific hypotheses individually.

10.2.1.2   *The Factual Component*

10.2.1.2.1   *Criticism on the basis of inaccurate projections*
The source of the FACTUAL CRITICISM of a scientific hypothesis is the inaccurate projections that can be made on the basis of the hypothesis. This point may be illustrated with reference to the biological investigation of the flight control mechanism of bats.

One of the hypotheses considered by Spallanzani in the previous century may be formulated as (8).

(8)   Bats control their flight in the dark by means of their taste.

On the basis of this hypothesis, Spallanzani made the prediction (9).

(9)   Bats of whom the tongue has been removed will lose the ability to fly collision-free in the dark.

Spallanzani then collected experimental data to test the accuracy of this prediction. In his experiment he released bats of whom the tongue had been removed in a dark space. This experiment produced the following data:

(10)   Bats of whom the tongue has been removed are just as able to fly collision-free in the dark after the operation as before.

From these data Spallanzani concluded that the hypothesis (8) is incorrect.

The logical basis of Spallanzani's conclusion may be reconstructed as the argument (11).

(11)   MaP : If bats control their flight in the dark by means of their taste, then bats of whom the tongue has been removed will lose the ability to fly collision-free in the dark.

MiP : Bats of whom the tongue has been removed do not lose the ability to fly collision-free in the dark.

C   : Bats do not control their flight in the dark by means of their taste.

A parallel formulation of this argument may be given by using the expression "If the hypothesis (8) is true", as the antecedent and adapting the conclusion accordingly.

The pattern of thought underlying the argument (11) may be represented schematically by means of the following argument:

(12)   MaP : If the hypothesis H is true, then the projections made on the basis of H will be correct.

MiP : One or more of the projections made on the basis of H are incorrect.

———————————————————————

C   : The hypothesis H is false.

Both the argument (11) and the argument (12) are instances of a DEDUCTIVE FORM OF ARGUMENT. Symbolically this form of argument may be represented as follows:

(13)   MaP : If p, then q
        MiP : Not q

———————————————

C   : Therefore not p

In (13) a proposition constituting the negation of the antecedent ("Not p") of a conditional proposition ("If p, then q") is deductively inferred from this conditional proposition and a proposition constituting the negation of its consequent ("Not q"). The form of argument represented in (13) is known as the *modus tollens*. Note that the *modus tollens* differs from the other deductive form of argument, the *modus ponens*, which was represented as (9) in §9.2.1.2.1.

A projection which can be confronted with factual data constitutes a TEST IMPLICATION of the hypothesis on the basis of which it is made. For instance, the prediction (9) is a test implication of the hypothesis (8). Factual data from which it appears that a projection made on the basis of a hypothesis is inaccurate, DISCONFIRMS, FALSIFIES or REFUTES the hypothesis. Such data constitute NEGATIVE INSTANCES of, or DISCONFIRMING/FALSIFYING/REFUTING EVI-DENCE for, the hypothesis. For instance, the data (10) constitute disconfirming evidence for the hypothesis (8). An argument in the minor premiss of which disconfirming evidence is presented for a hypothesis is known as a DISCONFIRM-ING/FALSIFYING/REFUTING ARGUMENT, The argument (11) above is a typical diconfirming argument. Against this background, the factual criticism of a hypothesis may be referred to as THE DISCONFIRMATION/FALSIFICATION/ REFUTATION OF THE HYPOTHESIS. At this point a terminological point has to be cleared up. Some philosophers draw a distinction between the meaning of the expressions "disconfirm", "falsify" and "refute". In our study we will use these expressions and their derivatives loosely as synonyms.

10.2.1.2.2   *Inconclusive nature of refutation*

In the previous chapter it appeared that the justification of a scientific hypothesis can never be conclusive. The arguments in which evidence is presented in justification of the hypothesis are nondemonstrative. The question which now arises is whether a hypothesis can be conclusively refuted. Can it be demonstrated that a hypothesis is, beyond all reasonable doubt, false? For many years scholars were of the opinion that this was indeed possible. Today, however, opinion is divided on this issue, as is clear from the articles in the volume *Can theories be refuted?* (1976a), edited by Sandra Harding. Let us try to establish why many philosophers of science and scientists are of the opinion that scientific hypotheses cannot be refuted conclusively.

The point of view that the refutation of a scientific hypothesis can be conclusive is based on the nature of disconfirming arguments. We saw in the previous paragraph that these arguments are by nature deductive. From this it follows that disconfirming arguments are demonstrative: given that the premisses are true, then the conclusion must necessarily be true. According to the traditional view, therefore, it is possible, within the framework of such arguments, to demonstrate conclusively that a hypothesis is false.

The problem with this point of view is that it is based on an unrealistically simple view of the factors involved in the refutation of a hypothesis. According to this view, only three factors play a role in refutation: the hypothesis, the test implication(s) of the hypothesis and the factual data from which it appears that the test implication(s) is/are correct. Schematically this view of the refutation of a scientific hypothesis may be represented as follows:

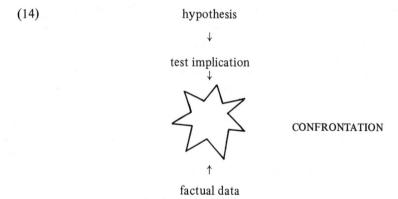

(14)   hypothesis

                          test implication

                                              CONFRONTATION

                          factual data

The view represented as (14) is oversimplified in that it does not show how indirect the refutation of a hypothesis in fact is. This indirectness results from the fact that, in addition to the three factors mentioned above, at least three more factors play a role in the refutation of scientific hypotheses.

The first additional factor is that of BACKGROUND ASSUMPTIONS. Scientific hypotheses normally do not exist as isolated entities, but are integrated into a theory with other hypotheses. It is generally the case that test implications cannot be derived from a hypothesis if the hypothesis is regarded as an isolated entity outside the context of this theory. Moreover, scientists have certain ideas about what would constitute reliable and valid tests for the hypotheses within their theories. These ideas also form part of the assumptions which form the background for the derivation of the test implications of a hypothesis. An obvious example of an assumption which forms the background for the derivation of the test implication (9) from the hypothesis (8), is that of (15).

(15)   The operation by which a bat's tongue is removed will not affect its balance, thereby making it impossible for the bat to fly collision-free in the dark.

Without the assumption (15), the test implication (9) cannot be derived from the hypothesis (8).

The second additional factor in the refutation of scientific hypotheses is that of AUXILIARY HYPOTHESES. It is the case with most hypotheses that the test implications which can be derived from the hypothesis and its background assumptions cannot be directly confronted with factual data. The claims asserted in the test implications do not have a direct bearing on the phenomena about which factual data are available. Let us call such test implications POTENTIAL TEST IMPLICATIONS. In order that the potential test implication may be confronted with factual data, it must be converted into an assertion which has a direct bearing on the phenomena on which the data in question bear. For the purpose of this conversion, one or more additional hypotheses are required which, in view of their function, are known as "auxiliary hypotheses". By "applying" an auxiliary hypothesis to a potential test implication, the latter is converted into a CONCRETE TEST IMPLICATION.

The test implication (9) is a concrete test implication. However, it is not derived directly from the hypothesis (8). Only the potential test implication (16) can be derived from the hypothesis in question.

(16)   Bats of whom the taste has been destroyed will lose the ability to fly collision-free in the dark.

The concrete test implication (9) can only be derived by assuming the following auxiliary hypothesis:

(17)   The bat's taste is localized entirely in its tongue.

"Application" of this auxiliary hypothesis to the potential test implication (16) produces the concrete test implication (9).

The third additional factor involved in the refutation of scientific hypotheses is that of IDEALIZATION. Recall that most scientific hypotheses make claims about an ideal or idealized reality. The factual data which the scientist has, more or less, at his direct disposal, however, are data about a nonideal reality. To be able to use these data to test his hypotheses about an ideal reality, the scientist has to idealize these data as well. In other words, data which have no bearing on his ideal reality must be eliminated as irrelevant. This process of elimination is based on what may be called IDEALIZING ASSUMPTIONS. Furthermore the accuracy of the data that are accepted as being relevant must be beyond reasonable doubt.

To give an explicit account of the role of the three additional factors discussed above, the schematic representation (14) of the refutation of a scientific hypothesis must be adapted as follows:

(18)

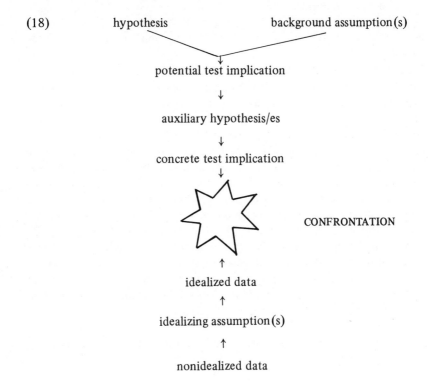

hypothesis   background assumption(s)

potential test implication

↓

auxiliary hypothesis/es

↓

concrete test implication

↓

CONFRONTATION

↑

idealized data

↑

idealizing assumption(s)

↑

nonidealized data

In view of the adapted representation of the refutation of an individual scientific hypothesis, it is quite clear why this refutation is considered to be inconclusive.

Suppose that a concrete test implication of a hypothesis were inconsistent with one or more of the idealized data with which it is confronted. This is a clear sign that something is wrong somewhere, but it is by no means obvious what it is that is amiss.

(19)   The concrete test implication may be inconsistent with the data in question

   (a)   because the hypothesis from which the potential test implication was derived is incorrect, and/or

   (b)   because the background assumption(s) providing a basis for the derivation of the potential test implication is/are incorrect, and/or

   (c)   because of auxiliary hypothesis/es in terms of which the concrete test implication was derived from the potential test implication is/are incorrect, and/or

   (d)   because the idealized data are either incorrect or irrelevant as a result of the fact that they were derived from the nonidealized data on the strength of one or more incorrect idealizing assumptions.

For an individual hypothesis to be conclusively refuted, it must be shown that the background assumption(s), auxiliary hypothesis/es and idealized data mentioned above are relevant as well as correct. However, in the previous chapter this was shown to be impossible. The justification for these background assumption(s), auxiliary hypothesis/es and claim(s) expressing the idealized data is in principle inconclusive, as it is given within the framework of nondemonstrative arguments.

Let us make this point more concrete: Spallanzani's data, presented as (10), conclusively refute the hypothesis (8) if and only if these data are both relevant and correct, if the background assumption (15) is correct and if the auxiliary hypothesis (17) is correct. The scientist has no logical means at his disposal by which to demonstrate conclusively that the data, the background assumption and the auxiliary hypothesis are correct. If the data, background assumption and auxiliary hypothesis are *in all probability* correct, i.e. well-justified, then the data show that the taste hypothesis (8) is *in all probability* false. However, the refutation of an individual scientific hypothesis is less inconclusive than its justification. Whereas a hypothesis is refuted within the framework of demonstrative arguments, it is justified within the framework of nondemonstrative arguments.

10.2.1.3   *The Systematic Component*

In addition to the factual component, the criticism of scientific hypotheses also has a systematic component. The defects that the hypothesis may have within the framework of the acceptability standards which we considered in §9.2.1.3 are pointed out in the SYSTEMATIC CRITICISM of a given hypothesis. In other words, systematic reasons are given why the hypothesis is hardly or not at all acceptable as the solution to a problem. These reasons could include one or more of the following:

(20)(a) The hypothesis expresses a claim which is inconsistent with the existing facts or knowledge [cf. (24) in §9.2.1.3].

(b) The hypothesis cannot be integrated into an existing, well-justified theory [cf. (25)(a) in §9.2.1.3].

(c) The hypothesis is not heuristically fruitful [cf. (25)(b) in §9.2.1.3].

(d) The hypothesis is over-complex conceptually [cf. (25)(c) in §9.2.1.3].

(e) The hypothesis postulates the existence of a unique entity.

The latter reason could, for example, be given for the nonacceptance of the hypothesis (11) in §9.2.1.2.1: the bat's flight in the dark is controlled by a sixth sense which it uniquely possesses. Hypotheses postulating unique entities, imply that reality is more chaotic than was expected. This is inconsistent with one of the major objectives of empirical inquiry, viz. to impose some sort of order on what seems to be chaotic, by discovering underlying regularities. Therefore, unless there are clear factual indications of the existence of a postulated unique entity, the hypothesis which postulates this entity is unacceptable.

This brings us to the interrelatedness of the factual and the systematic components of the criticism of scientific hypotheses. To put this question more precisely: why does this criticism have a systematic component in addition to its factual component? There are three reasons for this. Firstly, the factual criticism of an individual hypothesis is inconclusive. Although the factual criticism offers the strongest type of reason for rejecting the hypothesis, it offers no absolutely compelling reason for rejecting the hypothesis. Scientists therefore try to supplement their factual criticism with criticism of a systematic nature. Secondly, a hypothesis for which there is no factual disconfirming evidence, does not always offer an optimal solution to a scientific problem. A hypothesis postulating a unique entity would represent such a nonoptimal solution, even if it were impossible to present disconfirming factual evidence for the hypothesis. Thirdly, it is often the case that disconfirming evidence can be presented for both of two alternative hypotheses. This gives rise to the question of which hypothesis has the least merit. This question may be answered by determining what kind of systematic criticism can be brought against these hypotheses. The one against which the systematic criticism weighs heaviest is the one which, for the time being, does not deserve revision.

10.2.1.4   *The Nonobjective Component*

Factual and systematic criticism of an individual scientific hypothesis are both forms of objective criticism. As this criticism is not wholly conclusive, the possibility exists of supplementing it with criticism of a nonobjective nature. Although this cannot change the inconclusiveness of the objective criticism, it is possible that scientists who do not recognize nonobjective criticism as such may be persuaded by it to reject the hypothesis in question as unacceptable. The considerations underlying nonobjective criticism were discussed in §9.2.1.4. Against the background of those considerations, a scientist could be persuaded by nonobjective reasons such as those of (21) to reject a hypothesis as unacceptable.

(21)(a)   The justification for the hypothesis is poorly structured and/or badly presented [cf. (29)(a) in §9.2.1.4].

   (b)   The structure of the individual arguments for the hypothesis is opaque [cf. (29)(b) in §9.2.1.4].

   (c)   The scientist proposing the hypothesis is unknown or, for some nonobjective reason, has a low standing among other scholars in the field [cf. (30)(a) in §9.2.1.4].

   (d)   The hypothesis expresses a claim that is inconsistent with a prevailing *Zeitgeist*, intellectual trend or climate, cultural mood or social values [cf. (31) in §9.2.1.4].

Nonobjective considerations such as those of (21)(d) and (c) are rarely explicitly mentioned in the criticism of a scientific hypothesis. However, it does not follow from this that they do not play a very real role in the process by which scientists are persuaded of the unacceptability of a hypothesis.

10.2.2   Criticizing Scientific Hypotheses

It is clear from the preceding discussion that the criticism of scientific hypotheses involves several intellectual activities.

(22)   To criticize a scientific hypothesis involves

   (a)   presenting, within the framework of one or more demonstrative arguments, disconfirming evidence for the hypothesis, this evidence having been obtained by

     (i)   assessing whether the hypothesis is testable,

     (ii)   deriving concrete test implications from the hypothesis and the necessary background assumptions, via one or more auxiliary hypotheses,

     (iii)   collecting factual data with which the test implications may be confronted,

     (iv)   idealizing these data, if necessary, and assessing their correctness and relevance,

     (v)   comparing the claims expressed in the test implications and the assertions by which the idealized data are presented,

     (vi)   assessing the importance of the inconsistency between the data and the claims expressed in the test implications in such a way that it becomes clear whether it is the tested

hypothesis, the background assumptions, the auxiliary hypotheses or the idealized data that are probably incorrect;
(b)   presenting, within the framework of one or more demonstrative
arguments, systematic reasons why the hypothesis has little
merit as a solution to the problem in question;
(c)   NOT citing nonobjective reasons in an attempt to convince other
scientists that the hypothesis has little merit.

The points (i)–(vi) of (22)(a) will be further clarified in our discussion of the
activities involved in the criticism of grammatical hypotheses. The activities
indicated in (i)–(vi) of (22)(a) are conventionally known as the TESTING OF A
HYPOTHESIS. It is therefore clear that the testing of scientific hypotheses is
merely a part of the more comprehensive enterprise of criticizing such hypotheses.

A last general point remains to be made. Suppose that it were to appear from
the comparison referred to in (22)(a)(v) above that the claims made by the test
implications of the hypothesis are consistent with the (idealized) data about
reality. These data do not then reflect negatively on the tested hypothesis, but
actually represent positive instances of the hypothesis. Within the framework of
a reductive argument, these data may therefore be presented as confirming
evidence for the hypothesis. This point was discussed in detail in §9.3.2.2.2.

10.3   GRAMMATICAL INQUIRY

10.3.1   General

We are now better equipped to consider the nature of the criticism of grammatical hypotheses and the intellectual activities involved in criticizing these
hypotheses. An example of a fragment of such criticism was presented as (1)
in §10.1. Two further examples will serve to make the discussion more concrete.

Consider the grammatical prediction presented as (23)(a) in §8.3.1. Suppose
that it were to appear that the derived nominal *John's easiness to succeed* is in
fact acceptable. This fact could then be used as factual criticism of the grammatical hypothesis by which the prediction in question was made. The criticism
could be formulated as follows:

(23)   If the hypothesis that *easy* may not take a sentential complement is
true, then the derived nominal *John's easiness to succeed* will be
unacceptable. In this derived nominal *easy* has a sentential complement in the form of *to succeed.* And yet the derived nominal in
question is acceptable. Therefore, the grammatical hypothesis concerned is false.

Our second example is a fragment of another kind of criticism of a grammatical hypothesis. The grammatical hypothesis concerned is the transformationalist hypothesis about derived nominals in English.

(24) If a grammatical hypothesis is inconsistent with a well-justified general linguistic hypothesis, then the grammatical hypothesis is relatively unacceptable. The transformationalist hypothesis postulates the existence of a transformational rule which deletes deep structure elements in a nonrecoverable way. Consequently, the transformationalist hypothesis is inconsistent with the general linguistic hypothesis known as the recoverability condition on deletion transformations. Therefore, the transformationalist hypothesis is relatively unacceptable.

The criticism brought against the transformationalist hypothesis in (24) is based on an acceptability standard in which the concept *'ad hoc'* is of fundamental importance. (The standard in question was formulated as (73) in §9.3.2.3.2 above.) To say that the transformationalist hypothesis is inconsistent with the recoverability condition is to imply that, from a general linguistic point of view, this hypothesis has an *ad hoc* character. The expression "relatively" in (24) above is an abbreviation for "relative to the acceptability standard (73)".

10.3.2   Nature of Criticism of Grammatical Hypotheses

The criticism of grammatical hypotheses is similar to the justification of such hypotheses in that it is made up of three components, viz. a factual component, a systematic component and an external component. We shall consider each of these components individually.

10.3.2.1   *The Factual Component*

The fragments of criticism (1) and (23) above illustrate the factual criticism that can be levelled at grammatical hypotheses in their explanatory function. The source of factual criticism of a grammatical hypothesis is its negative instances. In other words, this criticism is based on linguistic data which show that certain projections that can be made on the basis of the hypothesis are incorrect. Such linguistic data constitute disconfirming evidence for the grammatical hypothesis in question. Generative grammarians commonly call these data COUNTER-EXAMPLES (FOR GRAMMATICAL HYPOTHESES).

10.3.2.1.1   *Structure of a fragment of factual criticism*
A fragment of factual criticism of a grammatical hypothesis is made up of several components. A first component of (1) is the grammatical hypothesis being criticized.

(25)   The lexicalist hypothesis: at the level of deep structure all derived nominals in English have the internal structure of NPs.

A second component of the fragment of criticism (1) takes the form of two grammatical background assumptions.

(26)(a)   *His criticism of the book before he read it* is a derived nominal.
　　(b)   This derived nominal includes a constituent of a VP, *before he read it*, as a structural component.

A third component of (1) is the potential test implication that can be derived from a combination of the lexicalist hypothesis and the two background assumptions mentioned above.

(27)   The derived nominal *his criticism of the book before he read it* should be an ungrammatical linguistic unit.

The test implication (27) is only a potential test implication as it cannot be directly confronted with linguistic data. This test implication expresses a claim about an abstract linguistic unit, while intuitive linguistic data are data about concrete utterances. In order to be testable the claim expressed in this potential test implication must be converted into a claim about concrete utterances. The conversion is done by means of an auxiliary hypothesis. This auxiliary hypothesis constitutes a fourth component of the fragment of criticism in question.

(28)   If a linguistic unit is ungrammatical, then the corresponding utterances will be unacceptable.

By "applying" the auxiliary hypothesis to the potential test implication (27) a concrete test implication can be derived. This concrete test implication forms a fifth component of the fragment of criticism (1).

(29)   The utterance *his criticism of the book before he read it* will be unacceptable.

A sixth component of the fragment of criticism (1) is a linguistic datum about an utterance. It takes the form of an intuitive acceptability judgment.

(30)   The ordinary native speaker of English finds the utterance *his criticism of the book before he read it* acceptable.

However, the test implication (29) does not express a claim about the nonidealized linguistic reality of ordinary native speakers of English. On the contrary, it expresses a claim about the idealized linguistic reality of the ideal speaker. Data such as that of (30) about a nonidealized linguistic reality cannot be directly used to test claims about an idealized linguistic reality. These data could, for instance, have a bearing on one or more of those aspects of the nonidealized linguistic reality which is not an aspect of the idealized linguistic reality as well. If this were actually the case, the data in question would be irrelevant with regard to the testing of the correctness of claims about the idealized linguistic reality. To enable him to use a datum about a nonidealized linguistic reality to test a claim about an idealized linguistic reality, the grammarian must idealize this datum as well. This implies that the datum in question must be shown to be relevant to the testing of claims about the idealized linguistic reality on the basis of an idealizing assumption. A seventh component of the fragment of criticism (1) is therefore an idealizing assumption.

(31)   Intuitive linguistic data about the nonidealized linguistic reality of ordinary native speakers of a language generally provide information about properties of the idealized linguistic reality of the ideal speaker of the language.

In terms of this idealizing assumption, the nonidealized linguistic datum of (30) can now be "converted" into the idealized linguistic datum of (32).

(32)   The ideal speaker of English finds the utterance *his criticism of the book before he read it* acceptable as well.

The idealized linguistic datum (32) represents an eighth and last component of the fragment of criticism (1).

In view of the various distinctions drawn above, the structure of the fragment of criticism (1) may be schematically represented as follows:

(33)   GRAMMATICAL HYPOTHESIS
        At the level of deep structure all derived nominals in English have the internal structure of NPs.

        BACKGROUND ASSUMPTIONS
        1. *His criticism of the book before he read it* is a derived nominal.
        2. This derived nominal includes a constitutent of a VP, *before he read it*, as a structural component.

POTENTIAL TEST IMPLICATION
The derived nominal *his criticism of the book before he read it* will be an ungrammatical linguistic unit.

↓

AUXILIARY HYPOTHESIS
If a linguistic unit is ungrammatical, the corresponding utterances will be unacceptable.

↓

CONCRETE TEST IMPLICATION
The utterance *his criticism of the book before he read it*
will be unacceptable.   ↓

CONFRONTATION

↑

IDEALIZED LINGUISTIC DATUM
The ideal speaker of English finds the utterance *his criti-cism of the book before he read it* unacceptable as well.
↑
IDEALIZING ASSUMPTION
Intuitive linguistic data about the nonidealized linguistic
reality of ordinary native speakers of a language generally
provide information about properties of the idealized
linguistic reality of the ideal speaker of the language.
↑
NONIDEALIZED LINGUISTIC DATUM
The ordinary native speaker of English finds the utterance
his criticism of the book before he read it acceptable.

Note that not all the components of (32) are *explicitly* represented in the fragment of criticism (1). It is characteristic of such fragments of criticism that
(some of) the background assumptions, the auxiliary hypothesis/es and the
idealizing assumption(s) are not explicitly mentioned. However, generative
grammarians do work with these two types of assumptions and auxiliary hypotheses implicity. Without them the argument within the framework of which the
criticism is presented would not constitute a coherent argument.

10.3.2.1.2   *Logical form of a fragment of factual criticism*
The form of argument characterized as *modus tollens* above is the logical "spine"
of a fragment of factual criticism such as (1). Within the framework of this form
of argument the fragment of criticism in question may be reconstructed as the
following disconfirming argument:

(34)   MaP : If
        (a)   the lexicalist hypothesis (25) is true,
        (b)   the background assumptions (26)(a) and (b) are correct,
              and
        (c)   the auxiliary hypothesis (28) is correct,
        then the utterance *his criticism of the book before he read it*
        will be unacceptable.

MiP : The utterance *his criticism of the book before he read it* is acceptable.

C   : The lexicalist hypothesis (25) and/or one or both of the background assumptions (26)(a) and (b) and/or the auxiliary hypothesis (28) is incorrect.

The simplest form of the *modus tollens* was symbolically represented as (13) in §10.2.1.2.1.

As a concrete case of the *modus tollens*, the disconfirming argument (34) is demonstrative. Yet the lexicalist hypothesis is not conclusively refuted within the framework of this argument. This is the result of the fact that it is not immediately clear what it is that the disconfirming evidence in the minor premiss shows to be incorrect: the lexicalist hypothesis and/or one or both of the background assumptions and/or the auxiliary hypothesis? Another possibility – for which no explicit provision is made within the framework of this disconfirming argument – is that the idealizing assumption does not hold in this particular case. If this could be the case, the disconfirming evidence would simply be irrelevant as it would provide no information about the (in)correctness of the lexicalist hypothesis and/or the background assumptions and/or the auxiliary hypothesis. The measure of conclusiveness of the disconfirming argument (34) is a function of the measure of justification for the background assumptions, the auxiliary hypothesis and the idealizing assumption in question: the greater the latter measure of justification, the larger the former measure of conclusiveness.

10.3.2.1.3   *Complexity of factual criticism*
The factual criticism of a grammatical hypothesis is complex in two ways. First, the fragments of which it is composed exhibit a complex internal structure. This point was illustrated in §10.3.2.1.1 above. Second, the factual criticism of a grammatical hypothesis may be composed of various fragments which are interrelated in an intricate way. This is the case when a whole series of auxiliary hypotheses is required in order to derive concrete test implications from a grammatical hypothesis (and background assumptions).

This point may be illustrated with reference to the series of supplementary arguments for the lexicalist hypothesis, which was represented as (52) in §9.3.2.2.4. These arguments were interrelated in the following way: to justify the aspect (35)(a) of the lexicalist hypothesis, the grammatical hypothesis (35)(b), among other things, was presented as evidence; to justify the grammatical hypothesis (35)(b), the grammatical hypothesis (35)(c), among other things, was presented as evidence; and to justify the grammatical hypothesis (35)(c), the evidential statement (35)(d) was presented.

(35)(a)   The possessive construction of the form NPs − N represents a base structure.

(b)   In the sense of inalienable possession, the expression *John's leg* (which is a possessive construction of the form NPs − N in which N is not a derived nominal) cannot be derived from the structure *N that NP has.*

(c)   The expression *leg that John has* does not have the sense of inalienable possession.

(d)   One cannot say in English "the leg that John has hurts" or "the leg that John has is weak from the climb".

For more details about the precise nature of the interrelatedness of the statements (35)(a)−(d), turn back to §9.3.2.2.4.

Suppose now that it were to appear that it is possible in English to say "the leg that John has hurts" and "the leg that John has is weak from the climb". Then the statement (35)(d) would be incorrect. This statement represents a test implication of the hypothesis (35)(c). So, if (35)(d) is false − given that the background assumption(s) and the auxiliary hypothesis in terms of which it is derived from (35)(c) are well-justified − then the hypothesis (35)(c) is probably false as well. The hypothesis (35)(c) represents a test implication of the hypothesis (35)(b). If the hypothesis (35)(c) is false − and given that the background assumption(s) and auxiliary hypothesis in terms of which it is derived from (35)(b) are well-justified − then the hypothesis (35)(b) is probably false as well. The hypothesis (35)(b) is a test implication of the hypothesis (35)(a). If the hypothesis (35)(b) is false − and given that the background assumption(s) and auxiliary hypothesis in terms of which it is derived from (35)(a) are correct − then the hypothesis (35)(a) is probably false as well.

Schematically the situation just described may be represented as follows:

(36)   (35)(a)   not (35)(a)
          ↓   ↑
        (35)(b)   not (35)(b)
          ↓   ↑
        (35)(c)   not (35)(c)
          ↓   ↑
        (35)(d)   not (35)(d)

It is possible in English to say "the leg that John has hurts" and "the leg that John has is weak from the climb".

It is quite clear from the diagram above that the refutation of an abstract grammatical hypothesis such as (35)(a) by means of a concrete intuitive judgment is highly complex. The greater the number of auxiliary hypotheses needed to derive concrete test implications from a grammatical hypothesis, the more complex the chain of inferences leading to the conclusion that the grammatical hypothesis in question is (probably) false. The complexity of this chain is further illustrated in the discussion of the nature of the grammatical predictions (34)(a) and (b) in §8.3.2.2.1.

The schematic representation (36) shows that both intuitive and hypothetical evidence can constitute disconfirming evidence for grammatical hypotheses. A case in which intuitive evidence plays this role is that of the intuitive linguistic judgment which refutes the hypothesis (35)(a). In (36) the probably false grammatical hypotheses (35)(b) and (c) represent disconfirming theoretical evidence for a grammatical hypothesis. Finally, a grammatical hypothesis may also be refuted by means of theoretical intuitive evidence. This is the case if the hypothesis expresses a generalization which is not linguistically significant according to the grammarian's theoretical intuitions. In §6.3.3.1.2 we mentioned McCawley's theoretical intuition which could be used to refute the hypothesis that 'specifier' represents a linguistically significant category of English.

10.3.2.1.4   *Evidential criteria in factual criticism*
In §9.3.2.2.5 we looked at two criteria for evidence which are used in the factual justification of grammatical hypotheses, viz. the criteria of evidential comprehensiveness and evidential independence. These criteria also play an important role in the factual criticism of grammatical hypotheses. The following points of factual criticism may be brought against grammatical hypotheses on the basis of these criteria:

(37)(a)   There is a comprehensive corpus of disconfirming evidence for the hypothesis.

  (b)   There is no comprehensive corpus of confirming and supporting evidence for the hypothesis.

  (c)   There is disconfirming evidence belonging to mutually independent types for the hypothesis.

  (d)   There is no confirming and supporting evidence belonging to mutually independent types for the hypothesis.

These points of factual criticism are presented within the framework of deductive arguments that are instances of the form of argument known as *modus tollens*. This form of argument was symbolically represented as (56) in §9.3.2.2.5.1.

In §9.3.2.2.5.1 we did in fact consider two examples of arguments in which factual criticism is presented for grammatical hypotheses. The criterion of evidential comprehensiveness is used in both these examples: cf. (37)(b). In the first example, (53), McCawley criticizes Chomsky's hypothesis that the relationship between derived nominals and their meaning is pure chaos. In the second example, (54), McCawley criticizes the hypothesis that neutral lexical entries play a role in the lexicon of the grammar of English. Both these examples involve the point of factual criticism given as (37)(b) above: the corpus of evidence for the grammatical hypotheses in question is insufficiently comprehensive.

The remaining points of factual criticism, (37)(a), (c) and (d), are used in a parallel way. As factual criticism, the point (37)(d) — that there is no independent evidence for a given grammatical hypothesis — weighs heavily against a grammatical hypothesis. It is therefore widely used by generative grammarians. An example of the way in which this point of criticism is used was implicitly given in §9.3.2.3.2. In (72) of that paragraph, Jackendoff (1974a:3—4) argues that the transformationalist hypothesis requires the postulation of a large number of idiosyncratic transformations. To say that these transformations are idiosyncratic is to imply, among other things, that the grammatical hypotheses in terms of which they are presented are without independent motivation. This, in turn, implies that the point of criticism (37)(d) may be levelled at these hypotheses.

The point of factual criticism (37)(c) weighs heavily against a hypothesis as well. Suppose that it were possible to criticize a given hypothesis on the basis of this point of criticism. This would indicate that thorough testing has shown the hypothesis to fail in various domains over which it applies. The philosopher of science, Ernest Nagel (1966:190), formulates the basis of this point of criticism as follows:

> Variety in the kinds of positive instances for a theory is a generally acknowledged factor in estimating the weight of the evidence. The reason for this is that experiments which are conducted in qualitatively different domains make it easier to control features of the theory whose relevance in *any* of the domains may be in question. Hence, by increasing the possibility of eliminating what may be simply accidental success of a theory under special or unanalyzed circumstances, the possibility of finding negative instances for the theory is increased. In this way of conducting experiments, the theory is subjected to a more searching examination than if all the positive instances were drawn from just one domain.

10.3.2.2   *The Systematic Component*

In addition to factual criticism, criticism of a systematic nature may be levelled at grammatical hypotheses. This entails putting forward systematic considerations from which it is clear that the hypothesis has defects as a solution to a grammatical problem. The defects in question are those which appear on appraisal of the hypothesis in terms of the grammatical acceptability standards that were discussed in §9.3.2.3.2.

In §10.3.1 above, a fragment of the systematic criticism which may be brought against the transformationalist hypothesis was presented as (24). The argument within the framwork of which this criticism is presented may be reconstructed as follows:

(38)   MaP : If a grammatical hypothesis is inconsistent with a given well-justified general linguistic hypothesis, then the grammatical hypothesis is relatively unacceptable.

MiP : The transformationalist hypothesis is inconsistent with the recoverability condition on deletion transformations.

C   : The transformationalist hypothesis is relatively unacceptable.

The argument (38) is a concrete instance of the deductive form of argument known as the *modus ponens.* In the minor premiss of this argument data about a metascientific property of the transformationalist hypothesis are presented as negative evidence for the hypothesis. Metascientific evidence can therefore be used in the criticism of grammatical hypotheses as well.

The major premiss of the argument (38) contains the acceptability standard on the basis of which the grammatical hypothesis in question is criticized. In view of the other grammatical acceptability standards discussed in §9.3.2.3.2, the systematic considerations of (39) may be presented as systematic criticism of a grammatical hypothesis.

(39)(a)   The grammatical hypothesis is at most consistent with certain linguistic data, but does not explain these data [cf. (67) in §9.3.2.3.2].

(b)   The grammatical hypothesis is defective in that its content is limited and/or unclear [cf. (68) in §9.3.2.3.2].

(c)   The grammatical hypothesis is not easily refutable [cf. (69) in §9.3.2.3.2].

(d)   The grammatical hypothesis can represent certain linguistic data, but does not explain these data [cf. (70) in §9.3.2.3.2].

(e)   The grammatical hypothesis is *ad hoc* in a language-specific sense [cf. (71) in §9.3.2.3.2].

(f)   The grammatical hypothesis requires an undesirable extension of the formal power of the general linguistic theory [cf. (74) in §9.3.2.3.2].

(g)   The grammatical hypothesis is heuristically unfruitful [cf. the discussion in connection with (75) and (76) in §9.3.2.3.2].

Notice, in passing, that in the argument (1) presented in §9.1, Chomsky criticizes the transformationalist hypothesis in terms of the consideration (39)(a). The consideration (39)(f) represents one of the strongest points of criticism that can be brought against a grammatical hypothesis. It weighs so heavily that it makes even a hypothesis for which no disconfirming factual evidence has been presented, unacceptable.

10.3.2.3   *The External Component*

10.3.2.3.1   *Criticism of the psychological reality of grammatical hypotheses*

The factual and systematic criticism which we considered above represents criticism of grammatical hypotheses in their explanatory function. However, grammatical hypotheses are criticized in their descriptive function as well. The purpose of such criticism is to show that a given grammatical hypothesis is probably not psychologically real, i.e. that it does not give a true representation of an aspect of the form of the linguistic competence. We saw in §9.3.2.4 that grammatical hypotheses are justified in their descriptive function on the basis of, among other things, external linguistic data. Likewise, external linguistic data are generally used to criticize grammatical hypotheses in their descriptive function.

10.3.2.3.2   *Nature of external criticism*

The external linguistic data on the basis of which grammatical hypotheses are criticized are data about objects or phenomena outside the grammarian's linguistic reality. Every external linguistic object or phenomenon about which projections can be made on the basis of a grammatical hypothesis, in conjunction with an additional bridge theory, is a potential source of diconfirming data. The nature of the external linguistic projects that are made about these objects and phenomena was dealt with in §8.4.3.4 and the paragraphs immediately preceding it.

We did in fact consider a fragment of external criticism of a grammatical hypothesis in §9.3.2.4.2 where we saw how Whitaker goes about criticizing the transformationalist hypothesis on the basis of neuropsychological evidence. If we have a closer look at the argument (82) which was presented in that paragraph, we see that it is a disconfirming argument. In the minor premise of the argument, neuropsychological data are presented from which it is clear that the transformationalist hypothesis makes incorrect projections about dynamic aphasia.

Note, however, that the reconstruction (82) of the argument in question is incomplete in an important respect. The background assumption which is needed in order to infer the consequent from a combination of the conditional statement and its antecedent is not stated in the major premise of this argument. This background assumption — which was cited on page 327 — is that the relation between the human mind and the human brain is one of identity. The complete major premise of the argument would therefore be as follows:

(40)   If
      (a)   the transformationalist hypothesis is psychologically real, and
      (b)   the relation between mind and brain is that of identity,
      then it should not be possible for a person's ability to use verbs and his ability to use the corresponding derived nominals to be affected by dynamic aphasia in a nonparallel way.

In disconfirming arguments presenting external evidence which reflects negatively on grammatical hypotheses, background assumptions such as (40)(b) play an exceedingly important role. Without these assumptions the external data cannot be qualitatively relevant to the grammatical hypothesis in question. Such background assumptions often represent components of a complex bridge theory about the relatedness of the linguistic competence, on which the grammatical hypothesis has a bearing, and the external linguistic objects or phenomena to which the data in question refer.

Bearing this in mind, it is quite easy to see why external data are even less conclusive as disconfirming evidence than internal data. As we saw in §10.3.2.2, the measure of conclusiveness of internal disconfirming evidence depends on, among other things, the extent of the justification for a few grammatical background assumptions. The measure of conclusiveness of external disconfirming evidence, by contrast, depends on the extent of the justification for an entire bridge theory. It is highly probable that part of such a bridge theory may be false. Moreover, bridge theories are generally far less well articulated and much more speculative than grammatical background assumptions (and auxiliary hypotheses). Consequently, the extent of the justification for a bridge theory is usually smaller than the extent of the justification for a single grammatical background assumption. In concrete terms, the disconfirming external evidence presented for the transformationalist hypothesis in (82) of §9.3.2.4.2 is highly inconclusive. The fact that this evidence apparently conflicts with a test implication of the transformationalist hypothesis could be considered to indicate rather that one of the hypotheses in Whitaker's neuropsychological bridge theory is false.

10.3.2.3.3   *A fragment of external criticism*
To illustrate the nature of external criticism of a grammatical hypothesis somewhat further, we shall consider one more fragment of external criticism. In her article "When does a test test a hypothesis, or, What counts as evidence?" (1975), Victoria Fromkin shows how external data about speech errors may be used to disconfirm grammatical hypotheses. One of the cases she discusses (pp.59–60) relates to the psychological reality of a simple phonological hypothesis.

(41)   In English /č/ and /ǰ/ each consists of two successive segments.

Fromkin contends that the test implication (42) may be derived from this phonological hypothesis.

(42)   In some speech errors involving /č/ and /ǰ/, it should be possible to separate the two segments of which each consists.

This test implication conflicts with the evidence about speech errors which Fromkin has at her disposal.

(43)   In the speech errors involving /č/ and /ǰ/, the two segments of which each consists are never separated.

For instance, speakers of English do not commit the speech error *pretty chilly* ⟶ *critty philly*, where the *c* in *critty* represents the first segment of /č/ and the *h* in *philly* represents the second segment of /č/. However, they do commit the error *pretty chilly* ⟶ *chetty prilly*, where the segment /č/ as a whole has been mistakenly reordered.

These data about speech errors can apparently be presented as disconfirming evidence for the hypothesis (41) within the framework of the following argument:

(44)   MaP : If in English /č/ and /ǰ/ each consists of two successive segments, then speech errors should occur in which these two segments are (mistakenly) separated.

MiP : No speech errors exist in which the segments in question are (mistakenly) separated.

C   : In English /č/ and /ǰ/ do not consist of two successive segments.

But an important component is missing from the major premiss of (44); a component without which it is impossible to infer the test implication of the consequent from the grammatical hypothesis of the antecedent. This is a theory of speech production in which it is shown, among other things, how a speaker applies his linguistic competence in producing utterances. Fromkin appears to accept implicitly a theory of speech production in which (45) is the central assumption.

(45)   The linguistic competence − as described by a generative grammar − forms a direct part of a speaker's speech production mechanism.

The major premiss of the disconfirming argument (44) should therefore be as follows:

(46)   If
(a)   In English /č/ and /ǰ/ each consists of two successive segments and
(b)   the linguistic competence − as described by a generative grammar − forms a direct part of a speaker's speech production mechanism,
then speech errors should occur in which these two segments are (mistakenly) separated.

By including (b) in the major premiss of (46) it becomes quite clear that the disconfirming evidence for the grammatical hypothesis in question is highly inconclusive. The reason for this is that the theory of speech production under-lying (b) is poorly worked out and highly speculative. In their book, *The psycho-logy of language* (1974:ch.5), psycholinguists such as Fodor, Bever and Garrett argue that the assumption expressed in (b) is false. If they are right, the external linguistic data in question are not relevant as disconfirming evidence for the phonological hypothesis (41). This is a further striking illustration of the in-conclusive nature of the external criticism of the psychological reality of gram-matical hypotheses. The main difficulty with this type of criticism is that it depends entirely on the existence of an appropriate bridge theory. In general, bridge theories are insufficiently developed and without strong justification. In their article "Linguistic theory and performance models" (1975), Donald Foss and David Fay offer an interesting discussion of this difficulty as it manifests itself with regard to bridge theories about speech production, speech perception and language acquisition.

10.3.3   Criticizing Grammatical Hypotheses

10.3.3.1   *General Characterization*

The principal intellectual activities involved in the criticism of a grammatical hypothesis may, in general terms, be characterized as follows:

(47)(a)   To criticize a grammatical hypothesis H in its *explanatory function* involves
  (i)   presenting factual criticism of H
    (α) by furnishing linguistic data, within the framework of *modus tollens* arguments, from which it is clear that the hypothesis serves as a basis for incorrect projections about properties of sentences of the language in question;
    (β) by furnishing metascientific data, within the framework of *modus ponens* arguments, from which it is clear that the hypothesis has the defects of $(37)(a)-(d)$ in terms of the evidential criteria of comprehensiveness and indepen-dence,
  (ii)   presenting systematic criticism of H by furnishing metascien-tific data, within the framework of *modus ponens* arguments, from which it is clear that the hypothesis is (relatively) un-acceptable in terms of grammatical acceptability standards.
(b)   To criticize a grammatical hypothesis H in its *descriptive function* — thereby further criticizing it in its explanatory function — involves, among other things, presenting external linguistic data, within the

framework of *modus tollens* arguments, from which it is clear that the hypothesis H, in conjunction with other nonlinguistic assumptions, serves as a basis for inaccurate projections about properties of objects or phenomena outside the grammarian's linguistic reality.

The criticism of (47) must of course be presented in the form of a clear, coherent case against H. Moreover, in criticizing a grammatical hypothesis, a grammarian may not resort to nonobjective considerations in order to give a misleading representation of the defects of the hypothesis being criticized.

10.3.3.2   *Testing Grammatical Hypotheses*

The intellectual activity described in (47)(a)(i)(α), which is generally known as THE TESTING OF A GRAMMATICAL HYPOTHESIS, constitutes the central activity in the criticizing of grammatical hypotheses. We shall therefore devote part of our discussion exclusively to this activity which, in turn, is composed of smaller components: assessing the testability of grammatical hypotheses, deriving test implications, collecting raw linguistic data, processing raw linguistic data, confronting the derived test implications with idealized linguistic data and interpreting the disconfirming evidence which may result from this confrontation.

10.3.3.2.1   *Assessing testability*
Only a grammatical hypothesis which is testable can in fact be tested. Thus, testing a grammatical hypothesis presupposes that its testability be assessed.

The question which immediately arises is this: under what circumstances can a scientific hypothesis, such as a grammatical hypothesis, be said to be testable? Scientists and philosophers of science have come up with various alternative answers to this question. One of the answers that is quite widely accepted is that given by the philosopher of science Carl Hempel in his book *Philosophy of natural science* (1966). Hempel (1966:30ff.) bases his answer on a distinction between testability-in-principle and testability-in-practice.

(48)   A hypothesis or theory is TESTABLE-IN-PRINCIPLE if
   (a)   precise test implications can be derived from it and
   (b)   it can be shown precisely what empirical data – if such were available – would indicate that the test implications are false.

EMPIRICAL DATA are data which have a bearing on reality and which have been collected by means of systematic, controlled observation. In the natural sciences, for instance, such observation is systematized and controlled experimentally.

This brings us to testability-in-practice.

(49)   A hypothesis or theory is TESTABLE-IN-PRACTICE if the empirical

data with which its test implications can be confronted are in fact available.

The criterion of testability-in-practice is stronger than that of testability-in-principle. Hempel (1966:30) elucidates the difference between testability-in-practice and testability-in-principle as follows:

> . . . no statement or set of statements T can be significantly proposed as a scientific hypothesis or theory unless it is amenable to objective empirical test, at least 'in principle'. This is to say that it must be possible to derive from T, in the broad sense we have considered, certain test implications of the form 'if test conditions C are realized, then outcome E will occur'; but the test conditions need not be realized or technologically realizable at the time when T is propounded or contemplated. Take the hypothesis, for example, that the distance covered in t seconds by a body falling freely from rest near the surface of the moon is $s = 2.7 \, t^2$ feet. It yields deductively a set of test implications to the effect that the distance covered by such a body in 1, 2, 3, . . . seconds will be 2.7, 10.8, 24.3, . . . feet. Hence this hypothesis is testable in principle, though it is as yet impossible to perform the test here specified.

In short: in order to be an empirical hypothesis, a hypothesis need only be testable-in-principle. Moreover, assessing the testability of a hypothesis implies assessing its testability-in-principle. When we refer to the testability of a hypothesis below, it has to be understood as testability-in-principle.

The testability of a hypothesis may be adversely affected by various factors. We shall consider three of these factors and their influence on the testability of grammatical hypotheses.

10.3.3.2.1.1   *Obscurity of content*   The content of a hypothesis is obscure if this content has vague, ambiguous or imprecise aspects. If the content of a hypothesis is obscure, it is impossible to establish exactly what the hypothesis is claiming. If this cannot be done, no precise test implications can be derived from the hypothesis. In other words, if a given hypothesis is obscure as regards its content, it is impossible to determine whether whatever the hypothesis claims about reality is (in)consistent with data about this reality. Obscurity of content is therefore a first factor which adversely affects the testability of scientific hypotheses.

The effect of this factor can be observed in the work of some generative grammarians, the testability of whose mentalistic hypotheses is adversely affected by obscurity of content. Recall that a linguistic hypothesis is a MENTALISTIC HYPOTHESIS in its descriptive function. Suppose that a grammarian of English wanted to determine whether the lexicalist hypothesis is psychologically real, in other words that he wanted to test this hypothesis in its descriptive function. Suppose further that this grammarian were to argue in the following, typical manner:

(50)   If the lexicalist hypothesis is psychologically real, then certain aspects of the form of the linguistic competence of speakers of English will correspond to the neutral lexical entries in the grammar of English.

The "then" part of (50) represents a test implication of the lexicalist hypothesis as a mentalistic hypothesis.

The question that arises is this: is it possible to confront this test implication with empirical data? One aspect of the test implication stands in the way of such a confrontation, viz. the aspect expressed by the term "correspond". Under what circumstances can an aspect of the form of the linguistic competence be said to correspond or not to correspond to a grammatical hypothesis? If this question cannot be answered satisfactorily, mentalistic hypotheses become nontestable-in-principle. Some critics of generative grammar do in fact claim that the correspondence aspect of the content of mentalistic linguistic hypotheses is obscure. This claim leads them to conclude that such hypotheses are not empirical hypotheses.

A discussion and appraisal of this criticism would cause us to deviate too far from the main point of this paragraph. However, we do quote the exposition given by Robert Schwartz (1969:187–188) of a general problem which arises when an attempt is made to interpret "correspondence" claims:

> The fact that we can specify S's competence in terms of a formal system of generative rules does not in itself imply that S has represented a *corresponding* system in him. In fact, the whole question of what would count as a corresponding system is a messy issue. An example may best make my point. Suppose we observe an input-output device that labels spheres '+' if their density is greater than 1.0 and '−' if their density is less. We would specify this output with the following equations:
>
> $$\text{Vol. of sphere} = \tfrac{4}{3}\,\pi\ \text{radius}^3 \qquad \text{Density} = \frac{\text{weight}}{\text{volume}},$$
> $$\text{Acceptable (+) density} = > 1.0$$
>
> but the device might not employ a set of principles anything like this. It might never determine the individual sphere's radius, weight, or volume; instead it might merely contain a liquid of 1.0 and label '+' any sphere that sinks in the liquid and '−' any that floats. Would it be reasonable to claim that our equations are internally represented in this machine? Although in some sense the liquid in the machine could be held to 'stand for' the equations, it seems less reasonable to claim that the analysis provided by the equations is mirrored in any interesting manner by the internal processes of the machine.

Thus, mentalistic linguistic claims are testable only if the content of the concept 'correspond to' is nonobscure.

10.3.3.2.1.2   *Nature of empirical data*   A second factor which affects the testability of a scientific hypothesis is the nature of the (empirical) data with which its test implications may be confronted. Not all data which are apparently inconsistent with these test implications constitute disconfirming evidence for the hypothesis. In order to qualify as disconfirming evidence, the data should, among other things, have the following two properties: they must be correct and they must be qualitatively relevant to the hypothesis. Suppose that it were not in principle possible to assess the correctness of the data with which the test implications of a hypothesis may be confronted. If these data are the only data with which the hypothesis in question can be confronted, the hypothesis is in principle nontestable. The same applies if it is in principle impossible to assess the qualitative relevance of the data.

Recall that the primary linguistic data with which the test implications of a grammatical hypothesis are confronted are linguistic intuitions. A number of scholars hold that grammatical hypotheses which can be tested only on the basis of linguistic intuitions are in principle nontestable. They base their view on the difficulties encountered in checking the accuracy of linguistic intuitions. The arguments for and against this controversial view are too complex to be discussed here. Discussions of problems in connection with the status of intuitive evidence may be found in Botha 1973: ch.5 and Ringen 1975.

10.3.3.2.1.3   *Protective devices*   A third factor which may have an adverse effect on the testability of scientific hypotheses is the presence of protective devices in a hypothesis or in the theory of which the hypothesis forms part. A PROTECTIVE DEVICE is a concept, conceptual distinction or hypothesis which has only one function, viz. to make it possible to interpret the data which could refute a hypothesis in such a way that these data are not inconsistent with the test implications of the hypothesis. The sole function of such a device, then, is to protect a hypothesis against potential disconfirming evidence. The presence of protective devices in a hypothesis or a theory of which the hypothesis forms part has the effect of rendering the hypothesis nontestable-in-principle. The nature and properties of protective devices – commonly known as "*ad hoc* hypotheses" in metascientific literature – will be discussed in §11.3.1.4.1 below.

Let us consider only one example of a protective device which has an adverse effect on the testability of grammatical hypotheses in their descriptive function. The protective device in question takes the form of a certain conceptual distinction which is at the root of the following criterion for psychological reality:

(51)   A grammatical hypothesis is psychologically real if the mental entity which it postulates plays a direct or an indirect role in the psychological mechanisms in terms of which speakers produce and/or perceptually process utterances.

The protective device in question is the distinction between a *direct* and an *indirect* role in the psychological mechanisms of (51).

Suppose that a grammarian found external linguistic data which indicated that neutral lexical entries play no role in the production or perception of utterances in English. These data would constitute potential disconfirming evidence for the psychological reality of the lexicalist hypothesis. However, in terms of the distinction mentioned above, the hypothesis could be protected against this disconfirming evidence. It could be argued, for instance, that what is clear from the data in question is merely that neutral lexical entries do not play a *direct* role in the production or perception of the utterances concerned. As long as the data do not exclude the possibility that the entries could play an *indirect* role in the production or perception of the utterances, the lexicalist hypothesis cannot be refuted in its descriptive function in terms of the criterion (51).

This argument is acceptable only if the distinction between a direct and an indirect role in linguistic performance is both clear and principled. It should be clear, for instance, in what sense a psychological entity can play an indirect role in the production or perception of utterances. If this role were not unambiguously defined, the distinction in question would serve no purpose other than that of protecting mentalistic hypotheses against disconfirming evidence. This would cause the protected hypotheses to lose their empirical status. For more details of an attempt to use the distinction in question in an acceptable way, see Foss and Fay's 1975 article. A second typical example of a conceptual distinction which may be used to protect mentalistic hypotheses against refutation is that between the psychological reality of rules and the psychological reality of structural descriptions. This distinction is discussed in some depth by Katz (1977:560–561).

To summarize our discussion so far: we have seen that the assessment of the testability of grammatical hypotheses has three parts.

(52)   To assess the testability of a grammatical hypothesis involves
    (a)   determining whether or not the content of the hypothesis includes obscure elements;
    (b)   establishing whether or not the data with which the test implications of the hypothesis may be confronted are empirical data;
    (c)   establishing whether or not the hypothesis is being protected against disconfirming evidence by means of concepts, conceptual distinctions or hypotheses that are *ad hoc.*

10.3.3.2.2   *Deriving test implications*

The second intellectual activity involved in the testing of grammatical hypotheses is the derivation of test implications from combinations of these hypotheses and indispensable background assumptions. It is clear from the example discussed in §10.3.2.1.1 above that this activity is also made up of several smaller components.

(53)   Deriving test implications from grammatical hypotheses involves

(a)   taking the grammatical hypotheses and the necessary background assumptions as premisses;

(b)   deriving one or more potential test implications from these grammatical hypotheses and background assumptions in terms of a rule of deduction;

(c)   deriving one or more concrete test implications from the potential test implication(s) by means of one or more auxiliary hypotheses.

The (a) and (b) parts of (53) were sufficiently illustrated in §10.3.2.1.1. Only one point remains to be stressed: it is most important that the background assumptions, without which the potential test implications cannot be derived, be explicitly recognized as such. We shall see in §10.3.3.2.6 that it is impossible to determine the implications of potential disconfirming evidence without knowing exactly what the background assumptions are.

Let us take a closer look at the role of auxiliary hypotheses in the derivation of concrete test implications from potential test implications. The fact that auxiliary hypotheses play the role of (53)(c) in the testing of grammatical hypotheses is the result of a certain fundamental distinction which the grammarian draws. This distinction in question is that between sentences as units of linguistic competence and utterances as units of linguistic performance. The grammarian's projections are primarily claims about the properties of sentences. By contrast, the intuitive linguistic data with which these claims must be confronted are primarily data about properties of utterances. An intermediate step is therefore needed to make it possible to use data about the properties of utterances in the appraisal of claims about the properties of sentences. This intermediate step involves establishing a systematic relationship between the two classes of properties. It is the function of the auxiliary hypotheses in question to establish this systematic relation.

A variety of grammatical auxiliary hypotheses are used in linguistic inquiry. We shall consider five typical examples.

(54)(a)   If a grammar specifies that a sentence (or part of it) is (un)grammatical, then the corresponding utterances will be (un)acceptable.

(b)   If a grammar specifies that a sentence (or part of it) is ambiguous — by assigning two or more semantic representations to it — the corresponding utterances will be interpreted in two or more different ways.

(c)   If a grammar specifies that two sentences are paraphrases of one another, then the utterances corresponding to these two sentences will be interpreted in the same way.

(d)   If a grammar specifies that a sentence is anomalous — by assigning no semantic representation to it – then the corresponding utterances will be noninterpretable or incomprehensible.

(e)   If a grammar specifies that two sentences are phonetically different, then the utterances corresponding to these two sentences will sound different.

It should be possible in principle to relate each individual grammatical property of a sentence to a property of corresponding utterances by means of one or a series of such auxiliary hypotheses. Metaphorically speaking, these auxiliary hypotheses may be regarded as the chains anchoring grammatical hypotheses to an empirical ground.

At a first glance it seems to be obvious that auxiliary hypotheses such as the five listed above must be true. This, however, is only an illusion. Grammatical hypotheses would have been obviously true only if linguistic competence and linguistic performance were related in a simple, direct way. But in fact no such relatedness exists. We have seen repeatedly that linguistic competence is but one of the many factors involved in linguistic performance. This means that, apart from the linguistic competence, various other factors contribute to the properties of utterances as products of linguistic performance. It then follows that if an utterance, as a product of linguistic performance, has a particular property it is not at all obvious that a sentence, as a unit of linguistic competence, should have a corresponding property, and the reverse is equally true.

We have in fact looked at the implications of the absence of a simple relationship between the properties of sentences and the properties of corresponding utterances in some detail in another context. In §7.4.6 we explained why an unacceptable utterance does not necessarily correspond to an ungrammatical sentence. By implication, it was shown why the auxiliary hypothesis (54)(a) is not obviously true. A sentence such as *The horse raced past the barn fell* is grammatical, i.e. formed in accordance with the syntactic rules of English. However, as the corresponding utterances are perceptually complex, these utterances are deemed to be unacceptable. The reverse is also true: by using an ungrammatical sentence in a special, appropriate context, the corresponding utterances may be felt to be completely acceptable. For similar reasons the remaining auxiliary hypotheses, (54)(b)–(e), cannot be considered to be obviously true. The problematic aspects of such grammatical auxiliary hypotheses should be dealt with in a course on substantive aspects of generative grammar.

10.3.3.2.3   *Collecting raw data*

A third component of the testing of grammatical hypotheses is the collecting of raw linguistic data with which the concrete test implications of grammatical hypotheses may be confronted. Raw data are primarily intuitive linguistic data. It will be shown in §10.3.3.2.4 in what sense these data are raw.

In many forms of empirical inquiry, raw data are obtained by conducting experiments. For a philosopher of science such as Bunge (1967b:251ff.) the

CONDUCTING OF AN EXPERIMENT is the carrying out of an organized series of intellectual and physical activities, often with the aid of instruments. The scientist's aim in conducting an experiment is deliberately to effect certain kinds of changes or to elicit reactions. The changes thus effected or the reactions elicited are observed, noted and interpreted against a certain background, viz. that of a cognitive aim. This cognitive aim is the appraisal of one or more scientific hypotheses. The activities performed in planning, conducting and evaluating experiments as well as in interpreting the experimental results are highly complex and will not be discussed here. In fact, in generative grammar experiments play only an insignificant role in the collecting of raw linguistic data.

Experiments and systematic, controlled observation techniques could play a role in the collecting of linguistic intuitions as primary linguistic data, but we saw in §4.3.2.2.2 that generative grammarians generally make no effort to elicit such intuitions from informants in a systematic, controlled way. To obtain these intuitions, the grammarian introspectively "consults" his own linguistic competence or "taps" that of his closest colleagues in an informal way.

Apart from phonetically oriented approaches to generative phonology, the role of experiment in generative grammar is limited to the collection of certain types of external linguistic data. These data are used to test the psychological reality of linguistic hypotheses. Experiments are conducted with the purpose of obtaining performance data about, for instance, speech errors, speech production, speech perception and the various forms of linguistic pathology. In the terminology of Harré (1961:67ff.), an experiment conducted with the purpose of obtaining such data may be called an ONTOLOGICAL EXPERIMENT. An ontological experiment is aimed at testing a claim that a certain mechanism exists at an underlying level of reality. The experiments by means of which Whitaker (1972) obtained the neuropsychological data of §9.3.2.4.2 and the experiments by which Foss and Fay (1975) tried to obtain certain performance data are typical examples of ontological experiments. The nature of such experiments is discussed in some detail – with reference to a certain type of psycholinguistic test – in *The function of the lexicon in transformational generative grammar* (Botha 1968: §3.5.4).

10.3.3.2.4 *Processing raw data*

The linguistic data – the collection of which was discussed in the previous paragraph – are RAW or unprocessed in two respects. On the one hand, their qualitative relevance to the grammatical hypothesis being tested has not yet been assessed. On the other hand, it has not yet been established that these data have the status of facts. For these reasons, testing grammatical hypotheses includes a fourth component, viz. processing raw linguistic data.

(55)   Processing raw linguistic data involves
    (a)   idealizing the data and
    (b)   assessing the factualness and accuracy of the data.

We shall consider these two points individually.

Idealizing raw linguistic data in a certain sense complements the derivation of concrete test implications from potential test implications. Raw linguistic data — and particularly intuitive linguistic judgments — are data about a nonidealized linguistic reality. However, these data are to be used to test grammatical hypotheses about an idealized linguistic reality, viz. that of the ideal speaker. The former linguistic reality has various aspects which have been idealized "out of" the latter linguistic reality. For example, the nonidealized linguistic reality includes phenomena such as idiolectal variation, dialectal variation, sociolinguistic variation, speech errors committed by ordinary speakers with finite physical and mental capacities, and so on. None of these phenomena occur in the idealized linguistic reality.

These differences between the nonidealized and the idealized linguistic reality have an important implication for testing grammatical hypotheses. This is that not every datum about the nonidealized linguistic reality is at the same time a datum about the idealized linguistic reality. Specifically, data about aspects of the nonidealized linguistic reality which have been idealized "out of" the reality of the ideal speaker cannot be used to test hypotheses about the latter reality. Such data are qualitatively irrelevant to the testing of these hypotheses. This is the reason for including the idealization of raw linguistic data in the testing of grammatical hypotheses. In idealizing raw linguistic data, the qualitative relevance of these data is assessed. Every raw datum about an aspect of the nonidealized linguistic reality which is not at the same time an aspect of the idealized linguistic reality is ignored as being qualitatively irrelevent. In terms of §4.3.2.2.2.2, this means that idealizing implies distinguishing between genuine and spurious linguistic intuitions. The concrete test implications of grammatical hypotheses can only be confronted with genuine linguistic intuitions. The idealizing of raw linguistic data clearly corresponds to the aspect of the evaluating of primary linguistic data which was discussed in §4.3.2.2.2.2.

The idealized linguistic data with which the concrete test implications of grammatical hypotheses are confronted may not of course be obviously inaccurate. For this reason the factualness or accuracy of the raw data underlying them must be assessed. In linguistic inquiry this assessment is hardly ever carried out in a systematic, conscious and explicit way. The problem is that generative grammarians do not have the criteria of accuracy and the corresponding strategies or techniques required for such an assessment at their disposal. In paragraphs 5.4.3 and 5.4.4 of *The justification of linguistic hypotheses* (Botha 1973), the limitations of the strategies used by a number of generative grammarians for the purpose of this assessment are discussed in some detail. In practice most grammarians assess the accuracy of the data in question in an informal way by directly asking close colleagues or a few linguistically untrained informants whether they agree with the content of the intuitive linguistic judgments in question. Agreement about the content of an intuitive linguistic judgment is regarded as an intersubjective indication that the judgment is correct.

10.3.3.2.5   *Confronting the test implications with the data*

The fifth component of the testing of grammatical hypotheses involves the confrontation of the concrete test implications with (the statements which represent) the idealized linguistic data. The question at issue is whether or not what is claimed in the test implications is consistent with the evidential statements representing the linguistic data. If both the former and the latter statements are nonobscure, the answer to this question is, on the whole, fairly obvious. Suppose, for instance, that it is asserted in a given concrete test implication that a certain utterance is acceptable and this assertion is confronted with the evidential statement that native speakers intuitively judge the utterance in question to be unacceptable. The fact that the former "acceptable" statement and the latter "unacceptable" statement are mutually inconsistent cannot be overlooked. This type of confrontation normally leads a grammarian to notice such obvious (in)consistencies.

10.3.3.2.6   *Interpreting disconfirming evidence*

Suppose it were to appear from the confrontation of a given concrete test implication with an evidential statement that the test implication and the evidential statement are mutually consistent. The linguistic datum represented in the evidential statement is then regarded as a positive instance of the tested grammatical hypothesis. Should it appear, however, that the test implication and the evidential statement are mutually inconsistent, a complex problem arises. The problem is that of the interpretation of the inconsistency of, or conflict between, the test implication and the evidential statement. Interpreting the implication of such a conflict constitutes the sixth component of the testing of grammatical hypotheses.

In his interpretation of the implication of such a conflict, the generative grammarian has to consider various possibilities. A first series of possibilities is that of (56).

(56)(a)   The test implication is false and the evidential statement is both qualitatively relevant and correct.

(b)   The test implication is true and the evidential statement is either qualitatively irrelevant or incorrect.

(c)   The test implication is false and the evidential statement is either qualitatively irrelevant or incorrect.

Without further investigation the grammarian cannot establish which of the three possibilities is responsible for the conflict.

Suppose the indications were that the conflict is the result of (56)(a). The linguistic datum in the evidential statement then acquires the status of a negative instance, counterexample or disconfirming evidence. But it is still not clear what this datum in fact refutes. A second series of possibilities now arises.

(57)   The linguistic datum in question is a counterexample or disconfirming evidence
(a)   either for the grammatical hypothesis from which the false test implication was derived,
(b)   or for one or more of the background assumptions by means of which the potential test implication was derived,
(c)   or for one or more of the grammatical auxiliary hypotheses by means of which the concrete test implications were derived from the potential test implication,
(d)   or for any combination of the grammatical hypothesis, the background assumptions and the auxiliary hypotheses.

It is once more impossible, without further investigation, to make a nonarbitrary choice from among these possibilities.

Suppose that further investigation were to indicate that the first possibility applied in a given case, i.e. the linguistic datum in question reflects negatively on the grammatical hypothesis. Even so it would be inadmissable to jump to the conclusion that the grammatical hypothesis is false. A third series of possibilities still exists.

(58)(a)   The counterexample in question is not a true counterexample but an exception.
(b)   The counterexample in question is a true counterexample and not an exception.

But what is the difference between a (true) counterexample and an exception? This distinction is drawn because the laws represented in grammatical hypotheses have a particular status, viz. that of rules that have undergone a historic development. This point is illustrated by Lightfoot's version (1974) of the history of the English base rules for AUX and VP. We shall consider a simpler example to illustrate the point.

The grammar of English contains a hypothesis which postulates phonological rules by which plurals are formed from a suffix with the phonological form /z/. On the basis of these rules it may be predicted that the lexical items *ox* and *child* will have the plural forms *oxes* and *childs* respectively. However, native speakers of English judge these plurals to be unacceptable. The acceptable forms, of course, are *oxen* and *children* respectively. The question is whether or not the plural forms *oxen* and *children* are to be regarded as counterexamples for the grammatical hypothesis in question. Grammarians of English say not. They argue that in the historical development of the relevant rules of plural formation, their nonextension to the items *ox* and *child* was purely accidental. On the strength of this argument, the plural forms *oxen* and *children* are accorded the status of EXCEPTIONS to the rules in question. By implication they deny these forms the status of counterexamples which would show the hypothesis to be false. A hypothesis cannot be refuted by historically explicable exceptions to the rule(s) it postulates. Thus, a linguistic datum must satisfy a certain requirement in order to be accorded the status of a TRUE COUNTEREXAMPLE for a grammatical hypothesis: the datum may not be a historically explicable exception to the grammatical rule postulated by the hypothesis. King's *Historical linguistics and generative grammar* (1969: §5.3) may be consulted for a brief discussion of the historical development of the English rules of plural formation. Note, in conclusion, that a potential counterexample for a hypothesis may not arbitrarily be accorded the status of an exception to the rule in question. This would be interpreted as protection of the hypothesis against refutation. A grammarian who claims that a given potential counterexample in fact represents an exception must furnish appropriate evidence to justify his claim. Historical evidence is the most obvious means of justifying such a claim. With that we have isolated another role that external evidence can play in linguistic inquiry.

10.4   GENERAL LINGUISTIC INQUIRY

10.4.1   General

This brings us to the criticism that can be levelled at general linguistic hypotheses. First of all, we shall consider three fragments of this type of criticism.

In §7.3.1 we had a look at Ross's Coordinate Structure Constraint. On the basis of this general linguistic hypothesis it can be predicted that the grammar of, say, English will not include a transformational rule which has the effect of moving a conjunct of a coordinate structure out of this structure. Let us now make the counterfactual assumption that the most highly valued grammar of English does in fact contain such a transformational rule T_x. This piece of evidence could be used as follows to criticize the general linguistic hypothesis in question:

(59)   If Ross's Coordinate Structure Constraint is true, then the most highly valued grammar of English will not include a transformational rule which moves a conjunct of a coordinate structure out of this structure. The most highly valued grammar of English includes the transformational rule T_x which moves a conjunct of a coordinate structure out of this structure. Therefore, the Coordinate Structure Constraint is false.

It will be shown in §10.4.2.1 below that (59) represents a fragment of factual criticism of a general linguistic hypothesis.

The second example of a fragment of criticism levelled at a general linguistic hypothesis represents systematic criticism of the hypothesis in question, this hypothesis being the $\overline{X}$-convention.

(60)   If a general linguistic hypothesis makes it possible to express linguistically nonsignificant generalizations about a particular language, then this hypothesis is unacceptable. According to McCawley, the $\overline{X}$-convention makes it possible to express linguistically nonsignificant generalizations about English in terms of the category 'specifier'. Therefore, the $\overline{X}$-convention is unacceptable.

The background of this fragment of systematic criticism is to be found in §§5.3.2.2 and 9.4.2.2.2.

In our final example of a fragment of criticism of a general linguistic hypothesis, external criticism is levelled at the $\overline{X}$-convention. The criticism arises from the projection about an impossible linguistic change in English which was presented as (48) in §8.4.3.2. Suppose that the projective statement of that projection should appear to be incorrect. This would give rise to the following criticism of the $\overline{X}$-convention:

(61)   If the $\overline{X}$-convention is true, then a linguistic change in English which changes (simplifies) one of the three rules of (46) in §8.4.3.2 without changing (simplifying) the other two rules in a parallel way will be impossible. English is undergoing the linguistic change T in which only rule (46)(a), and not rules (46)(b) and (c), is being changed (simplified). Therefore, the $\overline{X}$-convention is false.

Recall that for generative grammarians such as Kiparsky "false" in (61) has the meaning of 'not psychologically real'.

We can now consider two general points in connection with the criticism brought against general linguistic hypotheses in more detail. First, we shall focus on the nature of this criticism and, second, we shall try to gain an overall impression of the intellectual activities involved in the criticism of general linguistic hypotheses.

10.4.2   Nature of the Criticism of General Linguistic Hypotheses

As may be seen from the fragments of criticism (59)–(61), the criticism of general linguistic hypotheses is made up of three distinct components, viz. a factual, a systematic and an external component. The criticism of a general linguistic hypothesis and that of a grammatical hypothesis, then, have the same composition.

10.4.2.1   *The Factual Component*

In §8.4 it appeared that projections about the properties of individual human languages may be made on the basis of general linguistic hypotheses. Data about these properties which show these projections to be inaccurate constitute the primary source of factual criticism of general linguistic hypotheses. In other words, these data are the source of counterexamples or disconfirming evidence for general linguistic hypotheses.

10.4.2.1.1 *Logical form of a fragment of factual criticism*

The factual criticism of a general linguistic hypothesis takes the logical form of an argument of the form *modus tollens*. The fragment of criticism (59), for instance, may be explicitly reconstructed in the form of the following argument:

(62) MaP : If Ross's Coordinate Structure Constraint is true, then the most highly valued grammar of a natural language will not include a transformational rule which moves a conjunct of a coordinate structure out of this structure.

MiP : The most highly valued grammar of English includes the transformational rule T_x which moves a conjunct of a coordinate structure out of this structure.

C   : Ross's Coordinate Structure Constraint is false.

The argument (62) is demonstrative. Yet the Coordinate Structure Constraint is not conclusively disconfirmed within the framework of this argument. We shall now consider three factors which contribute to the inconclusive nature of a disconfirming general linguistic argument such as (62).

10.4.2.1.2 *Nature of disconfirming evidence*

A first factor that contributes to the inconclusive nature of disconfirming general linguistic arguments is the nature of the disconfirming evidence. The disconfirming evidence presented in the minor premiss of an argument such as (62) typically does not take the form of primary linguistic data about sentences of a particular individual language. This disconfirming evidence typically takes the form of a grammatical hypothesis about a property of (the grammar of) a particular language, in the case of (62) the hypothesis that the most highly valued grammar of English includes a certain movement transformation T_x. Note in particular that the hypothesis in question is not part of just any grammar of English. It is part of the *most highly valued* grammar of English.

General linguistic hypotheses cannot be directly tested with reference to primary linguistic data about individual human languages. They can only be tested via hypotheses that form part of the most highly valued grammars of the individual languages on which the data have a bearing. From this an important principle follows.

(63)   The measure of conclusiveness of the refutation of a general linguistic hypothesis can never be greater than the measure of conclusiveness of the justification for the grammatical hypothesis/es constituting the disconfirming evidence.

Recall that the justification of a grammatical hypothesis can, in principle, never be conclusive. In his article "On *wh*-movement" (1976:5), Chomsky puts it in a nutshell:

To find evidence to support or refute a proposed condition on rules [as a linguistic universal – R.P.B.], it does not suffice to list unexplained phenomena; rather, it is necessary to present rules, i.e., to present a fragment of grammar. The confirmation or refutation will be as convincing as the fragment of grammar presented.

Suppose now that, as is the case in (62), a test implication of a general linguistic hypothesis were inconsistent with a grammatical hypothesis about an individual human language. The general linguist could then reach one of two possible conclusions.

(64)(a)   The tested general linguistic hypothesis is false.
   (b)   The grammatical hypothesis constituting the disconfirming evidence is false.

Without further investigation, it is impossible to establish which of these conclusions should be accepted. The general linguist will not blindly accept the conclusion that the general linguistic hypothesis in question is false. He will first try to establish whether the grammatical hypothesis of (64)(b) is well-justified as part of the most highly valued grammar of the individual language in question. He will be particularly concerned with establishing whether no alternative for this grammatical hypothesis exists which is not inconsistent with the relevant test implication of the tested general linguistic hypothesis.

Let us consider this point with reference to the fictitious grammatical hypothesis that English has the transformation T_x. Suppose T_x to be the *Wh*-movement transformation. Suppose further that this transformation violates the Coordinate Structure Constraint, as would be indicated by the fictitious "fact" that the interrogative (b) sentences are acceptable in English.

(65)(a)   *Mary lives in New York and Chicago.*
   (b)   *Where does Mary live in New York and?*

(66)(a)   *Peter likes Margaret and Anne.*
   (b)   *Whom does Peter like Margaret and?*

(67)(a) *John works in the mornings and evenings.*
  (b) *When does John work in the mornings and?*

The general linguist will try to determine whether it isn't possible in the most
highly valued grammar of English to derive the interrogative (b) sentences by
some means other than the *Wh*-movement transformation. Suppose that this
were indeed possible and that it could be shown that this "other means" is well-
justified. The *Wh*-movement transformation would then no longer violate the
Coordinate Structure Constraint and would no longer constitute a counterexample for this general linguistic hypothesis. The point that must be stressed is
that only well-justified grammatical hypotheses that are part of the most highly
valued grammar of particular languages can constitute disconfirming evidence for
general linguistic hypotheses.

10.4.2.1.3 *Nature of linguistic universals*
Suppose, by contrast, that no other well-justified means of deriving the interrogative sentences (65)(b), (66)(b) and (67)(b) existed. This would mean that the
Wh-movement transformation retains the status of a transformation which
violates the Coordinate Structure Constraint. Despite this fact, some generative
grammarians would still not be prepared to accept the possibility (64)(a), i.e.
that the Coordinate Structure Constraint is false. Such generative grammarians
have another view of the nature of linguistic universals than the conventional
one we have been working with so far.
  The view of linguistic universals with which we have been working is known
as the ABSOLUTE VIEW. According to this conventional view, a given linguistic
principle is a universal only if it forms part of the grammar of every human
language. The general linguistic hypothesis that a given linguistic principle is a
universal can be refuted, according to this view, by showing that it plays no role
at all in the most highly valued grammar of at least *one* human language.
  Opposed to the absolute view of linguistic universals there is a RELATIVE
VIEW of such universals. The basis for this view is formulated in chapter 9 of
Chomsky and Halle's *The sound pattern of English* and is also expounded in
Chomsky's article "Conditions on transformations" (1973:234ff.). According
to the relative view, a linguistic universal need not form part of the most highly
valued grammar of *every* individual human language. A language in the grammar
of which a given universal plays no role at all can merely be regarded as less
highly valued than languages in the grammar of which the universal in question
does play a role. In terms of the relative view, the general linguistic theory as
a whole is essentially an EVALUATION MEASURE. In terms of its linguistic
universals, the general linguistic theory appraises the "typicalness", naturalness
or value of each human language as a human language. This value may be
expressed in terms of the concept MARKED. The lower the value of a language —
i.e. the greater the number of linguistic universals that play no role at all in the
most highly valued grammar of the language — the more marked that language.

Generative grammarians subscribing to the relative view of linguistic universals may refuse to accept the possibility of (64)(a). As far as they are concerned, the – fictitious – "fact" that English has a movement transformation which violates the Coordinate Structure Constraint indicates only one thing: that, as a human language, English is marked or less highly valued in a certain respect. A second factor, then, which contributes to the inconclusive nature of disconfirming general linguistic arguments is the possibility of subscribing to a relative view of linguistic universals. We shall consider an important consequence of this view in §10.4.3.2. It should be added that the relative view of linguistic universals has become the dominant view in Chomsky's most recent writings.

10.4.2.1.4   *General linguistic background assumptions*

A third factor which may contribute to the inconclusive nature of disconfirming general linguistic arguments is the role of background assumptions in such arguments. In general it is not possible to derive test implications from a general linguistic hypothesis without making additional background assumptions. It is difficult to illustrate this point in a simple manner with reference to the disconfirming argument (62). The general principle involved, however, is the same as the one that was illustrated with reference to grammatical hypotheses in §10.3.2.1.1. Within a general linguistic disconfirming argument, too, a counter-example or a piece of disconfirming evidence may have several implications.

(68)(a)   The general linguistic hypothesis from which the incorrect test implication was derived is false.

(b)   One or more of the background assumptions by means of which the incorrect test implication was derived is false.

(c)   Both the general linguistic hypothesis of (a) and one or more of the background assumptions of (b) are false.

The disconfirming evidence in question can only indicate that the tested general linguistic principle is false if a considerable measure of justification exists for the background assumptions mentioned above. The justification for these background assumptions can, in principle, never be conclusive. The refutation of a general linguistic hypothesis can never be more conclusive than the justification for the relevant background assumptions.

10.4.2.2   *The Systematic Component*

In addition to factual criticism, systematic criticism may be brought against general linguistic hypotheses. The source of systematic criticism of general linguistic hypotheses is the defects these hypotheses manifest when appraised in terms of general linguistic acceptability standards.

10.4.2.2.1 *Logical structure of a fragment of systematic criticism*

A fragment of systematic criticism of a general linguistic hypothesis was presented as (60) above. The $\overline{X}$-convention is criticized for a defect it manifests in terms of the acceptability standard (96) of §9.4.2.2.2. The logical form of such a fragment of systematic criticism is typically that of the *modus ponens* form of argument. As a concrete instance of this form of argument, the fragment of systematic criticism in question may be reconstructed as follows:

(69)   MaP : If a general linguistic hypothesis makes it possible to express linguistically nonsignificant generalizations about a particular language, then this hypothesis is unacceptable.

        MiP : According to McCawley, the $\overline{X}$-convention makes it possible to express linguistically nonsignificant generalizations about English in terms of the category 'specifier'.

        C   : The $\overline{X}$-convention is unacceptable.

Notice that the general linguistic acceptability standard (96) of §9.4.2.2.2 constitutes the major premiss of this argument. It is clear from a symbolic representation of this argument that it is a demonstrative argument.

10.4.2.2.2 *Points of systematic criticism*

The most important general linguistic acceptability standards used in linguistic inquiry were mentioned in §9.4.2.2.2. On the strength of these standards, the considerations of (70) may be presented as systematic criticism of a general linguistic hypothesis.

(70)(a)   The general linguistic hypothesis plays no role in the giving of grammatical explanations [cf. (90) in §9.4.2.2.2].

    (b)   The general linguistic hypothesis plays no role in the making of accurate grammatical predictions [cf. (94) in §9.4.2.2.2].

    (c)   The general linguistic hypothesis plays no role in the expression of linguistically significant generalizations by individual grammars [cf. (95) in §9.4.2.2.2].

    (d)   The general linguistic hypothesis deprives individual grammars of the ability to express certain linguistically significant generalizations [cf. (97) in §9.4.2.2.2].

    (e)   The general linguistic hypothesis entails an undesirable extension of the formal or descriptive power of the general linguistic theory [cf. (99) in §9.4.2.2.2].

One important consideration should be added to this list of points of systematic criticism that may be levelled at general linguistic hypotheses.

(71)   The formal or descriptive power of the general linguistic theory is unduly restricted.

This point of systematic criticism of a general linguistic theory may be interpreted in two ways.

On the one hand, the formal power of a general linguistic theory may be unduly restricted when it comes to expressing linguistically significant generalizations about individual human languages. To show that a general linguistic theory has this defect, the linguist must take two steps. First, he must show that, in the case of a particular language, linguistically significant generalizations exist which should be expressed in terms of the objectives of the general linguistic theory. Second, he must show that it is impossible to express these generalizations by means of the formal mechanisms made available by the general linguistic theory. For instance, it was shown in §5.3.2.2 that a general linguistic theory which does not include a formal mechanism such as the $\overline{X}$-convention does not have the power to express certain linguistically significant generalizations about the base rules of English.

On the other hand, the formal power of a general linguistic theory may be unduly restricted when it comes to giving grammatical explanations for problematic primary linguistic data about individual languages. To show that a general linguistic theory has this defect the general linguist must, likewise, take two steps. First, he must show that, in the case of a particular language, data exist that are problematic within the framework of the general linguistic theory. Second, he must show that it is impossible to give a grammatical explanation of these data by employing the formal mechanisms of this linguistic theory. In the recent history of linguistics, this consideration played an important role in, for instance, the criticism of nontransformational linguistic theories. Chomsky, for instance, argued that a general linguistic theory that does not include the formal mechanism of transformational rules lacks the power that would make it possible to give a grammatical explanation of the ambiguity of expressions such as *the shooting of the hunters*. In the history of linguistic inquiry the lack of sufficient formal power of general linguistic theories − in both the aforementioned respects − has often been raised as a point of serious criticism against these theories.

The most serious criticism that can be brought against a general linguistic theory is that it has too much or too little formal power. In both cases the general linguistic theory fails to give an accurate characterization of the concept 'possible human language'. If the formal power of the general linguistic theory is too restricted, there will be (possible) human languages that cannot be described as such within the framework of this theory. If the general linguistic theory is overly powerful, there will be systems that are not possible human languages, but that can be described as such within the framework of this theory. This point was extensively illustrated in preceding paragraphs, such as §§6.4.3.1.3 and 9.4.2.2.2.

General linguistic hypotheses can further be criticized in terms of acceptability standards that are not specific to linguistic inquiry alone. These standards apply to scientific hypotheses in general. A general linguistic hypothesis may, for instance, be criticized for not being easily refutable, for being heuristically unfruitful, etc.

In conclusion, it has to be stressed that the systematic criticism of a general linguistic hypothesis does not carry less weight than the factual criticism of such hypotheses. The reason is simply that a general linguistic theory is, in a particular sense, a theory about other — grammatical — theories. It then follows that, in the appraisal of a general linguistic theory, great value is attached to the (im)perfection of its relatedness to the grammatical theories for individual languages.

10.4.2.3   *The External Component*

As in the case of grammatical hypotheses, the criticism of general linguistic hypotheses may contain an external component. External criticism of a general linguistic hypothesis generally takes the form of criticism of the hypothesis in its descriptive function. The general tenor of such criticism is that the general linguistic hypothesis in question is probably not psychologically real. The nature of external criticism of general linguistic hypotheses does not differ from the nature of external criticism of grammatical hypotheses in any essential respect. The nature of the latter type of criticism was discussed fairly extensively in §10.3.2.3.2. We shall therefore not discuss the nature of external criticism of general linguistic hypotheses at any length.

10.4.2.3.1   *Criticism on the basis of false projections*
A first source of external criticism of general linguistic hypotheses is the false projections that may be made on the basis of these hypotheses and bridge theories about objects or phenomena outside the linguistic reality of the general linguist. Among these external linguistic objects and phenomena are (possible) linguistic changes, dialectal variation, sociolinguistic variation, speech production and perception, linguistic pathology, speech errors, and so on. The fragment of external criticism presented as (61) above is based on a false projection about an (im)possible linguistic change. In (61) the $\overline{X}$-convention is criticized as being psychologically unreal because it serves as a basis for a false projection about a linguistic change in English. It is important to note that this criticism carries weight only if the assumed bridge theory about linguistic change is well-justified. This point was discussed at some length in §10.3.2.3.2 with reference to a bridge theory about the relation between the human mind and brain.

10.4.2.3.2   *Criticism on the basis of unaccountable data*
Unaccountable external linguistic data constitute a second source of external criticism of general linguistic hypotheses. This point may be illustrated with reference to data about linguistic changes which took place in the history of

individual languages. Generative grammarians such as Kiparsky (1968a:188) and Lightfoot (1976b:2–5; in press) require the general linguistic theory, in conjunction with a theory of linguistic change, to serve as a basis for the explanation of historical data about documented linguistic changes. This point may be illustrated by an example.

Suppose that the three fictitious changes of (72) were documented as changes that took place simultaneously in the history of English.

(72)(a)   NPs such as *proofs John's of the theorem* are used instead of NPs such as *John's proofs of the theorem.*

(b)   VPs such as *prove will the theorem* are used instead of VPs such as *will prove the theorem.*

(c)   APs such as *ignorant even of the theorem* are used instead of APs such as *even ignorant of the theorem.*

Two facts suggest that these three changes may be related. Firstly, all three changes involve a change in the order of a specifying constituent with regard to a specified constituent. The order specifying constituent-specified constituent is reversed to that of specified constituent-specifying constituent. Secondly, these three structurally analogous changes take place simultaneously in the history of the language. To explain these changes it must he shown that they are surface manifestations of one and the same underlying change.

This brings us to the question of whether the general linguistic theory has the formal mechanisms required to formulate this single underlying change? Suppose that the general linguistic theory did not have the required mechanisms. The historical data would then be unaccountable and, therefore, a source of external criticism of the general linguistic theory. If the general linguistic theory did have the required formal mechanisms, the historical data in question would be accountable and, therefore, a source of external justification for the general linguistic theory.

It is clear that the data about the fictitious linguistic changes of (72) may be used as a basis for external criticism of a general linguistic theory which does not include a formal mechanism such as the $\overline{X}$-convention. Such a mechanism would be needed to formulate the single linguistic change underlying the three changes of (72). In terms of the $\overline{X}$-convention this single underlying change may be characterized as a change in the abbreviated rule schema representing the base rules for NP, VP and AP. A change in this rule schema will cause NPs, VPs and APs simultaneously to undergo structurally analogous changes. Supposing that changes such as those of (72) did take place in the history of English or another language, the historical data about these changes would constitute a source of external justification for the $\overline{X}$-convention.

Unaccountable historical data about linguistic changes are not the only source of external criticism of the general linguistic theory. Every kind of external linguistic datum that is qualitatively relevant to the general linguistic theory could in principle be used as a source of external criticism. An article by Ashley Hasting and Andreas Koutsoudas, "Performance models and the generative-interpretive debate" (1976), may be studied for an additional example of external linguistic criticism brought against a general linguistic theory. In this article they use data about speech production and perception as a source of criticism of the psychological reality of Chomsky's (extended) standard theory.

10.4.3 Criticizing General Linguistic Hypotheses

10.4.3.1 *General Characterization*

To criticize general linguistic hypotheses is to reason or to present arguments. The main components of this intellectual activity may be briefly characterized as in (73).

(73)(a) To criticize a general linguistic hypothesis in its *explanatory function* involves
  (i) presenting, as factual criticism, data from which it is clear that the hypothesis serves as a basis for inaccurate projections about the properties of the most highly valued grammars of individual languages;
  (ii) presenting, as systematic criticism, metascientific data from which it is clear that the hypothesis is (relatively) unacceptable in terms of general linguistic acceptability standards.

(b) To criticize a general linguistic hypothesis in its *descriptive function* involves
  (i) presenting external linguistic data from which it is clear that the hypothesis, in conjunction with a given bridge theory, serves as a basis for inaccurate projections about the properties of external linguistic objects or phenomena;
  (ii) presenting external linguistic data that are qualitatively relevant to the hypothesis or general linguistic theory but cannot be explained on the basis of this hypothesis or general linguistic theory, in conjunction with an appropriate bridge theory.

Point (73)(a)(i) represents what is conventionally known as the TESTING OF A GENERAL LINGUISTIC HYPOTHESIS. Two additional points in connection with this testing remain to be discussed.

10.4.3.2 *Refutability of "Relative Universals"*

In §10.4.2.1.3 a distinction was drawn between two views of linguistic universals:

the absolute view and the relative view. Within the framework of the absolute view it is reasonably clear under what circumstances a (general linguistic hypothesis postulating a) universal will be considered to be false. To falsify such a universal it is only necessary to show that there is one language in the most highly valued grammar of which the universal plays no role at all. Within the framework of the relative view, by contrast, it is not so clear when a proposed universal may be considered to be false. A "relative universal" cannot be refuted by indicating a language of which the most highly valued grammar does not include the universal in question. In short, within the latter framework, non-instantiation of the universal in an individual language is no indication of its incorrectness. It is merely an indication that the language in question is less highly valued.

This line of argument can be dangerous, however. If it were to be used freely, general linguistic hypotheses would lose their refutability. The distinction between an absolute and a relative view of linguistic universals could easily acquire the status of a mechanism of which the only function is to protect general linguistic hypotheses against disconfirming evidence.

But what can be done to prevent the distinction in question from becoming a mere protective device? This question has not yet been penetratingly and systematically discussed in the literature. The most promising answer is the one given by Lightfoot (in press: §1.5). He is of the opinion that the judgment that a given language is less highly valued in a certain respect – because it does not instantiate a particular universal – should itself be regarded as an empirical claim. In other words, such a claim should be refutable and must be justified. The judgment in question must be specifically tested and justified with reference to external linguistic data. This implies the following: if a given language is less highly valued in a certain respect, the fact of its being less highly valued must be reflected in data about, for instance, linguistic change, language acquisition, speech production and perception, linguistic pathology, and so on.

Consider the following value judgment:

(74)   English is less highly valued in the sense that it includes a *Wh*-movement transformation which violates the Coordinate Structure Constraint.

This judgment may be justified by means of various kinds of external linguistic data: data which show that the rule in question is in the process of changing, data which show that children have more difficulty acquiring this rule than other movement rules that do not violate the constraint in question, data which indicate that the rule is often wrongly applied in linguistic performance, data which indicate that the interrogative sentences generated by means of the rule are perceptually complex, data which show that in linguistic pathology this rule is one of the first to be lost, and so on. It is obvious that the same kind of external data could constitute disconfirming evidence for the value judgment (74) as well. By using external linguistic data in this way to test and justify value judgments such as that of (74), the concept 'less highly valued language' is given empirical content. At the same time the distinction between the absolute and the relative view of linguistic universals is prevented from acquiring the status of a protective device.

There is, however, an important point to be borne in mind. The various kinds of external linguistic data mentioned above may be used in the justification and refutation of value judgments only if the condition (75) is satisfied.

(75)   For every kind of external linguistic datum a bridge theory must exist which specifies the systematic relatedness between the external linguistic object or phenomenon on which the datum has a bearing and the ideal speaker's language acquisition faculty and linguistic competence.

In the absence of well-justified bridge theories, external linguistic data are simply irrelevant with regard to the appraisal of value judgments such as that of (74) about man's linguistic capacities. At present, the fundamental problem with the relative view of linguistic universals is the fact that such bridge theories have not yet been adequately developed.

10.4.3.3   *Refutability of "Absolute Universals"*

In the preceding paragraph, the impression was given that "absolute universals" are more easily refutable than "relative universals". This impression is essentially correct, but should be refined. It is based on the tacit assumption that all "absolute universals" are equally refutable. This assumption is false. In his article "Linguistics as chemistry: the substance theory of semantic primes" (1973), Arnold Zwicky shows that all general linguistic principles, i.e. our "absolute universals", are not equally refutable (and justifiable). According to Zwicky, general linguistic principles may be divided into three classes according to their refutability.

The first class of general linguistic principles includes Zwicky's ARGUABLE PROPOSITIONS. Among these arguable propositions Zwicky (1973:470) includes "universal hypotheses, most of them *exclusions,* restrictions on the use of certain notational conventions". In (76) five examples of Zwicky's arguable propositions are given.

(76)(a)   Braces (curly brackets) cannot be used in the abbreviation of syntactic rules.

(b)   Transformational rules may not insert material (= constituents) from one S into a lower S.

(c)   Rules that effect absolute neutralization in phonology are prohibited.

(d)   Syntactic rules cannot be conditioned by phonological features.

(e)   The phonological cycle is restricted to prosodic phenomena.

It is clear from these five examples in what sense arguable propositions are "exclusions". They exclude certain logically conceivable principles as impossible in human language. The recoverability condition and the Coordinate Structure Constraint are examples of arguable propositions.

This brings us to the refutability of arguable propositions. As a class they represent the most refutable — and most justifiable — general linguistic principles, according to Zwicky. In the preceding paragraphs, we were in fact concerned with the refutation and the refutability of arguable propositions. Nothing need be added here to the views expressed in those paragraphs.

The second class of general linguistic principles which Zwicky distinguishes includes his ORGANIZING HYPOTHESES. According to Zwicky (1973:471), organizing hypotheses are "high-level assumptions, fundamental empirical hypotheses". Let us consider three of the examples given by Zwicky.

(77)(a)   In the course of time phonological rules are reordered to reduce markedness.

(b)   Transformations do not change the meaning of the syntactic structures to which they apply.

(c)   Every semantic prime is realizable as a lexical unit — root, inflection, or derivational affix — in some human language.

For Zwicky (1973:471), organizing hypotheses as a class are less refutable than arguable propositions. He has the following to say about the former hypotheses:

> The most salient fact about such assumptions is that they are not easily given up, even in the face of apparent counterexamples, which will be treated as manifestations of minor complicating principles or as outright anomalies (. . .). It is this resistance to disproof that gives organizing hypotheses their 'field-defining' nature. They are testable, in some sense, and they can be abandoned after argument, but the tests are not simple nor the arguments straightforward.

Zwicky illustrates the lesser refutability of organizing hypotheses with reference to the so-called Post Office Principle, i.e. the organizing hypothesis (77)(b). This hypothesis is called the Post Office Principle on the grounds that it treats syntax as an elaborate delivery system: a system designed to get messages to an addressee without changing their content. It is difficult to find convincing evidence for or against the Post Office Principle as a typical example of an organizing hypothesis. For Zwicky (1973:473)

> the problem is that it is almost always possible to fix up a description so that it will conform to the principle. Accordingly, whether or not an analyst will make the required adjustments tends to depend on whether or not he believes in the Post Office Principle.

Zwicky's third class of general linguistic principles comprises his METHODOL-OGICAL PRINCIPLES. Zwicky's notion of methodological principles was already discussed in §5.3.3. For him (1973:468) they are rules of thumb which "suggest what the most likely state of affairs is in a given situation, in the absence of evidence of the usual sort". In §5.3.3 (28)(a)—(c) we considered the Majority Vote Principle, the Contrast Principle and the Surfacist Principle as examples of such methodological principles.

From the point of view of their refutability, methodological principles, unlike arguable propositions and organizing hypotheses, are not empirical propositions. Zwicky (1973:468) characterizes their epistemological status as follows:

Instead of being verified or falsified, methodological principles are judged as useless or useful, and the basis for the judgment is whether the descriptions they recommend are confirmed or not. To defend a methodological principle, one provides numerous illustrations of cases where it chooses a description that turns out to be well supported on other evidence. To refute a methodo-logical principle, one adduces cases where it selects a description that turns out to be unsatisfactory for independent reasons. In either direction, such arguments are not easy.

The initial impression concerning the refutability of "absolute universals" has therefore to be refined as follows: even within the framework of an absolute view of linguistic universals, there are (two classes of) general linguistic principles that are not at all easily refutable, viz. organizing hypotheses and methodological principles. This refinement has an important implication. In preceding paragraphs we concentrated on the criticism that may be levelled at the most refutable class of general linguistic hypotheses, viz. Zwicky's arguable propositions. It appeared that the criticism of these general linguistic hypotheses can but be inconclusive. But we have now established that there are two classes of general linguistic hypotheses that are even less refutable than arguable propositions. This shows clearly to what extent the conventional view that general linguistic hypotheses can be conclusively refuted is untenable.

SELECTED READING

Discussions of the criticism of scientific hypotheses normally form part of discussions of the justification of these hypotheses. Consequently, most of the literature cited at the end of chapter 9 applies to the present chapter as well. Only a limited number of additional biblio-graphical items are mentioned here. These are items which deal almost exclusively with the criticism brought against hypotheses.

Inquiry in General

General Discussion of Factual Criticism and Testing

Bunge 1967b:ch.15; Harré 1961:§6; 1967:ch.6; Hanson 1971:76—77; Hempel 1966:ch.2—3.

Nonfactual Criteria for Criticism

Bunge 1967b:§15.7; Caws 1966:ch.31; Harré 1967:ch.7; Hempel 1966:ch.4; Laudan 1978:ch.4.

Inconclusiveness of Refutation

Grünbaum 1971; Harding 1976b; all further articles in Harding (ed.) 1976a; Musgrave 1973.

Testability

Hempel 1965:§3.5; Popper 1965:ch.I, V, VI.

Truth, Theories of

Chisholm 1966:ch.7; Kaplan 1964:311—322; Woozley 1967:ch.5—7.

Linguistic Inquiry

Empirical Status

Protective Devices

Botha 1971:§5.2.3; Botha 1978; Sinclair 1977.

Empirical Status of Intuitive Data

Botha 1973:ch.5; Dretske 1974; Itkonen 1976; Labov 1972; Linell 1976; Ringen 1975; to appear a; to appear c; Sampson 1975b:ch.4; Wunderlich (ed.) 1976.

Relative View of Linguistic Universals

Chomsky 1978; Chomsky and Halle 1968:ch.9; Lightfoot in press; Postal 1968.

Testing of Linguistic Hypotheses

Cohen and Wirth (eds.) 1975.

CHAPTER ELEVEN

Reacting to Criticism of Linguistic Hypotheses

11.0 PERSPECTIVE

The criticism of linguistic hypotheses elicits reaction from generative grammarians. Reacting to criticism of linguistic hypotheses therefore represents a ninth main aspect of linguistic inquiry. It is on this aspect that we will be concentrating in chapter 11 of our study. In the first main section of this chapter a minimal metascientific background is presented as a basis for further discussion. A distinction is drawn between hypotheses, theories and approaches. This distinction serves as a basis for a further differentiation between seven types of reaction to the criticism brought against scientific hypotheses.

In the second main section of the chapter we take a closer look at the way in which six of these types of reaction are used in grammatical inquiry: rejecting the criticism brought against grammatical hypotheses or theories, taking no steps to accommodate apparently appropriate criticism of a grammatical hypothesis or theory, levelling countercriticism at alternative grammatical hypotheses or theories, protecting a grammatical hypothesis or theory against criticism, modifying a criticized grammatical hypothesis or theory and replacing a criticized grammatical hypothesis or theory with a better alternative. The circumstances in which each of these forms of reaction is appropriate and the effect each form of reaction has on further inquiry are subsequently discussed. Finally, a brief characterization is given of the various intellectual activities involved in reacting to criticism of grammatical hypotheses or theories.

The third main section of chapter 11 deals with a seventh type of reaction to criticism of linguistic hypotheses or theories, viz. revolution. In the context of general linguistic inquiry, this type of reaction is illustrated with reference to the Chomskyan revolution in linguistics. The circumstances which contributed to the revolution, its content and the types of consequences it had are discussed. In the discussion, an attempt is made to show clearly how drastic revolution is as a type of reaction to criticism of linguistic hypotheses and theories. In conclusion, a brief characterization is given of a counterreaction elicited by the Chomskyan revolution, viz. a possible empiricist counterrevolution.

11.1 INTRODUCTION

The lexicalist hypothesis may be criticized on the basis of data about the properties of pairs of derived nominals such as *the enemy's destruction of the city* and *the city's destruction by the enemy*. Jackendoff (1974a:10) formulates the general tenor of this criticism as follows:

(1)   "A second possible difficulty for the lexicalist hypothesis concerns the passive transformation. We observe that the relation of the derived nominals [26a] and [26b] seems to be the same as that between the active sentence [27a] and its passive [27b].

[26] a.   *the enemy's destruction of the city*
     b.   *the city's destruction by the enemy*
[27] a.   *the enemy destroyed the city*
     b.   *the city was destroyed by the enemy*

In order to capture the similarity of the two relations, the grammar should not have to state, in addition to the standard passive, a transformation having very similar effects to the passive, but in the domain NP. Within the transformational hypothesis this generalization is quite simple; all four phrases above are derived from the same underlying form, but [26a] undergoes nominalization, [27b] undergoes passive, and [26b] undergoes passive followed by nominalization. [26b] thus is the nominalization of a passive sentence. In the lexicalist hypothesis this solution is not available, since there is no nominalization transformation."

In "Remarks on nominalization", Chomsky anticipates this problem for the lexicalist hypothesis. He also proposes a solution of which Jackendoff (1974a:10) summarizes the main points as follows:

(2)   "Instead Chomsky suggests that, like the base rules and the projection rules, some transformations, in particular the passive, may apply over the domain NP as well as S. If this is the case, [26b] is derived from the same underlying form as [26a], but it undergoes the generalized form of the passive. Hence its relation to [26a] is the same as the relation of [27b] to [27a], precisely as required, and no extra rules need be added to the grammar."

What is present in (2) is in fact Chomsky's reaction to a point of criticism that may be brought against the lexicalist hypothesis. This brings us to a ninth main aspect of linguistic inquiry: reacting to criticism of linguistic hypotheses and theories.

Schematically this main aspect may be represented as follows:

(3)

| criticism of hypothesis or theory | → | activities of ninth main aspect | → | reaction to criticism |

This main aspect is as complex as the other main aspects of linguistic inquiry. We shall analyze it via the following two general questions:

(4) (a)   What are the general nature and specific types of generative grammarians' reactions to the criticism levelled at their hypotheses and theories?

(b)   What is involved in reacting to such criticism?

As regards scientific inquiry in general, only the outline of the answers to these questions will be sketched. More particulars will be given in the sections on linguistic inquiry.

11.2   INQUIRY IN GENERAL

11.2.1   Hypotheses vs. Theories vs. Approaches

The questions posed in (4) may be answered on the basis of a certain tripartite distinction, viz. that between a HYPOTHESIS vs. a THEORY vs. an APPROACH. In §§5.2.3 and 6.2.2.2 we looked at the distinction between hypotheses and theories. A hypothesis was characterized as an assumption about the possible regularity, structure, pattern, mechanism or cause underlying a problematic state of affairs. A theory, by contrast, was characterized as a set of interrelated hypotheses.

This brings us to the third member of the distinction, which was merely mentioned in §4.3.2.1.5. Within a given field of study there may be theories that are interrelated in the sense that they are all products of the same approach to the object(s) of inquiry.

(5)   An APPROACH to an object of inquiry is distinguished from other alternative approaches with regard to any number of the following aspects:

(a)   it pursues a distinctive aim with regard to the object;

(b)   it has a hard core of distinctive substantive assumptions about the object of inquiry;

(c)   it has a distinctive set of metascientific criteria for the significance of problems, the acceptability of solutions, the adequacy of descriptions and explanations, the strength of justifications and the weight of criticism;

(d)   it (often) has a distinctive (symbolic) language for the formulation of hypotheses and theories;

(e)   it has a distinctive long-term strategy of inquiry in terms of which it pursues the aim of (a).

As it is used here, "approach" is a neutral term denoting more or less what is common to the disciplinary matrices of Thomas Kuhn (1974: 462–463) and the scientific research programmes of Imre Lakatos (1970:133ff.). Kuhn's disciplinary matrices represent only one component of what he previously called "paradigms". It is not necessary for us to linger on the details of the differences between disciplinary matrices and research programmes, on the one hand, or between disciplinary matrices and paradigms on the other hand.

Theories that arise from the same approach are related in terms of the aspects (5)(a)–(d). They share a common distinctive aim, and common fundamental substantive assumptions and metascientific aspects. In addition, they are the products of the long-term strategy of inquiry of (5)(e). From a temporal point of view such theories may be related in two ways. On the one hand, they may form a series, $T_1, T_2, \ldots, T_n$, in time so that T_2 is an improved version of T_1, etc. On the other hand, they may exist at the same point in time as alternatives that do not differ fundamentally with regard to the aspects (5)(a)–(d).

An example may serve to clarify this point. Chomsky's lexicalist hypothesis, as the name indicates, is an example of an individual (grammatical) hypothesis. A specific grammar of English which includes this hypothesis is an example of an individual (grammatical) theory. Chomskyan transformational generative grammar is an example of a distinct approach (to the study of language in general and to the individual languages). As an approach, Chomskyan transformational generative grammar is realized as various related general linguistic theories and various (alternative) grammars for individual human languages.

11.2.2   Types of Reaction

The criticism levelled at scientific hypotheses and theories is fallible. In other words, a particular point of criticism brought against a hypothesis H or a theory T cannot be regarded as appropriate merely because it is offered as "criticism". Some points of criticism, factual and/or systematic, levelled at a hypothesis or a theory may be inappropriate, irrelevant or inaccurate. Such criticism, of course, does not reveal true defects of H or T. Other points of criticism levelled at H or T may be appropriate, relevant and accurate. Such criticism reveals true defects of H or T. In accordance with his judgment about whether or not a given point of criticism brought against his hypothesis or theory is appropriate, a scientist may choose one or more of seven fundamental types of reaction to the criticism.

(6) (a)   Indifference: the scientist implicitly or explicitly rejects the criticism brought against H or T as inappropriate.

(b)   Reasoned apathy: the scientist takes no direct steps to remedy the defect(s) of H or T, but provisionally retains H or T in an unrevised form.

(c)   Countercriticism: the scientist takes neither direct nor indirect

steps to remedy the defect(s) of H or T, but in turn criticizes
alternatives that have been proposed for H or T.

(d)   Protection: the scientist takes steps to protect H or T from the
criticism without eliminating its defect(s) in any direct way.

(e)   Modification: the scientist revises H or T in such a way that the
defect(s) is/are eliminated while the essence of H or T is retained.

(f)   Replacement: the scientist replaces H or T with an alternative
which differs from it in important respects.

(g)   Revolution: the scientist abandons the approach of which H or T
is the product in favour of another more promising approach.

One of the respects in which the various types of reaction differ concerns the
question of how drastic an effect each type of reaction has. Judged intuitively,
each type of reaction in (6) is more drastic than the preceding one.

Each of these types of reaction may be considered from various points of
view: that of the circumstances in which it is an appropriate type of reaction,
that of the logical mechanisms by which the reaction is expressed and that of
its implications for continued inquiry and the growth of scientific knowledge.
In the philosophical literature, various alternative theories about the growth of
scientific knowledge are proposed in which these types of reaction are considered
from the points of view just mentioned. These theories are interesting but highly
speculative. For this reason a discussion of their content, merits and defects falls
outside the scope of our study. The contributions of Paul Feyerabend (1970),
Thomas Kuhn (1970a; 1970b), Imre Lakatos (1970), Karl Popper (1970) and
Stephen Toulmin (1970) to the volume *Criticism and the growth of knowledge*
give a fair impression of the content of and problems attendant upon these
theories about the growth of scientific knowledge. We can do little more than
indicate how generative grammarians (have) use(d) the various types of reaction
of (6)(a)–(g). It is possible in principle to choose any of the seven types of reaction in both grammatical and general linguistic inquiry. However, to keep our
discussion within reasonable limits we shall consider the first six types of reaction in the context of grammatical inquiry and the seventh in the context of
general linguistic inquiry.

11.3   GRAMMATICAL INQUIRY

11.3.1   Nature and Types of Reaction to Criticism

11.3.1.1   *Indifference*

As a type of reaction to the criticism of a grammatical hypothesis or theory,
INDIFFERENCE implies rejecting the criticism as inappropriate, irrelevant or

inaccurate. Such criticism leaves the grammarian "indifferent" because it does not reveal a true defect or defects of the hypothesis or theory in question. The grammarian who rejects the criticism simply upholds the criticized hypothesis or theory in an unrevised form.

Normally, however, criticism of grammatical hypotheses cannot be merely rejected. The grammarian has to give reasons for his rejection. In other words, he has to give reasons for regarding the criticism as inappropriate, irrelevant or inaccurate. There are various possible reasons for rejecting criticism of grammatical hypotheses.

(7) (a)   The criticism is based on a misconception and/or a misrepresentation of the content of the criticized grammatical hypothesis.

(b)   The criticism is based on factual data that are qualitatively irrelevant: data about objects or phenomena which are not related to the linguistic competence in any specifiable way.

(c)   The criticism is based on inaccurate data: incorrect intuitive judgments or grammatical hypotheses.

(d)   The criticism is based on an inaccurate view of the aim of a generative grammar.

(e)   The criticism is based on an inappropriate acceptability standard or on a wrong application of an appropriate one.

(f)   The criticism is nonobjective in the sense of §10.2.1.4.

(g)   The criticism is presented in terms of logically incoherent statements which are therefore logically irrelevant to the criticized hypothesis.

(h)   The criticism is presented in terms of obscure formulations.

Within the narrow confines of our study it is impossible to illustrate each of these reasons for the rejection of criticism of a grammatical hypothesis by means of an example. Their content is, fortunately, reasonably clear. However, it may be interesting to look at one example which illustrates the first reason within the framework of the grammatical study of nominalization in English.

This example involves a point of criticism that Chomsky raises against the transformationalist hypothesis: the transformationalist hypothesis does not account for the fact that derived nominals have the internal structure of NPs. McCawley (1973:7–8) rejects this criticism on the strength of (7)(a) above. McCawley justifies his rejection of the criticism by pointing out that Chomsky misrepresents the content of the transformationalist hypothesis. According to McCawley, Chomsky's use of expressions such as "the transformationalist hypothesis/position/treatment" suggests that there is only *one* transformationalist hypothesis. In fact, there are several variants of the transformationalist hypothesis. According to McCawley (1973:7), at least one of these variants implies that derived nominals do indeed have an NP-like deep structure:

. . . a deep structure in which the sentence to be nominalized is part of a 'full'

NP, say, a relative clause modifying an 'abstract' head noun, which may be accompanied by any of the other matter that can appear in the deep structure of NP.

According to McCawley, the NP properties of derived nominals can be accounted for in terms of this variant of the transformationalist hypothesis. However, Chomsky does not accurately represent the content of this variant of the transformationalist hypothesis. For this reason McCawley rejects Chomsky's criticism on this particular point.

The foregoing is an example of a reasoned rejection of criticism levelled at a grammatical hypothesis. In certain circumstances such criticism is rejected with no reasons given. This happens when the criticism is so obviously inaccurate or irrelevant that any trained grammarian will recognize it as such. If the criticism is so irrelevant or inaccurate as to border on the ridiculous, it is not even explicitly rejected. It is usually merely ignored without comment.

11.3.1.2 *Reasoned Apathy*

Suppose now that a grammarian were to judge that a particular point of criticism levelled at one or more of his grammatical hypotheses is probably appropriate. The least drastic type of reaction to probably appropriate criticism of a grammatical hypothesis or theory is that of REASONED APATHY. This implies that the grammarian consciously takes no steps to remedy the defect(s) of the criticized hypothesis or theory. If the criticism takes the form of counterexamples, these are accorded the status of anomalies. An ANOMALY is a state of affairs, object, phenomenon, event, etc. of which the nature or properties are inconsistent with an internally consistent set of hypotheses, ideas, views or facts. An anomaly can never exist in an absolute sense, a fact which is stressed by Willard Humphreys in his book *Anomalies and scientific theories* (1968:81ff.). Anomalies always exist relative to some or other system of (potential) knowledge.

Let us consider an instance in which Chomsky reacts by adopting an attitude of reasoned apathy to possible factual criticism of the lexicalist hypothesis. Chomsky's reaction (1972b:58–59) stems from the negative reflection that the existence of mixed nominals could cast on the lexicalist hypothesis.

(8) The discussion so far has been restricted to gerundive and derived nominals, and has barely touched on a third category with some peculiar properties, namely, nominals of the sort illustrated in [56]:
[56] a. *John's refusing of the offer*
  b. *John's proving of the theorem*
  c. *the growing of tomatoes*
These forms are curious in a number of respects, and it is not at all clear whether the lexicalist hypothesis can be extended to cover them. That

it should be so extended is suggested by the fact that these forms, like derived nominals, appear to have the internal structure of noun phrases; thus the possessive subject can be replaced by a determiner, as in [56c]. On the other hand, adjective insertion seems quite unnatural in this construction. In fact, there is an artificiality to the whole construction that makes it quite resistant to systematic investigation. Furthermore, the construction is quite limited. Thus we cannot have *the feeling sad, the trying to win, the arguing about money, the leaving,* etc.

Chomsky proceeds to discuss specific problems which the mixed nominal *the growing of tomatoes* presents for the lexicalist hypothesis. However, he offers no suggestion as to how the lexicalist hypothesis may be extended to cover the class of mixed nominals as well.

This example serves to illuminate a number of properties of reasoned apathy as a type of reaction to criticism of grammatical hypotheses. Firstly, it is fairly clear that reasoned apathy is not a form of indifference. The grammarian does not indicate by his reasoned apathy that no difficulties exist with regard to the criticized hypothesis. Secondly, it appears that this type of reaction is not inherently unreasonable. It can be justified on the strength of various considerations. A first consideration is that the criticized hypothesis – the lexicalist hypothesis in this case – is an interesting, general hypothesis for which there is a reasonable measure of justification. A second consideration is that the criticism is based on properties of "artificial" phenomena – such as mixed nominals – i.e. phenomena that are not well understood. A third consideration is that the phenomena in question are quite limited in number.

It would indeed be unreasonable to modify or to abandon an interesting, general, reasonably well-justified hypothesis on the strength of data about a limited number of phenomena that are poorly understood. The fact that the phenomena are poorly understood makes it difficult to know what steps to take to improve or substitute the defective hypothesis. It is much more reasonable to accord the problematic phenomena the provisional status of anomalies. Kuhn (1967:80ff., 145) quotes interesting examples from the history of empirical inquiry which show that it is quite normal for anomalies to exist within the framework of general hypotheses and theories. It is also quite common for these anomalies to "resolve" themselves, so to speak, as further progress is made with the inquiry. However, it is obvious that a hypothesis or theory containing anomalies must be abandoned if an alternative is proposed within which these anomalies no longer exist. The latter hypothesis or theory may of course not have serious flaws that the former does not have.

11.3.1.3   *Countercriticism*

As a third type of reaction to criticism of a grammatical hypothesis, COUNTER-CRITICISM is related to reasoned apathy in at least two senses. Firstly, as in the case of reasoned apathy, the grammarian concedes that the criticism is probably appropriate. Secondly, as in the case of reasoned apathy, the grammarian does not take immediate steps to remedy the identified defect(s) of the grammatical hypothesis. Instead, he takes it upon himself to criticize the alternatives which have been proposed for the criticized grammatical hypothesis. The purpose of countercriticism is to show that these alternatives have essentially the same, or even more serious (kinds of) defects than the criticized hypothesis. He then argues that, for the present, there is no good reason why he should abandon his defective hypothesis in favour of one of the alternatives.

An example may elucidate this point. McCawley (1973:5) concedes that the transformationalist hypothesis wrongly predicts that the derived nominals *John's easiness/ease to please, John's certainty to win the prize, John's amusement of the children with his stories* will be grammatical. He thereby admits that a point of factual criticism brought against the transformationalist hypothesis by Chomsky is probably appropriate. McCawley then goes one step further by levelling countercriticism at the lexicalist hypothesis. He points out that, in its essential form, the lexicalist hypothesis also makes inaccurate predictions. For instance, it wrongly predicts that the derived nominal *John's eagerness to please* will be ungrammatical. The gist of McCawley's argument is presented in (9).

(9) The facts thus appear to conflict with both hypotheses: the lexicalist hypothesis implies that all nominalizations of structures derived by cyclic rules are ungrammatical; the transformationalist hypothesis implies that they are all grammatical; but in reality some of them are grammatical and some ungrammatical.

McCawley hereby implies that, in their essential form, the hypotheses in question suffer from the same kind of defect. In his view, therefore, the transformationalist hypothesis need not be abandoned in favour of the lexicalist hypothesis.

Countercriticism is an appropriate type of reaction if a domain of problematic phenomena is poorly understood and if it is not obvious what should be done to remedy the defect(s) of the criticized grammatical hypothesis/es. In the circumstances it would be unwise to make a "final" choice between alternative hypotheses. It is far wiser to try and delimit as sharply as possible the defects of the alternative hypotheses. However, countercriticism should not be used as a means of deception. For instance, it would be deceptive to detract attention from the fundamental defects of a hypothesis A by using countercriticism as a means of presenting trivial flaws in an alternative hypothesis B as serious defects.

11.3.1.4 *Protection*

The fourth type of reaction, protection, is more drastic than the first three.

PROTECTION implies that the grammarian tries to defend the criticized hypothesis or theory without effecting any internal changes. Thus, this type of reaction is also aimed at retaining the criticized grammatical hypothesis, but retaining
it by taking certain steps. These steps involve the formulation of auxiliary hypotheses which protect the defective hypothesis or theory from the criticism. If the
criticism is factual, the auxiliary hypotheses serve to make the criticized hypothesis or theory consistent with the linguistic data that were initially counterexamples. By using a large number of auxiliary hypotheses in this way, a
PROTECTIVE BELT, to use Imre Lakatos's terminology (1970:133), is drawn
around the defective hypothesis or theory. According to Lakatos, it is quite
normal for scientists to surround their most general and fundamental hypotheses
with such a protective belt. This use of auxiliary hypotheses may be either
objectionable or acceptable. Let us consider two examples from Chomsky's
"Remarks on nominalization" which illustrate this point.

11.3.1.4.1   *Ad hoc (auxiliary) hypotheses*

In (1) of §10.1 the intuitive judgment of (some) speakers of English, that the
derived nominal *his criticism of the book before he read it* is acceptable, was
presented as a point of factual criticism that may be brought against the lexicalist hypothesis. This derived nominal includes a structural element of a VP in
the form of the *before* clause. In terms of the lexicalist hypothesis, this is
impossible, as the hypothesis specifies that derived nominals have the internal
structure of NPs. The judgment of (some) speakers of English, that the derived
nominal *his criticism of the book because of its failure to go deeply into the
matter* is acceptable, likewise reflects negatively on the lexicalist hypothesis.

Let us consider Chomsky's reaction (1972b:27–28) to the criticism in question.

(10)   "The examples [15] (= *his criticizing the book before he read it
(because of its failure to go deeply into the matter, etc.)*) and [16]
(= *his criticism of the book before he read it (because of its failure
to go deeply into the matter, etc.*) raise interesting questions relating
to the matter of acceptability and grammaticalness. If the lexicalist
hypothesis is correct, then all dialects of English that share the analysis
of adjuncts presupposed above should distinguish the expressions of
[15], as directly generated by the grammar, from those of [16], as not
directly generated by the grammar. Suppose that we discover, however,
that some speakers find the expressions of [16] quite acceptable. On
the lexicalist hypothesis, these sentences can only be derivatively
generated. Therefore we should have to conclude that their acceptability to these speakers results from a failure to take note of a certain
distinction of grammaticalness. We might propose that the expressions
of [16] are formed by analogy to the gerundive nominals [15], say by
a rule that converts X-*ing* to the noun X *nom* (where *nom* is the

element that determines the morphological form of the derived
nominal) in certain cases."

In his reaction Chomsky takes certain steps to protect the lexicalist hypothesis
from the potentially disconfirming acceptability judgments. But what do these
protective measures involve?

Chomsky's protective measures involve his making at least four assumptions.

(11)(a)   Speakers generally have the ability to take note of properties of an
           underlying mental capacity, an internalized grammar (which is the
           level at which the aforementioned distinction of grammaticalness
           exists).

   (b)   Those speakers of English who find [16] acceptable have failed to
           take note of the distinction in question.

   (c)   Human language in general includes rules of analogy as a structural
           element.

   (d)   English has a rule of analogy which converts X-ing to X *nom* in cer-
           tain cases.

The assumptions (11)(a)–(d) form part of the protective belt drawn around the
lexicalist hypothesis. The question we have to ask ourselves is whether Chomsky's
protection of the lexicalist hypothesis is acceptable or objectionable.

In the article " 'The theory comparison method' vs. 'the theory exposition
method' in linguistic inquiry" (Botha 1976b: §3.4), Chomsky's full reaction to
the criticism in question is analyzed and his protective measures are found to be
objectionable. The essence of the objection to these measures is that the assumptions (11)(a)–(d) represent *ad hoc* (AUXILIARY) HYPOTHESES in the context of
Chomsky's *Remarks* article. This has two implications. On the one hand, no independent motivation is offered for the hypotheses in question in this article. On the
other hand, it is not indicated in the article what the test implications of the
hypotheses are on the basis of which they could be refuted. The hypotheses in
question – of which (11)(a) and (c) are general linguistic and (11)(b) and (d) are
grammatical hypotheses – are therefore merely protective devices in the sense of
§10.3.3.2.1.3 and do not contribute to the discovery of new facts about language
in general or about English in particular. From the point of view of the growth
of linguistic knowledge, the use of *ad hoc* hypotheses such as those of (11) results
in a "degenerating problemshift" in the terminology of Imre Lakatos (1970:118).
A DEGENERATING PROBLEMSHIFT is a problemshift which does not give rise to
further inquiry in which new discoveries may be made.

11.3.1.4.2   *Non-ad hoc auxiliary hypotheses*

It follows from the discussion above that the use of auxiliary hypotheses to
protect a criticized hypothesis or theory may, in certain circumstances, be
acceptable. Such circumstances exist if there is independent motivation for the

protective auxiliary hypotheses and if it is possible to derive refutable test implications from the protective auxiliary hypotheses. Non-*ad hoc* auxiliary hypotheses lead to a PROGRESSIVE PROBLEMSHIFT. The inquiry resulting from such a problemshift may give rise to significant new discoveries.

We have in fact looked at an example of the protection of a grammatical hypothesis by means of a non-*ad hoc* auxiliary hypothesis, viz. Chomsky's reaction presented as (2) in §11.1. In his reaction, Chomsky takes certain steps to protect the lexicalist hypothesis from the criticism that it precludes the possibility of giving a descriptively adequate account of the relatedness of an active nominal such as *the enemy's destruction of the city* and a passive nominal such as *the city's destruction by the enemy*. The gist of Chomsky's reaction involves the making of two assumptions.

(12)(a)   Cyclic transformations may apply in the domain of NP as well as that of S.

(b)   The passive transformation in English applies over the domain of NP as well as that of S.

Chomsky's proposed replacement of the passive transformation with two separate transformations, NP Preposing and Agent Postposing, is one of the consequences of the assumption (12)(b). We need not go into the details of this replacement.

What is important is that the protective general linguistic hypothesis (12)(a) and the grammatical hypothesis (12)(b) are apparently not *ad hoc*. Work such as that of Jackendoff (1974a) on the X̄-convention indicates that there is independent motivation for the former hypothesis. Jackendoff finds that, apart from the passive transformation, various other cyclic transformations and interpretation rules of English may be applied in the domain of both NP and S. Among these rules are Equi, Reflexivization, X̄-Gapping and X̄-Deletion.

John Bowers (1975:531ff.) finds that the domain of cyclic transformations — such as that of the rule which moves the S in a relative clause to the right of the head N in the surface structure — may even be extended to AP. In other words, he finds that the general linguistic hypothesis (12)(a) may be formulated in even more general terms.

With regard to the non-*ad hoc* nature of the grammatical hypothesis (12)(b), both Chomsky (1972b:39ff.) and Jackendoff (1974a:27ff.) argue that data exist that are unrelated to the data about the relatedness of active and passive nominals and that support this grammatical hypothesis. These data indicate that (the components of) the generalized passive transformation also apply in nonderived NPs. For this reason, the grammatical auxiliary hypothesis (12)(b) can be regarded as non-*ad hoc* as well. Chomsky's protective auxiliary hypotheses (12)(a) and (b) have therefore resulted in a progressive problemshift. These hypotheses gave rise to new general linguistic and grammatical discoveries and are therefore not merely protective devices in the sense of §10.3.3.2.1.3. This clearly shows that the protection of a criticized grammatical hypothesis need not necessarily be objectionable.

11.3.1.5   *Modification*

The aim of reasoned apathy, countercriticism and protection is to retain a criticized grammatical hypothesis or theory in an unrevised form. The fifth type of reaction, MODIFICATION, is directed at the criticized grammatical hypothesis or theory itself. To modify a criticized grammatical hypothesis or theory involves reformulating it in such a way that its defect(s) is/are eliminated while the non-problematic core is retained. A widely used method by means of which a grammatical hypothesis or theory may be modified is to formulate it in less general terms. In other words, the domain of the hypothesis or theory is restricted by, for instance, excluding the data on the strength of which it is criticized from this domain. However, the exclusion should not be effected in an arbitrary way. An example will serve to illustrate this point.

Many transformational rules in the grammar of English represent grammatical hypotheses that have been modified as indicated. Recall that gerundive nominals such as (13)(a)–(c) are transformationally derived from the structures underlying the sentences (14)(a)–(c).

(13)(a)   *John's being easy (difficult) to please*
     (b)   *John's being certain (likely) to win the prize*
     (c)   *John's amusing (interesting) the children with his stories*

(14)(a)   *John is easy (difficult) to please.*
     (b)   *John is certain (likely) to win the prize.*
     (c)   *John amused (interested) the children with his stories.*

However, in its most general formulation, the transformation of gerundive nominalization generates a number of unacceptable gerundive nominals. Chomsky (1972b:18, n.8) cites the following examples:

(15)(a)   **that John was here's surprising me*
     (b)   **its surprising me that John was here*
     (c)   **John's happening to be a good friend of mine*

The unacceptability of the gerundive nominals of (15) may serve as a basis for factual criticism of the most general formulation of the transformation of gerundive nominalization.

Generative grammarians such as Chomsky react to such criticism by placing restrictions on the transformation in question. Let us consider two of these restrictions.

(16)(a) The transformation does not apply if, as in the case of **that John was there's surprising me*, the subject is too complex to permit possessives.

(b) The transformation does not apply in the case of verbs which involve extraposition as in **its surprising me that John was here* and **John's happening to be a good friend of mine*.

To impose these two restrictions on the transformation in question is to modify the grammatical hypothesis which expresses it in a nonessential way.

Note that the modification is by no means effected in an arbitrary way. On the contrary, the domain of the grammatical hypothesis in question is limited in a principled manner by indicating that the counterexamples for the most general form of the hypothesis belong to two or more well-defined grammatical classes: in this case, the class of subjects that are too complex to permit possess-ives and the class of verbs that involve extraposition. The strategy employed involves the following: a given counterexample is excluded from the domain of the hypothesis by correlating an independent grammatical property with this counterexample. The strategy further entails that the modifications made to the hypothesis in question give rise to certain predictions. Let us consider two of these predictions.

(17)(a) A sentence of which the subject is too complex to permit possess-ives will have no corresponding gerundive nominal.

(b) A sentence of which the verb involves extraposition will have no corresponding gerundive nominal.

Modifications of grammatical hypotheses that give rise to refutable test implica-tions are unobjectionable.

By contrast, modifications that cannot in principle have such empirical con-sequences are by nature arbitrary and hence objectionable. This point may be illustrated with reference to the transformation of derivative nominalization. This transformation, in its most general form, produces many unacceptable derived nominals.

(18)(a) **the easiness to please John* (derived from the structure underlying *It is easy to please John*)

(b) **John's amusement of the children with his stories* (derived from the structure underlying *John amused the children with his stories*)

(c) **John's easiness to please* (derived from the structure underlying *John is easy to please*)

(d) **John's certainty to win the prize* (derived from the structure underlying *John is certain to win the prize*)

It is impossible to exclude all the derived nominals that are counterexamples for the transformation of derivative nominalization from the domain of the rule in a principled manner. If a grammarian wanted to retain this rule, he would have to specify the derived nominals in question as an unordered list of exceptions to the rule. This manner of modification has no refutable test implications and is therefore objectionable.

11.3.1.6 *Replacement*

The criticism brought against a grammatical hypothesis or theory may be so fundamental that neither reasoned apathy, nor protection, nor modification represents an adequate reaction. If this is the case, generative grammarians are forced to choose a sixth type of reaction, viz. replacement. REPLACEMENT involves abandoning the criticized hypothesis or theory in favour of an alternative in which not even the essence of the original is retained. Chomsky's choice of the lexicalist hypothesis as opposed to the transformationalist hypothesis is in fact an instance of this sixth type of reaction. On the strength of the criticism which we considered in §1.4, Chomsky replaces the transformationalist hypothesis, (19)(a), with the lexicalist hypothesis, (19)(b), in the grammar of English.

(19)(a) Derived nominals are transforms of underlying sentence-like structures.

  (b) Derived nominals are deep structure NPs.

In the formalized grammar this replacement entails the substitution of a transformation of derivative nominalization with changed base rules and associated neutral lexical entries.

It is clear from this example that replacement is a much more drastic type of reaction than modification. In the first place, not a single element of the content of the transformationalist hypothesis survives the replacement in the grammar. In the second place, the replacement in question has important consequences for the content of both the grammar and the general linguistic theory. On the one hand, the replacement entails the inclusion of, among other things, the hypotheses (75) of §9.3.2.3.2 in the grammar of English. On the other hand, the replacement requires the inclusion of, among others, the hypotheses (76) of §9.3.2.3.2 in the general linguistic theory.

The replacement of one grammatical hypothesis with another need not have the general linguistic implications described above. For instance, the passive transformation could be replaced with extended base rules in the grammar of English. The fact that in this case passive sentences would be generated as base structures and not as transforms would not necessarily require a change in the content of the general linguistic theory.

In his article "Consolations for the specialist" (1970:219ff.), Paul Feyerabend makes it clear that the replacement of one hypothesis or theory with another often has advantages as well as disadvantages. Schematically this point may be illustrated as follows:

(20)

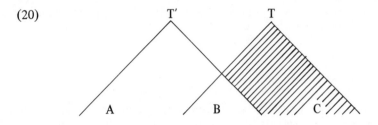

In (20) T represents the old, criticized theory and T' the new, substituting theory. B represents the domain of reality in which both T and T' are successful. A represents the domain in which T fails but T' is successful. A, then, represents what is to be gained by replacing T with T'. C represents the domain in which T was successful, but in which T' does not achieve success, in other words, the loss entailed by the replacement. To establish whether, by replacing T with T', any progress is made, the gain involved should be set off against the loss. The replacement of one hypothesis or theory with another often represents progress that may be described as taking three steps forward and one step back.

This last point may be illustrated with reference to Chomsky's replacement of the transformationalist hypothesis with the lexicalist hypothesis. What is gained by the replacement is, among other things, the fact that the lexicalist hypothesis can account for the internal structure, semantic irregularity and syntactic irregularity of derived nominals in a more illuminating way than the transformationalist hypothesis. However, McCawley points out that the replacement also entails certain losses. According to McCawley (1973:9), one of the disadvantages of the replacement is that the transformationalist, but not the lexicalist, hypothesis can serve as a basis for the explanation of the absence of a subject NP in agent nominalizations and for the absence of an object NP in object nominalizations. For instance, the transformationalist hypothesis, but not the lexicalist hypothesis, can serve as a basis for the explanation of the unacceptability of the agent nominalization *the inventor of dynamite by Nobel* and of the object nominalization *Newton's writings of treatises on theology.* For details of the content of this explanation, the aforementioned paragraph in McCawley's article may be studied. The important point is this: replacement of a criticized grammatical hypothesis with an alternative rarely represents only a gain.

11.3.2   Reacting to Criticism

This brings us to the question (4)(b) about the intellectual activities involved in reacting to criticism. In view of our discussion of the various types of reaction we can now give a general characterization of these activities.

(21) To react to the factual or systematic criticism brought against a grammatical hypothesis involves

  (a) remaining indifferent, i.e. rejecting the criticism by giving reasons why it is inappropriate, irrelevant or inaccurate; or

  (b) adopting an attitude of reasoned apathy, i.e. initially taking no steps to accommodate the criticism *and* giving reasons why this reaction should enjoy preference; or

  (c) initially retaining the hypothesis in an unrevised form, after having shown by means of countercriticism that the alternatives have the same or even more serious (kinds of) defects; or

  (d) protecting the hypothesis by means of non-*ad hoc* auxiliary hypotheses, in such a way that a progressive problemshift occurs; or

  (e) modifying nonessential aspects of the content of the hypothesis, for instance, by restricting its domain in a nonarbitrary way; or

  (f) replacing the hypothesis with an alternative, in such a way that the gain entailed by the replacement outweighs the loss.

Notice that the activities (21)(d)–(f) involve asserting new claims about the object of inquiry. Each of these new claims must in turn be justified and criticized. In other words, the grammarian choosing to react in one of the ways described in (21)(d)–(f) once again activates the EMPIRICAL CYCLE. A methodologist such as De Groot (1961:29ff.) regards the empirical cycle as a constant repetition of the acts of observation, induction, deduction, testing and evaluation. "Induction" is used in the sense of "the forming of hypotheses/theories".

11.4   GENERAL LINGUISTIC INQUIRY

11.4.1   General

Generative grammarians resort to all seven types of reaction described in (6) to accommodate criticism levelled at general linguistic hypotheses. The seventh type of reaction, revolution, will be discussed in detail in §11.4.2. Four of the remaining six types of reaction are each illustrated by an example.

Linguistic universals represent hypotheses of considerable generality and fundamentality. For this reason nondrastic types of reaction such as indifference, reasoned apathy and countercriticism are often chosen in reacting to criticism of universals. A single counterexample will generally not induce generative grammarians to protect, modify or replace a universal. Consider, for instance, Chomsky's autonomy thesis. The autonomy thesis is a general linguistic hypothesis which specifies, among other things, that transformational rules apply "blindly" to phrase markers of the appropriate form. This implies that transformational rules apply to phrase markers without taking into account the meaning and grammatical relations associated with them. McCawley (1973:88) points out two counterexamples for the autonomy thesis: in the grammar of English the Passive and Tag-formation transformations are not blind in this sense. Chomsky's reaction to these counterexamples appears to be that of reasoned apathy. The autonomy thesis is such a general and fundamental general linguistic hypothesis that one or two counterexamples are apparently considered to be too weak to affect the hypothesis in any way.

In §10.4.2.1.3 we saw how the fourth form of reaction, protection, may be used to accommodate criticism of general linguistic hypotheses. It appeared that it is possible to interpret a linguistic universal for which counterexamples exist in a relative way. Such a relative interpretation makes it possible to interpret the criticism brought against the universal as a less highly valued aspect of the language in the grammar of which the universal in question plays no role. Consider, for instance, the linguistic universal known as the "phonological cycle". In informal terms, this universal – which represents a mode of rule application – expresses two fundamental assumptions.

(22)(a)   The phonetic form of a complex linguistic unit is determined by the inherent properties of its elements and by the way in which these elements are combined.

(b)   The same phonological rules apply repeatedly to linguistic units of ever increasing complexity.

It seems probable that certain languages – agglutinative languages – do not make use of the phonological cycle. However, this does not force Chomsky and Halle (1958:25, n.12) to modify or abandon this principle. They opt for regarding those languages that do not adopt this principle as less highly valued in this respect. The hypothesis that the languages in question are less highly valued represents an auxiliary hypothesis with a protective function. If this auxiliary hypothesis can be justified on independent grounds, its use is unobjectionable. Examples of such independent grounds were given in §10.4.3.2. However, if it proves to be impossible to find independent evidence for the auxiliary hypothesis in question, it acquires the status of an *ad hoc* auxiliary hypothesis.

The literature on generative grammar abounds with examples of cases in which grammarians resort to the fifth type of reaction, modification, to accommodate criticism levelled at general linguistic hypotheses. Several examples of such modifications are given in chapter 9, "Revisions in transformational theory", of Emmon Bach's *Syntactic theory*. A simple example has to do with the general linguistic hypothesis that the terms in the structural description of a transformational rule must be finite in number. Bach (1974a:217) shows how the existence of transformations such as Gapping has forced generative grammarians to modify this general linguistic hypothesis. Gapping is an instance of a rule that is best stated in terms of an indefinite number of terms. We have also in fact considered a second example of the modification of a general linguistic hypothesis. The hypothesis in question is the one in terms of which cyclic transformations are applicable in the domain of S. Chomsky modified this hypothesis to the effect that these transformations may apply in the domain of both NP and S.

Of the sixth possible type of reaction to criticism of general linguistic hypotheses many examples are, likewise, to be found in the literature. In other words, it is fairly common for general linguistic hypotheses or larger fragments of the general linguistic theory to be replaced with more adequate alternatives. One striking example will serve to illustrate this point, viz. Chomsky's replacement of the standard theory with his extended standard theory. The fundamental difference between these two theories lies in their treatment of the relationship between syntax and semantics. The general linguistic hypothesis (23) represents the view expressed in the standard theory.

(23) The syntactic deep structure of a sentence fully determines its semantic interpretation.

In a more recent version of Chomsky's general linguistic theory (1975c:103ff.), i.e. the extended standard theory which includes the trace theory, this hypothesis is replaced with the following hypothesis:

(24) The syntactic surface structure of a sentence fully determines its semantic interpretation (where "semantic interpretation" is understood in the restricted sense of 'logical form').

The replacement of (23) with (24) represents a nontrivial modification of the general linguistic theory. It is a drastic revision which affects not only the syntactic (sub)theory but other components of the general linguistic theory, such as the semantic (sub)theory, as well. Moreover, this replacement necessarily has drastic consequences for the content and organization of the particular grammars constructed within the framework of the Chomskyan linguistic theory. However, the replacement does not entail a drastic revision or rejection of generative grammar as an *approach* to the scientific study of language.

11.4.2 Revolution

In his study *The structure of scientific revolutions* (1967), Thomas Kuhn shows that the growth of scientific knowledge is not always a gradual evolutionary or cumulative process. He points out that this growth may take the form of a scientific revolution. He (1967:91) regards scientific revolutions as "non-cumulative developmental episodes in which an older paradigm is replaced in whole or in part by an incompatible new one". In our terminology, then, a scientific revolution is the replacement of one approach by another. The seventh type of reaction to criticism of a general linguistic theory is that of REVOLUTION, i.e. the replacement of the approach to which the linguistic theory owes its existence by an alternative approach. This is the most drastic type of reaction to criticism levelled at a general linguistic theory.

11.4.2.1   *The Chomskyan Revolution*

It is the conventional view that generative grammar as an approach to the scientific study of language was born in a revolutionary way. In their article "The fall and rise of empiricism" (1974:1), Katz and Bever formulate this view as follows:

> The transformationalist revolution in Linguistics fits Thomas Kuhn's account of scientific revolutions. There was a prevailing (structuralist) paradigm, taxonomic grammar, in which grammatical analysis consists of segmentation and classification of actual speech into a form resembling a library catalogue. This paradigm failed to provide an adequate framework for explaining such phenomena as syntactic ambiguity, grammatical relations, ellipsis, agreement, stress, constituent equivalences, etc. The revolution that overthrew structuralism replaced it with the new paradigm of generative grammar, in which grammatical analysis is conceived of as the constructing and testing of theories about the speaker's internalized linguistic competence. In this paradigm, the grammatical analysis of a language is represented as a typical case in science of inference from behaviour to a theory about the unobservable system responsible for it.

The "transformationalist" or CHOMSKYAN REVOLUTION, therefore, consisted in the replacement of the taxonomic approach with the generative approach. The factor that triggered this revolutionary reaction was the criticism levelled at the neo-Bloomfieldian taxonomic approach. It will be impossible here to give a (critical) account of the comprehensive literature on the Chomskyan revolution. We are, in any case, not particularly interested in the finer details of this revolution. We want to focus on the nature of revolution as a type of reaction to criticism of linguistic theories. In other words, we want to determine, at a general level, the contributory circumstances that triggered the revolution, its general content and the most important kinds of consequences of the revolution.

11.4.2.1.1   *Contributory circumstances*

The circumstances directly contributing to the Chomskyan revolution are indicated in the passage quoted from Katz and Bever's work above: the approach at which the revolution was aimed, had failed over a wide spectrum of linguistic phenomena. It was impossible, within this approach, to give adequate grammatical explanations for data about phenomena such as syntactic ambiguity, grammatical relations, ellipsis, agreement, stress, constituent equivalences, etc. The circumstances that contributed to the Chomskyan revolution could therefore be characterized as explanatory impotence. Within the framework of the taxonomic approach the number and variety of counterexamples, anomalies and "recalcitrant" data were rapidly increasing. Details of these counterexamples, anomalies and "recalcitrant" data are given in most introductions to the substantive aspect of generative grammar.

11.4.2.1.2   *General content*

The general content of the Chomskyan revolution becomes clear when the fundamental differences between the generative and taxonomic approaches are considered. These differences concern objects, objectives, idealizations, the form of linguistic theories, criteria of adequacy and methods.

Objects.   The object of study of a generative grammar is a mental capacity: the linguistic competence which represents the ability to produce and interpret an infinite number of sentences. By contrast, the object of study of a taxonomic grammar is a finite collection or corpus of concrete utterances of a particular language. A generative grammar, therefore, is mentalistic in its choice of object. A taxonomic grammar, with its object of concrete products of linguistic performance, is behavioristic.

Objectives.   The central objectives of a generative grammar are description and explanation: description of the underlying linguistic competence and explanation of problematic properties of sentences. By contrast, the ultimate objective of a taxonomic grammar is classification: the compilation of an inventory or catalogue of classes of which (the parts of) the utterances of the corpus are members.

Idealizations.   We have seen that a generative grammar idealizes its object. In accordance with this idealization, it studies only one of the factors affecting the grammaticality of sentences, viz. the grammatical factor. A taxonomic grammar makes no such idealizations, with the result that the classification of utterances takes into account every factor that systematically affects the properties of utterances in the corpus. Because it makes the aforementioned idealization, a generative grammar is rationalistic – as was shown in §7.4.6.3. A taxonomic grammar, by contrast, is empiricist on this point.

Form.   In order to realize its objectives, a generative grammar must take the form of a finite system of rules (and a finite lexicon). A taxonomic grammar, by contrast, takes the form of a system of classes of utterances. Consequently, a taxonomic grammar lacks the lawlike aspect which is typical of a generative grammar.

Criteria of adequacy.   The fundamental criterion for a generative grammar is that of descriptive adequacy. A generative grammar must give a *true* representation of the content and organization of the underlying linguistic competence. By contrast, the criteria of adequacy adopted for taxonomic grammars are not formulated in terms of a concept 'truth'. Such grammars are essentially means of organizing a corpus of utterances. As such they may be more or less adequate in terms of criteria of simplicity, elegance, internal consistency, usefulness, and so on. The simpler, more elegant, more useful, etc. the classification for which a taxonomic grammar provides, the better the grammar.

Method. Within the generative approach, the aim of the general linguistic theory is to give a description of a mental capacity: the language acquisition faculty. This description is given in terms of linguistic universals specifying essential properties of possible human languages. This description serves as a basis for the explanation of the problematic properties of the grammars of particular languages. Within the taxonomic approach, the general linguistic theory has a completely different aim. It is not the aim of the taxonomic linguistic theory to describe an underlying mental capacity or to specify a system of linguistic universals which characterize the content of the concept 'possible human language'. Rather, it is the aim of the taxonomic linguistic theory to specify a series of methods by means of which grammars may be constructed for corpora of utterances. In other words, the aim of the taxonomic linguistic theory is to develop a system of procedures for the discovery of adequate classifications of corpora of utterances. These methods, which must, as far as possible, be mechanically applicable, include means of identifying, segmenting and classifying the units of which utterances are composed. The generative linguistic theory, on the other hand, does not specify procedures for the discovery of generative grammars. Insofar as it does specify "methods", these "methods" are used in the evaluation of alternative grammars to determine which one of a number of alternative grammars is the most highly valued grammar for a particular language.

Much has been written about the differences between the generative and the taxonomic approach. We have merely indicated how fundamental these differences are. The Chomskyan revolution was not concerned with the modification or replacement of one or two substantive notions about language in general or about individual languages. It involved the replacement of an entire, unproductive approach to linguistic inquiry by a more productive approach.

11.4.2.1.3   *Types of consequences*

Because the Chomskyan revolution, as a type of reaction, was concerned with such fundamental points, it is understandable that it had drastic consequences. Let us consider three types of consequences.

Consequences for linguistic inquiry. The first and most important type of consequence resulting from the Chomskyan revolution concerns the nature of linguistic inquiry. The nature of linguistic inquiry, as a kind of intellectual enterprise, underwent radical changes in the Chomskyan revolution. The most important respects in which linguistic inquiry has changed were indicated above with reference to objects, objectives, idealizations, the form of linguistic theories, criteria of adequacy and methods. A by-product of the revolution was a new symbolic language for the formalization of grammatical theories. These changes in the nature of linguistic inquiry contributed dramatically to the growth of linguistic knowledge. Within the framework of generative grammar, linguists gained many new and revealing insights into the nature of human language and into individual languages.

At this point it must be stated that the Chomskyan revolution was in a certain sense not complete. The rift between the generative and taxonomic approaches was incomplete in a substantive respect: an appropriately adapted version of certain neo-Bloomfieldian notions about the structure of human language continued to exist (at least initially) as part of the generative approach. Let us consider five examples.

(25)(a) Sentences are the fundamental units of linguistic structure (and a grammar is by definition a sentence grammar).

(b) The syntactic structure of sentences may be described in terms of purely formal concepts, i.e. without making use of semantic concepts (= the autonomy thesis).

(c) One aspect of the syntactic structure is constituent structure, another aspect is lexical structure.

(d) Transformations play an important role in the representation of the syntactic structure of sentences.

(e) A grammar describes the syntactic and phonological aspect of sentences, but not their meaning or aspects of their use.

The first four general linguistic hypotheses above are still part of the Chomskyan approach, while the last one was abandoned by generative grammarians in the mid-sixties. The repeated occurrence of notions such as those of (25) cause them to exhibit one of the characteristics of Holton's themas. It is themas such as these that ensure that the growth of linguistic knowledge shows a certain degree of continuity. In §6.3.2.2 we saw how such themas are expressed in one of the three components of the content of theoretical linguistic concepts.

Consequences for linguists. The type of consequence of the Chomskyan revolution discussed above is strictly objective. In other words, it affects linguistic inquiry as a nonpersonal intellectual enterprise. However, these objective consequences also affect the people who practise linguistic inquiry and the groups to which they belong. Indirectly, then, the Chomskyan revolution had a second type of consequence: personal and socio-scientific consequences.

This second type of consequence particularly affected the members of the "old guard" of taxonomic grammarians. A first group of them saw the sense of the revolution and (critically) accepted the new approach. They simply continued working as generative grammarians.

A second group of taxonomic grammarians pretend to have seen the sense of the Chomskyan revolution and to be working as generative grammarians. In fact, however, they do not understand the principles of generative grammar at all. In practice, they are still making classifications. These classifications are then misleadingly presented in the *terminology* of generative grammar. Ray Dougherty (1972:15) calls such a classification a "generative catalogue". Such a catalogue is given generative overtones

> (1) by adding some discussion of universals, cognitive psychology, semantics, etc., (2) by naming rules but not presenting them – thereby giving the impression that the rules could be formulated, and (3) by using terms from generative theory to delineate the classifications – for example, instead of saying he is establishing 'substitution classes', the linguist contends he is specifying 'lexical entries'. Of course, he never presents rules to indicate how these 'lexical entries' wend their way into actual sentences.

A third group of taxonomic grammarians could not or would not make the change to generative grammar and do not pretend to have become generative grammarians either. After an initial, unsuccessful, attempt to resist the revolutionary Chomskyans, these taxonomic grammarians either "died" an academic death or retired into relative isolation, there to continue practising their taxonomic grammar. Their position is a striking illustration of the view of the celebrated physicist Max Planck – quoted by Holton (1973:384) – that

> an important scientific innovation rarely makes its way by gradually winning over and converting its opponents: it rarely happens that Saul becomes Paul. What does happen is that its opponents gradually die out, and that the growing generation is familiarized with the ideas from the beginning.

The taxonomic grammarians belonging to this third group, unlike those of the second group, do not produce misleading research results. But their continued taxonomic inquiry can only accidentally provide new insights into the nature of human language.

Consequences for related disciplines.   The third type of consequence of the Chomskyan revolution affects related disciplines such as psychology and philosophy. Psychology was affected in two major respects. On the one hand, generative grammarians developed a notion of human language which refuted one of the most general psychological theories of our time, viz. the behavioristic learning theory. Generative grammarians have shown human language to be so abstract and complex as not to be learnable in terms of the behavioristic processes of learning which involve habit formation and association, conditioning and reinforcement. The behavioristic learning theory is a fundamental part of the behaviorist psychology. The fact that generative grammar found this theory of learning to be inadequate casts serious doubts on the behaviorist psychology in general.

On the other hand, Chomsky's distinction between linguistic competence and linguistic performance has proved to be a powerful stimulus for the development of psycholinguistics. This distinction served as a basis for the development of linguistically grounded theories about the perception and production of utterances. In chapter 8 of his book *Chomsky* (1970), John Lyons presents a highly readable survey of the psychological consequences of the Chomskyan revolution.

In the field of philosophy, the Chomskyan revolution rekindled the long-standing dispute between rationalists and empiricists. This dispute concerns the nature of the human mind and, in particular, the origin of human knowledge. RATIONALISTS hold that man possesses knowledge which he could not have gained through experience and which, furthermore, determines the form of the knowledge that is acquired by experience. EMPIRICISTS, by contrast, claim that the human mind is a *tabula rasa* which contains no knowledge that is not derived from experience. Moreover, the human mind places no restrictions on the possible forms that knowledge may take, barring the fact that these forms originate by means of mechanisms such as the building up of habits and associations by relating stimulus and response. Chomsky's view of man's language acquisition faculty as a form of innate, genetically determined linguistic knowledge supports the rationalist point of view and radically opposes that of the empiricists. More particulars of the philosophical implications of the Chomskyan revolution are given in a condensed form by Lyons in chapter 9 of his aforementioned book and by John Searle in §iv of his article "Chomsky's revolution in linguistics" (1974).

It is clear from the preceding discussion of the content and the consequences of the Chomskyan revolution that revolution represents an extremely drastic type of reaction to criticism of linguistic theories. It is therefore not to be wondered at that revolutions have not been an everyday phenomenon in the history of linguistic inquiry. In view of the scarcity of revolutions, the Chomskyan revolution has an interesting aspect: according to certain scholars, this revolution has elicited a counterrevolution. Let us briefly consider this possibility.

11.4.2.2   *An Empiricist Counterrevolution?*

Scholars such as Katz and Bever (1974:3) are of the opinion that not only political revolutions, but scientific revolutions too may elicit counterrevolutions. Such COUNTERREVOLUTIONS are "conflicts within the revolutionary camp itself, conflicts between what may be called the 'revolutionary old guard' and the 'counterrevolutionaries'". Katz and Bever claim that erstwhile followers of Chomsky – such as Paul Postal, John Ross, George Lakoff, James McCawley and Charles Fillmore – have launched a "counterrevolution" against Chomsky. These "counterrevolutionaries" are commonly known as generative semanticists. However, this "counterrevolution" is controversial in several respects. For instance, linguists have different opinions about whether there is in fact question of a "counterrevolution" at all, what such a "counterrevolution" would be aimed at and how successful it is/was. We shall assume, for the sake of convenience, that the generative semanticists' attacks on the Chomskyan approach do indeed represent a "counterrevolution" and will henceforth no longer use this expression with the inverted commas.

As was indicated above, grammarians have widely divergent opinions about what it is that the counterrevolution is aimed at. At the outset, the generative semanticists themselves indicated that they wanted to overthrow Chomsky's autonomy thesis. They were especially opposed to this thesis as embodied in Chomsky's notion of a level of syntactic deep structure which is distinct from a level of semantic representation. Generative grammarians argued that the deep structure of a sentence is identical with its semantic representation. This hypothesis has drastic implications for a large number of formal and organizational syntactic universals of the Chomskyan approach.

However, Katz and Bever (1974) argue that the counterrevolution in question is not so much aimed at Chomsky's view of the relationship between syntax and semantics, but rather at Chomsky's rationalism. As such it represents a return to a pre-Chomskyan form of empiricism. Generative semanticists such as George Lakoff are in fact rejecting Chomsky's distinction between linguistic competence and linguistic performance, with the inevitable result that the Chomskyan distinction between the grammaticality of sentences and the acceptability of utterances is abandoned. In so doing, they include every factor which systematically influences the acceptability of utterances in the domain of a grammar. A grammar is therefore subjected to the following condition: it must serve as a basis for the explanation of the (un)acceptability of every utterance that is (un)acceptable for a systematic reason. This condition does away with the distinction between genuine and spurious linguistic intuitions. Within the framework of generative semantics, therefore, a grammar has to be a much more comprehensive theory than within the framework of Chomskyan generative grammar. According to Katz and Bever, a grammar that has to cover such a large domain sacrifices much of its explanatory depth. It becomes little more than an inventory or a description of problematic linguistic data. Generative semanticists, then, become little more than practitioners of "The New Taxonomy". This point was already made in §7.4.6.3 in another context.

If the empiricist counterrevolution is indeed a revolution, it has properties that differ markedly from those of the original Chomskyan revolution. Several leading generative semanticists, such as McCawley, claim that they are still practising generative grammar — they are merely doing it better than the conventional Chomskyans. Moreover, the counterrevolution lacks a true intellectual leader who could play a role analogous to that of Chomsky in the original revolution. Lastly, the counterrevolutionaries are internally divided on various fundamental issues. It would perhaps be more appropriate to say that the generative semanticists — instead of launching a counterrevolution — have caused a FRAGMENTATION of the initially fairly homogeneous Chomskyan approach. Whatever the case may be, from our point of view, the empiricist counterrevolution is interesting for a very particular reason: it illustrates the radical nature of revolution as a type of reaction to criticism of linguistic theories. It is the radical nature of such a revolution which is responsible for creating an intellectual atmosphere in which counterrevolution, which is just as radical, appears to be an appropriate type of reaction.

SELECTED READING

Inquiry in General

General Reactions to Refutation
Musgrave 1973.

Anomalies
Humphreys 1968; Laudan 1977:26ff., 118–119.

Protection
Agassi 1975:ch.8; Botha 1978; Grünbaum 1976; Hempel 1966:§3.4; Lakatos 1970:111, 117, 133ff.; 1976:14–33; Laudan 1977:114ff.

Theories about the Growth of Scientific Knowledge
Feyerabend 1970; Holton 1973:391–395; Kuhn 1967; 1970a; 1970b; Lakatos 1970; Laudan 1977; Popper 1970; Scheffler 1967:74–89; Shaphere 1964; 1966; Suppe 1974b:6–56; Toulmin 1970.

Linguistic Inquiry

Ad Hoc (Auxiliary) Hypotheses
See "Protective devices" on p. 404.

Chomskyan Revolution
Bach 1965; Katz and Bever 1974; Lyons 1970; Percival 1976; Ruwet 1973:ch.1; Searle 1974.

Empiricist Counterrevolution
Dougherty 1972; Katz and Bever 1974; Lakoff 1974b; Maclay 1971; McCawley 1974; 1975; Searle 1974.

CHAPTER TWELVE

Integration and Diversity of Linguistic Inquiry

12.0 PERSPECTIVE

In this brief concluding chapter we shall consider two final general points regarding linguistic inquiry. On the one hand, the internal integration of linguistic inquiry as an intellectual enterprise will be viewed from two angles: that of the interrelationship of its various aspects and that of the inseparability of the aims of grammatical and general linguistic inquiry. On the other hand, a brief survey will be given of the various forms which individual linguistic investigations can take within the framework of generative grammar.

12.1 INTEGRATION

A second reading of the introductory "Perspective" preceding each chapter will reveal the complexity of linguistic inquiry. In order to come to grips with this highly complex intellectual activity, we have adopted the well-known strategy of divide and rule. Consequently we distinguished nine main aspects within linguistic inquiry; within each main aspect we distinguished a number of sub-aspects; within (most of) the subaspects we distinguished sub-subaspects; and so on. These ((sub-)sub-)aspects were viewed from three angles: that of inquiry in general, that of grammatical inquiry and that of general linguistic inquiry.

The strategy of divide and rule holds a potential danger: by concentrating on the various parts of a complex whole one may easily lose sight of the interrelationship, or the integration, of the parts within the whole. It is therefore important to gain a final overall impression of the way in which the various aspects and components of linguistic inquiry are integrated.

12.1.1 Integration of Aspects of Inquiry

In preceding chapters an effort has been made to show clearly how the ((sub-)sub-)aspects of linguistic inquiry are interrelated. Only the essence of this interrelationship will be considered here. Linguistic inquiry represents a search for insight into the nature of human language in general and into the nature of individual languages. Each ((sub-)sub-)aspect of linguistic inquiry is a logically distinguishable step in this search for insight. In other words, this search is manifested in each ((sub-)sub-)aspect of linguistic inquiry. So, within the choice of aims, this search for insight is manifested in the choice of certain objects, idealizations, objectives and criteria for linguistic knowledge; within the formulating of problems, this search for insight is manifested in the choice of criteria for well-formed and significant linguistic problems; in the making of discoveries, it is manifested, for instance, in the rejection of simple heuristic strategies of a taxonomic nature; in the giving of theoretical descriptions, it is manifested in the choice of criteria for linguistic theories, hypotheses and concepts; in the giving of explanations, it is manifested in the choice of criteria for linguistic explanations; and in the making of projections, the justification and the criticism of linguistic hypotheses and the reaction to criticism, it is manifested in anologous criteria. The SEARCH FOR INSIGHT into human language(s), therefore, is the integrating theme echoing through every aspect of linguistic inquiry. The various aspects are interrelated insofar as each aspect, in harmony with the others, is aimed at furthering this search.

In his search for insight the Chomskyan generative grammarian is guided by a small number of interrelated, fundamental philosophical principles. Four of these are: the principle of ontological realism (1)(a), the principle of phenomenological rationalism (1)(b), the principle of epistemological empiricism (1)(c), and the principle of methodological generality (1)(d).

(1) (a)   Reality is multileveled: problematic phenomena on the surface can be understood in terms of the properties of real objects on a deeper level.

 (b)   Specific phenomena on the surface of reality are often the result of the interaction of various (physical, psychological, biological, etc.) systems on the deeper level.

 (c)   The hypothetical statements describing the objects/systems mentioned above must be testable in principle and justified in fact.

 (d)   The hypothetical statements mentioned in (c) – and the theories within which they are integrated – must be of maximal generality.

In the nonexplicated form of (1)(a)–(d) the four principles in question may sound quite profound. As they stand, however, they are in fact without concrete content. This brings us back to the main point of this paragraph, which is that the various aspects of linguistic inquiry are integrated in the sense that they collaborate in giving concrete metascientific content to the four principles in question. Let us consider this point from the angle of grammatical inquiry.

The principle of realism (1)(a) is metascientifically instantiated, i.e. made concrete, in, for instance, the generative grammarian's choice of an object of inquiry on the underlying level of the linguistic reality; in his view that a pretheoretical grammatical description cannot be the final product of grammatical inquiry; in his view that a grammar is a theoretical description of the form of a mental mechanism, the linguistic competence; in his view that grammatical explanations must, in their lawlike generalizations, refer to theoretical grammatical descriptions; in his adopting the criterion that grammatical explanations must be real explanations; in his view that grammatical hypotheses require special (types of) justification in their descriptive function; in his view that grammatical hypotheses, in their descriptive function, must also be subjected to special (types of) criticism; etc. The principle of rationalism (1)(b) is metascientifically instantiated in, for instance, the generative grammarian's adopting the idealization of an ideal speaker; in his adopting the criterion that the intuitive judgments which are included in the corpus of primary linguistic data should represent true linguistic intuitions; in his attitude that a theoretical grammatical description can only be an approximate description of the linguistic competence of a nonideal speaker; in his view that a grammatical explanation must be more than a mere representation of a wide range of (pseudo-)linguistic data; in his view that, without the aid of an adequate bridge theory, no grammatical predictions can be made about extralinguistic phenomena; in his adopting the criterion of qualitative relevance for linguistic evidence; in his view that before raw linguistic data can be used to test grammatical hypotheses, these data must be idealized; in his view that criticism of grammatical hypotheses in terms of qualitatively irrelevant data is inadmissible; etc. Note that the principle of rationalism (1)(b) — which was also discussed in §7.4.6.3 — should not be confused with the rationalist point of view of §11.4.2.1.3 as regards the acquisition of human knowledge. The principle of empiricism (1)(c) is metascientifically instantiated in, for instance, the generative grammarian's adopting the criteria that grammatical knowledge must be testable and justified; in his adopting the criterion of complete explicitness for theoretical grammatical descriptions; in the material criteria which he adopts for grammatical explanations and predictions; in a variety of criteria of evidence and acceptability which he adopts for the justification and criticism of grammatical hypotheses; etc. The principle of empiricism (1)(c) must of course not be confused with either the empiricist point of view of §7.4.6.3 as regards the data of grammatical inquiry, or the empiricist point of view of §11.4.2.1.3 as regards the acquisition of human knowledge.

The various aspects of linguistic inquiry, therefore, collaborate very closely in giving metascientific substance to the general principles of (1) in order that these principles may indeed be applicable in practice. This point can be further elucidated with reference to the principle of generality (1)(d). In the diagram (2) examples are given of contributions made by the various main aspects of linguistic inquiry to the metascientific instantiation of the principle of generality.

(2)   METASCIENTIFIC INSTANTIATION OF THE
                    PRINCIPLE OF GENERALITY

		examples of contribution to instantiation
main aspects of linguistic inquiry	choice of aims for inquiry	criteria relating to the generality and systematic nature of grammatical knowledge
	formulation of problems	criterion that pretheoretical classes must be natural; generalization of correlations
	discovery	criterion of predictive power for hypothetical solutions to grammatical problems
	theoretical description	criteria that grammatical concepts must allow the expression of linguistically significant generalizations, must possess systematic grammatical content and must possess general linguistic content
	explanation	criterion that explanations must be based on (lawlike) generalizations; criterion of generality for lawlike generalization in explanans
	prediction	criterion that predictions must be based on (lawlike) generalizations
	justification	criteria of evidential comprehensiveness and independence; criteria requiring hypotheses to be non-*ad hoc* in both a language-particular and a language-independent respect
	criticism	criteria analogous to those given above for justification
	reaction to criticism	criterion relating to the non-*ad hoc* nature of protective auxiliary hypotheses; criterion that modifications of defective hypotheses must be principled (not *ad hoc*)

Two possible misconceptions which may arise in connection with this diagram must be cleared up here. Firstly: the diagram does not aim to be complete. The summaries given of the mechanisms in terms of which the various main aspects metascientifically instantiate the relevant principle of generality are in no way exhaustive. The diagram is merely illustrative of the way in which the main aspects of linguistic inquiry are integrated in a concerted effort to instantiate an abstract philosophical principle to the extent where it can be applied in the practice of linguistic inquiry. Secondly: when we say that a particular metascientific criterion contributes to the instantiation of the principle of generality, we are not claiming that *all* aspects of the content of the particular criterion have to do with generality. Aspects of the content of some of these criteria also have a bearing on one or more of the other three philosophical principles of (1). This is not so strange, since the principle of generality is but one of the fundamental principles by which the linguist is guided in his search for insight. What is more, the principle of generality is the least fundamental of the four principles stated in (1). A grammatical hypothesis which fails in terms of one or more of the criteria implicit in the principles of realism, rationalism or empiricism has no right of existence in a Chomskyan generative grammar – no matter how general this hypothesis may be. The principle of generality is in fact subservient to the other three principles of (1).

This automatically brings us to the nature of our study of linguistic inquiry. Linguistic inquiry within the framework of generative grammar is often described as in (3).

(3)   The purpose of linguistic inquiry is (simply) to make maximally general statements about language in general and about the particular languages.

Such statements are just as often made without any elucidation, as if they were crystal clear and obviously correct. Despite their ring of profundity, however, such statements are completely obscure. It is only when it has been clearly spelled out in metascientific terms how they are instantiated in the various aspects of linguistic inquiry that these statments can be said to have a clear and justified content. That is precisely what we have been trying to do in this book: to spell out in as precise and as detailed a way as possible in an introductory study, what exactly linguistic inquiry involves.

12.1.2   Integration of Aims

The internal integration of linguistic inquiry is further borne out by the interrelationship between the aim of general linguistic inquiry and that of grammatical inquiry. Schematically this relationship can be represented as follows:

(4)

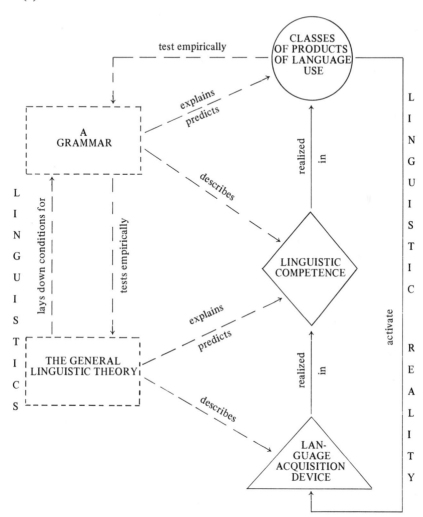

Every part of this diagram has been discussed in previous paragraphs. One general point, however, should be re-emphasized: every individual linguistic inquiry has two sides, a grammatical side and a general linguistic side.

On the one hand, every grammatical inquiry is undertaken within the framework of a general linguistic theory. Without the linguistic universals specified by such a theory, the grammarian is unable to distinguish between aspects of a language that are typical of human language in general and aspects of that language which characterize it as a particular individual language. By conducting his inquiry within the framework specified by the linguistic universals, the grammarian is at the same time testing the relevant general linguistic theory. From his inquiry it will be clear whether the proposed linguistic universals also apply to his particular individual language – as they should do according to the absolute view of universals. It should also be clear from the grammarian's inquiry to what extent the general linguistic theory allows linguistically significant generalizations about particular individual languages to be expressed.

On the other hand, every general linguistic inquiry is carried out with reference to at least one particular language. The general linguist cannot study language in general in isolation from the individual languages. This accounts for the grammatical side of his inquiry. The general linguistic theory must describe what is a possible human language and this description must be borne out by the available grammatical facts about individual languages. Therefore, when he attempts to formulate linguistic universals, the general linguist must "keep his feet on firm grammatical ground".

In his article "Problems of explanation in linguistics" (1970:428) Chomsky formulates the essence of this relationship between grammatical and general linguistic aspects of linguistic inquiry as follows:

> In practice, the linguist is always involved in the study of both universal and particular grammar. When he constructs a descriptive, particular grammar in one way rather than another on the basis of what evidence he has available, he is guided, whether consciously or not, by certain assumptions as to the form of the grammar, and these assumptions belong to the theory of universal grammar. Conversely, his formulation of principles of universal grammar must be justified by the study of their consequences when applied in particular grammars.

Chomsky uses the terms "particular grammar" and "universal grammar" to distinguish between the grammatical and the general linguistic aspects of linguistic inquiry as described above.

To call a given linguistic inquiry "grammatical" or "general linguistic" is to indicate the focal point of the inquiry. If its main concern is the formulation of the principles of a specific individual language, the inquiry is a "grammatical" one. If, on the other hand, its main concern is the formulation of linguistic universals, the inquiry is a "general linguistic" one. In his article "Settling on an underlying form: the English inflectional endings" (1975) Arnold Zwicky gives a striking illustration of the interrelatedness of grammatical and general linguistic aspects within a specific investigation.

12.2   DIVERSITY

Remember that the picture of linguistic inquiry, as it emerges from the preceding chapters, is a maximal one and that every INDIVIDUAL LINGUISTIC INVESTIGA-

TION need not exhibit all nine main aspects. Various types of individual investigations may be distinguished on the basis of those aspects which they do manifest. Three of these distinctive types are discussed briefly in the article " 'The theory comparison method' vs. 'the theory exposition method' in linguistic inquiry" (Botha 1976b: §3.5).

The first type of linguistic investigation is directed at problematic linguistic phenomena of which no penetrating study has as yet been made and which are therefore not well understood. Investigations of this type are mainly concerned with the formulation of a "first", new linguistic theory and with a first attempt at providing some degree of justification for this theory. Formulation of problems, theoretical description, explanation and justification are the research activities most prominently represented, while criticism and reaction to criticism are not characteristic of this type of investigation. Investigations of this sort are valuable in that they open up new perspectives and lines of inquiry.

The second type of linguistic investigation is directed at linguistic phenomena which have been studied so extensively that alternative linguistic theories have been proposed to account for them. The main purpose of such investigations is to determine the relative merit of the alternative theories. Most prominent among the research activities performed are those of justification and, above all, criticism. Formulation of new problems plays a minor role, or no role at all, in investigations of this type.

The third type of linguistic investigation has features of both the types described above. These investigations are directed at the modification or replacement of a proposed theory. The research activities carried out include, above all, criticism of the old theory and justification of the new alternative theory. Chomsky's *Remarks* investigation belongs to this type as it is directed at the criticism of an existing theory, the transformationalist hypothesis, the formulation of a new theory, the lexicalist hypothesis, and the justification of the latter theory.

It should be clear that the type to which a particular linguistic investigation belongs is partly determined by the degree of progress which has been made in the study of the problematic linguistic phenomena in question. It has been claimed that only those investigations which involve comparison of two or more alternative linguistic theories are truly generative in spirit. This is not true. Any individual linguistic investigation that represents a sincere attempt to contribute, directly or indirectly, to the realization of the aims of generative grammar should be looked upon as a potential contribution to the field. In the case of grammatical inquiry, this is an investigation that aims, directly or indirectly, at constructing a generative grammar — an explicit system of rules — for a particular language. In the case of general linguistic inquiry, this is an investigation that aims, directly or indirectly, at giving a restrictive description of what is a possible human language.

Bibliography

Achinstein, Peter
    (1968) *Concepts of science: A philosophical analysis*. Baltimore, Maryland: The Johns Hopkins Press.
    (1971) *Law and explanation: An essay in the philosophy of science*. Oxford: At the Clarendon Press.
Agassi, Joseph
    (1975) *Science in flux*. (*Boston Studies in the Philosophy of Science* XXVIII) Dordrecht/ Boston: D. Reidel Publishing Company.
    (1976) The Lakatosian revolution. In Cohen, Feyerabend, and Wartovsky (eds.) 1976: 9–21.
Alexander, Peter
    (1969) *An introduction to logic: The criticism of arguments*. London: George Allen and Unwin Ltd.
Anderson, J.M., and C. Jones (eds.)
    (1974) *Historical linguistics II: Theory and description in phonology*. (*Proceedings of the First International Conference on Historical Linguistics, Edinburgh, 2nd– 7th September 1973*) Amsterdam&Oxford: North-Holland Publishing Company.
Anderson, Stephen, and Paul Kiparsky (eds.)
    (1973) *A Festschrift for Morris Halle*. Cambridge, Mass.: MIT Press.
Aronoff, Mark H.
    (1976) *Word formation in generative grammar*. Cambridge, Mass.: MIT Press.
Austerlitz, Robert (ed.)
    (1975) *The scope of American linguistics*. (*Papers of the First Golden Anniversary Symposium of the Linguistic Society of America*, held at the University of Massachusetts, Amherst, on July 24 and 25, 1974). Lisse: The Peter de Ridder Press.
Bach, Emmon
    (1964) *An introduction to transformational grammars*. New York, etc.: Holt, Rinehart and Winston, Inc.
    (1965) Structural linguistics and the philosophy of science. *Diogenes* 51: 111–128.
    (1974a) *Syntactic theory*. New York, etc.: Holt, Rinehart and Winston, Inc.
    (1974b) Explanatory inadequacy. In Cohen (ed.) 1974: 153–171.
Bach, Emmon, and Robert T. Harms (eds.)
    (1968) *Universals in linguistic theory*. New York, etc.: Holt, Rinehart and Winston, Inc.
Baker, Carl L.
    (1978) *Introduction to generative-transformational syntax*. Englewood Cliffs, N.J.: Prentice-Hall.
Bar-Hillel, Yehoshua
    (1964) Neorealism vs. neopositivism: a neo-pseudo issue. *Foundations of Language* 2: 394–399.
    (1971) Out of the pragmatic wastebasket. *Linguistic Inquiry* II: 401–407.

Barker, S.F.
    (1957) *Induction and hypothesis: A study of the logic of confirmation.* Ithaca: Cornell University Press.
Baumrin, B. (ed.)
    (1963) *Philosophy of science (The Delaware Seminar* 1) New York: Interscience Publishers.
Beerling, R.F., S.L. Kwee, J.J.A. Mooij, en C.A. van Peursen
    (1972) *Inleiding tot de wetenschapsleer.* Utrecht: Byleveld.
Benjamin, A. Cornelius
    (1965) *Science, technology, and human values.* Columbia: University of Missouri Press.
Bever, Thomas A.
    (1974) The ascent of the specious or there's a lot we don't know about mirrors. In Cohen (ed.) 1974: 173–200.
    (1975) Functional explanations require independently motivated functional theories. In *Papers from the Parasession on Functionalism,* Chicago Linguistic Society, 580–609.
Bever, Thomas G., Jerrold J. Katz, and D. Terence Langendoen (eds.)
    (1977) *An integrated theory of linguistic ability.* Hassocks, Sussex: The Harvester Press.
Black, Max
    (1970) Comment on Chomsky 1970. In Borger and Cioffi (eds.) 1970: 452–461.
Blackburn, Simon
    (1973) *Reason and prediction.* Cambridge: At the University Press.
Bocheński, J.M.
    (1965) *The methods of contemporary thought.* Dordrecht: D. Reidel Publishing Company.
Bogdan, Radu J., and Illka Niimiluoto (eds.)
    (1973) *Logic, language and probability.* Dordrecht: D. Reidel Publishing Company.
Borger, Robert, and Frank Cioffi (eds.)
    (1970) *Explanation in the behavioral sciences.* Cambridge: At the University Press.
Botha, Rudolf P.
    (1968) *The function of the lexicon in transformational generative grammar (Janua Linguarum, Series Maior* 38) The Hague: Mouton.
    (1970) *The methodological status of grammatical argumentation (Janua Linguarum, Series Minor* 105) The Hague: Mouton.
    (1971) *Methodological aspects of transformational generative phonology. (Janua Linguarum, Series Minor* 112) The Hague: Mouton.
    (1973) *The justification of linguistic hypotheses: A study of nondemonstrative inference in transformational grammar. (Janua Linguarum, Series Maior* 84) The Hague: Mouton.
    (1976a) On the analysis of linguistic argumentation. In Wirth (ed.) 1976: 1–34.
    (1976b) 'The theory comparison method' vs. 'the theory exposition method' in linguistic inquiry. Reproduced by the Indiana University Linguistics Club.
    (1976c) On the Rosetta Stone Strategy or How to camouflage nonvalid arguments. Reproduced by the Indiana University Linguistics Club.
    (1976d) 'Gut feelings' in generative grammar. Reproduced by the Indiana University Linguistics Club.
    (1977) *On the logic of linguistic research. (Utrecht Working Papers in Linguistics* 2) Utrecht: RUU, Instituut voor Algemene Taalwetenschap.
    (1978) Protecting general-linguistic hypotheses from refutation. Paper presented at the Round-Table Discussion of "Linguistics as an empirical science", XIIth International Congress of Linguists, Vienna, 29th August–2nd September 1977. *Stellenbosch Papers in Linguistics* 1: 1–38.

(1979a) External evidence in the validation of mentalistic theories: a Chomskyan paradox. *Stellenbosch Papers in Linguistics* 2: 1–38. (To appear in *Lingua* 48, 1979 as well.)

(1979b) *Methodological bases of a progressive mentalism. (Stellenbosch Papers in Linguistics* 3). (To appear in *Synthese* 43, 1980 as well.)

Bowers, John S.

(1970) A note on remind. *Linguistic Inquiry* 1: 559–560.

(1972) Grammatical relations. Ph.D. Dissertation, MIT, Cambridge, Mass.

(1975) Adjectives and adverbs in English. *Foundation of Language* 13: 529–562.

Braithwate, R.B.

(1964) *Scientific explanation: A study of the function of theory, probability and law in science.* Cambridge: At the University Press.

Bresnan, Joan

(1976) Toward a realistic model of transformational grammar. Mimeographed.

Broad, C.D.

(1919) Mechanical explanation and its alternatives. *Proceedings of the Aristotelian Society* 19: 85–124.

Brody, Baruch A. (ed.)

(1970) *Readings in the philosophy of science.* Englewood Cliffs, N.J.: Prentice-Hall.

Bunge, Mario

(1959) *Metascientific queries.* Springfield, Ill.: Charles C. Thomas.

(1967a) *Scientific research I: The search for system.* Berlin, etc.: Springer-Verlag.

(1967b) *Scientific research II: The search for truth.* Berlin, etc.: Springer-Verlag.

Bunge, Mario (ed.)

(1964) *The critical approach to science and philosophy: In honour of Karl R. Popper.* London: Free Press of Glencoe.

Carden, Guy

(1970) *Logical predicates and idiolect variation in English. (Report NSF–25 to the National Science Foundation)* Cambridge, Mass.

Carnap, Rudolf

(1952) Empiricism, semantics, and ontology. In Linsky (ed.) 1952: 208–228.

Caws, Peter

(1966) *The philosophy of science: A systematic account.* Princeton, N.J.: D. Van Nostrand Company Inc.

(1969) The structure of scientific discovery. *Science* 166: 1375–1380.

Chapin, Paul G.

(1967) On the syntax of word-derivation in English. Ph.D. Dissertation, MIT, Cambridge, Mass.

Chen, Matthew

(1973) Predictive power in phonological description. *Lingua* 32: 173–192.

Chisholm, Roderick M.

(1966) *Theory of knowledge.* Englewood Cliffs, N.J.: Prentice-Hall.

Chisholm, Roderick M., *et al.*

(1965) *Philosophy.* (Second printing). Englewood Cliffs, N.J.: Prentice-Hall.

Chomsky, Noam

(1957) *Syntactic structures (Janua Linguarum* IV) The Hague: Mouton.

(1962a) Explanatory models in linguistics. In Nagel, Suppes, and Tarski (eds.) 1962: 528–550.

(1962b) A transformational approach to syntax. In Hill (ed.) 1962a: 124–158.

(1962c) Discussion with Sledd. In Hill (ed.) 1962b.

(1964) *Current issues in linguistic theory. (Janua Linguarum, Series Minor XXXVIII)* The Hague: Mouton.

(1965) *Aspects of the theory of syntax.* Cambridge, Mass.: MIT Press.

(1966) *Topics in the theory of generative grammar. (Janua Linguarum, Series Minor LVI)* The Hague: Mouton.

(1967) The formal nature of language. In Lenneberg 1967: 397–442.

(1968) *Language and mind.* New York, etc.: Brace and World.

(1970) Problems of explanation in linguistics. In Borger and Cioffi (eds.) 1970: 425–451, 462–470.

(1972a) *Studies on semantics in generative grammar. (Janua Linguarum, Series Minor 107)* The Hague: Mouton.

(1972b) Remarks on nominalization. In Chomsky 1972a: 11–61.

(1972c) Deep structure, surface structure and semantic interpretation. In Chomsky 1972a: 62–119.

(1972d) Some empirical issues in the theory of transformational grammar. In Chomsky 1972a: 120–202.

(1973) Conditions on transformations. In Anderson and Kiparsky (eds.) 1973: 232–286.

(1974) Discussing language with Herman Parret. In Parret 1974: 27–54.

(1975a) *The logical structure of linguistic theory.* New York: Plenum Press.

(1975b) New introduction to *The logical structure of linguistic theory.* In Chomsky 1975a: 1–53.

(1975c) *Reflections on language.* New York: Pantheon Books.

(1975d) Questions of form and interpretation. In Austerlitz (ed.) 1975: 159–196.

(1975e) On cognitive structures and their development. Mimeographed.

(1976) On the biological basis of language capacities. In Rieber (ed.) 1976: 1–25.

(1977) On *Wh*-movement. In Culicover, Wasow and Akmajian (eds.) 1977: 71-132.

(1978) A theory of core grammar. *Glot* 1: 7–26.

Chomsky, Noam, and Morris Halle.

(1965) Some controversial questions in phonological theory. *Journal of Linguistics* 1: 97–138.

(1968) *The sound pattern of English.* New York, etc.: Harper and Row, Publishers.

Chomsky, Noam, and Jerrold J. Katz

(1974) What the linguist is talking about. *The Journal of Philosophy* LXXI: 347–367.

Chomsky, Noam, and Howard Lasnik

(1977) Filters and control. *Linguistic Inquiry* 8: 425–504.

Chomsky, Noam, and George A. Miller

(1963) Introduction to the formal analysis of natural languages. In Luce, Bush, and Galanter (eds.) 1963: 269–322.

Christie, W. (ed.)

(1976) *Proceedings of the Second International Conference on Historical Linguistics, Tucson, January 1976.* Amsterdam, Oxford: North-Holland Publishing Company.

Clark, Herbert H., and Susan E. Haviland

(1974) Psychological processes as linguistic explanation. In Cohen (ed.) 1974: 91–124.

Cohen, David (ed.)

(1972) *Limiting the domain of linguistics. (Papers from the UWM Linguistic Group First Annual Symposium)* Milwaukee: UWM, Linguistics Department.

(1974) *Explaining linguistic phenomena.* Washington, D.C.: Hemisphere Publishing Corporation.

Cohen, David, and Jessica R. Wirth (eds.)

(1975) *Testing linguistic hypotheses.* Washington, D.C.: Hemisphere Publishing Corporation.

Cohen, L. Jonathan
(1950/51) Teleological explanation. *Proceedings of the Aristotelian Society* 51: 225–292.
(1970)   *The implications of induction.* London: Methuen.
Cohen, R.S., P.K. Feyerabend, M.W. Wartovsky (eds.)
(1976)   *Essays in memory of Imre Lakatos.* (*Boston Studies in the Philosophy of Science,* Vol. XXXIX) Dordrecht/Boston: D. Reidel Publishing Company.
Colodny, Robert G. (ed.)
(1966)   *Mind and cosmos: essays in contemporary science and philosophy.* Pittsburgh: University of Pittsburgh Press.
Copi, Irving M.
(1965)   *Symbolic logic.* (Second edition). New York: Macmillan.
Crothers, John
(1971)   On the abstractness controversy. *Project on Linguistic Analysis, Second Series* 12: CR1–CR29.
Culicover, Peter W., Thomas Wasow, and Adrian Akmajian (eds.)
(1977)   *Formal syntax.* New York, etc.: Academic Press.
Derwing, Bruce L.
(1973)   *Transformational grammar as a theory of language acquisition: A study in the empirical, conceptual, and methodological foundations of contemporary linquistics.* Cambridge: At the University Press.
Derwing, Bruce L., and Peter R. Harris
(1975)   What is a generative grammar?. In Koerner (ed.) 1975: 297–314.
Dinneen, F.P. (ed.)
(1974)   *Georgetown University Round Table on Languages and Linguistics 1974.* *Washington: Georgetown University Press.*
Dougherty, Ray C.
(1972)   Generative semantic methods: a Bloomfieldian counterrevolution. Reproduced by the Indiana University Linguistics Club.
(1974)   What explanation is and isn't. In Cohen (ed.) 1974: 125–151.
(1975)   The logic of linguistic research. Mimeographed.
(1976)   Argument invention: the linguists's feel for science. In Wirth (ed.) 1976: 111–165.
Dretske, Fred
(1974)   Explanation in linguistics. In Cohen (ed.) 1974: 21–41.
Dubin, Robert
(1969)   *Theory building.* New York: The Free Press.
Edwards, Paul (ed. in chief)
(1967)   *The encyclopedia of philosophy.* New York and London: Macmillan.
Elliot, Dale, Stanley Legum, and Sandra Annear Thompson
(1969)   Syntactic variation as linguistic data. *Papers from the Fifth Regional Meeting Chicago Linguistic Society:* 52–59.
Edmonds, Joseph E.
(1976)   *A transformational approach to English syntax: Root, structure-preserving, and local transformations.* New York, etc.: Academic Press.
Evers, Arnold
(1976)   Onderzoeksprogramma's en het transformationele onderzoeksprogramma. In Koefoed en Evers (ed.) 1976: 82–110.
Fain, Haskell
(1963)   Some problems of causal explanation. *Mind* 72: 519–532.
Feigl, Herbert
(1950)   Existential hypotheses: realistic versus phenomenalistic interpretations. *Philosophy of Science* XVII: 35–36.

(1965) What is philosophy of science?. In Chisholm et al. 1965: 470–539.
Feigl, Herbert, and May Brodbeck (eds.)
(1953) *Readings in the philosophy of science.* New York: Appleton Century Crofts.
Feigl, Herbert, and Grover Maxwell (eds.)
(1962) *Minnesota studies in the philosophy of science Vol. III: Scientific explanation, space and time.* Minneapolis: University of Minnesota Press.
Ferguson, Charles A.
(1971) Absence of copula in normal speech, baby talk, and pidgin. In Hymes (ed.) 1971: 141–150.
Feyerabend, Paul K.
(1964) Realism and instrumentalism: comments on the logic of factual support. In Bunge (ed.) 1964: 280–308.
(1970) Consolations for the specialist. In Lakatos and Musgrave (eds.) 1970: 197–230.
Fodor, J.A., T.G. Bever, and M.F. Garrett
(1974) *The psychology of language: An introduction to psycholinguistics and generative grammar.* New York, etc.: McGraw-Hill Book Company.
Fodor, Janet Dean
(1977) *Semantics: theories of meaning in generative grammar.* Hassocks: The Harvester Press.
Foss, Donald J., and David Fay
(1975) Linguistic theory and performance models. In Cohen and Wirth (eds.) 1975: 65–91.
Foster, Marguerite H., and Michael L. Martin (eds.)
(1966) *Probability, confirmation, and simplicity.* New York: The Odyssey Press Inc.
Fraser, Bruce
(1970) Some remarks on the action nominalization in English. In Jacobs and Rosenbaum (eds.) 1970: 83–98.
Fromkin, Victoria A.
(1975) When does a test test a hypothesis, or, what counts as evidence. In Cohen and Wirth (eds.) 1975: 43–64.
Galambos, Robert
(1942) The avoidance of obstacles by flying bats: Spallanzani's ideas (1974) and later theories. *Isis* 34, Pt 2, No. 94: 132–140.
(1943) Flight in the dark: a study of bats. *The Scientific Monthly* 56: 155–162.
Galambos, Robert, and Donald R. Griffin
(1942) Obstacle avoidance by flying bats: the cries of bats. *Journal of Experimental Zoology* 88: 475–490.
Gingerich, Owen (ed.)
(1975) *The nature of scientific discovery.* Washington: Smithsonian Institute Press.
Gleason Jr., H.A.
(1969) *An introduction to descriptive linguistics.* (Revised edition). London, etc.: Holt, Rinehart, and Winston.
Griffin, Donald R., and Robert Galambos
(1941) The sensory basis of obstacle avoidance by flying bats. *Journal of Experimental Zoology* 86: 481–505.
Groot, A.D. de
(1961) *Methodologie: Grondslagen van onderzoek en denken in de gedragswetenschappen.* The Hague: Mouton, (English translation available).
Grossman, Robin E., L. James San, and Timothy J. Vance (eds.)
(1975) *Papers from the parasession on functionalism.* Chicago Linguistic Society. Chicago.
Grünbaum, Adolf
(1971) Can we ascertain the falsity of a scientific hypothesis?. In Nagel, Bromberger, and Grünbaum 1971: 69–129.

(1976) *Ad hoc* auxiliary hypotheses and falsification. *The British Journal for the Philosophy of Science* 27: 329–362.

Halle, Morris

(1959) *The sound pattern of Russian.* The Hague: Mouton.

Hanson, Norwood R.

(1959) On the symmetry between explanation and prediction. *The Philosophical Review* 68: 349–358.

(1965) *Patterns of discovery: An inquiry into the conceptual foundations of science.* Cambridge: At the University Press.

(1969) *Perception and discovery: An introduction to scientific inquiry.* San Francisco: Freeman, Cooper and Company.

(1971) *Observation and explanation: A guide to philosophy of science.* London: George Allen and Unwin Ltd.

Harding, Sandra G. (ed.)

(1976a) *Can theories be refuted? Essays on the Duhen-Quine Thesis.* Dordrecht: D. Reidel Publishing Company.

Harding, Sandra G.

(1976b) Introduction to Harding (ed.) 1976a: IX–XXI.

Harman, Gilbert (ed.)

(1974) *On Noam Chomsky: critical essays.* Garden City, N.Y.: Anchor Press/Doubleday.

Harré, R.

(1961) *Theories and things: A brief study in prescriptive metaphysics.* London and New York: Sheed and Ward.

(1967) *An introduction to the logic of the sciences.* London, etc.: Macmillan.

(1972) *The philosophies of science: An introductory survey.* London: Oxford University Press.

Hartridge, H.

(1920) The avoidance of objects by bats in their flight. *Journal of Physiology* 54: 54–57.

Hastings, Ashley J., and Andreas Koutsoudas

(1976) Performance models and the generative-interpretive debate. In Wirth (ed.) 1976: 187–216.

Hempel, Carl G.

(1952) *Fundamentals of concept formation in empirical science.* (*International Encyclopedia of Unified Science, Foundations of the Unity of Science* I–II) Chicago: University of Chicago Press.

(1965) *Aspects of scientific explanation: And other essays in the philosophy of science.* New York and London: The Free Press, etc.

(1966) *Philosophy of natural science.* Englewood Cliffs, N.J.: Prentice-Hall, Inc.

Hempel, Carl G., and Paul Oppenheim

(1953) The logic of explanation. In Feigl and Brodbeck (eds.) 1953: 319–352.

Henkin, L., P. Suppes, and A. Tarski (eds.)

(1959) *The axiomatic method.* Amsterdam: North-Holland Publishing Company.

Heringer, James T.

(1970) Research on negative-quantifier dialects. *Papers from the Sixth Regional Meeting Chicago Linguistic Society:* 287–296.

Hesse, Mary

(1967a) Laws and theories. In Edwards (ed. in chief) (1967) 4: 404–410.

(1967b) Models and analogy in science. In Edwards (ed. in chief) (1967) 5: 354–359.

(1974) *The structure of scientific inference.* Berkeley: Unversity of California Press.

Hildebrand, Joel H.

(1957) *Science in the making. New York: Columbia University Press.*

Hill, Archibald A. (ed.)
(1962a) *Proceedings of the Third Texas Conference on problems of linguistic analysis in English.* Austin: Texas University Press.
(1962b)*Proceedings of the Second Texas Conference on problems of linguistic analysis in English.* Austin: Texas University Press.
Hoepelman, J.P., en B. Willink
(1971) Linguistiek en methodologie. *Studia Neerlandica* 6: 179–188.
Holton, Gerald
(1973) *Thematic origins of scientific thought. Kepler to Einstein.* Cambridge, Mass.: Harvard University Press.
Hook, Sidney (ed.)
(1969) *Language and philosophy.* New York: New York University Press.
Humphreys, Willard C.
(1968) *Anomalies and scientific theories.* San Francisco: Freeman, Cooper and Company.
Hutchinson, Larry
(1974) Grammar as theory. In Cohen (ed.) 1974: 43–73.
Huygens, Christiaan
(1945) *Treatise on light.* Chicago.
Hyman, Larry
(1970) How concrete is phonology?. *Language* XLVI: 58–76.
Hymes, Dell (ed.)
(1971) *Pidginization and creolization of languages. (Proceedings of a conference held at the University of the West Indies, Mona, Jamaica, April 1968)* Cambridge: At the University Press.
Itkonen, Esa
(1976) *Linguistics and empiricalness: answers to criticisms. (Publication No. 4 of the Department of General Linguistics. University of Helsinki).*
Jackendoff, Ray S.
(1974a) Introduction of the $\overline{X}$–convention. Reproduced by the Indiana University Linguistics Club.
(1974b) Morphological and semantic regularities in the lexicon. Reproduced by the Indiana University Linguistics Club.
(1976) Towards an explanatory semantic representation. *Linguistic Inquiry* 7: 89–150.
Jacobs, Roderick A., and Peter S. Rosenbaum
(1968) *English transformational grammar.* Waltham, Mass.: Blaisdell Publishing Company.
Jacobs, Roderick A., and Peter S. Rosenbaum (eds.)
(1970) *Readings in English transformational grammar.* Waltham, Mass.: Ginn and Company.
Kaplan, Abraham
(1964) *The conduct of inquiry: Methodology for behavioral science.* San Francisco: Chandler Publishing Company.
Katz, Jerrold J.
(1964) Mentalism in linguistics. *Language* 40: 124–137.
(1977) The real status of semantic representations. *Linguistic Inquiry* 8: 559–584.
Katz, Jerrold J., and Thomas G. Bever
(1974) The fall and rise of empiricism. Reproduced by the Indiana University Linguistics Club.
Kimball, John (ed.)
(1973) *Syntax and semantics* 2. New York and London: Seminar Press.
King, Robert D.
(1969) *Historical linguistics and generative grammar.* Englewood Cliffs, N.J.: Prentice-Hall.

Kiparsky, Paul
  (1968a) Linguistic universals and linguistic change. In Bach and Harms (eds.) 1968: 171–202.
  (1968b) How abstract is phonology? Reproduced by the Indiana University Linquistics Club.
  (1972) Explanation in phonology. In Peters (ed.) 1972a: 189–227.
  (1975) What are phonological theories about? In Cohen and Wirth (eds.) 1975: 187–209.
Koefoed, Geert
  (1974) On formal and functional explanation: some notes on Kiparsky's 'Explanation in phonology'. In Anderson and Jones (eds.) 1974: 227–293.
Koefoed, G. en A. Evers (eds.)
  (1976) *Lijnen van taaltheoretisch onderzoek.* Groningen: H.D. Tjeenk Willink.
Koerner, E.F.K. (ed.)
  (1975) *The transformational-generative paradigm in modern linguistic theory.* Amsterdam: John Benjamins B.V.
Körner, Stephan (ed.)
  (1975) *Explanation.* New Haven: Yale University Press.
Koutsoudas, A.
  (1966) *Writing transformational grammars: an introduction.* New York: McGraw-Hill.
Kuhn, Thomas S.
  (1967) *The structure of scientific revolutions.* Chicago and London: The University of Chicago Press.
  (1970a) Logic of discovery or psychology of research? In Lakatos and Musgrave (eds.) 1970: 1–23.
  (1970b) Reflections on my critics. In Lakatos and Musgrave (eds.) 1970: 231–278.
  (1974) Second thoughts on paradigms. In Suppe (ed.) 1974a: 459–482.
Kyburg, Jr., Henry E.
  (1968) *Philosophy of science: a formal approach.* New York: The Macmillan Company.
Labov, W.
  (1972) Some principles of linguistic methodology. *Language in Society* 1: 97–120.
Lakatos, Imre
  (1970) Falsification and the methodology of scientific research programmes. In Lakatos and Musgrave (eds.) 1970: 91–195.
  (1976) *Proofs and refutations: The logic of mathematical discovery.* Edited by John Worrall and Elie Zahar. Cambridge, etc.: Cambridge University Press.
Lakatos, Imre, and Alan Musgrave (eds.)
  (1970) *Criticism and the growth of knowledge.* Cambridge: At the University Press.
Lakoff, George
  (1967) Lexicalism. Mimeographed.
  (1969) On generative semantics. Reproduced by the Indiana University Linguistics Club. (Also published in Steinberg and Jakobovits (eds.) 1971: 232–296.)
  (1970) *Irregularity in syntax.* New York, etc.: Holt, Rinehart and Winston, Inc.
  (1974a) Discussing language with Herman Parret. In Parret 1974: 150–178.
  (1974b) Humanistic linguistics. In Dinneen (ed.) 1974: 103–117.
Lakoff, Robin T.
  (1974) Pluralism in linguistics. In Dinneen (ed.) 1974: 59–82.
Lambert, Karl, and Gordon G. Brittan
  (1970) *An introduction to the philosophy of science.* Englewood Cliffs, N.J.: Prentice-Hall, Inc.
Laudan, Larry
  (1977) *Progress and its problems: Towards a theory of scientific growth.* London: Routledge and Kegan Paul.

Leatherdale, W.H.
(1974) *The role of analogy, model and metaphor in science.* Amsterdam/Oxford: North-Holland Publishing Company.
Lees, Robert B.
(1957) Review of Chomsky 1957. *Language* 33: 375–408.
(1965) Two views of linguistic research. *Linguistics* 11: 21–29.
(1966) *The grammar of English nominalizations.* (Fourth printing). The Hague: Mouton.
Lenneberg, Eric H.
(1967) *Biological foundations of language.* With appendices by Noam Chomsky and Otto Marx. New York: Wiley, and Sons.
Levelt, W.J.M.
(1974) *Formal grammar in linguistics and psycholinguistics III: Psycholinguistic applications. (Janua Linguarum, Series Minor* 192/3) The Hague: Mouton.
Lightfoot, David
(1974) The diachronic analysis of English modals. *Montreal Working Papers in Linguistics* 3: 115–145.
(1976a) The base component as the locus of syntactic change. Paper presented at the Second International Conference on Historical Linguistics, Tucson, January 1976. Mimeographed. (To appear in Christie (ed.) 1976).
(1976b) Syntactic change and the autonomy thesis. Paper presented at the Santa Barbara Symposium on the Mechanisms of Syntactic Change, May 1976. Mimeographed.
in press   Principles of diachronic syntax. (Page references are to the manuscript)
to appear   Explaining syntactic change. In Lightfoot and Hornstein (eds.).
Lightfoot, David, and Norbert Hornstein (eds.)
to appear   *Explanation in linguistics.*
Linell, Per
(1976) Is linguistics an empirical science? *Studia Linguistica* XXX: 77–94.
Linsky, Leonard (ed.)
(1952) *Semantics and the philosophy of language: A collection of readings.* Urbana: University of Illinois Press.
Losee, John
(1972) *A historical introduction to the philosophy of science.* London, etc.: Oxford University Press.
Luce, R.D., R. Bush, and E. Galanter (eds.)
(1963) *Handbook of mathematical psychology II.* New York: John Wiley and Sons.
Lyons, John
(1970) *Chomsky.* London: Fontana/Collins.
Maclay, Howard
(1971) Overview. In Steinberg and Jakobovits (eds.) 1971: 157–182.
Martinet, André
(1960) *Elements of general linguistics.* Translated by Elisabeth Palmer. London: Faber.
Maxwell, Grover
(1962) The ontological status of theoretical entities. In Feigl and Maxwell (eds.) 1962: 3–27.
McCawley, James D.
(1971) On the role of notation in generative phonology. Reproduced by the Indiana University Linguistics Club.
(1972) On interpreting the theme of this conference. In Cohen (ed.) 1972: i–vi.
(1973) Review of Chomsky 1972a. Reproduced by the Indiana University Linguistics Club.
(1974) Discussing language with Herman Parret. In Parret 1974: 249–277.
(1975) Discussions on Ray C. Dougherty's 'Generative semantic methods: a Bloom-

fieldian counterrevolution'. *International Journal of Dravidian Linguistics* IV: 151–158.
Morgenbesser, Sidney (ed.)
    (1967) *Philosophy of science today*. New York: Basic Books.
Musgrave, A.E.
    (1973) Falsification and its critics. In Suppes, et al. (eds.) 1973: 393–406.
Nagel, Ernest
    (1961) *The structure of science: Problems in the logic of scientific explanation*. London: Routledge and Kegan Paul.
    (1966) Probability and degree of confirmation or weight of evidence. In Foster and Martin (eds.) 1966: 184: 194.
    (1967) The nature and aim of science. In Morgenbesser (ed.) 1967: 3–13.
Nagel, Ernest, Sylvain Bromberger, and Adolf Grünbaum
    (1971) *Observation and theory in science*. Baltimore and London: The Johns Hopkins Press.
Nagel, Ernest, Patrick Suppes, and Alfred Tarski (eds.)
    (1962) *Logic, methodology and philosophy of science*. Stanford: Stanford University Press.
Northrop, F.S.C.
    (1966) *The logic of the sciences and the humanities*. (Sixth printing). Cleveland and New York: The World Publishing Company.
O'Hala, John J.
    (1974) Phonetic explanation in phonology. In *Papers from the Parasession on Natural Phonology*. Chicago Linguistic Society, 1974: 251–274.
Pap, Arthur
    (1962) *An introduction to the philosophy of science*. With an epilogue by Brand Blanshard. New York: The Free Press of Glencoe.
Parret, Herman
    (1974) *Discussing language*. (*Janua Linguarum, Series Maior* 93). The Hague: Mouton.
Percival, W. Keith
    (1976) The applicability of Kuhn's paradigms to the history of linguistics. *Language* 52: 285–294.
Perlmutter, D., and J. Oreznik
    (1973) Language particular rules and explanation in syntax. In Anderson and Kiparky (eds.) 1973: 419–459.
Perloff, Michael, and Jessica R. Wirth
    (1976) On independant motivation. In Wirth (ed.) 1976: 95–110.
Peters, Stanely
    (1970) Why there are many 'universal' bases. *Papers in Linguistics* 2: 27–43.
Peters, Stanley (ed.)
    (1972a) *Goals of linguistic theory*. Englewood Cliffs, N.J.: Prentice-Hall, Inc.
Peters, Stanley
    (1972b) The projection problem: how is a grammar to be selected? In Peters (ed.) 1972a: 171–188.
Popper, Karl R.
    (1965) *The logic of scientific discovery*. New York and Evanston: Harper and Row Publishers.
    (1966) *Conjectures and refutations: The growth of scientific knowledge*. (Third edition revised). London: Routledge and Kegan Paul.
    (1970) Normal science and its dangers. In Lakatos and Musgrave (eds.) 1970: 51–58.
Postal, Paul M.
    (1966) Review of Martinet 1960. *Foundations of Language* 2: 151–186.

(1968) *Aspects of phonological theory.* New York, etc.: Harper and Row Publishers.

(1970) On the surface verb 'remind'. *Linguistic Inquiry* 1: 37–120.

(1971) *Crossover phenomena.* New York, etc.: Holt, Rinehart and Winston, Inc.

(1976) Avoiding reference to subject. *Lingustic Inquiry* 7: 151–182.

Prideaux, Gary D.

(1971) On the notion 'linguistically significant generalization'. *Lingua* XXVI: 337–347.

Prince, Alan

(1974) McCawley on formalization. Mimeographed.

Rescher, Nicholas

(1958) On prediction and explanation. *British Journal for the Philosophy of Science* 8: 281–296.

(1970) *Scientific explanation.* New York: The Free Press.

Rieber, R.W. (ed.)

(1976) *The neuropsychology of language: Essays in honor of Eric Lenneberg.* New York and London: Plenum Press.

Ringen, Jon D.

(1975) Linguistic facts: a study of the empirical scientific status of transformational generative grammars. In Cohen and Wirth (eds.) 1975: 1–41.

to appear Transformational generative grammars as descriptions of idiolects. Paper pre-
a sented at the LSA Summer Meeting, Amherst, Massachusetts, July 28, 1974.

to appear Linguistic intuition and introspective "observation". Paper presented at the
b LSA Winter Meeting, San Francisco, December 28, 1975.

to appear On evaluating data concerning linguistic intuition. Paper presented at the Fifth
c Annual UWM Linguistics Symposium, University of Wisconsin-Milwaukee, March 28, 1976.

Ross, John Robert

(1967) Constraints on variables in syntax. Ph.D. Dissertation, MIT, reproduced by the Indiana University Linguistics Club.

(1972) Upstairs primacy. Paper presented at the NELS Meeting, October, 1972.

Rudner, Richard S.

(1966) *Philosophy of social science.* Englewood Cliffs, N.J.: Prentice-Hall, Inc.

Ruwet, Nicholas

(1973) *An introduction to generative grammar.* (*North-Holland Linguistics Series* 7) Translated from the French by Norval S.H. Smith. Amsterdam and London: North-Holland Publishing Company.

Rijen, J.B.M. van

(1974) Transformationeel-generatieve grammatika's als verklarende theorieën. *Spektator* 4: 42–52.

Sadock, Jerrold M.

(1976) On significant generalizations: notes on the Hallean Syllogism. In Wirth (ed.) 1976: 85–94.

Salmon, Wesley C.

(1963) *Logic.* Englewood Cliffs, N.J.: Prentice-Hall, Inc.

(1965) The status of prior probabilities in statistical explanation. *Philosophy of Science* 32: 137–146.

(1967) *The foundations of scientic inference.* Pittsburgh: University of Pittsburgh Press.

(1975) Theoretical explanation. In Körner (ed.) 1975: 118–145.

Sampson, Geoffrey

(1975a) Theory choice in a two-level science. *British Journal for the Philosophy of Science* 26: 303–318.

(1975b) *The form of language.* London: Weidenfeld.

(1976) Review of Cohen (ed.) 1974. *Journal of Linguistics* 12: 177–182.

Sanders, Gerald A.
  (1974) Introduction to Cohen (ed.) 1974. In Cohen (ed.) 1974: 1–20.
Schane, Sanford A.
  (1972) Natural rules in phonology. In Stockwell and Macaulay (eds.) 1972: 199–229.
  (1976) The best argument is in the mind of the beholder. In Wirth (ed.) 1976: 167–185.
Scheffler, Israel
  (1963) *The anatomy of inquiry.* (First printing). New York: Alfred A. Knopf.
  (1967) *Science and subjectivity.* Indianapolis: Bobbs-Merrill Company.
Schwartz, Robert
  (1969) On knowing a grammar. In Hook (ed.) 1969: 183–190.
Scriven, Michael
  (1963) The temporal asymmetry of explanations and predictions. In B. Baumrin (ed.) 1963: 97–105.
  (1970) Explanations, predictions, and laws. In Brody (ed.) 1970.
Searle, John
  (1974) Chomsky's revolution in linguistics. In Harman (ed.) 1974: 2–33.
Shaphere, Dudley
  (1964) The structure of scientific revolutions. *Philosophical Review* 73: 383–394.
  (1966) Meaning and scientific change. In Colodny (ed.) 1966: 41–85.
Sinclair, Melinda
  (1977) The refutability of Emonds's structure-preserving constraint. M.A. Thesis, University of Stellenbosch.
Skinner, B.F.
  (1972) *Beyond freedom and dignity.* New York: Albert A. Knopf.
Smart, J.J.C.
  (1968) *Between science and philosophy: an introduction to the philosophy of science.* New York: Random House.
Stegmüller, W.
  (1969) *Probleme und Resultate der Wissenschaftstheorie und analytischen Philosophie: Bd. I, Wissenschaftliche Erklärung und Begrundung.* Berlin, etc.: Springer Verlag.
Steinberg, Danny D.
  (1975) Chomsky: from formalism to mentalism and psychological invalidity. *Glossa* 9: 218–252.
Steinberg, Danny D., and Leon A. Jakobovits (eds.)
  (1971) *Semantics: an interdisciplinary reader in philosophy, linguistics and psychology.* Cambridge: At the University Press.
Stich, Stephen P.
  (1975) Competence and indeterminacy. In Cohen and Wirth (eds.) 1975: 93–109.
Stockwell, Robert P., and Ronald K.S. Macaulay (eds.)
  (1972) *Linguistic change and generative theory.* Bloomington, etc.: Indiana University Press.
Stockwell, Robert P., Paul Schachter, and Barbara Hall Partee
  (1973) *The major syntactic structures of English.* New York, etc.: Holt, Rinehart and Winston, Inc.
Suppe, Frederick (ed.)
  (1974a) *The structure of scientific theories.* Urbana, etc.: University of Illinois Press.
Suppe, Frederick
  (1974b) The search for philosophic understanding in scientific theories. In Suppe (ed.) 1974a: 3–241.
Suppes, Patrick (ed.)
  (1973) *Logic, methodology and philosophy of science IV. (Proceedings of the Fourth*

International Congress for Logic, Methodology and Philosophy of Science, Bucharest, 1971) Amsterdam, London: North-Holland Publishing Company.

Theobald, D.W.
(1968) *An introduction to the philosophy of science.* London: Methuen and Co. Ltd.

Toulmin, Stephen
(1961) *Foresight and understanding: An inquiry into the aims of science.* New York, etc.: Harper and Row Publishers.
(1965) *The philosophy of science: An introduction.* London: Hutchinson and Co.
(1970) Does the distinction between normal and revolutionary science hold water? In Lakatos and Musgrave (eds.) 1970: 39–47.

Vanek, Anthony L.
(1971) The psychological reality of g/h and its implications for the theory of grammar. *Papers in Linguistics* IV: 379–388.

Vennemann, Theo
(1973) Explanation in syntax. In Kimball (ed.) 1973: 1–50.

Wang, J.T.
(1973) On the presentation of generative grammars as first order theories. In Bogdan and Niimiluoto (eds.) 1973: 302–316.

Weigl, Egon, and Manfred Bierwisch
(1970) Neuropsychology and linguistics: topics of common research. *Foundations of Language* VI: 1–18.

Whitaker, Harry A.
(1970) Linguistic competence: evidence from aphasia. *Glossa* IV: 46–53.
(1972) Unsolicited nominalizations by aphasics: the plausibility of the lexicalist model. *Linguistics* 78: 62–71.
(1974) Is the grammar in the brain? In Cohen (ed.) 1974: 75–89.

Wirth, Jessica R.
(1975) Logical considerations in the testing of linguistic hypotheses. In Cohen and Wirth (eds.) 1975: 211–220.

Wirth, Jessica R. (ed.)
(1976) *Assessing linguistic arguments.* Washington, D.C.: Hemisphere Publishing Corporation.

Woozley, A.D.
(1967) *Theory of knowledge.* London: Hutchinson.

Wunderlich, D.
(1976) *Die Wissenschaftstheorie der Linguistik.* Frankfurt/M: Athenäum.

Ziman, J.M.
(1968) *Public knowledge. An essay concerning the social dimensions of science.* Cambridge: At the University Press.

Zwicky, Arnold M.
(1973) Linguistics as chemistry: the substance theory of semantic primes. In Anderson and Kipasky (eds.) 1973: 467–485.
(1975) Settling on an underlying form: the English inflectional endings. In Cohen and Wirth (eds.) 1975: 129–185.

Index

Only the fundamental concepts used in this study have been included in the index. For the definition of most of the concepts, the reader is referred to only one page.

163 3
98